# APPLES

### New and Updated

## BY GAIL GIBBONS

HOLIDAY HOUSE · NEW YORK

# To Vicki and Dennis Schooley

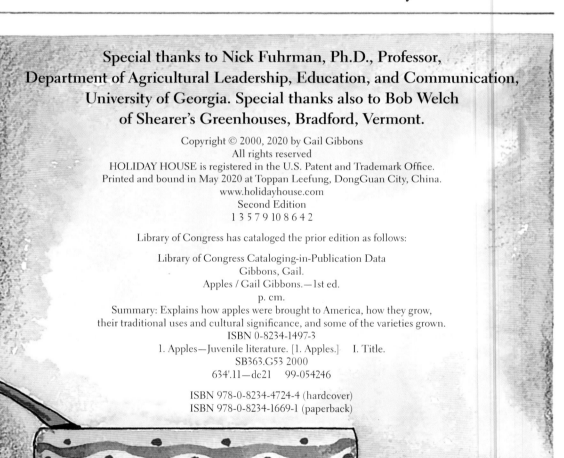

**Special thanks to Nick Fuhrman, Ph.D., Professor,
Department of Agricultural Leadership, Education, and Communication,
University of Georgia. Special thanks also to Bob Welch
of Shearer's Greenhouses, Bradford, Vermont.**

Copyright © 2000, 2020 by Gail Gibbons
All rights reserved
HOLIDAY HOUSE is registered in the U.S. Patent and Trademark Office.
Printed and bound in May 2020 at Toppan Leefung, DongGuan City, China.
www.holidayhouse.com
Second Edition
1 3 5 7 9 10 8 6 4 2

Library of Congress has cataloged the prior edition as follows:

Library of Congress Cataloging-in-Publication Data
Gibbons, Gail.
Apples / Gail Gibbons.—1st ed.
p. cm.
Summary: Explains how apples were brought to America, how they grow,
their traditional uses and cultural significance, and some of the varieties grown.
ISBN 0-8234-1497-3
1. Apples—Juvenile literature. [1. Apples.]    I. Title.
SB363.G53 2000
634'.11—dc21    99-054246

ISBN 978-0-8234-4724-4 (hardcover)
ISBN 978-0-8234-1669-1 (paperback)

An apple is a fruit. It grows on an apple tree. Apple trees grow in more parts of the world than any other fruit tree. They have been in existence for about two million years.

A SEEDLING is a very young, small tree.

The first American colonists brought apple seeds and seedlings with them from England.

Many times during the early 1800s, John Chapman traveled throughout the wilderness of Ohio, Pennsylvania, and Indiana planting apple seeds. Also, he gave seeds and seedlings to the settlers there. He became known as Johnny Appleseed.

Nowadays, some apples are grown at home . . .

and some are grown commercially.

A group of apple trees is called an APPLE ORCHARD.

Each year, about 250 million bushels of apples are grown in the United States, and about 28 million bushels are grown in Canada.

An apple is a firm, crisp fleshy fruit with a hard center called a core. The core has five seed chambers.

In the springtime, flowers called apple blossoms begin to bloom on the apple trees.

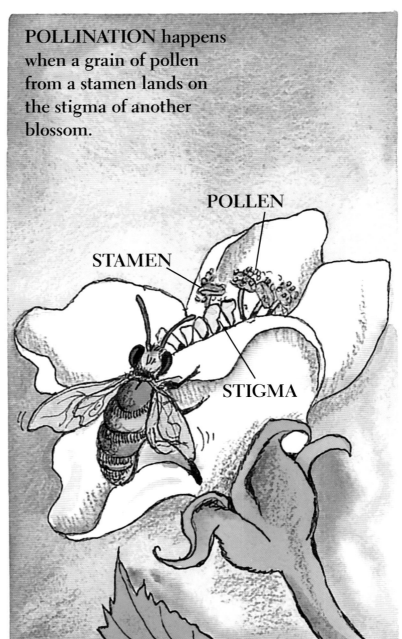

**POLLINATION** happens when a grain of pollen from a stamen lands on the stigma of another blossom.

POLLEN

STAMEN

STIGMA

Each blossom has to be pollinated in order for an apple to grow. The blossoms are usually pollinated by insects or by the wind.

The leaves capture sunlight, which helps the tree to grow. After a while the blossoms begin to die and apples start to grow.

Throughout the warm summer the little apples grow bigger and bigger.

GOLDEN DELICIOUS

During the late summer or early fall the apples ripen.

14

When the trees are loaded with ripe apples, it is harvest time. Workers pick the apples by hand.

Some are shipped to stores. Some are used to make apple juice, apple cider, apple jelly, applesauce, and lots of other apple products.

Some are sold in baskets at roadside stands.

During the fall, it is fun to go apple picking.

Also, there are country fairs. Awards are given to the best-looking apples, the best-tasting apple pies, and the most delicious applesauce. There is apple cider, too.

During Halloween, there are caramel apples and candy apples.

Some people bob for apples.

DORMANT means alive
but not actively growing.

When winter arrives, the apple tree branches become bare. The trees
will become dormant until the next spring . . .

22

when the trees will produce a new crop of apples!

# SOME COMMON APPLES GROWN IN

ROME BEAUTY

McINTOSH

RED DELICIOUS

GOLDEN DELICIOUS

Apples have many tastes, ranging from sweet to tart.

# NORTH AMERICA

JONATHAN

STAYMAN

YORK

GRANNY SMITH

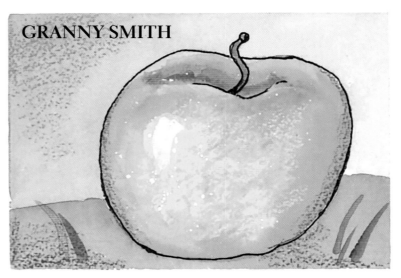

All apples are different shades of yellow, green, and red, or a mix of those colors.

# HOW TO PLANT AND CARE FOR AN APPLE TREE

**1.** It is best to plant a seedling in the fall.

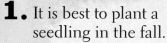

**2.** Dig a hole that is big enough to give the seedling's roots room to grow.

**3.** After placing the seedling into the hole, add topsoil.

**4.** Pack down the soil to give the seedling support.

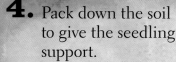

**5.** Water the seedling. It will need about ten gallons of water each week during the first few months after planting.

An apple tree will not grow apples until it is about five to eight years old. Each spring the tree branches are trimmed. This is called pruning.

Most apple trees grow to be about 20 feet (6m) tall. The soil around the trees should be fertilized. The pruning and fertilizing help produce lots of good apples.

# AN APPLE A DAY . . .

**1.** Place dough for the bottom crust into a pie pan and trim off the edges.

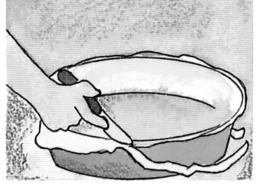

**2.** Peel and slice six to eight apples. Granny Smiths and Jonathans are good to use for apple pies, because they are tart and stay firm when they are baked. Remove the cores. Put the slices into the pie pan.

**3.** Mix ½ cup (118 ml) brown sugar, ¼ teaspoon (1.23 ml) salt, ½ teaspoon (2.46 ml) cinnamon, and ¼ teaspoon (1.23 ml) nutmeg. Sprinkle mixture over the apples.

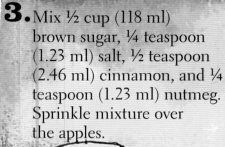

**4.** Put a layer of dough on top. Pinch down the edges and remove any extra dough. Poke little holes in the top.

**5.** Bake for 50 minutes at 425°F (228°C).

Make your own apple pie with the help of an adult.

# THEY ARE GOOD FOR YOU

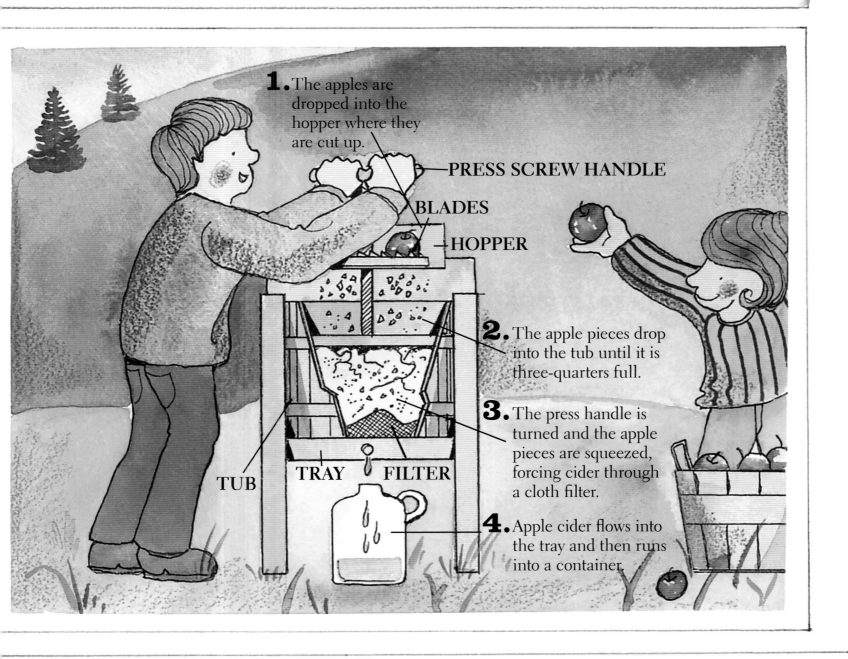

**1.** The apples are dropped into the hopper where they are cut up.

PRESS SCREW HANDLE

BLADES

HOPPER

**2.** The apple pieces drop into the tub until it is three-quarters full.

**3.** The press handle is turned and the apple pieces are squeezed, forcing cider through a cloth filter.

TUB    TRAY    FILTER

**4.** Apple cider flows into the tray and then runs into a container.

Here's how an apple cider press works.

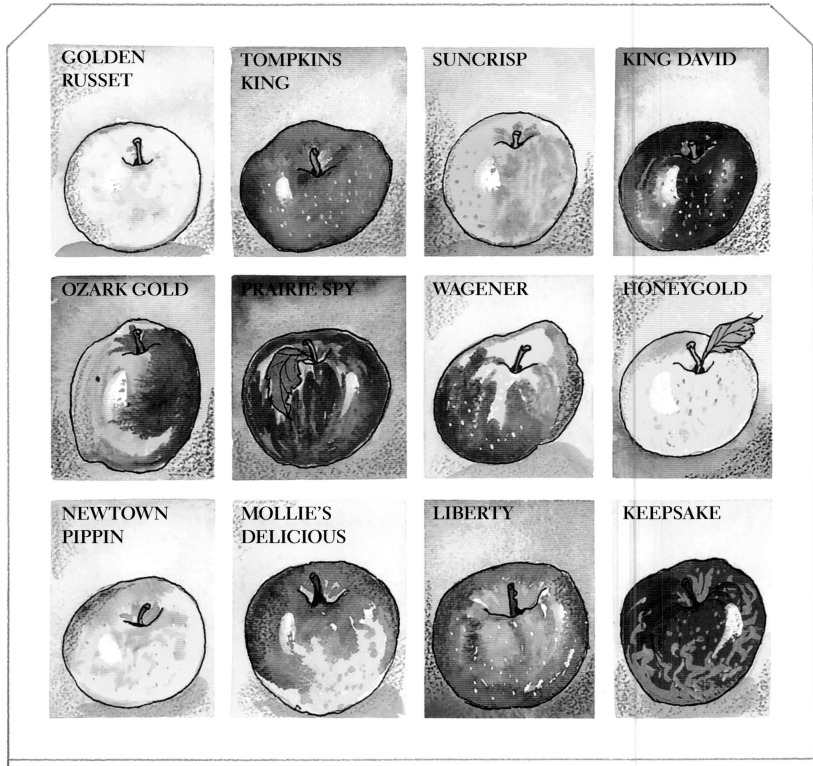

GOLDEN RUSSET

TOMPKINS KING

SUNCRISP

KING DAVID

OZARK GOLD

PRAIRIE SPY

WAGENER

HONEYGOLD

NEWTOWN PIPPIN

MOLLIE'S DELICIOUS

LIBERTY

KEEPSAKE

There are thousands of varieties, or kinds, of apples.

They are nutritious and delicious.

# APPLES...APPLES...APPLES...

The smallest apples are crab apples. They make good apple jelly.

The most popular apple in the United States is the Red Delicious, which originated on a farm in Iowa about 1881.

The states of Washington, New York, Michigan, Pennsylvania, and California produce the most apples in the United States.

Johnny Appleseed was born in Leominster, Massachusetts, and died in Ft. Wayne, Indiana.

Some people say when they like someone, "You're the apple of my eye!"

One apple, the Arkansas Black, is reddish purple and becomes nearly black by the end of the season.

The apple blossom is the state flower of Arkansas and Michigan.

There are over 7500 varieties of apples grown worldwide and 2500 varieties grown in the United States.

If you store your apples in a cool and dry place, they can last for months.

The McIntosh apple was introduced in 1870 in Ontario, Canada. A monument marks the site of the first tree. Also, the Canadian provinces that grow the most apples are British Columbia, New Brunswick, Nova Scotia, Ontario, and Quebec.

# MAMMALS
## OF THE CANADIAN WILD

BY ADRIAN FORSYTH

**CAMDEN HOUSE**

Canadian Cataloguing in Publication Data

Forsyth, Adrian
  Mammals of the Canadian wild

Bibliography: p.
Includes index.
ISBN 0-920656-40-4.

1. Mammals – Canada.   2. Mammals –
United States.   3. Wildlife conservation.
I. Title.

QL715.F67  1985   599.097   C85-099483-7

Trade distribution by
Firefly Books
3520 Pharmacy Avenue, Unit 1-C
Scarborough, Ontario
Canada M1W 2T8

Colour separations by
Herzig Somerville Limited
Toronto, Ontario

Printed in Canada by
RBW Graphics
Owen Sound, Ontario, for

**Camden House Publishing Ltd.**
7 Queen Victoria Road
Camden East, Ontario
K0K 1J0

# CONTENTS

# INTRODUCTION

One night not long ago, I awoke suddenly and found myself sitting bolt upright in bed. A full moon poured light through the window, and from the end of the driveway, I heard a sharp yip, followed by a drawn-out eerie wail. A coyote, probably detecting the scent of a dog we were watching for vacationing neighbours, was reestablishing claim to our property.

As I lay in bed, unable to go back to sleep, it struck me that the patch of land we call our property isn't ours at all. We share our small acreage with dozens of other mammals, which, like the coyote, regard it as their territory.

Only a day earlier, a red squirrel had leapt off a fencepost near the driveway and pursued a grey squirrel almost under the wheels of my truck. Near the house, chipmunks and meadow voles are consuming substantial portions of the garden, the squirrels preferring flowers and the voles competing with my wife and me for the kohlrabi and bean shoots. Three muskrats and two groundhogs conduct a running battle over claim to a patch of yellow sweet clover growing around the pond in front of the house, and the patter of the feet of the deer mice resident in the house have become a familiar nocturnal sound.

We have some help keeping these rodents at bay from transient carnivores that pass through the property. A long-tailed weasel and a red fox patrol the area regularly, and the resident short-tailed shrews feast on meadow voles.

Deer leave their cloven hoofprints all along the path from the pond. I surprised a jumping mouse in the grass one evening and watched it bound away like a tiny kangaroo. Skunks root in the compost pile for eggshells to lick, and a mink and a raccoon pounce on frogs along the pond margin. At the lake nearby, a beaver noses its way across the surface leaving a V-shaped wake.

If we lived in a remote wilderness cabin, this rich diversity of backyard mammal life might be expected. But we occupy a middle-class house a comfortable morning's drive from large Canadian cities such as Montreal, Toronto and Ottawa and within a day of Boston, New York and other large metropolitan areas of the eastern United States. Few Canadians and residents of the northern states are ever far from a rich array of wild mammals. No other area in the world has such a diverse, large, healthy population of native mammals or the vast areas of wilderness necessary to support them.

Little wonder that in the last two decades, the printing of field guides has become a minor growth industry. But while bookstore shelves now offer the naturalist identification guides on everything from fungi to tropical fish, from insects to whales, few books take the next logical step — to introduce the public to the scientific way of contemplating nature.

Recent Darwinian insights into the lives of mammals have remained trapped in the dry, dense and jargonladen prose of scientific journals. This book, then, was written with two goals: to provide a basic natural history of northern wild mammals and to present a modern biological way of thinking about nature.

To this end, in addition to containing information about the basic biology of mammals, I have also included small essays which address questions that behaviourists, ecologists and evolutionary biologists are asking. The most profitable way of asking these questions is simply to examine how a behaviour or physical characteristic affects an individual mammal's reproductive success. Looking at each mammal as an individual can turn a pleasant walk through a meadow or forest into a fascinating adventure in a world inhabited by creatures far more sophisticated and interesting than could have been imagined a few decades ago.

A colony of ground squirrels, for instance, might seem bland and uninteresting compared with the majesty of a bull moose or a blue whale. But the application of modern biological principles to ground squirrels has revealed that the small rodents have evolved a remarkably complex social system tied to close blood relationships. They are able to identify each other by smell and to distinguish between relatives and strangers. They emit shrill warning calls if a predator approaches when their kin are nearby but not if strange squirrels are present. Mother ground squirrels battle with strangers over scarce burrow sites but pass their territory on to their daughters.

The key to making sense out of the complex and seemingly contradictory behaviour and ecological relationships of mammals is found in the theory of natural selection, although calling it a theory is to invite argument from biologists. That evolution through natural selection occurs is as much a theory as is the theory of gravity or the theory that the Earth orbits the sun.

The logic behind natural selection is simple: Individuals may differ genetically, which may result in some having more offspring than others. Over time, individuals that have the greatest reproductive success will dominate. The complex dam-building behaviour of the beaver, the grotesque nose sac of the hooded seal and the fierce disposition of the wolverine can be seen as the result of genes that have been sifted and culled by a long and hard history of selection by natural forces: predation, competition, starvation, heat, cold, parasitism, anything that affects an individual beaver's, seal's or wolverine's reproductive contribution to future generations.

Behavioural biologists often talk about strategies. The behavioural strategy of the male bighorn sheep, for example, is said to be one in which large, powerful males fight to defend a harem and lesser males attempt to sneak copulations while avoiding fights. The biologist does not mean to imply that a male bighorn is able to ponder the costs and benefits of fighting as opposed to sneaking. Strategy in this context refers to the behavioural or ecological programme that is competing with an alternative pattern. By approaching behaviour in this way, biologists can measure and compare the genetic costs and benefits of different behaviours and physical traits.

Although biologists spend careers gathering the reams of data needed to answer the questions of mammal behaviour, anyone who enjoys the natural world is free to contemplate and speculate on why mammals do what they do. Something as small as the inch of black fur that appears on the snow-white tail of a long-tailed weasel in the winter but not on the closely related least weasel provides plenty of fodder for the speculation of a naturalist. Why does the least weasel lack the tip? What are the costs and benefits of the black tail tip? The black tip may deflect the aim of a diving hawk or owl, whose talons would otherwise strike a more critical part of the weasel's body. But for the small least weasel, which lives in the North, the cost of keeping a long tipped tail warm may outweigh the benefits of predator protection. To appreciate the depth and sophistication of nature, one must see organisms not as static perfection but as the constantly changing products of compromise and conflict.

The evolutionary perspective allows the naturalist to appreciate the design problems that have been so beautifully solved by natural selection. A person truly understands nature when he or she knows that the graceful pronghorn antelope, which rockets across the grasslands at speeds of up to 61 miles per hour, evolved from the low-slung waddling ancestors of the pig. One can marvel at the elegance with which a dolphin has adjusted to a life in the oceans when one realizes that its ancestors plodded on four legs across dry land.

Humans must come to a deeper understanding of wildlife — and soon. All over the world, the marvels wrought by millions of years of evolution are disappearing into extinction before they can be recognized as the masterpieces they are. In most parts of the world, wildlife has already been replaced by grainfields, highways, slums and skyscrapers. It has been eaten, poisoned and otherwise consumed by the demands of the nearly five billion humans that occupy the Earth. Much of the destruction has been unnecessary, brought about not by greed or willful vandalism but by simple ignorance. This destruction continues — and it will continue until government planners, schoolteachers, corporate executives, politicians and the average citizen come to appreciate more fully the virtues of living creatures and to value each as a work of art to be enjoyed as much as any Mona Lisa or statue of David.

Thomas Huxley, an eloquent Victorian biologist, once wrote: "To a person uninstructed in natural history, his country or seaside stroll is a walk through a gallery filled with wonderful works of art, nine-tenths of which have their faces turned to the wall."

This book will have achieved its goal if it turns some of those faces the other way.

Adrian Forsyth
July 17, 1985

**Preceding page**, *a bull elk bugles a warning to intruders approaching his harem. Horns and inaccessible terrain,* **right**, *protect solitary mountain goats from predators and competing males.*

# CLOVEN-HOOFED MAMMALS
## Artiodactyla

From a human perspective, artiodactyls are the world's most important wild mammal. As man evolved from a hunter to a farmer, he selected several artiodactyls for domestication — goats, camels, pigs, oxen, cattle, buffalo and sheep — and over time, these animals have provided humans with important sources of food and muscle power. The history of humanity has been shaped by these animals more than by any other — their value assured by their ability to harvest and digest great volumes of vegetation that is unpalatable and indigestible to humans.

The artiodactyls first appeared some 54 million years ago. Then, they were small animals with relatively short legs and generalized teeth. Most species weighed less than 11 pounds and were omnivorous, eating various fruits and vegetation, probably scavenging the occasional bit of meat or small animal, a tendency retained by the pigs and their close relatives, the hippopotamus and the peccary. This line of artiodactyls has retained short legs and a squat body. Their teeth still include large canines, and pigs, at least, are still highly omnivorous. But the main artiodactyl group evolved long legs, an efficient foot and body plan designed for running, and teeth and a stomach capable of handling a purely vegetarian diet.

These ruminant artiodactyls have lost or reduced their upper canines and have evolved a long set of broad molars with complicated crescent-shaped ridges along their surface. This is an adaptation for cutting and grinding vegetation. Their stomach has developed into a multichambered fermentation device that uses microorganisms to break down hard-to-digest molecules and convert them into useful forms.

The shift from omnivory to browsing and grazing resulted in the evolution of different body forms. The limbs of a vegetarian are of little use in catching or manipulating food, as artiodactyls can accomplish this using a flexible neck and lips. Their callused tongue pushes vegetation against the lips and roof of the mouth, while the lower teeth shear it off.

Meanwhile, the limbs became superb instruments of locomotion. As artiodactyls' legs became specialized solely for walking and running, their feet took on a new shape. All species walk on their third and fourth toes, whose tips have become sheathed in a strong hoof material, and their side toes have been reduced. Numerous other adaptations, which lengthened the stride and increased the ability to run, also evolved.

Artiodactyls are often active in exposed places, and they have well-developed senses of sight and smell to deal with predators. Many of them are gregarious and rely on herding to reduce the probability of being eaten by predators. They tend to have large, precocial offspring, born one at a time and ready to run soon after birth.

Woodland deer, by contrast, have well-camouflaged altricial young that are relatively helpless for several weeks and must pursue a "hider strategy" for survival. Open-habitat animals, such as bison or caribou, have precocial young that are able to walk within a few hours, joining their mother as she moves around. This is the "follower" strategy.

*Artiodactyls, such as this moose, evolved flexible necks and lips in their transition from omnivores to grazers.*

# *Deer* Cervidae

Deer are woodland browsers. They have the typical long-legged and long-necked grace of open-plains grazers, but most deer are associated with wooded areas and limited amounts of open habitat. They will graze in meadows and grasslands, but when danger threatens, they retreat to cover. Much of their food is twigs and leaves clipped from trees and shrubs, rather than grasses. Most of the world's deer species are found in subtropical forests or forest-edge habitats. A few, such as the caribou, spend much of their lives beyond the trees, and some — the tiny Asian water deer, for example — live in reedy marshland. Others, like the mule deer, range well into open grassland or other open habitats. Some species, such as Asian musk deer, are only the size of an average dog, while others, such as the moose, are larger than a horse.

Deer evolved in Eurasia, probably in the heavy north temperate and subtropical forests, eventually coming to North America and then moving into South America. Some species, such as caribou, are found around the northern hemisphere, and some, like elk, are recent immigrants. Deer have never reached Australia and have never penetrated Africa because of the barrier posed by the Sahara or because of competition from other grazing mammals. In the New World, deer replaced a wide variety of deerlike browsers and grazers that had arisen in other now extinct groups. Deer are among the most sought-after game animals, but as yet, there is not even agreement on exactly how many species exist. Recent estimates range from 19 to 53.

Deer are distinguished by their antlers. All species but one (a small Asian deer) have these bony growths on the skull. Antlers are important in mating and courtship behaviour. Most deer tend to be polygynous, with harem formation and male-male combat using antlers. Only in caribou do the females also have antlers.

The herd size of deer varies greatly from one species to another. White-tailed deer and moose, which live in dense forests, are far less gregarious than open-habitat species, such as caribou or elk. Being part of a herd has distinct advantages in open areas where highly visual predators, such as wolves and coyotes, are a threat. In this sense, herding behaviour is much like the schooling behaviour of minnows and other fish that are food for larger predators. Entering into a group is a way for individuals to lessen the chances of a predator's singling them out for attack. Individuals that are vulnerable because of injury, illness or age may conceal themselves in the crowd. A group also has more eyes for detecting the approach of predators. This enables each individual to devote less time to watching and more time to feeding.

Large herds of grazing mammals may actually encourage the growth of preferred species of food plants by heavily cropping an area. This has been shown to occur in African savannas where large herds of grazers are found. The heavy cropping of the herds maintains grassland communities and prevents less palatable shrubs from taking over. Conceivably, this could also be true of the North American caribou, although the idea has yet to be tested.

By contrast, more solitary species, such as deer, that depend on shrubby browse are known to be unable to control the growth of the forest when they are at their naturally low densities. Under natural conditions, they depend on fires and severe storms to open up new stands of brush habitat.

Deer family herds are often segregated by sex, females occurring with other females and immature offspring and males banding together in bachelor herds that are usually composed of males of similar age. This segregation may serve several purposes. Since wolves single out and attack individuals that appear to be abnormal, it would pay an individual to join a group as similar to itself as possible. For that reason, antlered males that are exhausted after the fall rut would be conspicuous and vulnerable if they were to join a group of antlerless females. When bachelor males join a group of peers, it is probably necessary for them to develop the sparring skills that will be used in combat for mating territories later in life. Females may benefit from joining with other females because older females will have learned the whereabouts of good feeding areas and locations that offer defence from predators.

The herding instinct of some species of deer suits them to domestication. It would be very difficult to farm solitary species, such as moose, but deer such as red deer and reindeer are farmed in Europe. Herds are managed to provide meat and milk products, and the velvet from the antlers is sold to the Orient as an aphrodisiac.

*A prime bull elk displaying his antlers typifies the majesty of the deer family, the only animals that grow a new set of antlers every year.*

## *Caribou* Rangifer tarandus

**Mammal:** *Rangifer tarandus* — caribou, reindeer; the only genus of deer family in which both sexes are antlered

**Meaning of Name:** *Rangifer*, from the Old French word *rangifère* (reindeer); *tarandus* (reindeer or an animal of northern countries)

**Description:** compact, heavyset; unusually large crescentic hooves; large, blunt well-furred muzzle and short, broad, heavily furred ears; long ventral mane on throat; antlers are extremely variable and are never a mirror image of each other on one animal; both sexes grow these slender palmate antlers (not all does have them), which are mahogany brown in colour and have one prominent tine down over the nose; colour varies with subspecies and according to season but is basically chocolate brown, darker on the face, chest and dorsal tail surface; creamy white neck and mane; white belly, rump and ventral tail surface; brown legs with narrow white ''socks'' just above hooves

**Total Length:** male, 5.2 to 7.5 feet; female, 4.5 to 6.7 feet

**Tail:** male, 4.5 to 6 inches; female, 3.9 to 5.5 inches

**Weight:** male, 134 to 400 pounds; female, 138 to 260 pounds

**Gestation:** 215 to 240 days

**Litter Size:** usually 1 (sometimes twins)

**Age of Maturity:** male may be excluded from mating by older males until the third year; female, 16 months

**Longevity:** average in the wild is 4.5 years (maximum is 13 years); maximum in captivity is 20 years 2 months

**Diet:** browser and grazer; lichens are a mainstay of diet, especially in winter

**Habitat:** prefers mature coniferous upland habitats surrounding the Arctic tundra and taiga zones; also found in remote alpine meadows; uses semi-open and open bog more in winter

**Predators:** man is chief predator; also wolf, grizzly bear, wolverine and lynx; golden eagle may prey on young

**Dental Formula:** 0/3, 1-0/1, 1/3, 3/3 = 32 or 34 teeth

Caribou are the dominant grazers of the tundra and far northern forest. In Lapland and Russia, they have been domesticated as reindeer, making them the most northerly of all domesticated animals. They show the greatest adaptation of all cervids to a life that is spent walking on snow, on boggy tundra and in cold air. Their feet are the widest of all the deer; the normally defunct toelike dew claws are well developed to help bear the weight of the animal atop deep snow. The hooves show a distinct seasonal cycle of adjustment from the winter demands of walking on snow and ice to summer's tundra. In summer, the foot pads are soft and widespread, while in winter, the hoof pads grow hard, and dense hair grows between the toes to protect the toe pads from abrasion by ice and crusted snow. These stiff hairs also prevent skidding and slipping on icy surfaces.

One of the most unusual features of caribou is that females have well-developed antlers. They are not as large as the males' but are still impressive. Moreover, females retain their antlers until calving time in the spring, while males shed theirs just after the autumn rut. Females may use their antlers for social/sexual status, but they represent a severe drain on their carrier's supply of minerals. There is some evidence that females can use antlers as a mineral bank and reabsorb nutrients from them as their pregnancies progress, but this is likely to account for only a small recouping of the total nutrient diversion.

There are clearly dominance relationships between members of a caribou band, but exactly what benefits females achieve with their antlers is not clear. Possibly, they increase a female's winter access to food, as caribou dig deep craters in the snow in their search for sustenance. This food is particularly important to pregnant females.

Caribou are gregarious animals that typically herd together and travel as seasonal nomads over long distances.

*Of all the deer species, caribou range farthest north, to the very tip of the Arctic archipelago. They are the only kind of deer in which both males and females have antlers, **left**. Some caribou herds undertake spectacular migrations, **above**, with tens of thousands of animals following traditional routes across hundreds of miles of northern wilderness.*

Most herds have summer and winter ranges that they move between, often travelling 600 or more miles. Generally, they move south to better cover in the northern taiga forests in winter and into more open habitats in summer. When selecting their summer grounds, the caribou tend toward windswept areas to avoid the biting flies that may otherwise torment them and their newborn calves. There are several nonmigratory populations, such as the herds on Peary Island in the high Arctic and the Shickshock Mountains in the Gaspé. The woodland caribou of the boreal forest do not move as extensively, and in keeping with their forest habitat, they live in smaller groups. In open areas, such as the barren-grounds, the coalescing bands may form into herds of 10,000 caribou streaming across the countryside. They wear great trails in the landscape and tend to follow traditional routes, fording and swimming great rivers in their journey.

The spring movement toward calving grounds is led by the older pregnant females. Pregnant females are hostile to others and separate from the group to calve alone, possibly in an attempt to reduce the likelihood of attracting predators. A single well-developed precocial calf is born, able to run within hours of birth.

During the summer, caribou are grazers, rather than browsers, and feed on grass, sedge, moss and lichens, a favourite food. Even in the more southerly woodlands, where plant life is diverse, caribou eat lichens that they glean from trees. Because lichens are full of complex chemicals, the reindeer gut has special bacteria to digest them. Unfortunately, lichens collect radioactive fallout from atomic testing, and reindeer concentrate it in their bodies. An adult caribou has radioactive fallout from tons of lichens, and the Inuit who eat caribou have been found to have radioactive compounds in their bodies at concentrations several hundred times that found in urban North Americans.

During winter, the caribou's diet also includes browse from shrubs, such as willow and birch. Reindeer

*Dozens of pounds of minerals and large quantities of energy go into the construction of a male caribou's antlers, whose coating of velvet is thrashed off against shrubbery prior to the autumn rut.*

will also eat lemmings when they are plentiful and the cast-off antlers that litter the tundra.

While a lot of the summer's nutrient growth is put into fat stores for the winter, much of it is devoted to the development of antlers. In males, antler development starts in early spring and continues until late summer, when large males will have produced racks 4 feet wide. As the animals move south and toward treed areas, the antlers harden and their velvet coating is thrashed off against the shrubbery. Females begin developing their antlers in summer and do not rub the velvet off until late autumn. Some females do not develop antlers, and it may be that they either have too few nutrients for the task or are following a different nutrient-investment strategy.

Male caribou do not maintain a harem in the sense that elk do, being closer to moose in their reproductive strategy. Bulls follow a single female at a time as she approaches oestrus, although prime bulls may interrupt one another to fight over a female. After the rut, large weakened males are prime targets for wolves; one reason females retain their antlers may be to distinguish themselves from males that are the objects of selective wolf predation.

Wolves are the dominant predators of both calves and adult caribou, and many biologists feel that wolves are able to regulate caribou populations effectively. When human hunters become involved as well, certain caribou populations cannot withstand the onslaught. Caribou have been eliminated in the southern areas of their range, while in parts of the north, hunting pressure is progressively weakening stock. Some wolf-control programmes have been established in an effort to perpetuate traditional hunting and to preserve caribou populations.

The success of highly migratory herds may depend on the existence of well-travelled routes. Oil pipelines and related developments are threats to herds with set migration patterns, and hydroelectric dams in Quebec have recently been cited as the cause of large kills of tens of thousands of migrants.

Despite these problems, caribou remain one of the most important animals for northern peoples, and they have scope for further sustained use in the Canadian Arctic.

## Antlers As Status Symbols

*Humans display a reverence for horns and antlers. Traditionally, the ceremony used by many societies to crown their royalty is implicit recognition of the power and status that a full set of horns and antlers brings to its bearer.*

*In the deer family, antlers are a clear indicator of a male's reproductive status. The size of the antlers provides a reliable cue for females and other males as to the quality and vigour of an individual. The same is true of the horns of bovids. Both horns and antlers are bony outgrowths from the skull, their chief difference being that antlers are shed yearly while horns stay on the animal, enlarging each year. Castrated males from either family will fail to grow horns or antlers or will lose them.*

*Antlers are dependable clues to the health and vigour of their bearer because they are so costly to produce. The physical cost to an adult male of producing antlers or large horns is greater than that incurred by females during pregnancy or lactation. Production of*

*Male caribou assess the strength of their rivals in antler-wrestling contests.*

antlers or horns may cause the male to lose calcium and other minerals from his skeletal system so that the size of the antlers reflects a male's ability to forage more and to range farther — ample proof of his health and abilities. Antlers are not a signal that can be easily faked.

In theory, an individual could build large, impressive but hollow and weakly reinforced antlers or horns, but such duplicity would not go undetected. Male bighorn sheep and other horned and antlered mammals often aggregate in groups that seem to be display and assessment arenas where antlers and body size are compared. To assess status and dominance, males engage in direct tests of each other's vigour. Often, they use sparring matches, such as the antler wrestling of elk and caribou. In rather formalized encounters, males wave and lower their antlers in a display that emphasizes their size. If that is unconvincing to either rival, they lock antlers in a pushing and twisting sparring match in which the weaker male, having assessed his opponent, can withdraw before the fight escalates.

If either party is not subdued by the other's performance, he may decide to charge and fight seriously, an action that usually leads to severe injuries and sometimes even death.

Since mating success is closely tied to success in male-male dominance contests, antlers and horns have been designed for success in that endeavour, rather than for fighting and repelling predators. In fact, much evidence suggests that huge horns or antlers are more of a hindrance than a help. Female deer do not usually have antlers, and the males shed theirs after the rut is over. In sheep and goats, males' horns are usually much larger than those of the females, which again suggests that the horns'

main use is in male-male competition and not in predator defence.

The size of the antlers of different species of deer and sheep is a reliable indication of how polygynous the species is. Harem-breeding species, such as elk, have huge horns, and the acquisition of a harem is a high-yield, high-cost system. Males that are able to pay the price of large antlers get to father a large number of offspring. On the other hand, there are species of deer in which females are so dispersed that there is little opportunity for assembling a harem and little value in a large rack of antlers. Males may get more mates by searching widely or by simply following a single female until she is ready to mate. This is the pattern shown by small forest species of deer that live where antlers are more of a physical liability than they are to open-habitat species. In any case, less polygynous forest deer have smaller antlers.

## Mule Deer *Odocoileus hemionus*

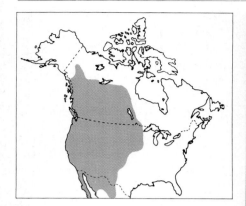

**Mammal:** *Odocoileus hemionus* — mule deer

**Meaning of Name:** *Odocoileus* (hollow tooth) refers to well-hollowed teeth; *hemionus* (a half-ass, a mule) refers to the fact that it has very large ears, like a mule

**Description:** body is larger and stockier than white-tailed deer; large metatarsal gland (2 to 6 inches) is surrounded by stiff brown hairs; dichotomously branched antlers on males are not prongs from a main beam; in summer, pelage varies from reddish to tawny brown above with a dark brown forehead; white face with black muzzle; rump patch, thighs, belly, throat and inside of ears are white; tail is either black-tipped or black on top; winter coat is dark or grizzled brown

**Total Length:** male, 4.7 to 6.2 feet; female, 4.5 to 5 feet

**Tail:** male, 5.9 to 7.9 inches; female, 4.5 to 7.9 inches

**Weight:** male, 110 to 473 pounds; female, 69 to 159 pounds

**Gestation:** 195 to 212 days

**Litter Size:** 1 to 3 (usually 2)

**Age of Maturity:** female, 1.5 years

**Longevity:** seldom more than 10 years in the wild; 25 years in captivity

**Diet:** browser; feeds mostly on evergreen twigs, saplings and shrubs; also grasses, forbs, herbs, mushrooms, nuts and lichens

**Habitat:** open coniferous forests, subclimax brush and shrubs, chaparral, shrubby grasslands, steep broken terrain and river valleys

**Predators:** mountain lion, wolf, coyote, lynx, bobcat, bear; golden eagle may prey upon fawns

**Dental Formula:** 0/3, 0/1, 3/3, 3/3 = 32 teeth

The mule deer is a western version of the white-tailed deer, although it is larger and adapted to more open and arid habitats. The mule deer does not have the raised white tail flag of the white-tail, and its run is a stiff-legged gait that contrasts with the more graceful bounds of the white-tail. Males have antlers that branch into four prongs on either side when they reach full size.

In keeping with its occupation of more open areas where sound travels over long distances, male deer have larger ears than white-tailed deer, hence their name. They are also more gregarious and seek safety in herd numbers to increase their ability to detect predators. In winter, when bucks have lost their antlers, they join with females and juveniles, forming

*The mule deer gets its name from its widespread mulelike ears, an adaptation for detecting predators.*

large bands of several dozen individuals. Like other western cervids, these bands move with changing snow conditions and follow an altitudinal migration in mountainous areas. Their distribution and movement may be most influenced by the availability of water or of lush grazing that would fulfill their water needs.

Mule deer have the typical autumn rut, with large males attempting to attract a harem of females. The females give birth in spring, usually to twins. It is not clear whether the mule deer fawns are more precocial at birth than white-tails, which their use of open habitats would predict.

## Sexual Selection

*Darwin's most famous book is his* Origin of Species, *the massive tome in which he carefully laid out his theory of evolution and natural selection. Most of an animal's traits, such as the spotted coat of a deer fawn or the strong jaws of a wolverine, seem obviously beneficial to the individual that bears them. Darwin had no difficulty in explaining how these adaptations could be developed and refined through the process of natural selection. But there were many features of animals that troubled him, features such as the gross red bladder that the hooded seal blows out of its nose or the massive racks of antlers on the head of the male elk.*

*How could natural selection have favoured these bizarre traits? They seem like vulnerabilities that would increase the risk of being noticed by predators, increase the effort of locomotion and decrease the animals' abilities to forage efficiently. To answer the problem posed by these ornaments, Darwin wrote another massive book,* The Descent of Man and Selection in Relation to Sex, *in which he developed the theory of sexual selection. Its main intent was to explain the evolution of the many strange traits and behaviours that would seem to lower, not raise, the survivorship of an animal.*

*Darwin noted that the most elaborate and bizarre traits were associated with courtship. They tended to be more highly developed in males and occurred only rarely in females. For example, outside of the breeding season, males tended to throw off their antlers, to tone down their roaring and scent marking and to begin acting and looking like females. Darwin suggested that certain traits could evolve if they increased an individual's success at courtship, mating and producing offspring, even if the traits resulted in a lowering of the individual's rate of survival. What really mattered was whether they raised or lowered the total number of descendants the individual left. Thus, even though a male's antlers and rutting behaviour might make it more vulnerable to wolves after the rut, these traits*

*Male and female mule deer pursue different reproductive strategies that have led to the evolution of the small female body and the large male antlers.*

*would help the male to father more offspring, which would favour the same features in the evolutionary process.*

*Darwin recognized two ways in which males might increase their reproductive success through sexual selection. They could evolve characteristics to increase their ability to conquer other males in combat over access to females or they could increase their attractiveness to females.*

*Females tend to produce offspring at a high physical cost. They have relatively large eggs, long pregnancies and high child-rearing responsibilities, and the total number of offspring that they can expect to produce in a lifetime is low compared with what a male could potentially father. This means that males, with their billions of available sperm, must compete for a limited number of female eggs. Conversely, females tend to be selective about which males father their few offspring. This sets the general conditions for the evolution of male weaponry that is designed for use against male competitors rather than predators and for displays that indicate the male's health and freedom from defects.*

*Sexually selected traits will continue to evolve if they give an individual an advantage in mating until they are opposed by some stronger selective pressure, such as predation. Thus it is a mix of these various selective pressures that determines the appearance of an animal. Judging by male rutting and display behaviour, sexual selection is clearly a potent evolutionary force. For male artiodactyls, antlers and horns must have more advantages than disadvantages.*

*As a result of sexual selection, we see vast differences in the male and female approach to courtship — the males often being aggressive, singing and performing elaborate rites, displays and contests, while the females remain aloof and selective about their mates, repelling the advances of young untested males. These patterns are the result of sexual selection, a process set in motion not long after the evolution of life itself.*

## White-tailed Deer  Odocoileus virginianus

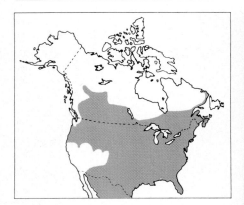

**Mammal:** *Odocoileus virginianus* — white-tailed deer

**Meaning of Name:** *Odocoileus* (hollow tooth) refers to well-hollowed teeth; *virginianus* (of Virginia); Virginia was the locality of this deer in the original description

**Description:** preorbital glands and pear-shaped tarsal glands on the inside of the hocks, which are surrounded by stiff white hairs; males have antlers that spread slightly backward, outward and then directly forward, curving inward on an almost horizontal plane, with several sharp unbranched tines; in summer, coat is reddish tan on back, with white on belly, throat and eye ring; in winter, coat is grizzled grey on the upperparts; in both seasons, head is marked with black nose, tawny fringed ears and black spot on each side of white chin

**Total Length:** male, 6 to 7 feet; female, 5.2 to 6.5 feet

**Tail:** 5.9 to 11 inches

**Weight:** male, 151 to 311 pounds; female, 90 to 210 pounds

**Gestation:** 195 to 212 days

**Litter Size:** 1 to 4 (usually 2)

**Age of Maturity:** male, 1 year, but does not get a chance to mate until older and stronger; female, most at 1 year (a few at 7 months)

**Longevity:** up to 16.5 years in the wild, but seldom past 10; 20 years in captivity

**Diet:** browsers; in winter, buds and twigs of shrubs and saplings as well as needles and leaves of evergreens; in summer, grasses, fruits, forbs and green foliage of shrubs and saplings, needles of evergreens, mushrooms

**Habitat:** forests and forest edges, cedar swamps and swamp edges, open brushy areas; on the prairies, found in wooded coulees during the day and forage on open prairie in the evening

**Predators:** carnivores (coyote, wolf, lynx, bobcat, black bear and feral dogs)

**Dental Formula:** 0/3, 0/1, 3/3, 3/3 = 32 teeth

White-tailed deer are far more solitary than other northern cervids, such as elk and caribou. They are creatures of the forest whose lives are based on concealment to avoid the attention of predators. In many respects, this species' life history resembles that of the cottontail rabbit. The white-tailed deer occupies a small section of forest and is far less migratory than the other cervids. Often, a home range of only 40 to 200 acres is used. This enables the individual to become familiar with the terrain and with all of the possible escape routes.

Females do not band together either at birthing time or when their calves are maturing, pursuing their hiding strategy to the extreme. They give birth to one or two fawns over a wider seasonal range than most large herbivores, anytime from early spring to late summer. Occasionally, in some protected spots, three or four fawns may be born. Like the cottontail, the mother disperses her fawns if she has more than one to minimize the chances of a predator finding all of them. She returns to nurse them only a few times a day to avoid drawing attention to them.

The fawns are born in a relatively helpless state, unable to travel for sev-

*Born helpless, speckled white-tailed fawns nurse for as long as three months, the only prolonged social contact in the life of these deer.*

eral days after birth. They rely on their stillness, reduced odour and highly speckled coat for concealment, and only after three weeks do they begin to travel with their mother. The early association of the fawns with their mother seems to be the only form of prolonged social contact in white-tailed deer. They nurse for as long as three months and continue to associate with the mother even after weaning. Males may leave their mother at the fall rutting season to join up with a few other yearling males, or they may defer this until the spring. Female fawns stay with their mother over the winter and may remain with her for as long as four seasons, although the mother may leave for a while at the time of the rut. Whether this extended female association results in the inheritance of territory or is merely a way of passing on maternal experience is not known.

Like all cervids, male white-tailed deer grow antlers in preparation for the attempt to acquire a harem of breeding females. In autumn, they rub trees with their scent glands and thrash the vegetation with their antlers to mark out territories, which they defend from other bucks. There is little vocalization except a baa-ing as a male follows a female, and generally, the rut seems less intense than that of the elk. Similarly, the horns of this species are less spectacularly enlarged than in many cervids from more open habitats. Males may also stay with a single female over a period of several days to several weeks, and it may be that mate guarding is an alternative to trying to establish large harems. The intensity of predation and the lack of visibility in the forest may have constrained the white-tailed male's polygynous tendencies.

Outside of the rutting season, white-tails are silent animals, hard to hear and hard to see in the forest. When surprised, they make use of their bounding leaps to sail over logs and brush and to outdistance most pursuit predators. The larger cats, such as the puma and the lynx, rely on surprise to catch adult white-tails, and wolves normally depend on favourable snow conditions and pack hunting to run them down.

The white-tail is a relatively southerly deer whose range extends into South America, but recently, the species has been expanding its range northward. It is a generalized browser, favouring shrubbery of all sorts, so that clearing and cutting and subsequent regrowth of northeastern forests has been favourable to white-tails, as has the extermination of many large carnivore populations. What seems to limit the northern deer populations is a combination of snow conditions and adequate food. In northern areas, deer are forced to yard up in thick stands of conifers to gain protection from the wind. Often, they will remain sheltered from the wind and snow rather than venture out to forage, as their coats are not very thick and their small hooves are not designed to handle soft or lightly crusted deep snow. To escape from wolves, for example, they rely on a series of crisscrossing hard-packed trails that radiate from the deer yard. Without these, they would flounder and tire in chest-deep snow, and wolves could easily run them down.

The restriction of activity and feeding range that results from the reliance

on these winter trails leads to dominance patterns. Older females establish priority and are able to reach the food first to snip off favoured browse.

The weapons of the female white-tail and the male without horns are the forefeet. Capable of inflicting hard blows, female white-tails have caused broken bones and severe injuries to lone wolves that they have attacked.

Deer hunting is the major mortality factor controlling white-tailed deer populations. Two million are shot each year in North America, and in urban areas, car-deer collisions account for as many kills as do hunters. Feral and unleashed domestic dogs are another important mortality agent accounting for up to 10 percent of the winter kill. Nevertheless, the multiple litters and early age of reproduction allow white-tails to remain one of the most abundant of all large-game animals.

*The size of a male's antlers is a clear indicator of his age and strength.*

## Why Wave a Flag?

*Surprise a white-tailed deer, and its usual response is to snort, turn tail and run. As it does, it lifts its long white tail, which then flashes conspicuously as the animal bounds away. This seems an unlikely behaviour for a forest animal that is cryptically coloured and secretive in its other movements. Why should it wave a flag at predators?*

*There is a multitude of possible explanations. It might act as a startle display at close range, the sudden flare of white causing the predator to hesitate, allowing a crucial split-second headstart. This sort of startle display is well developed in various insects and frogs, so it is at least a potentially plausible idea. But most*

mammalian predators, such as puma or wolves, should be undeterred by such a display, especially after they have seen it a few times.

Another possibility is that the flag warns other deer about the approaching predator. This could be valuable in several ways. It might cause other deer to startle and reveal themselves to the predator, reducing the probability that the signaller would be attacked. This sort of selfish manipulation might be more expected in groups of unrelated animals, but if the deer is surrounded by kin or its own offspring, it might simply be a mutually beneficial warning. Related to this is the idea that the raised white tail might enable offspring to follow their mother as she bounds through the forest. But the signal is not used so selectively. Lone animals wave their flags the same way that social animals do.

The third possibility is that the signal is a direct communication between the deer and the predator. The deer, in effect, signals, "I have seen you. I know you are a predator." This could be beneficial to the waver in two ways. It might help resolve any uncertainty the deer has about whether the predator is hunting — the deer can settle any confusion by exposing itself to test the intentions of the predator. Alternatively, it might be an attempt to discourage the predator by indicating that the deer is aware of its enemy and can probably outrun it. Most predators must rely on an ambush or surprise attack to capture a deer.

It is this last idea that has received the most support. The flag is useful to the predator, since the predator can save itself the unprofitable stalk and chase if the deer knows it is there. The deer, of course, is not signalling to save the predator from exertion, it merely seeks to prevent an attack.

A test of these ideas revealed that deer flag when they are alone, not just when they are in groups, and that the flag is directed toward the threat, not other deer. This suggests that the warning hypothesis is not a strong possibility. Interestingly, not all

The bright upright tail of a fleeing white-tail may be a signal designed to discourage predator pursuit by indicating that the deer is alert to the predator's presence.

deer flag. Those that are surprised at close distances or see a predator making a second approach to resume a chase do not flag but simply get going. The simplest interpretation of this fact is that the deer realizes the tail has failed to discourage the predator.

In the test, the deer most likely to flag were those that saw the predator approach from afar and had time to make their exit. This suggests that discouraging pursuit is why it may sometimes pay to wave a flag.

# *Moose* Alces alces

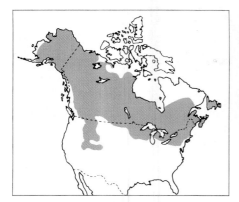

**Mammal:** *Alces alces* — moose; the largest living member of the deer family

**Meaning of Name:** *Alces* (elk); moose is derived from the Algonkian word *moos* (eater of twigs, or he strips off bark)

**Description:** prominent drooping snout and a dewlap, or "bell," hanging from throat; males have large palmate (shovel-shaped) antlers that are flat and have small prongs projecting from the borders; brittle, stiff pelage; reddish brown to black with grey legs; lower belly and underside of legs are whitish; males have more brownish foreheads, females more greyish; first year, animals are more reddish

**Total Length:** male, 7.5 to 9.2 feet; female, 6.5 to 8.5 feet

**Tail:** 2 to 4.7 inches

**Weight:** male, 849 to 1,800 pounds; female, 727 to 873 pounds

**Gestation:** 226 to 264 days

**Litter Size:** 1 (sometimes 2, rarely 3)

**Age of Maturity:** male, 2 to 3 years, but rarely has the opportunity to breed until 5 or 6 years old; female, 2 to 3 years

**Longevity:** up to 27 years

**Diet:** primarily a browser; in winter, twigs and shrubs, bark of saplings; in summer, leaves from upland plants, large quantities of water plants, forbs, grasses and foliage

**Habitat:** wooded areas and early successional stages of evergreen forests; swamps, lakeshores adjacent to forests, muskegs and streams of great boreal forests; also tundra; in winter, it is found in mosaics of mature and young coniferous, deciduous and mixed stands

**Predators:** wolf is major predator; grizzly bear, black bear, wolverine and puma prey on calves

**Dental Formula:** 0/3, 0/1, 3/3, 3/3 = 32 teeth

The moose is the largest cervid, reaching a weight of 1,800 pounds. Next to the bison, moose are the largest land animals in North America.

The moose is a boreal-forest specialist. It is not common in mature coniferous forests, which are dark and support little shrubbery in the undergrowth. Instead, the moose favours a forest mixture with open areas as well as the edges of watercourses. Its name is an Algonkian word meaning twig eater or bark stripper. The moose is indeed a browser that clips a wide variety of trees and shrubbery along its forest-edge habitat. However, in winter, when there is heavy snow and

*Moose spend much of their summer wading and swimming in the lakes and rivers of the boreal forest.*

weather, the moose will search the thick mature coniferous forest because the understorey is relatively clear of snow and well shielded from the wind.

The long legs of the moose seem to be adaptations for snowy winters. Moose can high-step their way through deep snow, and their broad hooves provide good support in boggy, wet areas. The boreal forest is crisscrossed with lakes and rivers,

and moose are excellent swimmers. They will take to the water to outswim predators, such as wolves, and they feed heavily on water plants in summer. Moose have even been seen diving and swimming underwater in search of water plants.

Like other creatures of the boreal forest, the moose is solitary. It is more of a loner than any other North American cervid. Although a few moose may yard together in favourable spots during winter, they travel alone for most of the year. In spring, females give birth to a single calf, which they defend with great vigour. The calf is

weaned by autumn and stays with the mother through the winter until she gives birth again. Females may tolerate the presence of the calf for as long as a year, but otherwise, they solicit company only during the autumn rut. Unlike other cervids, such as elk, the female moose takes the most vocal role in the rut. She bawls out a loud and long moan that calls in any bulls in the area. The call is effective and has long been imitated by hunters.

Since moose are generally widely dispersed, males do not attract and defend a harem of females as do open-habitat cervids like elk. Instead, the

*The thick network of blood vessels needed to grow antlers is clearly visible in the velvet this bull moose is shedding from his new rack.*

bull patrols the area, advertising his presence with urine and other scent marks, thrashing the vegetation with his antlers and creating wallows. If he encounters a male, he attempts to chase him out of the area, and if he encounters a female, he either mates with her, if she is receptive, or stays with her and waits up to several weeks for her to come into oestrus. The dispersion of the females limits a male's opportunity for polygyny. Nevertheless, successful mating seems to depend heavily on the male's ability to defend a mating territory. In some areas, small groups of males and females may congregate for mating, but this has not been well documented.

Moose have some of the most massive antlers of all animals: some may stretch 6 feet and weigh over 70 pounds. They represent a tremendous investment of nutrients, even though they are cast off every season. To support and wield their antlers, bulls develop huge neck muscles. They may increase their weight by almost a third before the rut, and it will drop down to 10 percent less than normal after the rut. During the rut, males can be extremely belligerent and will charge humans and even cars.

The range expansion of white-tailed deer has brought them into a dangerously increased contact with moose. White-tails are host to *Parelaphostrongylus tenuis*, the meningeal worm, which is a parasite of little consequence to deer but which attacks the moose's nervous system and will cause paralysis and eventual death. Contact between white-tails and moose can fuel dangerous infections and lead to serious moose-population decline.

## A Taste for Salt

*It's a good bet that moose would like the taste of junk food, especially potato chips, as most herbivores in the North have a difficult time getting enough salt. The mammalian body uses the sodium molecules of salt in all sorts of jobs: for transmitting electrical impulses along nerves, for maintaining pressure within cells and for effecting the movement of compounds through membranes. Meat eaters get plenty of salt in their diet, but northern herbivores usually have to eat twigs and bark all winter long. These are low in sodium, so by the time spring arrives, the animals' salt reserves are extremely low.*

*This accounts for some strange browser behaviour; it explains why porcupines love to eat canoe seats, outhouses and virtually anything that has come in contact with salty sweat and urine. It is why sheep and deer will travel many miles to salt licks,*

*even though they are exposed to predators along the route. And it explains why moose go swimming and diving during the summer. Moose have been seen to dive 15 feet deep in a lake looking for the salt to be found in underwater plants.*

*Aquatic plants concentrate salt and other minerals. Some species, such as milfoil and the* Potamogeton *pond weeds, have sodium at concentrations 10 to 400 times that of the woody plants moose browse on during the winter. Moose exhibit definite preferences for these over other kinds of water plants, and they have favourite lakes that they visit, to the exclusion of others. The ideal lake for a salt-hungry moose is shallow, with a high mineral content and a good flow of water in and out of it. These features and the density of water plants determine how much salt a moose can acquire over the summer. There is some suggestion that they may build up a reserve of sodium to try to get through the winter. They seem to store sodium in their large rumen, whose fluids make up 15 percent of their total body weight. Over the winter, they deplete this reserve.*

*It has also been suggested that the need for sodium and the intense use of aquatic plants may cause population cycles in moose. In years of moose abundance, the moose eat, trample and otherwise destroy*

*Accomplished swimmers, moose will venture far into lakes and rivers in search of water plants that are rich in sodium salts.*

*aquatic-plant populations. They also strip the sodium-rich bark from trees and eventually kill them. Thus the moose population declines until the plant populations recover.*

*Not all of the foraging ecology of moose revolves around sodium. They must meet other nutrient demands for protein, vitamins and carbohydrates. When aquatic plants are available, the moose pursue a foraging strategy that maximizes their energy intake as opposed to minimizing the time they spend feeding. This energy-maximizing strategy might be expected in large adult moose faced with building up fat reserves. Compared with smaller mammals, moose have few predators to fear aside from wolves, and a healthy adult can usually fend off wolves in summer months. Mothers with calves, however, must compromise. They often swim out to islands without wolves and feed in areas with less energy- and sodium-rich plant material. Thus cows with calves are considering the risk of predation in their foraging tactics.*

# Elk  *Cervus canadensis*

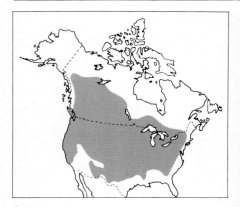

**Mammal:** *Cervus canadensis* — elk, wapiti; the second largest animal in deer family

**Meaning of Name:** *Cervus* (Latin for deer or stag); *canadensis* (of Canada); wapiti is from a Shawnee Indian name meaning ''white rump''

**Description:** widely branching majestic antlers arise from large burrs high on the head; each antler consists of one heavy beam sweeping up and back from the head and over the shoulder with several tines; tawny brown in summer; darker on face, belly, neck and legs; prominent pale-coloured patch on rump and buttocks; in winter, darker brown head, neck, belly and legs contrast with paler brown on back and sides; males have long dense mane

**Total Length:** male, 7.5 to 8.9 feet; female, 5.9 to 7.9 feet

**Tail:** male, 4 to 7 inches; female, 4.5 to 7 inches

**Weight:** male, 584 to 1,100 pounds; female, 414 to 660 pounds

**Gestation:** 249 to 262 days

**Litter Size:** 1 (sometimes 2)

**Age of Maturity:** male, 2 years but must wait until 4 or 5 years when it can challenge other stags; female, 2.5 years

**Longevity:** 14 to 26 years

**Diet:** largely grasses and herbs but also a variety of woody plants; if grasses and shoots are scarce, it will strip bark from trees

**Habitat:** woodlands and open lands, mountain meadows, foothills and plains; frequents swamps, coniferous forests and cuttings

**Predators:** mountain lion, wolf, lynx and coyote; wolverine, bobcat, black bear and golden eagle will kill unprotected young

**Dental Formula:** 0/3, 1/1, 3/3, 3/3 = 34 teeth

*Newborn elk are defenceless and have spotted coats for camouflage.*

The elk, or wapiti, is one of the most vocal of all mammals, and the sound of bugling elk epitomizes the Canadian autumn wilderness. Some attribute it to Europe and Russia as well, but there is no firm agreement on whether the elk is a different species from *Cervus elaphus*, the red deer of Europe. The two are at least close relatives that may have been genetically in contact as recently as the last Ice Age when the Bering Strait land bridge connected this continent with Russia. But since the two are now geographically separated, most people consider the elk a different species.

The elk is generally larger than the red deer, but its bugle is higher-pitched, a difference that is a reflection of their dissimilar habitats. As forest animals, red deer require a call designed to travel through vegetation — a deep low-frequency bugle that is not muffled by thick greenery. Elk, which frequent forest-edge and open habitats, use a higher-frequency sound that travels well across unobstructed open space.

Elk are harem breeders, and the bugle is an advertisement designed to lure females into the harem, broadcasting the size and strength of the bugler male. Studies have shown that bugling and roaring are honest advertisements of male strength as they demand large amounts of energy. Thus the most vocal males do have the highest reproductive success.

Because bugling is a valid test of male vigour, females are attracted to those that bugle the loudest and most often. A bugling male may be of higher genetic quality than a noncaller, and at the very least, he is unlikely to be weakened by diseases that are potentially contagious or hereditary. Subdominant males that try to bluff by bugling are immediately challenged by a dominant territorial male and attacked if necessary. Thus the bugle is a reliable cue that females can use to choose a mate.

There is considerable anecdotal evidence that in this species, it is the female that chooses the male and not vice versa. A male may try to herd females and to keep them in the harem with threat displays and even antler attacks, but this tends to be more a demonstration of his prowess than an effective tactic, as a female can easily leave when the male is preoccupied with male rivals or courting.

It is to the female's advantage to examine as many males as possible and to use as many criteria as possible to assess their qualities as mates. Antlers are used to impress females, and males deprived of their antlers are unable to attract and hold mates, regardless of their size. Antlers reach weights close to 30 pounds with spans of 5 feet and require special strengthening of the neck muscles.

Males advertise their reproductive state and territorial position with

*The harem-breeding system of elk has favoured males evolving huge antlers and the powerful neck and chest muscles necessary to defeat rival males.*

smells given off by their urine and by a facial gland. Human observers may find the idea repulsive, but since reproductive hormones are excreted in the urine, it also makes a reliable signal of reproductive conditions. Males spray their belly, mane and face with urine, often spreading it further by urinating on the ground and wallowing in it until mud and urine become caked on the fur and face. This is mainly an activity of large bulls, and the smell of their wallows excites young male elk and cows.

The cost of all this male advertising is high, and it dictates important changes in the feeding and movement strategies of bulls. During summer, they must feed more than females, moving greater distances searching for browse if they are to accumulate the fat and muscle needed to withstand the fall rutting season. Bulls in summer are less sociable than females. In open habitats, however, they may band together to gain added protection from predators.

After the rut, bulls are energy-de-pleted, and their antlers make them conspicuous to predators such as wolves, which are adept at cutting out the most vulnerable animals. In forest habitats, males may lose their antlers and forage alone, while in open areas, they tend to retain their antlers for a longer time because they are used in dominance contests for access to food.

Females tend to be highly social. They depend on herd living to reduce predation on themselves and their calves. A group of females, for example, will attack and kick coyotes, and they will run as a unit from more serious predators, with older, more experienced animals acting as leaders. Females, however, do not entrust the welfare of their newborn calves to group defence. Calves are born away from the herd by lone females that seek out some protected area of cover. This seems a clear example of the origins of elk as forest animals that have only recently become herding animals in the semiopen areas of North America. Their calves are born with a speckled coat used as camouflage in the

*The loud bugling call of a bull elk at rutting season carries for miles, luring females and discouraging rival males.*

dappled light of the forest, and unlike plains-adapted animals, such as bison or pronghorns, the calf of the elk is relatively helpless and slow to begin running.

The "hider" strategy of the mother elk requires some elaborate precautions. She meticulously eats the afterbirth and even the soil and leaf litter in the area of the newborn calf to minimize scents that predators might pick up. She may even eat the feces and urine of her offspring as an additional precaution. The mother visits her calf only half a dozen times a day to nurse it, keeping separate from yet close enough to the calf to hear it bleat. She will attack smaller predators, such as coyotes, and may decoy larger predators away. A distinctive female alarm bark will cause the calf to crouch and remain still. The calf may stay in seclusion for as long as three weeks before it joins a nursery herd of mothers, calves and yearlings.

The mothers, calves and juveniles herd together, separate from the bulls, until the autumn rut. Both groups shift with the snow melt, moving to higher and cooler ground as the summer progresses. Elks are generalized grazers and browsers, feeding on a wide variety of grasses, shrubbery and other vegetation.

Elk have been eliminated from most of their southern and eastern range, but in the western mountain and plains areas, they are still abundant, with herds totalling some 400,000 or more. In the West, hundreds of thousands of sportsmen hunt elk each autumn; their numbers have increased several hundred percent since the 1950s. But naturalists also search out elk, and both groups exert pressure on elk populations. It has been shown, for example, that cross-country skiers may influence winter elk movements at a season when movement is a potentially large drain on energy reserves. As elk users increase, management plans that have traditionally met the needs of humans will have to deal with the reduced range for elk. Urban expansion, mining, logging and housing and recreational developments continue to diminish the amount of wilderness every year.

### What's in a Name?

*The use of Latin binomials, such as* Odocoileus virginianus *to name the white-tailed deer, does not sit well with many people. Latin is a dead language, and few people ever study it — not even biologists. Scientific names and the system of nomenclature stand as a barrier between nature and those who would contemplate it. Rare is the nature lover who will go to the trouble of learning what the difference between an order and genus is or what the artiodactyls are. Such pleasures are usually reserved for university students training to become professional biologists. Nevertheless, anyone who enjoys observing and thinking about nature will find Latin names worth the small amount of trouble they take to learn. Few things help more in understanding and appreciating the diversity of living creatures.*

People have always classified living organisms. The essence of the system has been a lumping of like with like: chairs look like chairs, and tables look like tables. Biologists approached animal classification with the same method for many centuries. However, with the discovery of the principle of evolution, biological classifiers known as taxonomists, or systemicists, became obsessed with developing a classification system that reflected the evolutionary process and the different evolutionary relationships that exist between different kinds of organisms.

Splitting things into categories is the simplest way to handle information, and that is how biological identification proceeds. When we look at an organism, we subject it to a series of questions designed to sort it into categories that are ever more finely divided.

The most fundamental category — the kingdom — is easily grasped. Is it within the plant kingdom or the animal kingdom? Even this general classification is a bit more complicated than it used to be, since there are now five recognized kingdoms (including ones for bacteria, protozoans and fungi).

Groupings, such as kingdoms, are based on shared characteristics, with biologists looking for similarities and differences between groups. The differences between plants and animals are obvious, and the similarities within the groups are also clear. But as we proceed through the classification system looking for ever smaller groupings, the characteristics are less obvious and require careful study.

The animals are next divided into groups called phyla. Mammals are members of the phylum Chordata, which means they have an internal skeleton and a large nerve cord in the back. Thus birds, reptiles, amphibians, bony fish and several other groups, along with the mammals, are all chordates. To the evolutionary biologist, the significance of such shared features as a nerve cord or internal skeleton is that all the chordates had a common ancestor from which they diverged.

The next major division is the class. Mammals form the class Mammalia. All the members have fur, mammary glands and some other less obvious shared features. They are a neat grouping, clearly separated from other classes, such as the reptiles. The class Mammalia can then be divided further. For example, all the mammals that have shearing carnassial teeth are placed in the order Carnivora. The order is then divided into families, such as the cats, the dogs and the bears. All the members of the dog family share certain common features which indicate that dogs, wolves and foxes had a common ancestor and that they are different from bears or cats.

A distinct organism, such as the wolf, has two Latin names, Canis lupus, that refer to the next two divisions, the genus and the species. The genus is a grouping of closely related species (coyotes, dingoes, domestic dogs and jackals are all members of the genus Canis), while the second part of the binomial, the species name, distinguishes the individual within the genus. Thus the wolf is Canis lupus, while the coyote is Canis latrans.

All living things can be traced through this hierarchical structure from the species we see today back through groups that reflect a long and diverging evolutionary history. The wolf provides an apt example of the classification process: kingdom, Animalia; phylum, Chordata; family, Canidae; genus, Canis; species, lupus.

*The neat system of biological classification breaks down with some species, such as the pronghorn, a graceful dryland runner that shares a common ancestor with the pig.*

This is certainly not an easy system to absorb quickly, and some species do not fit neatly into it. Biologists still disagree, for example, on whether pandas are members of the bear or raccoon family, and many fossil records are incomplete, with only bits and pieces of evidence that could fit an animal equally well into different categories. Categories are often hard to assess, and there is constant debate on the merits of classifying a group as a separate family. Is the pronghorn different enough from other artiodactyls that it should be placed in its own family, or is it better placed in Bovidae, along with bison and cattle? These kinds of questions will always be there awaiting refinement of our knowledge. But the system is worth learning now.

The organization of diversity is the first step toward understanding and enjoying the animal kingdom fully. Things are certainly clearer if one uses Latin binomials when deciding whether the brush wolf is a grey wolf, a timber wolf or a coyote. It is definitely Canis latrans, a close relative of Canis lupus, the grey wolf. And from the evolutionary perspective, we can appreciate the graceful beauty of a pronghorn a little more once we know that it shared a common artiodactyl ancestor with the pig.

# *Sheep, Oxen & Goats* Bovidae

Bovids are grassland animals that originated in Europe and later invaded Africa, Asia and North America. A few species have become creatures of the high mountains and tundra. Yaks, muskox and mountain goats dominate the top of both the Old and New Worlds.

Another group, the antelope, radiated to tropical savannas. During the Ice Ages, when the boreal forest progressed southward, most bovids moved with it into dry parts of Africa and India. This geographical area remains the centre of diversity today, where antelope, kudu, eland, wildebeest and buffalo dominate the natural landscape. Few species have penetrated into North America, because the passage through the Bering land bridge filtered out groups that were not adapted to cold conditions. Many of the species that did exist in North America, such as giant bison and many kinds of antelope, became extinct in the Pleistocene epoch, one million years ago.

Bovids differ from cervids in several distinct ways. Instead of antlers, they have horns that are never shed and are usually found on both sexes. The family is more a grazing than a browsing family, but goats are excellent browsers of shrubs.

The world supports 111 different species of bovids. The northern part of this continent is home to several species that represent distinct radiations within the families. The mountain goat, or mountain antelope, follows the typical goat pattern of being restricted to cliff areas with limited amounts of meadow grazing. The sheep graze in meadows and grasslands, retreating to rocky areas when danger threatens. United by their fear of predators, sheep are more social

than goats, which tend to be less concerned with predators and territorially defensive about food.

The muskox is a type of goat antelope that has become adapted to the far northern tundra. Bison are allied with a recently evolved and advanced grassland lineage that has given rise to cattle, yaks and African buffalo. The pronghorns are a relatively distinct group found only in North America, the equivalent in design of the African antelope. North America used to host many other kinds of bovids, but they became extinct during the last Ice Age.

## Born to Run

One of the best ways to deal with a problem is to run away from it. That discovery has been made by many successful lineages but especially by the artiodactyls, which count in their membership some of the world's fastest land animals. The ancestors of speedsters, such as antelopes or pronghorns, were slow, squat piglike animals, and the evolution of today's running animals was in response to the new demands and opportunities offered by the open plains. In order to become fleet-footed, artiodactyls had to evolve from a body suited for a life close to the ground, rooting and grubbing much as hogs do now.

The most obvious design simplification came in the feet. The number of toes was reduced to produce a compact hoof so that only the tips of the toes make contact with the ground. This has several advantages. On uneven ground, there is the danger of breaking a wider foot. Reducing the size of the foot also means that the body weight will be more cleanly distributed on the bearing surface, and more importantly, by reducing the size and

weight of the foot, less energy is required to move the foot back and forth.

Moving a heavy foot at the end of a long limb is analogous to lifting a large weight with one's arm extended. The energetic cost of extending the long artiodactyl limb is also reduced by making the shin lean and economical. The lower legs of antelopes, like those of racehorses, look almost absurdly thin, as though they have no strength at all. In fact, they are tightly bound with ligaments and tendons that run to the large upper-leg muscles. Most of the power in the leg comes from the muscles on the upper area close to the body, which has the advantage of keeping the centre of gravity near the body so that the runner can leap and manoeuvre around obstacles and still retain its balance.

The length of the stride is one of the two basic determinants of a runner's speed. Artiodactyls have eliminated the clavicle, or collarbone, allowing the shoulder blade to shift forward and lengthen the stride by as much as 20 percent. The backbone is also used to increase the stride. Fast runners, such as the pronghorn or cheetah, have a spine that is extremely flexible. It bends and curves in on itself in a concave shape as the hind legs reach forward so that the hind hooves are actually ahead of the forelimbs. Then as the forelegs lift up and reach ahead with the back legs pushing, the backbone and spinal muscles unleash, shoving the animal's entire forequarters ahead. This coiling and unleashing of the backbone with the hind legs swinging ahead of the forelimbs is the hallmark

The muskox is the most northern of all the widely dispersed bovids.

Pronghorns are the fastest middle-distance runners on Earth, reaching speeds of 61 miles per hour.

of the fastest mammals.

But speed comes only partly from the length of the stride. The second basic adaptation is the rate of the stride. The bones have been reduced in number to allow more rapid movement, but the number of flexible joints has actually increased. An animal cannot move faster than its feet, and the rate at which the foot moves ahead is determined by how many joints are moving it. Adding another moving joint with muscles to pull the limb ahead increases the rate at which the end of the limb moves. Not only do the moving spine and shoulder blades act as extra joints, but the artiodactyl's foot has another moving joint within the toes. The heel of the animal is raised off the ground, freeing the toes to act as units of propulsion.

There is a special ligament called the "springing ligament" that is attached to the toes and runs backward behind the shinbone. When the animal puts weight on its foot, the foot lowers and stretches the toes into a horizontal position, pulling the ligament out like an elastic band. As the weight is released, the elastic

ligament flicks the foot back, a characteristic obvious to anyone who has watched trotting horses. This flexible strip gives the foot a final bit of thrust as it leaves the ground, without the expense and weight of a muscular unit pushing and pulling.

Artiodactyls also have a ligament to lighten the neck. Grazers with long, striding legs need a long neck. This, coupled with the weight of antlers and horns, would normally require a huge and heavy set of neck muscles. But instead, artiodactyls have a long neck ligament, the nuchal ligament, that runs along the back of the neck to the vertebrae between the shoulder blades. This makes it easy to maintain various postures of the head without excessively heavy neck muscles.

Finally, as every human runner knows, it is impossible to sprint with a full belly. The fastest North American mammal, the pronghorn, has a very small stomach — half the size of slower grazers — and proportionately larger lungs and heart. This smaller stomach means that the pronghorn, like other specialized athletes, has a more selective diet that includes the most nutritious plants on the range.

# *Pronghorn* Antilocapra americana

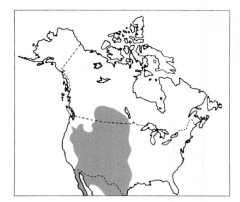

**Mammal:** *Antilocapra americana* — pronghorn, antelope

**Meaning of Name:** *Antilocapra* (horned animal — probably an antelope — and she-goat); perhaps a corruption of *antholops*, which seems to refer to the beautiful eyes of the animal; *americana* (of America)

**Description:** very large eyes; males and females have black horns with an anterior prong and curved tips; horns are covered by a layer of skin with specialized hairs; tan back with a creamy white rosette on the rump; bucks have black face that extends as far as the base of the horns; does have black on muzzle only, with the rest of the rostrum brown, fading to pale grey about the horns; 2 white throat bars

**Total Length:** 4.1 to 4.8 feet

**Tail:** 2.3 to 7 inches

**Weight:** male, 100 to 150 pounds; female, 71 to 104 pounds

**Gestation:** 230 to 252 days

**Litter Size:** 1 to 3 (usually 2)

**Age of Maturity:** 1.5 years (however, males cannot mate successfully until they are 3 years old)

**Longevity:** usually 4.5 years in the wild (maximum 14 years)

**Diet:** both browser and grazer; wide variety of weeds, shrubs, forbs, grasses, cacti and other plants; likes sagebrush

**Habitat:** gently to strongly rolling plains, prairies and foothills; prefers areas with water and an abundance of low-growing vegetation

**Predators:** coyote is main predator; also bobcat and grizzly bear; bobcat, golden eagle and raven prey upon newborn

**Dental Formula:** 0/3, 0/1, 3/3, 3/3 = 32 teeth

Pronghorns are among the fastest animals in the world. They have been clocked at 61 miles per hour, slightly slower than a cheetah, but a cheetah gives out after less than a mile, while a pronghorn can run at least 4 miles at a steady 45 miles an hour. It is probably the world's fastest middle-distance mammal.

The speed of the pronghorn is an adaptation to the open plains. A large male weighs less than 150 pounds, and like many small animals, its only defence against most large carnivores, such as wolves, is to outrun them. Its skill at doing so has made the pronghorn a relatively incautious animal, more likely to investigate a strange intrusion than to retreat immediately. The first settlers of the grasslands found that by waving flags, they could

*With large males weighing only 150 pounds, the pronghorn's only defence from predators is running.*

attract pronghorns within easy rifle range, and the pronghorn population followed the same pattern as the buffalo's. North American herds of some 20 million to 40 million were reduced to fewer than 30,000 animals.

Pronghorns also resemble the bison in their migratory habits. As the seasons progress, they are constantly on the move, adjusting their position along a circuit according to the snow and the availability of food. The range may cover a couple of hundred miles, as the pronghorn is a selective grazer that seeks out high-energy food — nutritious forbs and shrubby browse. It does not do well on coarse grasses.

*Unlike other bovids, male pronghorns shed their horns after the rut.*

Pronghorns have a polygynous breeding system. Larger males may scent-mark a territory and try to attract a group of females to it, although there have been reports that in some areas, males try to join and guard a harem instead. This difference appears to depend on the quality of the forage. If the forage is lush and worth defending, males will set up territories, opting to join a harem if it is not.

After the rut, males join up with mixed-sex herds for the winter. During winter, various bands may coalesce to form large herds of several thousand individuals.

Females that are about to give birth in spring pursue a hider strategy that is somewhat out of keeping with their open-plains habitat. They leave the group and search out some protected spot where, in most cases, they give birth to twins. These kids stay hidden for up to three weeks, even though they can stand within hours after being born. Because pronghorns offer no group defence to predators, relying on their speed to escape, kids that join the group too early could be cut out from the herd by coyotes and attacked.

Mothers and young kids band together into nursery herds for the summer. The young males disperse the next spring and travel in all-male bands until they can achieve territorial status.

Pronghorns are unusual in that males shed their horns after the rut, whereas other bovids retain theirs. This characteristic has led some taxonomists to classify pronghorns as a separate family, the American antelopes of Antilocapridae. North America used to be home to more than a dozen different species of pronghorns, but all except one of them have become extinct. The prevailing opinion is that the pronghorns are a part of the bovid family and represent a separate radiation, or subfamily, within it.

Pronghorns have now recovered to population levels of around half a million animals.

## Spreading the Risk

*When it comes to hunting, most mammalian carnivores are creatures of habit. Once they have discovered a prey item and a means of finding it, they will specialize in that until it becomes scarce. Artiodactyl fawns make an ideal prey for many carnivores, as they are tender, are easily carried and put up little resistance. Wolves, coyotes, bobcats and grizzlies all eat fawns and calves of grazing animals during the birthing season.*

*This tendency of intelligent carnivores to specialize on particular prey at certain seasons is said to be responsible for the phenomenon of birth synchrony, whereby females give birth around the same time. The young of females that give birth late*

*suffer higher predation because they attract the attention of predators that have learned how to find infants. Females that give birth early, before predators develop their taste and skills, do much better. Females that force the birthing season back into early spring find that bad weather becomes a greater risk than predation.*

*An example of birth synchrony is seen in bison. Eighty percent of the calves are born within a three-week period, and the same is true for elk and some deer; the periods for pronghorn, caribou and mountain sheep are even shorter.*

*The synchronous birthing of large herding animals has the potential of swamping predators. During much of the year, no vulnerable fawns or calves are available, and the predators exist at relatively low numbers dispersed over a wide area, so that at calving season, there are more calves than they can harvest. Thus the young of mothers that time their birthing at the height of the season will suffer the lowest predation. Unfortunately for this idea, nonherders or those in small bands, such as white-tails and sheep, show the same amount of synchrony as large herders such as buffalo.*

*There is a difficulty with the idea that birth synchrony in these species is an antipredator adaptation. Wolves and grizzlies live a long time, and they have good memories, while naïve individuals represent a small segment of the population. Certainly predators soon learn when the calving season is and are then able to exploit it annually for the rest of their lives. It seems more likely that mothers birth synchronously according to the demands of the climate and use other behavioural measures to spread their risk and reduce the return to predators so that they will search for alternative food items.*

*The crucial time for an artiodactyl is from birth until the young animal can run with its mother and the herd. In this period, the mother can spread the risk using several different tactics. Deer with more than one fawn hide them in different locations. Caribou have been known to deal with wolf and bear predation by*

dispersing into the mountain areas to increase the effort that wolves and bears must expend, making their search for alternative prey more economical.

This hiding strategy has been studied in pronghorn antelope. Coyotes seem to be the main predators of young pronghorns, and new mothers will stand guard within sight of their fawns' hiding places, occasionally attacking predators, running patrolling coyotes down and trying to kick them. But the pronghorn mother using the hider strategy must make a complex tactical decision. She must remain close enough to her young to be aware of danger to them, yet not so close as to reveal their location to intelligent predators, such as the coyote. Females try to stand about 70 yards away from their young, just far enough to make it unprofitable for coyotes to search the surrounding area. A coyote would have to search

a large area around the mother, providing a lower average return on its efforts than it could get hunting ground squirrels.

Females also have a second defence. In theory, a coyote could simply follow a mother going to feed her calves, but mothers stay away from their young for so long that, once more, coyotes have more to gain by hunting ground squirrels.

Mother pronghorns are not in complete control of the situation. In order to keep track of their young, they have to look at them, at the risk of revealing the fawns' location to predators. A patient coyote that can narrow the search by observing the direction of the mother's most frequent gaze can potentially obtain twice the energy it gets from ground squirrels, making the effort worthwhile.

Eighty percent of bison calves are born within a three-week period each spring. Such synchronous birthing may reduce the risk of predation.

# *Bison* Bison bison

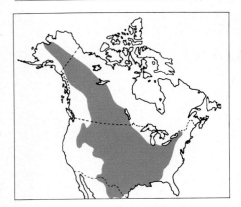

**Mammal:** *Bison bison* — bison, buffalo; the largest terrestrial mammal

**Meaning of Name:** *Bison* (wild ox or buffalo)

**Description:** massive head and forequarters, which appear out of proportion to its slim hindquarters; massive hump on shoulders; tail has terminal hair tassel; short black horns on the side of the head; large nostrils; slate-blue tongue; matted, woolly undercoat; head, shoulders and forelegs are covered with a shaggy dark brown mane; hindquarters are coppery brown; head and beard are almost black

**Total Length:** male, 9.9 to 12.5 feet; female, 6.5 to 7.5 feet

**Tail:** male, 17 to 32 inches; female, 18 to 21 inches

**Weight:** male, 1,014 to 2,000 pounds; female, 794 to 1,100 pounds

**Gestation:** 270 to 300 days

**Litter Size:** 1 every 1 or 2 years

**Age of Maturity:** male, 2 to 3 years; female, some as yearlings but usually 2 to 4 years

**Longevity:** 20 years in the wild; potential may be 40 years

**Diet:** grazer; mainly grasses, forbs, sedges and other ground forage

**Habitat:** wide range of habitats; open, arid plains, open forests, grasslands and meadows, river valleys and mountainous areas

**Predators:** grizzly bear, grey wolf, puma; predators usually forced to prey upon young or old as even a pack of wolves cannot easily overcome a lone bison

**Dental Formula:** 0/3, 0/1, 3/3, 3/3 = 32 teeth

In the last century, bison numbered between 40 and 60 million in North America. The first white explorers to reach the western grasslands reported great herds blackening the plains as far as the eye could see.

The bison, also called the buffalo, was the mainstay of the Plains Indians, but neither they nor wolves and silver-tipped grizzly bears constrained its numbers. A full-grown bull weighs 1 ton and stands 6 feet high at the shoulder, the largest land animal in North America. A pack of wolves or a grizzly no doubt found the bull too formidable a foe to bother and probably took only calves, the old and the

*Winter starvation is one of the few natural threats an adult bison faces.*

injured. Winter kills in blizzards were likely the main sources of mortality.

The Plains Indians made use of the bison's stampeding behaviour. When they hunted, they would run the bison over cliffs or into box canyons for easy dispatches. But the Indians themselves were subject to population limits, disease, starvation and warfare, and they never threatened the abundance of buffalo.

It was the arrival of the settlers from Europe, along with railroads and pro-

fessional buffalo hunters, that quickly reduced the buffalo to bleaching bones on the prairies. Eventually, even the bones were picked by the destitute Plains Indians, who sold them by the trainload to be ground into fertilizer. In less than a century, the millions had been reduced to fewer than 1,000. It was only the existence of a few isolated populations that kept the buffalo from going the way of the passenger pigeon.

Ironically, much of the shortgrass prairie where the buffalo once thrived was suitable only for livestock grazing. The irony persists today. Buffalo grow better on a natural range and have a more efficient digestion system than cattle when they are eating native vegetation. Cattle are only more efficient under feedlot conditions or when being fed high-quality hay. A bison is also better able to withstand the winter of the plains and to deal with predators.

Bison are compact and coated with a thick shaggy fur that once enabled them to range as far as the Northwest Territories. However, it is unlikely that their fine adaptation to the grasslands will ever be exploited on a scale comparable to what existed in the past. Bison are migratory, moving hundreds of miles with the season. Their routes were often traditional, involving hundreds of thousands of animals that wore deep paths across the landscape. Some of these traditional buffalo routes are still visible from the air.

Bison had a great effect on local conditions within the grasslands. Their wallows became temporary ponds in spring and home to salamanders and other aquatic organisms. They often frequented prairie dog towns, browsing on the plants that prairie dogs avoided. Their hoof marks and dung then favoured the growth of the grasses used by the prairie dogs. The system of grasses extracting soil nutrients and being continuously cropped and turned into dung by bison is thought to have been a major factor in building the deep, rich organic soils of the prairies. Bison grazing is thought to have encouraged many shortgrass species that tend to

*Bison rid themselves of old fur, flies and skin parasites by wallowing in the dust.*

become extinct locally when there is nothing to keep the vegetation short and open. Cowbirds followed the herds, eating the insects that the bison disturbed.

If populations were stable at about 50 million and the average female reproduced every two years, it can be calculated that there were at least a billion pounds of buffalo being recycled every year by predators, parasites, scavengers and decomposers.

Bison are sexually dimorphic, the males being much larger than the females, and bulls attempt to mate with as many females as possible in the late summer and autumn. The rut is extremely loud, and the roars of the bulls may be heard five miles away. They use a variety of snorts, foot stamps, urination and other threats to intimidate rivals and to attract females. The strategy of a bull is not to assemble a harem but to follow and defend a female until she is ready to mate and to repel the advances of other bulls. Contesting males stand side by side, comparing sizes. If contestants are evenly matched and the threatening, roaring matches escalate into a fight, the males will charge and ram each other with their heads. This accounts for the bull's massive front end. They use their relatively short horns to try to gore their opponent in the belly or flanks if he should falter.

Females usually give birth to a single calf in spring or summer. The calf is well adapted for life on the open plains. It is able to stand within half an hour and to run after three or four hours. The calf stays with the mother in a nursery herd and trails close by for a period of three weeks. It may then mix with other young calves in the herd, but it continues to recognize its mother and may not be weaned for almost a year. A mother, and sometimes the entire herd, will defend a calf against intruders. But large herds usually respond to danger by stampeding away. Individual bison can be dangerously aggressive, even outside the rutting season, and have been known to kill humans who fail to respect their wild and powerful character.

## Rumination

*People who become strict vegetarians soon learn that they have to devote a lot of effort toward food selection. They must devise schemes to obtain adequate protein and B vitamins, or they must rely on commercial preparations. The reasons for this are simple. Humans are omnivores with a physiology designed for a diverse diet that includes some animal protein and vitamins. A diet of only plants is a low-nutrient diet. Much of a plant is composed of structural support molecules, tough items that make up the bulk of plant biomass and act as the plant skeleton. The generalized mammalian stomach is inefficient at breaking down and processing these molecules and liberating what nutrients they do contain.*

*Artiodactyl grazers have devised a solution to the problem posed by such a bulky low-nutrient hard-to-digest diet; they have evolved a large multichambered gut. Their stomach has enlarged and divided into several*

*chambers, one of which is known as the rumen.*

*The rumen is part of a system of mechanical and chemical breakdown in which the grazing ruminant swallows, without chewing, fresh and relatively tough vegetation. The saliva that follows the food down helps control its moisture content and the acidity of the gut. The fresh and coarse material passes into the rumen, where digestive enzymes mix with the material in a great soup of fluids, saliva, plant material and fermenting microorganisms.*

*There is a sieve-like structure that skims off coarse particles, now softened by the enzymes in the gut, and the mass of material can be regurgitated back into the mouth several hours later. The animal then chews its cud, as it is called. This allows the animal to adjust its feeding time so that harvesting is done when weather is better or there is greater visibility for predator detection. The time-consuming job of shredding material and grinding it finely is left for a time when the animal is resting in a safe and comfortable spot.*

*The rumen is a fermentation chamber, home to distinct and specialized microorganisms. They do the difficult chemical work of digesting plant molecules, such as cellulose and lignin, the plant material from which lumber and paper are made. Once the nutrients of the finely shredded material are extracted, they can pass through the*

*sieve and continue their passage along the other chambers of the stomach and down the intestine. The digested plant products and any of the fermenting organisms that move down this route can then be further digested and absorbed into the bloodstream. Where the small intestine turns into the large intestine, there is a final large fermentation chamber, the cecum, that finishes the extraction process.*

*The result of this system is that ruminants not only break down plant material efficiently, but they also obtain many vitamins that are synthesized by the fermenting bacteria. The heat given off by this fermentation may also be of some use in cold climates. Cold- and dry-climate artiodactyls also enjoy an additional digestive advantage over grazers that use different digestive systems. They can recycle nitrogen wastes from the bloodstream into the rumen. The mammalian body is continually breaking down proteins that produce urea in the blood — a chemical that the kidneys filter out and excrete as urine. In winter, in order to cut their body-heat requirements, northern mammals minimize the amount of snow and ice they eat, which reduces the amount of hot urine they must excrete.*

*Ruminants can recycle urea from the blood into the rumen where microorganisms feed on it, somewhat like fertilizing an internal compost pile to get the microorganisms working more effectively. This has a wide-ranging implication: it has allowed ruminant grazers to dominate the high Arctic and the driest deserts, both climates that place a premium on water conservation.*

*The other large mammalian grazers are from the order Perissodactyla, which includes horses, tapirs and rhinoceroses. While they lack a rumen, they use a hind-gut digestive chamber. There are advantages and disadvantages to both the artiodactyl and perissodactyl systems. A ruminator, such as a cow, can extract two-thirds of the nutrients from its food, whereas a horse extracts less than half. Horses, however, can pass the food through the system, making room for more in as little as two days. A cow may take close to four days to pass the same meal through its system. This is why horses are known as ''hay burners.'' They have evolved a less efficient but higher rate of extraction.*

*The difference in the two systems probably accounts for the different body sizes and species diversities of the groups. Ruminants can specialize on certain plants that hind-gut digestors cannot. A ruminant, being more efficient, needs a smaller volume of food, so it can select rarer but more nutritious species. Ruminants can afford to be small-bodied, like the pronghorn antelope, since they exist on relatively less food. This is why ruminants are ecologically more diverse than hind-gut fermenters. On the other hand, if both a ruminant and a hind-gut fermenter are forced to exist on the same amount of vegetation, the ruminator could grow larger, since it gets the most out of its food.*

*The largest grazers, such as elephants, are hind-gut fermenters that can process huge volumes of coarse woody material quickly. They follow a quantity-not-quality strategy and therefore must be large and must range widely. Hind-gut fermenters also have more control over their rate of gut clearance — the more they eat, the faster it passes through, so they can adjust behaviourally to the quality of the forage. Ruminators ruminate at a*

*slow steady rate and cannot vary their rate of digestion.*

*Since body size affects so many other traits, such as predator resistance and cold tolerance, the development of the rumen has had profound implications for humans. It is the ruminators that humans have specialized in domesticating, and it is the ruminating gut that is the model for much of our existing food production, such as bread, cheese, beer and yogurt. Much of modern biotechnology is based on the fermentation process that artiodactyls have been using for millions of years.*

The efficient digestion of vegetation by rumination allows bison, **left**, to live at high densities in dry grasslands and mountain goats, **above**, to survive on thinly vegetated cliffs.

# *Mountain Goat* Oreamnos americanus

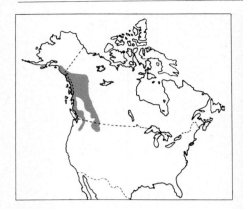

**Mammal:** *Oreamnos americanus* — mountain goat

**Meaning of Name:** *Oreamnos* (mountain lamb); *americanus* (of America)

**Description:** short, black recurved horns with basal annulations and smooth shiny tips; pair of black glands at base of horns; creamy white; sometimes brownish dorsal line or yellow wash; black lips, nostrils, horns and hooves

**Total Length:** male, 5.1 to 6.7 feet; female, 3.9 to 5.2 feet

**Tail:** male, 3.7 to 5.5 inches; female, 3.5 to 4.7 inches

**Weight:** male, 143 to 249 pounds; female, 100 to 212 pounds

**Gestation:** 147 to 178 days

**Litter Size:** 1 or 2 (occasionally 3)

**Age of Maturity:** male, 39 months; female, 27 months

**Longevity:** 12 years in the wild (maximum is 14 years for males, 18 years for females)

**Diet:** part grazer, part browser; feeds on various high-mountain vegetation such as grasses, mosses, lichens, woody plants and herbs; salt licks are important

**Habitat:** rugged mountains with steep slopes; prefers steep grassy talus slopes at the base of cliffs in alpine tundra or subalpine areas; associated with low temperatures and heavy snowfall

**Predators:** mountain lion, eagle, grizzly bear, wolverine, wolf, coyote; eagles prey upon the young

**Dental Formula:** 0/3, 0/1, 3/3, 3/3 = 32 teeth

The mountain goat is the most skilled rock climber of all North American mammals. It moves with confidence along ledges barely wide enough to accommodate it. Mountain goats will leap from ledge to ledge across deep chasms without hesitation and have a repertoire of manoeuvres that would excite the most skilled mountain climbers. Goats have been seen in virtual free-falls, descending steep, two-sided rock chutes by bouncing from wall to wall to break their speed as they go. One goat that walked far out along a thin ledge above a 400-foot drop found the ledge petering out and executed a cartwheel to turn around — planting its front feet on the ledge and walking its back legs up along the cliff face until it was turned and could retreat.

A mountain goat's legs are short and muscular, with hooves designed to take the impact and wear of rock while still providing spring and traction. The two-toed hoof has a stiff outer rim with a flexible pebbled pad on the central surface. The dew claws (thumbs) provide a grip when moving down against a steep surface.

Goats are at home where predators are unable to roam, but they pay a price for this security as there is little grazing on the cliffs they inhabit. This makes mountain goats far less social than mountain sheep, which travel in bands for protection. Mountain goats are more solitary and, unlike sheep, will vigorously defend feeding areas in times of food shortage.

*A calm disposition and fearless agility make mountain goats skilled rock climbers.*

The horns of the female mountain goat are almost the same size as the male's, and both sexes will use them to defend feeding areas. They do not bother with a drawn-out ritual of horn comparison, as do the more social sheep, but put interlopers to flight as soon as possible, trying to drive their sharp lancelike horns into their opponent's flanks and belly. Sometimes, they will try to butt each other over cliffs. Males are not dominant over large nannies that are able to hold their own feeding territories.

Horns also serve as weapons against predators. They tend to be better weapons than antlers, and this may be one reason why bovid females have horns. A mother goat will stay with her kid for up to a year and will defend it aggressively against lynx, wolverine and other predators. Predation seems to be a relatively minor pressure on mountain goat populations, and only when adults venture into meadows to feed do they become vulnerable to predators, such as grizzlies. Golden eagles have been seen trying to knock adults from their ledges, and they do take the occasional kid, but they are not an important mortality factor. By far the major sources of death are winter avalanches, falls and sometimes starvation in severe blizzards.

Males are polygynous, as are the other artiodactyls, defending rutting territories in autumn and engaging in vicious fights. Mountain goats are not true goats in the narrow sense of the word, actually belonging to a group known as mountain antelope, but nevertheless, the males carry the typical goat odour. They make copious glandular secretions behind their horns to wipe around their territory. They also urinate and ejaculate frequently on their goatee, wearing the smell as testimony to their maleness.

This musky taint in their meat makes mountain goats virtually inedible. As a result, they have been little

*Nearly vertical cliffs offer mountain goats a safe haven where no predators dare to follow.*

hunted except by those who wish to mount their heads as trophies. The biggest threat to their populations is the development of roads leading to increased human activity in their habitats, although their remote terrain makes them less vulnerable than are many other North American mammals.

# *Bighorn Sheep* Ovis canadensis

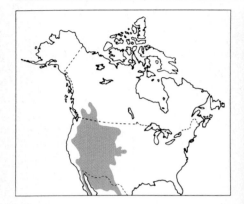

**Mammal:** *Ovis canadensis* — bighorn sheep

**Meaning of Name:** *Ovis* (sheep); *canadensis* (of Canada); although not confined to Canada

**Description:** massive brown spiralled horns have many annulations; horns grow from the skin over a concealed bony core and are not shed; ewes' horns are shorter; pelage has a thick grey fleece underneath and is composed of an outer coat of long brittle bone-white guard hairs with brown tips; brown back, darker on chest, face and legs; brown tail; belly, backs of legs, muzzle and large rump patch are ivory-white

**Total Length:** male, 5.2 to 6.1 feet; female, 4.6 feet

**Tail:** male, 4 to 6 inches; female, 4 inches

**Weight:** male, 287 to 344 pounds (one female weighed 139 pounds)

**Gestation:** 171 to 178 days

**Litter Size:** 1 (occasionally twins)

**Age of Maturity:** male, 3 years but does not breed until 7 years due to social factors; female, 2 to 3 years

**Longevity:** 15 years in the wild

**Diet:** grazer and browser; grasses and sedges are the staple food; also forbs and browse plants; mineral licks containing salts are sought primarily in spring and summer

**Habitat:** mountain slopes with sparse growth of trees, rugged terrain and alpine meadows; requires dry slopes with less than 60 inches of snowfall since it cannot paw through deep snow to feed

**Predators:** bobcat, mountain lion and eagle can attack on rocky slopes; wolf, puma, coyote, bear and lynx may take newborns or diseased sheep

**Dental Formula:** 0/3, 0/1, 3/3, 3/3 = 32 teeth

The mountains of the west are a safe haven for agile climbers like the bighorn sheep. Their life is a compromise between the security offered by rocky ledges and rugged terrain and the better meadow feeding grounds available on flatter and more exposed terrain. While goats have specialized in cliff life, with occasional excursions into meadows, sheep tend to gravitate to open meadows, using the rocky areas when they need protection.

Mountain sheep live in bands to give themselves added protection from predators. The composition of the band centres on the ewes. Normally, there are several older females that provide leadership to younger ewes, immature males and lambs that travel and forage together. Rams that are reaching sexual maturity, around the age of 3, band together in all-male groups led by older males. These older males separate from the females in spring, when the males begin their summer feeding in preparation for the autumn rut.

In summer, the bands are continually on the move, grazing and clipping along traditional routes with well-marked trails. They follow a typical altitudinal migration from the valleys in winter, where large groups of up to a hundred individuals may herd together. In spring, the males set off for higher ground, followed by the female bands. Their movement may follow as many as six different ranges and seasonal phases, as determined by the snow, lambing season, rutting and the need to visit mineral licks.

Female bands may contain more than 15 individuals, many of which are close relatives, while male bands are smaller, usually around half a dozen individuals of varying ages and sizes. The males sort themselves out into a dominance hierarchy, a situation that inevitably leads to compromise. While an animal might raise its status by joining a smaller group where it will have a greater opportunity for leadership, it will feed less efficiently, as sheep in small groups spend much more time scanning for predators than grazing.

Predator pressure comes in many forms. Mountain lions, wolves, coyotes, lynx, bobcats, bears and golden eagles all prey on sheep. The response

of the sheep is usually to flee to rocky terrain, but larger rams may turn to fight lone coyotes. The spring lambing time is a period of major mortality. Even though lambs are born on rocky ledges inaccessible to most predators and are hidden until they are a week old and able to walk, golden eagles still take a heavy toll.

The aggregation of females into bands creates conditions favourable to harem-guarding males. In the autumn rut, males attempt to control access to and to mate with all of the receptive members of a female band. This produces the spectacular head-cracking duels between the largest bighorn males. The force of two rams charging full speed into each other creates a loud crack like the sound of a gunshot and may break the horns and skull of smaller males. There is also a great deal of subtle interaction between males. They seem to gather in groups to compare horns and body size. They also use homosexual mountings to express dominance, the subdominant male being forced to submit to mounting by a more dominant male or else risk an escalated attack.

The male physiological investment in big horns and fighting seems to be ultimately limited by a higher rate of mortality. A survey of sheep skulls

*The massive curling horns of male bighorn sheep, **left**, are used in ritualized displays and violent head-smacking duels, **above**, that determine dominance and access to females.*

*Wild and rocky terrain is the habitat of bighorn sheep, but they will range further into open grasslands and tundra than mountain goats will.*

has shown that the rate of horn development is correlated with a higher death rate. Males that spend more time and effort than average in rutting may have a higher mating success, but eventually, they face exhaustion and increase their susceptibility to starvation and predation in the winter.

Females take an active role in the courtship proceedings. They will fend off the attempts of young subordinate males and will actively seek out large males. Nevertheless, some younger males are able to sequester

females and force them to mate. In such cases, a female may copulate simply to reduce the amount of time she has to spend with a subordinate male. Once she is free of him, she can seek out a preferred male. A female will generally mate with several different rams during the same rutting season, and there are always surplus males ready to replace an older, tired male.

# *Dall's Sheep* Ovis dalli

**Mammal:** *Ovis dalli* — Dall's sheep
**Meaning of Name:** *Ovis* (sheep); *dalli* (named after W.H. Dall, an American zoologist)
**Description:** slender horns (compared with other sheep) that have a more corrugated keel on the outer curl than occurs on bighorn sheep; northern race is creamy white with a few dark hairs along the spine and tail; southern race is slate brown except for a white rump patch and muzzle and white on inside of hind legs and on forehead; between these 2 races are populations with integrated colours, such as the saddle-backed sheep of eastern Yukon Territory
**Total Length:** southern race male, 4.3 to 5.8 feet; female, 4.5 feet; northern race male, 4.5 to 5 feet; female, 4.5 feet
**Tail:** southern race male, 3 to 4.3 inches; female, 3 inches; northern race male, 3.5 to 4.5 inches; female, 3.9 inches
**Weight:** southern race male, 200 pounds; northern race male, 165 to 198 pounds; female, 126 pounds
**Gestation:** slightly less than 6 months
**Litter Size:** 1 (sometimes 2)
**Age of Maturity:** male, probably 18 to 36 months; female, probably 18 to 30 months
**Longevity:** 14 years
**Diet:** primarily grasses and sedges
**Habitat:** in summer, rough terrain, alpine tundra slopes; in winter, lower, drier southern-facing slopes
**Predators:** lynx, wolverine, coyote, grizzly bear, wolf and golden eagle; wolves prey on them primarily during migration when they cross flat stretches of tundra
**Dental Formula:** 0/3, 0/1, 3/3, 3/3 = 32 teeth

The Dall's sheep is a more northerly and graceful species than the bighorn sheep. It lives along the highest mountains of North America and ranges into the tundra. Its habitat, especially in winter, when it moves down the mountain slopes, is more open than that of the bighorn. When Dall's sheep pass through large expanses of tundra without protective rocky areas, they are vulnerable to wolves, which encourages a more social herding instinct. As winter sets in, snow forces them into open areas, where food is more accessible — their winter range then becomes a compromise between foraging grounds and predation.

*Exposure to predators in the open Arctic alpine habitat of Dall's sheep favours the formation of large bands during migration.*

This sheep's rut is similar to that of the bighorn. Males use a stand-up display, rising high on their hind legs before they charge, a forceful signal designed to warn the opposing male of its attacker's size.

## The Overkill

*Magnificent as it may appear, the mammal world of modern-day*

Male bighorn sheep's preoccupation with other males during dominance contests makes them easy prey for hunters and predators.

Canada and the northern United States would seem pathetic to humans of an earlier time. Just 10,000 or 11,000 years ago, North American humans had a much richer array of species to contemplate. There were giant beaver the size of bears, woolly mammoths, elephantlike mastodons, sabre-toothed tigers, lions, yaks, camels, horses, giant ground sloths, llamas, antelopes, tapirs, peccaries and giant hyenalike dogs. All in all, several dozen different genera, entire families and many hundreds of species became extinct in the last Ice Age.

The vision conjured up by the list of extinct mammals is reminiscent of present-day Africa, with its big-game fauna of elephants, hyenas, jackals and large predatory cats feeding on a rich array of grazers.

Why so many North American fauna were lost is an intriguing question, especially as Africa lost so few species by comparison. There are two schools of thought: one blames the loss on climatic changes;

the other, on human hunters.

The first idea is a difficult one to test, as the extinct animals are not available for study. The second idea is somewhat more easily considered since an answer would be based on the time that human hunters contacted the New World fauna, which can be determined by archaeological digs. The essence of the "overkill hypothesis," as it is known, is that when humans first arrived from Siberia across the Bering Strait and spread down through the Americas, they hunted the big-game animals into extinction.

This may seem farfetched, as it is hard to imagine how hunters with a technology no more sophisticated than spears, bows and arrows could have dispatched mammoths, lions and sabre-toothed tigers. Nevertheless, there are some compelling patterns that fit the hypothesis and are not readily explained by the notion of climatic change.

Many small mammals have become extinct over the last three

million years, but they did so gradually, without any sharp upsurge in the decline rates. By contrast, the larger mammals disappeared suddenly, many in the last 10,000 years, soon after the arrival of the hunters. In that period, 65 to 75 percent of large North American animal species died off, while in Africa, there was only a 10 percent decline. The basis of the theory is that in Africa, man and big-game animals had a history of contact over millions of years. The human hunting rules and territories that evolved over this period limited the hunt, even after the advent of more sophisticated hunting technologies, and prevented the overkill. Interestingly, compared with North America, Australia has an even greater extinction rate, as does New Zealand, and the extinctions peaked just after the arrival of humans.

This still begs the question of how early hunters could achieve such a devastating overkill. Evidence indicates that 11,000 years ago, the Clovis people used buffalo drives to send animals by the hundreds to their death over cliffs and that mammoths were also killed efficiently. Many of the grazers, such as the giant ground sloth, were defenceless, as were other larger mammals, such as horses, camels and yaks. Once weakened, the remnants of those populations could have been eradicated by carnivorous cats that then starved for lack of prey. But why did some animals, such as bison, survive the overkill?

Proponents of the overkill hypothesis suggest that the animals that survived were virtually all recent immigrants from Siberia, such as moose, muskox, caribou and grizzlies — animals that had already had a long evolutionary interaction with the hunters from Asia.

And what ended the killing? The establishment of tribal territories with hunting taboos and the development of agriculture are possibilities, and in any case, no large mammal is known to have become extinct in the 8,000 years before the European conquest of North America.

The cycle began anew with the European colonists, a new race with new technologies and a lack of experience with the new fauna. Only

rising human populations with diverging interests conspired to prevent the colonists from hunting large mammals, such as the bison, pronghorn, elk and even the white-tailed deer, to extinction.

The development of modern hunting technology has created new pressure on bighorn sheep populations. Today, their survival is as dependent on intensive management and government regulation as it is on natural forces.

# *Muskox* Ovibos moschatus

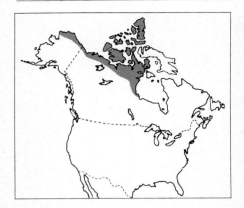

**Mammal:** *Ovibos moschatus* — muskox
**Meaning of Name:** *Ovibos* (sheep + cow); *moschatus* (musky) refers to preorbital glands that secrete a musky odour
**Description:** bulls have massive keratinous horns with only a narrow groove separating their cores (females' horns are not as large); horns sweep downward close to the skull, then tips turn upward and outward; an overcoat of long guard hairs hangs about the body; dark brown to blackish; creamy yellowish saddle and stockings; females and juveniles have lighter foreheads; fur is short and greyish on muzzle and legs
**Total Length:** male, 6.5 to 8.1 feet; female, 6.5 feet
**Tail:** male, 4.5 to 6.5 inches; female, 2.5 to 6 inches
**Weight:** male, 580 to 1,450 pounds; female, 617 to 650 pounds
**Gestation:** 8 to 9 months
**Litter Size:** usually 1 (twins are rare) every 1 or 2 years
**Age of Maturity:** 3 to 5 years (as early as 18 months in captivity)
**Longevity:** 20 to 25 years
**Diet:** browser and grazer; willow, tundra grasses, forbs and sedges
**Habitat:** Arctic tundra with sufficient forage; in summer, moist habitats such as river valleys, lakeshores and seepage meadows; in winter, hilltops, slopes and plateaus
**Predators:** wolf is main natural predator and usually preys on lone animals; also grizzly bear
**Dental Formula:** 0/3, 0/1, 3/3, 3/3 = 32 teeth

The muskox may look like a great shaggy ox, but its closest relative is a goatlike species found in the Himalayas. The muskox evolved into its characteristic ox form when it invaded the cold Asian grasslands and spread north into Siberia and later across the Bering land bridge into North America.

The muskox is not as big as it looks. Under its shaggy coat, it is a relatively small animal when compared with the bison. Bulls usually reach weights of roughly 750 pounds, with 1,450 pounds being the maximum recorded for an animal fed and raised in captivity. The massive fur coat is composed mainly of long threads of extremely fine-quality wool, thought to be the highest-quality wool in the world. The outer coat is overlain with long, coarse guard hairs, which may be 2 feet long. Heat-losing extremities, such as the tail and ears, are buried in the coats, an adaptation that allows muskox to survive at the very limit of the tundra, where snow lies on the ground 10 months out of 12.

Muskox can weather temperatures of minus 40 degrees F without increasing their metabolism. They are slow-moving in the deep of winter and probably conserve energy by being relatively inactive, reducing their intake and excretion of water to avoid the energy drain of converting cold snow to warm urine.

The muskox is not a migratory animal but limits itself to local areas of

*The finest-quality wool on Earth blankets the muskox and enables it to live at the northernmost limits of the tundra.*

well-vegetated tundra where wind, drainage and snow accumulation provide reasonable growing conditions. Muskox browse and graze most of the Arctic shrubs, sedges, grasses and forbs, but they do not eat the quantities of lichens that caribou do. The depth of snow is a primary restraint on their diet, as taller plants, such as willows, are more easily dug out in winter.

The basic social unit of the muskox is a band of females, their juvenile offspring and a single bull that treats the band as a harem, staying with them for most of the year. The dominant bull provides leadership, taking the lead in repelling predators, setting routes and fording rivers. Within the herd of cows, there is also a dominance hierarchy, and when the bull is absent, certain females assume the leadership role. In spring, bulls leave their herd and either join with bands of younger animals or forage alone. As the late-summer and autumn rut approaches, they become aggressive and fight to assume leadership of a band of females. Their horns are larger than those of the females, and they grow together in a heavy band across the forehead, which is used in head butting.

A female bears a calf every spring or two according to her physical condi-

tion. The calf is a precocious type, up and following its mother around on the first day. Females form stable groups that include the young of the year as well as immature males and older females. It is likely that many females remain in the mother's group. This could account for the coordinated group defence of muskox.

The band of females and offspring, with or without a bull, is an integrated unit that cooperates in defence against predators. Their most famous protective strategy is an outward-facing circle of adults ringing around the herd's calves. Their cooperative nature extends to the preservation of energy, as they lie together for warmth and break trails for one another in snow.

The only serious predators of muskox are wolves, which may dash into a herd to pull down a calf or sometimes try to kill a lone adult. An adult in good condition, though, is difficult prey, for muskox are capable of goatlike agility. Their broad hooves have a sharp outer rim and a soft inner area that enables them to grip, turn and scramble about on ice and rocky substrates. Their skull is massively

reinforced, and the horns are lethal weapons. Being strong swimmers, lone muskox will wade into water when harassed, where they are virtually invulnerable.

The greatest source of mortality is the stress of overwintering. On Bathurst Island in 1973, a winter storm that left a coat of frozen snow and ice over the vegetation killed half of the area's muskox population.

Muskox are now protected in the Canadian Arctic, but their preserves remain open to mining and oil development, which may prove disastrous for such sedentary and easily disturbed animals. Muskox in a defence ring are easily shot, and many regional populations have been extinguished, although efforts have been made to reintroduce them. Southern sport hunters pay as much as $6,000 for the chance to shoot a muskox, providing an occasional source of income for Northern peoples. One alternative — increasing the size of muskox herds and using them for wool production — is under study. Approximately 10,000 muskox currently inhabit the continent.

*Although effective against wolves, the defensive ring of muskox makes them vulnerable to predators with guns.*

# WHALES, DOLPHINS & PORPOISES *Cetacea*

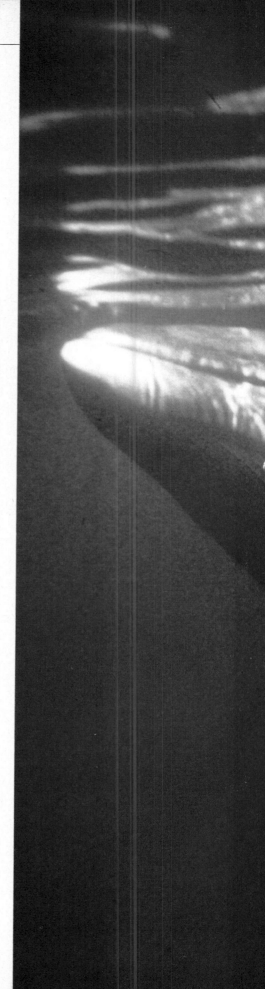

Whales' ancestors once plodded around on land. They had fur, legs and, presumably, all the features of land mammals. The ancestral whale probably came from the same stock that gave rise to the ungulate mammals such as deer, cow, hippopotamus and elephant. It may have been a resident of marshy areas. One scenario for the evolution of whales begins 60 million years ago in an area now filled by the Mediterranean and Arabian Seas. The large semiaquatic reptiles such as the plesiosaurs and ichthyosaurs were dying out, and the habitats they occupied — marshes, swamps and shallow-water estuaries — became available to ancestral whales.

The first recognizable cetaceans, the Archaeoceti, or archaic whales, appeared 50 million years ago. They were highly elongated, with long snouts and tiny hind legs, thus showing adaptive trends that modern whales continued to develop. This ancient group of whales became extinct some 7 million years ago. Two other suborders of cetaceans came to dominate: the Odontoceti, or toothed whales, and the Mysticeti, the baleen, or whalebone, whales. These whales continued the trends of body streamlining, head elongation, shift of the nostrils into blowholes and loss of the hind limbs. In the 60 million years since whales' ancestors entered the sea, they have lost all but the smallest traces of the features of land mammals. And in their redesign, we see some of the most complete and elegant examples of adaptation to a life in water.

Water is an unforgiving element and demands great modification of the basic mammalian body plan. It is viscous, hundreds of times denser than air. To move through water is costly for all but the smooth and streamlined. Water has a tremendous capacity for absorbing calories, and warm-blooded animals must deal with the perpetual and high rate of energy drain imposed by cold oceans.

Some of the redesign that has taken place in whales is obvious from a glance at any photograph or accurate drawing. Hind limbs have been lost, except in rare individuals that have a few protruding bones. The forelimbs have been reduced, and the skin and muscle have grown into flippers used for steering. Only a few bristles of hair remain, and the skin has lost its sweat glands. Whales' eyes have been reduced in size and fixed in position. The ear opening is just big enough to admit a matchstick. Larger whales swim with such power that water resistance could snap flexible neck vertebrae. Although small cetaceans, such as dolphins, have retained unfused neck vertebrae and some flexibility of the neck and head, most whales' neckbones are fused. No neck or shoulder structure is obvious. Instead, the body is moulded into a smooth, streamlined, fusiform shape. The skull has been "telescoped," with the jawbones drawn far out ahead of the position of the nostrils. Positioning the blowholes at the top of the head enables the whales to breathe while swimming largely submerged. Genital organs have been moved inside a slit along the body, to be exposed only during mating. The breasts have a special set of muscles that pump the milk outward, so a large ex-

*The sei whale displays a superbly streamlined body that gives little hint that ancestral whales were once four-legged land animals.*

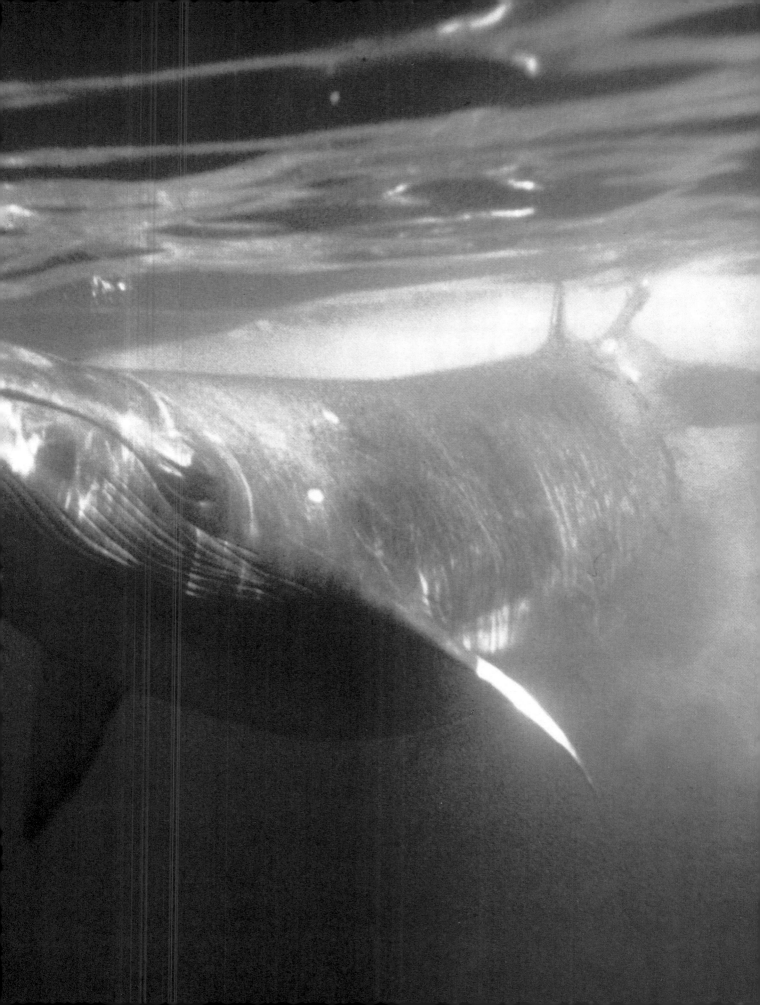

*Dolphins, such as the Pacific white-sided dolphin,* **above,** *often travel in large herds.* **Right,** *a grey whale ploughs the bottom to feed.*

ternal nipple is unnecessary for feeding. All of these are adaptations required for movement through water.

Less obvious but no less critical to life in an aquatic environment are some of the changes in the whales' physiological and sensory capabilities. In order to allow whales to spend great stretches of time submerged between breaths (some species can stay down for more than an hour), their muscles contain huge amounts of myoglobin, a protein like haemoglobin, which absorbs oxygen. Whale muscle can absorb twice as much oxygen as terrestrial-mammal muscle. Whale blood contains twice as many red blood cells as that of a terrestrial

mammal, increasing the whale's ability to transport oxygen through its body. Whales have a high tolerance of carbon dioxide and lactic acid in the blood, waste products that must eventually be disposed of through exhalation. This allows whales to go longer without exhaling than land mammals. When a land mammal breathes, it uses only 4 percent of the oxygen in the air. Because of the greater efficiency of its lungs and blood, a whale uses 12 percent.

Anyone who has felt the eardrum-piercing pain of even a shallow dive in a backyard pool knows that water exerts a great pressure. At a depth of 33 feet, a body is subjected to twice the pressure it is on the surface, yet some whales, such as sperm whales, can dive as deep as 9,000 feet and experience 300 times the surface pressure with no ill effects. When humans go

scuba diving, they breathe compressed air, which keeps the lungs inflated in spite of the crushing pressure of the water. The disadvantage of this system is that it can cause caisson disease, or the bends. Under pressure, the nitrogen gas that makes up about three-quarters of the air dissolves and enters the blood and tissues. If the pressure is suddenly released during a fast ascent, this nitrogen comes boiling out, like the soda in a bottle that has been shaken and opened. It can damage the tissues and organs of the body. To prevent this, whales have a single collapsible lung that compresses, forcing the air up into the nasal passages and windpipe. There, thick linings prevent the transfer of nitrogen into the blood and tissues. For whales, large permeable lungs would be a liability, not an asset, which explains the observation that

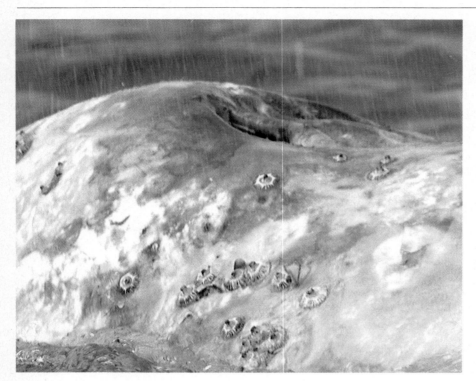

*Like the oceangoing ships they resemble, whales, such as the grey whale, become encrusted with barnacles and other parasitic organisms.*

the deepest-diving whales actually have relatively small lungs compared with those of shallow-water whales.

Another major adaptation to the water is the development of sonar, or echolocation. The toothed whales emit sounds and listen to the echoes that return. These echoes enable them to navigate and locate objects in the murkiest of water. In fact, one species of river dolphin is entirely blind. Harbour porpoises can use echolocation to detect a wire as thin as 1/50 inch. Dolphins can spot a sphere the size of a large marble 10 feet away, a baseball at 20 to 30 feet and a school of mackerel at 100 to 350 yards.

Researchers still disagree about what actual structure whales use to perceive sounds. Some cetaceans have a strange oil-filled sinus, called a melon, in the forehead. The melon could focus sound waves, like an acoustic lens comparable to the human eye lens, which focuses light. Other researchers argue that the melon is actually a hydrodynamic and orientation device that enables the animal to assess depth and direction. The same function is thought to be served by the huge sinus cavities and sinus hairs of whalebone whales. There is also disagreement about how whales generate the sounds they make. Cetaceans lack true vocal cords and use other structures, such as the blowholes, air sacs and larynx, for sound production. Their sounds may vary from high-frequency clicks to low rumbles. These have different transmission and reflection properties, with the high-frequency sounds being used for object location and lower-frequency sounds for orientation.

All whales have a reduced sense of smell, with no olfactory surface and a reduced olfactory lobe in the brain. Thus there is probably no chemical communication among cetaceans. They have taste buds, however, and can taste their food.

Although the small eyes of cetaceans are of little use underwater, there is evidence that they are useful above water. They may act like pinhole cameras. In bright light, the pupil shuts down to a tiny slit, which would give a very sharp image of distant objects and may enable whales to recognize landmarks such as coastlines. Dolphins may scan the horizon looking for flocks of feeding seabirds as a clue to the whereabouts of schools of fish. Migratory whales, in particular, may use their eyes to plot directions from the positions of sun and moon. Many whales take advantage of their ability to see great distances above water by raising their heads out of the water and looking around, a behaviour called "spy hopping."

There is considerable variation in aquatic adaptation of the various whales, dolphins and porpoises. The skull, for example, varies substantially among different families and reflects the degree of divergence from the skull design of the ancestors of whales.

The two living suborders of whales are easily distinguished by their feeding apparatus and blowholes. The baleen whales have two external blowholes but no teeth. The toothed whales have one blowhole and peglike teeth. Baleen whales consist of 10 species in 3 families; toothed whales consist of roughly 66 species in 6 families.

Baleen is a series of plates that grow from the mouth. These plates are not teeth but are built of a protein somewhat like that in human fingernails. The baleen has a smooth outer surface and an inner surface that is rough and coated with bristles of hairlike structures. The plates are arranged in series, like the teeth of a comb, with one row running along each side of the mouth. The bristles on the inside of the comb run in toward those from the opposite side and make a sievelike structure used for filtering fine particles of food.

Baleen whales filter feed on a variety of organisms, ranging from plankton no bigger than a grain of sand to shrimplike krill and medium-sized fish. The baleen is used in a variety of ways. The whale may swim, letting water flow past the bristles and plates, which strain continuously. Other whales gulp a huge load of water containing prey, then force the water out through the plates. Still others suck up a mixture of food and water. Baleen whales do not seem to use echolocation to find food, which is appropriate since their food is often a cloudy soup of tiny zooplankton. By feeding low on the food chain, baleen whales have access to the huge food resources of the open ocean, an ecological niche that has enabled them to become the largest creatures on Earth.

The toothed whales are generally smaller and use echolocation to hunt prey such as fish and squid.

# *Beaked Whales* Ziphiidae

## *Northern Bottlenose Whale* Hyperoodon ampullatus

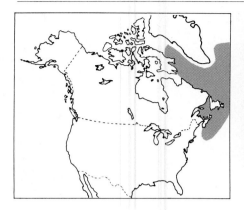

**Mammal:** *Hyperoodon ampullatus* —
northern bottlenose whale
**Meaning of Name:** *Hyperoodon* (palate
+ tooth); the first specimen described
supposedly had tiny teeth in the palate
(this is misleading as they have 2 teeth in
the lower jaw); *ampullatus* (provided with
a flask or bottle) refers to the long snout
in front of the bulging forehead
**Description:** robust, narrow, cylindrical
body with a short beak; adult male has
bulbous forehead, or melon, rising
abruptly from the beak; blowhole is an
indented area behind the forehead;
usually 2 throat grooves present
**Colour:** young whales are blackish
brown and lighter below, and older ones
are light brown with light blotches on the
back and sides that increase with age;
very old whales are yellowish brown with
whitish beaks and heads
**Total Length:** male, up to 32 feet;
female, up to 26 feet
**Weight:** male, 8,000 pounds; female,
7,000 pounds
**Gestation:** 1 year
**Litter Size:** 1 every 2 or 3 years
**Age of Maturity:** male, 7 to 11 years;
female, 8 to 12 years
**Longevity:** at least 37 years
**Diet:** Arctic squid (*Gonatus fabricii*);
bottom-dwelling echinoderms, such as
sea stars and sea cucumbers; and fish
**Habitat:** pelagic; frequents cold, deep
(usually more than 3,300 feet deep)
Arctic waters of the northern Atlantic
Ocean; generally well offshore; may
approach the polar ice packs during the
summer
**Predators:** killer whale
**Dental Formula:** 2 + teeth

Beaked whales range from 9 to 36
feet long and swim in all oceans, but
they are the least known of the whales.
Indeed, they have been called the
most poorly known of all mammalian
families. Beaked whales do not normally occur within sight of land or
even on the continental shelf, and
there are few observations of living
specimens. They seem to be deep-
ocean specialists capable of diving for
bottom organisms and squid. Eigh-
teen species have been described, and
it is likely that there are other species.

Most species of beaked whales are
difficult to identify. As a group, they
can be recognized by their small
heads, slim bodies tapered at both
ends and elongated jaws forming a
beak. Tail flukes lack a distinct notch
to separate the right from the left. The
dorsal fin is small and set far back toward the tail. Beaked whales' flippers
are short and rounded.

The elongated jaws from which the
beaked whale derives its name appear
to be designed for squid catching, an
adaptation that may explain the diversity of the group. Squid are abundant
and vary greatly in their species diversity and ecological distribution. The
richness of beaked whale species may
reflect the variation in squid ecology
as different beaked whale species feed
on different squid populations. The
beak itself is an unlikely apparatus,
being virtually toothless, but it is apparently able to clamp down on slip-
pery squid. A rough palate keeps the
squid in place.

Some beaked whale species are still
hunted for food and oil, but fortunately for the whales, the meat and oil
appear to have laxative properties.
The natives of the Kamchatka Penin-

*The oil-filled forehead of the bottlenose
may be an adaptation for deep diving.*

sula in Soviet Asia used it "as a treat
for undesirable guests."

Most of what is known about
beaked whales is based on these
hunted species. They can stay submerged for two hours and descend
1,500 feet per minute. Some species
may be unusual in having extremely
long gestation periods, up to 17
months, the longest of any whale.

The northern bottlenose is the best
known of all beaked whales, a distinction it unfortunately owes to commercial whaling. This is one of the larger
bottlenose species, with males reaching a length of more than 27 feet.
Robust and heavy-bodied for beaked
whales, male bottlenoses may have a
girth of 20 feet and weigh 3 to 4 tons.
The Norwegian whaling industry in
particular has sought out bottlenoses.
These whales are unlike most members of the family in that they are not
elusive and shy. Instead, they often
approach ships seemingly out of curi-
osity. In addition, bottlenoses are
among the more social of beaked
whales, occurring in pods of 4 to 10
animals, which may represent a family group. In any case, when one
member of the pod is harpooned, the
others remain with it until it is dead,
becoming easy targets themselves.

The northern bottlenose has a distinctive sexual dimorphism. Not only
are males usually one-third larger
than females, but they also have a
massive, bulging forehead. This forehead melon is oil-filled, like that of the
sperm whale, and may be an adaptation for deep diving or a sexual trait.

# *Sperm Whales* Physeteridae

## *Sperm Whale* Physeter catodon

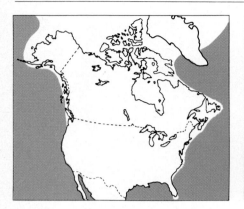

**Mammal:** *Physeter catodon* — sperm whale; the largest toothed mammal in the world and the most sexually dimorphic of all cetaceans

**Meaning of Name:** *Physeter* (blow pipe or bellows) refers to the blowhole on the top of the head; *catodon* (a tooth down below); the lower-jaw teeth are functional

**Description:** enormous squarish head, one-quarter to one-third of body length; the huge spermaceti organ is filled with up to 500 gallons of waxy oil; blunt, squarish snout projects far beyond the lower jaw tip; only one blowhole that is situated on the left side near the tip of the snout; small spout projects forward at a sharp angle; the usual dorsal fin is replaced by a hump that is followed by a series of bumps; ventral keel

**Colour:** the back is brownish grey and appears shrivelled; ventrally, it is lighter with white splashes at the navel and on the lower jaw; older animals often have a pale grey whorl on the snout

**Total Length:** male, 36 to 61 feet (usually 50); female, 26 to 40 feet

**Weight:** male, 77,000 to 110,000 pounds; female, one-third as much as male (25,500 to 36,500 pounds)

**Gestation:** 14 to 17 months

**Litter Size:** 1 calf (rarely twins) born every 4 years

**Age of Maturity:** female, 7 to 12 years; male, reaches puberty at 9 years, is sexually mature at 19 but has no opportunity to breed until 25 to 27 years

**Longevity:** up to 77 years

**Diet:** primarily squid, including giant species, but also several species of sharks and other deep-sea fish

**Habitat:** pelagic; in temperate and tropical oceans along the edge of the continental shelf or near oceanic islands, usually at depths of 3,000 to 6,000 feet, or farther out to sea

**Predators:** man

**Dental Formula:** 34 to 58 teeth

Of the three species in Physeteridae, the giant sperm whale, the great white whale of *Moby-Dick*, is the best known. Smaller, and mainly residents of warm-water regions, the pygmy and dwarf sperm whales are otherwise similar in many respects to the better-studied giant sperm whale.

Because they have been heavily hunted for so long, sperm whales may be the best known of all whales. Unfortunately, most of what has been discovered is based on corpses.

The giant sperm is the largest of all toothed whales. It is easily identified by its huge squarish head, which makes up a third of its length. The giant sperm whale's blowhole is S-shaped and produces a distinctive spout that shoots forward at a 45-degree angle and to the left of the animal. This species has rippled, wrinkled-looking skin. The blocky shape of the giant sperm whale's head accommodates the spermaceti organ, an oil-filled cavity bound with ligaments, veins, arteries and nerves and connected to one of the nasal passages. The high-quality spermaceti oil, once used as fuel for lamps, gave the sperm whale its common name.

The exact function of the spermaceti organ remains unknown. It might act as an acoustic lens for focusing incoming and outgoing sounds used in echolocation. The lens could even enable the sperm whale to produce enough sound to stun its prey at close range. Another theory holds that the organ absorbs nitrogen during diving or is involved in lung evacuation. Some researchers say that it controls buoyancy. Flooding the head cavities

*Sperm whales are deep divers that prey on giant squid up to 60 feet long which live thousands of feet below the surface.*

with cold ocean water causes the oil to solidify into dense wax that pulls the whale down like a weight during the dive. To ascend, the whale pumps hot blood around the cavity, liquefying the oil, which then acts like a float. Unfortunately, none of these ideas has been proved.

What is known is that sperm whales are formidable divers. They stay down for at least 80 minutes and eat bottom-dwelling sharks in an area where the ocean is more than two miles deep. Most sperm whale hunting probably involves echolocation, and sperm whales vocalize with clicks when diving.

The long, deep dives of sperm whales make them difficult to observe, and relatively little is known about their behaviour, except as it relates to whaling. True to Herman Melville's whaling epic, large lone bull males do attack whale boats, which they may mistake for other male sperm whales. Mature males attack and tooth-rake each other, producing long slashes in the skin. Sperm whales are the most sexually dimorphic of all whales, with males more than three times as heavy as females at maturity. Females are sexually mature at 7 to 12 years, but in males, maturity is delayed until age 9 to 19, and status as a dominant male with access to a female group may not occur until age 26.

Males probably compete for access to the basic social unit of sperm

whales, the nursery school. This so-cial unit seems to consist of 10 to 40 adult females, their calves, and juve-niles of both sexes. Mature males as-sociate with a nursery school during breeding season but are solitary most of the rest of the year, although they do sometimes join together in schools based on size. Males tend to move more than females, migrating as far north as 70 degrees latitude, while females stay within 40 degrees of the equator. At high latitudes, the males are usually solitary.

Sperm whale groups exhibit co-operative behaviour. When one is wounded, the others form a circle around it, a trait exploited by whalers who then proceed to harpoon the defenders.

Although sperm whales eat a wide variety of deep-sea fish, they prefer squid, battling even giant squid, the world's largest invertebrate with a length of 60 feet. The giant squid's suction-cupped tentacles leave scars the size of dinner plates on the skin of sperm whales. Perhaps this ex-plains why sperm whales more often

eat smaller squid, consuming up to 28,000 at a time.

But even small squid have a horny indigestible beak. Sperm whales coat masses of these beaks with a waxy substance and excrete them as a lump called ambergris, sometimes found floating on the ocean or washed ashore. Ambergris is used as a fixative by the perfume industry. For centu-ries, perfume wearers have anointed themselves with a potion based on this sperm whale dung.

Sperm whales also accumulate large quantities of fat, up to a third of their weight. This store of blubber may be important in the migration of sperm whales, which winter in warmer tropical regions and move to the high latitudes to feed during sum-mer. Ironically, it was this life-sus-taining fat, rendered into whale oil, that made sperm whales so attractive to the whaling industry. Sperm whales have been heavily hunted for centuries and continue to be hunted by onshore whaling operations, but they are not considered endangered. Nonetheless, the great battle-scarred

*Sperm whales form nursery herds of adult females and calves. Bachelor males gather in their own pods.*

bulls that inspired the legend of Moby-Dick have all been killed.

# *White Whales* Monodontidae

## *Narwhal* Monodon monoceros

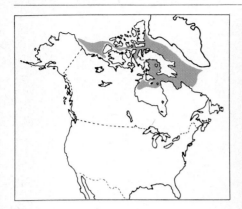

**Mammal:** *Monodon monoceros* — narwhal

**Meaning of Name:** *Monodon* (single tooth); *monoceros* (single horn) refers to the fact that the canine in the male develops into an enormous horn; narwhal, meaning corpse whale, comes from Old Norse — the whale's pallid colour is said to resemble that of a floating corpse

**Description:** short, blunt, rounded head; no dorsal fin; the striking feature is a long, spirally twisted horn that projects through the upper lip of the male (its maxillary tooth); series of 2-inch-high bumps visible along the dorsal midline from the middle of the back to the tail

**Colour:** adults are dark bluish grey or brownish with slate-grey blotches on the back and sides; newborns are slate-grey and become lighter with age

**Total Length:** male, 20 feet; female, 14 feet

**Weight:** male, 3,500 pounds; female, 2,000 pounds

**Gestation:** 14.5 months

**Litter Size:** 1 (rarely twins) every 2 or 3 years

**Age of Maturity:** male, 8 or 9 years; female, 4 to 7 years

**Longevity:** 40 years

**Diet:** squid, fish (Arctic cod, halibut, flounder and skate), cephalopods and crustaceans

**Habitat:** deep waters of the high Arctic along the edge of land-fast ice and ice floes; avoids shallow seas and bays

**Predators:** Inuit hunters, killer whale and the rogue bull walrus

**Dental Formula:** 1 or 2 teeth

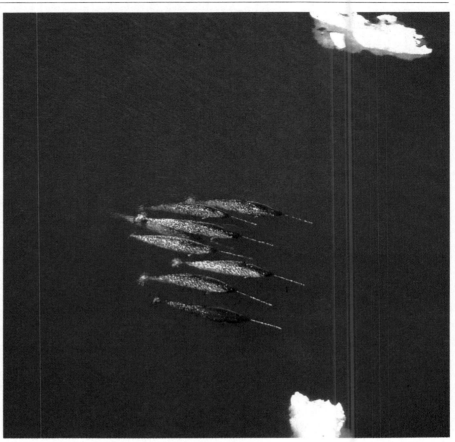

This family has only two members, both distinctive: the narwhal, with its spiralling tusk, and the beluga, made unmistakable by its brilliant white colour. Though they appear different at first glance, belugas and narwhals have much in common: both are high-Arctic specialists and have thick layers of blubber; both travel in spectacular herds and aggregations.

Possessing the world's largest tooth, the narwhal is credited with being the inspiration for the legend of the unicorn. The spiral tusk is one of the male narwhal's two teeth. It begins to erupt from the male's upper lip when it reaches about 1 year of age and grows as long as 10 feet. In the past, it has been wrongly suggested that the tusk is an adaptation for hunting food, attacking predators and making breathing holes in the ice. The tusk's true function is suggested by sexual dimorphism. Females lack this tusk, except as rare individuals. Male nar-

*The 10-foot-long tusk of the male narwhal is a specialized tooth used in battles over mates.*

whals have been observed crossing tusks, and it is likely that the tusks are used in the same way as the horns and antlers of other male mammals. They enable males and females to assess age and territorial status and are perhaps used in male-male combat. Males often have scars on their heads, and broken tusks are not uncommon.

In winter, narwhals, like belugas, move through pack ice to deep-water regions of the high Arctic, but unlike belugas, narwhals remain offshore or in deeper inlets in summer and do not bottom feed extensively. They can dive several hundred yards and are faster swimmers than belugas. They eat fish such as flounder, halibut and cod, along with squid, octopus and other invertebrates. They are also

highly gregarious and vocal. Males grow larger and take twice as long to mature as females. This, and the tusk, suggest intense male-male competition. Large groups do occur, but smaller groups of 20 or so individuals segregated by age, size and sex are more common.

Pack ice dictates the range and movement of narwhals. Fast-forming ice may occasionally trap and kill them, and whales in pack ice may be more easily preyed upon by polar bear and even walrus. The human desire for ivory is a potential threat to narwhals, although the Canadian government regulates the Inuit trade in narwhal tusks.

## Bioconcentration

*A beluga calf shot by hunters in the St. Lawrence River in 1973 had 800 parts per million of PCBs and 827 parts per million of DDT in its blubber. In mammals such as beef cows, concentrations above a few parts per million would be cause for alarm. DDT is an agricultural chemical that was banned long ago in Canada, and PCBs, used in the chemical industry, are also strictly controlled. How did they show up in a marine mammal in such concentrated amounts?*

*Compounds such as DDT, which*

*are chemically synthesized, are highly stable. Few organisms have the enzymes needed to break them down and detoxify them, since these chemicals have never existed in nature. This explains both the effectiveness of DDT as a poison and its persistence. What is less obvious is why it should become concentrated in animals such as belugas. This concentration is an inevitable result of the way food chains work and of the tendency of many pesticides and pollutants to dissolve in or adhere to organic material, rather than disperse evenly through water. DDT, for example, sticks to organic detritus such as decaying plant and animal remains on the bottoms of ponds and other bodies of water. When this detritus is eaten by insects or fish, the DDT dissolves in the fat of the animal.*

*It takes 10 pounds of insects to make 1 pound of fish muscle, so the concentration of chemicals increases dramatically with each step in the food chain. A typical pattern of this concentration has been worked out for a freshwater food chain in which the water itself contained only 0.00005 parts per million of DDT. In plankton, the concentration rose to 0.04 parts per million; in minnows, it had increased to 0.94 parts per*

*Even though it will live in the remote Arctic, this young narwhal will accumulate large quantities of industrial and agricultural pollutants.*

*million; predatory fish also had 0.94 parts per million; and the fish-eating cormorant birds had 26.4 parts per million, an increase of a million times above the initial level of DDT in the water.*

*Pesticides and pollutants that bioconcentrate and are slow to break down may be under control in developed countries such as Canada and the United States. However, large quantities continue to be used in the Third World. Pesticide pollution of the oceans is increasing, and these pollutants are being carried to the farthest reaches of the Arctic. Now that commercial whaling is controlled, pollution of the ocean stands as one of the greatest long-term threats to the whales that sit at the top of the food chains.*

# *Beluga* Delphinapterus leucas

**Mammal:** *Delphinapterus leucas* — beluga, white whale

**Meaning of Name:** *Delphinapterus* (finless dolphin); *leucas* (white); beluga is derived from *belyi*, which is Russian for white

**Description:** fusiform body tapers to a distinct "neck"; small head and short beak; upper jaw protrudes slightly ahead of the melon; back has a narrow ridge of small bumps behind the middle; no dorsal fin; blowhole is crescentic

**Colour:** the smooth, thin skin is creamy white in adults, brown in young calves and various shades of grey in juveniles; adults have brown eyes

**Total Length:** male, up to 16 feet; female, up to 13 feet; size depends on particular stock

**Weight:** male, 3,300 pounds; female, 3,000 pounds

**Gestation:** 13 to 14 months

**Litter Size:** 1 every 2 or 3 years

**Age of Maturity:** male, 8 or 9 years; female, 4 to 7 years

**Longevity:** 25 to 30 years

**Diet:** an opportunistic feeder, it eats many species of fish, including cod, herring and capelin, as well as octopus, squid, crab, shrimp, clams and worms

**Habitat:** cold seas of Arctic zone along coasts in shallow bays and estuaries and mouths of rivers; also occurs in deep offshore waters and can survive and feed in warmer waters

**Predators:** man, killer whale, polar bear

**Dental Formula:** 32 to 40 teeth

Belugas are highly social, producing sounds variously described as screams, moos and trills in a range that humans can hear. Whalers called them "sea canaries." Russians, who gave them their common name, meaning whitish, also have an expression, "screaming like a beluga," for noisy people. Unlike most whales, the beluga has a fairly flexible neck and mouth, and its face is capable of a wide range of expressions.

The beluga is a shallow-water specialist, using its mobile neck and face for bottom feeding on a wide variety of invertebrates and fish. It may even use its flexible lips to suck prey off the seafloor. The beluga has a thick skin and a thick blubber coat. Up to 40 percent of a beluga may be blubber, versus 15 percent for warm-water dolphins. Both adaptations are useful for a life lived close to Arctic pack ice.

In winter, pack ice forces belugas to deeper, open water, where they may be seen together with narwhal; but in summer, belugas head toward shallow estuaries for feeding and breeding. Sometimes, this involves migrations of several hundred miles through pack-ice areas to the mouths of large rivers in the Arctic. There are also some relatively stationary populations, such as the one in the mouth of Quebec's Saguenay River. Belugas sometimes swim up large rivers for great distances, travelling 600 miles into the Yukon and even up the Rhine into Germany. In some areas, this may be to feed on runs of fish such as young salmon. This habit, combined with their eye-catching white colour and gregariousness, makes belugas one of whale watching's most spectacular sights.

Belugas normally travel in large herds that are densely aggregated

*The white beluga can be wrapped in a coat of blubber that may constitute 40 percent of the animal's weight.*

during the breeding season. In some areas, such as the Mackenzie River estuary, thousands of belugas may come together to breed. The complete social structure within these large herds has not been established, but there is segregation by sex and age. Pods can be made up of males only or of mothers and calves only. Males grow larger than females and have multiple mates, so some harem activity seems possible. Females segregate from the herds to calve in quiet bays. They are ready to breed between 4 and 7 years old and calve every 2 or 3 years. Calves are dark, not white, and remain with their mothers for 2 years.

Belugas are thought to have the richest vocal repertoire of all whales, in keeping with their intensely social nature. This gregariousness, coupled with their preference for shallow estuaries, makes belugas vulnerable to pack-hunting killer whales, polar bears and humans, who have been particularly hard on belugas. The Quebec government bombed belugas in the St. Lawrence River in the 1930s to protect the cod fishery, and the Manitoba government allowed the promotion of beluga sport hunting during the late 1960s and early 1970s. Various commercial fisheries have also concentrated on beluga harvesting. A major fishery operated at Churchill, Manitoba, producing meat for prairie fur farms. In the Northwest Territories, another fishery produced canned *muktak*, the blubbery skins sought after by the Inuit as food. These fisheries shut down when it was learned that belugas contained dangerously high concentrations of mercury.

At present, only native hunting of belugas is permitted, though netting for aquariums also takes place. Belugas are not endangered, but certain populations are threatened by over-hunting, and others are vulnerable to developments such as river damming, oil terminals and oil spills.

## Swimming Isn't Easy

*Swimming through water involves a difficult feat of engineering. If an animal or boat produces turbulence — swirling and eddying of the water — it will expend a great deal of energy. Dolphins, for example, can swim at the rate of 15 knots for long periods of time. If they produce turbulence, the effort required to swim that fast is comparable to the effort it would take a human being to climb 17,680 feet in an hour, a level of exertion beyond possibility. How is it, then, that dolphins can produce bursts of speed calculated at 24 miles per hour, blue whales are able to cruise at 23 miles per hour and killer whales can reach 36 miles per hour, faster than most oceangoing ships?*

*When a body moves through water, a boundary layer of water forms around it. The thickness and turbulence of this boundary layer determine the amount of friction and drag there will be. If the water around the body slows down due to friction, the boundary layer is disrupted, and a large swirling wake forms and creates drag behind the animal or ship. When the boundary layer flows smoothly, there is little wake and little drag. A streamlined shape minimizes the breakup of the boundary layer, but it is not enough to allow high-speed swimming. For this, the surface of the shape must allow the water to move in a laminar fashion — in smooth sheets instead of turbulent eddies.*

*Researchers once thought dolphins had a special skin that rippled under pressure and reduced turbulence, but attempts to demonstrate this have failed. They may, however, use a special muscular shiver to shed turbulence and reduce drag when moving at high speed.*

*Dolphins are not especially fast swimmers — they just seem fast.*

*Actually, large whales such as the 60-to-90-foot fin or blue whales can swim as fast as any dolphin. There is a peculiar paradox involved in the speed of these largest whales. For a wide range of sizes, there is a good correlation between how large a fish or whale is and how fast it can swim: the larger, the faster. There are also two types of speed: that of active swimming and that reached during brief bursts of full power. A dolphin swimming at full power reaches 33 feet per second, a speed that is merely the active cruising speed for a blue whale. In theory, blue whales could reach a speed of 270 miles per hour, but they never do, probably because such high speeds are of no use to them.*

Belugas are among the few whales with flexible faces that enable them to produce complex sounds and to forage in the bottom sediments.

# *Dolphins* Delphinidae

With 32 species found in all oceans and many tropical rivers, Delphinidae — the dolphins and their relatives — is the dominant family of cetaceans. The group originated recently, during the last 10 million years. The youth of Delphinidae and the high rate of speciation is reflected in the incomplete genetic isolation of dolphin species. Hybrids between supposedly distinct species are sometimes found in nature, and in captivity, crosses between members of different species and even members of what are considered different genera or families have occurred.

In size, dolphins range from the yard-long tropical-river dolphin to the massive seven-yard-long killer whale. All members of this group, however, have a highly streamlined shape, with a central sickle-shaped dorsal fin and well-developed teeth in both jaws. Many species also have a prominent forehead and a beaklike mouth. As a group, Delphinidae exhibit striking colour patterns that differ greatly from one species to another. These colour patterns may be used as social signals and species identification by dolphins, since they often occur in mixed schools and are more gregarious and visual than other cetaceans. Peglike teeth distinguish dolphins from porpoises, which have flattened teeth.

Much of what is known about dolphin behaviour and physiology is based on studies of the bottlenose dolphin, a species of warmer temperate and tropical waters. It is the best known dolphin, the species most often used as a performer in aquaria and in films. This species, which comes with a built-in smile, is capable of spectacular leaps. It is highly social, a superb imitator and one of the few cetaceans that can survive and breed in captivity. Some, but not all, of the observations of the bottlenose are typical of the dolphin family.

Bottlenoses, like many dolphin species, are opportunistic hunters, and the prey they select appears to influence their social groupings. Dense fish schools may attract herds of hundreds to thousands of dolphins. Herman Melville, author of *Moby-Dick*, called the aggregations "hilarious shoals, which upon the seas keep tossing themselves to heaven like caps in a Fourth of July crowd."

Subgroups of several to a few dozen individuals appear frequently within large herds. There is some segregation by sex and size. Large adult males, for example, rarely occur with subadult males. Young males may form bachelor groups or join adult females. And females with calves may group together. But, in general, the herd composition and structure is loose, and there may be little long-term association among family members except between mothers and offspring. Although calves are weaned after 18 months, they continue to associate with their mothers for as long as 6 years. Dolphin groups that stay together can coordinate their hunting activities and work together to repel sharks, chasing them away aggressively. Observations of those in captivity have also revealed that bottlenoses are obsessively sexual, much to the embarrassment of some aquarium audiences. While many cetaceans mate only at specific times, dolphins mate throughout the year. Males begin making sexual advances when they are only a few months old, attempting to copulate with everything from sea turtles to other dolphins, of either sex. Their penises are rich in nerve endings and are capable of coordinated movements, which seem to allow the penis to act as a tactile organ for feeling and exploring objects.

During courtship, dolphins bite and nip each other, often gently, but in adults, this may escalate to violent play involving leaps from the water, rushing at each other and smashing heads and bodies together. This activity between a male and a female usually ends in copulation.

Similar smashing contact often occurs between males, with older, larger males attempting to damage smaller ones. Males tend to have many scars in their genital region, presumably from attacks by other males. Aquarium operators acknowledge male-male aggression as one of the problems of keeping dolphins together. In the battle to establish dominance, one male may rape another. According to one account, when first put together, two large male Atlantic bottlenoses began with the usual open-mouthed threats and ended with sexual pursuit and two successful intromissions by the victor and somewhat reluctant submission by the loser. The entire episode lasted one hour, terminated, and was not seen again. The loser, who had been the dominant animal in the community, never again established himself nor was he seen to try. Whether this tactile aggression also occurs in wild dolphins is not known.

The bottlenose and other dolphins have sophisticated sound production and echolocation abilities. Bottlenoses send out clicking sounds and then read the echoes to determine the size, range, shape and even the substance of underwater objects. Using only echoes, they listen and interpret

---

*As the dominant family of cetaceans, the dolphins range in size from the 3-foot-long river dolphins of the tropics to massive 25-foot-long killer whales.*

*A pod of killer whales travelling in formation can encircle and trap schools of salmon or even sea lions.*

with enough subtlety to distinguish between objects differing by only 0.004 of an inch in thickness, between shapes such as cubes or cylinders and between cylinders made of different metals. To process sound so precisely requires large numbers of neural circuits and no doubt accounts for the huge size of the dolphin's brain.

## Cooperative Hunting

*Cetaceans have developed sophisticated forms of cooperative hunting. Bottlenose dolphins use their intelligence to coordinate the herding and trapping of fish. One extreme example of this was observed in a salt marsh in Georgia. Pairs of dolphins herded fish into the shallows until waves stranded the fish on shore. The dolphins then swam onto the land to eat and returned to the water with the next wave.*

*Humpback whales often form groups of three to seven to concentrate fish such as herring. They use a sophisticated technique known as the bubble net. Herring are*

*minuscule compared with humpbacks, so concentrating is necessary to make them a profitable prey item. One or two humpbacks dive below a herring school and begin releasing a trail of air bubbles as they swim around in a great closing spiral. The rising bubbles frighten the herring, and they draw to the centre. Finally, the humpbacks lunge together, swallowing herring by the thousands. There is probably some auditory communication used to coordinate the lunge.*

*The most skilful of all coordinated hunters are probably killer whales. Unlike humpbacks and most other dolphins, killer whales live in stable social groups in which the individuals are closely related, and they stay together and communicate among themselves for many years. Thus, like lion prides, packs of wolves and African wild dogs, a pod of killer whales has all the ingredients necessary for developing into a highly skilled unit capable of harvesting prey items far too hefty or swift for an individual to manage. The fastest fish, dolphins, large whales, sharks, sea turtles and sea lions all fall prey to packs of killer whales.*

*Author Erich Hoyt witnessed a*

*remarkable salmon hunt by a killer whale pod off British Columbia, a hunt so well coordinated that it is imitated and used by commercial fishing boats to find and catch salmon. The pod of 16 individuals, 60 to 100 feet apart, moved slowly up the coast in a line, herding salmon by shooting out of the water and whacking their heads down or smacking their flukes. The noises spooked the salmon and forced them to move. Gradually, the orcas joined into a circular formation, a living seine net, and then began to close in. Soon, the salmon school was packed together, jumping and boiling, and the killer whales began to feed. One at a time, they rushed in to gulp salmon while the others maintained the circular formation.*

*Cooperative food gathering in cetaceans, as in other mammals, may be one of the driving forces of sociality. It enables those who forage cooperatively to harvest a greater range of food, and in the case of killer whales, it is a means whereby younger and smaller family members receive the benefit of an increased food supply.*

# *Orca* Orcinus orca

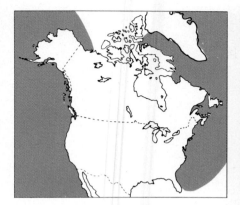

**Mammal:** *Orcinus orca* — orca, killer whale
**Meaning of Name:** *Orcinus* (whalelike); *orca* (whale)
**Description:** powerful streamlined body without much of a neck; large, blunt head with very small beak on upper jaw
**Colour:** shiny black above and white below; white ventral band extends from the lower jaw and widens at the base of the pectoral fins; it then narrows to form a three-pronged trident-shaped mark with the central prong running mid-ventrally to the base of the flukes; the other 2 prongs reach around to the posterior flanks; oval white patch just above and behind the eye and a grey indistinct saddle behind the dorsal fin
**Total Length:** male, up to 32 feet (usually 25); female, up to 26 feet
**Weight:** male, 19,800 pounds; female, 12,000 pounds
**Gestation:** 12 to 16 months
**Litter Size:** 1 every 10 years (some reproduce at 3-year intervals)
**Age of Maturity:** male, 16 years; female, 8 to 10 years
**Longevity:** male, 50 years; female, 100 years
**Diet:** an opportunistic feeder; consumes fish (salmon, cod, herring), squid, baleen whales and other smaller cetaceans, pinnipeds, sea turtles, penguins and other aquatic birds
**Habitat:** upper layers of cooler seas; prefers coastal, rather than pelagic, waters; often enters shallow bays, estuaries and mouths of rivers
**Predators:** man
**Dental Formula:** 40 to 56 teeth

Killer whales are the biggest and most formidable of all dolphins. With adult males reaching lengths of 32 feet and weights of 9 tons (as much as two elephants), orcas are the largest predators in the world, perched at the pinnacle of the oceanic food chain. As adept in the water as they are sizable, killer whales can reach speeds of 30 miles an hour and leap so that their mouth is 40 feet above the surface. They can, and do, eat the largest animals of the oceans, including other whales, seals, sharks, sea lions, sea turtles and a great variety of fish.

Many researchers compare orcas to wolves. Like wolves, orcas are not only top-level carnivores but are also highly social, intelligent and cooperative. Orcas and wolves have both been vilified and maligned because they are carnivores and were once thought of as a threat to both human life and economics. The public has now discovered that orcas are not to be feared and persecuted but to be admired. Numerous observers have reported that orcas are strangely loath to attack humans either in the water or in boats. In captivity, orcas have proved to be gentle subjects, and in the wild, they live in an orderly manner, usually displaying little of the ferocity attributed to them by earlier writers. In the words of biologist Richard Ellis, "The killer whale is not a murderer; neither is it a jolly circus clown to be made to jump through hoops for our entertainment. The real

*The killer whale is the top-level carnivore in the ocean, able to eat whales and other large marine mammals.*

orca lies somewhere between these extremes."

Orcas are no more deserving of the name "killer" than a baleen whale that kills and eats billions of krill. Orcas, however, are capable of attacks that provoke negative visceral reactions, and it is easy to see why witnesses have found some predation incidents overpowering and shocking. A film crew once photographed orcas ripping apart a young blue whale in a coordinated manner, with a few orcas herding the blue whale on the sides, others preventing it from diving too deeply and some forcing it down just far enough below the surface to interfere with breathing. Simultaneously, other orcas shredded the blue's tail flukes and tore away the dorsal fins. Large bull orcas ripped chunks of blubber and flesh away and dug a 6-square-foot cavity in the whale's side. The event was surrounded by much blood and gore. But the hunt of the killer whale, like that of wolves, wild dogs or chimpanzees, is simply an adaptation that allows the animals to harvest prey far larger than themselves. It is an adaptation that humans have employed in a similar fashion throughout evolutionary history, and it counts as one of the driving forces favouring the evolution of social behaviour.

*These killer whales are rubbing their skins underwater to scrape away parasites.*

The social system of orcas is based on groups known as pods, extended family groupings with amazing stability in membership. It appears that a killer whale stays in its pod for life. Perhaps when a pod grows too large — with more than 50 individuals — it becomes inefficient, and a mature female may leave to start her own pod. In smaller pods, sons and daughters may remain together with their mothers and dominant males for many years. Calves associate with their mothers for as long as 10 years, possibly much longer. Some researchers describe the orca social system as a matriarchy that grows and then splits off smaller matriarchal groups.

Members of a pod communicate with sound, and each pod appears to have its own dialect. It is likely that different pods compete with each other, at least indirectly. Larger pods appear to maintain better foraging areas, for example, in regions of high salmon density. Smaller pods are forced into the role of transients that range farther and take less profitable food items. Some researchers believe that these transient herds perpetrate most of the attacks on large whales and that these whales are not preferred prey. From time to time, several orca pods join together temporarily in large aggregations whose significance is unclear. The gatherings may simply

be the result of prey concentration. But even when in the company of outsiders, pods maintain their integrity. The possession of distinctive dialects probably facilitates this.

Male orcas may live 50 years and females for as long as 100 years. Because these long-lived whales remain together, they have an opportunity as well as the genetic incentive to develop highly cooperative behaviours, especially those requiring learning and teamwork among group members.

Killer whales are sexually dimorphic. Males grow larger than females and mature at a later age — 16 years as opposed to 8 to 10 for females. The dorsal fin of the male is close to twice the size of the female's, reaching a height of 6 1/2 feet, and may be used as a signal of size and age. During the breeding season, large bulls may be pugnacious, and it is likely that a harem system operates in the pod, with each large bull having access to three or four females. Normally, there are far fewer females than males available for mating because of the long birth interval. Females may give birth every third year in theory, but in nature, a calf once every 10 years is more typical.

*The powerful tail flukes of the killer whale,* **top**, *can be used as a clubbing weapon to stun prey as large as sea lions. The orca's size, fierce reputation and intelligence make it a popular public-aquarium attraction,* **bottom**.

## Pacific White-sided Dolphin *Lagenorhynchus obliquidens*

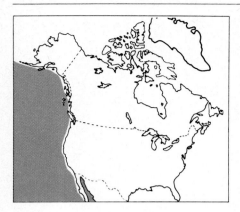

**Mammal:** *Lagenorhynchus obliquidens* — Pacific white-sided dolphin
**Meaning of Name:** *Lagenorhynchus* (bottlenose); *obliquidens* (slanted) may refer to sharply hooked dorsal fin
**Description:** cylindrical fusiform body; small beak; slender hooked dorsal fin; keeled slender tail stock
**Colour:** black back fading to grey on the flanks, fins and flukes; white underparts; tip of lower jaw is black; 2 pale grey or white stripes on each flank and another pair on the tail stock; a narrow dark strip between corner of mouth and flipper is continuous with dark lips
**Total Length:** up to 7.5 feet
**Weight:** 180 to 300 pounds
**Gestation:** 10 to 12 months
**Litter Size:** 1
**Age of Maturity:** male, 6 feet long; female, 6 feet long
**Longevity:** 20 to 30 years
**Diet:** wide variety of small fish and squid
**Habitat:** cool offshore temperate to sub-Arctic waters; also occurs on the outer edge of the continental shelf or close to shore near deep canyons
**Predators:** none recorded (probably killer whale and sharks)
**Dental Formula:** 116 to 128 teeth

*Pacific white-sided dolphins, like their Atlantic cousins, are small, gregarious and athletic. Not only do they bow ride with boats, but they seem to seek out the company of larger whales along with small companions such as Dall's porpoises, common dolphins and even sea lions.*

## Atlantic White-sided Dolphin *Lagenorhynchus acutus*

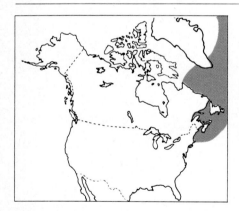

**Mammal:** *Lagenorhynchus acutus* — Atlantic white-sided dolphin
**Meaning of Name:** *Lagenorhynchus* (bottlenose); *acutus* (sharp, pointed) may refer either to the dorsal fin or to the short distinct beak
**Description:** robust body
**Colour:** black above and white below; sides are variable with zones of grey, tan and white; long white band on the sides runs below dorsal fin to above anus; black stripe from corner of mouth to junction of pectoral fin; black beak
**Total Length:** 6 to 9 feet
**Weight:** 400 to 515 pounds
**Gestation:** 10 to 12 months
**Litter Size:** 1 every 2 or 3 years
**Age of Maturity:** male, older than 4 to 6 years; female, older than 5 to 8 years
**Longevity:** male, 22 years; female, 27 years
**Diet:** fish (herring, hake, mackerel, smelt, anchovies), small squid, crustaceans, whelks
**Habitat:** pelagic species occurring in cool offshore waters
**Predators:** sharks, killer whale
**Dental Formula:** 120 to 132 teeth

*The Atlantic white-sided dolphin cavorts throughout the North Atlantic in schools numbering in the thousands. Its aerial performance includes graceful arcing leaps with spins and lobtailing.*

## How Smart Are They?

*The brain of the bottlenose dolphin is as large as a human's, and a sperm whale brain, at 11 pounds, is four to five times as large. Brain size, in combination with the ability of dolphins to imitate and to learn complicated tricks in captivity, leads some to suggest that dolphins possess an intellect comparable to that of humans. But it is difficult to get scientists to agree on a definition of intelligence for our own species; attempting to define and measure intelligence for another species is all but impossible.*

*Intelligence is often defined as the ability to solve problems and use reason. However, this begs two questions: What are the problems to be solved, and how do we measure success? Problems that involve visual memory would prove that dolphins are dumb indeed. In nature, dolphins have less use for visual information than for other kinds of signals. Their streamlined and rigid facial structure means that they use facial expressions relatively little, and although they see well, sound is a much better medium for detecting and sending signals. The same animals tested on problem solving with sounds would seem much more intelligent.*

*Researchers cannot study intelligence independently of the environment in which a species lives. It may be difficult to conceive of the kind of problems that would reflect dolphin intelligence, simply because we know so little about what they do in the wild and how they perceive their world. For example, problems involving variables such as the size of a fish school, the species in the school and the rate at which it is moving are what the large dolphin brain is designed to solve. Dolphin brains are not designed to communicate with humans.*

*Many researchers have assumed that intelligence depends on language and that language is necessary for ordered thought and reasoning. Because dolphins use a variety of complicated sounds, people have often assumed or attempted to show that dolphins use language in the same way humans do. Some have even said that*

*Atlantic white-sided dolphins often use their intelligence to hunt cooperatively by herding fish with coordinated tactics.*

*dolphins can learn to speak to humans. Again, there is no ecological reason to expect dolphins to use a human-style system to solve their radically different aquatic communication problems. There is also no evidence that dolphins have evolved a language system with syntax and structure like that of humans.*

*A more objective definition of intelligence may be to compare the capacity of different brains for processing information. The volume of the brain is correlated with the amount of information it is able to store and decipher. On this scale, dolphins do rank as intelligent, although not as intelligent as humans. This still leaves unanswered the question of what dolphins use their large brains and intelligence for. One possibility is that processing the echolocation signals for distances, speed, textures and other measures from a barrage of echoes uses a large amount of the brain. Bats, however, do not have such large brains, though they are faced with a similar echolocation information-processing task. A more likely explanation is that dolphins use large amounts of brain circuitry in communicating with each other and in solving prey-capture problems.*

*Most dolphins are long-lived generalized feeders, encountering hundreds of different prey items in almost infinite permutations and combinations, and they depend on*

*group coordination for prey capture. They probably rely on learning and remembering behaviours used by older, more experienced dolphins to catch food.*

*One of the features of captive dolphins that has impressed humans is their superb ability at imitation and mimicry. Bottlenose dolphins in captivity have picked up a piece of tile and used it to scrape algae off the tank window after watching human tank cleaners scraping away algae. A 6-month-old aquarium dolphin that saw someone puff cigarette smoke against the glass observation window swam off to her mother, collected a mouthful of milk, swam back to the observation window and puffed out her own cloud of milk. It is safe to say that these are actions never performed in the wild. However, when animals live a long time, are social and must handle a great variety of prey, the ability to copy what others are doing must be highly adaptive. Dolphins are like primates in this respect; possibly both groups have developed large brains for that reason.*

## *Long-finned Pilot Whale* Globicephala melaena

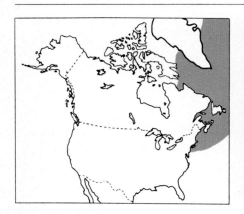

**Mammal:** *Globicephala melaena* — long-finned pilot whale, Atlantic pilot whale, pilot whale, pothead
**Meaning of Name:** *Globicephala* (bulbous head), due to large rounded melon; *melaena* (black); the colour is black except for the white throat
**Description:** slender robust body with thick bulbous head, sometimes squarish in front; very long "sicklelike" pectoral fins
**Colour:** black with an indistinct dark grey saddle behind the dorsal fin and small dark grey spot behind each eye; pearl grey anchor-shaped patch running from the throat to the anus
**Total Length:** male, 13 to 23 feet; female, 11 to 17 feet
**Weight:** 1,800 pounds (maximum of 6,000 pounds)
**Gestation:** 15 to 16 months
**Litter Size:** 1; female bears 5 or 6 calves in a lifetime (possibly every 3 years)
**Age of Maturity:** male, 12 to 13 years; female, 6 years
**Longevity:** maximum is estimated to be 40 to 50 years
**Diet:** squid are exclusive food, and fish (especially cod) are only eaten if squid are not available
**Habitat:** generally pelagic but may occur in inshore waters in the summer; often found on the edge of the continental shelf, where water depths quickly descend from 600 feet to the ocean floor, where there are plenty of squid
**Predators:** no known predators aside from man
**Dental Formula:** 36 to 48 teeth

Long-finned pilot whales are larger than all dolphin family members except the killer whale. Males may reach a length of 23 feet and females 17 feet, with weights of 2 to 3 tons for the largest individuals. Males mature at age 12 and females at age 6. Pregnancy lasts 15 to 16 months, and females nurse their calves for as long as 20 months, which gives the pilot whale a low reproductive rate. There are strong bonds between mothers and offspring and possibly among other relatives. When one pilot whale is wounded, it is usually attended by other members of the school.

The long-finned pilot whale can be distinguished by its dark black-brown colour and by its protruding forehead, which gives it the common name of pothead. This forehead melon may function in the echolocation of squid schools. Potheads eat both squid and fish and also rummage along the bottom. However, their main food is squid, and the behaviour and ecology of this food source appear to influence the behaviour of these dolphins. Rather than having any rigid or pronounced migration system, they aggregate and follow the activity of the squid.

A large population of pilot whales once existed around Newfoundland, and heavy whaling there has supplied much information on this species. In Newfoundland, potheads begin arriving at inshore waters in June and July and remain there, feeding, until October and November, when they head offshore to areas washed by the warm Gulf Stream currents. This movement duplicates that of the squid species *Illex illecebrosus*, which moves inshore during the summer to feed on capelin, herring and mackerel. *Illex illecebrosus* has an explosive growth

*The gregarious pilot whale has well-developed social bonds and may assist other pilot whales in distress.*

pattern. Young squid are spawned offshore at the edge of the continental shelf in late autumn, and their parents die after spawning. The young squid feed mainly on krill and other plankton over the winter. At the start of summer, when they weigh a few ounces, they move inshore and begin eating capelin, mackerel, herring and other fish and grow at a phenomenal rate, reaching a weight close to a pound by the end of the summer. These squid provide the bait for line fishing of cod and are a major food for seals, seabirds (such as fulmars and shearwaters) and pilot whales, which can each eat as much as 10 tons of squid per year.

Some pilot whales live year-round at the edge of the continental shelf where squid are constantly available. It is the ability of these dolphins to track the squid following the fish that earns them the name pilot whales. Fishermen, as well as seabirds and other dolphin species, rely on sightings of pilot whales to guide them to fishing or squid-jigging grounds.

Pilot whales are highly gregarious, which again may reflect the concentrated schools of squid the whales feed on. Aggregations of pilot whales in the hundreds and thousands have been reported. When not feeding, pilot whales often lie floating together, almost touching, like log rafts. This herding may have evolved in response to shark and killer whale attacks. Pilot whales seem to respond to threats in a coordinated manner, following leaders and emitting individual distinctive distress calls. This, unfortunately, has made the species vulnerable to stranding and mass slaughter. Frequently, hundreds of pilot whales become stranded along beaches and usually die. The cause is unknown, and none of the possible explanations — such as disorientation due to storms, parasites disrupting the sonar navigation, frenzied feeding or stress-induced suicide — are plausible.

Regardless of the cause, mass stranding appears to be related to the intense cohesiveness of pilot whale schools. The Newfoundland pilot whalers once put this behaviour to use and herded large schools into bays and ran them aground to be butchered. In 1956 alone, 10,000 pilot whales were killed in Newfoundland, and whale meat was sold for pennies a pound to mink farms. This led to a serious depletion of the pilot whale stocks in the area until whaling was banned in 1972.

*Pilot whales migrate according to the seasonal movements of squid and capelin, often coming into shallow bays during summer months.*

## White-beaked Dolphin *Lagenorhynchus albirostris*

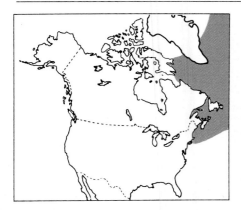

**Mammal:** *Lagenorhynchus albirostris* — white-beaked dolphin
**Meaning of Name:** *Lagenorhynchus* (bottlenose); *albirostris* (white snout)
**Description:** robust, streamlined body with very small beak; high, slender dorsal fin
**Colour:** dark grey to black above and white or light grey below; flanks have 2 greyish areas in front of, behind and below dorsal fin; pale band across beak, but lips outlined in black
**Total Length:** up to 10 feet
**Weight:** male, 440 pounds; female, 400 pounds
**Gestation:** 1 year
**Litter Size:** may give birth to 2 or more

calves, but usually only 1 survives
**Age of Maturity:** unknown
**Longevity:** unknown
**Diet:** squid, fish (cod, herring, mackerel, capelin, anchovies), crustaceans, whelks, octopus
**Habitat:** pelagic in offshore cold Arctic waters
**Predators:** no known predators other than man
**Dental Formula:** 88 to 100 teeth

A northern specialist, the white-beaked dolphin is distinguished by a thick coat of blubber and a willingness to venture farther north in the Atlantic than other dolphins. White-beaked

*The white-beaked dolphin is one of the few dolphins specialized for a life in the cold North Atlantic.*

dolphins are also athletic leapers. Groups range from 10 to 1,500 animals. Even though white-beaked dolphins have fewer teeth than many other dolphins, they eat a wide variety of food, ranging from hermit crabs and snails to fish. The preferred fare, however, appears to be soft-fleshed squid, which might account for their shortage of teeth.

# *Porpoises* Phocoenidae

### *Dall's Porpoise*  Phocoenoides dalli

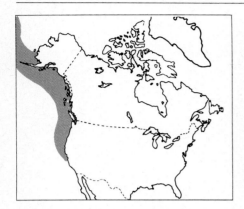

**Mammal:** *Phocoenoides dalli* — Dall's porpoise

**Meaning of Name:** *Phocoenoides* (porpoise); *dalli* (after William H. Dall, an American naturalist)

**Description:** extremely robust with small head and flukes; short, straight mouth with poorly defined beak

**Colour:** slate-grey to shiny black overall; white blaze on belly extends onto the sides as large oval white patch, sometimes with faint dark spots below and behind the dorsal fin; the flippers, the posterior margin of the tail stock and the tip of the dorsal fin may be pale grey or blotched

**Total Length:** male, 6 to 7 feet; female, 5 to 7 feet

**Weight:** male, 210 to 290 pounds; female, 150 to 330 pounds (up to 480 pounds)

**Gestation:** 11.4 months

**Litter Size:** 1 every 3 years

**Age of Maturity:** male, 8 years; female, 7 years

**Longevity:** a few have lived more than 16 years

**Diet:** deep-sea fish, squid and crustaceans

**Habitat:** in cool waters usually well offshore and beyond the outer edge of the continenal shelf; occasionally found in deep inshore waters

**Predators:** killer whale, sharks and man

**Dental Formula:** 44 to 52 teeth

Of the world's six porpoise species, two occur in North America and, at 5 feet long, are the continent's smallest cetaceans. Their uniform body plan includes a reduced dorsal fin, small jaws, blunt snout and the flat teeth that distinguish them from dolphins. All porpoises seem to be generalized fish- and squid-feeders that pursue their prey at high speed.

The Dall's porpoise speeds through the deep waters along the west coast of North America. With a huge heart and a powerful body capable of driving the animal along at 30 knots, the Dall's porpoise is a pursuit predator of many kinds of fish. Whale watchers delight in seeing these brightly marked animals, with their splotches of black and white, throwing up shearing wakes as they make sharp turns. Dall's porpoises rarely breach but frequently ride bow waves. Most of their feeding is thought to take place in medium-depth water of less than 650 feet, making them neither creatures of the deep open ocean nor of shallow bays. Instead, they most often occur near the edge of deep water and probably dive to feed on bottom fish.

Dall's porpoises travel in small groups, and little is known of their social behaviour. With adult males reaching 7 feet, they are among the largest porpoises and have a long breeding and weaning interval, calving every 3 years and weaning after 2 years. Even though abundant, the Dall's porpoise is at risk when deep drifting gill nets are in use.

*The squat, thick body form of the Dall's porpoise makes it a powerful swimmer that sends up "rooster-tail" sprays of water when it zigzags in pursuit of fish.*

# *Harbour Porpoise* Phocoena phocoena

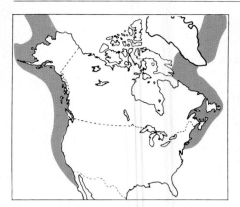

**Mammal:** *Phocoena phocoena —* harbour porpoise
**Meaning of Name:** *Phocoena* (porpoise)
**Description:** features that distinguish them from dolphins include blunt, short beak and spade-shaped teeth (rather than conical, as in dolphins); stout body and blunt head; triangular dorsal fin with 6 small tubercules on its leading edge
**Colour:** dark grey or black above, fading to light greyish brown on sides (may be speckled in overlap zone); white belly; black stripes run from flippers to corners of mouth and lower lip
**Total Length:** usually 5 feet, but up to 6 feet
**Weight:** up to 140 pounds
**Gestation:** 10 to 11 months
**Litter Size:** 1 every 1 or 2 years
**Age of Maturity:** 3 to 6 years
**Longevity:** 6 to 10 years; rarely exceeds 13 years
**Diet:** schooling fish (herring, hake, pollack, capelin, whiting), bottom-living fish, squid, octopus and crustaceans
**Habitat:** subarctic and cold temperate waters; generally inshore in shallow waters along the continental shelf and often in bays, harbours, estuaries and the mouths of large rivers
**Predators:** man, killer whale and large sharks
**Dental Formula:** 44 to 52 teeth

Measuring only 5 feet long when fully grown, harbour porpoises are the smallest cetaceans in northern North American waters. These shy animals are often seen but difficult to study. Perhaps their size makes them vulnerable to and wary of predatory sharks and killer whales.

Harbour porpoises are shallow-water specialists and feed on a wide variety of prey. Their group sizes and movements are closely linked to the movements of the fish they eat. Sometimes, harbour porpoises are seen alone or in groups of a few individuals, but on the East Coast, large groups of up to 50 form. Little is known about harbour porpoises' social life except that it seems unstructured, possibly to allow the porpoises to adjust to changing fish dispersions. Sex-segregated groups, with mature males in some bands and females with calves and juveniles in others, occur.

The harbour porpoise has a low reproductive rate for its small size. It takes 3 to 6 years to mature, and females probably give birth only every other year, since gestation takes 10 or 11 months and weaning another half-year or more.

Because they feed in shallow bays, harbour porpoises are sensitive to pollution. In the Bay of Fundy, harbour porpoises suffer from high levels of DDT, PCBs, mercury and other chemical pollutants. In large areas of Europe, harbour porpoise populations have been decimated, possibly

*Harbour porpoises are among the smallest of cetaceans, usually less than 6 feet long.*

because of pollution. There are locations in North America where the Indian practice of hunting porpoise for food continues. This, however, is less harmful to harbour porpoise populations than the mortality caused by monofilament gill nets set for fish. There are no reliable population estimates to determine if harbour porpoises are seriously threatened, but they are declining.

# *Grey Whale* Eschrichtidae

## *Grey Whale* Eschrichtius gibbosus

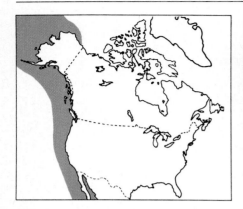

**Mammal:** *Eschrichtius gibbosus* — grey whale

**Meaning of Name:** *Eschrichtius* (named in honour of D.F. Eschricht, a Dutch zoologist); *gibbosus* (humped) refers to the fact that in place of the dorsal fin, there is a row of 9 or 10 small humps

**Description:** fusiform body that looks tapered at both ends when viewed from above; relatively small, triangular-shaped head slopes down at a sharp angle from a pair of blowholes; large mouth curves slightly upward; in place of the dorsal fin, there is a low hump, beginning two-thirds of the distance along the back, followed by a serrated ridge; irregular rows of hair on upper and lower jaws, especially on lips; 138 to 174 yellow baleen plates on each side of mouth

**Colour:** mottled grey; heavily flecked with white scars caused by whale lice and barnacles embedded in the hide

**Total Length:** male, 40 to 50 feet; female, 46 to 50 feet

**Weight:** 44,000 to 81,400 pounds

**Gestation:** 11 to 13 months

**Litter Size:** 1

**Age of Maturity:** 5 to 11 years (average 8 years)

**Longevity:** 70 years

**Diet:** mainly benthic organisms (amphipods are staple of their diet), crustaceans, mollusks, worms and small fish

**Habitat:** coastal temperate waters along shallow continental shelves and closer to shore than any other large cetacean

**Predators:** killer whale, large sharks

**Dental Formula:** 0

With no fossil record and only one living species, Eschrichtidae is distinct from all other baleen whale families. The grey whale has only two to four throat grooves, and its baleen plates are the shortest of all baleen whales, only 1 foot long, compared with the 12-foot-long plates of some other species. Greys have more hair than other whales, with rows of bristles around their lips. All of these differences are probably adaptations for bottom feeding. Grey whales are also the only baleen whales with distinctly grey mottled skin and no dorsal fins.

Unlike other baleen whales, the grey feeds on the bottom of the ocean and has poorly developed throat grooves, the expandable pleats that enable other species to swallow and sieve a huge mass of plankton or fish. The grey whale has a different feeding strategy. It dives to the bottom, rolls sideways and ploughs its head through the mud, sucking up sediment. This mass of mud and bottom-dwelling animals is then filtered by the grey whale's short baleen plates. Feeding whales often surface with muck and water streaming out of their mouths and are attended by seabirds that pick out scraps the whales miss or reject. The gouges left in the mud are selectively depleted of small amphipod crustaceans, and it is thought that grey whale foraging has an important role in regulating the bottom-dwelling invertebrate communities of the shallow northern seas. The huge population of barnacles and whale lice carried by the grey whale are responsible for its unique mottled pattern.

Grey whales hug the west coast,

*A conservation success story, grey whales exhibit "friendly" behaviour to whale watchers, appearing alongside boats to be scratched and petted.*

bringing them within easy range of whale watchers and researchers, and as a result, they are well understood. Greys are best known for their long migration, said to be the longest of any mammal. Some may travel from the high Arctic seas to tropical Mexican lagoons, an annual circuit of 12,500 miles.

A conflict between their feeding requirements and calving requirements prompts greys to migrate. Cold Arctic waters, particularly in the Bering and Chuckchi Seas, are highly productive in summer and ideal for feeding, but they are poor for calving. Relatively small when born, young grey whales lack an insulating blubber coat necessary to withstand constant submersion in Arctic seas. Tropical waters produce less food, but they are mild and do not stress the young calves.

The migration is segregated by sex and size. Late-term pregnant females start south in the autumn. Adult males follow, and immature animals leave last. Pods of up to 16 whales move along at top speeds of 4 to 5 miles per hour and cover roughly 60 miles per day. The whales seem to travel 24 hours a day and apparently do not sleep during the entire journey, which takes from 2 1/2 to 3 months. Greys winter for 2 or 3 months in shallow lagoons off California and Mexico. The lagoons are so shallow that greys are occasionally stranded at low

tide. However, they remain calm and simply wait for high tide to float them again.

Females give birth from January through March in sheltered lagoons and stay segregated from males. Females with calves leave the southern waters later in the spring than males. The mothers and young whales also travel more slowly than males. Mothers defend calves strongly and continue to nurse until the calves are as old as nine months.

Courtship takes place in the winter lagoons, and because roughly half of the females are pregnant or lactating, there are several males for every receptive female. Although females have been seen rolling and splashing in the company of three or four males, male-male combat is not overt.

Migrating greys are thought to feed little, but this is uncertain. They do, however, remain close to the coast, which once made them vulnerable to all manner of coast-based fisheries. However, it was only when 19th-century whalers began killing pregnant and nursing females in their calving lagoons that the population began to crash. Grey whales were hunted almost to extinction along the west coast of North America, and currently, they are on the verge of extinction in Korean waters. They once existed along the coast of Europe but became extinct, presumably because of overhunting by Basque whalers. Fortunately, in North America, they are now thought to be approaching their previous population densities.

Some conservation measures have

*Found close to shore along the West Coast during the summer, grey whales migrate 12,500 miles each year to calve in Mexican waters.*

worked successfully for this whale. The grey whale, in turn, has proved a good ambassador. It entertains thousands of whale watchers, thereby increasing public concern and awareness of the problems confronting other whales. Grey whales are even reported to exhibit ''friendly'' behaviour to whale watchers, with some individuals appearing regularly alongside boats to be scratched and petted. This may be because greys are itchy from their heavy infestations of barnacles and whale lice, but it may mean something more.

# *Rorquals* Balaenopteridae

The Balaenopteridae family contains six species, distributed throughout the oceans. In contrast to right whales, rorquals are streamlined. They also have distinctive ribbed skin folds along their throats. They have a bowed jawline and feed using baleen sieving, but different species take different sized prey. The skin folds act as expanding pleats, allowing the whales to gulp massive loads of seawater, krill and fish. They then force the seawater out, straining the food with their baleen. All species except the tropical Bryde's whales follow a north-south migration, giving birth in warm areas and moving to the high latitudes to feed during summer. These are large, long-lived whales. Some species live 100 years. They tend to have long pregnancies of roughly 1 year and nurse their calves for 6 to 7 months. Many rorquals have yet to recover from near extinction caused by whaling, and they remain threatened.

## Migration

*Researchers have found surprising parallels between the migrations of the giant whales and those of birds. Whales and birds might seem as different from each other as any two animal groups could be, but they do have important energetic similarities that make long-distance migration economically attractive.*

*Long-distance migrants, be they whales, birds, bats or fish, normally store food before migration and feed relatively little en route.*

*Whales can travel huge distances because they store and move cheaply a massive amount of energy-rich fat. Birds can migrate far because the most efficient flying velocity is very fast. A bird burns energy at a high rate, but it also covers distance at a high rate. A 2-ounce bird can carry enough fat to fly 600 miles without feeding. A larger bird with a higher optimum flight speed and lower transport cost can fly even farther. Whales must travel at slower speeds, since the most efficient swimming velocity is much lower than that of flying. However, whales burn their fuel at a very slow rate. So a whale can migrate as far as a bird simply by taking longer and by accumulating a huge store of fat.*

*Birds and whales seem to migrate for the same reasons. Mortality rates during winter are lower in warmer areas, and so is the cost of maintaining body temperature. Food, however, is less plentiful. Migratory birds rear their young in the Arctic because of the tremendous explosion of insect and other food sources during the summer months. Twenty-four hours of daylight allow foraging to continue for much greater periods in the Arctic than in the tropics. Similarly for whales, the great amounts of sunlight and the upwelling of nutrients in the cold oceans cause massive blooms of planktonic plants that, in turn, produce population explosions in the animals and fish that feed on the plants. Plankton densities in the summer Arctic may exceed those in the tropical wintering grounds by a hundred times. Migratory whales generally calve in the warmer wintering grounds, but this is not the time of greatest energy costs for the female. Breast-feeding is usually more costly than pregnancy, and the young calves continue to breast-feed and grow at great rates during the Arctic summer months.*

*Climatic history has played a key part in the migration of whales. Whales probably evolved in warm-water regions when much of the world had a similar climate. As the Earth became more polarized with greater temperature extremes and the continents continued drifting apart, whales began to move and breed seasonally, extending their range until extreme journeys such as the 12,500-mile migrations of the grey whale had evolved.*

*The cues that whales use to migrate are even less well understood than those of migratory birds. It is thought that whale migration is stimulated by day-length changes that cause hormonal changes. Some observers believe grey whales follow bottom topography along the coast. Radio-tracking studies of dolphins off the coast of California indicate that dolphins also follow undersea floor features. When grey whales encounter a strange region of the ocean floor, such as a deep canyon, they may "spy hop," that is, raise their heads entirely out of the water vertically and then look around, possibly for landmarks. How deep-water whales such as blue and sei find their way is not known. Like birds, they may use the sun and the stars to plot directions. In any case, it is likely that young whales depend on following older whales to learn migration routes. By selectively taking the largest, oldest and most knowledgeable whales, human whalers have probably depleted a valuable information pool. The loss of information about where and when to travel may be one reason why some of the migratory whales have been so slow to recover.*

The expandable throat pleats of rorquals, such as this humpback, allow the whales to gulp in and strain massive volumes of water.

## *Fin Whale* Balaenoptera physalus

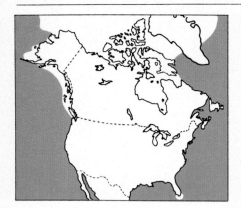

**Mammal:** *Balaenoptera physalus* —
fin whale, fin-backed whale
**Meaning of Name:** *Balaenoptera* (whale
with a strong dorsal fin); *physalus* (pipe
or wind instrument) refers to the
blowhole through which the whale
breathes and makes whistling sounds
**Description:** long, sleek body tapering
posteriorly; V-shaped snout with single
median dorsal ridge; 60 throat grooves
extend from tip of lower jaw to navel;
dorsal fin is high and strongly hooked
behind; posterior to dorsal fin, the back
is distinctly ridged
**Colour:** slate-blue above and white
below; right side of face is paler than left
side; right-front baleen plates are pale
grey, and the rest are striped with
alternating yellowish white and blue-
grey; the left plate of the baleen is blue-
grey behind; there is a greyish white
chevron behind the head
**Total Length:** 60 to 70 feet (up to 88
feet)
**Weight:** up to 99,000 pounds
**Gestation:** 11 to 12 months
**Litter Size:** 1 every 3 years
**Age of Maturity:** 4 to 12 years
**Longevity:** some have been estimated
to have lived up to 114 years
**Diet:** various kinds of small fish, krill and
other pelagic crustaceans and squid
**Habitat:** pelagic; seldom found in water
less than 700 feet deep; occurs in both
inshore and offshore waters
**Predators:** killer whale, man
**Dental Formula:** 0

Fin whales are the second largest whales and the most abundant baleen whales. They are known for their inexplicable head coloration, with the right side white and the left side dark grey. One theory is that fins may use the white to scare and herd fish and the dark as camouflage. Fin whales eat a variety of plankton as well as fish, which they may locate with low-frequency echolocation. Like many fish eaters, fins are capable of spurts of speed up to 20 miles per hour, and they are one of the deeper-diving baleen whales, descending to 750 feet. A fin whale tagged with a radio transmitter has been recorded travelling 180 miles in a day. They migrate north to south in groups of two to seven or alone. Little is known about their behaviour.

### Undercrowding: The Allee Effect

*Undercrowding may be as great a threat to survival as overcrowding. The ecologist W.C. Allee demonstrated that some organisms may have actually reduced survival rates if they become too rare. He showed that fish, for example, are less able to survive stress as individuals than as members of a group. Whales are probably particularly vulnerable to the Allee effect. Many species rely on cooperative hunting to gather much of their food; others rely on the learning and experience of older group members to migrate successfully; and those whales that exist dispersed over the high seas must expend more time and effort in*

*Fast and large, fin whales are able to travel 180 miles in a day.*

*mate finding when they are rare than when they are common.*

*Many populations typically go through phases of population growth: a fast growth at intermediate densities; a slow, stable birth-and-death rate at high densities; and a lag phase at low densities where both birth and death rates are low. It might be possible for a species to get stuck in a lag phase, especially if predation continually crops the population. This may be one reason for the slow increase of some of the larger baleen whales even though they are no longer hunted. The bowhead population of Hudson Bay, an immense area of water, has declined to a few hundred whales. The right whale population is limited to a few hundred in the northern Atlantic and Pacific. It is conceivable that this results in low pregnancy rates or possibly decreased calf survival to the point that the birth rate is cancelled by the death rate.*

## *Sei Whale* Balaenoptera borealis

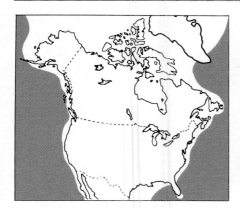

**Mammal:** *Balaenoptera borealis* — sei whale

**Meaning of Name:** *Balaenoptera* (whale with a strong dorsal fin); *borealis* (of the north)

**Description:** heavier body form than the other rorquals; relatively short pectoral flippers; large dorsal fin situated relatively forward; 40 to 62 pinkish throat grooves that only extend midway between the base of the flippers and the navel

**Colour:** bluish grey dorsally; bands of grey on sides extend from lower jaw backwards and meet on the abdomen; belly is greyish white near the ventral grooves; irregular white splotches on throat and chest

**Total Length:** male, 26 to 60 feet; female, 36 to 57 feet (up to 69 feet)

**Weight:** 60,000 pounds

**Gestation:** 10 to 12 months

**Litter Size:** 1 every 2 or 3 years

**Age of Maturity:** 6 to 12 years

**Longevity:** up to 74 years

**Diet:** small planktonic crustaceans, such as copepods (*Calanus* spp), and several species of krill as well as fish

**Habitat:** pelagic species, primarily in temperate open seas far from shore; migrates to subtropical waters for winter

**Predators:** killer whale, man

**Dental Formula:** 0

Sei whales are unpredictable. They migrate, but with an irregular rhythm, so their movements cannot be accurately predicted the way grey whales' can. The word sei comes from the Norwegian term for the pollack fish that arrive off the coast of Norway at the same time as the whales. It is possible that both pollack and whales feed on the same plankton. When sei whales swim, they veer erratically and travel at speeds of up to 30 miles per hour, faster than any other member of their family. They feed at or near the surface. Seis have the most finely fringed baleen of all whales, with bristles only 1/250 inch in diameter, and are capable of taking tiny planktonic organisms. But true to their unpredictable character, they will also gulp fish. Seis are strictly pelagic and rarely come close to shore to feed.

The seis' broad diet, irregular occurrence and lack of a heavy blubber coat meant that whalers ignored them until the other large rorquals had been decimated. Sei populations were then heavily hunted even though almost nothing was and is known about them. Commercial whaling of seis has now ceased, and they seem to be recovering.

In water, the sei can be distinguished from blue and fin whales by its more forward and erect dorsal fin and heavier body form. Its social behaviour is still largely unknown, except that it tends to travel in small groups of two to five.

*Sei whales are open-ocean specialists whose delicate baleen plates sieve out the finest sizes of plankton.*

## *Minke Whale* Balaenoptera acutorostrata

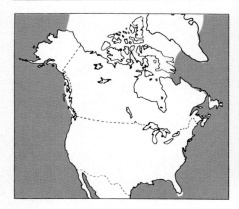

**Mammal:** *Balaenoptera acutorostrata* — minke whale; smallest baleen whale in North America

**Meaning of Name:** *Balaenoptera* (whale with a strong dorsal fin); *acutorostrata* (sharp or pointed beak) refers to the fact that this whale has a more pointed snout than other whales

**Description:** streamlined body tapering posteriorly; medially ridged and pointed rostrum and small mouth; 40 to 70 throat pleats terminate halfway between the tip of the flippers and the navel; tall falcate dorsal fin; 270 to 348 yellowish white baleen plates

**Colour:** dark grey to black with white underparts from the lower lip to flukes; a major diagnostic feature is a diagonal white band on the upper surface of the pectoral flippers

**Total Length:** 20 to 30 feet (up to 35 feet)

**Weight:** maximum of 22,000 pounds

**Gestation:** 10 to 11 months

**Litter Size:** 1 every 1 or 2 years

**Age of Maturity:** 7 to 8 years

**Longevity:** 50 years

**Diet:** small fish, some squid, krill and copepods

**Habitat:** open polar and temperate seas over the continental shelf; seldom found farther than 100 miles from land; often enters bays and estuaries; moves farther into polar ice fields than any other rorqual

**Predators:** killer whale

**Dental Formula:** 0

Measuring 26 feet when full-grown, the minke whale is the smallest rorqual. Smallness made minkes unattractive to whalers when larger whales were available, so relatively little is known about the species. Some populations are highly migratory in the typical baleen whale fashion. Others seem to stay in one area for most of the year. Migrant minkes can travel far into the breaking pack ice and are occasionally trapped there. Minkes are usually solitary or in groups of only a few individuals, except in rich feeding grounds, where several hundred may concentrate to feed. They eat small fish and krill and often engage in lunge-feeding and breaching. Like humpbacks, their pursuit of schools of fish is bringing them into conflict with fishermen. They are often killed in fish traps and nets, and they are now the target of commercial whalers. Unlike other rorquals, minke whales have a tendency to approach ships, and they are reported to be relatively acrobatic, breaching and rolling belly-up. They have a distinctive V-shaped head, and in northern regions, they often have a white band running diagonally across their flippers.

### On Being Big

A single blue whale is as massive and burns as much energy as the entire human population of a 2,000-resident North American town. A mature blue whale is longer than three railrcad boxcars, weighs between 150 and 200 tons (as much as 40 bull elephants) and can eat 4 tons of food and burn 1½ million calories a day. The blue whale is the largest, longest and heaviest animal that has ever lived on Earth. Its large size is made possible by the freedom and buoyancy provided by seawater.

*Minke whales are the smallest of all rorquals, and until recently, they were ignored by commercial whalers.*

For land animals, gravity makes large size a liability and a constraint. The cost of falling, for example, goes up sharply as the weight of an animal increases. The great evolutionary biologist J.B.S. Haldane expressed it graphically: "You can drop a mouse down a 1,000-yard mine shaft, and on arriving at the bottom, it gets a slight shock and walks away, provided that the ground is fairly soft. A rat is killed, a man is broken, a horse splashes."

The laws of physics dictate that large, heavy animals hit the ground with a greater speed and force than small animals. Because small animals have a large surface area relative to volume and weight, the forces of friction and turbulence in the air when falling come close to cancelling the force of gravity.

Larger animals have other problems associated with their relatively small surface area. They may have trouble radiating enough of the heat that their body chemistry generates. By living in cold ocean waters, whales can dissipate large amounts of heat because of water's efficiency as a conductor and heat absorber. And by floating in seawater, which provides support against gravity, whales can become long and thin with relatively delicate bones. Only creatures as small as worms and snakes, whose bodies usually rest on the ground, can be long and skinny on land. For larger animals, the strain of gravity is too great.

# Blue Whale *Balaenoptera musculus*

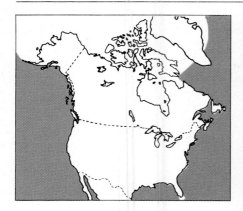

**Mammal:** *Balaenoptera musculus* — blue whale; the largest living animal
**Meaning of Name:** *Balaenoptera* (whale with a strong dorsal fin); *musculus* (little mouse) could be a tongue-in-cheek description
**Description:** torpedo-shaped body with an extremely small dorsal fin; 70 to 118 ventral grooves present; scattered rows of short hairs on lips, rostrum and around the nares and a beard at the tip of the lower jaw; 250 to 400 short, coarse baleen plates
**Colour:** bluish grey above, mottled with grey or greyish white oval spots on flanks, back and belly; undersurfaces of flukes and flippers are pale; may be yellowish blotches on throat and navel
**Total Length:** 70 to 85 feet (maximum of 100 feet)
**Weight:** up to 392,000 pounds
**Gestation:** 10 to 12 months
**Litter Size:** 1 (rarely twins) every 2 or 3 years
**Age of Maturity:** approximately 10 years; male, 74 feet; female, 79 feet
**Longevity:** possibly up to 110 years
**Diet:** krill (planktonic crustaceans), usually of the genus *Euphasia*, is their exclusive food
**Habitat:** open water of polar and temperate seas; sometimes found in shallow inshore waters; occurs in places where deep water, rich in nutrients, upwells to the surface and nourishes phytoplankton
**Predators:** occasionally a pod of killer whales
**Dental Formula:** 0

The blue whale is the largest creature ever to live on this planet. Almost every statistic on this animal is remarkable. The calf is almost 23 feet long at birth and weighs 3 tons. It grows at the rate of 8.8 pounds an hour. The largest recorded blue was a 100-foot-long female weighing an estimated 150 tons. Blues are migratory and largely solitary whales, sometimes found in pairs. They feed in shallow areas, gulping as much as 8 tons of krill per day.

The only small statistic associated with the blue whale is the number of its population. Blue whales were brought to the point of extinction and today number only about 11,000. The destruction of blue whale populations deprived humans of another valuable resource. George Small, who has documented the history of the blue whales' slaughter, writes: ''The failure of the International Whaling Commission to protect the blue whale destroyed a large and perpetual source of food. At an optimum population level — about 60,000, according to the population experts hired by the Whaling Commission — the blue whale could have supplied man in perpetuity with a sustainable yield of some 6,000 whales annually. Six thousand blue whales with an average length of 80 feet could produce some 580,000 long tons of raw material. From that, man could produce 105,300 tons of oil, enough to supply 2.5 ounces of margarine or edible oil a day every day for a year to 4,138,000 adult human beings. In addition, 189,000 long tons of meat could be produced, enough for a 6-ounce steak every day for a year for 3,090,000

*At weights of up to 160 tons, blue whales are the largest animals that have ever lived.*

adult human beings. That food supply has been destroyed.''

But the significance of the near extinction of the blue whale is more than just another case of shortsighted resource exploitation. It is a lesson and a warning: When an international resource is exploited by nations competing selfishly against other nations for a larger share of a limited resource, the resource will be squandered. It is signficant that harvesting of the large baleen whales ceased only after they became so rare that they were of minor economic importance. In every instance, the countries with the largest stake in the industry continued to exploit the resource the longest. Whale populations are on the increase in many cases, but as the world's human population grows and nations are forced into more intense competition for food, we may expect whales to be again subject to self-serving nationalistic exploitation.

# *Humpback Whale*  Megaptera novaeangliae

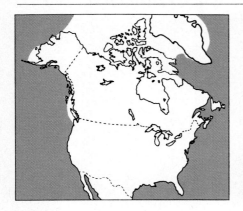

**Mammal:** *Megaptera novaeangliae* — humpback whale

**Meaning of Name:** *Megaptera* (big fin) refers to the unusually large flippers; *novaeangliae* (of New England) — the first specimen described scientifically was obtained along the Maine coast in New England

**Description:** short, stout body; the long scimitar-shaped flippers are unique as they carry a string of fleshy knobs and indentations on the forward edge; these knobs are randomly distributed on the top of the head and lower jaw; distinctive rounded projection on tip of lower jaw; ventral pleats are spaced relatively far apart and extend from the rim of the lower jaw to the navel; blow is wide and balloon-shaped; 320 to 360 black baleen plates (on each side) with pale grey bristles

**Colour:** usually black above and white below; forward edges and undersurfaces of flippers and flukes are white

**Total Length:** male, 36 to 47 feet; female, 38 to 48 feet (maximum is 59 feet)

**Weight:** 66,000 pounds

**Gestation:** 11 to 13 months

**Litter Size:** 1 every 1 to 3 years

**Age of Maturity:** 6 to 12 years

**Longevity:** up to 77 years

**Diet:** krill and other planktonic crustaceans and small schooling fish

**Habitat:** usually along the coast either on the continental shelf or along island banks or in bays and estuaries; sometimes found in open seas

**Predators:** killer whale

**Dental Formula:** 0

Humpbacks are known as singing whales or as "gentle giants." Only the former description is accurate. Humpbacks do sing one of nature's most complex songs. It is now known that singing is a form of male-male competition. Humpbacks also use more direct forms of combat. Docile around divers and whale watchers, male humpbacks smash and slash each other with their tails, frequently drawing blood.

Observation and interpretation of humpbacks' elaborate songs became possible only through great efforts made to photograph and sex the species. The variegated black-and-white markings, particularly on the tail flukes, can be used to identify each individual humpback. Studies have revealed that singers are males courting females and that fights often occur between lone males and those escorting females.

Like other baleen whales, humpbacks migrate to high-latitude waters in summer for feeding and return to tropical areas in winter to mate and calve. Their preferred habitats are shallow shelf and bank areas, rather than deep ocean, and they are readily seen along both the east and west coasts of North America. They may congregate in groups of several hundred while feeding on dense fish and krill schools. Within these large congregations, several whales may forage cooperatively. On the breeding grounds, usually only two or three individuals occur together, and these groups often consist of males escorting females due to come into oestrus.

Humpbacks are stout, stocky whales compared with other members of their family. Although slow swimmers, they are by far the most

*Humpback whales sing the longest and most complex courtship song of any wild mammal.*

acrobatic rorquals. Their spectacular breaches, "spy hopping" and fluke-slapping make them one of the mainstays of the whale-watching industry. Their acrobatic abilities are put to use during feeding. Humpbacks are known to eat larger-sized prey items, inch-long krill and schools of small fish such as capelin, herring, anchovy, sardine and Arctic cod. They take the cod by rushing dramatically into schools. One humpback was found with six cormorants in its stomach; the birds were probably engulfed accidentally during a lunge for cod.

The feeding behaviour of humpbacks has led to conflict in the shallow coastal waters where both humpbacks and humans fish. Humpbacks often become entangled in nets to the detriment of both whales and fishermen. Entanglements may be the result of overfishing of capelin. Large European fleets have fished the Grand Banks capelin heavily for human food as well as for livestock feed and dog food. As capelin have declined on the Grand Banks, humpbacks may have been forced inshore to feed on shallow-water capelin. In the shallows, the whales run into gill- and seine-net operations.

Humpbacks have several distinctive features besides their stocky body form. Their 16-foot flippers are longer than those of other whales. They also exhibit a series of curious lumps on their upper and lower jaws. These protuberances each contain a coarse hair and probably act as tactile sensory organs with such functions as measuring water currents. Humpbacks also have crusty white and

pinkish growths on the face, throat and fins. Called callosities, these blotches can be used to identify individual humpbacks. Callosities are parasitic infestations of barnacles and whale lice. They may be unpleasant for the whales, which could explain why humpbacks enter river mouths to bask in fresh or brackish water. The change in salinity may kill the parasites.

In addition to the whale lice and barnacle incrustations, humpbacks' skin is often marked with oval scoop-shaped scars, possibly the marks of a 2-foot-long shark, *Issistius brasiliensis*, the cookie-cutter shark, which bites neat oval chunks of blubber out of various whales and dolphins.

## Aquatic Songsters

*It makes sense to use sound as a means of underwater communication. Light travels only a few hundred yards underwater at best, and chemicals are easily dispersed in the ocean. Sound travels at a high speed — five times as fast as in air — and it travels far. The explosion of a depth charge*

*in Australian waters has been registered in Bermuda, 12,000 miles away. Whale songs can be detected at least 115 miles from the singer.*

*Every cetacean studied produces sounds. Whales and dolphins use their larynx, or voice box, and possibly their lips, blowholes and air sacs in the head to produce chirps, clicks, grunts, barks, squeaks, moans and whistles as well as extremely complicated singing. While the songs of animals like crickets, frogs and birds are specifically for mating, whales use their songs for a number of purposes. Dolphins, for example, use pure-tone whistles for a variety of messages unrelated to courtship. These whistles can act as signatures, allowing dolphins to recognize one another. They may communicate moods such as excitement, distress or aggression, and they also give information on the location of the individual sending the signal. But singing is normally thought of as a courtship device, used by mammals and birds to advertise their territorial status and to court mates and repel rivals.*

*Humpback whales prefer the shallow waters of the continental shelf to the deep ocean, feeding on the water's krill and schools of fish.*

*In whales such as the humpback, this sort of behaviour has evolved into an extremely sophisticated performance, possibly the most complicated serenade in the animal kingdom. The song of the humpback whale is an intricate sequence of sounds that may take over half an hour to sing. It has a beginning and an ending, and the sequence of chirps, bleeps, moans and other strange noises that make up the song follows a definite order repeated in the same manner time after time. The song consists of syllables that are organized into recurring groups, and these groups, known as motifs, are used to produce six basic themes. Each whale sings its own distinctive variation, but at any one time, the whales in a given area sing a song that is recognizably the same. If a whale is interrupted in its singing, it will pick up the melody later where it left off.*

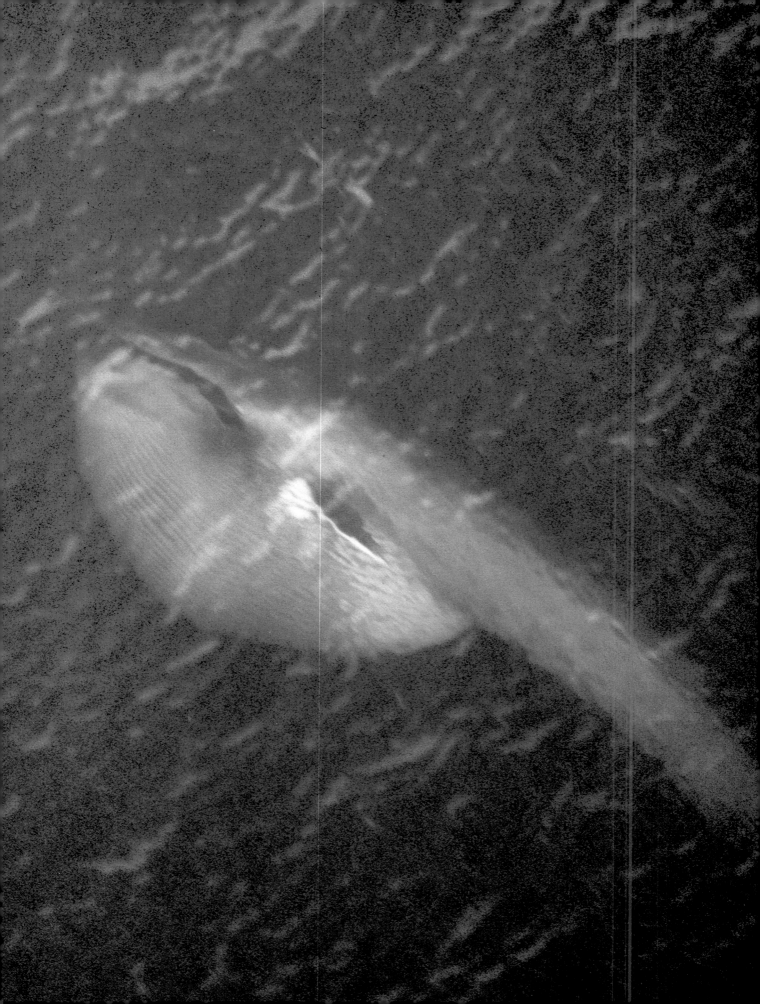

Only male humpbacks sing and only on the breeding grounds. Their songs appear to be primarily a courtship device. One possible explanation for their complexity is that they provide useful information to the female and to rivals about the experience and learning ability of the singer. This notion is reinforced by the observation that the songs are not static. Over a period of years, the songs in an area change, sometimes radically. When the whales sing, they do not sing together. Several whales may be singing at the same time, but each individual is singing his own song at his own pace. Since humpbacks are social and live to an old age and since males engage in combat, recognition of individual males by their songs may be valuable to both the singer and the audience. Poorly matched rivals will avoid fighting, losers may avoid whales that have beaten them, victors may advertise their prowess and identity, and females and young males may listen and act accordingly.

## Food Webs

Ecologists use the term food web to symbolize the interconnections, both indirect and direct, that exist among a great diversity of organisms. One of the main tasks of ecology is to determine what organisms are part of a food web and how changes in the abundance of one species will affect other members of the web. Even the simplest of food webs is highly complex. The Arctic has far fewer species than temperate or tropical regions, and ecologists wrongly assumed that Arctic food webs would be easy to understand. In some ecological systems, it is possible to determine what effect the abundance of one animal has on another, but usually only in hindsight, after the change has taken place.

Baleen whales were a conspicuous part of the oceanic food web, and their destruction, especially in the Antarctic, has provided biologists with an unpleasant but interesting large-scale experiment. The presence or absence of a baleen

whale obviously affects hundreds of species, ranging from whale lice and barnacles that live on the whale to seabirds and dolphins that join it during feeding, to orcas and humans that feed upon the whale. However, the most obvious impact that the loss of these whales had was on the population of krill and other plankton. When the whales were devastated, large quantities of krill were left unharvested and available to other predators. Baleen whales in the Antarctic probably harvested 180,000 tons of krill annually, but their decline meant that only one-sixth as much was being consumed. In the Antarctic, this seems to be having unexpected effects. Fur seals were virtually destroyed in the Antarctic by the turn of the century — only a tiny remnant stock survived, clinging to existence for several decades. These seals eat krill, and when the whales were destroyed, fur seal populations exploded, doubling every four to five years. There are now close to 1,000,000 Antarctic fur seals.

That might sound like unqualified good news. But the seals' increase has hurt other species. Breeding female seals, for instance, erode grassy shoreline areas where seabirds, such as albatross and petrel, nest. Nest sites are reduced in number, and the lack of grassy cover means that predatory birds such as skuas, which eat nestlings and eggs, are better able to hunt. Crab-eating seals — which, despite their name, feed heavily on krill — are also experiencing population increases and so are the leopard seals, which prey on crab eaters. Penguins may be on the rise because some of the fish they prey on eat krill. All of these changes may prevent the recovery of the krill-eating whales.

Who could have predicted that a Victorian taste for thread-waisted women squeezed by corsets and girdles of baleen and the invention of oil lamps would have affected the fortunes of Antarctic albatross in the late 20th century? One of the most basic principles of ecology is illustrated in these transformations: all the world is ultimately joined in one large food web, and altering parts of it will have unpredictable consequences.

The bulging throat and mouth of a blue whale can capture tons of plankton.

# *Right Whales* Balaenidae

All three species of right whales reside in temperate and northern waters but are absent from tropical and Antarctic regions. They nearly became absent from all regions. Their common name, the right whale, was given to them by whalers looking for the best species to harpoon.

The pygmy right whale is found only in southern temperate oceans, the northern right whale is found in the North Atlantic, and the bowhead is a resident of the Arctic. None of these species migrates far. All of them are chunky, heavy whales, and all share certain anatomical features that separate them from other baleen whales. Right whales have no throat grooves. They have a deeply curved jawline, and their baleen plates are long and thin. The baleen of right whales was used to make corsets, umbrellas and anything else that required a flexible springy rod. A single whale yielded up to a ton of baleen. Right whale baleen plates are adapted for sieving tiny copepods and krill in the surface waters. This is slow, steady work, and these whales rarely dive. This and their 2-foot layer of valuable blubber made them the "right" whales to hunt. They are so blubbery that they even float after harpooning, a further attraction for whalers.

## It's Lonely at the Top

*Every ecosystem is made up of three components: producers, usually plants; consumers, such as herbivorous animals, that eat the plants; and secondary consumers that eat the herbivorous animals. Primary producers use the energy in sunlight to build large, complex organic molecules from commonplace raw materials such as carbon dioxide and simple nitrogen compounds. All other trophic levels in a food chain consume either primary producers, other consumers or the organic detritus resulting from the death and decay of primary producers and consumers.*

*The image of a food chain is used by ecologists to explain the passage of food energy from the sun into plant biomass and then through various types of animal consumers. Each time a given amount of food is eaten, digested and turned into a new form of plant or animal, a large proportion of the chemical energy stored in the food source is given off as heat. Transformation of one species into another via digestion and molecular synthesis requires energy to break and re-form chemical bonds.*

*Relatively little energy from one trophic level can be turned into biomass at a higher trophic level because so much of the energy involved in biomass conversion is lost as heat. Different levels vary in their efficiency. Insects may convert as much as 60 percent of their food into making more insects, whereas a warm-blooded predator turns only 3 percent of food energy into duplicating its kind. A ballpark figure for energy conversion is usually around 10 to 20 percent. In other words, each time biomass passes along the food chain from one level to a higher level, 80 to 90 percent of the energy is lost as waste heat. So 1,000 pounds of phytoplankton plants will support 100 pounds of plankton-eating fish, which will support only 10 pounds of a fish-eating predator such as a seal. The seal, in turn, will support only 1 pound of another higher-level predator. Most food chains have only four to five links.*

*This inefficient conversion sets a limit on the length of food chains and explains the size and population limits set on large predators. It also explains why killer whales are not very abundant, certainly not as abundant as filter-feeding whales that feed lower down in the food chain. A baleen whale eating phytoplankton and krill has hundreds of times more food energy available to it than a killer whale.*

*Conversion inefficiency also explains why there are no "super" killer whales as large as blue whales. Killer whales are large compared to other dolphins, but they only weigh one-tenth as much as the baleen whales. In addition, a sizable predator must bear the cost of both building and maintaining its bulky warm-blooded body. The bigger the animal gets, the greater that cost becomes, which means there is even less energy available for reproduction. This is why killer whales are rare and why they have not evolved to a larger size. They are already big enough to eat anything that swims in the ocean. Growing would simply increase their maintenance costs.*

*Only a few hundred of the docile and playful right whales survive, even though commercial hunting of right whales ceased half a century ago.*

# Bowhead Whale   *Balaena mysticetus*

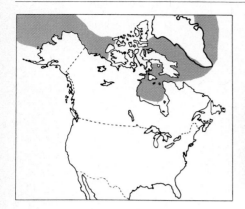

**Mammal:** *Balaena mysticetus* —
bowhead whale
**Meaning of Name:** *Balaena* (whale);
*mysticetus* (whale with a moustache)
refers to the sheets of whalebone or
baleen plates that hang down from the
upper jaw
**Description:** resembles a huge tadpole
with an enormous head (one-third of the
body length); the mouth forms a trough
from the front, cradling the narrow
depressed snout inside the arched lower
lip; lips and snout have rows of short
white bristles; very long, narrow baleen
plates; approximately 360 plates on each
side, the longest being in the middle —
they are dark grey or black, sometimes
with whitish front edges
**Colour:** mainly black; chin is unevenly
white, sometimes with a series of greyish
to black spots; also some white flashes
on belly and a pale grey area on tail
stock
**Total Length:** average is 57 feet (up to
66 feet)
**Weight:** maximum of 152,000 pounds
**Gestation:** 10 to 13 months
**Litter Size:** 1 every 2 or 3 years
**Age of Maturity:** 4 years
**Longevity:** possibly 40 years
**Diet:** mainly zooplankton (copepods,
amphipods, euphausiids and pteropods)
**Habitat:** primarily an Arctic species
found in association with ice floes and in
shallow waters; frequents bays, straits
and estuaries in summer
**Predators:** killer whale
**Dental Formula:** 0

The bowhead is named for its huge
head — up to one-third of the body
length — and for the great curve of its
lower jaw. This accommodates the
bowhead's 360 thin bristle-coated
baleen plates, which measure up to 14
feet long. These plates skim out small
planktonic animals, which bowheads
normally take by swimming at the
surface with their mouths open. They
also stir up sediments in shallow
regions, and recent observations suggest that they feed extensively in the
water column. Still, as a rule, they do
not dive deeply, and they usually
resurface within 20 minutes. Bowheads sometimes feed cooperatively,
with as many as 14 individuals moving along in formation like a series of
combines.

Like other Arctic whales, bowheads
migrate with the ice pack, south in the
winter to open water and north along
the melting ice when summer comes.
Usually, they travel alone or in small
groups segregated by sex. Little is
known about bowheads' social interactions, but they are probably much
like those of the northern right whale.
As with most baleen whales, females
grow larger and mature later than
males, usually around 4 years of age.

Bowheads were hunted to the brink
of extinction by the turn of the 19th
century. They probably owe their survival to the advent of spring steel,
which replaced baleen. Today, 4,000
survive, at most, and despite a commercial whaling ban, the populations
are not increasing adequately. With
the pace of Arctic oil development
accelerating, concern for the bowhead
has increased. There is also concern
about the continued hunting of bowheads by Alaskan Inuit. The native
hunt has been a traditional part of the
culture and economy, but it is now
being conducted with modern technology, including grenade-tipped

*Bowhead whales have a curved lower
jaw to accommodate baleen sheets that
are up to 14 feet long.*

harpoons, which makes its justifica-
tion on traditional cultural grounds
questionable.

## Sperm Competition

*Male mating strategies take many
forms. Some males increase their
offspring by attempting to acquire
harems; others may use a mating
plug or intense monogamy to gain
exclusive access to a single female.
Males may also court females with
elaborate displays, or they may
succeed in the breeding game
primarily through sperm competition.*

*Researchers have observed a
correlation between testes size and
the amount of sperm competition and
promiscuity in a species' mating
system. This relationship was first
described for primates: monkeys,
gorillas and humans. The ratio of
testicle weight to body weight is
extremely high for chimpanzees.
Chimps have a promiscuous mating
system in which males and females
may copulate several times an hour
for several days every month. By
contrast, gorillas have a harem
mating system in which the huge
silver-backed male excludes all other
males and gains exclusive access to
a harem. Males in this sort of mating
system typically invest heavily in
weaponry used to repel other males
but put little effort into sperm
production. In the case of the gorilla,
copulation rates are very low
compared with those of
chimpanzees, and accordingly, the
gorilla has a very low testes-to-body-
weight ratio. (Humans are
intermediate between the two.) This
same correlation has been found in*

The promiscuous mating system of the right whale explains why these whales have evolved the world's largest testicles — half a ton each.

animals ranging from mountain sheep to sandpipers. Promiscuous species have large testes weights; in monogamous species or those in which a female has several mates (polyandry), the male invests little in testes development.

The same sort of differences appear to exist in whales. Male harem defenders, such as dolphins and other odontocetes, tend to be much larger than females. Grey whales and other baleen whales show the reverse trend, with females being the larger sex. This suggests that male-male combat is not particularly important in their mating strategy. Males in a promiscuous system, such as that of the northern right whale, typically attempt to copulate with as many females as they can and as often as possible. In such a system, there is probably a good correlation between the amount of sperm produced and the number of offspring a male will sire. This may account for the huge size of the northern right whale testicle, a half-ton sperm factory.

# Northern Right Whale Eubalaena glacialis

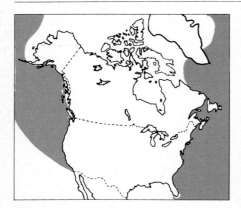

**Mammal:** *Eubalaena glacialis* — northern right whale, right whale
**Meaning of Name:** *Eubalaena* (right or true whale); *glacialis* (of the ice) is inappropriate, as they are not confined to Arctic seas but are also found in southern oceans
**Description:** rotund whale with large paddle-shaped pectoral flippers; no dorsal fin or throat grooves; large head comprises approximately one-quarter of the body length; jaw is highly arched and curves upward along the side of the head; large, yellowish oval rugose callosity, known as the bonnet, at tip of the snout; other smaller warty protuberances on snout, lower lip and above the eyes; 228 to 259 dark brown to dark grey baleen plates on each side
**Colour:** brown to black, mottled overall with irregular white splashes on chin and belly
**Total Length:** male, 36 to 48 feet; female, 31 to 60 feet
**Weight:** male, 49,000 pounds; female, 51,000 pounds
**Gestation:** 11 to 12 months
**Litter Size:** 1 every 2 to 4 years
**Age of Maturity:** 10 years
**Longevity:** not known
**Diet:** primarily planktonic crustaceans (especially copepod — *Calanus* spp), krill and some small fish
**Habitat:** temperate seas along coasts in shallow water; prefers the continental shelf habitat and sometimes occurs in large bays
**Predators:** killer whale, man
**Dental Formula:** 0

Northern right whales are similar in many respects to bowheads. They, too, have large heads with long baleen plates and chunky bodies and exhibit a tendency to occur alone or in small groups and to swim near the surface where they skim copepods and krill. But northern right whales differ in many respects from bowheads. Northern rights' baleen is only half as long, they prefer temperate waters, and they have been brought even closer to extinction.

A distinctive feature of right whales is their callosities — warty, rough incrustations in specific spots near the eyes, jaws and other parts of the head, throat and belly. These are infested with whale lice (cyamid amphipod crustaceans), barnacles and worms. The callosities may be pure white or various shades of yellow, orange and pink. Their function is not known. It is not simply parasitism, because evidence of incipient but uninfested callosity patches are seen in embryos. It is almost as though the whales' skin is designed to be colonized by parasites. Callosities could act as splash deflectors. Males, which have larger callosities than females, might use them to scrape each other. Regardless of their function, they serve the purpose of allowing whale identification. Each right whale has a slightly different pattern.

Another unique aspect of right whale anatomy is the huge size of the male testes. One testis weighed 1,157 pounds, five times the weight of testes in larger blue and grey whales. This suggests that the mating strategy of male right whales may involve considerable sperm competition. Rather

*The deep thick head of the right whale holds the long sheets of baleen that made this whale sought-after by 19th-century corset makers.*

than sequester females by fighting and mate guarding, males may compete by inseminating females with more sperm and more often. Mating is indeed reported to be promiscuous for this species. A female may be surrounded by two to six males attempting to copulate with her. The female remains on the surface, and the male mates from below, belly to belly, holding on with his front flippers.

Females probably reproduce only every three years, so there may be a low availability of mates for males. Impregnable females become much sought after. Unreceptive females go to great lengths to dissuade males. They may lie on their backs, keeping their genital regions up in the air and inaccessible to males, who still attempt to roll them over. This may also explain why a right whale may sometimes be observed in a headstand with its tail emerging straight from the water. An alternative suggestion is that the whale is "sailing," using the flukes to catch and travel with the wind while resting.

Females with calves segregate themselves from males when they are on the winter breeding grounds, probably because of male harassment. Aggregations appear to be loose and based on food availability.

Right whales are highly acrobatic for their size and are capable of bending their head to their tail. Since they feed by placid filter skimming, swim slowly and usually dive for only a few

minutes at a time, it is unlikely that feeding requires this flexibility. Again, it may reflect their mating system. Right whales frequently breach and tail slap. They utter deep belchlike groans. They are reportedly playful and have been seen cavorting with navigation buoys, sea lions and dolphins. Their docile, approachable nature made hunting them easy for whalers. Only a few hundred northern right whales remain, and many of those depend on areas such as the Bay of Fundy, which is perpetually at risk from the development of oil terminals, hydroelectric dams and other disruptions.

Even though right whale whaling ceased a half-century ago, these whales have not recovered. There may simply be too few spread too thinly and exposed to too many environmental problems for them ever to come back.

*Northern right whales are marked by distinctive patches of barnacles and whale lice.*

# SEALS & SEA LIONS
# *Pinnipedia*

Pinnipeds lead a double life. Seals and sea lions live part of their lives in the water and part on land or ice. Most species court, mate and give birth out of the water, and all of them swim and dive for their food. This double life means that pinnipeds must cope with two very different sets of environmental problems.

The most obvious adaptation to aquatic life is streamlining. The penis, testes and nipples have moved inside the body, and the ears have greatly shrunk, providing the pinniped with a smooth, obstruction-free shape. The limbs have been reduced and converted into flippers, and the tail shortened. The neck is long, and the spine is flexible, which allows for undulating swimming motions and agile underwater turns. Manoeuvrability is also enhanced by the loss of the collarbone and the very small size of the pelvis. The fur of the true seals and the walrus has been trimmed. Instead, they depend on a thick layer of blubber for insulation from the cold sea water. The skin is rich in oil glands.

Pinnipeds are active mammals. Northern species maintain a body temperature that is 100 Fahrenheit degrees warmer than the aquatic environment for much of the year. This requires rapid food digestion. Seals can pass a meal through the digestive tract in as little as six hours. This is not to suggest any wasteful haste. Instead, they may be extremely efficient digesters, since their intestines are among the longest in the world relative to their body length. One Steller sea lion's intestine measured 264 feet long, a remarkable 38 times its body length.

Feeding underwater has required special design features for vision. The large rounded eye is shaped like that of a fish. It features a well-developed tapetum lucidum, a mirrorlike membrane that runs along the back of the eye. This increases visual sensitivity in the low-light conditions underwater. The receptor cells in the mammalian eye consist of cones that detect colours in bright light and rods that are sensitive to the difference between dark and light. Scientists believe the eye has a switch system that uses cone vision in bright light, alternating with rod vision as the light dims.

The pinniped's double life also requires a good thermostat. In cold water, the need is to conserve heat. While on land — lazing in the hot summer sun or fighting or breeding in the local rookery — the problem is staying cool. Seals use their flippers as heat radiators. The blood system is designed like a counter-current heat exchanger. The hot seal can shunt blood cooled by the environment back into the body. Alternatively, while underwater, it can allow the flipper to absorb heat from arterial blood before returning it directly into the body to conserve heat.

The pinnipeds — including seals, eared seals and the walrus — have a distinctive look. True seals developed from a separate carnivore ancestor, probably an ancient relative of the sea otter. This lineage is different from the ancestor that gave rise to the walrus and eared seals. Moreover, seals are more recent, having originated 15 million years ago. By contrast, walruses and eared seals emerged about 25 million years ago.

---

*The evolutionary history of pinnipeds, such as these Steller sea lions, is one of compromise between adaptations for a life on land, where they mate and give birth, and for a life in the sea, where they feed.*

# Eared Seals Otariidae

## Northern Fur Seal Callorhinus ursinus

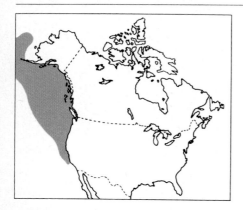

**Mammal:** *Callorhinus ursinus* —
northern fur seal, Alaska fur seal
**Meaning of Name:** *Callorhinus* (beautiful
hide); *ursinus* (bearlike)
**Description:** large hind flippers that are
turned forward when moving on land;
thick underfur, unlike the true seals;
bulls are black dorsally, brownish red
ventrally and have a grizzled grey mantle
on neck and shoulders; cows are grey
above and reddish below, but pelage
looks darker in the water; pups are born
with a shiny black pelage that is shed
and replaced by a silver coat
**Total Length:** male, 6.2 to 7 feet;
female, 3.5 to 4.5 feet
**Tail:** male, 2 inches; female, 2 inches
**Weight:** male, 330 to 600 pounds;
female, 84 to 119 pounds
**Gestation:** 1 year (including a 4-month
period of delayed implantation)
**Litter Size:** 1 (there is a record of twins)
**Age of Maturity:** male, 4 to 5 years, but
does not breed until 10 years of age;
female, 3 to 5 years
**Longevity:** male, 15 years; female, 22
years
**Diet:** squid and fish (capelin, herring,
anchovy, salmon, sand lance, rockfish)
are major food; sometimes eats birds;
stomach often contains rocks
**Habitat:** mostly pelagic; spends 6 to 8
months of the year at sea; young
animals are found in coastal waters
during the winter; rookeries are formed
on rocky beaches
**Predators:** large sharks, killer whale,
man
**Dental Formula:** 3/2, 1/1, 4/4, 2/1 = 36
teeth

The eared seals — including fur seals and sea lions — are the most recent offshoot of the enaliarctids, extinct doglike carnivores. Unlike most of the walrus family, which also arose from this stock, the eared seals have not suffered extinction. Indeed, the group is more diverse than ever. The fact that they retain external ear flaps and have a face that is less telescoped than that of true seals also indicates that this group is a recent arrival in the marine environment. Eared seals are considered conservatives in evolutionary terms, with most species having the same body plan and life-history pattern. Their hind limbs point forward. They use their front flippers for swimming and moving around on land, where they are able to amble and scrabble about in a way that true seals would find impossible.

In comparison with true seals, whose sleek, streamlined bodies are insulated with a thick coat of blubber, eared seals keep warm with a coat of thick fur that traps air bubbles. The lack of blubber may mean that otariids are less well adapted to cold ocean waters. They must keep swimming to maintain their body temperatures in frigid conditions where some phocid seals are lolling about comfortably motionless without cooling off. Otariids are extremely vulnerable to spills of oil, which reduce the insulating properties of their fur coat.

The northern fur seal is highly pelagic, a creature of the open ocean. It fishes at dusk and at night and rests on the surface during the day. This aquatic life is made possible by the seal's dense fur, which traps air bubbles, adding buoyancy as well as insulation. Fur seals are migratory, moving south along the coast to California in North America and to Japan in Asia. Their distribution probably changes according to the movements of fish.

At sea, fur seals are largely solitary. Only during the summer breeding season do they congregate at rookeries on islands along the coast of Alaska. Fur seals utilize the typical harem system of mating, with a large bull defending groups of females. Females remate a week after giving birth. Having mated, the mother returns to the sea to feed for five to six days, leaving the pup to survive on the fat it was able to accumulate during the previous week's suckling. Pups disperse at the end of summer.

Though fur seals have endured centuries of harvest for their rich coats, populations are presently healthy. Increased oil pollution and Arctic fishing may place them at risk.

*Recently evolved from land mammals,
eared seals, such as this northern fur seal,
lack insulating blubber layers and must
keep warm with thick coats of fur.*

## *Steller Sea Lion* Eumetopias jubatus

**Mammal:** *Eumetopias jubatus* —
Steller sea lion, northern sea lion; largest
of the eared seals
**Meaning of Name:** *Eumetopias* refers to
broad forehead; *jubatus* (having a mane)
refers to the male's shaggy mane
**Description:** largest of the eared seals;
the cow is slim, but the bull has massive
forequarters and a swollen neck;
whiskers are approximately 20 inches
long and are stiff, pale and mystacial;
large flippers; pelage lacks an
undercoat; bulls are buffy above, reddish
brown below, dark brown flippers; bulls
have a mane, cows are uniformly brown
**Total Length:** male, 8.8 to 10.5 feet;
female, 6.1 to 7.8 feet
**Weight:** male, over 1,986 pounds;
female, 606 to 805 pounds
**Gestation:** 1 year (includes 4-month
delayed-implantation period)
**Litter Size:** 1
**Age of Maturity:** male, 4 to 6 years, but
not effective breeders until 9 to 15 years;
female, 3 to 6 years
**Longevity:** 17 years
**Diet:** wide variety of invertebrate marine
life, especially squid
**Habitat:** chiefly marine but sometimes
goes up rivers; spends most of its life in
a narrow belt of coastal water; breeds on
islands, rocky outcrops, boulders,
cobblestone and coarse sand beaches
**Predators:** man, killer whale, large
sharks
**Dental Formula:** 3/2, 1/1, 4/4, 1/1 = 34
teeth

Weighing in at a ton, a male Steller sea lion is the heaviest of all the eared seals. Steller sea lions are slightly less gregarious than other otariids. They feed in inshore waters on fish and bottom invertebrates, possibly causing local depletions of fish. This is certainly the opinion of West Coast fishermen, who periodically call for bounties on these animals. On the other hand, given the variety of a Steller's diet, it is questionable how much they will reduce a fish population when other more common foods are available. In one case, two sea lions that were killed in the midst of a salmon run proved to have only lampreys in their stomachs.

A more important problem may be the effect these large, powerful animals have on fishing gear. Sea lions rip great holes in gill nets as they pillage them for fish. Fishermen complain about sea lion damage all along the British Columbia coast. In response, the government has sponsored programmes to reduce sea lion populations to a few thousand. Only in the northern limits of their range — the ice-free Alaskan islands and coast — are there large populations of some 200,000 individuals.

*Weighing up to one ton, the male Steller sea lion may guard a harem of as many as 30 females.*

Steller sea lions form dense breeding colonies. Males control territories during summer, a task that precludes feeding for several months. They occupy rocky areas along the seashore, where females come to give birth. A male may guard up to 30 females. Females, however, may move from one harem to another. They remate only a week after giving birth to a single pup. Though the pups may be suckled for as long as a year, they leave the rookery at the end of the summer.

Females mature at 3 to 6 years. Males mature at 6 years but require at least a decade to attain the huge size of a harem bull.

Killer whales have been observed preying on Steller sea lions. In one case, wildlife biologists watched as a pod of orcas penned in a pair of sea lions by encircling them. The sea lions were helpless, unable to escape. Eventually, a large male orca swam into the circle, approached them and swatted them with its flukes, hard enough to knock one of the sea lions into the air. Neither sea lion escaped.

# *California Sea Lion* Zalophus californianus

**Mammal:** *Zalophus californianus* — California sea lion
**Meaning of Name:** *Zalophus* (high crest) refers to the high sagittal crest on the male's skull; *californianus* (of California)
**Description:** fusiform body; hind flippers trail when swimming, but rotate forward when resting on land; has a high forehead; small pointed ears; stiff long, mystacial whiskers; bulls have a bony crest on the crown of the head; pelage does not have an undercoat; looks black when wet and buff to brown when dry
**Total Length:** male, 6.5 to 8.2 feet; female, 4.9 to 6.5 feet
**Tail:** male, 4.5 inches; female, 3 inches
**Weight:** male, 441 to 661 pounds; female, 110 to 220 pounds
**Gestation:** 11.5 to 12 months (includes a 3.5-month period of delayed implantation)
**Litter Size:** 1
**Age of Maturity:** male, 5 years; female, 3 years
**Longevity:** 18 to 25 years in captivity
**Diet:** mainly squid, octopus and a variety of fishes such as herring, sardines, rockfish, hake and ratfish
**Habitat:** rookeries and hauling-out spots are usually sandy or boulder beaches backed by cliffs and sometimes sea caverns; a shore-living and coastal seal, not usually farther than 100 miles out to sea
**Predators:** man, killer whale and large sharks
**Dental Formula:** 3/2, 1/1, 4/4, 2/1 = 36 teeth

As the name suggests, this is a more southerly sea lion than the Steller sea lion. The California sea lion is smaller and more graceful, sociable and playful than the Steller, making it the normal choice of aquarium trainers. Being eared seals, they are highly adept with their flippers, but why they are so willing to catch thrown objects in their mouths is unknown. This may mimic an action they use underwater for grabbing fish that swim by. In fact, most of their performing behaviour, such as flipper slapping and even trumpet blowing, appears to re-create actions used in normal sea lion life.

The California sea lion's breeding traits are very similar to the Steller's, except that the large males are constrained by overheating problems. California sea lions breed as far south as Mexico. During the summer breeding season, males are exposed to the hot sun and are forced to make frequent dives into the water to cool off. This leaves the female vulnerable to the intrusions of nonterritorial males who may try to sneak a copulation. A prime territory, then, is one that allows quick entry and exit to and from the water. Sleeping lowers the California sea lion's heat production by 25 percent, which is still not adequate protection in bright sunlight. California sea lions try to stay in areas where breaking waves and wind will increase evaporative heat losses. When necessary, they may urinate on themselves and wave their flippers to simulate the process. Sweating ac-

*Familiar to anyone who has watched a seal show at an aquarium, the California sea lion is both social and playful.*

counts for only 12 percent of their heat loss.

The breeding season of the California sea lion is shorter than that of the Steller. This may be a consequence of the male's smaller body size and reduced capacity to rely solely on stored body fat.

The California sea lion feeds in the same style as the Steller. The two species would probably compete, if their ranges were not, for the most part, separate. Lately, there has been a rise in the number of California sea lions moving into British Columbia waters for winter feeding. This may be a result of population reductions of Steller sea lions.

# *Walrus* Odobenidae

## *Walrus* Odobenus rosmarus

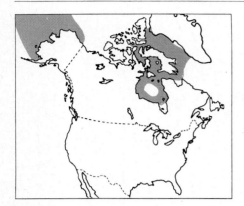

**Mammal:** *Odobenus rosmarus*
— walrus

**Meaning of Name:** *Odobenus*
(tooth + walk) — the walrus has been
seen dragging itself along the ice using
its tusks; *rosmarus*, from Norwegian and
earlier Scandinavian words meaning
whale horse or walrus

**Description:** largest North Atlantic
pinniped; skin is beige-brown in colour
and is sparsely covered with short wiry
reddish brown hairs; it is very thick and
wrinkled; colour changes to more of a
reddish brown at the belly and at the
base of the flippers; has quill-like
whiskers set in 2 well-developed pads on
the upper lip; the most characteristic
feature is the long tusks, which are
actually enormously elongated canine
teeth; has short limbs; the tail is
enclosed in a fold of skin

**Total Length:** male, 8.3 to 12.1 feet;
female, 7.5 to 9.6 feet

**Weight:** male, 2,000 to 2,432 pounds;
female, 1,250 to 1,629 pounds

**Gestation:** 15 months (including a
3-month period of delayed implantation)

**Litter Size:** 1 (rarely 2) every 2 or 3 years

**Age of Maturity:** male, may mature at 6
years but usually 9 to 10; female, 4 to 7
years

**Longevity:** 16 to 35 years, possibly up to
40 years in the wild

**Diet:** clams are the principal food; also
eats whelks, sea cucumbers,
crustaceans, worms and small polar cod

**Habitat:** open northern waters near the
edge of the polar pack ice; finds shelter
on isolated rocky coasts, islands and ice
floes (especially those floating over
shallow shellfish beds)

**Predators:** primarily man; killer whales
or polar bears may prey on the young or
infirm

**Dental Formula:** 1/0, 1/1, 3/3, 0/0 = 18
teeth

Twenty million years ago, a family
of large bearlike carnivores ambled
into the shallow bay waters of the
northern Pacific Ocean. Eventually,
they diverged from the now extinct
ancestral family, the Enaliarctidae,
and gave rise to the walruses and fur
seals. Walruses speciated widely and
once dominated the warm coastal and
temperate waters of the Pacific. Gradually, walrus species have become extinct, and the walrus is the sole surviving member of the family.

The walrus cannot be mistaken for
other pinnipeds. Its upper canines are
stretched into huge ever-growing
tusks up to a yard long in males and
two-thirds of a yard in females. The
walrus has a small head with a dense
set of facial whiskers set on a swollen
wrinkly body that is virtually naked of
fur.

The body of the walrus is adapted
for grazing along the bottom of cold
northern oceans. The tusks are not
used so much for clam digging as for
dragging the walrus around when la-
bouring on the bottom or hauling-out
onto ice floes. The generic name, in
fact, means "tooth walker." The walrus is able to blow powerful jets of water out of its mouth. One possible way
of feeding is for the walrus to use its
tusks to anchor itself headfirst in the
sediments and then to expose nearby
clams by blowing away the mud. The
walrus seems to plough and root in a
piglike fashion, leaving a messy trail
of churned mud and debris across the
ocean bed. Occasionally, when a male
decides to dine on seals or beluga
whales, its tusks are used as weapons.

The walrus's weak cheek teeth are
unable to crush mollusk shells efficiently. Instead, it is thought that the
walrus holds the shell in its lips and
uses its powerful tongue like a piston
moving up and down in its cylinder-
shaped mouth. This creates a strong
suction capable of extracting the clam
or snail from its shell.

The tusks are probably most used to
deliver social signals in disputes over
status and mating. This would explain why males have larger tusks
than females. Walruses are gregarious
animals. They haul-out on ice or shore
in a dense pack. During the winter
breeding season, females form small
bands roughly a dozen strong. The
males follow these groups and energetically advertise their presence
using underwater sounds and specific
calls. Some of the noises produced
with a special throat sac have a bell-
like quality that contrasts with the
usual barking walrus voice.

Males use their tusks to establish
dominance over other males. The
tusks are displayed in threat encounters similar to those used by bighorn
sheep. Since the size of the tusks increases with the age and weight of the
male, they are probably a reliable signal of fighting ability. If the rival male
is not convinced just by looking, the
tusks may be used as weapons in an
escalated fight. The male's swollen
neck is coated with a thick, lumpy

*Tusks up to a yard long are used to drag
the walrus along the ocean bottom and
to pull it onto ice floes.*

hide that seems to be a form of protection against the jabs and stabs of rivals.

Females may use their tusks to protect their offspring from predators and to establish a position within the herd. The only animals posing a potential threat to the adult walrus are polar bears and killer whales. Sometimes, the role changes. Groups of walruses have been seen threatening a polar bear by slapping their flippers as they advance toward it. In the water, a milling, agile herd of walruses could easily damage a bear. Groups of walruses are known to attack Inuit boats. The Inuit claim that walruses will also attack the killer whale. When Inuit in boats are approached by killer whales, they cup their hands and bellow into the water, imitating the sound of an enraged bull walrus. This drives the killer whales away.

The walrus shows an interesting adaptation to Arctic waters. Its skin functions as a heat sink and radiator. During a cold-water dive, the walrus is able to maintain a stable internal temperature almost 100 Fahrenheit degrees warmer than the surrounding water by shunting blood away from the skin and blubber layer. When the walrus hauls-out and basks in the sun, it faces a serious overheating problem. It then shunts blood back to the surface layer and turns a bright reddish brown. In this case, the hairless corrugated skin acts as a radiator, releasing excess body heat.

Unlike many Arctic mammals, the walrus has an extremely low reproductive rate. Females give birth to a single calf — rarely two — in spring. The calf is relatively helpless, suckling for half a year and depending on contact with its mother for warmth. The calf will remain with its mother for two years. This means that females breed only every two to three years or at even greater intervals. Juveniles disperse and segregate with others of the same sex and age. Females may be ready to reproduce at age 4 to 7, but males usually need 10 to 15 years to reach the size of a harem-controlling bull.

Walruses are migratory. Like most Arctic marine mammals, they must

*To keep warm during dives, the walrus shunts blood away from its skin, which causes a distinctive white coloration.*

move with the ice. Different populations move at different times and over varying distances according to the pattern of freezing and thawing. Some walrus populations were once resident as far south as the Magdalen Islands, Sable Island and possibly into New England. These have been wiped out by overhunting. Walruses now number 200,000 or less in the Pacific and 25,000 in the Atlantic, a small fraction of their previous populations. Inuit continue to depend on the walrus as a source of meat, oil, leather and ivory tusks for use in carving. Proposals for massive clam-dredging operations and Arctic oil development are the greatest threats to the walrus.

## Pinniped Polygyny

*Pinnipeds exhibit some of the most extreme cases of sexual dimorphism in the animal kingdom. Males of some pinniped species may be three* times the size of females and display strange protuberances from their noses, utter violent roars and comport themselves in a ferocious manner. On the other hand, some seal species have males which look much the same as females and which are relatively quiet and mild-mannered — even at breeding time. The degree of dimorphism is closely correlated with the kind of breeding system each species has developed.

The largest, most ferocious and most vocal males occur in the harem-breeding species such as sea lions, fur seals, walruses and elephant seals. The benefits to harem masters are obvious. Some have harems that contain as many as 100 breeding females. Harem masters obviously have a much higher reproductive rate than a monogamous male would. This begs the question as to why other pinnipeds — especially the true seals — lack harem-breeding behaviour. Similarly, why do some pinnipeds — such as grey seals — have a reduced form of polygyny?

The presence or absence of harem polygyny appears to depend on the dispersion of females. In species such as the ringed or bearded seal, the female's birthing dens or birthing sites are dispersed. The female does not tolerate the near presence of another female. From the standpoint of males, such behaviour means that females are not a defensible resource. By contrast, the females of harem-breeding species are usually forced to come to a crowded space for giving birth. Species that give birth on beaches or rocky shores have limited numbers of sites available to them. The location must have good water access and be difficult for terrestrial predators, such as bears, to reach. Whenever females concentrate, there is a potential for males to evolve harem-breeding behaviour, meaning the attempt to gain exclusive access to a group of females. In the highly mobile fur seal, this may involve actively herding and controlling the movement of the females. In heavy and less mobile species such as elephant seals and Steller sea lions, the male may simply defend a prime piece of real estate from other males and mate with whichever females decide to use the area.

The otariids, including eared seals and the walruses, are highly polygynous harem breeders. This may have resulted from their dependence on dry land, which, in turn, stems from their use of fur, rather than blubber, for insulation. A young otariid cannot leave the rookery to nurse while in the water until its fur moult is complete. This means that a male otariid can economically defend a harem of females who are forced to stay in one area with their pups. If the females were free to come and go at the time they were about to come back into oestrus, it would be more difficult for a single male to defend them. By contrast, true seals nurse their pups for short periods and tend not to be harem breeders. An exception is the elephant seal, an extreme harem breeder. Female elephant seals nurse their young for about a month, somewhat longer than most other true seals.

Those seals that are not harem breeders are not necessarily monogamous in the conventional sense. The males do not remain with a single mate or provide parental care. Instead, they are like displaying birds whose males sing and dance for the approval of females. Males are chosen or rejected on the basis

The largest and most ferocious male pinnipeds occur in harem-breeding species, such as walrus. Harems may contain up to 100 breeding females.

of the effectiveness of their courtship. Species such as the harbour seal use a variety of twisting jumps, splashes and complex vocalizations to pay court to the females. Male-male competition plays a role in this system: dominant males may intimidate smaller, younger males and prevent them from displaying.

The breeding system of pinnipeds strongly depends on the actions of females. Either females control the amount of harem formation that occurs by how aggressive or tolerant they are of other females or they control the amount of polygyny in the species by choosing the most effective suitors over others.

# *Earless Seals* Phocidae

Earless seals are the most highly aquatic of the pinnipeds. Absence of an external ear is evidence of how completely they have evolved for life in the water. Swimming is carried out almost entirely by the hind flippers along with the undulation of the hind end of the body. To reduce drag, their forelimbs are kept close to the body except for manoeuvring. Earless seals are ungainly on land. The specialized forelimbs and backward-pointing hind flippers are of little use to phocids for locomotion. On land, the forelimbs serve mostly for heat radiation and social gesturing. Some earless seals are so streamlined that their fusiform cigar shape is similar to that of the fast-swimming tuna and dolphins. Certain species use their speed to rocket several yards out of the water, then land on the ice to bask. The earless seals use a caterpillarlike undulation to get around when out of the water. This action clearly distinguishes the family from the eared seals, which use their fore flippers for both swimming and walking.

Among the pinnipeds, the earless seal is the richest family, with 19 species found along the coastlines of the northern and southern hemispheres. They have the greatest variation in body size, breeding biology and ecology. The elephant seal may reach a weight of 3 tons, while the ringed seal weighs only 100 pounds. Some earless seals are polygynous, while others are monogamous breeders. Some species are specific to freshwater lakes or Caribbean islands. Most earless seals are equipped with simple cheek teeth to feed on fish, squid and mollusks. Two species are filter feeders and have highly complicated cheek teeth. Most species have peglike teeth adapted for catching and killing fish. The leopard seal of Antarctica has

huge sharklike teeth adapted for its predatory life of eating penguins and other seals.

Most phocid species are long-lived, usually attaining 30 and, in some cases, up to 56 years. Their reproductive rate is slow, with single-pup litters born on ice or land. Females mate soon after giving birth, but implantation is delayed. Many Arctic phocid species spend months on the ice fasting during favourable weather and feeding at other times, accumulating large stores of blubber.

## Mammals and Milk

*Breasts, which are unique to mammals, are modified sweat glands. The advantages of liquid milk help to explain the marvellous success enjoyed by mammals. The mother is often more mobile and a better feeder than her offspring. She can store up nutrients and feed them to her young as milk, allowing them to grow faster than if they had to find their own food. As well, by providing milk, the mother allows her offspring to postpone the eruption and development of teeth.*

*The mammalian tooth is encased in rigid enamel. As a consequence, teeth cannot continue to enlarge as the mammal grows. Milk feeding enables tooth development to be postponed until the animal's jaws have reached adult size. Some mammals solve this problem by having the teeth emerge in a sequence as the animal grows.*

*Mammals are able to alter the nutritive quality of their milk according to their particular life history. Seals, whose pups are subjected to extreme cold stress, have placed a premium on rapid development. Half of the seal's milk may be fat, as opposed to 4 to 10*

*percent butterfat content in the milk of dairy cows. Mammals such as the large grazers, which require the young to develop muscles and be highly mobile soon after birth, produce milk that contains less fat and more protein.*

*Besides being nutritious, milk is an important source of antibodies — a means by which mothers can transfer resistance to infection to their young. Many antibody molecules are too large to cross the uterine membrane that links the mother and fetus.*

*The breast-feeding of a young mammal makes extreme demands on the mother. In small rodents, a lactating female must eat 240 to 330 percent more food than normal. A mother may lose up to half of her skeletal calcium while lactating unless she has a rich supply of calcium in her food. The mother who is trying to maximize her lifetime reproduction often engages in weaning conflict with offspring that would suckle longer. While individual offspring would benefit from longer feeding, the mother's chance of having future offspring would eventually decrease.*

*A body as streamlined as that of a fast-swimming fish and the absence of an external ear are both evidence of the extreme adaptation to aquatic life of earless seals, such as the harbour seal.*

# Harbour Seal *Phoca vitulina*

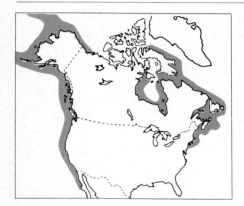

**Mammal:** *Phoca vitulina* — harbour seal
**Meaning of Name:** *Phoca* (seal); *vitulina* (sea calf)
**Description:** profile resembles a dog's; large convex eyes are dorsally placed to provide good underwater vision; from the front, the nostrils form a broad V, almost meeting at the bottom; mystacial whiskers; colour is extremely variable but is essentially bluish grey on the back with irregular dark brown spots, streaks or blotches; silvery white belly with scattered dark spots
**Total Length:** male, 4 to 6 feet; female, 4.5 to 5.5 feet
**Weight:** male, 160 to 198 pounds (maximum, 249 pounds); female, 128 to 198 pounds (maximum, 245 pounds)
**Gestation:** 10 to 11 months (including a delayed implantation)
**Litter Size:** usually 1 (rarely twins)
**Age of Maturity:** male, 3 to 6 years (usually 5); female, 2 to 5 years (usually 3 or 4)
**Longevity:** probably 40 years
**Diet:** primarily fish (herring, alewife, flounder, hake, smelt, cod); also mollusks, such as squid, octopus and clams, and sometimes crayfish, crab and shrimp
**Habitat:** coastal waters of the northern oceans in bays, harbours estuaries, mud flats and even some accessible lakes if certain features are present
**Predators:** polar bear, walrus, killer whale and sharks; golden eagle may prey on young
**Dental Formula:** 3/2, 1/1, 4/4, 1/1 = 34 teeth

Harbour seals range the coasts of the northern hemisphere from the southern edge of the temperate zone to the high Arctic. They are the most widespread seal in northern waters and tolerate a wide range of salinities and water temperatures. Harbour seals swim up large rivers and have travelled as far inland as Lake Ontario. There are also several landlocked harbour seal populations in lakes in British Columbia and Quebec.

Harbour seals are wary animals and require secure haul-out areas on rocks, sandbars and mud flats with easy access in and out of deep water. Hauling-out in groups permits a bit more relaxation. Studies have shown that harbour seals spend less time scouting for predators when they are in a group than when they are alone. Usually, they haul-out and rest at low tide and reenter the water to feed during the incoming tide. In winter and stormy weather, harbour seals spend most of their time in the water.

Harbour seals are extremely common but rarely occur in groups of more than a hundred. Larger gatherings may have difficulty finding enough food. Harbour seals are generalized fish eaters, feeding on a broad spectrum of species. They will dive to 980 feet and remain submerged for up to 23 minutes. They can eat smaller fish while they swim underwater, but larger catches are brought to the surface.

The harbour seal's appetite can lead

*Born either in, or out of, the water, a harbour seal pup is weaned after four weeks but may remain in the care of its mother for three months.*

to conflict with man, as the seals can eat 9 pounds of fish daily. Since there may be hundreds of harbour seals along certain bays, their catch may total several tons a day in an area where humans are also competing for fish. Sometimes, harbour seals feed heavily on the salmon runs, and they may foul fishing gear or rob fish traps. This has led to the harbour seal's extermination along parts of the coastline. Human vengeance is often unjustified. During much of the year, harbour seals have a small impact on fishing profits since they feed on noncommercial fish species.

The breeding system of the harbour seal is poorly understood. Most reports indicate that the mating is promiscuous and is conducted in shallow water near the haul-out spots in late summer and autumn. Males perform jumps and flips for females. Females delay implantation for several months and give birth in early summer to a single pup or, rarely, twins. Harbour seal pups are born onshore or in the water. They are fairly precocious, able to dive after a week and crawl onshore. Females wean them after only four weeks, though for the next few months, the pup is cared for and accompanied by the mother. Maturity is not reached until 5 to 6 years, and the harbour seal may live to be 40.

# *Grey Seal*  Halichoerus grypus

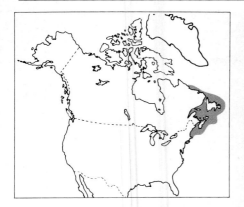

**Mammal:** *Halichoerus grypus* — grey seal

**Meaning of Name:** *Halichoerus* (sea pig); *grypus* (hook-nosed)

**Description:** flexible forelimbs and long slender claws increase its mobility on land; bulls have swollen, scarred, wrinkled necks and broad, distinctive "Roman noses"; male pelage has overall brownish grey or black tone with obscure lighter marks on neck and flanks; female's pelage is a lighter grey to tan colour and silver or whitish underneath; pups have a long, crinkly white coat that they moult at the age of 3 or 4 weeks to a dark grey, spotted juvenile coat

**Total Length:** male, 8 to 9.8 feet; female, 7 to 7.5 feet

**Weight:** male, 617 to 798 pounds; female, 400 to 551 pounds

**Gestation:** 11.5 months (including a 3-month delayed-implantation period)

**Litter Size:** 1

**Age of Maturity:** male, 3 to 7 years; female, 3 to 4 years

**Longevity:** male, 35 years; female, 45 years

**Diet:** primarily a coastal feeder, eating whatever is abundant and available; cod, flounder, skate, pollack, mackerel, whiting and rockfish, as well as squid and pelagic crustaceans

**Habitat:** along exposed rocky coasts, cliffs and caves of remote islands, reefs and shoals

**Predators:** man, killer whale

**Dental Formula:** 3/2, 1/1, 4/4, 1/1 = 34 teeth

The grey seal has a relatively limited range, generally staying north of Cape Cod and south of the Arctic. It is an inshore fish eater and frequents the same areas as harbour seals. One of the larger seals along the Atlantic coast, the grey probably takes bigger fish than its cousins the harbour seals do, feeding on large flatfish and crabs as well as migratory schools of herring, mackerel and salmon. The grey seal is a more accomplished walker than the harbour seal and will breed farther from water. Where the two species occur together, the grey seal displaces the harbour seal from haulouts (onshore gathering places).

Grey seals breed in dense, noisy aggregations and have evolved a polygynous breeding system. Males are able to guard a group of up to 10 females. The polygynous nature of males is reflected in their larger body size and possibly in their longer snout, which may be used in aggressive vocalizations. Female grey seals are aggressive to other females and repel them during breeding season. On occasion, this behaviour forces males into monogamy. The origin of

*Grey seals have been observed napping on the ocean bed, occasionally rising to breathe while still asleep.*

female territoriality could be their tendency to return year after year to the spot where they previously gave birth. This, in turn, suggests that females are competing for nesting spots of varying quality.

Females give birth to a precocious white pup that is weaned after three weeks and then deserted.

Grey seals have been observed napping on the bottom of the ocean bed, occasionally rising to breathe while still asleep and then gently sliding back to the bottom.

## *Bearded Seal* Erignathus barbatus

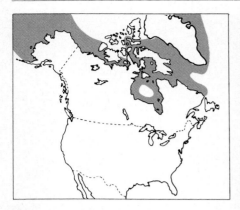

**Mammal:** *Erignathus barbatus* — bearded seal

**Meaning of Name:** *Erignathus* (very + jaw) refers to the rather deep jaw; *barbatus* (bearded) refers to the seal's abundant whiskers

**Description:** characteristic long white whiskers resemble a prominent bushy moustache; external opening of ear is large, pigmented and easily seen; square spadelike foreflippers due to the fact that the middle digit is the longest; 4 mammae (which are not found in other Arctic phocids); pelage is composed of stiff hairs; smoky grey with a darker brown cap and dorsum

**Total Length:** 6.9 to 9.5 feet

**Weight:** 551 to 716 pounds (maximum, 875 pounds)

**Gestation:** 10.5 to 11.5 months (includes a 2.5-month period of delayed implantation)

**Litter Size:** 1 or 2 every second year

**Age of Maturity:** male, 7 years; female, 6 years

**Longevity:** up to 31 years

**Diet:** mollusks (whelks and cockles) form much of the food along with other bottom-living animals (shrimp, crab, holothurians, octopus) and fish such as sculpin, polar cod and flounder

**Habitat:** found along coasts and ice floes in the Arctic Ocean and adjoining seas; prefers shallow coastal waters that are ice-free in the winter along with gravel beaches and ice floes that are not too far out to sea

**Predators:** killer whale and polar bear

**Dental Formula:** 3/2, 1/1, 4/4, 1/1 = 34 teeth

The bearded seal has a thick set of whiskers used when browsing on the seabed for food. Large claws on the front flippers are probably useful for digging through mud and silt. The bearded seal eats crab, shrimp, various fish and probably most other species encountered in the bottom sediments. On occasion, this seal's stomach is found to contain mud and pebbles. The bearded seal's method of feeding restricts its range to areas of the Arctic Ocean where the water is less than 650 feet deep. Winter populations must move to the Bering Sea or south toward the Gulf of St. Lawrence to avoid heavy pack ice.

The bearded seal is unsociable. Both sexes seem not to tolerate others of their species near their onshore sites. Males are probably less polygynous than other pinnipeds because of female territoriality.

The bearded seal's reproductive biology is unusual. Females have two pairs of teats and give birth to twins. The pups are relatively helpless (altricial) and stay with their mother for longer than is common among the pinnipeds. Females only breed every other year because of the long time before weaning. As a result, despite their fecundity, their long-term reproductive rate is the same as most seals. Producing twins might be an adaptation to capitalize on particularly productive feeding years when females have accumulated large stores of fat.

Males and females both reach 660 pounds. The meat, blubber and hide

*Thick whiskers enable the bearded seal to browse the seabed for food.*

of the bearded seal has been an important resource for both the Inuit and polar bears.

### Devices for Diving

*Seals are capable of some amazing underwater achievements. Though they do not dive as deep or for as long as whales, they may reach depths of 2,000 feet and remain submerged for an hour. Because seals are easier to study than whales, their special adaptations are better understood.*

*Seals perform their diving feats with a lung capacity little greater than that of a human. When a dive starts, the seal's circulatory system is slowed down and reorganized. The objectives while underwater are to maintain an oxygen supply to vital organs such as the brain, while directing carbon dioxide and other waste products to less essential areas of the body.*

*The face of the seal has nerves that trigger a diving reflex when submerged. On receiving this signal, the heartbeat drops immediately from 150 beats per minute to 8 to 12 beats per minute. Veins are constricted, reducing blood supplies to many muscles, organs and noncritical parts of the body. The kidneys stop filtering blood, while the brain remains well supplied.*

The seal has a larger volume of blood in its body than most land mammals. Its blood is rich in red cells, which carry oxygen. The seal's muscles contain large quantities of myoglobin, a molecule that carries oxygen. This enables the muscles to coast along, utilizing stored oxygen while they are cut out of the circulatory system. The seal is insensitive to the breathing response in humans triggered by the buildup of carbon dioxide in the blood.

When the seal surfaces, its heartbeat shoots as high as 250 beats per minute. It more fully clears its lungs as it exhales and inhales than does a land-based mammal.

During the dive, decreased oxygen-burning activity by much of the muscle and tissue mass results in reduced generation of body heat. To maintain the temperature of blood feeding the heart, brain and other vital organs while submerged in cold water, the seal has veins that run through brown fat tissue, a special set of cells that generates heat.

The seal must also contend with high pressures underwater and the risk of bends when surfacing. Since water pressure could cause body cavities and sinuses to collapse, most sinus cavities in the skull have been eliminated. To prevent crushing of the chest, the ribs are flexibly attached. The lung cavity is not attached to the body wall. Thus water pressure can flatten the chest and lungs of the seal without tearing tissue or breaking bones. The bends are caused by nitrogen gas in the lungs being absorbed by tissues under pressure and then boiling out, like a carbonated soft drink, as the seal shoots to the surface. To avoid this potentially fatal problem, the seal exhales before it dives. The walls of the breathing channels are lined with cartilage, which absorbs little gas. Finally, there are pockets of fat in the sinuses and along the lung walls. Fat absorbs and releases nitrogen without causing the bends.

The high pressure of the dive also creates problems for the seal's heart and circulatory system. To avoid pressure becoming too intense, a large bulb in the aorta — the main exit channel from the heart — balloons during the dive as a sort of

safety valve. This eases the pressure on the rest of the system.

The seal's ear has a dual protective system. Membrane and muscle close it off as required. Blood sinuses engorge to reduce the volume of gas in the ear canal and simultaneously increase sound transmission from the water through the sinus to the inner ear.

These adaptations exhibit many parallels with those of whales. This is another case where two unrelated organisms have evolved similar adaptive designs to deal with the same kind of environmental problems.

Pinnipeds, such as the California sea lion, have evolved respiratory and circulatory systems that enable them to dive to great depths. Some species can go as deep as 2,000 feet and stay down for one hour.

# Harp Seal *Phoca groenlandica*

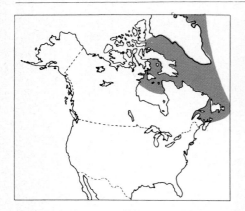

**Mammal:** *Phoca groenlandica* — harp seal

**Meaning of Name:** *Phoca* (seal); *groenlandica* (of Greenland)

**Description:** resembles harbour seal in head and body form but is proportionately stockier in the thoracic region; colour varies considerably and depends on the sex and on a sequence of immature coats from newborns to adults; males have a silvery background colour; head is dark grey or black to just behind the eyes; small dark irregular splotches develop into a dark saddle along the flanks and over the back as the seal grows older; female is similar, but face and saddle are lighter (greyish brown); pups are born with a white coat that begins to shed after about 1 week and, in 3 to 4 weeks, is completely replaced by a silvery coat with small, dark, irregular splotches

**Total Length:** male, 4.5 to 6.5 feet; female, 4.6 to 6 feet

**Weight:** up to 401 pounds

**Gestation:** 11.5 months (including 4.5 months of delayed implantation)

**Litter Size:** 1

**Age of Maturity:** male, 3 to 8 years (perhaps 1 or 2 years later); female, 3 to 7 years (usually 4.5 years)

**Longevity:** approximately 30 years

**Diet:** mainly fish (especially capelin and polar cod); to a lesser degree, crustacean macroplankton; young pups start to feed on euphausiid shrimp and amphipods

**Habitat:** pelagic species; inhabits the edge of the Arctic pack ice and the sub-Arctic waters of the North Atlantic

**Predators:** man, sharks, killer whale and polar bear

**Dental Formula:** 3/2, 1/1, 4/4, 1/1 = 34 teeth

The harp seal is a controversial pinniped. The merits and demerits of the commercial harvest of the harp are fiercely disputed on an international scale. The harp seal is specialized to live on the unstable edge of the North Atlantic ice pack. Females about to give birth gather at special haul-out sites on the ice sheets. Though aggregations numbering in the thousands are common, losses to natural predators are very low. Harp seals appear to whelp out of the usual range of polar bears. But since the ice sheet drifts as far south as Newfoundland and the Magdalen Islands, the remarkable density of harp seal aggregations makes them highly attractive to the sealing industry.

Harp seals have a migratory life cycle determined by the ice and the season. In late September, as the bays of the high Arctic begin freezing, they commence the southward migration. Harp seals stream out of Hudson Bay and from around Greenland and the Arctic archipelago, moving through Hudson and Baffin Straits and south along the coast of Labrador. Some harp seals travel into the Gulf of St. Lawrence, while others head for the Grand Banks. They feed through the winter until the ice sheets have reached their farthest southern extension. Harp seals become very fat from a rich diet of oceanic fish along with larger crustaceans such as krill. In spring, they haul-out to give birth and then breed.

The haul-out sites are situated along

*Just born, this baby harp seal will do virtually nothing but nurse for the first two weeks of its life, growing from 7 to more than 100 pounds.*

particular channels and holes providing inroads through the ice. Rough, hummocky ice is often chosen, and the large aggregations may help keep the holes open. Females defend a small patch of ice adjacent to where they whelp, while males haul-out and wait for females to wean their pups and commence the new year's mating. Fasting during the haul-out period results in a stoppage of growth and leaves annual rings on the teeth. Like tree rings, these marks provide a convenient way to determine the age of harp seals.

In the whelping grounds, up to 6,000 females per square mile each give birth to a snow-white pup. Doing virtually nothing but nurse, the precocious harp seal pups grow rapidly, from a birth weight of 7 to 9 pounds to 90 to 105 pounds within two weeks. They are then weaned, an expedient aimed at getting the pups into the safety of water as soon as possible. Their weight growth represents a serious depletion of the mother's nutrient reserves. A harp seal mother can recognize her own offspring by its smell. She will repel attempts to nurse by orphaned or abandoned pups.

Being born onto the ice comes as quite a shock for the pups. To combat hypothermia, skeletal muscle heat is generated through extensive shivering and through the use of brown fat tissue that is specialized for producing heat from fatty compounds. The white coat acts like greenhouse glazing, allowing the pup's body to soak up and retain solar energy.

Weaned pups are deserted by their mothers about the time they begin to moult from white and grow into the mottled juvenile coat. Juveniles move to the ice edge and eventually begin feeding on krill and other animals when they are a month old. By that time, their weight has fallen by 50 percent, forcing them to feed for themselves or starve. The harp seal matures within 3 to 10 years and lives as long as 30 years.

Having weaned their pups, female harp seals are ready to breed. Males compete for their attentions by putting on swimming and jumping displays and waving their flippers. The males vocalize underwater using 16 different calls. Copulation takes place in the water. Mating seems to be promiscuous, with no pair-bonding, mate-guarding or harem formation. It is probable that the female's choice of mates is based on the quality of the male's courtship.

## Conserving the Cute

*Animal conservationists appear to have their favourites. The World Wildlife Fund uses a panda bear's face for its logo. Greenpeace spends money to prevent the clubbing and skinning of the undeniably cute harp seal pup. Burros receive a tremendously expensive helicopter airlift out of canyon country that is being destroyed by their overgrazing. There is public outrage over the harvesting of wild horses.*

*This concern for the welfare of wildlife, even for species introduced by humans in the first place, is heartening. However, it is interesting and perhaps shortsighted that there is little public concern for rare shrews, a species with limited distribution, or for threatened species of bat. Nor is the public clamouring for wolverines to be reestablished in their former haunts. There may be a pattern to the expression of popular concern. This is of great concern to scientists because it means that conservation decisions and the availability of funding are made for reasons that are often more*

*emotional than biological.*

*Konrad Lorenz, the famous German student of animal behaviour, has suggested a reason that might explain why the public worries intensely about harp seals, which are not at all endangered, and yet cares virtually nothing about the fortunes of small rodents and shrews whose biology remains virtually unknown. Lorenz noted that there is an "infant schema" that instinctively tugs emotional strings in the human observer. Large rounded heads, receding chins and big eyes are the signals which make puppies irresistibly appealing and which evoke human sympathies. Many people get the same kind of reaction when they see a human infant, which explains the evolutionary origins of the reaction.*

*Harp seal pups epitomize the infant schema at its most extreme. Anyone who can bring himself to club a harp seal pup while its large trusting eyes stare up probably has a family to support and strong cultural encouragement for doing the job. Perhaps it is unfortunate that harp*

Cute and controversial, the harp seal pup and other emotionally attractive animals have been able to secure scarce conservation resources, while more threatened animals are ignored.

*seals are harvested. More critical is a situation in which limited resources are being invested in protecting harp seals and other emotionally attractive animals, while less cute species move closer to extinction.*

*Harp seal populations are thought to total between 2 million and 3 million. They are hunted along their migration route from the high Arctic to the whelping grounds in the Gulf of St. Lawrence. Recently, the harvest of the harp seal pups has been a subject of emotional controversy. There is some historical precedent for opposition to the hunt. On several occasions, they have been seriously overhunted, but government protection has allowed the harp seal stock to recover to levels healthy enough to pose occasional competition for the fishing industry. In response, some governments have moved to limit their numbers. Each harp seal eats about a ton and a half*

of food each year. Thus 3 million harp seals must eat close to 9 billion pounds of fish and krill annually.

The economic value of harp seals is not particularly great to the nation as a whole. Canadians earn about $5.5 million from the annual harvest, making it a small contributor to total revenues from the luxury-fur industry. However, the global and national perspective does not alter the fact that for many of the people who live near the harp seal's migratory routes, the harvest is an important material and cultural practice. Suggested employment alternatives, such as aquaculture or expansion of the conventional fishery, could prove to be more environmentally destructive, though socially more acceptable. In most cases, the people who have traditionally depended on seal hunting have had little impact on harp seal populations. Instead, large corporations and government management — or mismanagement — have caused serious depletions of the harp seal population.

Most of the current protest over the harvest of harp seals focuses on the killing of the appealing snow-white pups. From a biological standpoint, though, this is the appropriate stage to harvest the animal. Natural mortality would kill many of the pups. In a way, the hunt maximizes the overall productivity of the population. A controlled harvest at current levels does not threaten the harp seal. But reaction to killing the pups is often strongly emotional.

There are several biological management issues. Is there enough data to manage the species? What level of harvest will ensure a healthy harp seal population? What level of harvest will alter ecological relationships in the harp seal's habitat? What impact will more extensive fishing have?

Whether or not harp seal killing should continue, even in a rational and humane way, is a philosophical and emotional issue rather than a biological one. Can it be argued that a mammal deserves not to be harvested in a sustainable fashion simply because it is more appealing than a chicken or more intelligent than a lettuce? The danger of an

From a biological standpoint, the appealing snow-white phase of the harp seal pup is the appropriate stage at which to harvest the animal.

argument based on emotive reaction to the killing of a cute pup is that it diverts attention from the problem of acquiring data needed to solve existing management problems.

Management problems, the intensity of the harvest and ecological pressures on the harp seal will inevitably increase. Human population growth and competition for fish, increasing oil pollution, industrial residues and pesticides will exert greater pressure on the harp seal. As the human population inexorably increases, exploitation of animals such as the harp seal will intensify rather than abate. In the face of this virtual certainty, perhaps the best we can do for the harp seal is to manage its harvest properly and to establish the methodologies needed to prevent the severe depletions that have been inflicted on their populations in the recent past.

# *Ringed Seal* Phoca hispida

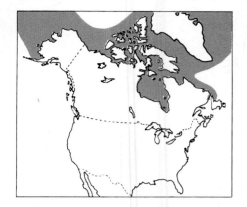

**Mammal:** *Phoca hispida* — ringed seal, the smallest of the pinnipeds
**Meaning of Name:** *Phoca* (seal); *hispida* (rough, hairy or bristly) could refer either to the coarse hair texture or to the whiskers
**Description:** resembles a small harbour seal; pelage colour is quite variable; dorsally, it is brown to bluish black in the background, with irregular creamy rings with dark centres; silver belly; pups have a soft, crinkly, white coat
**Total Length:** 4 to 5.5 feet
**Weight:** 110 to 249 pounds
**Gestation:** 10.5 to 11 months (including 3.5-month period of delayed implantation)
**Litter Size:** 1
**Age of Maturity:** male, 5 to 7 years; female, 4 to 6 years
**Longevity:** up to 43 years, but 20 to 25 years is more usual
**Diet:** primarily shrimplike organisms and, to a lesser degree, small fish such as polar cod, herring, whiting, eulachon and smelt; also a few crabs and prawns and, in deeper water, krill
**Habitat:** land-fast ice or the solid ice cover of the Arctic Ocean, where it occurs in the shifting leads and pressure ridges; usually in fiords and bays but also in some lakes and estuaries; infrequently in drifting ice floes of open seas
**Predators:** man, polar bear, sharks, killer whale and occasionally walrus
**Dental Formula:** 3/2, 1/1, 4/4, 1/1 = 34 teeth

Usually less than 5 feet long and weighing under 225 pounds, the ringed seal is the smallest pinniped. Nevertheless, this seal has been important prey for both Inuit and polar bears. Populations are estimated at close to 5 million, making the ringed seal the most abundant marine mammal in the Canadian Arctic and one of the most important elements in the high Arctic coastal ecosystem.

Ringed seals restrict their range to the Arctic ice packs. Their adaptations to this habitat include strong claws on their front flippers for scraping breathing holes through the ice. In winter, the ringed seal's blubber layer accounts for 40 percent of body weight, which explains their popularity with predators.

The ringed seal's diet changes with the seasons and its travels on the pack ice. Such Arctic crustaceans as krill, shrimp and other larger planktonic organisms compose their main diet. Ringed seals also eat smaller fish, such as Arctic cod and capelin. At midsummer, ringed seals enter a curious period of fasting when they haulout on the ice for a couple of months to laze in the sun and shed their coats.

The ringed seal's mating system is poorly understood, though it seems to be monogamous or weakly polygynous. Mating occurs under the ice, and males may protect underwater territories. In the spring breeding season, males are sometimes scarred, possibly from fighting. Still, dispersed distribution of females may prevent much

*The most abundant marine mammal in the Canadian Arctic, the ringed seal is popular with predators because of its thick blubber layer.*

harem building. If monogamy exists among the ringed seals, it is not associated with male parental care.

Denning of female ringed seals is unique. In spring, the females excavate tunnels and chambers in the snow on the pack ice where they give birth to their pups. When the thick winter ice begins to buckle and form pressure ridges, females swim underneath, searching for a crevice that will lead through the ice into the snow. There is a single underwater entrance to the den, which is several yards long. For safety, they may build multiple dens to reduce the chances of a bear or Arctic fox excavating the one containing their pup. The male dens are avoided due to an unpleasant musky smell that polar bears, sled dogs and Inuit uniformly dislike.

Ringed seal pups are less precocial than those of the slightly larger harbour seal. They do not leave the den and are not weaned for at least two months. As the pup grows, it builds itself numerous tunnels under the snow, increasing its chances of escaping predators. Pups are born with a snow-white coat that is difficult for an animal peering into a tunnel to notice. Despite these precautions, polar bears may find half a year's crop of pups. Ringed seals fortunate enough to survive to maturity may live 43 years.

# *Hooded Seal* Cystophora cristata

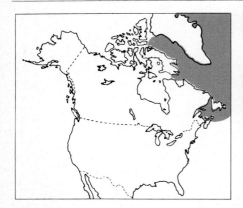

**Mammal:** *Cystophora cristata* — hooded seal

**Meaning of Name:** *Cystophora* (bladder-carrying); *cristata* (crested); the male has a peculiar pouch, which forms a crest on the nose, that can be inflated like a bladder

**Description:** the nasal apparatus is the most remarkable feature (part of the elastic nasal cavity can be inflated to form a distensible hood that runs from the crown to the upper lip, which it overhangs, proboscislike, in older animals; an inflatable nasal membrane can be extruded to form a bubble-gum-like balloon when the hood deflates); general background colour is steel-grey with irregular black patches that become smaller in size on the neck and belly; face is black to just behind the eyes; young are born with a distinctive slate-blue coat dorsally, shading abruptly to light silver-grey on the sides and belly (therefore called bluebacks); an earlier whitish foetal coat is shed before birth

**Total Length:** male, 6.5 to 9 feet; female, 5.8 to 7 feet

**Weight:** male, 904 pounds; female, 595 pounds

**Gestation:** 11 months

**Litter Size:** 1

**Age of Maturity:** 4 to 6 years

**Longevity:** 20 to 32 years

**Diet:** octopus, squid, shrimp, mussels, starfish, herring, capelin, cod, redfish, Greenland turbot

**Habitat:** pelagic species; inhabits the edge of the drifting Arctic pack ice; rarely found on firm ice

**Predators:** man, polar bear, sharks and killer whale

**Dental Formula:** 2/1, 1/1, 4/4, 1/1 = 30 teeth

Among true seals, there is usually little difference in size and appearance between males and females. But with hooded seals — and their close relatives, the elephant seals — males have evolved comparatively large bodies and some flamboyant displays. The male hooded seal has the unusual and, some would say, gruesome habit of blowing the inner nasal sac out through his nostril so that it emerges looking like a bright red bladder. The nasal bladder may also be pumped up when it is drawn into the head, thus creating a large facial bulge that looks less like a hood (the basis for the seal's name) than a massive swollen black blister.

These bizarre displays are examples of what mate selection on the basis of male displays can produce. Males blow their nasal bubble when they are hauled-out on the breeding grounds and trying to guard a female, and often her pup. The bladder is some kind of threat and may indicate the size of the male. Older males are more likely than the young to blow out the blood-red bladder, while immature males lack the ability. Female aggression to other females may prevent polygyny, even though haul-outs are densely aggregated, a pattern of behaviour that is often associated with harem-style breeding. Males are very aggressive at breeding time and will threaten human intruders. At 880 pounds, a large male must be taken seriously.

Hooded seals follow the same mi-

*When guarding females, a male hooded seal threatens other males by inflating a large inner nasal sac.*

gratory pattern as harp seals, since they both use pack-ice edge areas for breeding. The hooded seal is larger than the harp seal, dives deeper and feeds on larger fish and organisms such as starfish and octopus.

The hooded seal population is thought to be roughly half a million.

## *Northern Elephant Seal* Mirounga angustirostris

**Mammal:** *Mirounga angustirostris* — northern elephant seal; the largest pinniped

**Meaning of Name:** *Mirounga,* derived from *miouroung,* an Australian native name for the seal; *angustirostris* (narrow snout)

**Description:** a rather obese seal; large head, long broad snout and thick creased neck; short thickened foreflippers and bilobed hind flippers; males have a remarkable proboscis that hangs over the mouth but can be inflated, at which point it curves downward into the mouth; nostrils are located at the tip of the proboscis; proboscis is actually an extension of the nasal cavity and is divided by the nasal septum; short, dense pelage is dull brown to yellowish grey, lighter on belly

**Total Length:** male, 18 to 19.7 feet; female, 10.2 to 12.1 feet

**Weight:** male, 8,157 pounds; female, 1,984 pounds

**Gestation:** 11.3 months (including a delayed-implantation period of 3 months)

**Litter Size:** 1

**Age of Maturity:** male, 4 to 5 years (becomes territorial breeding bull at 9 or 10 years); female, 3 to 5 years

**Longevity:** 15 years in captivity

**Diet:** deep-water bottom-dwelling marine life (ratfish, sharks, dogfish, eel, rockfish and squid)

**Habitat:** pelagic species found in warm temperate seas, except during breeding, which takes place on deserted beaches off the coasts of subtropical continental and oceanic islands

**Predators:** large sharks (especially white shark) and killer whale

**Dental Formula:** 2/1, 1/1, 4/4, 1/1 = 30 teeth

When feeding, northern elephant seals range as far as Alaska. However, breeding activity is limited to the coasts of California and Mexico. Elephant seals dive deeply, up to 650 feet, feeding on rays, sharks and other organisms they encounter in the inshore waters.

During the winter breeding season, elephant seals congregate on sandy beaches — a spectacle that ranks as one of the most bizarre and extreme expressions of sexual selection and male-male combat in the animal kingdom. The name elephant refers to the male's huge size, great snout and bellowing roars. Males are three times larger than females, reaching a length of nearly 20 feet and a weight of 8,000 pounds or more, far heavier and longer than the average loaded pickup truck. Elephant seals are the largest of all the pinnipeds.

The elephant seal's long proboscis can be inflated. When the tip of this snout extends into the mouth and the nostrils point toward the voice box, the whole affair acts as an echo chamber, magnifying the sound of the bellows. These roars can be heard a mile away and signify the ferocity of a mature bull. Males fight fiercely for control of a harem, pounding their massive chests into each other and gashing their foe's face and proboscis. The neck of the mature male is coated with a rough thick hide as a defence against bites from rivals. Though only a tiny fraction of male elephant seals gain harems, the rewards for success-

*During the breeding season, female elephant seals accompanied by their pups gather on beaches. In the mating frenzy that follows, 10 percent of the pups are crushed to death.*

ful combat are great, as 5 percent of the males enjoy roughly 90 percent of all the matings. A male may inseminate 100 different females in a single mating season.

The intensity of physical combat is such that while elephant seals may be sexually mature after 5 years, they are generally unable to acquire a harem until age 10. Even then, the effort of warding off rivals means that harem masters are soon exhausted. Males rarely survive more than four years of harem ownership. During the breeding season, which may extend for two months or more, males do not leave the harem to feed. They must fight and breed, depending on stored body fat as an energy source.

At the time when female elephant seals are receptive to mating, they are accompanied by young pups ready to be weaned. The furious charges of fighting males crush 10 percent of the pups and may also injure many females. Males are also heedless about the wishes of females. They try to copulate with any and every female that comes within reach. Sexually immature females, pregnant females, females with newborn pups and receptive females all receive equal treatment. The elephant seal male grabs the female by the neck with his jaws,

*By inflating its proboscis and inverting its nostrils so they point into the mouth and toward the voice box, a male elephant seal,* **above,** *can emit a roar audible one mile away. Females,* **right,** *weigh only one-third as much as males, who attain weights in excess of 8,000 pounds, making them the largest of the pinnipeds.*

throws himself down and mates with her. Females that resist are slapped and bitten into submission. When a female wishes to leave the harem and enter the ocean to feed, subdominate males hovering at the edge of the breeding harem waylay them and try to copulate. Subdominate males are so intent that they may inadvertently kill females that attempt to bypass them.

Female elephant seals give a characteristic scream when mating. This might simply be the consequence of being set upon by 8,000 pounds of male elephant seal. However, it has also been interpreted as an adaptation. The female is best served by mating with a proven male, the harem keeper that has survived many years of feeding and fighting and that is obviously free of serious genetic defects or diseases. By screaming, the female may prevent a subdominate and less proven male from copulating. Her scream alerts the harem master, who rushes over to attempt to throttle the intruder. After breeding season, males and females disperse to feed. They tend to return to the same breeding grounds each year.

During the 19th century, hunters slaughtered virtually all elephant seal populations. By the time they were given complete protection, only 50 animals survived. Since then, populations have grown to roughly 45,000, but the recolonization of their former range has been slow. Now that they are protected from human predation, only sharks and killer whales prey on this seal. Fortunately, populations continue to rebound at a high rate.

# MEAT EATERS *Carnivora*

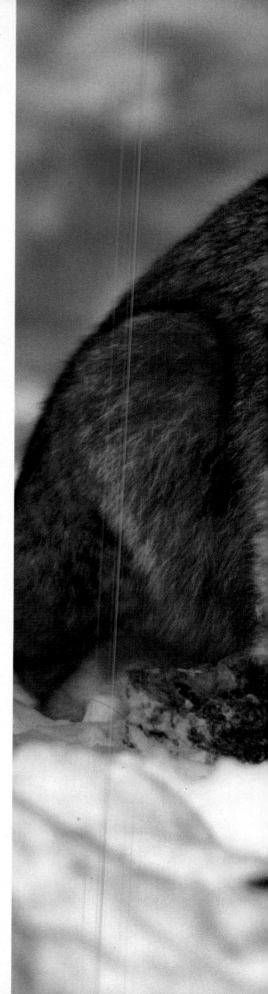

Carnivores are killers. Most of the species in this order live by killing and eating other mammals, their predilection for red meat reflected in a unique type of teeth that carnivores possess. All carnivores, from the giant grizzly bear to the smallest weasel, have four teeth specially adapted for eating meat — an upper and lower pair of premolars and molars. These are the so-called carnassials, and they act as shearing blades that cut against each other as the mouth opens and closes. This slicing mechanism evolved more than 50 million years ago when a group of primitive insectivores began to eat fewer insects and more mammalian meat.

By the time the first carnivores appeared, mammals had already existed for more than 100 million years and had evolved into a number of orders called herbivores, omnivores and insectivores. The new specialization of meat-eating predators was a successful evolutionary innovation, and the group proliferated and radiated explosively into the diversity of forms we now recognize as bears, weasels, cats, raccoons, mongooses and dogs. It is hard to believe that animals so different in size, body form and behaviour could all have descended from the same ancestor. Yet this common ancestry is reflected in many adaptations, the most important of which — like the carnassial teeth — relate to their lives as predators.

In addition to slicing and shearing meat, carnivores must be able to deliver a killing bite, normally with large incisor teeth. The powerful movement of the mouth as it opens to deliver that bite is unlike that involved in closed-mouth chewing. Therefore, two entirely different sets of muscles are required to deliver biting power both when the mouth is open (the temporalis) and when the mouth is closed (the masseter). Because large expanses of bone are needed as an anchoring place for these muscles, most carnivores have several bone ridges running along the skull. These crests are especially well developed in the largest carnivores, such as pumas and grizzly bears.

The bodies of carnivores have adapted to their predatory life style in several ways. Because carnivores must be flexible enough to roll, twist and contort while making a kill, they have evolved a body plan with little fusion of bones, except in the feet. To strengthen the feet for rough-terrain running, most species have fused wrist and ankle bones. Likewise, the clavicles, or collarbones, of carnivores are drastically reduced in comparison with other orders because of their method of running down prey with a straight forward and backward stride. With little need for tight control of the forelimbs' side-to-side movement, there is no need for a well-developed clavicle.

While the meat of vertebrates is a concentrated source of energy, as opposed to plant or insect material, it is relatively hard to acquire. Therefore, carnivores have had to develop prey-sensing mechanisms, and the order has invested heavily in eyesight, hearing and smelling. As a corollary, their well-developed senses have predisposed carnivores to make use of a rich array of sensory communication devices, including complicated chemical signals, vocalizations and facial expressions. Only primates exceed carnivores in the sophistication of their communication.

*Carnivores such as the lynx are built for a life of stalking, killing and eating other animals.*

# Foxes & Wolves *Canidae*

Canids are long-distance runners. More than 50 million years ago, when the family began to evolve in North America, its members had short, stubby legs, broad five-toed forepaws and long, thin bodies: they looked more like weasels than wolves. Subsequently, their legs became longer, compact toes and toe pads developed to absorb the shock of running, and bones in the forelegs fused to keep them from twisting as the animal ran.

The incisors — front teeth adapted for cutting — grew larger, and the muzzle lengthened so that the canid could slash open-mouthed at running prey and bite penetratingly when it fell. The long muzzle also featured enlarged and highly convoluted spiral bones, coiled like turbines to filter air as it passed through the nose and to provide a huge sensory surface for smelling prey. More importantly, the turbinate bones enabled the long-distance runner to conserve moisture lost through high ventilation rates and, in extreme weather, to warm or cool the air before it reached the lungs. The development of carnassial teeth — adapted for tearing flesh — and the crushing molars allowed canids to eat a more varied diet than members of families that have reduced molars.

These adaptations were most useful on the open grasslands, and the fossil record indicates that the family diversified on the dry plains of North America, reaching a zenith there some 20 million years ago with 42 different genera. Some of these canids were extremely large and muscular. For example, the bone-eating dogs of the genus *Borophagus* were sometimes as large as bears and had huge crushing jaws. Palaeontologists think that they were the North American equivalent of hyenas, scavenging much of their food and cracking the bones left from the kills of other carnivores.

Today, only 10 to 15 genera and 35 species of canid remain. Nevertheless, these represent a tremendously successful family that thrives on every continent except Antarctica. The wolf, dingo, African wild dog and coyote are still dominant mammals in their respective habitats, ranging over vast expanses of open country.

The family seems to allow great adaptability in body form — witness the wide variety of shapes and sizes of domestic dog. Nature has also generated a broad range of hunting strategies. For example, although most canids belong to the open country, roaming the grasslands, tundra, dry mountains and deserts, there are certain foxes, bush dogs and raccoon dogs that have a lower body form and hunt alone, often in forested habitats, in search of small prey.

None of the canids is very large. The fennec, a small Saharan fox, weighs only 2 pounds; at the other extreme is the largest species, the timber wolf, that weighs only 176 pounds. Yet the social flexibility of canids allows them a great breadth of diet, with some of them hunting mammals as large as the moose and buffalo while others consume rodents and insects. The small African hunting dog weighs only 55 pounds, but by hunting in a group, it is able to prey on adult lions. In general, the pack hunters are highly carnivorous and prey on large mammals, while solitary species, especially the smaller ones, are omnivorous and may eat large amounts of vegetable matter.

Canids depend heavily on their eyes, and many species hunt during the day. Also, most members of the family have a large bushy tail and large erect ears that are used for communication with other members of their species. The face itself is highly flexible and expressive of emotional states. Wolves, for example, are able to display at least 13 facial expressions, many of which resemble those of the even more expressive primates — including monkeys, apes and human beings. Back arching, paw raising and groin presentation are also used socially.

The canids have excellent hearing and a rich vocal repertoire consisting of as many as eight kinds of signal. The nose of a dog is estimated to be 100 times more sensitive than that of a human being, and canids are also able to communicate by smell. Thus the sniffing of genitals or scent-marking with urine are important means of giving and receiving information. The dog that urinates on a fire hydrant leaves a signature that indicates identity, sex, reproductive state and, possibly, other information. Urine is also used to mark territorial boundaries.

## Howling and Scowling

*The sound of howling wolves and coyotes is a wild one that sends a shiver down the spine. One longtime student of wolves described it: "The cry of the lobo is entirely unlike that made by any other living creature — it is a prolonged, deep, wailing howl, perhaps the most dismal sound ever heard by man. The best comparison I can give would be to take a dozen railroad whistles, braid them together and then let one strand after another drop off, the last peal so frightfully piercing as to go through your heart and soul."*

*Intelligent and curious, canids such as this grey wolf are among the most social of all mammals.*

Wolves do not howl at the moon, and their howling is not some canine expression of melancholy. They howl at each other as a way of scowling — a canine kind of warning.

Wolves and coyotes kill members of their own species. Often, the victim is a lone individual killed by a group of strangers whose realm he has invaded, but even full-fledged packs may fight each other, especially if food is scarce. (There is, however, a well-documented case from Riding Mountain National Park, Manitoba, of one pack's being displaced by another even though there was abundant food in the area for both packs.)

A conflict between two wolf packs is similar in some ways to a conflict between two nations armed with nuclear weapons. If mutually fatal conflicts are to be avoided, communication must be maintained so that each will have advance warning of the other's intentions. Such communication springs not from concern for the other group but from the need for self-protection, as lethal fights may be detrimental to both parties.

Wolves scent-mark the borders of their territories so that wanderers are warned when they move into foreign territory and may expect to be attacked. Howling is another way of establishing territoriality and sending out long-distance signals of location. Wolves howl all through their own territory, not just at the borders, to define their space for the benefit of surrounding wolf packs.

When wolves hear other wolves howling, they usually reciprocate, for howling is an expression of strength, and silence — an admission of weakness — could invite intrusions. Wolves guarding a kill will howl to protect their meal, and breeding wolves at their dens almost always respond to the howling of distant packs. When one member of a pack howls, all the rest join in, to indicate the location of the pack as well as its strength. A medium-sized pack will howl 50 percent more than a small pack, but lone wolves on the move rarely ever howl since this would constitute a direct broadcast of their location and vulnerability.

In Superior National Forest in northeastern Minnesota, intruding packs have made direct forays into the home sites of others, killing some individuals and, in one case, forcing the victimized pack to disband and disperse. It may be that the amount of howling and its strength enabled intruders to assess the weakness of their neighbours before they made their move.

Howling is one way wolves send and receive information about territory boundaries, pack size and location of intruders or competing wolf packs.

# *Grey Wolf* Canis lupus

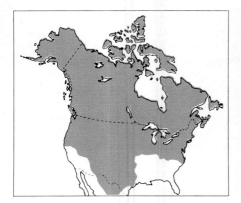

**Mammal:** *Canis lupus* — grey wolf, timber wolf

**Meaning of Name:** *Canis* (dog); *lupus* (wolf)

**Description:** covered with bristly hair; colour is extremely variable, from white to black and all intermediate degrees of cream, grey, brown and orangish black; grey tones are the most common (with yellow and reddish hues usually lacking)

**Total Length:** 4.9 to 6.7 feet

**Tail:** 13.8 to 23.6 inches

**Weight:** male, 44 to 176 pounds; female, 40 to 121 pounds

**Gestation:** 63 days

**Litter Size:** 1 to 11 (usually 6 or 7)

**Age of Maturity:** male, 3 years; female, 2 years

**Longevity:** may live 16 years, but usually not more than 10 years in the wild; 18 years is the record in captivity

**Diet:** carnivore; primarily big game (moose, caribou, deer, wapiti, bison, muskox and mountain sheep); also smaller game (rabbits, shrews, voles, mice, squirrels, beavers, muskrats), birds, fish, berries, fruit, insects, grass and crayfish

**Habitat:** shows little preference for special habitats, frequenting all habitats and travelling along game trails, forest edges and lake shorelines

**Predators:** man, grizzly bear; eagle, black bear, bobcat and lynx may eat unattended pups, but this is probably unusual

**Dental Formula:** 3/3, 1/1, 4/4, 2/3 = 42 teeth

The grey wolf is the largest of the dogs. A pack of wolves is the continent's most formidable predatory apparatus, capable of hunting down even the largest mammals.

For hundreds of years, grey wolves ranged over the entire northern hemisphere, from the farthest reaches of Siberia south to China, from Lapland to Spain, from Greenland to Mexico. But as agriculture spread, their southern ranges disappeared. Man's hatred of the wolf has ancient roots and is mainly due to the fact that the wolf, in pursuit of big game, effectively competed with rural human populations. When humans began to keep livestock within the range of the wolf, the antipathy intensified. Although there is good evidence that European wolves sometimes preyed on humans, it is competition and not fear that best explains this widespread aversion. Wolves that have attacked humans almost certainly suffered from rabies, since healthy wolves, made cautious

*The life of the wolf is an unending cycle of hunting, feeding and then moving on in search of prey.*

by centuries of wolf-hunting, tend to avoid people.

Individual wolves are not physically formidable. They rarely stand more than 3 feet high at the shoulder, weigh less than the average adult human and have neither great speed nor stamina. This means, surprisingly, that although wolves can sprint faster and bite harder, humans are more dangerous long-distance predators. Wolves normally pursue their prey at speeds of less than 25 miles an hour, and since they rarely run for more than 20 minutes at a time, they do not cover great distances in a chase. (The longest chase on record is 13 miles.) Humans can run as fast and can often go farther. Plains Indians used to make a sport of running down wolves on foot, and a Canadian, Thomas Kessick, is credited with running one down in 1865 be-

*The social life of wolves involves battles over positions of dominance within the pack.*

tween Fort Pelly and the Touchwood Hills in Saskatchewan. The 100-mile chase ended when Kessick killed the exhausted wolf with his knife.

The success of the wolf as a large-game predator is a factor in its social relationships. Almost 80 percent of grey wolves belong to packs of animals that travel, hunt and den together; only a few individuals live largely solitary lives. The pack is a kind of extended family, centred on a breeding pair, which produces an annual litter of some half-dozen young. These cubs may stay with their parents as they grow older to form the basis of an average eight-member pack, although at maturity, some may be forced to leave the pack to seek breeding partners. Wolves mature at almost 2 years of age and usually breed in their third year.

Wolves have a well-developed hierarchy that affects breeding privileges, and normally, only the dominant male and female breed.

Eventually, one of the adult breeding pair will be challenged by a stronger wolf in a courtship which may extend over months or even a year and which requires the establishment of dominance. Fighting may be a part of the process, but often, more subtle behaviour is involved. For example, aggressive males with designs on leadership may tackle dangerous prey or an intruder such as the grizzly bear, or they may stand guard while other members of the pack rest.

Females often take the active part in courtship. There is one recorded case of a wild female courting a tame male already paired with a tame female. The wild female killed her rival and mated with the tame male.

Breeding takes place in the winter. One aspect of the breeding of wolves and close relatives such as the domestic dog is the baffling copulatory tie. During copulation, the male's penis becomes locked in the female vagina, and he is held in a seemingly awkward position straddling the female for as long as half an hour. Some biologists claim that this is a way of ''cementing the pair bond.'' Others hold that since the male is putting himself in a very vulnerable position, the tie effectively ensures that only the dominant male will risk copulation.

The mother seeks out a rocky, protected den before the birth of her altricial (helpless) pups. They take 10 months to reach adult size. During the first few months, when the pups are unable to hunt and forage, other members of the pack help the breeding female to feed and care for them.

Being at the top of the predatory chain, wolves are not subject to predation, but they are food-limited, meaning that the size of litters and packs, and the overall population density, is clearly tied to the abundance of game. To obtain enough food, packs range over wide areas, and hunting grounds may cover anywhere from 400 to 5,000 square miles, depending on the availability of food. Wolves tend to move along a circuit, covering as much as 50 miles a day.

Packs are territorial and hostile to nonpack members — lone wolves are usually attacked and killed. Wolves are also hostile to other large carnivores and have often been known to tree mountain lions, to harass bears and to kill wolverines and coyotes.

The prey of the wolf is as varied as the habitat it occupies. It feeds heavily on Arctic hare on Ellesmere Island, caribou in the barren-grounds, moose in the boreal forest, deer in deciduous forests and, in earlier times, buffalo on the plains. Smaller animals — such as beaver, foxes, ground squirrels and rodents — are also consumed from time to time.

Wolves suffer from a perpetual cycle of feast and famine and can go for two weeks or more without feeding. When a kill is finally made, a wolf is able to eat as much as 20 pounds of meat, swallowing huge chunks with virtually no chewing.

Biologists disagree as to whether wolf predation seriously affects the abundance of big game. However, it is reasonable to assume that the effect on slow-growing herbivore populations, such as moose and elk, would be significant. This fear has led many governments to embark on campaigns that have seen wolf populations hunted and poisoned into extermination throughout most of their former range. Only in Canada and Alaska do large wolf populations still exist.

## Tactics

*Wolves are not invincible predators. The deer and moose that they feed on have developed ways of protecting themselves from attackers; in response, wolves have developed ways to increase their effectiveness. Both the hunter and the hunted use certain tactics to play on the weakness of their adversary.*

*Wolves are not fast runners. Over the long haul and under favourable ground conditions, both deer and moose can outrun them, and moose can outswim them. Wolves have responded by relying heavily on the value of surprise. They stalk their prey, approaching from the upwind side so that their quarry is not warned by their scent. When they have managed to creep close to the unsuspecting deer or moose, they rush to the attack.*

*Small, agile prey, such as the*

white-tailed deer, may respond to the rush by bounding rapidly away. They are capable of simply outrunning the wolf and are also able to leap through low brush that impedes their pursuer. In winter, the long-legged deer plunge easily through the soft snow while their enemies bog down behind them. Wolves may respond to the superior agility and speed of the deer by setting up an ambush and actually driving the prey toward hidden members of the pack. This phenomenon has not been rigorously studied, but it is certainly possible in rolling, open terrain. Wolves live for as long as two decades, often remaining in a single area, and they may learn enough of the topography and behaviour of game to predict the probable course of a chase.

Not all prey run from wolves. Muskox will stand and fight as a group, and so will individual moose. The way in which wolves tackle a moose seems to depend on the moose's reaction. A well-documented study on the outcome of moose-wolf encounters in Isle Royale National Park in northern Michigan found some clear patterns. Of 131 moose discovered by wolves, only 6 were killed. Sometimes, the moose became aware of the approaching wolves before it was spotted and was able to avoid them. Even when the wolves saw the moose and pursued it, the moose simply outran the wolves in half of the cases. Sometimes, however, the moose was surprised and stood at bay or, after an initial pursuit, was forced to turn and face its attackers.

Most moose that turned to fight were successful. In all of the 36 recorded cases where the moose decided to fight, the wolves very quickly gave up. Fights were as brief as half a minute, and the longest battle was over in only five minutes. The principal weapons of the moose and other hoofed animals are not the antlers but rather the forefeet. The moose whirls and lashes out with bone-breaking blows. In only a few minutes, the wolves are able to get an indication of their quarry's abilities. If it appears strong and able to mete out punishment, they abandon the attack and move off in search of easier prey. On the other hand, if the wolves can

panic the moose into bolting, they have an immediate advantage and will run alongside, ripping at its belly and legs. Often, one wolf will attempt to clamp its teeth onto the moose's nose, while the others attack its body.

The white-tailed deer, lacking the strength and fierceness of the moose, is forced to protect itself by strategy. This they do by using the territorial nature of wolves to their own advantage. Since wolf packs defend their territories against other wolves and since trespass is severely punished, there is often a kind of buffer zone, a ''no-wolf's-land,'' between adjacent territories. Neither pack tends to hunt close to the territory of another because of the threat of aggression, and deer tend to establish their yards in this neutral ground. Such deeryards usually last until there is a shift in the wolf population. Wolves in the surrounding territories feed on surplus deer that

*By relying on the tactic of surprise, wolves can stalk and kill large-game animals such as deer.*

may be forced out of the buffer zone by competition.

These buffer zones have been compared to the no-man's-land that used to exist between hostile Indian tribes. Such areas supported relatively high densities of game and acted as a source of replenishment for areas that were continually being cropped by hunting and predation. Similarly, modern-day moose gravitate to camping and recreational areas in national parks, which the wolves avoid. Wolves leave a buffer zone around their main competitors — humans —and the moose make use of it.

# *Coyote* Canis latrans

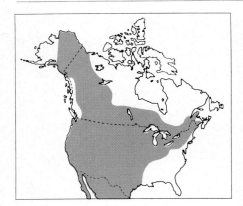

**Mammal:** *Canis latrans* — coyote
**Meaning of Name:** *Canis* (dog); *latrans* (barking); coyote is from the Aztec name *coyotl*
**Description:** colour varies from grizzled grey to rufous; muzzle, outside of ears, forelegs and feet are reddish brown to yellow; white throat and belly; prominent dorsal stripe and a dark cross on shoulders formed by black-tipped guard hairs; fawn-coloured tail (lighter underneath) is black at tip; scent gland above base of tail
**Total Length:** 3.4 to 4.5 feet
**Tail:** 11.4 to 15.7 inches
**Weight:** male, 18 to 51 pounds; female, 15 to 40 pounds
**Gestation:** 60 to 63 days
**Litter Size:** 1 to 9 (usually 6)
**Age of Maturity:** female, 1 year; male, slightly older
**Longevity:** usually 6 to 8 years in the wild (maximum of 14.5 years); one animal lived almost 22 years in captivity
**Diet:** opportunistic feeder, but small rodents and lagomorphs, along with carrion, form a major part of diet; also white-tailed deer, birds, eggs, insects, snakes, turtles, frogs, fish, acorns, fruit and plants
**Habitat:** open grasslands and plains, mixed forest and cleared environments, agricultural areas, burned-over woodlands, lowland conifers and brush and occasionally upland hardwoods
**Predators:** man, wolf, lynx, puma, black bear, grizzly bear, golden eagle and domestic dog
**Dental Formula:** 3/3, 1/1, 4/4, 2/3 = 42 teeth

*Possessing great stamina, coyotes are able to run for hours in search of prey.*

A natural target of the grey wolf, the coyote has historically tended to populate areas beyond the wolf's range — opting for the arid grasslands and deserts of North America, while the wolf prospered to the north. Wolves are known to kill coyotes, but with the gradual extermination of wolf populations, the coyote has steadily expanded its range to the north and east. Human activity, while tending to eliminate the wolf and big game, has enhanced the population of smaller mammals, providing coyotes with a steady food supply.

Coyotes do not hunt big game. They have smaller bodies and smaller social units than wolves and are far more catholic in their feeding habits, eating any mammal they can kill — usually ground squirrels, rabbits and, more rarely, deer, but also mice, voles and even fruit and insects.

The male-female pair is the basic social unit of the coyote, although they often operate within a pack made up of other males and females — probably siblings or offspring — if adequate range and prey are available. The breeding biology of coyotes — a single breeding pair — is similar to that of the wolves, and both males and females help raise the pups with the assistance of other pack members. The coyote young usually disperse at the age of 1 year, especially in habitats that do not support large-game animals. The extreme social flexibility of coyotes enables them to survive both in virgin wilderness and on the outskirts of large cities where they kill rodents and scavenge for garbage.

Coyotes are adept at solving unusual foraging problems, and their wily reputation is well deserved. Coyotes have been seen to go fishing, wading out into the water, plunging their heads below the surface and emerging with carp gripped between their teeth. They also catch crayfish that crawl along the bottom of streams, and on Pacific coast beaches, they search for and excavate sea turtle eggs. Coyotes often follow a badger around as it searches for ground squirrels. When the badger digs into the burrow, the coyote positions itself at one of the side entrances ready to pounce on any squirrels that take the emergency exit.

Coyotes work in pairs to sneak up on prairie dogs and other rodents. While one approaches from a conspicuous position, thus attracting the attention of the prairie dog, the other stalks it from behind. They also follow vultures and ravens in search of carrion and prey on domestic sheep.

Farmers' efforts to control coyotes have usually been fruitless, as the coyote can climb fences 6 feet high and burrow under electric fences. Poisoning programmes often have resulted in the killing of other species, and the coyote continues to flourish despite the intensive efforts to reduce its numbers.

## Social Economics

*Students of social behaviour among animals have long been fascinated by the coyote and the grey wolf. Sometimes coyotes live in packs, sometimes in pairs, and often alone. Grey wolves are more social, but the size of the pack ranges from 3 or 4 to as many as 20. The conventional explanation is that sociality in canids is related to the size and abundance of the prey that they hunt.*

*Small canids, such as foxes, always eat small mammals, insects or fruits, hunt alone and are not social. This same lack of sociality is seen in arid grassland coyotes, which feed on rodents, probably because a large group of predators may be more easily seen and avoided than the more efficient individual or pair. However, individuals or pairs would be unable to catch and kill a larger animal, such as the white-tailed deer. In some areas, coyotes appear to subsist on large mammal carcasses — not killed by them but, rather, found as carrion. In such cases, a large group size allows the defence of the meat against other coyotes and scavengers.*

*There is clearly a general correlation between the group size of canids and the size of their prey. But among coyotes and, perhaps, wolves, the correlation may be the result of social behaviour rather than a cause of it. If pack size is determined by foraging efficiency, then the amount of meat caught by each individual ought to increase*

*with an increase in group size. The size of the pack ought, therefore, to stabilize at the point at which per capita meat yields are maximized. In fact, however, packs are usually larger than simple efficiency would dictate. In other words, there are more animals in the pack than are strictly necessary to handle the kill. There is also evidence that when food is limited, the birth rate declines as the group size increases.*

*In fact, cooperative hunting efficiency may not be the only factor controlling group size. Foraging efficiency is definitely part of the equation, but individual resistance to leaving the pack may be just as important. Increases in pack size are usually the result of delayed dispersal of the younger wolves or coyotes. Young canids might delay dispersing while they help to raise their young kin, at the same time acquiring much-needed breeding skills. Also, membership in an existing pack brings with it the benefits of an established territory. If the habitat is saturated and prospects for establishing a new territory are slight, the individual is faced with a long, hazardous journey away from its pack.*

*Saturation of the habitat and competition between packs may contribute to the creation of groups that are larger than the optimum foraging size. The threat of annihilation by competing wolves may encourage packs to prolong*

By travelling in packs of between 3 and 20, grey wolves increase the size of game they can kill, which in turn increases the amount of food each pack member receives.

*their association with unnecessary members, even though the pack would eat better if it were smaller. If this is true, then pack size should increase as competition between groups increases.*

*The social economics of coyotes and wolves depend on more than just the size of the prey they feed on. Competition within and between group members, the genetic relationship of members, the longevity of individuals and groups, the cost of dispersal and the difficulty of establishing new groups are all part of a complex equation. That complexity may be the reason for so much variation in the sociality of coyotes and wolves.*

# *Arctic Fox* Alopex lagopus

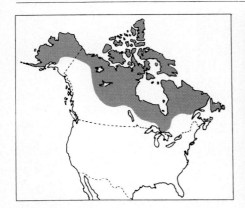

**Mammal:** *Alopex lagopus* — Arctic fox; the smallest Canadian wild canid

**Meaning of Name:** *Alopex* (fox); *lagopus* (hare + foot) refers to the fact that, like a hare, the fox has hair on the soles of its feet, probably to prevent slipping on the ice

**Description:** soles of feet are well furred; 2 colour phases in winter — white and blue (varies from blue-black to pearl grey; there is a higher proportion of blue foxes in populations living in marine areas); both phases are similar in summer with dark brown on the back, tail and outer sides of the legs and yellow-white to buff on belly and flanks

**Total Length:** male, 2.9 to 3.9 feet; female, 2.5 to 2.8 feet

**Tail:** male, 11 to 13.4 inches; female, 10.4 to 12.6 inches

**Weight:** male, 7.1 to 8.8 pounds; female, 5.5 to 7.3 pounds (can reach 19.8 pounds)

**Gestation:** 49 to 57 days

**Litter Size:** 1 to 14 (usually 5 or 6); up to 25 have been recorded

**Age of Maturity:** 9 to 10 months

**Longevity:** one captive lived 15 years, but most young do not survive first 6 months; few live more than several years in the wild (can live 8 to 10 years)

**Diet:** scavenger; eats any available animal food (alive or dead); prefers lemmings, Arctic voles and ground squirrels; also ground-nesting birds, carrion (follows wolves and polar bears to clean up their prey carcasses as well as eating stranded marine mammals), fish, mollusks, crabs and sea urchins

**Habitat:** primarily in Arctic and alpine tundra, usually in coastal areas; can be found in the boreal forest border during winter and will venture onto frozen seas

**Predators:** besides man, wolf is chief predator; also polar bear, grizzly bear, snowy owl, peregrine falcon, golden eagle, wolverine, weasel and red fox

**Dental Formula:** 3/3, 1/1, 4/4, 2/3, = 42 teeth

The Arctic fox lives at the top of the world in a ring of tundra that circles the northern parts of Russia, Alaska and Canada. The small carnivore is superbly designed for northern conditions, with a compact body, furry feet and a huge bushy tail.

In extremely cold weather, the Arctic fox is able to maintain its body temperature at up to 200 Fahrenheit degrees above the ambient temperature. Thus, even when Arctic winters bring minus 80 degrees, the fox keeps itself at a steady 104 degrees, its normal temperature. A thick insulating coat and the ability to increase its metabolic rate when temperatures drop below minus 60 degrees mean that the fox can function effectively during even the most severe northern winters.

*In its summer coat, the Arctic fox blends in with the mosses and sedges of the tundra.*

The feet of the Arctic fox are warmed by a countercurrent blood-circulation mechanism. As cool blood returns to the body from capillaries in the toes and feet, it picks up heat from fresh warm blood being pumped from the heart and warm body core. This heat is then carried back into the feet. Thus the feet stay at a temperature just a degree or two above freezing even though the fox is standing on ice or snow.

The Arctic fox, like many northern animals, turns white in winter. This is a form of camouflage that varies with the environment: on islands or along the open coast — in Iceland, for example — the coat of the Arctic fox has a bluish cast.

The breeding biology of the Arctic fox has also been modified for life in the harsh Arctic weather. For example, the litter size averages 20 during years of abundant food, which is two to four times the size of red or grey fox litters. The average Arctic fox litters contain 6 to 12 offspring; the largest have 25. These large litters allow the fox to exploit years when lemmings are plentiful and to protect the family from extinction in years of severe weather and scarce food.

Arctic foxes are monogamous and breed once a year in the spring. After the female gives birth, she remains in the den with her cubs for the first few days, while the male brings food. Almost from the beginning, the cubs tend toward strong sibling rivalry, and during times of scarce food, the weaker members of the litter may be killed by the stronger. Although they are born blind, naked and helpless, the cubs develop rapidly, and by the time they are 2 weeks old, they have been weaned and are ready to venture outside the den. By late summer, the male stops caring for them; very soon, the female follows suit. The young then disperse, leaving the male — and most females — ready to breed again by the next spring.

Arctic foxes are not extremely territorial, though males tend to exclude other males from their den sites during the breeding season. Thus, although the dens may be scattered far and wide — as few as one in every 22 miles — they may also be clumped together in good sheltered spots.

Dens remain in use for long periods of time, and some are known to have been inhabited for up to 60 years. Foxes avoid areas of permafrost and try to situate their dens in high, well-drained areas where the soil is light and easily excavated. More rarely, foxes burrow into rock piles. Their dens are dug as a system of tunnels with many entrances and exits — usually a dozen or so but sometimes as many as 100. During low years in the population cycle, many dens may be empty; in years of high population density, good dens may be scarce.

Dens are often recognizable from afar as islands of lush grass among the prevailing shrubs and mosses. The digging of foxes tends to stimulate the

growth of vegetation, which is also enriched by the nutrients excreted near the entrance of the den.

Small rodents, particularly lemmings and voles, are the most important food of the Arctic fox, and breeding pairs with pups may eat as many as 4,000 lemmings during the denning season. However, populations of small mammals on the tundra tend to wax and wane every three to five years, and the foxes are tied to the same wheel. Like lemmings, foxes tend to migrate in huge numbers when their food source disappears. Some amazing journeys have resulted: one fox was tagged in Russia and caught in Alaska; another was tagged and released in Ontario, only to be caught two years later 700 miles away.

The hunting success of the Arctic fox depends on a keen sense of smell, which it uses to locate lemmings in their burrows under the snow. Foxes have been known to venture out onto the pack ice, where they are able to sniff out the presence of seal pups under 2 feet of snow. Arctic foxes forage within a 1-to-8-mile radius of the den, depending on the abundance of prey. When small mammals are scarce, the foxes feed on nesting birds; in winter, they trail wolves or polar bears and feed on the remains of their kills. They must, of course, be very cautious, since wolves and bears are — with humans — the major predators of the Arctic fox.

Some Inuit depend heavily for their livelihood on trapping the Arctic fox. Other predators are the snowy owl, large hawks and, in the southern part

*In the Arctic fox's winter phase, its coat conceals it from predators and prey.*

of the range, wolverines, weasels and red foxes. In recent years, red foxes have been moving farther into the range of the Arctic fox and have inflicted increasing damage.

Like the red fox, the Arctic fox is subject to rabies, and in epidemic years, up to 20 percent of the population may succumb to the disease.

# *Red Fox* Vulpes vulpes

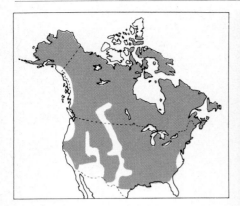

**Mammal:** *Vulpes vulpes* — red fox
**Meaning of Name:** *Vulpes* (fox)
**Description:** long silky fur; 3 distinct colour phases — 1. red fox: face, top of head and nape are yellow to rusty red; back is yellowish red or fulvous; lips, chest, abdomen, inside of ears and tip of tail are creamy white; back of ears and anterior portions of legs are black; 2. cross fox: greyish brown, long black guard hairs form a cross from shoulder to shoulder; 3. silver fox: totally black except for white tips on tail and a variable amount of frosting; also a black phase, which is black all over
**Total Length:** 3 to 3.6 feet
**Tail:** 13.8 to 16.5 inches
**Weight:** 7.9 to 15 pounds (up to 30.9 pounds)
**Gestation:** 51 to 53 days
**Litter Size:** 1 to 10 (usually 5 to 7); 1 litter per year
**Age of Maturity:** 10 months
**Longevity:** few live more than 3 to 4 years; has potential to live 12 years
**Diet:** omnivore, but more a carnivore as it prefers animal matter; small rodents, frogs, insects, birds, snakes and plant material such as acorns, grasses, corn, fruit
**Habitat:** open regions such as farming areas, prairie, alpine and Arctic tundra, meadows, bushy fence lines, woody stream borders and forest clearings, low shrub cover and along beaches bordering larger lakes
**Predators:** man is chief predator; also wolf, coyote, dog, lynx, bobcat; occasionally bear or wolverine, as well as hawks and owls
**Dental Formula:** 3/3, 1/1, 4/4, 2/3 = 42 teeth

The red fox enjoys the largest geographic range of any living carnivore. It is found, probably as a single species, throughout the northern parts of both the Old and New Worlds, wherever the habitat is relatively undisturbed.

The red fox has only recently become common throughout North America. It is now found everywhere from the high Arctic to the deep south, except in the dry plains and deserts. The fox may not be native to the continent, however. Some scientists believe that North American red foxes are descended from the European species introduced into New England in 1750, but fossil skeletons have been found that predate that import. Thus other scientists argue for a relatively rare breed of native red fox that may have interbred with the European import. The resulting hybrid may have then proliferated; alternatively, the formerly rare native fox may have spread in the wake of increased human activity.

The diet of the red fox is limited only by what it can find or catch. Scientists, prodded by hunters suspicious of fox depredations on game birds and small animals, have learned

*Large ears and a pointed muzzle make the red fox a formidable predator by enabling it to hear and catch small rodents in thick vegetation.*

a great deal about the fox's diet. They have discovered, for instance, that most foxes are omnivorous: when wild grapes, blueberries, cherries and other small fruits are in season, they may eat nothing but fruit; at other times, they feed primarily on small mammals up to the size of cottontails and groundhogs. At all times, the diet is supplemented with insects, frogs, snakes, birds and bird eggs. They also scavenge the carcasses of large animals that they would be unable to kill themselves.

The red fox's habitat ranges from tundra and boreal forest all the way to prairie. However, they are rarely found deep in mature forests, preferring to roam the open country and to live at the edge of forests.

Red foxes breed as monogamous pairs once a year, appropriating the burrows of other small mammals — such as the groundhog — for dens where their cubs can be born. In spring, the females give birth to about five cubs. There is a lot of variation in social and breeding behaviour, but at

least in some areas, the male stays with the family and assists in rearing the young. However, when many den sites are clumped together, males may mate with more than one female and neglect to provide parental care.

As the cubs grow older, the parents begin to bring them half-dead animals to play with, and so begins their education as hunters. Soon, the young begin to accompany their parents on foraging trips where they acquire the skills they will need for survival. By the end of summer, the new generation of foxes disperses, and by spring, they are themselves ready to breed.

Except during the reproductive season, foxes are solitary and hunt alone. They stay very definitely in one home range, marking the boundaries with scent and urine; and yet, though males may exclude other males during the breeding season, they are not overtly territorial.

In habitats shared with coyotes, there may be antagonism between the two species. An adult fox will approach and bark at coyotes that come too close to its breeding den; coyotes respond by chasing the agile fox, but they are seldom able to catch it. However, pressure from coyotes causes foxes to favour denning close to human habitation, since foxes tolerate human disturbance much better than coyotes do.

Red foxes are the main carriers of rabies in eastern North America, and

their population periodically suffers epidemic outbreaks of the disease. Rabies is often transmitted to attacking dogs or to livestock and thus to humans. Recent attempts to inoculate wild foxes against the disease have involved dropping medicated meatballs from airplanes. Experiments have shown that most foxes in a given area will come across one of these meatballs and eat it. This has made it possible, for the first time, to control the scale of rabies epidemics.

*The burden of rearing fox pups, **top**, is occasionally shared by the male, who sometimes brings half-dead game for the pups to play with. In spite of trapping, **bottom**, hunting and rabies, the red fox now has the greatest geographic range of any carnivore.*

# Swift Fox *Vulpes velox*

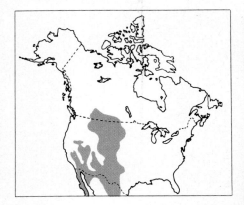

**Mammal:** *Vulpes velox* — swift fox, kit fox

**Meaning of Name:** *Vulpes* (fox); *velox* (quick, swift); called swift fox because of its speed

**Description:** in winter, pelage is long and dense; mainly buffy grey above and orange-tan on the sides and legs; the cylindrical tail is also tan and is tipped with black; the throat, chest, underparts and the inside of the ears are creamy white; there are 2 prominent black spots on each side of the snout, below the eyes; in summer, the fur is short, coarse and more reddish grey

**Total Length:** 2.8 feet

**Tail:** 8.9 to 13.8 inches

**Weight:** male, 3.7 to 6.6 pounds; female, 3.5 to 4.6 pounds

**Gestation:** 50 to 60 days

**Litter Size:** 1 to 8 (usually 4 or 5); 1 litter per year

**Age of Maturity:** male, first year; female, 10 months (not all females breed the first year)

**Longevity:** 8 to 10 years in the wild; have lived up to 12 years 9 months in captivity

**Diet:** omnivore; however, jackrabbits, cottontails and carrion are the most important food items — also eats rodents, birds, insects and a few lizards and fish; some vegetable matter, including grasses and berries

**Habitat:** open plains and prairies and shrubby deserts with sparse grasses of short and medium height

**Predators:** coyote, wolf, eagle, red-tailed hawk and rough-legged hawk

**Dental Formula:** 3/3, 1/1, 4/4, 2/3 = 42 teeth

The swift fox has adapted to life on the dry prairies. Like other desert foxes, it is small — only half the weight of a red fox — and has large ears. Many large-eared foxes are insectivores, and indeed, often half of the swift fox's summer diet is made up of grasshoppers. However, it is also a competent predator on mammals, taking its name from the speed with which it runs down rabbits. The swift fox has been clocked at 37 miles an hour, which is the speed of the fastest jackrabbit.

The swift fox lives primarily in the shortgrass prairie and desert, where it preys on small mammals, principally jackrabbits, rodents and some ground-nesting birds.

The swift fox is too small to be a threat to livestock. Nevertheless, it was poisoned almost to extinction in Canada in the 1930s, along with many other grassland predators and rodents. Habitat destruction also played its

*With large ears and a small body, the swift fox relies on a single food source — grasshoppers — for up to half of its summer diet.*

part in wiping out this fox as the prairie was gradually ploughed under. South of the border, however, the swift fox survived, and it is now being reintroduced to Canada.

## Olfactory Sophistication

*Carnivores — including cats and dogs — have the most highly developed noses of all mammals. They use their sense of smell not only to find food but also to communicate with each other.*

*Among the carnivores, humans are probably most familiar with the dog's remarkable sense of smell. Dogs have been observed to recognize members of a family by smell alone and are able to distinguish even genetically identical twins. They can recognize the smell of human* fingerprints that have been left on a glass slide for six weeks. They can trail a human on the run even when the person wears rubber boots or rides a bicycle. Dogs can even follow odours left scattered on vegetation or trailing in the air. That is why the dog has been used to track escaped prisoners or to search for contraband and bombs.

Since the domestic dog is a very recent descendant of the grey wolf, it is likely that wolves and other canids have a sense of smell at least as acute as the dog's, and possibly more so. In the wild, this sensitivity allows canids and other carnivores to locate prey that is still out of sight and to follow it unerringly, even when the trail is hours old.

The carnivore's highly developed sense of smell also plays an important social role, as the canid nose registers signs left by other members of its species. Most carnivores scent-mark with urine and glandular secretions, often as a way of setting territorial limits. Recent wolf studies show that breeding wolves, both male and female and especially newly formed pairs, scent-mark their territory, and the process is probably an important part of establishing their dominance. Lone wolves do not scent-mark.

Carnivores have a pouch of receptor cells, called Jacobson's organ, on the roof of the mouth, and this sometimes connects with the nasal passages. The function of this pouch is unclear, but it may serve to analyze hormones excreted in the urine of other individuals. It is thought that when a male tastes the urine of a female, pulling his lips back from the gums in a prolonged grimace as he does so, he is able to activate these sensitive cells to distinguish females in a reproductively receptive state.

Wolf urine is made up of a mixture of volatile compounds called ketones and sulphids. These vary in type and proportion according to the sex of the wolf and the time of the year, and each compound has a distinctive smell. A series of long-chain aldehyde molecules is also present in the urine, and they are subject to change with the hormonal state of the animal. That is why wolves are probably able to read a great deal in the smell of urine; the Arctic fox has a

much simpler set of compounds in its urine and is, by way of contrast, a much less social animal.

Cats mark their territory by spraying urine widely over vegetation, rather than marking a series of single spots. This increases the power of the scent and improves the status of the individual. Cats also rub their cheeks against the ground to leave a trail of glandular secretion, but it is not known what information is thus conveyed.

Urine may also be used as a reminder. Recent studies of fox and coyote food caches show that the animals will not urinate in the area until the food has been entirely consumed. Then they deliberately urinate on the cache site, perhaps to serve notice that the cache is exhausted of usable food even though the area still reeks of good meat.

So insensitive is the human nose that we have been slow to recognize the importance of smell in the lives of the carnivores. It may be that even more olfactory sophistication lies undiscovered, right under our noses.

The highly developed sense of smell of canids such as this grey fox enables them to locate prey that is still out of sight and to follow it unerringly, even when the trail is hours old.

# *Grey Fox* Urocyon cinereoargenteus

**Mammal:** *Urocyon cinereoargenteus* — grey fox

**Meaning of Name:** *Urocyon* (tailed dog); *cinereoargenteus* (silvery grey)

**Description:** pelage is denser and coarser than that of the red fox; the upper pelage is pepper and salt, due to white bands and black tips on guard hairs; underfur is buffy; legs, cheeks and chest are ochraceous; upper lip, throat and belly are whitish; black nose with a muzzle patch forming a line of black fur extending to and around each eye; long thick brush; tail has a black tip

**Total Length:** 2.5 to 3.5 feet

**Tail:** 10.8 to 17.5 inches

**Weight:** male, 8 to 13 pounds; female, 7.5 to 11.9 pounds

**Gestation:** 51 to 63 days

**Litter Size:** 1 to 7 (usually 4)

**Age of Maturity:** female, usually during first year of life

**Longevity:** 6 to 10 years in the wild; over 13 years in captivity

**Diet:** omnivore; small mammals (especially cottontails), birds, insects, fish, fruits, nuts and grains; takes more plant food than other foxes do

**Habitat:** primarily wooded and brushy country in rocky or broken terrain; also in marshes

**Predators:** bobcat and coyote; great horned owl may eat young

**Dental Formula:** 3/3, 1/1, 4/4, 2/3 = 42 teeth

The grey fox is roughly the same size as a red fox, and it shares much of the same geographic range. The two species are separated, however, by habitat preferences and by behaviour. Grey foxes avoid the open agricultural land that red foxes thrive on, preferring to range through shrubby woodland with hilly and rocky terrain. Like the red fox, grey foxes are omnivorous, but they tend to eat more plants and many more insects than other foxes in the same area.

The biggest and most obvious difference between the two species is the ability and inclination of the grey fox to run up trees and even to jump from the branches of one tree to another — possibly a survival mechanism favoured by long interaction with predatory coyotes. That is part of the reason why 18th-century colonists in New England, frustrated to find that their hounds could not follow the trail of the grey fox, decided to import the more convenient European fox.

Grey foxes sometimes establish their dens in animal burrows and rocky cavities; more often, however, they tend to nest in thick brush or high

*Grey foxes prefer rocky, brushy terrain,* **right,** *and avoid the agricultural habitats used by red foxes. They den not only in the ground,* **above,** *but also high up in hollow trees.*

up in hollow trees. This may limit the animal's northern distribution, although in the other direction, it extends well into South America. In fact, the grey fox may well have originated in the warm habitats of the south.

The reproductive and social behaviour of this fox appear similar to those of its red cousin. However, few detailed studies of grey foxes in the wild have been carried out.

# *Bears* Ursidae

Bears, the largest land-hunting carnivores, have grown far away from their many agile, fleet-footed relatives among the cats and dogs. Large and ponderous, with a heavy, flat-footed gait and teeth more suited to crunching and grinding than to stabbing and biting, they have tended to turn from meat as a primary source of food.

The Indian sloth bear, *Melursus ursinus*, has become a virtual anteater and is one of the more extreme examples of the bear's movement away from meat. In order to feed on termites and ants, it has developed specialized teeth, none of which are incisors. It also has naked, flexible lips and a long, thin tongue for sucking up insects. At the other end of the spectrum is the polar bear, most carnivorous of all, with well-developed carnassial teeth for slicing meat. Grizzly and black bears take the middle ground, with an intermediate tooth structure, some generalized incisors, well-developed canines and large molars for masticating vegetable food.

The largest bears are those found in the North — the black, grizzly and polar bears. The large size of northern species is an adaptation to winter, when the bears den up and spend months in dormancy without eating. The low metabolic rate associated with their large size means they can live for long periods on their stored body fat. One of the costs of being so large is having to patrol a large feeding territory. Northern bears require hundreds of square miles of foraging territory to support themselves. Bears are territorial and rarely congregate except at particularly rich feeding grounds, such as salmon runs and garbage dumps.

In spite of their large size, bears often eat small food items. Their strength enables them to flip over boulders and to tear apart logs to get at ants and insect larvae that are denied to other mammals. Their large size also renders them immune to predation. Grizzlies and polar bears appear to have no natural enemies aside from man. Black bears are rarely killed, but accounts of predation by wolves and grizzly bears exist.

The ancestor of the modern bear was a small foxlike animal related to the dog, and this form gave way quite recently to the larger bears we know today. The grizzly and the polar bear, for example, evolved only in the last two million years. The grizzly, or brown bear, developed in Asia and spread to North America less than 70,000 years ago. The polar bear is an even more recent development and is thought to have split off from the brown bear in the middle of the last Ice Age, about 10,000 years ago.

Despite their massive skulls and heavy bones, all bears are fast sprinters, able to keep pace with a horse and to outrun a man, at least over a short distance. Many are good tree-climbers, even though their short tails are of little use for balance — or, incidentally, for social signalling. Some tropical bears, such as the sun bear, forage extensively in the trees of Southeast Asia, and they all have large, nonretractable claws that they use as foraging tools. On the whole, bears tend to have small eyes and ears compared with other carnivores, and they depend less on sight and hearing for communication and hunting. However, since much of their foraging is done at night, a keen sense of smell is vital.

Up until 10,000 years ago, the most powerful land predator in North America was a giant, long-legged bear called *Arctodus simus*, built for speed and equipped with the large canines and carnassials that are associated with big-game predation. However, when the large grazing animals disappeared, this great killer was also doomed to extinction. The bears that survived were the smaller, more flexible omnivorous bears, the black, the brown and the polar bear, which had adapted for unrivalled dominance in the Arctic habitat.

Bears never penetrated south of the Sahara into the African continent, and that failure may have had a positive effect on human evolution. Some scientists argue that it was lack of competition from large, intelligent and omnivorous bears that allowed the tree-dwelling primates to evolve into large, intelligent and omnivorous terrestrial apes — including man.

*Bears such as this silver-tipped grizzly are the strongest land carnivores, and they use their strength for flipping boulders over and ripping logs open in search of food.*

# Grizzly or Brown Bear *Ursus arctos*

**Mammal:** *Ursus arctos* — grizzly bear, brown bear

**Meaning of Name:** *Ursus* (classical Latin word for bear); *arctos* (classical Greek word for bear)

**Description:** prominent hump on shoulders is formed by muscles of massive forelegs; face is dish-shaped; very long claws; pelage varies in colour from pale yellowish to dark brown or almost black; white tips on hairs give it a frosted or grizzled effect

**Total Length:** 8.5 feet

**Tail:** 2.4 to 8.3 inches

**Weight:** 322 to 842 pounds

**Gestation:** 180 to 266 days

**Litter Size:** 1 to 4 (average 2); every third year

**Age of Maturity:** 5 to 6 years or older (can breed at 3 years)

**Longevity:** about 25 years in the wild, possibly up to 50 years

**Diet:** omnivore, but plants and vegetation make up most of the diet; new grass, sedges, roots of legume *Hedysarum* (probably the most important food in much of the range), fruits, salmon, insects, fungi, roots, moss, mice, marmots, ground squirrels, newborn elk, moose, deer and caribou

**Habitat:** variety of habitats; prefers open areas; alpine tundra, high mountains, subalpine forests, alpine meadows and along coastlines; requires some areas with dense cover

**Predators:** no natural enemies apart from man

**Dental Formula:** 3/3, 1/1, 2-4/2-4, 2/3 = 34 to 42 teeth

*Female grizzly bears defend and tutor their cubs for two years.*

The grizzly bear, in terms of size, range and diet, stands midway between the polar and black bears. It is larger and more carnivorous than the black bear, yet smaller and with a more varied diet than the polar bear; it has a narrower distribution than the black but ranges more widely than its Arctic cousin. Yet in terms of range, the grizzly is not what it was: this bear used to roam throughout the Great Plains and prairies of North America and all along the western coast of the United States; now it survives only in the western mountains and in the tundra of the North.

Like the black bear, the grizzly is highly omnivorous, but there are parts of the year when its diet is mainly meat. During the spring calving season, for example, it eats young elk, deer and caribou. All during the summer, the bears dig for rodent species, and during the salmon runs, they turn into effective fishermen. In late summer, berries are its most important food, along with nuts, herbs and grasses. They feed selectively but use some 200 different species of plants to make up roughly half of their yearly intake of food.

The size of the grizzly's home range has been found to vary as much as 10,000 to 27,000 square miles, depending on the abundance of food and probably on the character of the individual bear. Males typically roam farther than females do. They also emerge from hibernation much earlier in the year than the females, and they tend to remain active much later.

In late summer, grizzlies begin to fatten up, preparing for hibernation. Like the black bears, they spend the entire winter holed up in dens that they dig into well-drained slopes where drifting snow accumulates to act as insulation. While living in their winter dens, females may give birth to one to four cubs (usually two). Females can begin to breed at 3 years of age, but they do not normally reproduce until their fifth year. The father provides no parental care, and the cubs remain with their mother until the second summer.

Many males and females may congregate during the breeding season, and mating is entirely promiscuous. Copulation, according to one observer, is "prolonged and vigorous," ranging from 10 to 60 minutes in duration. Females may mate many times with as many as four males over a two-day period; males will copulate with as many females as they can gain access to. Ovulation is induced by copulation and, as with other bears, the mating success of the male depends on establishing a territory that overlaps those of several females.

Adult males are territorial and will fight to gain or defend a home range. Young bears that still have to win a territory are particularly prone to engage in fierce, mauling fights, whereas mature males within established ranges tend to leave each other alone. Females with cubs are also dangerous and likely to attack anything that threatens them. A startled black bear may climb a tree or disappear under cover when it feels endangered; however, a grizzly seems to hold that "the best defence is a good offence."

Sport hunting has accounted for the death of many grizzlies. However, increasingly, the conflict of bears with food-laden campers and backpackers who trespass on a bear's territory, leaving a trail of garbage behind them, has meant the shooting of many grizzlies. Grizzlies have a strong homing instinct and are difficult to transplant from the areas that the public wishes to enjoy in their pursuit of wilderness. But people must realize that the grizzly, with all its ferocity and power, epitomizes the wilderness. Campers and hikers must learn to move safely through the wild parts of this continent without attempting to destroy the animals that make it what it is.

## Bear Attacks

*Bear attacks human! These are the headlines, redolent with the terror and pain of the victim, that horrify the public from time to time. The usual result is the shooting of one or more bears. Conflict with humans now constitutes one of the major pressures on grizzly populations. Painfully little is known about the cause of attacks, though one authority writes that "such improbable stimuli as severe thunderstorms, forest fires, perfume, cosmetics and menstruating women have been suggested."*

*More probably, aggression is simply a normal part of the lives of most bears. Bears are not always instinctively aggressive toward humans or toward other bears. Their reactions depend on many factors — health, sex, the timing of the breeding season, the possible presence of young cubs or a source of food and, indeed, the personality of the bear. The context of the encounter is also important: was the bear surprised or hungry and following the scent of food?*

*Bears must defend their territories from other bears. Males must fight*

*rivals for food and the right to breed. Females must defend their cubs. Unfortunately, bears and humans do not understand the signals that each gives to the other. Humans are roughly the same size as bears, and they hold themselves in the upright posture, which is threatening to bears, conveying aggression and readiness to fight. Humans, for their part, when they see bears, fail to recognize the posture and sounds of hostility. On the other hand, if they are frightened, they may run, thus taking the vulnerable role of a subordinate bear or acting like an item of prey. Even if the bear is merely irritated and intends to discourage this strange competitor, the moderate bite or blow he delivers may be enough to wound or kill a human.*

*Attacks on humans by wild bears are exceedingly rare, usually taking*

Both male and female grizzly bears are territorial, and they settle disputes with wrestling matches.

*place in campgrounds where bears are conditioned to eat garbage and food that is reeking with the human scent. These campground bears have lost their fear of humans and, when hungry, may treat them as competitors or, indeed, as items of prey. It is public ignorance, and not the bear, that is at fault. It is a failure of respect for potentially dangerous animals coupled with poor management of human recreation that every year results in more injuries to humans and more dead bears. It may be, in the course of nature, that bears and people cannot coexist without conflict. It is clear, however, that proper management of human-bear interaction would eliminate the vast majority of attacks.*

# Black Bear *Ursus americanus*

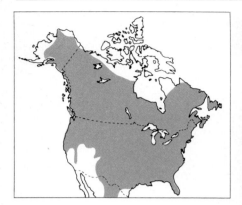

**Mammal:** *Ursus americanus* — black bear

**Meaning of Name:** *Ursus* (bear); *americanus* (of America)

**Description:** dense, coarse pelage; usually black with cinnamon-brown muzzle and white V on chest; cinnamon-coloured bears occur in western Canada; other colour phases include white and blue and are restricted to locations on the Pacific coast.

**Total Length:** male, 4.5 to 5.9 feet; female, 3.9 to 4.9 feet

**Tail:** male, 3.5 to 4.9 inches; female, 3.1 to 4.5 inches

**Weight:** male, 249 to 595 pounds; female, 203 to 449 pounds

**Gestation:** 210 to 220 days (including delayed implantation)

**Litter Size:** 1 to 5 (usually 2); 1 litter every other year (sometimes every 3 or 4 years)

**Age of Maturity:** male, 5 to 6 years; female, 3.5 to 5 years

**Longevity:** 25 to 30 years in the wild, but usually less than 10; up to 30 years in captivity

**Diet:** omnivore; berries, fruit, nuts, twigs, leaves, tubers, roots, insects and their larvae, eggs, carrion, honey and small mammals; also garbage (garbage eating is a fixation with many bears, and natural-food foraging becomes secondary)

**Habitat:** mainly forested areas; also swamps, marshes and thickets in several plant successional stages; may occur on tundra and in mountainous areas

**Predators:** man, grizzly bear; grey wolf may attack young or a pack of wolves may kill females

**Dental Formula:** 3/3, 1/1, 2-4/2-4, 2/3 = 34 to 42 teeth

*Black bears, such as this one investigating a beaver lodge, eat far more plant material than meat.*

The black bear is the success story of its kind. Less spectacular than the polar bear or the grizzly, it is undeniably more prosperous. While threatened grizzly and polar bear populations have needed strict controls to prevent them from being harvested out of existence, the black bear puts up with an annual hunting toll of 30,000 without significant effect. The black bear's secret is its wide-ranging tastes in food and its ability to thrive in virtually any kind of forest habitat. In both deciduous and coniferous forests from the tundra tree line all the way into Mexico, wherever there is enough natural forest to sustain it, the black bear continues to inhabit almost all of its former range. Only in the densely settled east of North America has it disappeared.

The black bear is the most omnivorous of all bears and, indeed, of all carnivores. For much of the year, it browses on twigs, buds and berries, switching to nuts and roots in the autumn, and three-quarters of its food consists of vegetable matter. It makes up the rest of the menu by looking for grubs and worms under rocks and rot-

ting logs and will not turn up its nose at carrion. The bear also hunts mice, birds and other small mammals. By feeding lower on the food chain, the black bear has freed itself from a dependence on big game. The result is that forests can support a much higher density of black bears than other large carnivores, such as the puma or even the grizzly.

Black bears are mainly nocturnal and begin to forage at dusk. However, as winter approaches, they may spend more time feeding, both day and night. Because they are mainly vegetarian, most of their food disappears with the first snowfall. It is crucial, therefore, that they accumulate sufficient fat during the late summer and fall to support them through a winter-long period of dormancy.

The bear's dormant state causes a reduction in metabolic rate so that less fuel is burned than by an active bear. However, the long fast —in some areas, lasting almost half a year — uses up great reserves of fat, sometimes as much as 40 percent of the bear's autumn body weight.

Females, from the age of 3.5 to 5 years, begin to breed every other year. They usually give birth to two cubs — occasionally three or four — during the denning period. The young bears stay with the mother when she leaves the den and return with her to spend the next winter in her den. The following summer, they disperse, and

the female breeds again.

In northern areas, the den takes the form of a sheltered cave, a hollow tree or an excavated hole that is often lined with vegetation.

Black bears have few natural enemies, although grizzlies will charge and kill them on occasion, and grey wolves will attack weakened adults or young cubs if they find them alone. The black bear might have been much more vulnerable in the past, however, as it evolved together with the giant bears and canids of the Pleistocene. Its fast and skilful tree-climbing may have been a protective strategy developed in that era.

Black bears are solitary creatures, marking out their territories with excretions. Claw marks on scattered trees, set high and deep to show the

*Most omnivorous of all carnivores,* **top,** *black bears can exist at much higher densities than other more carnivorous bear species.* **Above,** *black bears have several colour phases, including black and cinnamon.*

size and strength of the bear, may also be a means of marking territory.

Bears use a wide range of vocalizations, moaning and teeth chattering as well as posturing to threaten members of their own species. Females with cubs are notably aggressive, but otherwise, few black bears attack people. However, there are populations of bears growing up around campgrounds and garbage dumps that have learned to associate humans with food — mostly as competitors, and sometimes as items of prey. The consequences can be fatal.

## *Polar Bear* Ursus maritimus

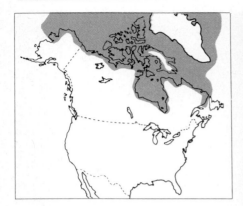

**Mammal:** *Ursus maritimus — polar bear*
**Meaning of Name:** *Ursus* (bear);
*maritimus* (of the sea)
**Description:** pure white in winter; in
summer and autumn, the coat is thinner
and has a yellow wash or is almost a
golden colour; soles of the feet are
bordered with dense fur to insulate them;
pale silvery blue eye shine
**Total Length:** 6.5 to 9.8 feet
**Tail:** 3 to 5 inches
**Weight:** male, 660 to 1,760 pounds;
female, 330 to 660 pounds
**Gestation:** 195 to 265 days (including a
period of delayed implantation)
**Litter Size:** 1 to 4 (usually 2) every 2 to 4
years
**Age of Maturity:** male, 4 years; female,
3 to 7 years
**Longevity:** 20 to 35 years in the wild; up
to 40 years in captivity
**Diet:** primarily the ringed seal (also harp,
bladdernose and bearded seals and
young walrus); also seabirds, eggs,
carcasses of stranded marine mammals
and other carrion; fish, mussels, crabs,
grasses, seaweed, lichens, mosses and
sedges
**Habitat:** prefers pack ice that is subject
to periodic fracturing in combination with
open water and land (barren rocky
shores and islands)
**Predators:** man is major predator;
occasionally a male walrus, a killer whale
or a wolf may kill one, but this is probably
rare
**Dental Formula:** 3/3, 1/1, 2-4/2-4,
2/3 = 32 to 42 teeth

The polar bear, which can weigh as much as 1,760 pounds, is the largest terrestrial carnivore. Yet although they are larger than the grizzly, polar bears, with their long legs and necks and their lean bodies, tend to look much less massive. Even the polar bear's muzzle is long and pointed.

The polar bear is designed for operating in snow and ice. The long legs and neck permit the wide-reaching blows and bites the bear uses to capture seals. Its legs also allow it to rear up high in the deep snow. The thick white coat is another Arctic adaptation, and one that goes far beyond camouflage. Mixed with the deep fur are many hollow hairs that trap warm insulating air and also act as solar collectors. The ears of the polar bear are relatively short, and the hearing is dull. However, polar bears have much better eyesight than most bears, since good vision is a vital tool in the open Arctic habitat. They are often seen standing high on their hind legs, obviously scanning the landscape. And, like all carnivores, they have a keen sense of smell.

In fact, the polar bear's sense of smell is vital to its success as a hunter. In the spring seal-breeding season, for example, polar bears forage both on the land-fast pack ice and on ice floes surrounded by open water. On land-fast ice, they sniff out the dens of ringed seals hidden beneath the ice and eat the seal pups.

Bears also stalk the ringed and bearded seals that haul themselves up

*Polar bears are skilled swimmers that have been seen stalking and killing seals in the open ocean.*

onto the ice. Sometimes swimming underwater, the bear works its way through a mix of ice and open water until it comes within range and is able to make the final rush. Polar bears also search out the breathing holes of seals and wait there, ready to hook out the seal with long, sharp, curving claws that seem custom-made for the task. Since the seals' breathing holes usually have a thin covering of ice or snow with just a tiny air hole, the bears have to excavate them, and they run the risk that the seals will be warned away by increasing light at the hole. But the polar bear has learned to fool the seal by leaning its head on the hole to darken it.

Stalking bears rely on their white colour for camouflage. They seem to be aware of its value and have even stooped to trickery to take advantage of it. Some bears have been seen to cover their black noses with a paw while hunting. Seals can easily outswim a bear, but while their eyes function well underwater, they do not have good visual judgment when they surface. One polar bear was seen pretending to be an ice chunk while he stalked an adult ringed seal in open water. The bear was first observed about 230 feet from the seal as it rested on the ice and began swimming strongly toward it; whenever the seal went underwater, the bear immediately stopped swimming and floated motionless; when the seal surfaced, the bear resumed its swim, gradually closing the distance between them. Finally, the seal surfaced right beside the bear, apparently mistaking it for a floating chunk of ice. The bear killed it with a sudden lunge and a single bite.

When polar bears kill a seal, they often eat only the skin and a layer of blubber, leaving the meat virtually untouched. Thus bear kills are a windfall for the Arctic foxes and ravens that follow the bears. Many of them subsist entirely on scavenged leftovers.

Polar bears also sniff out and eat the carcasses of dead whales and walruses, and as many as a dozen bears may congregate around a dead sea mammal. In a similar way, the bears also gather at man-made dumps to pick over the bones of civilized life, and this has brought them into direct conflict with Northerners who have established dumps in bear country. Moving the bears provides only temporary relief, since they seem to have a strong homing instinct. Bears that have been moved 300 miles away from Churchill, Manitoba, have returned within weeks.

Polar bears will eat almost any meat for which they can profitably forage. They have been known to attack anything from beluga whales that venture into shallow water to seabirds and small mammals. They eat some berries and a little grass and seaweed when the season allows; even that small vegetable component in their diet supplies some vital vitamins and trace elements.

Polar bears do not always, or even ordinarily, hibernate in winter — especially the males — though the degree of inactivity in winter may depend on the weather, the state of the ice pack and the fat reserves of the bear. However, in November and December, pregnant females consistently retreat to their dens, which are deep hollows dug into snowdrifts, to give birth to their cubs. The purpose of denning seems to be more to protect the young bears than to conserve the energy of adults. Unlike black bears, the meat-eating polar bear can hunt all winter long and does not need to conserve its energy for the reburgeoning of vegetable life.

Females breed between the ages of 3 and 7 at two- to four-year intervals. In the fall, when they come into oestrus, their scent is likely to attract a number of males, and after mating, the females retreat to their snowy dens to give birth to one or two cubs. The mother and cubs will break out of the den in March, and they will stay together for the next two years.

Animals as large and thickly furred as the polar bear tend to suffer in the warm Arctic summers. Some summer dens have been found around the southern end of Hudson Bay where the bears have dug burrows up to 20 feet long into the permafrost in search of coolness. Some of these dens appear to have been in use for hundreds of years.

Polar bears are dangerous animals. As solitary hunters stalking and killing large mammals for their subsistence, they are even prepared to fight members of their own species to protect, or to gain access to, a kill. Also, polar bears do kill people. Often, it is the young bears that are the killers — the aggressive male youngsters that ritualistically spar with each other

*Reaching weights close to a ton, polar bears are the largest of all bears and normally lead solitary lives. Groups do, however, gather around large food sources, such as dead whales and garbage dumps.*

during the autumn. Yet any one of those playful bites or irritable blows would be enough to kill a human.

## Rules of the North

*If one examines the localities where the largest individuals of a species — the biggest grey wolf, brown bear, moose or deer — are recorded, a pattern emerges. The biggest animals seem to come from the extreme northern limit of their ranges. The same is true when closely related species are compared. Wood rats that live in the north or at high altitudes are 300 percent larger than species from hot desert areas. This pattern is known as Bergmann's rule, which states that the average size of a mammal increases as one moves toward colder regions.*

One explanation for this pattern is that larger mammals have a slower rate of heat loss relative to body weight than smaller individuals. However, the total amount of heat being lost still goes up as the animal's body size increases. So even if it is more efficient at heating itself, a larger animal will burn and require more food than a smaller one. To explain Bergmann's rule, it is necessary to find some other absolute rather than a relative advantage of large body size. One possibility is that larger animals can fast or hibernate for longer periods than small ones, living off stored body fat. This effect becomes greater as the average temperature drops. Thus a large mammal can wait out a week-long northern blizzard or an extended period of hibernation better than a small mammal. But it will still have to consume more food to acquire the fat stores needed to do so.

One reason for larger body size might be that it enables the animals to feed on a wider variety of food sources, but it is difficult to see how this correlates with latitude. Certainly there is no evidence that larger wolves or bears in the north are more efficient hunters than those in the south.

The benefit of larger litter sizes in the north as a hedge against unpredictable weather has also been suggested, but this would be reflected only by larger female body

*Large size may be favoured in northern animals such as grizzly bears because it increases the length of time they can go without eating.*

size. However, this idea is ruled out because both sexes exhibit the tendency toward largeness.

A survey of 47 different mammal species showed that only 32 percent of them followed the trend predicted by Bergmann's rule. In other words, most species do not follow Bergmann's rule. The records of huge northern mammals may be more a measure of the health and the size of wilderness mammal populations than of Bergmann's rule.

Another rule that has been applied to northern mammals is Allen's rule, which states that as one moves north, the size of the extremities, such as ears, feet and other exposed areas, is reduced. The explanation for this is that by reducing unnecessary body surface area, animals can reduce heat losses. Grey wolves in the North have such shortened muzzles that their teeth grow cramped together. This may reflect a compromise between the need for long turbinate bones to warm incoming air in the nasal passages and the need to reduce heat loss through the facial area.

Arctic foxes are also cited as examples of the effect of Allen's rule. They have short, stubby legs, a reduced muzzle and short ears. But

again, the validity of this generalization is open to question. The body form of bush dogs in the South American tropics is not unlike that of the Arctic fox. Allen's rule, like Bergmann's, has yet to be tested and demonstrated with convincing data. It may be that adaptive forces other than minimizing heat radiation have shaped the mammals of the north.

## Energy Conservation

One of the ecological advantages that mammals enjoy is the maintenance of a high body temperature that enables them to stay active in extremely cold environments. Animals such as reptiles, whose body temperature fluctuates with the environment, are forced into inactivity by cold weather. In the north, a snake or lizard spends more than half of its life doing nothing because it is too cold to move. By contrast, many mammals can boost their metabolic rate to compensate for increased cold and can thus stay busy, which is why mammals, not reptiles or amphibians, have colonized the cold regions of the Earth.

But mammals must pay a high heating cost for maintaining their body temperature. A mammal at rest burns three times the number of calories that a lizard does, and during winter, an active mammal expends far greater amounts of energy. This is no problem for mammals that have a constant supply of food; rodents that burrow beneath the snow can feed on grasses and sedges, making use of the insulating properties of the snow, and the weasels that eat those rodents can likewise stay active. But mammals that feed on herbaceous forbs or on berries and fruits may find it impossible to get enough food to meet their heating costs. Some, such as pikas, mountain beaver and other rodents, must build up a winter food store, while others have evolved the ability to hibernate or to go torpid.

Deep hibernation is the most extreme energy-conservation strategy, as it involves profound changes in the metabolism. As the deep hibernator settles into its winter sleep, its heartbeat slows. The *jumping mouse's heart beats at a rate of 500 to 600 times a minute when it is active, but in deep hibernation, it slows to 30 beats a minute or less. Similarly, its oxygen consumption drops to a level only 5 percent of what it is when the mouse is active. The body temperature falls until it is just four degrees above freezing to further reduce the amount of heat burned by the body. Some mammals, such as the red bat, may even lower their body temperature to 23 degrees F without sustaining frost damage. Some mammals simply rely on torpor, a less extreme slowing of the metabolism. A bat, for example, may allow its body temperature to decline from close to 104 degrees F to around 77 degrees each day after it finishes foraging, allowing it to rise again as the evening's activity period approaches. This sort of torpor is used by many smaller mammals, such as chipmunks, which may remain torpid for periods of up to five days.*

*Small mammals that stay active during winter can use other adaptations to reduce heat loss. Rodents that eat bark and dried stems and seeds during winter are forced to eat snow as a water supply. The energy cost of melting snow in the body is substantial, so some small northern rodents, such as the red-backed vole, concentrate their urine during winter to reduce their water loss. This saves energy in two ways: warm urine carries heat from the body when it is excreted, and the snow required to replace it is a further energy drain.*

*The deepest hibernators are small rodents with a high surface area relative to their body mass and quantity of stored fat. Larger animals do not need such a radical lowering of body temperature. Bears, for example, den up for the winter, but their reduction in body temperature is less severe. The body temperature of a denning bear may be only a few degrees lower than when it is active, which, for years, led some researchers to claim that bears were not deep hibernators. The distinction is somewhat misleading. Bears are extremely efficient hibernators, and their higher body temperature simply reflects their lower rate of heat radiation relative to their size and fat*

*stores. They do not need to be cooler.*

*One of the advantages of staying closer to the active state is that the bear is more easily aroused and ready to move if necessary. The black bear's heartbeat drops from 40 to 10 beats a minute, and its oxygen consumption is cut by half, but a disturbed bear can make a coordinated response, something deep hibernators are incapable of doing.*

*As a large mammal that evolved in the tropics, man does not have any hibernating abilities, although some of us do seem to get fatter and sleepier in winter. But hibernators such as the black bear may provide us with valuable medical insights. Bears that are burning their winter fat have cholesterol levels in the blood that are twice as high as when they are active and twice as high as the normal human level. But black bears do not suffer the heart and circulatory diseases that many doctors believe are linked to high cholesterol in the bloodstream.*

*Bears can also go without*

Although an efficient hibernator, the black bear maintains a near normal body temperature even in the depths of winter and is easily aroused and ready to move if necessary.

*urinating for as long as 100 days. Researchers interested in kidney disease are studying the mechanisms that bears use to avoid the buildup of too much urea and urine. Apparently, some hormones may cause the urea in the urine to be reabsorbed and converted back into protein to rebuild muscles and other tissues. This is the way science progresses. An interest in the energy-conservation adaptations of mammals may lead to a treatment for gout or kidney disease in humans.*

# Raccoon Family Procyonidae

## Raccoon  Procyon lotor

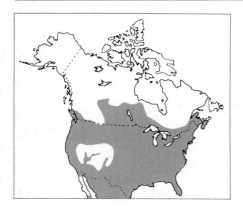

**Mammal:** *Procyon lotor* — raccoon
**Meaning of Name:** *Procyon* (before + dog) refers to the fact that the raccoon was considered to be close to the ancestral stock of dogs; *lotor* (washer) alludes to the raccoon's habit of wetting its food prior to eating; the name raccoon is from Algonkian *arathcone*, which can mean either "he scratches with his hands" or "least like a fox"
**Description:** approximately the size of a fat cat with a long fine coat; has a short bushy tail with 4 to 6 prominent rings; the general colour is grizzled grey, giving a salt-and-pepper effect; the sides are greyer than the back, and the underparts are brownish with a whitish wash; a black mask extends across the cheeks, eyes and nose; also has pale grey bars above and below the large eyes
**Total Length:** 2.5 to 3.1 feet
**Tail:** 8.5 to 10.2 inches
**Weight:** 12 to 30 pounds (up to 55 pounds)
**Gestation:** 60 to 73 days (average of 63)
**Litter Size:** 1 to 7 (usually 3 or 4); 1 litter per year
**Age of Maturity:** male, 2 years or older; female, 40 percent breed as yearlings
**Longevity:** 13 to 16 years in captivity (record is 22 years); often live over 4 years in the wild
**Diet:** omnivore; fruits, berries, acorns, sweet corn, crayfish, crabs, other arthropods, June beetles, grubs, grasshoppers, crickets, frogs, fish, small mammals and birds (including poultry and pheasants) as well as eggs
**Habitat:** wooded areas along waterways, river valleys, timbered and brush areas
**Predators:** bobcat, red fox, coyote, wolf, fisher, great horned owl; ravens prey on young
**Dental Formula:** 3/3, 1/1, 4/4, 2/2 = 40 teeth

The procyonids are not northern animals, and only the raccoon is familiar to temperate zone North Americans. The other members of the group are limited to more southern climates: coatimundis and ringtails to the dry American southwest and kinkajous to the forests of Central and South America. They are small- to medium-sized animals, not much larger than a small dog. Many spend much of their time climbing trees or foraging in forest habitats. Most species are nocturnal.

The Procyonidae family split off from the canids roughly 20 million years ago. Their bodies reflect adaptations to a forest environment: they have long tails, which are prehensile in some species and used for gripping tree limbs; their claws are long and sharp, and the forepaws are highly coordinated and capable of sophisticated manipulations. Many species have faces reminiscent of the smaller canids, such as foxes, but in keeping with their omnivorous diet, procyonids lack specialized carnassial and canine teeth. Their claws are nonretractile, and they walk on the soles of their feet.

The pandas are considered by some to be members of this family in spite of their bearlike appearance. Other taxonomists split the pandas off as a separate family, since the two panda species are obligate herbivores found in Asia while the other 15 procyonids are all omnivorous and found only in the Americas. None of the procyonids are endangered, but only the common raccoon and coatimundi have been well studied in the field.

The masked bandit hardly needs any introduction. Raccoons have profited from human contact and have become familiar animals to most humans, even those living in large cities. They are one of the few larger wild mammals that have done well in urban areas, and the only limit to their success has been a failure to tolerate the cold winters of the boreal forest and tundra regions.

The recent success of the raccoon results from the fact that it is omnivorous and intelligent. The raccoon readily incorporates novel foods into its diet and, because of manual dexterity, is able to handle items as diverse as crayfish, sweet corn, watermelon, snakes and the contents of well-closed garbage cans. The list of food items that have been eaten by raccoons would run into the thousands. In nature, they eat almost every edible fruit, berry and nut within their range as well as insects, worms, slugs, snails, mussels, oysters, seafood of all kinds, small mammals, birds as large as geese, bird eggs, rabbits, turtles, lizards, frogs, many kinds of fish and carrion and have even been known to kill sheep.

Not surprisingly, handling this array of food items requires a brain capable of problem solving and learning. Many food items are handled not through instinct but after watching the mother, which indicates that foraging techniques may be culturally transmitted from one generation to the next. For instance, the offspring of

*Raccoons are always found close to water, where they hunt and also bring their food to be washed.*

*Intelligent and omnivorous, raccoons eat almost any kind of animal as well as hundreds of plants. They readily learn to handle new varieties of food.*

the first raccoon to discover how to eat watermelon may have learned the technique from their mother without having to evolve or having to discover the behaviour by themselves. Intelligence tests show that raccoons are smarter than cats but are not smarter than rhesus monkeys.

Although some procyonids form social groups, raccoons are not social — the only extended social contact is between a mother and her offspring. Females mate in spring and give birth in summer to a litter of one to seven offspring. These stay with the mother and den with her during winter, dispersing the following summer. Under good conditions, they may reproduce the same year that they disperse. The male provides no parental care, and the female aggressively excludes males from the den area.

Normally, raccoons den and forage in areas that have water. Dens are located in hollow trees, rock crevices, abandoned animal burrows or any reasonably well-protected cavity. Winter den sites may be occupied for as long as four months, but raccoons are not deep hibernators. They put on large fat stores of which they may lose 50 percent over the winter. They sleep during most of the cold season, but their temperature and metabolic rate do not drop to the extent that they do with deep hibernators. Sometimes, groups of raccoons den together in an attempt to reduce winter heat losses. The home ranges of raccoons may run for a few miles, depending on the productivity of the habitat. The ranges overlap extensively, and there is little territoriality, although they may fight over food when it is concentrated in one area.

Raccoons are eaten by raptors and large mammals such as the puma, wolf and coyote. On the East Coast, these predators have been largely extinguished, and there are few checks on raccoon populations other than hunting, road deaths, starvation and disease. In some areas, raccoons are so common that they destroy almost all waterfowl nests.

## North Meets South

*We think of the jaguar and the ocelot as cats of the Amazon and South America; porcupines and raccoons, on the other hand, are known to be northern mammals. The fact is that each had its origin in the hemisphere opposite its present home.*

*Long ago, the continents of North and South America were separated by a sea channel some 250 miles in width, and the mammals of north and south evolved in isolation. Then, some three to five million years ago, the Panamanian land bridge rose out of the ocean, and the fauna and flora of the two continents began to mix. Among the northern mammals that went south were the peccaries, the skunks and a number of canids, including wolves and foxes. Cats, bears, deer, shrews, squirrels, kangaroo rats and rabbits also travelled south, as did the mastodon, which is now extinct on both continents. Horses, also later extinct on both continents, went with them as did tapirs, which died out in the*

are thought to be responsible for the sudden extermination of the sabre-toothed marsupials.

An interesting result of the exchange is that many formerly North American groups, such as dogs and mice, suddenly flowered in South America and split into many species. It may have been the great diversity of tropical plants and the richer and more specific habitats that encouraged more specialization and speciation. Certainly, the few South American groups that penetrated deep into the north have not diversified. Instead, a few species, such as the porcupine, have become extraordinarily successful and have taken up wide geographic ranges.

north while thriving in the south. Camels, which originated in North America, are now extinct here, but they survive as llamas in the Andes.

Southern mammals also made inroads into the north, with armadillos, opossums and porcupines moving into North America, while monkeys, anteaters and various rodents penetrated only as far as Central America. The exchange was symmetrical: 14 of today's 35 South American families came from North America, while 12 families from South America were added to the 35 North American families. As a result of the exchange

*Although this young raccoon is perfectly at home in the birches of a northern forest, its ancestors evolved in South America and migrated north some three to five million years ago.*

and the symmetrical extinction that followed, the two continents came to share 22 families. Where they were once totally dissimilar, they are now more alike than different.

The number of families remained roughly the same after the exchange, and that suggests to biogeographers that the immigration was responsible for the extinction. For example, the sabre-toothed cats that went south

# Weasels, Badgers, Skunks & Otters Mustelidae

The weasel family is a highly carnivorous group of some 67 species found on every continent but Australia and Antarctica. The group has penetrated every terrestrial habitat and many aquatic ones: martens hunt in the trees of northern, temperate and tropical regions; weasels frequent the cracks, crevices and tunnels of terrestrial habitats; otters have invaded oceans and freshwater ecosystems; and wolverines are powerful scavengers of the boreal forest.

This diversity is recognized by taxonomists, who divide the family into five subfamilies — skunks, otters, true weasels, badgers and honey badgers — each of which is clearly different from the others.

Most mustelid family members have evolved a mouth with fewer but more specialized teeth, many having large, sharp canines for slicing, cutting carnassials (incisors capable of fatal bites) or, in the case of omnivorous badgers, heavy crushing molars. Mustelids usually kill their prey with an instinctive bite to the base of the skull, their incisors slipping between the neck's vertebrae to sever the spinal column. Their elongated and triangular face is like a cat's, with a shortened muzzle that enables them to apply a tenacious neck bite and keep breathing.

Mustelids have long, streamlined bodies relative to their short limbs, and their long tails further enhance movement, acting as balancing devices for running and making sharp right-angled turns.

They have well-developed anal glands that figure prominently in communication and defence. They use the glands to mark territories or express discontent and hostility. Normally, the mustelids are solitary animals, predators that hunt alone, and most species exhibit little social behaviour. Many species are pugnacious and will hiss and threaten at the approach of intruders. Being intelligent, mustelids are quite curious and, in some cases, highly playful animals.

## Fur Appeal

*Sable, ermine, mink, otter, beaver — the best furs come from animals that nature has had to protect from the cold. The quality of fur comes from its value as insulation to the animal that produced it, and the long, thin weasels and other mammals that spend their lives in cold water have the finest, thickest fur coats. Take the sea otter: it spends its life in the cold northern seas and once provided the most expensive fur in the world. Single pelts sold for $1,000 at the turn of the century, at a time when well-paid workmen earned a dollar a day.*

*Of course, there is some fur-trapping in the southern hemisphere. It is no accident, however, that most of the tropical animals whose furs command a high price are river otters or high-altitude rodents. The trade in spotted-cat furs is an exception, but it has more to do with fashion novelty than fur quality. These decorative furs were developed by the animals more for camouflage than for insulation.*

*Mammal fur is usually made up of two distinct kinds of hair: long, coarse guard hairs in the outer coat and short, fine underhairs in the inner coat. Often, the hair has been further modified so that guard hairs have become spines (as in porcupine quills or pig bristles) or awns (which are the common guard hairs in most mammal fur). These are coarse hairs,*

*usually with a flattened tip and a narrow base. The underhairs may be velus (extremely fine, downy hairs) or fur (short, dense and fine) or wool (long and curly).*

*The guard hairs of aquatic mammals, such as beavers and otters, have a broad, flat shape and lie closely overlapping on the densely curled underfur. In between these two kinds of fur is an insulating layer of air bubbles to prevent heat loss to the highly conductive water. Such mammals spend a great deal of time grooming and oiling their coats, and beavers even have a special split toenail for that purpose. If the fur were not cleaned and oiled, it could not do its insulating work.*

*Some guard hairs are particularly prized for a special texture. The fur of the wolverine, for example, is widely used in the North for the lining of parka hoods and cuffs because the hairs shed rime frost and snow.*

*Northern mammals usually have a winter and summer coat, the latter being much thinner. In fact, some large mammals, such as sheep, show no sign of underwool development until September.*

*In some animals, there has had to be a trade-off between insulation and mobility. The insulating value is a function of the length and density of the coat, and some small mammals, such as the lemming, have very long fur relative to their body size. For animals like the weasel, however, a thick coat would limit its ability to forage in narrow crevices. Similarly, many aquatic animals cannot afford*

Inquisitive and intelligent, members of the weasel family, such as this sea otter, have exploited both terrestrial and aquatic habitats.

The fine waterproof pelt of the mink suits it to a semiaquatic foraging strategy.

to sacrifice mobility for warmth. Seals, for example, have lost their underfur completely and rely on blubber for insulation. Streamlining also takes precedence over other functions for aquatic animals, and both seals and sea otters have lost the erector muscles that ''raise the hackles'' of cats and dogs and make them look large and ferocious when threatened.

In winter, some increase in fur density is also achieved by a shrinking of the skin as the animal loses weight. The difference in fur density between a fat summer shrew and its thin winter self may be as much as 31 percent.

Like the rhinoceros, humans evolved in tropical Africa and lost most of their fur in the process. In our journey northward, however, we have had to borrow the furs of other mammals to keep us warm. In fact, it was the fur trade that gave impetus to the discovery and exploration of much of Canada. Only recently in human history have we come to rely on plant fibres and synthetic textiles made from petrochemicals; ironically, at the same time, the demand for fur as a luxury item has resulted in the extinction of some animals and the threatened extinction of others.

The problem is one of poor management, and the wise culling of overextended populations —the lynx, for example, when it has expanded beyond the resources of the snowshoe hare — would serve a useful purpose by preventing disease and starvation. Fur is a natural renewable resource, and its harvest is potentially less destructive than the conversion of nonrenewable petrochemicals into clothing. Even the production of natural textiles, such as cotton, has meant the wholesale destruction of valuable forests and grasslands.

Unfortunately, there are many times more humans than there are of most species of wild mammals, and it is unlikely that fur can ever be worn by more than a tiny fraction of the world's population.

## *Spotted Skunk* Spilogale putorius

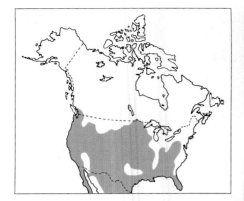

**Mammal:** *Spilogale putorius* — spotted skunk

**Meaning of Name:** *Spilogale* (stain or spot + marten-cat or weasel); *putorius* (bad smell)

**Description:** black with 6 white stripes running down the back, flanks and rump; stripes may be broken into spots for part of their length; a white spot on forehead and more white spots in front of the ears; the long tail has a black tip and a white plume

**Total Length:** male, 13.9 to 18.1 inches; female, 12.7 to 17.3 inches

**Tail:** male, 4 to 6.2 inches; female, 3.5 to 5.5 inches

**Weight:** male, 1.5 to 1.9 pounds

**Gestation:** 120 ± days

**Litter Size:** 4 to 7

**Age of Maturity:** male, 5 months; female, year of birth

**Longevity:** approximately 10 years

**Diet:** omnivore; in summer, mainly vegetable matter and insects; in winter, rodents and other small mammals; also birds and their eggs, carcasses, lizards, snakes and frogs

**Habitat:** brushy, rocky and wooded habitats, scrubland, farmland, along streams and among boulders; avoids heavy forests and wetlands

**Predators:** great horned owl, domestic dog and cat

**Dental Formula:** 3/3, 1/1, 3/3, 1/2 = 34 teeth

The spotted skunk is a slimmer version of its striped relation, and it has the same powerful spray and black-and-white warning pattern. Unlike the striped skunk, however, this species can spray while performing the threatening headstand display. It walks on its forelegs toward its target and sprays by arching its back.

The spotted skunk prefers a drier habitat such as the western scrubland and canyons where the striped skunk is less common. It is more agile and athletic than the striped skunk and is able to climb trees. Though highly omnivorous and adapted for digging and grubbing for invertebrates, the spotted skunk is more carnivorous than its insect-loving cousin. In other respects, however, it seems to share much of the life history and breeding behaviour of the striped skunk.

*The black-and-white colouring of the spotted skunk serves as a warning signal to predators.*

# *Striped Skunk* Mephitis mephitis

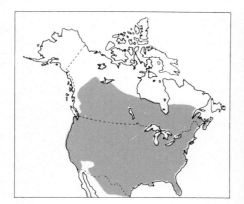

**Mammal:** *Mephitis mephitis* — striped skunk

**Meaning of Name:** *Mephitis* (noxious smell)

**Description:** shiny black pelage with a narrow frontal white stripe between the eyes and two broad white dorsal stripes running from the nape of the neck to the base of the tail; the underside, legs and feet are blackish; there may be white blotches on the chest; the tail may or may not have a white tip; each foot has 5 slightly webbed toes with claws

**Total Length:** male, 20.6 to 26.8 inches; female, 20.2 to 25.6 inches

**Tail:** male, 7 to 11 inches; female, 6.9 to 10.5 inches

**Weight:** male, 2.8 to 9.9 pounds; female, 2.1 to 8.5 pounds

**Gestation:** 59 to 77 days (probably some delay in implantation)

**Litter Size:** 1 to 10 (usually 4 to 6); rarely may be a second litter

**Age of Maturity:** female has first litter at 9 months to 1 year

**Longevity:** one lived 42 months in the wild; average approximately 6 years in captivity (up to 13 years)

**Diet:** omnivore; eats rodents and other small mammals and vertebrates; insects, grasses, leaves, buds, grains, nuts and carrion; may eat birds' eggs and nestlings; also mollusks

**Habitat:** prefers areas of mixed woods, grasslands and open prairie, usually close to water; also found in mixed agricultural and tree-cleared land; thrives in suburban areas

**Predators:** birds of prey, bobcat, fox, fisher, badger, lynx, golden eagle, coyote and puma

**Dental Formula:** 3/3, 1/1, 3/3, 1/2 = 34 teeth

All mustelids have anal musk glands that are used to express aggression and displeasure, but skunks have developed this capacity to the extreme. The musk glands of the striped skunk, about the size of a grape, are surrounded by powerful sphincter muscles. When the skunk is annoyed or frightened, those muscles force the fluid musk down a duct and out through a kind of nipple that can be protruded from the anus. The skunk has considerable muscular control over the spray and is able to produce a fine cloud of mist or to direct a concentrated stream of spray on objects as far as 16 feet away. At distances of 6 to 10 feet, the aim of the skunk is accurate enough to score a hit on most large mammals.

The musk gland contains about a tablespoon of an oily solution of sulphur alcohol called butylmercaptan, enough to produce half a dozen sprays. When eaten, the musk poisons the nervous system and can cause death; as an external spray, however, it has only temporary, although intensely nauseating and irritating, effects. Skunks are not immune to their

*Skunks spend most of their time rooting and grubbing through the upper soil layers in search of insects.*

own spray and will try to avoid spraying if they are likely to be soiled as a result. Probably the high physiological cost of manufacturing the musk also makes them hesitant to spray. The skunk has evolved a very conspicuous black-and-white colouring to deter its enemies.

A skunk also uses a wide range of behavioural threats to frighten its predators away before it resorts to the spray. The skunk arches its back and walks toward the intruder. It hisses, clicks its teeth, stamps its front feet and does headstands with the tail raised in a very clear warning. Some skunks can spray from the headstand position, but the striped skunk bends its body into a U-shape with head and anus pointed in the same direction.

Predation is probably less of a problem for skunks than for other mustelids. However, the skunk's defensive system does not render it immune from attack. Great horned owls kill and eat skunks as do a whole range of

large mammals — no doubt very hungry ones — including puma, coyotes and fishers.

Skunks, unlike most other mustelids, are omnivorous and will eat virtually anything they can catch or find. That includes a wide variety of berries and fruits, small mammals, birds' eggs and nestlings, young rabbits and frogs. Insects, however, are the most important part of their diet, and skunks grub extensively in the upper soil layers and under rocks and logs. They are especially significant predators of social insects such as hornets and bumblebees. The skunk digs into the nest, and as the insects emerge to defend the colony, the skunk grabs and kills them by rolling them between its tough palms. This means that skunks are a minor pest of the honeybee yard. They scratch at hives, and as the bees emerge, they kill them and stuff them into their mouths. The rolling technique is also used to process hairy caterpillars.

Skunks, since they like a mixture of open space interspersed with pockets of cover, have profited by human settlement. They also eat many of the fruits, insects and small mammals associated with disturbed habitats. In some areas, they have become so common that they are the major predator of waterfowl eggs and nestlings, young rabbits and ground-nesting game birds.

Skunks, when foraging, tend to stick close to their dens, which may be hollow trees, rock cavities or abandoned animal burrows. They stay in dens above the ground in summer, but when winter comes or when females are pregnant or newly delivered of a litter, they prefer to hide away below ground. They line the winter burrow with vegetation, and there they spend several months in a dormant state, although they do not hibernate. Sometimes, several skunks den together for the winter.

Northern skunks breed in spring. Females begin to breed at the age of 9 months, and each year, they give birth to a single litter of 1 to 10 kits. The males provide no parental care and are probably polygynous. The young remain with the mother all summer, foraging with her until the autumn, when some of them disperse. Others may den with the mother for the first winter and leave her in the spring.

*The skunk is normally a night-active animal that searches for food using its keen sense of smell.*

# Wolverine Gulo gulo

**Mammal:** *Gulo gulo* — wolverine
**Meaning of Name:** *Gulo* (glutton); probably eats no more than other carnivores, but it has a reputation for greed
**Description:** dark yellow-brown to almost black, darkest on the mid-dorsal saddle, feet and tail; paler on the cheeks and forehead; two pale buff or yellowish to light brown stripes run along the flanks and meet at the base of the tail; underparts are dark brown with some irregular creamy-white spots on the chest and throat
**Total Length:** male, 3.1 to 3.5 feet; female, 2.5 to 3.1 feet
**Tail:** male, 7.8 to 10.2 inches; female, 6.5 to 9.8 inches
**Weight:** male, 25 to 36 pounds; female, 14.5 to 33 pounds
**Gestation:** 215 to 273 days (includes delayed implantation)
**Litter Size:** 2 to 5 (usually 2 or 3); 1 litter every second to third year
**Age of Maturity:** second or third year
**Longevity:** probably several years in the wild; up to 17 years in captivity
**Diet:** omnivore, but primarily a scavenger; small game and some larger game animals (white-tailed deer, caribou, moose), carrion, eggs of ground-nesting birds, edible roots and berries
**Habitat:** tundra and taiga zones; in mountains near treeline; among rocky outcrops and steep canyon sides or on open plains
**Predators:** man is a major enemy; also wolf packs and large bears
**Dental Formula:** 3/3, 1/1, 4/4, 1/2 = 38 teeth

*More scavenger than hunter, the wolverine treks for dozens of miles searching for carrion.*

The wolverine is an animal of superlatives. It is the most powerfully built of all the weasels, with a massive, bony skull, a wolflike jaw and a bone-crushing bite very like that of the African hyena. Though it can bring down an adult caribou, it is better known as a robber and a scavenger. Any creature that tries to cache food in the North — including grizzlies, foxes, wolves and humans — has to reckon with the strong nose and paws of this weasel. Their huge claws and powerful forearms enable them to dig into soil, flip large rocks and tear through logs.

For all its fierce appearance, the wolverine is more of a scavenger than a hunter. Trackers have found that, rather than hunt, it will travel great distances in search of carrion or a food cache. Most hunting weasels tend to zigzag back and forth in their search for food, but the wolverine follows a characteristically straight trail. In areas where big game is common, it lives mostly on the carrion from large mammal carcasses and patrols a large home range that, depending on the habitat, varies from 115 to 770 square miles. Males typically range farther than females.

The wolverine seems to prefer to live in the snowy regions, and its large, flat and heavily furred feet are designed to bear it up, like snowshoes, on deep snow. Thus it remains active at times of the year when bears are hibernating and wolves move only with difficulty. In winter, when deer and caribou flounder in the deep snow, they are vulnerable to the attack of the more mobile wolverine. Wolverines habitually cache the meat from their kills, either by burying it or pulling it up into a tree. The wolverine also pounces on small game or digs out burrow-dwelling animals, and Arctic foxes, ptarmigan and ground-dwelling squirrels form an important part of their diet. During the summer, however, when competition is fiercer from other predators and the prey is fleeter, the wolverine may be forced to feed on wasp nests and berries.

The wolverine can be a tireless traveller, moving as far as 20 miles in the course of one night's foraging. A hunted wolverine, moving without rest, has been trailed for 40 miles. It is feats of endurance like these that have given rise to legends about the powerful wolverine.

The wolverine needs to control an extensive territory in order to find enough large game to support itself, and in the course of regular hunting patrols, it marks its range intensively. Wolverines not only scent-mark with their large glands, wiping the foul scent on boulders and on branches, but like bears, they also rake and scar trees in passing. One wolverine was found to have marked 26 trees in one night. Both sexes are territorial in that

they occupy well-defined areas. Although there is considerable overlap in some territories, conflict is avoided by the carefully timed patrols of different animals, and they do not usually run into each other. It may be that territorial marking is used not to establish exclusive access to a piece of land but rather to prevent individuals from using the same area at the same time. The powerful nose of the wolverine is able to detect the territorial musk over wide distances. Thus direct physical contact is minimized, and wolverines have not been seen fighting to establish territories. However, the fact is that wolverines have been heavily trapped in the areas where they have been studied. It is possible that in the absence of predation and trapping, adults would resort to aggression in order to prevent juveniles from establishing conflicting territories.

Males tolerate and mate with females during the spring and summer. Implantation is delayed, however, and the females do not give birth to

their two to five kits until the next spring. The den site is usually dug into snow or established in a rocky crevice. The mother feeds the young by herself, takes them on foraging excursions and allows them to den with her over their first winter. When spring comes, they disperse. It has been suggested that female wolverines will allow their daughters to take up a territory within or adjacent to their own, but information is still sparse. Studying the social behaviour of such wide-ranging animals would require a heroic, long-term effort. In the future, however, it may be possible to follow radio-collared animals via satellite to gain information not only on the movement of individuals but also on their interaction with others of their own species.

It is likely that many juvenile wolverines die at the time of dispersal. Otherwise, there are few animals that will attack an adult wolverine. There is a record, however, of a wolverine being attacked and killed by wolves

*Wolverines are strong enough to pull down and kill animals as large as caribou, and they use their keen noses to locate newborn calves.*

and of another being apparently raked and wounded by a puma. The long reach and agility of the puma would enable it, unlike most animals, to deal efficiently with a wolverine. There seems to be no animal that eats wolverines.

Many people fear the wolverine as a fierce predator. Trappers hate them because they sniff out and destroy meat set out along traplines. Thus they have been shot at, trapped and poisoned and, as a result, have disappeared from much of their southern and eastern range.

## Walking Softly

*The foot of the northern mammal is caught in a bind. The problem is that it has to perform a whole range of conflicting functions. In summer, it must carry the animal swiftly over*

Although the wolverine's large furry feet tend to slow it down in the summer, they act as snowshoes in the winter, allowing it to thrive in deep, powdery snow.

hard surfaces. It may have to help it climb trees or scramble over rocks. Then winter comes, and the foot must deal with an unstable mix of snowy powder, slush and ice.

Since winter is a time of high heating costs — and that means extra rations of food for mammals that are active in the cold — the way in which the animals deal with snow is crucial to their survival. Many northern carnivores, such as the lynx and the wolverine, are actually very efficient at moving through the deep powdery snow, and winter is the time of their prosperity. They have feet that act like snowshoes, with a large surface area relative to their body weight. In summer, however, their large furry feet tend to slow them down. Other species, like the wolf, have feet adapted for running over hard ground, and these tend to flounder through the drifts when winter comes.

The hoofed animals — such as

deer, antelope and elk — have feet primarily designed to absorb the stress of heavy bodies pounding over solid ground. The snows of winter can both help and hinder these animals, for although food is much harder to find, predators are more easily avoided. Caribou, in particular, because they have a larger dew claw than most artiodactyls, are buoyed up on the snow by very wide hooves. In winter, they travel mostly on hard-packed caribou trails. When they see a wolf pack, however, they jump off the trail into the deep snow. Even if the wolves choose to follow them, which they usually do not, the predators will soon bog down in the deep snow, and the caribou will easily leave them behind.

Moose are not so fortunate. They have about the same ratio of weight to surface area of foot as do their predators. Therefore, moose sink just as deeply into the snow as wolves do. Probably for that reason, moose

*Hunting success and techniques of carnivores such as this long-tailed weasel shift according to the change in the depth and texture of the snow.*

will often stand and fight in winter, rather than run from wolves.

The less powerful deer cannot fight wolves, so they try to stay in the shallow or hard-packed snow where their superior speed can be used to defeat the predator. This is probably why deer gather together in winter in what are known as deer yards. Together, they create a dense maze of hard-packed trails that crisscross the area around the yard. Then, when wolves approach, the escape route is ready. In soft snow, a wolf sinks in less than a deer, which is forced to bound high over the drifts in order to escape being bogged down. Often, however, when the snow reaches chest height, the deer becomes exhausted. In such conditions, the wolverine, which has the lightest tread of all the predators, can kill deer and even caribou.

It is probably the deep snows that limit the northern range of the deer. In periods of warming, such as the present one, deer tend to move farther north; correspondingly, in colder periods — in the so-called "little ice age," for example, from 1350 to 1800 — caribou have moved

south to take over the abandoned range of the deer.

Species such as bison and antelope have relatively small feet in relation to their weight, and they are restricted primarily to open prairie, where the wind blows areas clear of snow. In Wood Buffalo National Park in northern Alberta and the southern Northwest Territories, where the snow falls thickly, wolves can kill even the biggest buffalo in winter when the large bulls are unable to manoeuvre. In many species of deer and bovid, there is a selection for heavy male body size, which increases the prowess of males in fighting for control of the harem. Ironically, the increase in weight that contributes to breeding success probably means more winter mortality. Among artiodactyls, it may be the need to walk softly in winter that limits the tendency toward greater and greater size.

## *Long-tailed Weasel* Mustela frenata

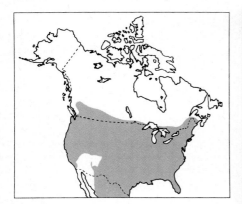

**Mammal:** *Mustela frenata* — long-tailed weasel

**Meaning of Name:** *Mustela* (weasel); *frenata* (bridle) refers to the bridle-like mask characteristic of weasels of this species from the more southern parts of its range

**Description:** in summer, the coat is cinnamon brown above and buff-coloured ventrally; there is a black tip on the end of the tail; in winter, it is pure white (including the whiskers), except for the black terminal quarter of the tail

**Total Length:** male, 13.8 to 18 inches; female, 11 to 14.3 inches

**Tail:** male, 4.1 to 6 inches; female, 3.3 to 4.7 inches

**Weight:** male, 6 to 9.5 ounces; female, 2.5 to 4.5 ounces

**Gestation:** 205 to 337 days (this includes a 7-month period of delayed implantation)

**Litter Size:** 3 to 9 (usually 6)

**Age of Maturity:** male, late spring following birth; female, 3 to 4 months

**Longevity:** probably up to 3 years

**Diet:** primarily rodents and other small mammals; also eats some birds, insects and, occasionally, snakes, fruits and berries

**Habitat:** prefers open brushy or grassy areas near water; land-use practices have not affected it, and it occurs in croplands, fallow fields, fencerows, small woodlots and even suburban residential areas

**Predators:** grey fox, red fox, coyote, grey wolf, bobcat, lynx, hawks, owls and man

**Dental Formula:** 3/3, 1/1, 3/3, 1/2 = 34 teeth

The long-tailed weasel is the largest of the true weasels. Despite its size, its diet is no different from that of the other weasels, consisting mainly of rodents. Like the larger weasels, this species consistently kills cottontails, water fowl, muskrats and ground squirrels.

The geographic range of the long-tailed weasel extends farther to the south than those of the closely related least weasel and ermine. It ranges from southern Canada all the way down into northern South America, preferring the open habitats of grasslands and semidesert.

Mating occurs in spring and summer, with implantation and birth delayed until spring. The litter is usually half a dozen kits that are born blind and helpless. Males offer no parental care, and the young remain with their mothers only until autumn. Females that are smaller than males mature in their first spring, but males may take another year to reach sexual maturity.

The long-tailed weasel shares with the ermine a black tip on its tail that is most conspicuous when its winter

*The skinny body and short legs of the long-tailed weasel enable it to pursue mammals in their burrows and along runways.*

coat has turned white. The southern populations of the long-tailed weasel stay brown all winter, but northern populations of this species, and of ermine, turn snow-white. The reason their tail tip remains black while the rest of their fur is white may be that it deters predators. Experiments using hawks trained to attack forms resembling weasels showed that the black tail tip caused confusion — the birds often directed their strikes to the tail tip, as if it were the head, and not to the hind end of the body. Hawks missed in their attacks on black-tipped models more often than on models that were all white or had the black mark in the middle. This raises the question of why the least weasel does not retain a black tail tip. One possibility is that with its small size and northerly location, it would be unable to keep a long-tipped tail from freezing.

# *Ermine*  Mustela erminea

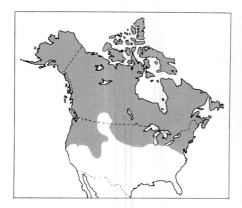

**Mammal:** *Mustela erminea* — ermine, stoat, short-tailed weasel

**Meaning of Name:** *Mustela* (weasel); *erminea*, from *ermine*, the Old French word for the white winter colour phase (in the brown summer pelage, it is referred to as stoat)

**Description:** in summer, this animal is rich brown dorsally; on the outer sides of the legs, flanks and the ventral surface (including lips and underside of legs and toes, it is creamy white; the tail is tipped with long stiff black hairs; a white line runs down the hind legs, connecting the white of the underparts with that of the toes; in winter, the coat is pure white except for the black tip of the tail

**Total Length:** male, 9.9 to 13 inches; female, 8.5 to 10.2 inches

**Tail:** male, 2.5 to 3.5 inches; female, 1.5 to 2.8 inches

**Weight:** male, 2.4 to 5 ounces; female, 1.5 to 2.5 ounces

**Gestation:** 10 months (including delayed implantation)

**Litter Size:** 4 to 9 (average 6); 1 litter per year

**Age of Maturity:** male, about 10 months (February or March following birth); female, 60 to 70 days

**Longevity:** maximum longevity in the wild is about 7 years

**Diet:** eats mainly small rodents; also earthworms, reptiles, amphibians, fish, birds, eggs, insects and carrion

**Habitat:** wide range from open tundra to deep forest; prefers areas with vegetative or rocky cover; also found in coniferous or mixed forests, tundra, shrub borders, lakeshores and meadow boundaries

**Predators:** coyote, badger, fox, marten, wolverine, fisher, black snake, domestic cat, hawks and owls

**Dental Formula:** 3/3, 1/1, 3/3, 1/2 = 34 teeth

Ermine is that luxuriant white fur that once lined the cloaks and sleeves of a mediaeval European aristocracy. It starts off, however, as the winter coat of a small weasel that ranges widely throughout the northern hemisphere. The ermine is found in most kinds of northern forest, in mountain meadows and right across the tundra, everywhere except on the shortgrass prairie and in marshland.

The ermine thrives on small rodents whose burrows it usurps as a residence. Its size limits it to small prey, however, and unlike the long-tailed weasel, it is rarely able to kill rabbits and hares.

Like all weasels, the ermine has three vocalizations — a trill, a screech and a squeal. The trill is used for communication among weasels, especially between mother and offspring or between siblings. The screech is used to startle prey and predators and may be followed by a lunging bite. Squealing, as in other mammals, expresses pain or distress.

The breeding behaviour of the ermine resembles that of the long-tailed and least weasels.

*The deer mouse being eaten by this ermine,* **top,** *is a typical prey species for weasels. Alert and intense, the voracious ermine,* **above,** *stalks small rodents in northern forests.*

# *Least Weasel* Mustela nivalis

**Mammal:** *Mustela nivalis* — least weasel
**Meaning of Name:** *Mustela* (weasel); *nivalis* (snowy) refers to its colour in winter
**Description:** resembles a long, slender mouse; in summer, the coat is brown dorsally and white ventrally, sometimes splotched with brown spots; the feet are whitish with furred soles; in winter, it is completely white except for a few black hairs at the tip of the tail
**Total Length:** male, 7.2 to 8.5 inches; female, 6.5 to 7.1 inches
**Tail:** male, 1 to 1.5 inches; female, 0.87 to 1.1 inches
**Weight:** male, 1.2 to 2.2 ounces; female, 0.88 to 2.0 ounces
**Gestation:** 35 to 37 days
**Litter Size:** 3 to 10 (usually 4 or 5); 2 or more litters per year
**Age of Maturity:** male, 8 months; female, 4 months
**Longevity:** approximately 1 year
**Diet:** almost entirely small rodents; also eats amphibians and insects
**Habitat:** open woodlots, cultivated fields, meadows, brush areas, mixed forests, fencerows, marsh edge and streamside vegetation
**Predators:** long-tailed weasel, grey fox, red fox, domestic cat, snakes, hawks and owls
**Dental Formula:** 3/3, 1/1, 3/3, 1/2 = 34 teeth

The least weasel is the smallest of the true carnivores. It specializes in small rodents such as mice, voles and lemmings as well as insectivorous shrews and moles. Often, it will take over the burrow system of one of its victims and use it as a home base. The tiny weasel will drag victims home to cache in its central burrow, plucking the fur of its prey to line and insulate its burrow.

Insulation is very important, for with its long and skinny small body, the least weasel has a metabolic rate equivalent to that of some shrews. In their Arctic range, they may elevate their metabolic rate by 400 percent to stay warm, burning food equal to half their body weight daily.

The least weasel's range is less than 2 acres. It feeds on small mammals that do not hibernate and are available all winter long, which may account in part for the least weasel's unusual life history. It has a continuous breeding system — females become mature within a few months of birth and may breed several times in a year. Unlike other weasels that have delayed implantation, the least weasel's pregnancy starts after mating and lasts

*The smallest of the true carnivores, the least weasel is able to pursue voles, lemmings and other rodents into their retreats.*

roughly 35 days. A litter of 3 to 10 kits is born and weaned after four weeks.

The male offers no parental care, and when food is scarce, it may drive the female out of its territory.

## Long and Skinny

*There are advantages to being long and skinny. Weasels can slip down crevices and crannies in the rocks in pursuit of small prey or follow shrews and pikas into their burrows. When it is their turn to be pursued, they can retreat to those same cracks and holes to escape the larger, fatter carnivores that prey on them.*

*There is, of course, a catch: the long and skinny shape of a weasel may enable it to catch more food, but it also allows it to lose more heat than rounder, more compact animals. In effect, the weasel needs to consume more food to keep the fires burning.*

*Weasels, like many small mustelids, have a resting metabolic*

rate 10 percent higher than is usual for mammals of their weight. The Arctic least weasel is an even more extreme example, with a resting metabolic rate 400 percent above average. That is the cost of staying active all year in the North if one happens to be long and skinny. Such animals have to be able to generate great quantities of heat to make up for the heat they lose. Not all mustelids demonstrate this metabolic pattern. For example, burrowing mustelids such as badgers and skunks have compact bodies and metabolic rates that are actually lower than normal for their body mass. It is the long, skinny carnivores and not mustelids in particular that have evolved these high metabolic rates.

Weasels can exploit their high metabolic rate by staying busy when prey is abundant. The proverbial and supposedly improvident weasel that kills every last chicken in the henhouse is not engaging in a wasteful, murderous spree. Rather, it is gathering food for its stockpile. Caches of more than a hundred rats and mice have been found, and these supplies allow the weasel to stay in the insulated warmth of its grass-lined, snow-covered burrow in the very cold weather and to keep itself warm by slow, steady feeding.

Weasels, when they sleep, curl up into a ball to cut down on radiated heat loss. In effect, they are changing their shape from long and skinny to round and compact.

The problem of the weasel's skinniness is compounded by the small size of its stomach. Studies have shown that a weasel is restricted to eating less than an

The long, thin body of the pine marten enables it to hunt along narrow branches but increases the amount of heat the animal loses.

ounce or so of meat at a time and can only have one meal every few hours. On the other hand, the weasel has to eat every few hours in order to survive. That means that if it is to eat regularly, the caching of food is an absolute necessity. It is ironic: the long, slender shape of the weasel makes it an effective hunter but an ineffective eater; yet because it loses heat at a high rate, it must eat more, and more often, than other mammals do just to stay warm.

# Pine Marten *Martes americana*

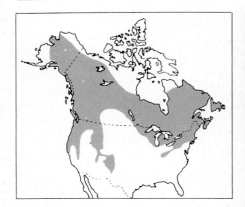

**Mammal:** *Martes americana* — pine marten

**Meaning of Name:** *Martes* (marten); *americana* (of America)

**Description:** long, lustrous pelage; varies in colour from pale buff to reddish and dark browns; ears are pale and edged with white; head is lighter than the rest of the body; underparts are pale brown with irregular creamy or orange-coloured breast spots; unlike other members of the Mustelidae family, it has semiretractable claws

**Total Length:** male, 21.7 to 25.4 inches; female, 19.3 to 23.7 inches

**Tail:** male, 6 to 8.5 inches; female, 5.5 to 7.8 inches

**Weight:** male, 1.5 to 2.9 pounds; female 1.3 to 1.7 pounds

**Gestation:** 220 to 275 days

**Litter Size:** 1 to 5 (usually 3 or 4)

**Age of Maturity:** 15 to 24 months

**Longevity:** 5 or 6 years in the wild; 18 years in captivity

**Diet:** mostly rodents and other small mammals; also birds, fruits, insects, carrion, amphibians, reptiles, fish and shellfish

**Habitat:** found in climax coniferous forests; in the west, it occurs in stands of spruce and fir (mostly mature trees), and in the east, it occurs in cedar swamps and mixed stands of both conifers and hardwoods; since man has disturbed its natural habitat, it also is found in cutovers, around logging camps, picnic sites and dumps

**Predators:** loggers and trappers are major predators; also fisher, bobcat, wolf, lynx, coyote; the great horned owl preys upon them to a limited extent

**Dental Formula:** 3/3, 1/1, 4/4, 1/2 = 38 teeth

The pine marten is a weasel of the northern coniferous forest. Unlike other weasels, it has semiretractable claws that can be extended for better tree climbing. It feeds on smaller prey items, preferring small rodents to rabbits and hares. Its ability to run through the trees along limbs proves useful at selected times — when birds are nesting, squirrels are abundant or there is heavy competition from fishers. In winter, it acts in the conventional weasel fashion and follows tunnels in the snow in pursuit of rodents such as voles and mice. The meat diet is supplemented in summer with fruits, berries and insects, but even then, 80 percent of its food remains animal prey. Yellowjacket hornets are eaten in autumn.

The pine marten is much smaller than the fisher, with a more pointed and delicate face. Males are larger

*The pine marten is able to pursue squirrels and other rodents through the treetops with a skill unmatched by other weasels.*

than females and, unhindered by parental duties, range farther than females. Although both exclude members of the same sex from their territories, they are more abundant than fishers, and given the pine marten's smaller territories, a forest can support a sizable marten population. Marten populations do not follow a 10-year cycle, and as the many species of small rodents they prey on may have independent population cycles, the marten food supply is steady.

Like the fisher, females produce a litter of roughly three kits in spring, using a tree hollow as a den. The young marten mature in their second year.

# *Black-footed Ferret*  Mustela nigripes

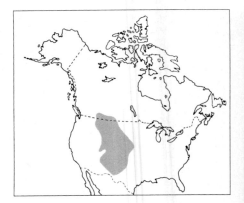

**Mammal:** *Mustela nigripes* — black-footed ferret
**Meaning of Name:** *Mustela* (weasel); *nigripes* (black foot)
**Description:** creamy white to buffy or yellowish brown; has a dark brown mask across the eyes; also has dark brown cheeks, feet, legs and end of tail
**Total Length:** male, 1.7 to 1.9 feet; female, 1.6 feet
**Tail:** male, 4.5 to 5.5 inches; female, 5 inches
**Weight:** 2.1 to 2.5 pounds
**Gestation:** 42 to 45 days
**Litter Size:** 1 to 5 (usually 4)
**Age of Maturity:** male, 1 year; female, 1 year
**Longevity:** 12 years in captivity
**Diet:** probably eats mainly prairie dogs; also other small mammals, ground-nesting birds and snakes
**Habitat:** mainly arid short mixed-grass prairies, closely associated with prairie-dog towns
**Predators:** hawks, owls
**Dental Formula:** 3/3, 1/1, 3/3, 1/2 = 34 teeth

The black-footed ferret, a large weasel that had the misfortune to develop a specialized taste for prairie dogs, is now the rarest mammal in North America. Massive poisoning campaigns organized by ranchers and farmers to wipe out the prairie dog have almost eliminated its even more vulnerable predator. The tide may have turned, however. As a result of recent efforts to protect the prairie dog, populations are growing; consequently, there is hope that the black-footed ferret will be saved from extinction. However, ferret populations — numbering only a few individuals in most known localities — have yet to show any signs of increase.

Ferrets are confined to the short-grass prairie where the prairie dog thrives. Like badgers, after killing and disposing of a prairie dog, they modify the chambers of their victim's burrow and move in. Also like badgers, they will eat a generalized diet of small mammals, birds and even young antelope. Almost nothing is known of other aspects of their behaviour.

*The black-footed ferret is the rarest North American mammal because its principal prey, the prairie dog, has been subject to poisoning campaigns.*

# *Fisher* Martes pennanti

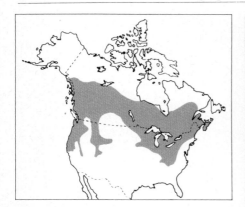

**Mammal:** *Martes pennanti* — fisher
**Meaning of Name:** *Martes* (marten); *pennanti* (named in honour of T. Pennant, an English zoologist)
**Description:** thick, glossy coat; grizzled grey mantle due to tricoloured guard hairs; rump, tail, feet and belly are glossy brown to black; irregular white or cream patches on the chest, in underarm region and around the genitals; in winter, the colour ranges from deep brown to black, with light-coloured hairs around the face and shoulders
**Total Length:** male, 2.8 to 3.5 feet; female, 2.5 to 3.1 feet
**Tail:** male, 13 to 15.5 inches; female, 10 to 14.5 inches
**Weight:** male, 5.5 to 12 pounds; female, 3 to 7 pounds
**Gestation:** 338 to 358 days
**Litter Size:** 1 to 6 (average 2 or 3)
**Age of Maturity:** male, 2 years; female, 1 year
**Longevity:** 7 years is average life span in the wild (10 years is upper limit); may live longer than 10 years in captivity
**Diet:** generalized carnivore; will eat any animal that it can overpower; eats all carrion; birds, fish, snakes, toads and insects; does eat some plant material — fruits, seeds, berries, and fern tips; one of the few predators that feeds on porcupine
**Habitat:** prefers continuous forest in the vicinity of water courses; always in areas of extensive overhead canopy; avoids open areas
**Predators:** man is the major predator; possibly wolf, but a fisher would probably be too agile
**Dental Formula:** 3/3, 1/1, 4/4, 1/2 = 38 teeth

*Fishers climb readily and use tree holes high off the ground for dens and as sites for rearing their young.*

The fisher is a large, powerful mustelid found in the northern coniferous forest, a habitat shared with the marten. The fisher is larger than the marten, about the size of a fox, with a relatively massive skull, and as a result, it tends to be most effective hunting on the ground. It is, however, well equipped for tree climbing, with semiretractable claws that will extend from the paw, a long bushy tail for balance and a special muscle that attaches to the shoulder blade for added climbing power. The wrist and foot joints are flexible, and the hind foot can swivel 180 degrees to allow fishers, and the closely related marten, to ascend and descend trees headfirst.

Fishers are voracious hunters and will eat virtually any vertebrate they are capable of killing. Rabbits and rodents form the bulk of their diet, but they will climb trees in pursuit of squirrels and in search of bird nests. They swim well and often forage along streams and ponds to feed on muskrat and even mink. Fishers have a reputation for eating mainly porcupine, but actually, they have a greater diversity in their diet than martens do, eating any mammal or bird they can kill, scavenging carrion and, in summer, feeding to a limited extent on berries.

The most famous item in their diet is the porcupine, an animal that few other predators besides pumas eat. To kill such prickly prey, the fisher continuously circles the porcupine for up to half an hour, biting it in the head until it is immobilized. Finally, the fisher flips it over and attacks its unprotected belly. The porcupine's tendency to retreat to a tree limb is of some hindrance, but a fisher can quickly scale trees and attack from above because of its ability to descend headfirst. On the ground, the low-slung fisher is able to deliver its bite to the head without stooping, which enables it to avoid the flailing tail of quills. The quills are dangerous weapons, and some fishers are reported to have died of quill wounds. Large porcupines and porcupines in dens are able to fend off fisher attacks.

The fisher's circling attack seems

instinctive, as captive fishers without the benefit of parental guidance or previous experience can kill porcupines. Fishers are reported to use a special searching technique when they are seeking porcupines. When hunting rabbits, fishers zigzag back and forth through the underbrush until they flush a victim and then run it down. For porcupines, however, they travel long distances in a straight line until they pick up a porcupine trail or a den. Anecdotal evidence from areas where fishers have been restocked suggests that they can reduce large porcupine populations (and the tree damage they inflict), but no one has yet proved this conclusively.

The fisher's territory is a regular hunting circuit of up to 18 miles in diameter, which it travels around every 4 to 12 days, moving approximately one to three miles a day, depending on the abundance of food. Males travel over larger areas than females, but the lighter females tend to forage more in the trees and to avoid open areas.

Like most weasels, fishers stay active all winter long. They may remain in their dens in severe weather, especially after eating a large meal, but they do not stay inactive for longer than a couple of days. They are most active at night but will venture out during the day at times.

Fishers show a tendency toward sexual dimorphism, with males being twice as large as the females. Males provide no parental care and are thought to be polygynous, their large size being used to exclude other males from their range. The anal glands are used to scent-mark posts around their territories, especially at breeding time, although it is different from the potent and foul anal musk released during fighting or when threatened.

In keeping with the pattern of sexual dimorphism, males do not breed until the age of 2, while females may breed at 1 year. Breeding takes place in early spring, but the embryos do not implant and begin to grow until the next winter. Pregnant fishers den high up in hollow trees and usually give birth to litters of three altricial (helpless) kits. The kits stay with the mother for three to four months and then disperse.

Fishers show some tendency to fol-low a 10-year population cycle, lagging a year or two behind the snowshoe hare, especially in areas where hares are the main prey. Because they are such wide-ranging and actively curious animals, fishers are easily trapped in areas where furbearers are heavily harvested and become victims of traps set for other furbearers. As a result, they have been extinguished in the southern end of their range.

*The strongly built fisher is the only North American mammal able to eat large numbers of porcupines.*

# Mink  Mustela vison

**Mammal:** *Mustela vison* — mink
**Meaning of Name:** *Mustela* (weasel); *vison* is of obscure origin — either from the Icelandic or Swedish word *vison* (weasel) or possibly from the Latin word *visor* (scout)
**Description:** thick, soft and lustrous pelage; the guard hairs are glossy and somewhat oily; the colour varies from rich brown to black; it is paler ventrally, with white splashes on lower lip, chest, lower abdomen; has a white chin patch
**Total Length:** male, 19.3 to 24.4 inches; female, 16.5 to 23.5 inches
**Tail:** male, 6.2 to 8.3 inches; female, 5 to 8 inches
**Weight:** male, 1.5 to 5 pounds; female, 1.7 to 2.6 pounds
**Gestation:** 39 to 78 days (due to varying period of delay in implantation)
**Litter Size:** 2 to 10 (usually 5); 1 litter per year
**Age of Maturity:** male, 18 months; female, 12 months
**Longevity:** 3, possibly 4, years in the wild; 10 years in captivity
**Diet:** primarily a carnivore; small mammals, fish, frogs, crayfish, insects, worms and birds — eats some plant material
**Habitat:** along streams and lakes in swamps and marshes; if it occurs away from the water, it prefers second-growth cover of mixed shrubs, weeds and grasses and the edges of cultivated fields and pastures
**Predators:** hunters and trappers are their major enemies; also great horned owl, bobcat, red fox, coyote, wolf, black bear and domestic dog
**Dental Formula:** 3/3, 1/1, 3/3, 1/2 = 34 teeth

Mink are wetland weasels, most commonly found in marshes and near the shores of lakes and streams, where they hunt both along the shore and underwater. With short, stubby legs and a sturdy, pointed face, minks tend to resemble most other weasels, except that they are semiaquatic and have partially webbed feet. Their fine lustrous fur is thick and oily and was designed by nature to insulate them for a life in the cold northern waters.

In terms of foraging strategy, they are also like other weasels, patrolling a circuit, investigating likely spots and rushing in to scare up small animals. On land, the mink hunts mainly small rodents, but it will also take frogs, snakes, shrews, rabbits and birds. Underwater, they eat mostly fish and some crayfish and salamanders. Male mink, which are larger than females, are able to kill muskrats

*Mink are able to dive underwater to catch fish and other aquatic organisms that are unavailable to most weasels.*

and rabbits, and in some areas, these may be a major food item. Females often take over muskrat dens for their own use.

The foraging circuit usually encompasses one-half to two miles of shoreline. Much smaller circuits are reported, however, for west coast mink because they forage in the intertidal zone where every tide brings in plentiful new food. The male, like other mustelids, ranges over a wider area than the female. Both sexes seem to be territorial and to mark their boundaries with strong excretions from scent glands.

Adult mink are solitary for most of the year. When the breeding season arrives, however, the males begin to roam in search of receptive females. Courtship ends with a prolonged and violent mating during which the male may savagely bite the female's neck. Copulation, which induces ovulation, is repeated several times daily for a few days.

A gestation period of approximately one month ends with the birth of anywhere from 2 to 10 kits, although the average is usually five. The kits stay with the mother for the summer and disperse in autumn. The male provides no parental care.

Contamination has begun to be a major problem for wild mink. Because they feed so heavily on fish that absorb and concentrate pesticides, mercury and PCBs, they are exposed to high levels of waterborne pollutants. Wild mink populations have been shown to suffer from mercury poisoning and PCB levels that either kill them or prevent them from reproducing. Most of the fur for mink coats now comes from mink ranches. Unpolluted areas still yield several hundred thousand mink each year, however, and trapping is the only major control of mink populations.

Canada used to be home to another species, the sea mink, M. macrodon. This animal was once common along the Atlantic coast, but it was exterminated by trapping even before scientists had a chance to describe it. The last sea mink was trapped at Campobello Island in New Brunswick in 1894.

## Embryos on Hold

*A black bear sow may mate, ovulate and fertilize her eggs in June. The fertilized egg begins to divide and to grow into a fetus. Then, suddenly, progress stops. In most mammals, the fetus would, at this point, implant itself in the wall of the mother's uterus, where it would be able to absorb nutrients from the mother through the placental membranes. Over the months, it would grow and develop into the form of a new animal. In the black bear, however, the embryo may be held in limbo, without any development at all, for as long as half a year.*

*Black bears and many of their close relatives are not the only mammals able to delay implantation. Several kinds of bats, weasels and*

*deer, as well as seals, the armadillo and a few other unrelated species, seem to have evolved this ability independently. Though the groups are unrelated, it is probable that each was subject to similar ecological conditions favouring this strategy.*

*For some species, the delay is obligatory, while for others, it is facultative (dependent on circumstances). The facultative delay is believed to be used by some rabbits and rodents when excessive nursing demands are already being made on the mother by an existing litter. If she has a large family that is literally draining her nutritional reserves, she may delay implantation and even abort the embryos. In the obligatory delay, the hiatus occurs regardless of the mother's nutritional state and may be an adaptation to allow a period of physiological assessment.*

*In bears, it is probable that implantation is delayed until the summer and autumn fattening period has passed. If it has been a scarce year, with few acorns and fruit, most females do not bear young, even if they have mated and are carrying embryos. The female must have enough fat not only to sustain herself during the winter but also to produce milk for the cubs. Delayed implantation prevents her from investing in a pregnancy before her food reserves are established. Once that is done, implantation occurs, and the pregnancy proceeds. Similarly, in weasels that stay active over the winter, implantation is delayed until the end of winter, when*

*Unpredictable winter-food availability may be why animals such as mink delay the development of their embryos until spring.*

*female fat reserves have met the test of the most severe winter conditions.*

*But why not simply delay mating and fertilization, instead of implantation, to save the loss of even partially developed embryos? Many female bats store sperm for the entire winter, only allowing their eggs to be fertilized when spring has clearly arrived. For them, mating in autumn seems to be more convenient and efficient than in spring.*

*That is not true of bears. For them, autumn is a crucial time for the laying on of winter fat. Courtship and mating at that time would tend to deplete their physical resources disastrously and impinge on their winter survival. Also, when females have an extended period of oestrus — in grizzlies, for example, it is two to five weeks in duration — they may mate at a time that will result in a far from optimum date of birth. If sperm do not store well, then delayed implantation is a solution.*

*The phenomenon of delayed implantation is, in some species at least, widely variable. Some weasels, for example, delay the development of their embryos, and some do not. The delay may represent the attempt of the female to time the birth of her young; it may equally well relate to an assessment of nutrient reserves. No widely accepted theory exists to explain it, and more study is needed.*

# American Badger *Taxidea taxus*

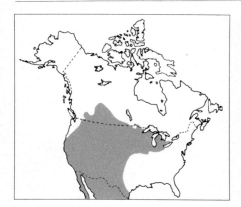

**Mammal:** *Taxidea taxus* — American badger

**Meaning of Name:** *Taxidea* (badgerlike), because of its general resemblance to the common badger of Eurasia; *taxus* (badger)

**Description:** has a shaggy pelage, longer dorsally, especially on the flanks where a fringe is formed (may be as long as 3.5 inches); back has a grizzled appearance; underparts are creamy, legs are brown, and feet are blackish; tail is covered in stiff light brown hairs; head has a distinct pattern — the muzzle, crown and hind neck are dark blackish brown with a white mid-dorsal stripe running from the muzzle to the shoulders; white cheeks; ears are white trimmed with black; behind the eyes on each cheek is a black crescentic spot

**Total Length:** 2.4 to 2.8 feet

**Tail:** 4.7 to 6.2 inches

**Weight:** 7.9 to 26.5 pounds

**Gestation:** 6 to 9 months (including period of delayed implantation)

**Litter Size:** 2 to 5 (usually 4)

**Age of Maturity:** male, second breeding season following birth; female, first breeding season following birth

**Longevity:** 4 or 5 years in the wild (maximum of 14); in captivity, one lived 23 years, 8 months

**Diet:** ground squirrels are a major component of its diet; also eats other small mammals, birds, birds' eggs, reptiles, arthropods and carrion

**Habitat:** dry, open prairies, grasslands, farmlands and parklands; clay or sandy soils are suitable for their burrows

**Predators:** man, coyote, golden eagle, and grizzly bear

**Dental Formula:** 3/3, 1/1, 3/3, 1/2, = 34 teeth

Badgers are diggers. They have taken the mustelid tendency to pursue rodents into their burrows one step further by evolving the bones and muscles necessary to dig them out. The badger has a heavy-boned body, flattened so that it can slip into small burrows. The forelimbs are armed with long, stout claws for digging, while the claws on the hind legs are short and shovel-like for scooping away dirt that the foreclaws have loosened. The eyes are small and protected from dirt by a special membrane.

Badgers dig for many kinds of rodents, some of them larger than the usual rodent prey — ground squirrels, pocket gophers, marmots and prairie dogs. Some of their digging techniques are quite sophisticated. When they go after ground squirrels, for example, they may plug all the doors but one before they proceed to dig the squirrel out. Alternatively, they may dig a connecting tunnel into the one remaining entrance to the burrow and just wait for the ground squirrel to leave.

In order to protect themselves from

*The badger is a fierce fighter with formidable claws and jaws that protect it from all but the largest predators.*

coyotes and grizzlies, badgers tend to dig very large burrows for themselves, often up to 10 feet wide and 30 feet deep. To save on the cost of construction, they may take over and renovate a prairie dog burrow after, of course, they have eaten the occupants.

The badger is a great fighter and is not easily killed, even when taken by surprise. The compact body and powerful claws and teeth mean that any predator smaller than a grizzly must take care with its attack. The badger uses any hesitation on the part of the attacker to dig itself into the soil. It can almost miraculously disappear into the earth in less than a few minutes.

The morphology and feeding habits of the badger suggest that it evolved on the grasslands, where the soils are deep and ground-dwelling rodents are abundant. Normally, badgers are restricted to a dry, open habitat, such as the prairies; however, they have been able to colonize some farmland in southern Ontario. The large bur-

rows of the badger tend to interfere with agriculture, and in much of their range, badgers are hunted or poisoned. They also suffer from the extermination of the ground squirrels and prairie dogs on which they live.

## Playing to Win

*Most mammals play. But why? The concept of play is difficult enough to define; it is almost impossible to study. Of course, pleasure is implicit in the notion of play, and animals at play seem to perform certain actions simply for the enjoyment of them. Often, however, these actions are actually a light-hearted imitation of more serious behaviour, and most biologists have come to believe that play is functional. The animal at play is rehearsing the behaviour on which his success will one day depend. The pleasure of playing is simply nature's way of encouraging the animal to practise and develop its skills.*

*Behaviourists distinguish between play and exploration, which is the investigation of an object in an attempt to understand what it is and what it does. They also distinguish between play and problem-solving, where the animal has a specific goal. Play is more complex: through it, the animal learns how to interact with its environment. It also learns how to experiment and to adjust its tactics in the face of new situations. In play, there is no fixed goal but merely a*

*toying with optional actions and outcomes. In the real world, play — a shadow of the life-and-death contests of later life — translates into much cavorting and romping.*

*Play is much more highly developed in mammals that are large, long-lived, intelligent and social. Shrews, for example, do not seem to play much; otters, on the other hand, play frequently and with great gusto. In fact, most aquatic mammals seem especially playful, probably because of their long, intelligent lives, rather than because of their environment.*

*In some mammals, the forms of play are relatively predictable. Foxes play by racing around and knocking each other down as they will later do in earnest when hunting. Squirrels also play by running in circles, making sharp turns and leaps and by going through the motions of courtship. People who entertain a kitten by dragging a string across the floor or by dangling it and making scratching noises with their fingers are mimicking the sounds and movements of small mammals, and the kitten is learning to hunt in its play.*

*In more sophisticated animals, play is more complex, flexible and wide-ranging. Monkeys, for example, use play to discover new behaviours, new foods to eat and new ways to handle it. It has been found that when a strange food is introduced to*

Badgers can burrow faster than any other mammals, and they use their digging ability to excavate ground-dwelling grassland rodents.

*a troop of monkeys, it is the youngest monkeys that learn to incorporate it into their diet. Play tends to promote this flexibility, and once mature animals have put playful learning behind them, they are less apt to learn. Hence the expression, ''You can't teach an old dog new tricks.''*

# River Otter *Lutra canadensis*

**Mammal:** *Lutra canadensis* — river otter
**Meaning of Name:** *Lutra* (otter);
*canadensis* (of Canada), because this
species was first described from Canada
**Description:** muscular streamlined body
with broad, flattened head; legs short
and powerful with fully webbed toes and
furred soles; short, oily pelage has a
dense underfur and rich brown guard
hairs; throat has a silvery sheen
**Total Length:** male, 3.1 to 4.5 feet;
female, 2.9 to 3.8 feet
**Tail:** male, 13.5 to 20.1 inches; female,
12.5 to 17.5 inches
**Weight:** male, 15 to 30 pounds; female,
10 to 25 pounds
**Gestation:** 245 to 380 days
**Litter Size:** 1 to 6 (usually 2 or 3)
**Age of Maturity:** male, mature at 2
years but are not successful breeders
until their fifth year (young males are
often rejected by females); female, 2
years (are known to breed when 1 year)
**Longevity:** 13 years in the wild; 14 to 20
years in captivity (maximum of 23 years
in captivity)
**Diet:** fish constitute bulk of diet; aquatic
invertebrates, amphibians, mammals
and birds are also eaten
**Habitat:** extensive water is the principal
component of their habitat; marshes,
points of land extending into water and
wooded stream banks are preferred;
found in all types of inland waterways as
well as estuaries and marine covers
**Predators:** bobcat, lynx, coyote; wolves
may catch otters migrating overland;
also bald eagle, great horned owl and
large game fish may take young
**Dental Formula:** 3/3, 1/1, 4/3, 1/2 = 36
teeth

The river otter is a freshwater mustelid. This almost completely aquatic
animal is found in rivers and lakes in
virtually all parts of North America,
from the edge of the tundra to the Gulf
of Mexico. It has adapted to its watery
environment in much the same way as
the sea otter, and it has developed the
same dense fur, large lungs, webbed
feet, short legs and heavy crushing
molars. Unlike its seagoing cousin,
however, the river otter dens on land
and forages along the shore; it has
been known to travel over large expanses of land. Also, unlike the sea otter, the river otter uses scent glands to
mark the banks of its river territory.

Otters breed in late winter or early
spring. Implantation is delayed so
that after a pregnancy that probably
lasts only two months, the female

*The streamlined form of the otter makes
it a fast and agile underwater predator
able to catch almost any kind of
freshwater fish.*

gives birth to one to six kits in the
spring. Otters are not equipped for
digging, and the female usually seeks
out an abandoned beaver lodge or the
burrow of some other animal on the
banks of a stream or lake. Failing that,
she may settle into a hollow tree.

Like other den nesters, the otter has
altricial kits — that is, kits that are
born blind and helpless. Sea otter kits
have opened their eyes and are swimming at the age of 2 weeks, but the
small river otters remain blind until
the age of 3 weeks and do not swim
until they are 6 to 9 weeks old. It takes
two years for the pups to mature sexu-

ally and to disperse. The otters continue to grow for several years, however, with males eventually reaching a larger size than females.

Otters, both male and female, tend to establish separate territories, although competition among the males prevents many of them from holding a breeding territory until they are at least 5, and perhaps 7, years old.

Although the mother initially cares for the kits without assistance from the male, he may rejoin the female later to assist in raising the young. The otter family spends a lot of time in play, and their games are a means of teaching skills to the young and helping them to develop the coordination they will need for an independent life.

Otters, like all successful pursuit predators, are intelligent enough to catch and handle a wide variety of prey. Indeed, their ingenuity is sometimes remarkable. They have been known to punch holes in beaver dams, and then, as the waters in the beaver pond recede, they wade in to feast on the trapped fish and frogs. They are also fast and versatile: they dash after fish; they dig into the mud of the river bottom in search of crayfish, frogs and

salamanders; they launch submarine attacks on floating waterbirds; and they plunder birds' nests. The otter is also a fighter. It will follow a muskrat into its burrow and kill it, and it is one of the few animals that may be able to kill a beaver in its lodge. In winter, otters have been seen fishing for bluegills under the lake ice. When they seize one, they bring it to a hole and flip it out onto the ice where it can be consumed at leisure.

Few animals have the opportunity

*The river otter,* **top***, usually comes ashore to eat prey that it pursues underwater with its eyes open,* **above***.*

to prey on the swift, agile otter as it darts through the water. However, wolves and coyotes may sometimes surprise them and kill them on land.

The playful, social nature of young otters and their intelligence means that they are easily trained in captivity. Otters have even been used to catch fish for human consumption.

# *Sea Otter* Enhydra lutris

**Mammal:** *Enhydra lutris* — sea otter
**Meaning of Name:** *Enhydra* (otter), derived from *enhudro*, which means living in the water; *lutra* (otter)
**Description:** extremely well adapted to aquatic environment, so much so that it resembles the pinnipeds — short, weak limbs with completely webbed feet and long webbed toes forming long flippers; short, fleshy naked ear pinnae; brownish black with white-tipped guard hairs on the head and neck, giving it a grizzled appearance; paler on the throat, chest and head
**Total Length:** male, 4.2 to 5.5 feet; female, 3.5 to 4.2 feet
**Tail:** male,14.2 inches; female, 10.2 to 11 inches
**Weight:** male, 48.5 to 99.2 pounds; female, 33.1 to 70.5 pounds
**Gestation:** 6.5 to 9 months (probably delayed implantation)
**Litter Size:** 1 (can have young every year but probably do so at greater intervals)
**Age of Maturity:** male, capable at 5 to 6 years but probably not successful breeders until several years later; female, 4 years
**Longevity:** approximately 8 years
**Diet:** slow-moving fish, marine invertebrates such as sea urchin, abalone, crab, starfish, octopus and mollusks; eats some seaweed as well
**Habitat:** in seas off rocky reefs, inlets, rocky coasts and soft-sediment communities; rarely more than a half-mile from shore; rests on kelp beds and rocky shores
**Predators:** man, killer whale, sharks and bald eagle
**Dental Formula:** 3/2, 1/1, 3/3, 1/2 = 32 teeth

Sea otters are the largest and most completely aquatic of all mustelids. In fact, they are the most completely aquatic of all carnivores. Only seals and whales have adapted more completely to life in the watery world.

Sea otters are now found mostly in the richly productive inshore waters of the Pacific coast of North America, but they formerly ranged all around the northern Pacific rim, from Japan northward to the Bering Sea and Alaska all the way south to Baja California. Before the turn of the century, by which time overhunting had reduced them to a few tiny, isolated populations, the northern distribution was probably limited only by the ice pack, and the southern distribution by the low productivity of tropical waters. In recent years, sea otter populations have begun to recover, however, and there are now several thousand of them along the Pacific coast.

The sea otter has adapted very distinctively to its environment and is distinguished in a number of ways from terrestrial mustelids. For example, since chemical communication is of limited value in the ocean, the sea otter has lost the anal scent gland of other otters. Retractile claws in the forepaws are used for grabbing fish and shellfish that require extensive manipulation. Webbed hind feet with elongated toes act as flippers, and while these enable the otter to scull efficiently even while floating on its back, they also make it a very slow and

*The sea otter often carries a stone on its chest that is used as a tool for smashing open shellfish and sea urchins.*

awkward runner on land. The sea otter does not have a thick insulating layer of blubber to keep it warm. Rather, it depends on its thick fur coat — made up of as many as 800 million tightly packed hairs — to keep the water from touching its skin. The sea otter is also adapted for swimming underwater. It has small ears with valvelike flaps that keep the water out and a stout muscular tail to act as a rudder.

Sea otters tend to live in fairly shallow water, around 200 feet in depth, although they have been known to dive as deep as 300 feet. They feed mostly on bottom-dwelling mollusks and sea urchins, and their jaws and teeth have been massively adapted for crunching shells. When the shell is very hard, however, the otter resorts to tools. Floating on its back in the water, it places a shellfish on its chest and pounds at it with a rock until it breaks.

Abalone is one of the otter's favourite foods, as are crabs, squid, rock fish and clams. In fact, this animal's taste for abalone has resulted in conflict between sea otters and fishermen. After the sea otter was made extinct along the California coast, the abalone population expanded, and a new and lucrative fishery came into being. However, the otters are back now and competing with humans for the abalone.

Most of the life of the sea otter is lived in the water. They mate in the water, and the single pup that results is probably born in the water. In the southern part of the range, at least, pups can be born at any time of year. The newborn pup is somewhat more precocious than other mustelids, but still, it is unable to swim or dive before it reaches the age of 2 weeks. The mother provides all the parental care and carries the pup with her on her chest and back. The pup remains with the mother for roughly a year and depends on her for food for most of that time.

Sea otters are eaten by killer whales, sharks and possibly by bald eagles, but none of these predators is thought to exert a major effect on populations. In fact, even though hunting has ceased, it is still man who is the greatest threat to the sea otter. This time, the danger comes in the shape of major oil spills. Since oil reduces the insulative value of the fur, an oiled sea otter will die of cold within a day or two.

*Composed of 800 million tightly packed hairs, the sea otter's thick coat keeps water from touching its skin.*

## Community Control

*There are not many good things that can be said about the extermination of an animal population. Often, however, there is one benefit that arises from the carnage — and that is knowledge. In a few cases, extermination by overhunting and trapping has acted like a giant experiment through which ecologists are able to see and understand the role played by one species in its relationships with others. The sea otters have given scientists just this kind of opportunity.*

*Off the west coast of North America, there are two island chains — the Rat Islands and the Near Islands. The islands are similar in topography, both with the same rocky coast, set in the same sea, with the same climate. The Rat Islands have sheltered an abundant colony of sea otters for the last 30 years; otters were hunted out in the*

*Near Islands, however, and only very recently have a few animals reappeared there.*

*There is one other difference: the Rat Islands are surrounded by thick beds of kelp, and the Near Islands are not. Great underwater forests of the giant algae grow in the intertidal area of the Rat Islands out to a depth of some 250 feet, and they support a rich array of marine organisms. So thick are these stands of kelp that they also reduce wave action and water turbulence along the shores of the Rat Islands. The Near Islands have virtually no kelp to protect them and nourish life forms in the surrounding sea.*

*Sea urchins — which graze on kelp — make up much of the otter's diet. Where sea urchins are free from sea otter predation, as on the Near Islands, the ocean floor is literally carpeted with them. In fact, they have become so abundant there that they have grazed away and destroyed the kelp forest. On the Rat Islands, by way of contrast, the sea otters eat all the biggest sea urchins. Only the smaller shellfish remain, thinly scattered throughout the kelp.*

*Of course, there are disadvantages to the kelp. The reduced turbulence allows the settling of sediment, and bottom-dwellers such as mussels are buried and smothered. In the Near Islands, however, thick mussel beds and stands of barnacles have grown up, in the order of 1,000 for every square yard, compared with only 5 in the same area off the Rat Islands. Nevertheless, on the whole, the kelp forests are considered to be among the most biologically productive environments on Earth. For example, fish thrive there, and thus islands with sea otters and kelp are also rich in fish-eating seals and bald eagles. Needless to say, there are few seals and eagles at the Near Islands.*

*This is an example of an extremely simple community: otter eats sea urchin; sea urchin eats kelp; kelp supports invertebrates; seals and eagles eat invertebrates. In more complex communities, however, the web of ecological interaction is less straightforward. No one can guess in advance with any certainty what impact the elimination of one species will have on the others.*

# *Cats* Felidae

Cats are the most specialized of all carnivores. This means that adaptations to teeth and claws have been taken to their most extreme development as aids for the capture and devouring of meat. Large canine teeth and reduced molars allow the cat, when it has stalked its prey and seized it, to kill with a single lethal bite.

The most extreme and ferocious examples of feline killers were once the sabre-, scimitar- and dirk-toothed cats, and these have been extinct since the last Ice Age. The sabre-toothed tiger was as large as the lions that roamed the plains of Canada and the United States until some 10,000 years ago and are now found only in Africa. These cats preyed on slow-moving herbivores, using their long, flattened canines like daggers. These knifelike blades were more than 8 inches long in some species and had serrated edges for severing tendons, muscles and arteries in the neck of their prey. Most of the ancient cats had long necks to facilitate striking and long forelimbs to reach up and grapple with the animals they attacked.

The large herbivores — the mammoths, mastodons, camels and horses — became extinct in North America at the end of the last Ice Age, though some of them survived in altered form in Africa and Asia. Their disappearance from the western hemisphere also meant the end of the large cats, at least on this continent. The largest surviving cat worldwide is the Siberian tiger, which weighs as much as 850 pounds. Its teeth are not as specialized as those of the species that became extinct, so it was able to vary its diet and to survive the disappearance of giant game.

Similarly, in North America, the cats that survived were the less specialized ones, such as the puma, bobcat and lynx, which eat smaller prey. Unlike the mustelids or the canids, the felines show little diversity of form, and all of the surviving cats have a catlike appearance. This reflects a uniformity in the way they move and hunt and what they eat. Cat species differ primarily in body size, habitat and range of prey.

Cats are not long-distance runners like the canids. Some of them are extremely fast sprinters, however — the cheetah, over distances under a mile, is the fastest land mammal on Earth. The paws and claws of the cat are therefore distinctively designed not for running but for climbing trees and attacking prey. Three-quarters of the world's cats live in forests, and most species — even those that hunt in the savanna, are able to climb trees. Thus cats have retractable claws that can be extended to grip bark or to claw prey. When cats are on the move, the claws are withdrawn into the paw so that a cat print looks very different from that of a dog. Only in the cheetah, a species specialized for running over grasslands, have the claws become incompletely retractive and somewhat doglike.

Cats also have relatively short muzzles compared with canids and a reduced nasal cavity. This allows a cat to breathe as it bites and buries its teeth into the neck and throat of its prey.

Cats are distinguished by a remarkable sense of balance that allows them to climb trees and to leap and twist through the air. A cat, as the saying goes, always lands on its feet. It is not only the supple body and fine coordination that allow this graceful orientation but a kind of gyroscope in the inner ear. As the cat twists through the air, the sensitive inner ear directs the brain and neck muscles to pull the head into a horizontal position, and the rest of the body follows suit.

Most cats hunt at night and have large eyes and acute vision. In bright daylight, cats see just as well as humans; in the dark, however, their eyes are six times as sensitive as ours. The bright shine of cat eyes caught in the beam of car headlights is caused by reflection off a membrane — the tapetum lucidum — at the back of the eyeball. This membrane catches any light not absorbed by the retina and bounces it back into the eye so that it can be read again. Cats have huge irises, which open at night to let in the maximum amount of light; during the day, the irises close to cat's-eye slits to protect the sensitive retina. The cat's whiskers are also adapted for night hunting, and they serve as sense organs to guide the animal around obstructions. The cat's hearing is as sensitive as our own, but smaller cats — like dogs — are able to hear a range of high-pitched sounds to which we are deaf. This aids them in locating rodents and insectivores that use ultrasound for hunting communication.

Cats rely on a combination of vision, hearing and smell to find their prey, but after an animal has been identified and located by sound or scent, and after the cat has stalked it or set up an ambush, it is the eyes that guide the final attack.

Most cats, except for lions and male cheetahs, are solitary hunters, eating only those animals that they can subdue alone. This limits the size of their

*With large canine teeth and reduced molars, cats such as this puma kill prey by slipping their teeth between the victim's vertebrae and severing its spinal cord.*

prey to animals of roughly the predator's size or slightly larger. The large cats are an exception, and they use specialized killing techniques to take grazers much heavier than themselves. They are the only carnivores able to do so.

Most cat attacks follow the same pattern. The cat slink-runs toward its prey, holding its body close to the ground and moving quickly. The cat then freezes to watch its prey, assessing its vulnerability. Even as the otherwise motionless cat watches, the tail twitches back and forth, and it may knead the ground with its feet. Then it may slink-run again or step slowly forward in a low crouch. Finally, the cat rushes forward, still crouched, to launch its final attack.

While anchoring itself firmly to the ground with its hind legs, the cat seizes the prey by the forequarters and delivers a killing bite to the animal's neck, just behind the head. The sharp canine teeth slip between the spinal vertebrae to sever the spinal cord, and the hunt is over. On larger prey, especially those with horns, the bite may be delivered to the throat so as to sever the windpipe, and the animal suffocates. Cats that eat smaller prey, such as birds, use their forepaws to bat and scoop the prey toward them before they kill it.

Of the 35 species of cat found throughout the world, 28 are small tropical cats, and these have the most diverse feeding habits of all. They eat not only small mammals and birds but also frogs, insects, snails, turtles and fish.

Even the smallest cats are formidable predators, able to kill species larger than themselves. They feed high in the food chain, and like all top-level carnivores, they demand a lot of room for their hunting activities and tend to have a dispersed distribution. They also defend their territories tooth and claw. Few species of cat — except for lions and cheetahs — belong to complex societies. As every cat owner knows, a cat likes to go its own way.

## Why Eat Meat?

At first glance, vegetarians seem to have it all over the carnivores. To begin with, their food grows all around them, and it does not run away or kick or claw in self-defence;

The specialized hunting techniques of this puma enable it to bring down deer and other big game.

an obligate carnivore spends its whole waking life trying to find enough meat to live. And when it does find its prey, there follows a demandingly energetic chase, often followed by a dangerous battle during which the hunter may be kicked, clawed, bitten or otherwise injured. The obvious question is, why bother?

The answer is that plants are not as defenceless as they look: many of them contain toxins that are indigestible by most mammals and that, in effect, act as biochemical weaponry. For example, the caffeine found in coffee and various other plants, or the nicotine of tobacco, are natural insecticides that will upset the metabolism of most mammals. People use modest amounts of sage in cooking because they like the strong and aromatic essential oils; in nature, however, these oils poison the vital gut bacteria of horses and other grazers.

Literally thousands of these defensive plant compounds exist. Herbivores deal with them somewhat by grazing selectively, but their bodies have also had to evolve sophisticated enzymes to break down and excrete toxins. Caribou and squirrels, for example, can eat the Amanita *mushroom that poisons a human being, but they pay a high*

physiological price for the manufacture of these enzymes.

Meat acts as a filter, and thus carnivores do not need to produce such costly protective enzymes. They eat meat that is free of poison, and because it is almost identical to their own body in composition, it is easy to digest and to convert into useful compounds.

The nutrient content of plants is low, and most of their energy is bound up in hard-to-digest cellulose and lignin molecules. Herbivores must enlist the services of bacteria to break down much of the woody material of plants, and they typically have huge stomach sacs where these processes are carried out. The carnivore's stomach and gut is, by comparison, small and compact.

The lack of mineral salts in vegetation is another problem that confronts herbivores, and they have to search long and hard for plants with a high salt content. That is why flocks of wild sheep and herds of cattle are often seen congregating at rare salt licks. Carnivores are much more fortunate in getting trace elements of minerals directly from meat.

Meat may be relatively scarce and hard to catch, but many species have found that the pursuit pays off.

## *Bobcat* Lynx rufus

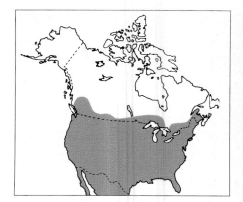

**Mammal:** *Lynx rufus* — bobcat
**Meaning of Name:** *Lynx* (lamp, to see) describes the animal's bright eyes and keen sight; *rufus* (reddish) describes the general coloration of the body
**Description:** coat is tawny brown above with numerous black spots, especially along the midline from the head to the base of the tail; tip of the tail is blackish above and white below, with subterminal black bars; underparts are white with black spots; tawny limbs have black horizontal bars on them; a prominent streaked ruff on each cheek extends down the side to below the lower jaw; short blackish ear tufts
**Total Length:** male, 2.5 to 4.1 feet; female, 2.5 to 3.1 feet
**Tail:** male, 5.1 to 6.7 inches; female, 5 to 6.5 inches
**Weight:** male, 14.1 to 40.3 pounds; female, 9 to 33.7 pounds
**Gestation:** 50 to 70 days
**Litter Size:** 2 to 5 (usually 3); in southern part of range, 2 litters per year
**Age of Maturity:** female, 1 year but does not mate until second year
**Longevity:** 12 to 14 years in the wild; maximum in captivity has been 32 years 4 months
**Diet:** primarily a small-game predator (rabbits, rodents and birds); larger prey such as deer are occasionally taken; also eats reptiles, insects and snails; will eat untainted carrion
**Habitat:** hardwood forests, mountainous areas, semideserts, brushland, rocky hillsides and swamps; occupies agricultural lands and the outskirt of cities; only requirement is woody cover
**Predators:** puma, coyote, wolf and man
**Dental Formula:** 3/3, 1/1, 2/2, 1/1 = 28 teeth

The bobcat is the slightly smaller southern counterpart of the lynx. Since it lacks the long legs, very wide feet and long ear tufts that make the lynx such an admirable winter hunter, it tends to prefer less snowy terrain. Its fur has a distinctively mottled pattern that disguises it in the brushy scrubland where it is commonly found.

Lynx and bobcat do not share the same territory. Where bobcats have been introduced into the range of the lynx — as on Cape Breton Island — they have tended to segregate, with the bobcats gravitating to the low coastal areas where winter snows are light and the lynx moving up into the snowy highlands.

What snowshoe hare is to lynx, cottontail rabbit is to bobcat — that is, the most important element of its diet and the basis of its prosperity. However, the bobcat is much less specialized than the lynx, both in terms of food and habitat. Bobcats are found everywhere from the dry deserts of the southwestern United States well into the cold boreal forests, the wet bogs and the mountain meadows of the north. However, bobcats do not thrive in deep snow, and they prefer rough terrain with rocky caves and ledges for their dens. Nevertheless, where these are lacking, they are flexible enough to set up housekeeping in dense, protective clumps of brush.

*Bobcats' flexibility in prey and habitat selection has allowed their populations to expand when most other cat populations are declining.*

Bobcats eat mostly rabbits and hares, but they supplement their diet with large numbers of birds and small mammals, and occasionally, they prey on young white-tailed deer and pronghorn antelope. Rabbits are commonly ambushed as they pass along well-travelled game runs, while deer are usually attacked when they have bedded down. There are records, however, of the bobcat leaping down on its prey from tree limbs. It is the flexibility of the bobcat, both in terms of food and habitat, that has allowed this species to increase its range at a time when most other cat populations are declining.

The social behaviour of the bobcat is similar to that of the lynx, especially when it comes to territoriality. There is one record of a female bobcat killing a juvenile, apparently a trespasser on her home range. She killed the intruder and ate it.

The breeding of bobcats follows the pattern of other solitary cats. Males are polygynous, offering no parental care, and they drive other males away from the oestrous female. Sometimes, several males will contest for one female, and many bobcats wear battle scars from the breeding season.

# Lynx Lynx canadensis

**Mammal:** *Lynx canadensis* — lynx
**Meaning of Name:** *Lynx* (lamp, to see) describes the animal's bright eyes and keen sight; *canadensis* (of Canada)
**Description:** prominent ruff around face; pointed ears are tipped with long pencils of black hairs; colouring can be fawn, yellow-orange or blue tone; guard hairs give the coat a frosted appearance; underparts are buffy; short tail with black tip; black stripes on forehead and around facial ruff; large feet have dense growth of coarse hairs during winter
**Total Length:** male, 2.5 to 3.5 feet; female, 2.5 to 3.2 feet
**Tail:** male, 2 to 5.5 inches; female, 3 to 4.8 inches
**Weight:** male, 14.8 to 37.9 pounds; female, 11.2 to 25.6 pounds
**Gestation:** 60 to 65 days
**Litter Size:** 1 to 5 (usually 2 or 3)
**Age of Maturity:** male, 33 months; female, 21 months
**Longevity:** up to 24 years in captivity
**Diet:** rabbits and hares form major part of diet, especially snowshoe hares; also rodents, birds, fish, deer and other ungulates; carrion is an important winter food
**Habitat:** primarily in dense climax forests with heavy undergrowth; may range into mountains, rocky areas, tundra and the edge of the Arctic prairie
**Predators:** man, coyote, wolf; large owls and eagles will prey on kittens
**Dental Formula:** 3/3, 1/1, 2/2, 1/1 = 28 teeth

The lynx is an animal that has adapted very precisely to a particular environment — namely, the boreal forest. More accurately, it has adapted to the snowshoe hare that lives there. The lynx is an active, mobile predator that hunts successfully throughout the long, dark winters of the North. Indeed, studies show that the lynx's hunting efficiency actually increases in winter. This it owes to a number of very special adaptations.

The lynx has wide furry paws that act like snowshoes to distribute its weight over the snow and long legs to carry it unimpeded through the deep white powder. The fine, thick fur of its coat has a soft grey-brown colour that fades into the gloomy forest colours. Sounds are muffled in the snow-choked forests, and it is thought that the lynx's long ear tufts amplify sound. The tail is short so that it does not drag in the snow.

The lynx, although it is able to kill animals as large as deer and will also eat smaller mammals and birds, prefers to prey on the snowshoe hare whenever it is available. In fact, the prosperity of the lynx is so intimately linked to that of the snowshoe hare that it shares with it a 10-year cycle of boom and bust. The increase in the number of hares is closely followed by an increase in the number of lynx; then, as the hares deplete their food resources and begin to dwindle, the lynx also decline.

During the low part of the hare's population cycle, the number of lynx

*The wide furry paws of the lynx act like snowshoes, making it an extremely efficient predator in deep snow and allowing it to kill animals as large as deer and moose.*

pregnancies drops, and the survival rate of kittens plummets. This is a pattern that is as old as the lynx itself and it is not inherently dangerous to either species. That was true, at least until man entered the picture. Now, trapping and loss of habitat mean that high mortality rates among lynx during the low part of the cycle may prevent them from rebounding to take advantage of subsequent hare abundance. Therefore, lynx populations are newly vulnerable and have declined in the last century, with each 10-year peak being lower than the one before it.

Fur-trading records of the Hudson's Bay Company dating back some 200 years show that in peak years, lynx used to be 70 times as abundant as in low years; now, the rebound brings them to a level only six times higher than the low point. Wildlife biologists are now seeking a trapping moratorium during the low part of the lynx cycle, but high fur prices at times of low abundance — perhaps as much as $1,000 for a single pelt — provide a strong economic incentive to the contrary. Thus the lynx, like many spotted cats of the tropics, is threatened by the luxury-fur trade.

Another problem confronting the lynx is human settlement and the

*Lynx kittens learn hunting techniques from their mother.*

clearing of forests. The lynx, if it is to find enough food to sustain itself, must have a large home range. In fact, recent studies in Manitoba established that each lynx ranges through 60 to 85 square miles. Researchers were forced to conclude that even Riding Mountain National Park in southern Manitoba — all 1,136 square miles of it — was ''not large enough to sustain a viable lynx population over time.''

Some lynx move considerable distances — one, for example, moved 300 miles before being trapped. It is possible, therefore, that some lynx will migrate from overcrowded areas to those where there is more room and better food. But lynx will not cross large areas of cleared land, so it would be difficult for them to recolonize many of the areas from which they have been eliminated.

Lynx are shy, solitary animals. Except for the female with kittens, they do not hunt together. They breed once a year, in spring, and the female produces a litter of from one to five kittens, which she raises without assistance from the male. The den site is primitive, often a simple crevice hidden in the brush or in a hollow log. The young stay with the mother until she is ready to mate again the following year. The young may also breed that year, especially if it is a time of abundant snowshoe hares.

The social relationships of lynx are not clear. Some researchers report that males exclude other males from their territory yet tolerate females; other scientists report the opposite pattern. It may be that the territoriality of the lynx varies with the abundance of prey and that several home ranges may overlap in times of plenty.

The lynx has few natural enemies, though wolves may kill a lynx if they catch it in the open and wolverine may drive it away from a kill. Some lynx have even been injured by deer that lacerate them with sharp hooves.

## *Puma* Felis concolor

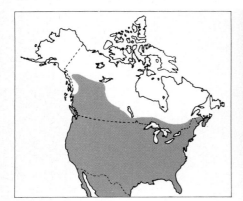

**Mammal:** *Felis concolor* — puma, cougar, mountain lion, panther

**Meaning of Name:** *Felis* (cat); *concolor* (of the same colour)

**Description:** distinct long tail; adult colour varies from reddish tawny to tawny grey to chocolate brown; darker on the mid-dorsal line; belly is pale buff; chest and throat are white; backs of ears, tip of tail and stripes on muzzle are black; pink nose pad is bordered by black, which extends to the lips; a vertical black stripe over each eye disappears with old age

**Total Length:** male, 5.5 to 9 feet; female, 5 to 7.5 feet

**Tail:** male, 26 to 35.4 inches; female, 20.9 to 32.3 inches

**Weight:** male, 147.7 to 227.1 pounds; female, 79.4 to 132.3 pounds

**Gestation:** 90 to 96 days

**Litter Size:** 1 to 6 (usually 3 or 4)

**Age of Maturity:** male, 3 years; female, 2 to 3 years (do not breed successfully until situated in a home area)

**Longevity:** 8 years or more in the wild; 19 years in captivity

**Diet:** carnivore; deer is most consistently important food; also eats other large cervids and bovids, porcupine, beaver, snowshoe hare, mice, squirrel, muskrat and raccoon; occasionally preys on domestic stock and even eats fish and snails

**Habitat:** highly adaptive; occupies a variety of habitats from swamps and wooded river valleys and lowlands to dense coniferous forests and high mountains; basic requirements include some woody cover and an abundant supply of prey animals, especially members of the deer family

**Predators:** man is major predator; young may be attacked by larger carnivores, eagles and large hawks (male pumas will eat kittens too)

**Dental Formula:** 3/3, 1/1, 3/2, 1/1 = 30 teeth

The puma (also known as cougar and panther) is now commonly called a mountain lion — an undeserved name and one that reflects only the very recent and much reduced range of this great cat. For the puma, still found in remote mountainous terrain from Tierra del Fuego to the Yukon, used to range from east to west in North America, in every kind of habitat, wherever the deer and elk were found. The eastern populations have long since been hunted and poisoned out of existence, and only a few small, isolated populations in Florida and the prairies testify to the onetime range of the puma.

Only a careful, deliberate reintro-

*The puma often waits motionless for hours in a tree above a game trail and then drops down onto the back of a passing deer, elk or moose.*

duction would reestablish the puma populations in the east, but no public outcry has so far been heard, and the government has taken no action. Perhaps there is an element of fear in the reluctance to promote this feline, for pumas grow to a great size. The heaviest on record is the 220-pound cat shot by Teddy Roosevelt, but it is believed that many individuals grow much larger.

Although pumas are shy, secretive animals, they can be very dangerous

to humankind. Starving cats have been known to maul humans, and they will often prey on livestock within their range. Ordinarily, however, they tend to prey on deer, and it is here that they come into direct competition with man. The deer-hunting lobby strongly resists programmes that may result in fewer deer for them to shoot or less area for them to hunt. Yet the demands of the puma are large: a single cat requires a range of 40 to 200 square miles. That means that a huge hunting reserve would have to be set aside if a viable, self-sustaining population of pumas were to be reintroduced in the east. Public education would be basic to the success of such a programme.

Western populations are still subject to hunting pressure, although every state and province regulates it in some way. However, the biggest threat to the puma comes not from the hunter's gun but from habitat destruction that follows in the wake of agriculture, forestry, mining and virtually any

*An appetite for big-game animals has brought the puma into conflict with human sport hunters.*

other form of human development.

The puma's diet, principally deer, elk and moose, tends to be very selective, and they can only survive in areas that support these large herbivores. However, the puma will turn to porcupines, beaver and other small mammals when big game is scarce. In fact, the porcupine is a fairly common prey of the puma. It probably flips the porcupine with its paw, stunning it, and then bites into the unprotected underside. It cannot be an easy skill to learn, and young pumas are known to have died from porcupine quill wounds.

The home range of the puma shifts with the season and the availability of food. In summer, the ranges are larger and tend to expand as the elk and deer migrate to higher summer grazing lands. In winter, the ranges contract as the deer move down into

sheltered valleys. Males have larger ranges that tend to overlap those of several females.

The larger size of the male and the larger range are tied to polygynous breeding biology, since males will fight each other for breeding rights. Like all cats, resident breeding males mark their territories. The puma does this with urine and excrement and by scraping the soil where debris is piled and marking it with scent from a gland in the foot pad. Males also rake the trees with their forepaws, just as the domestic cat does.

Female pumas do not come into heat at a given time, and oestrus appears to be controlled by the abundance of food. This means that the males, if they are to mate, must be consistently vigilant. In cats, ovulation is induced by copulation, and the first male that copulates with a female is the father of her offspring. Copulation lasts less than a minute but may take place several times during the daylong period of female oestrus.

The female bears her kittens in a simple den, perhaps in a rocky cave or under a fallen tree in the dense brush. The one to five kittens are weaned at 4 to 5 weeks of age, but they may stay with their mother for as long as two years — the length of time necessary for them to learn the complicated hunting techniques that they will need for survival. They have to learn how to deliver a fast, efficient killing bite while they avoid being kicked, gored or dragged and smacked into tree limbs by their fleeing prey. It is not uncommon for pumas to be killed by their prey. Young, inexperienced adults and pumas that are too old and weak to pursue their natural prey will kill livestock.

The young animals disperse after two years but do not breed until they are 3 years old.

Females often have to defend their cubs from male pumas, particularly when a new male takes over the range of another cat. If the new resident is able to kill the cubs that were fathered by the other male, the female will come into oestrus sooner.

# RODENTS Rodentia

Rodents have chewed, chiselled and gnawed their way to the top of all the mammal orders so that today, they form the most populous mammal group. Nearly 40 percent of all mammalian species are rodents; they are found in almost every terrestrial habitat on every continent. All rodents are fairly similar in design. They have small bodies, but they owe their biological success to their chisel-like, perpetually growing incisors.

Rodent classification is largely based on their gnawing and chewing abilities. Different families of rodents have developed different dental, skull and muscle patterns according to how and what they eat. They are basically vegetarians and can gnaw through the toughest tree bark and crack open the hardest nuts with their teeth. The sharp cutting edge of their incisors is formed by the chewing motion itself. A hard enamel layer, which is often increased by red and orange iron compounds, coats the front of these teeth. But the back portion is soft and uncoated. As the rodent gnaws, the back of the tooth wears away faster than the front, a process that forms the tooth edge into a sharp chisel.

To make gnawing easier, rodents can pull their lips out of the way of their sharp incisors. They have a large gap between these teeth and their molars, and they curl their lips backward into this gap while chewing. This behaviour also permits the rodent to exclude such unwanted debris as wood, nut hulls and soil from its diet.

Rodents' molars are also highly specialized, although the type of specialization varies among species. In some rodents, the molars grind with a complicated but efficient rotary action, enabling them to chew hard plant products. In others, the molars as well as the incisors are renewed by constant growth.

The earliest known rodents were squirrel-like creatures called *sciuromorphs* that lived more than 50 million years ago. They were apparently less efficient at gnawing and chewing than are their descendants. For example, they had weakly developed jaw muscles (known as masseters) and so could not pull the lower jaw forward effectively. By comparison, such rodents as the guinea pig of the Caviomorpha family have much larger masseters for more efficient gnawing. Mouselike rodents, the Myomorpha, have the largest masseters of all and are, consequently, the most efficient gnawers of the three basic rodent groups.

The fossil record indicates that rodents have recently experienced an explosive diversification. Unlike many of the large mammal groups, they have suffered few extinctions, and their evolution into different species has been so rapid and extensive that the classification of rodents remains unclear.

*The most populous of any mammal group, rodents, such as the beaver, owe their biological success to their chisel-like, perpetually growing incisors, which allow them to exploit tough tree bark and other difficult-to-eat vegetation.*

# *Mountain Beaver* Aplodontidae

## *Mountain Beaver* Aplodontia rufa

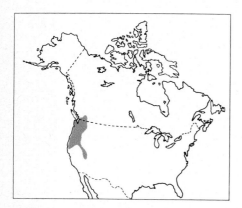

**Mammal:** *Aplodontia rufa* — mountain beaver
**Meaning of Name:** *Aplodontia* refers to simple cheek teeth; *rufa* (red or ruddy)
**Description:** stout; small rounded ears, short legs and plantigrade feet with fleshy soles and long claws; coarse, dark blackish brown coat; no apparent tail
**Total Length:** male, 13.2 to 14.9 inches; female, 13.8 to 14.1 inches
**Tail:** male, 1.2 to 1.4 inches; female, 0.9 to 1.3 inches
**Weight:** 2 to 3.3 pounds
**Gestation:** 28 to 30 days
**Litter Size:** 2 to 6 (usually 3); 1 litter per year
**Age of Maturity:** 2 years or older
**Longevity:** 5 to 10 years in the wild
**Diet:** strictly herbivorous; summer, forbs and deciduous plants; winter, bark, twigs, needles and leaves; reingests special green feces
**Habitat:** dense, wet thickets and forests; often found in initial seral stages after a forest has been clear-cut
**Predators:** puma, lynx, coyote, fox, wolf, bear, skunk, mink, fisher, weasel, eagle, hawks and owls
**Dental Formula:** 1/1, 0/0, 2/1, 3/3 = 22 teeth

The sole surviving species of this ancient rodent family, the mountain beaver is one of the world's most primitive living rodents. The mountain beaver's family originated some 50 to 65 million years ago in North America and spread to Europe and Asia. At that time, there were several different genera within the family, but all except the mountain beaver became extinct. This may have happened because of the species' need for moist habitats, which became scarce during the dry episodes of the Tertiary period.

Aside from the fact that both are rodents, mountain beavers are not related to the common beaver. They are terrestrial animals found only in the mild, moist forests of the Pacific coast.

The mountain beaver requires a wet environment because it cannot efficiently regulate its body moisture or its cooling system. At temperatures above 84 degrees F, it begins to suffer heat stress, and if the temperature goes as high as 90 to 95 degrees, it will die within two hours.

The mountain beaver cannot cope with drought either. Its kidneys are primitive in design, and consequently, the mountain beaver excretes a large volume of water in its urine.

*Aplodontia rufa*, however, does have several behaviours that enable it to overcome problems of heat stress and water conservation. For example, it constructs extensive systems of underground burrows and runways, which provide it with a cool, stable and humid environment. The tunnels of an individual may encompass an area 100 yards in diameter.

The mountain beaver is a vegetarian and meets its water needs from the great variety of succulent plants it consumes. Exiting from its tunnel, it harvests grasses, twigs and shrubs, then drags them back into its burrow to eat. This behaviour further reduces possible environmental stress and minimizes the animal's exposure to predators. The mountain beaver climbs trees to clip off branches and twigs, and it also makes hay piles. Both fresh and wilted vegetation are cached in the central feeding chamber. As much as a bushel of material may be stored in this chamber, enabling the mountain beaver to spend virtually all of autumn and winter below ground.

Mountain beavers have a unique defecation system: they extract each dung pellet with their teeth as it emerges from the anus, then store them in piles in special chambers. Like rabbits and pikas, they eat some of this dung — presumably to extract nutrients such as the B vitamins produced by microbial fermentation.

The mountain beaver's slow speed makes it easy prey for a wide variety of predators including wolves, coyotes, weasels, hawks and owls. Given the beaver's penchant for living in loose soils, even bears find them readily available with a bit of digging.

*One of the world's most primitive rodents, the mountain beaver is found only in the mild, moist forests of the west coast.*

# Squirrels *Sciuridae*

Squirrels must count as the most familiar of animals. Every continent, except Australia, is home to a rich array of squirrels. Squirrels are often active in daylight; they frequently live in large, conspicuous colonies and are tolerant of the presence of humans. In tropical regions and in the grasslands and open habitats of temperate areas, squirrels are often the dominant mammals. Many people rarely see other common small mammals, such as shrews, bats, mice and moles, but almost everyone is acquainted with some kind of squirrel.

Squirrels have very generalized features that have enabled them to spread into a wide variety of habitats and to develop numerous species. They first appeared some 30 million years ago in North America but soon spread to the Old World where they radiated in Africa and Southeast Asia.

There are three basic groups of squirrels: ground squirrels, arboreal, or tree-dwelling, squirrels and nocturnal flying squirrels. Ground squirrels are diurnal and tend to live in colonies that often have highly developed social systems. Almost all of them are seed eaters and grazers. Tree squirrels are also diurnal but usually live solitary, territorial lives. They feed largely on nuts and fruit.

Of all the small mammals, squirrels have the largest brains relative to their body size. This is reflected in their diverse diets, complicated vocalizations and tendency to develop complex social systems. Squirrels are among the most intelligent of rodents.

## Territorial Economics

*Some species of squirrels are aggressively territorial, others are not. During the breeding season, some males may exclude other males; pregnant and lactating females tend to exclude all intruders. In some species, territorial exclusivity may even extend beyond the reproductive period and is probably related to defence of foraging territories and food caches.*

*Although territoriality has its benefits — a secure food pile and mating area — it also has it costs. As squirrels battle for territory, they expose themselves to predators and expend great amounts of energy. Territoriality can only evolve when the benefits exceed the costs.*

*Among the western chipmunk species, territoriality depends on such factors as habitat, food supply and climate. The alpine chipmunk is strongly territorial, primarily because the foraging season is short and food is limited. With a territory of boulder fields, where rocks and crevices offer ready refuge from predators, the dangers of an alpine chipmunk's territory defence are relatively low. The yellow pine chipmunk, which lives lower down in the pine forest, is also strongly territorial and can safely defend a rich nut crop in an area with abundant cover from predators.*

*In contrast to these species, the least chipmunk is not territorial at all. It lives in hot, dry habitats where the cost of territorial chases and disputes is physiologically high. It is active only during the cool of early morning and probably has little time for defensive disputes. The lodgepole pine chipmunk is also nonterritorial. Presumably, it could defend nut trees like the yellow pine chipmunk does, but in its habitat, there is little protective shrubbery for hiding from predators. Defending nut trees would probably result in a high predation rate.*

*Similar observations on the costs and benefits of territoriality have been made for red squirrels. In the central and northern parts of their range, these squirrels are aggressively territorial. But where they overlap in the south with grey squirrels, their territorial system breaks down. The larger grey squirrels do not respond to their aggressive behaviour, making territoriality a waste of time and energy for the red squirrel. Douglas' squirrels stop their territoriality when the pollen-rich male Douglas fir cones are ready for harvesting. These cones last only a few weeks and do not store well; also, there are so many cones available at that time, there is no benefit in defending a tree. The most economical tactic is simply to keep quiet and eat as many of the cones as possible.*

*With broad appetites, a high degree of intelligence and generalized body plans, members of the Sciuridae family, such as this red squirrel, rank among the most successful of rodents.*

# *Groundhog* Marmota monax

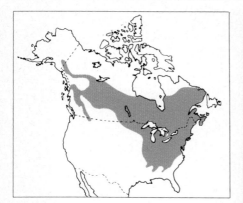

**Mammal:** *Marmota monax* —
groundhog, woodchuck
**Meaning of Name:** *Marmota* (mountain
mouse or rat); *monax* (solitary);
woodchuck is a corruption of an Indian
name used by trappers in northern
Canada
**Description:** heavy-bodied and short-
legged; buffy tips on guard hairs give the
animal a grizzled appearance; the colour
is highly variable and contains a number
of shades from pale buff to black; bushy
dark brown or black tail; black or dark
brown feet
**Total Length:** 18 to 25.7 inches
**Tail:** 4.1 to 6.4 inches
**Weight:** 4.9 to 14 pounds
**Gestation:** 31 to 33 days
**Litter Size:** 1 to 9 (usually 4); 1 litter per
year
**Age of Maturity:** may breed as
yearlings, but most breed for the first
time as 2-year-olds
**Longevity:** 4 to 6 years in the wild;
10 years in captivity
**Diet:** primarily a grazer; eats vegetative
parts of plants, bark and twigs if no
green leaves available; fond of fruits
and vegetables; consumes a few
insects and young birds of ground-
nesting species
**Habitat:** well-drained open woods,
pastures, fields, clearings and rocky
ravines; the deforestation of eastern
North America has helped it to prosper
**Predators:** hawks and rattlesnakes eat
young; bobcat, coyote, fox and domestic
dog are only predators that have not
been exterminated in its range
**Dental Formula:** 1/1, 0/0, 2/1, 3/3 = 22
teeth

Marmots are the largest of the North American squirrels. Unlike other groups of squirrels, the five species of marmots are grazers.

The groundhog, or woodchuck, is an eastern marmot species. It is the most widely distributed and best known of all the marmots. Like other marmots, the groundhog has a large, thickset body adapted for digging deep burrows. Its limbs are short and stout, and it has a short tail and a neck that is as thick and wide as its head. Its jaws and incisors are large and power-ful, adapted for cutting down large volumes of vegetation. Since wood-chucks are grazers, they prefer open areas and forest edges rather than the closed-canopy mature forests that are home to other squirrels. By clearing the eastern forests, humans have turned the woodchuck from a rela-tively uncommon animal into one of the most common.

Woodchucks are diurnal, foraging early in the morning and in late after-noon, especially on sunny days. Colder days find them most active when the sun reaches its peak. Some-times, they climb fenceposts or small trees where they sprawl across a high branch to sun themselves. At other times, they sit up at their main burrow entrance, watching alertly for preda-tors and competitor groundhogs.

*Heavyset, with strong forelimbs, the groundhog is built for digging extensive burrows that can be up to 50 feet in length and 16 feet deep.*

Groundhogs run for their burrow at the slightest hint of danger. Their bur-row is a fortress and may have 50 feet of tunnels running as deep as 16 feet underground. Each burrow has a main entrance, which the groundhog selects for its view of the surrounding area. There may be three or four al-ternative entrances, which provide both access and exit when the wood-chuck is chased by a predator. One of these entrances is usually a plunge hole with a vertical drop of more than 2 feet. A groundhog that is being chased can drop quickly down this hole and disappear. Normally, the plunge hole is inconspicuous and does not have a large pile of dirt around it — two factors that increase its effectiveness as an unexpected es-cape route.

All of the larger carnivorous mam-mals and raptors will eat groundhogs if given the opportunity. When cor-nered, the groundhog is a formidable biter. Its large incisors can slice flesh with ease. Most predators, therefore, rely on stalking to catch the ground-hog unaware. Stealthy hunters, such as foxes, coyotes and bobcats, take

*One of the largest of the deep hibernators, the groundhog usually spends winter in a dormant sleep living off its store of body fat but can awaken to search for food.*

more groundhogs than other predators do. It is too dangerous and too energy-intensive for predators to attempt to dig a groundhog out of its burrow.

Woodchucks may build two dens: a deep one for wintering that is located within the shelter of the forest and a shallow summer one situated in open areas close to foraging. The benefits of having two burrows seem to outweigh the extra energy required to dig them. With its summer home close to forage, the woodchuck spends less energy travelling to and from its food source and also has a quick escape route from predators. Its deep winter burrow keeps it warmer, thus reducing the energy output required for hibernating.

The groundhog is a true deep hibernator. It accumulates fat all summer long until shorter autumn days and foliage-killing frosts send it down into its burrow where it becomes dormant. It hibernates in a sealed chamber situated below the frost line. In deep hibernation, its body temperature drops from the normal summer temperature of 95 degrees F to 43 to 46 degrees. Its

heartbeat slows from 100 per minute to 15 per minute, and its oxygen consumption falls to one-tenth the normal rate. The woodchuck may breathe only once every six minutes when it is in deep hibernation. Hibernating animals lose 30 percent of their weight by burning off body fat to keep from freezing. This is a large weight loss, but it is only one-seventh the amount of energy used over the same time period by active animals. Hibernation is, therefore, an effective way to pass the winter, and it frees groundhogs from having to store food as do nonhibernating squirrels.

Groundhogs and other marmots are able to hibernate partly because of their large size. They may weigh as much as 14 pounds at full size, which gives them a slower metabolism than that of smaller rodents. The larger the animal, the longer it can last on the same percentage of body fat. This is clearly seen by comparing the overwinter weight loss in groundhogs of different ages and sizes. First-year groundhogs normally lose 50 percent of their body weight during hibernation and are probably severely stressed by springtime. Older and larger groundhogs may lose only a quarter of their body weight and so emerge from hibernation in much better condition.

Their large size and their need to endure the long winter hibernation may explain groundhogs' prolonged

growth period. Unlike most other squirrels, which reach adult size at the end of their first summer, groundhogs continue to grow for three years and usually do not reproduce until their second year.

The territorial nature of groundhogs may also have contributed to their larger size. Groundhogs defend their burrows and foraging areas from other groundhogs. They are normally solitary creatures except during the spring mating season when females will tolerate males. Males may fight with other males and often bear head wounds from bites. Groundhogs have a wide range of aggressive signals including hisses, growls, shrieks and teeth chattering.

Females give birth in spring to a litter of one to nine helpless offspring. They are weaned six weeks later, but they may remain with the mother until late summer, when they disperse to find their own territory. Females may sometimes stay with their mother until the next year, following a pattern similar to that of other ground squirrels. A daughter that inherits the maternal burrow is freed from having to expend the energy required in such extensive excavating.

Empty burrows are quickly occupied by other groundhogs or used by rabbits, skunks, foxes and other denning mammals, as well as hibernating snakes, lizards and arthropods.

# *Hoary Marmot* Marmota caligata

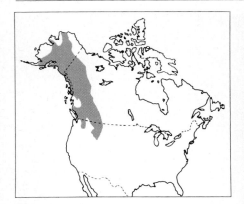

**Mammal:** *Marmota caligata* — hoary marmot; largest of the Sciuridae
**Meaning of Name:** *Marmota* (mountain mouse or rat); *caligata* (wearing boots); lower legs and feet are black, giving the appearance of boots; hoary indicates a greyish white coat
**Description:** head and shoulders are black and white; black "cap"; dark streaks on sides and white patch on muzzle; lower back and rump are grizzled grey, washed with yellow; black feet; greyish white underparts
**Total Length:** 26.8 to 29.5 inches
**Tail:** 7 to 9.8 inches
**Weight:** 7.9 to 19.8 pounds; maximum of 28.7 pounds
**Gestation:** 28 to 30 days
**Litter Size:** 4 or 5
**Age of Maturity:** at least 2 years, possibly 3 years
**Longevity:** not known (probably 4 to 6 years)
**Diet:** herbivore; alpine grasses and forbs, roots, wild flowers and berries
**Habitat:** subalpine areas with lots of vegetation or rolling alpine meadows, rocky taluses and cliffs; also in the forest edge where clearings provide food, and rock piles provide shelter
**Predators:** grizzly bear, black bear, wolf and golden eagle; predators must be strong enough to dig a marmot out of its den
**Dental Formula:** 1/1, 0/0, 2/1, 3/3 = 22 teeth

The hoary marmot is a huge squirrel, twice as large as a groundhog and the largest of all North American squirrels. Its large size is an adaptation for its life at high altitudes and in the far northern Rockies. The hoary marmot may spend two-thirds of its life hibernating. It pads itself with a layer of fat that may account for 20 percent of its weight and sleeps seven to eight months of the year, when the mountain meadows are covered with snow. Like the yellow-bellied marmot, it dens under boulders and rockfalls as protection against digging bears. Hoary marmots are preyed upon by golden eagles, and they are extremely wary, giving a loud police-style whistle whenever they detect a potential predator.

Males establish polygynous harems similar to those of the yellow-bellied marmot. They seem to pursue a mixture of mate guarding and promiscuity, a combination that one observer has called "gallivanting." To maximize the number of females inseminated, they leave their core territory area and copulate with females associated with other males. Male marmots provide no parental care.

*Wrestling and nuzzling are regular parts of the social life of the hoary marmot, **top**. Male marmots try to control access to a harem of females until they are eventually ousted by a new and stronger rival. The largest squirrel in North America, the hoary marmot has a thick silvery fur coat that adapts it for the cold climate of the western mountains, **above**.*

## *Yellow-bellied Marmot*  Marmota flaviventris

**Mammal:** *Marmota flaviventris* — yellow-bellied marmot

**Meaning of Name:** *Marmota* (mountain mouse or rat); *flaviventris* (yellow belly)

**Description:** heavy-bodied; overall yellowish brown colour with buffy yellow neck, hips and belly; yellow patches on each side of neck; creamy coloured bar across bridge of nose and about the lips; pale brown feet; grizzled brown tail

**Total Length:** male, 18.4 to 26 inches; female, 19.1 to 25 inches

**Tail:** 5.2 to 7 inches

**Weight:** male, 4.9 to 11.5 pounds; female, 3.5 to 8.7 pounds

**Gestation:** 30 days

**Litter Size:** 3 to 8 (usually 5); 1 litter per year

**Age of Maturity:** 2 years, but most do not mate until their third year

**Longevity:** at least 3 years

**Diet:** herbivore; selective with respect to the species of plant and parts of plant consumed; eats native forbs, grasses, sedges, clovers and alfalfa; can be cannibalistic

**Habitat:** rocky slopes or outcrops; on sides of mountains or other subalpine areas adjacent to lush meadows

**Predators:** eagle, badger, grizzly bear, wolf and puma (usually take immature animals)

**Dental Formula:** 1/1, 0/0, 2/1, 3/3 = 22 teeth

Yellow-bellied marmots live in mountain meadows. They choose a nest site among a pile of boulders, at the base of a talus slope or rockfall. They work their nest and burrow system into soil found under and between boulders to prevent badgers and grizzly bears from digging them out. They also excavate a system of auxiliary burrows away from the main burrow system. These burrows are shallower and shorter, running only a yard or two. They provide temporary refuge for marmots away from the main burrow.

The yellow-bellied marmot is similar to the groundhog in its diet and deep-winter hibernation but differs in its breeding and social system. Where groundhogs are solitary for most of their adult life, this species has a harem system. A male defends a territory that excludes other males and includes territories of a variable number of females. Some males are unable to acquire a high-quality territory and

*The yellow-bellied marmot digs its burrow at the edge of mountain meadows under boulders too large for badgers or even grizzly bears to move.*

exist as "satellites" without attracting any females.

In spring, females give birth to a clutch of three to eight altricial offspring. They spend the summer with their mother and may hibernate with her. They may begin hibernating as early as August in high mountain areas. Such an early hibernation gives these marmots very little time to deposit the huge fat stores needed for the long winter. The largest old males are usually able to hibernate first, followed by the adult females and finally the young of the year, which begin hibernating a month or two after the older males have settled in. Hibernation dens are usually located in areas with heavy snow cover. Adults in a harem hibernate communally.

## Harems: To Join or Not to Join

The breeding system of the yellow-bellied marmot provides an example of how male and female reproductive strategies often conflict. Females seek to exclude other females — a strategy that will lower the reproductive success for the resident male. And males seek to increase their mating opportunities through polygyny, which is disadvantageous to the females.

Male yellow-bellied marmots practise resource-defence polygyny. This means that they defend a resource that females find useful and, by excluding other males from the resource, gain exclusive access to the females. For example, one male may have a territory containing one to four females that he both defends and has exclusive sexual access to.

Genetically, the male harem master benefits from polygyny because the more females he can mate with, the more offspring he will produce. However, the reverse is true for the females. Females must forage within the territory of the male. The more females within a harem, the fewer the food resources that are available per female. This ratio is borne out by birth-rate statistics. As the harem size increases, the male reproductive success rate goes up, but the female reproductive success rate goes down. Marmot females who live monogamously produce

*Female marmots, such as these yellow-bellied marmots, may decide to become part of a harem, but defend their own individual territories within the larger male territory.*

several times as many offspring as the average female in a four-member harem because females must compete for resources within the harem. Yet there is a 1-to-1 sex ratio among marmots — just as many males as females. Why, then, do females join harems? Why aren't they monogamous? Because all males and all male territories are not equal. Prime territory sites with good forage, lookouts for predators and burrow sites are limited, and only some of the males are vigorous enough to control access to them. Females may find it more advantageous to join a harem in a high-quality territory than to join a solitary male in a territory of low quality. Members of a group also benefit from the protection afforded by other members. When a predator is spotted, marmots give an alarm whistle, alerting other marmots. In spite of this added protection, it would probably still be better for a female's reproductive success rate to be the only female in a territory, be it good or bad.

Females are aggressive toward other females from outside of the group; within the group, they form dominance hierarchies and harass subordinates. Sometimes, a

dominant female will try to bury a subordinate by plugging and stuffing a burrow entrance and may possibly kill the subordinate's offspring. Within the harem, females have a range of territorial strategies. Some females have exclusive territories, others have overlapping territories. The amount of overlap may reflect differences in the females' status. Probably only dominant females are able to have an exclusive territory. Strife between females within a territory is usually less if they are close genetic relatives, such as sisters.

Females compete primarily for good den sites, ones that are well protected and close to prime foraging areas. These are, of course, in short supply. Long-term observations of yellow-bellied marmot colonies have shown that few new burrows are created in any year. The older, more established burrows usually occupy the prime sites and are improved each year. An individual that opts to leave the colony or is forced out must build a new burrow, usually in a marginal site, or must undertake a long, dangerous journey to uncolonized areas.

Marmots have a long prereproductive period of two or three years. After they are 1 year old, the young males are driven out of the territory by the resident male. Females may drive young females out, but some may remain to become resident females. Roughly half of the females are forced to leave the colony. They then must try to join another male's harem or set up a den in a single male's territory.

## *Vancouver Island Marmot* Marmota vancouverensis

**Mammal:** *Marmota vancouverensis* — Vancouver Island marmot

**Meaning of Name:** *Marmota* (mountain mouse or rat); *vancouverensis* (of Vancouver Island)

**Description:** glossy chocolate brown; dirty white ring on muzzle and white patch on forehead; white streaks along chest and abdomen

**Total Length:** 24.9 to 28 inches

**Tail:** male, 7.9 to 11.8 inches

**Weight:** male, 7.7 pounds (may double or even triple their weight from May to September); female, 8.3 pounds

**Gestation:** not known (probably about 30 days)

**Litter Size:** 3; probably only reproduce every second year

**Age of Maturity:** most do not breed until their fourth summer

**Longevity:** not known (probably 4 to 6 years)

**Diet:** herbivore; berries, roots and bark in spring and winter; leaves, flowers and berries in summer and fall

**Habitat:** tree line and beyond in subalpine slopes, meadows or forest openings; favours steep slopes with a southern exposure

**Predators:** golden eagle, red-tailed hawk, puma and black bear

**Dental Formula:** 1/1, 0/0, 2/1, 3/3 = 22 teeth

The Vancouver Island marmot is a close relative of the hoary marmot. It is restricted to Vancouver Island and probably speciated there when the island population of marmots was isolated from the mainland population. Colonies are located in subalpine areas on steep and windswept slopes. In such areas, avalanches clear away the snowpack and open up early spring grazing areas for hungry marmots.

This marmot is biologically similar to the hoary marmot. It is, however, an endangered species. There are probably fewer than 1,000 individuals, making the Vancouver Island marmot vulnerable to logging, hunting and other forms of environmental disturbance.

*Numbering fewer than 1,000 individuals, the Vancouver Island marmot — found only on Vancouver Island — is a species that is highly vulnerable to extinction.*

# Black-tailed Prairie Dog *Cynomys ludovicianus*

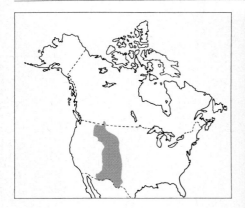

**Mammal:** *Cynomys ludovicianus* — black-tailed prairie dog
**Meaning of Name:** *Cynomys* (dog mouse); *ludovicianus* indicates that the animal was found in the state of Louisiana; known as prairie dog due to its sharp barking alarm call
**Description:** pinkish tan colour dorsally; whitish or pale buff underparts and lower part of face; short ears may be hidden in fur; larger and stouter and have shorter tails than squirrels
**Total Length:** 14.2 to 16.3 inches
**Tail:** 3 to 4 inches
**Weight:** male, 3 pounds; female, 2.5 to 2.8 pounds
**Gestation:** 30 to 35 days
**Litter Size:** 2 to 8 (usually 5)
**Age of Maturity:** 2 years; some mature as yearlings but have smaller litters
**Longevity:** 3 years in the wild; 7 to 8.5 years in captivity
**Diet:** primarily forbs and grasses; some animal matter; opportunistic but does select for certain plants according to nutritional requirements
**Habitat:** dry, open upland prairies and shortgrass plains; likes river flats and coulee bottomlands
**Predators:** rattlesnake, burrowing owl, eagles, hawks, badger, coyote and black-footed ferret
**Dental Formula:** 1/1, 0/0, 2/1, 3/3 = 22 teeth

Prairie dogs are among the most social of North American squirrels, and their behaviour is the most elaborate of all. One prairie dog town in Texas contained an estimated 400 million inhabitants and covered 25,000 square miles.

Named for their barklike warning call, black-tailed prairie dogs are at the extreme end of the scale of ground squirrel evolutionary tendencies. They are stouter than their cousins, they remain active except during the very coldest winter weather, and instead of using cheek pouches to carry and cache seeds, they eat large quantities of leafy vegetation and have evolved bigger incisors and molars for the job.

The densely packed "towns" in which they live alter the landscape of western grasslands. Before poisoning campaigns exterminated wholesale numbers of prairie dogs, their towns used to reach staggering sizes. Such large colonies may have had a mutually beneficial relationship with the vast bison and pronghorn antelope herds that ranged the same areas. The herds are thought to have grazed plants that the prairie dogs shunned, and the buffalo wallows encouraged the grassy and herbaceous vegetation favoured by the dogs.

*Being part of a strong family group is the key to success for a prairie dog. Extended families cooperate to outcompete other prairie dogs for grazing and burrowing territory.*

Prairie dogs' feeding habits and mound building leave their mark on the landscape. Their selective grazing favours the growth of certain species of woody shrubs, and sometimes, a town can be spotted miles away by the silvery blue shine of sage growing in the colony. Grass and broad-leaved herbs are so heavily cropped that towns are often depleted of favoured foods. In such cases, prairie dogs will also dig roots and eat insects.

The burrow of a prairie dog is unmistakable. Its entrance is in the crater of a volcano-shaped cone built of soil removed from the tunnel system. The cone serves as both a lookout perch and a dyke to prevent surface water from pouring down the entrance. The burrow is a remarkable excavation that begins with a straight plunge of 9 to 15 feet, a depth requiring that towns be located in areas of deep and malleable soils. The burrow then turns sideways and runs horizontally for 50 or more feet. It has short side tunnels that lead to nesting chambers or tunnels used for defecation, and it may have multiple exits. Burrow systems are usually 25 to 50 yards apart.

Towns are organized into extended female kin groups called coteries. A coterie typically consists of a single adult male, three to four adult females (often sisters or cousins) and larger numbers of juveniles of both sexes. A male maintains more or less exclusive sexual access to the breeding females in one coterie, but his territory may expand to include a second. In this case, the females of one coterie remain loyal to their own and are hostile to females of the other. A male's behaviour is thus subject to the outcome of female-female interactions.

Cooperation, sociability and egalitarianism are the most striking features of a coterie. The members usually sleep communally. They greet each other with a hug, placing their forepaws around each other. Their social gestures also include nose or teeth touching and tail flicking. And they all give alarm calls, defend their territory and build the burrow system. Neither males nor females in a single coterie dominate relationships with each other through violence or threats. However, as in any group, there is a mix of cooperation and competitiveness. Some subtle forms of competition may exist among females, because not all females within a group breed and because the average reproductive success per female declines as the size of the group increases. If such competition does exist, more obvious cooperative behaviour generally overshadows it. For example, nonbreeding females assume more than their share of colony defence. Mothers may also feed infants that are not direct descendants. On the other hand, pregnant and lactating females defend their nests against other members of the group. Females may also kill the offspring of other females within the group.

Both males and females breed at 2 years of age. Breeding occurs in late winter. The litter size is small as ground squirrels go — an average of three pups weaned per female. The pups first emerge above ground in May and June. Female pups will remain in the group for life, and males will disperse in the next summer, at the age of 12 to 14 months. Why males disperse is not clear. It may be because

the residents evict them, because females refuse to breed with closely related males or because the males are genetically encoded to disperse to avoid inbreeding.

After dispersing, a male must set up his own burrow system and attract females. Only the largest coteries have more than one breeding male. A male tolerates another male, and they may even groom each other and share burrows, but one male fathers the bulk of the offspring.

Colonies expand as mature males move to the periphery. Food depletion is lower there, but pioneering males and the females that they attract face a greater risk from predators, such as coyotes and hawks, than are the centrally located residents. Like all ground squirrels, prairie dogs give alarm calls, providing advance warning to interior residents. The warning

*Prairie dogs are choosy grazers that alter the entire plant community around the prairie dog town. Bison and pronghorn antelopes eat the plants that prairie dogs shun.*

call is one of at least nine vocalizations that the black-tailed prairie dog uses. Among its other greetings, threats and social signals is the territorial "bark," from which it derives its common name.

Many carnivorous mammals and raptors feed on prairie dogs. Badgers are sometimes able to excavate them, and coyotes working in pairs can sometimes catch them. The endangered black-footed ferret used to feed mainly on prairie dogs, but the poisoning campaigns that eradicated most prairie dog towns destroyed most of the ferrets as well. Rattlesnakes and burrowing owls also eat

*Because prairie dogs live in large, dense colonies that contain many closely related individuals, incest can become a problem. Special behavioural adaptations have evolved to prevent it.*

prairie dogs and use their burrows. The owls nest in them and the snakes den and overwinter in them.

The black-tailed prairie dog does not hibernate, although it sometimes becomes inactive during very cold spells. This is attributed to its ability to meet all its water needs from grazing plants. By contrast, the white-tailed prairie dog, which has a relatively high water requirement, is an obligate hibernator. In winter, it minimizes its water needs by turning its metabolism down and sleeping the season away.

## Incest: How to Avoid It

*Animals that live in dense colonies run a high risk of incest. Incest is mating with a close relative. In most animals, it results in a phenomenon that geneticists call inbreeding repression.*

*Every mammal has two sets of genes, one set from each parent. Some of these genes may be defective, but if the copy from either parent is functional, it can mask the effect of the defective gene. For example, an animal might inherit from*

*its father a defective skin-pigment gene, but if the copy of the gene it receives from its mother is functional, the animal will grow up to be normally pigmented.*

*Defective genes that are not expressed when a functional copy of the gene exists in the same body are called deleterious recessives. They are hidden, transmitted from generation to generation, and are exposed and removed by natural selection only when an individual receives two identically defective copies, one from each parent. An albino organism might be the result of such a pairing.*

*Mammals carry large numbers of deleterious recessives, and their effects on an individual's fitness vary. A gene that reduces fitness and reproductive success by 50 percent is half a lethal equivalent. Humans carry an average of two lethal equivalents, and if expressed, they could cause death. Other species have been shown to have similar numbers of deleterious genes hidden in their gene pool, and virtually every study of every mammal subject to inbreeding has shown severe costs when these genes are expressed.*

*Inbreeding increases the chance that both copies of a gene are identical. If an animal carrying the defective gene breeds with a brother*

*or sister or one of its parents, the chances are 50-50 that the mate carries the same defective genes. Simple laws of probability predict that the resulting offspring are highly likely to express a defective trait. For example, a deleterious recessive gene in humans can produce a genetic disease called phenylketonuria, which suppresses production of a metabolic enzyme and can cause severe mental retardation and grave illness. The gene occurs in 1 person in 100, but it is carried and transmitted from generation to generation, mostly in the recessive state. Individuals who carry the defective gene are unaware of its presence, because they usually also carry a working copy of the gene that produces the necessary enzyme. Under the laws of probability, the chance that an individual will inherit two copies of the gene from parents who are not related is 1-in-100 times 1-in-100, or, in other words, 1 in 10,000. Inbreeding between brothers and sisters increases 500-fold the chance that their offspring will receive a defective copy from each parent and express the disease.*

*How can prairie dogs living in such densely populated towns avoid inbreeding? One study found several answers. Newborn males disperse from their coterie before they reach breeding age, and their sisters and female cousins remain behind. This eliminates incest between siblings of the same age. A father also usually leaves the coterie before his daughters begin mating. If a father remains, the daughters tend not to come into oestrus. (Nine percent of the offspring in this study were sired by a male from outside the coterie, so females do have some chance of recruiting an unrelated mate if necessary.) And finally, if a female does come into oestrus when one of her close male relatives is around, she will avoid mating with him. This avoidance is based on the ability to distinguish kin from nonkin by their scent — which may explain why prairie dogs spend so much time hugging and grooming each other.*

*Two cases of inbreeding did occur in this study. No birth occurred in one instance. In the second, the litter died shortly after weaning. The avoidance of incest, then, appears worthwhile.*

# *Richardson's Ground Squirrel* Spermophilus richardsonii

**Mammal:** *Spermophilus richardsonii* — Richardson's ground squirrel

**Meaning of Name:** *Spermophilus* (seed lover); *richardsonii* (named after Sir John Richardson, who discovered the species in 1820)

**Description:** plump squirrel with long tail and small internal cheek pouches; smoky grey dorsally with yellowish cheeks, shoulders, flanks and thighs; cinnamon-buff head; brown transverse bars on rump; submarginal black band on tail, which is bordered with white or buff; eyes set high in skull to permit it to spot airborne predators with only the crown of its head sticking out of burrow

**Total Length:** 10.9 to 12 inches

**Tail:** 2.6 to 3.3 inches

**Weight:** 14.2 ounces in spring; increases to 17.1 ounces in autumn prior to hibernation

**Gestation:** 22.5 to 28 days

**Litter Size:** usually 6 to 8, but 2 and 11 have occurred; 1 litter per year

**Age of Maturity:** 11 months

**Longevity:** 3 to 4 years

**Diet:** mainly herbivorous; roots, leaves and seeds of native grasses and forbs as well as crop plants; also carnivorous, eating insects and carrion; partly cannibalistic

**Habitat:** open prairie and plains with gravelly or sandy soils; also sagebrush grassland near water

**Predators:** hawks, burrowing owl, weasel, ferret, badger, fox and coyote

**Dental Formula:** 1/1, 0/0, 2/1, 3/3 = 22 teeth

The ground squirrels, like the western chipmunks, are an extremely diverse genus. At least 13 species of ground squirrel inhabit a relatively small geographic range, yet most live within their own specialized habitats.

Richardson's ground squirrels are prairie specialists. They form colonies not because they are social but because they inhabit areas with short vegetation, easily worked soils and good drainage. Colonies are densest in virgin prairie areas, with about eight individuals living together per acre. Each adult digs its own burrow system. These consist of as many as eight entrances leading to an extensive system of tunnels as well as storage, nest-

*In the dry west, ground squirrels such as the Richardson's are among the most diverse mammals.*

ing and hibernation chambers. The tunnels may run for 15 yards and extend to a depth of 6 feet. The ground squirrels pile the excavated earth outside their burrows, forming observation mounds. Despite their tendency to live in dense colonies, Richardson's ground squirrels are solitary animals, and each adult defends his or her own burrow.

These squirrels are also diurnal and omnivorous. Their diet consists mainly of herbaceous prairie plants,

*Mother-and-daughter Richardson's ground squirrels cooperate to defend their territory against the assaults of foreign male and female squirrels.*

but they also eat large numbers of insects, such as grasshoppers, and will eat carrion when they get the chance. They cache seeds in their burrows to eat when their fat stores are depleted at the end of their seven-month hibernation. Hibernation takes place in one of their deepest chambers, which they plug and seal with soil to reduce the risk of being dug up by a predator. They also insulate this chamber with a lining of dried plants. Males begin and end their hibernation before females. They may begin hibernating as early as July and emerge in January in an attempt to mate with as many females as possible. Although the earliest emergent males may increase the number of potential matings, they risk being weakened by cold weather and limited foraging opportunities. Thus, when the peak of the female emergence occurs, they may be less successful in vying with other males for mates. Males fight and wound each other in their battles over females and sometimes die from their wounds. They also lose weight during the mating season, while females gain weight — which is another indicator of the high cost of the males' wide-ranging combative activities.

During the breeding phase, males intrude on female territories. However, when the mating season is finished, females oppose and exclude them, as they do other females. Males are passive while the females are bearing their young. Females give birth to a single litter in spring after a short pregnancy of only 24 days. The young are weaned and active outside the nest five weeks after birth. They remain with their mother for several more months and participate in defending the territory from intrusions by other colony members. By late summer, they reach adult size and disperse. The young of a given year can identify their siblings after they emerge from hibernation, an important mechanism for avoiding inbreeding.

Ground squirrel burrows interfere with agriculture, and wide-scale poisoning and bounty programmes have been sponsored to reduce the species. Ground squirrels also carry ticks and fleas that harbour Rocky Mountain spotted fever and a type of bubonic plague. At least one squirrel bounty hunter has died of the plague, presumably from handling dead squirrels.

## What's in a Warning?

*A colony of ground squirrels has a predatory warning system. The squirrel that sees a hawk, for example, whistles loudly, alerting other squirrels in the area to take cover in their burrows. This sounds simple and straightforward, but it is not.*

*A social group is rife with conflicting interests. There are kin groups, which ought to cooperate closely, living side-by-side with unrelated, competing individuals. Besides, there are other individuals representing a whole set of intermediate degrees of relationships. Thus an alarm call will affect the survival not only of the caller but of all the variously related squirrels that hear the call.*

*A successful behaviour increases the reproductive success of the individual exhibiting the behaviour. It is thus passed on to future generations. At the same time, the success of a particular individual is measured by his or her reproductive rate, with successful individuals reproducing at a higher rate than the average individual. So why should a squirrel give an alarm call that alerts other squirrels?*

*There is, after all, a risk that the call will attract the predator's attention to the caller, which would lower the caller's reproductive success directly. If the call increases the survival rate of unrelated squirrels, it will also lower the relative reproductive success of the caller. But biologists do not expect alarm calls to benefit a group of random individuals.*

*There are, then, two fundamentally different ways of looking at alarm calls. One view argues that alarm calls are a form of manipulation and selfishness. In this view, the caller causes other individuals to respond to a warning and to run or otherwise escape, thereby creating a diversion so that the caller will be less likely to be selected by the predator. The caller, it is believed, has the advantage of knowing where the predator is and of taking advantage of the action and confusion created by the call to escape.*

*The alternative and competing hypothesis is that alarm calls benefit relatives in the vicinity of the caller. By increasing the survival and reproductive success of his or her close kin, the caller increases the spread of the genes that control alarm-calling behaviour.*

*Ground squirrels are the ideal organisms with which to test these two views, both because they make alarm calls frequently and because their social system and dispersal patterns produce an asymmetric*

pattern of genetic relatedness. Sons disperse and generally end up in areas surrounded by nonrelatives. By contrast, daughters often set up near their mothers, producing clusters of closely related female kin.

Studies of Richardson's, Belding's and thirteen-lined ground squirrels have all ended up supporting the kin-selection explanation of alarm calls. The individuals that call the most are female. Most often, they are mothers that have offspring or closely related kin nearby. Furthermore, the studies of Belding's ground squirrel revealed that there was a real cost to alarm calling. The Belding's ground squirrels that called were more frequently attacked by predators than were noncallers. Females with relatives nearby, however, called in spite of this. They were also more likely to call than either males or females with no close kin nearby. This provides strong evidence that nepotism — the favouring of kin — has been the selective force behind alarm calling.

Ground squirrels greet intruders and alert their relatives with a loud, shrill whistle, **above** and **left**. When relatives are nearby, ground squirrels are more likely to give the warning call.

# *Columbian Ground Squirrel* Spermophilus columbianus

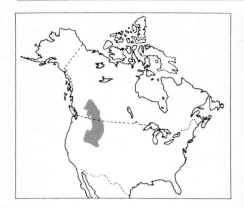

**Mammal:** *Spermophilus columbianus* — Columbian ground squirrel
**Meaning of Name:** *Spermophilus* (seed lover); *columbianus* (part of geographical range includes the basin of the Columbia River)
**Description:** mottled grey head and neck; pale ginger flanks and underparts; dark reddish feet and legs; bushy tail has a rufous base, a brown brush and a creamy terminal band
**Total Length:** 12.9 to 14.8 inches
**Tail:** 3 to 5 inches
**Weight:** 12 to 28.6 ounces, depending on whether it is entering or emerging from hibernation
**Gestation:** 24 days
**Litter Size:** 2 to 4; 1 litter per year
**Age of Maturity:** 2 years
**Longevity:** 4 to 6 years
**Diet:** roots, bulbs, stems, leaves and flowers; cultivated crops and some animal food, including insects, dead fish and mice
**Habitat:** open meadows, sagebrush plains or cultivated fields with a southern exposure and light sandy soil
**Predators:** diurnal avian predators, weasel, badger, coyote, fox, bobcat, puma, grizzly bear, skunk and wolf
**Dental Formula:** 1/1, 0/0, 2/1, 3/3 = 22 teeth

The Columbian ground squirrel lives in mid- to upper-elevation intermountain basins in open habitats characterized by light soil. Its relatively large size reflects its adaptation to these higher elevations. Like the Richardson's ground squirrel, it lives in colonies because of the local soil and habitat conditions. The Columbian ground squirrel is a generalized grazer as well as a predator of insects and, possibly, mice. It also stores seeds in its burrow system, especially if it is a large, early-emerging male.

This ground squirrel has a relatively small litter size, perhaps because of its large physical size and the intensity of its social competition. Dominance is achieved by fighting, and a larger squirrel is apt to be a more successful fighter. Litter size declines as altitude increases, suggesting that the squirrels balance their fecundity against the length of the growing season. The survival of juveniles over winter is higher in this species than in other ground squirrels, an indication that their reduced fecundity results in more vigorous offspring.

The Columbian ground squirrel requires two summers to achieve its full body size, whereas Richardson's ground squirrels are fully grown at the

*The Columbian ground squirrel is a large and slow-to-mature species in which size plays an important role in winning battles over territories.*

end of their first summer. In addition, the young do not disperse until their second summer. Males move away, while females tend to remain near the nest where they were born. Resident females are more likely to vacate their territory if they have a young daughter ready to inherit the site. The clusters of female kin interact in a more amicable manner than do female Richardson's ground squirrels.

Males fight to secure territories that overlap those of several females. After mating, males produce a copulatory plug that ranges from a hard crystalline substance to one that is white and rubbery. The plug is anchored firmly in the vagina and prevents other males from inserting sperm for at least a day, minimizing the chance that territorial males will lose paternity rights to intruding males. The thirteen-lined ground squirrel and the prairie dog also form these plugs. Other species of ground squirrels, such as Belding's, have a high rate of multiple paternity — that is, a litter from a single female is fathered by several different males. In these species, males do not form mating plugs, and a receptive female may mate with as many as five different males when she is in heat. As a result, more than three-quarters of the litters have two or more fathers. Such behaviour decreases the relatedness of the litter mates and also limits the chance for cooperative behaviour to develop among offspring. It may be that cooperative interactions between Columbian ground squirrel sisters evolved because of the use of mating plugs by their fathers. Therefore, the offspring usually have the same father and are close genetic relatives.

Sometimes, the weaned litters of several females of Columbian ground squirrels blend and interact, whereas the siblings of Richardson's ground squirrels only tolerate each other.

*Like most other squirrels, Columbian ground squirrels are omnivorous, and when the opportunity presents itself, they will attack and eat animals such as this bull snake.*

---

## *Franklin's Ground Squirrel* Spermophilus franklinii

**Mammal:** *Spermophilus franklinii* — Franklin's ground squirrel
**Meaning of Name:** *Spermophilus* (seed lover); *franklinii* (named in honour of Sir John Franklin)

**Description:** long bushy tail; olive brown dorsally with grey to white or tawny underparts; grey head with frosting of silver-tipped hairs and a white eye ring; grey feet

**Total Length:** male, 14.3 to 16.9 inches; female, 14.4 to 16.1 inches
**Tail:** male, 4.7 to 6.1 inches; female, 5 to 6.1 inches
**Weight:** male, 1 pound; female, 1.1 pounds
**Gestation:** 28 days
**Litter Size:** usually 7 to 9 (can be 2 to 12); 1 litter per year
**Age of Maturity:** after emergence from their first hibernation
**Longevity:** 8 to 10 years
**Diet:** omnivore
**Habitat:** transition zone between high coniferous forests and grassy areas;

*Shy and quick to retreat into the cover of its bushy habitat, the Franklin's ground squirrel is a solitary creature except during the mating season.*

areas with low trees but dense ground cover
**Predators:** hawks, badger, fox, coyote and weasel
**Dental Formula:** 1/1, 0/0, 2/1, 3/3 = 22 teeth

## Thirteen-lined Ground Squirrel *Spermophilus tridecemlineatus*

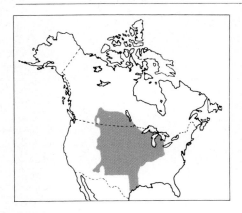

**Mammal:** *Spermophilus tridecemlineatus* — thirteen-lined ground squirrel

**Meaning of Name:** *Spermophilus* (seed lover); *tridecemlineatus* (thirteen-lined) refers to the dorsal stripes characteristic of this species

**Description:** 7 dark brown stripes separated by 6 narrow buff stripes on back; each of the brown stripes is enclosed by a row of buff squares; brown and buff specks on top of head; cinnamon nose, eye ring, cheeks, feet and underparts; yellowish brown tail has submarginal black band tipped with beige hairs; cheek pouches open into the sides of the mouth

**Total Length:** male, 10.1 to 11.7 inches; female, 8.9 to 10.7 inches

**Tail:** male, 3.6 to 4.4 inches; female, 3.5 to 3.9 inches

**Weight:** male, 5.8 ounces (maximum of 8.8 ounces); female, 4.9 ounces

**Gestation:** 27 or 28 days

**Litter Size:** 3 to 13 (usually 8); possibly a second litter if first one lost

**Age of Maturity:** 11 months

**Longevity:** maximum of 8 to 10 years in the wild

**Diet:** true omnivore; consumes more insects than most other ground squirrels; fresh green foliage and seeds, berries, domestic grain and garden produce; occasionally eats meat and carrion and even its own young

**Habitat:** transitional zone between grassland and forest with low grass, weeds or shrubby vegetation; also golf courses, abandoned overgrown fields, meadows and along fence lines between cultivated fields

**Predators:** hawks, shrike, crow, badger, weasel, coyote, fox, skunk and domestic cat

**Dental Formula:** 1/1, 0/0, 2/1, 3/3 = 22 teeth

One of the most beautifully patterned of all the mammals, the thirteen-lined ground squirrel becomes camouflaged amidst the sun and shadow of grassland vegetation.

## Golden-mantled Ground Squirrel *Spermophilus lateralis*

**Mammal:** *Spermophilus lateralis* — golden-mantled ground squirrel

**Meaning of Name:** *Spermophilus* (seed lover); *lateralis* (of the side) refers to prominent stripes on each side of body

**Description:** ears are quite large for a ground squirrel; diamond-shaped glandular area of thickened skin between the shoulders; 2 broad white lateral stripes running from shoulders (not cheeks, as in chipmunks) to rump, each side of which is bordered by narrow black stripes; a mantle that varies from tawny to russet brown covers head, neck and shoulders; white crescents above and below eyes; buff underparts, feet and legs

**Total Length:** 10.6 to 12.4 inches

**Tail:** 2.5 to 4.7 inches

**Weight:** 5.8 to 9.7 ounces

**Gestation:** 28 days

**Litter Size:** 2 to 8 (usually 4); 1 litter per year

**Age of Maturity:** the spring following birth

**Longevity:** 11 years in captivity (probably less in the wild)

**Diet:** omnivore; seeds, fungus, leaves, flowers, fruits, roots, eggs and arthropods

**Habitat:** mountain slopes and foothills; in alpine tundra beyond tree line

**Predators:** hawks, golden eagle, bobcat, fox, coyote, weasel, skunk and grizzly bear

**Dental Formula:** 1/1, 0/0, 2/1, 3/3 = 22 teeth

The golden-mantled ground squirrel lives at the very edge of the tree line in the western mountain ranges.

## Social Life of Squirrels

Some squirrel species are social, others are solitary. People are also social creatures and are understandably interested in what ecological and evolutionary forces cause an animal to be social. Studying animals like squirrels, where species vary considerably in the degree of sociality, has helped us to understand the factors that contribute to this behaviour. Such studies must use closely related organisms, ones that have not had a very long genetic separation. Animals that are related but have lengthy evolutionary histories may be social or not social for different reasons. The study of such closely related species as the squirrels minimizes this problem. For example, the woodchuck is a solitary creature, while the prairie dog is highly gregarious. What factors cause these differences? How much does sociality depend on genetics, and how much of it is caused by the environment?

Of course, no species is always antisocial or always gregarious; there is a continuum of behaviour between these two extremes for every species. Ground squirrels have such a variety of social systems that scientists have classified them into five grades, representing transitions along the solitary/social continuum. They have created these classifications from observations of the animals' family life, the basic unit of sociality in mammals. How long do family members remain together, do they cooperate, do they pass on and inherit resources, do they defend a territory together and do their descendants continue to associate? Such analyses are also concerned with territoriality, because all ground squirrels are territorial. Who, then, shares a territory, and who has to leave at maturity?

Gail Mitchener, a devoted student of ground squirrels, proposes this classification of their social systems from her observations:

1. ASOCIAL: In this system, there is no sharing of territories by males and females. The young disperse soon after weaning. Family members defend their territories and are as

When young male Richardson's ground squirrels mature, they leave their mother's territory and defend one of their own.

antagonistic toward each other as they are to unrelated individuals. In short, it is everyone for him- or herself. Social interactions and cooperation are limited to mating and the rearing of infants. This kind of system is typical of groundhogs and Franklin's ground squirrels.

2. SINGLE-FAMILY FEMALE KIN CLUSTERS: In this system, males and females also have separate ranges and territories, but mothers and daughters live near each other and may share a home range. Daughters often remain close to their mother for life. The kin group of mother and daughters is hostile to other groups of females. The sons leave home at maturity, and each establishes his own territory. This system is exhibited by Belding's ground squirrels, Richardson's ground squirrels and white-tailed prairie dogs.

*There is an interesting asymmetry between the sexes in this system. Males, because they disperse widely, are rarely closely related to the individuals around them. Females, on the other hand, live in closely related groups. The territory that males defend is used only during the mating season, so the resources within a male's territory have little long-term value to the females.*

*3. FEMALE KIN CLUSTERS WITH MALE TERRITORIALITY: In this system, the males' territories overlap those of several females and their daughters, and males defend their territories past the mating season. Such behaviours are typical of Arctic ground squirrels and Columbian ground squirrels and lead to more cooperation and interaction. Females rear their litters alone in their own burrows, but they all defend a part of their area included in the large territory of the male. Nevertheless, they have separate breeding areas and do not all live entirely within a single male territory, nor do they cooperate in defending the male's territory as a whole. There are more interactions among juveniles from several different litters. And, as in the other systems, males disperse while females remain near their mother.*

*4. POLYGYNOUS HAREMS WITH MALE DOMINANCE: In this system, which is practised by marmots, males are territorial and their territory contains one to four females. (Polygyny is the practice in which a male has more than one mate.) Again, females have daughters that tend to stay near them while their sons disperse. Males must patrol their territory to keep rival males from their harem, and fights between males are common. As a result, harem masters are short-lived. They are evicted or eaten by competitors every two to three years. Females, by contrast, live as long as 11 years, usually in the same harem with their sisters or close cousins. Yet they do not assist the male in defending his territory as a whole since they have their own activity areas and interact more with females. They are subordinate to the male.*

*5. EGALITARIAN POLYGYNOUS HAREMS: Olympic marmots and black-tailed prairie dogs are among*

The pinnacle of social complexity is seen in the towns of prairie dogs. One prairie dog town in Texas had 400 million inhabitants.

*the most social of rodents. They have few aggressive dominance interactions. Females are not subordinate to males. Males maintain harems in which the juvenile offspring — both males and females — may reside for as long as two years. Harem masters are not aggressive toward young males after the mating season has passed and do not mind their associating with the harem. All members of the extended-family group defend the family's territorial boundaries against the incursions of other families. This behaviour is different from that of yellow-bellied marmots, where a single male is charged with excluding other males. These marmots and prairie dogs do share the same dispersal pattern: daughters remain in the family unit when the mating season begins, whereas sons disperse to found their own unit or perhaps to invade an established unit.*

*Ground squirrels' social systems thus range from completely separate male and female territories to male territories that include some females to a system of an extended family where the territory of a male and some females are identical and defended in an egalitarian manner. In other words, as social complexity increases, male-female cooperation and especially female (mother-daughter-sister) cooperation increases. This latter feature is due to the asymmetrical dispersal of the sons and daughters and the resulting advantages and disadvantages to each.*

*Dispersal is a risky business. It increases one's chances of being eaten by a predator or damaged in a fight for territory. The mortality rates for females are thus lower because they typically do not have to disperse. A daughter also benefits because she inherits the extensive burrow system controlled by her female ancestors. Burrow sites are often limited and require a great deal of energy to dig. Females also need a more extensive burrow system than males do in which to raise their* young. Yet there are benefits to dispersing, the chief one being that the males are placed in a population of unrelated genetic individuals. A male that remained at home would end up mating with sisters or other close relatives, increasing the chances of genetic defects within the population. Thus it is to the parents' advantage to pass their territory and burrows along to their daughters while encouraging their sons to disperse.

This does not, however, answer the question of why woodchucks are nonsocial while prairie dogs congregate in dense colonies. Congregating has a cost. It increases the spread of disease and causes local food shortages and competition for space. Probably the key benefit is that many eyes are better than two. Social rodents are much more effective at spotting predators and warning each other about the danger. There appears to be a relationship between such social systems and their habitats. Social squirrels typically live in exposed, open habitats with a high vulnerability to visual predators. The less social woodchuck and tree squirrels are forest species and so may benefit less from a predator lookout system. There would also be more competition for food resources from an increased local population.

Many pressures can destabilize the social system. Female competition within a male's territory could drive other females out, reduce cooperation and raise the cost of territory maintenance, which might, in turn, make it more likely that both female and male young would disperse. A male might aggressively persecute his male relatives if they are potential competitors for mates within his territory. At high altitudes and high latitudes, animals may grow larger, because a large body is more efficient at storing fat needed for overwintering. This means, however, that the offspring will be large and will require a longer time at home before they disperse to fend for themselves. Consequently, parents will have a reduced reproductive rate.

There are thus many trade-offs in the sociality equation. The costs and benefits of sociality differ for every species according to environment, food resources, predators, dispersal problems and nest-site requirements. But the ultimate denominator is what behaviour contributes most to the spread of an individual's genes, either directly through his or her own mating or indirectly through the reproductive success of relatives who share a portion of their genes. This is the final determinant of which forms of social behaviour succeed.

## Fox Squirrel  Sciurus niger

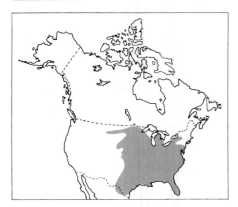

**Mammal:** *Sciurus niger* — fox squirrel; longest and bushiest tail of Canadian Sciuridae
**Meaning of Name:** *Sciurus* (shade tail), from habit of lying sprawled on a horizontal limb with tail held over its back as a sun shade; *niger* (black), based on black colour phase
**Description:** soft, dense pelage with heavy underfur and long, coarse guard hairs; three colour phases (black, grey and red) have a geographical pattern of distribution; grey phase is dominant in the northern population (each hair is tricoloured, giving a grizzled effect); pale fulvous to buffy ears, cheeks, feet and underparts; reddish bushy tail with a subterminal black border and cinnamon tips; no cheek pouches
**Total Length:** 19.7 to 22.4 inches
**Tail:** 8.3 to 10.6 inches
**Weight:** 1.6 to 1.8 pounds
**Gestation:** 44 days
**Litter Size:** 1 to 6 (usually 3 or 4); 2 litters per year
**Age of Maturity:** female, 1 litter as yearling; male, matures more slowly
**Longevity:** 6 to 10 years in the wild
**Diet:** omnivore; nuts, acorns, seeds, buds, flowers, catkins, fleshy fruits, insects, fungi, bird eggs and cambium beneath the bark of small branches
**Habitat:** suburbs; open hardwood woodlots with clearings interspersed; along shrubby fencerows
**Predators:** red-tailed hawk, great blue heron, owls, osprey, coyote, grey fox, weasel, raccoon and dog
**Dental Formula:** 1/1, 0/0, 1/1, 4/3 = 20 teeth

*The largest of the tree squirrels, the fox squirrel was originally a resident of southern oak and hickory forests but has extended its range northward with agricultural development.*

# *Arctic Ground Squirrel* Spermophilus parryii

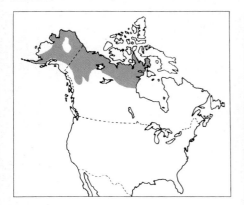

**Mammal:** *Spermophilus parryii* — Arctic ground squirrel, the largest of the ground squirrels

**Meaning of Name:** *Spermophilus* (seed lover); *parryii* (named by Sir John Richardson after American botanist and explorer Dr. C.C. Parry, 1823-90)

**Description:** cinnamon and tawny head, cheeks and shoulders; buff eye ring; greyish to buff brown nape and back flecked with white spots; tawny flanks, legs and underparts; tail is a combination of browns and black-tipped hairs, tawny below; black terminal brush

**Total Length:** male, 14.8 to 17.1 inches; female, 13.7 to 16.7 inches

**Tail:** male, 4.1 to 5 inches; female, 3.5 to 5.3 inches

**Weight:** male, 1.7 to 2 pounds; female, 1.5 pounds

**Gestation:** 25 days

**Litter Size:** 4 to 8 (usually 6); 1 litter per year

**Age of Maturity:** the spring following birth (approximately 11 months)

**Longevity:** maximum of 8 to 10 years in the wild

**Diet:** tundra vegetation such as leaves, seeds, stems, flowers and roots of grasses, forbs and woody species; also fruit, carrion, eggs and nesting birds

**Habitat:** tundra regions beyond the tree line and clearings within northern forests; usually beside water on eskers, moraines and in brushy meadows

**Predators:** Arctic carnivores (ermine, wolf, Arctic fox and grizzly bear), as well as some airborne predators (rough-legged hawk, peregrine falcon, gyrfalcon and snowy owl)

**Dental Formula:** 1/1, 0/0, 2/1, 3/3 = 22 teeth

The Arctic ground squirrel is the largest species in this genus and is also found the farthest north. It has a large litter size, usually six young, which is typical of animals adapted to Arctic habitats.

Arctic ground squirrels dig burrows, but permafrost limits the depth of these to less than 3 feet. They form colonies, and their mazes of burrows and tunnels often intersect those of other squirrels. Females disperse less than males, and sisters often live adjacent to one another, a behaviour that results in the formation of female kin clusters. These closely related females interact in a relatively friendly manner with each other but are hostile to unrelated females.

Males are polygynous and attempt to control an area that contains more than one female. Males will also kill young Arctic ground squirrels. When the males disperse, they move into areas inhabited by nonrelatives, so infanticide costs them little. Indeed, it may provide them with food, as well as increasing the opportunities of their future daughters to find territo-

*In the brief far northern summer, the Arctic ground squirrel must grow from infancy to a size larger than any other species of ground squirrel.*

ries. Females may form kin clusters in response to such infanticide, as a group of females is more capable of defending its young than several single, uncooperative females would be.

Males continue to defend their territories even after the mating season is finished and often do so with increased vigour — perhaps in an effort to defend their young against the cannibalistic tendencies of intruding males. As a result, unlike other male ground squirrels, those of the Arctic hibernate after the females.

The young disperse the same season that they are born. They are nearly full-grown before autumn, and after their winter hibernation, they are ready for mating. Such rapid maturation reflects the tremendous productivity of the summer Arctic.

These squirrels feed on a wide variety of plants as well as carrion, eggs and nesting birds.

# *Grey Squirrel*  Sciurus carolinensis

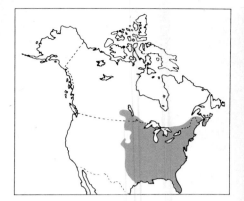

**Mammal:** *Sciurus carolinensis* — grey or black squirrel

**Meaning of Name:** *Sciurus* (shade tail), from habit of lying sprawled on a horizontal limb with tail held over its back as a sun shade; *carolinensis* (of Carolina) was originally described in Carolina

**Description:** soft dense pelage is grizzled grey with more yellowish brown tones on head, midback, sides and upper feet; whitish to brownish yellow underparts; whitish eye ring and spot behind ears; long thick pelage in winter; upperparts are washed with silver; ears are silver-tipped; other colour phases are common black, red and mixtures of these; some albinos have been reported

**Total Length:** 16.5 to 21.1 inches

**Tail:** 7.9 to 9.8 inches

**Weight:** 11.9 to 23.8 ounces

**Gestation:** 40 to 44 days

**Litter Size:** 1 to 6 (usually 2 to 4); 2 litters per year (only 20 to 40 percent have 2 litters)

**Age of Maturity:** female, 30 to 36 weeks (only females over 2 years will breed in both breeding seasons)

**Longevity:** 3 to 6 years in the wild (some have been found to be 13 years); 15 to 20 years in captivity (23.5 years maximum)

**Diet:** buds, flowers, seeds, nuts, fruits, fungi, some insects and occasionally a clutch of bird eggs; deer antlers, bones and turtle shells for calcium

**Habitat:** forest stands of eastern hardwoods or mixed forests; beech/maple, hemlock hardwoods, red and white pine; along streams (especially where there is a wide river-bottom habitat) and in suburban areas

**Predators:** hawks, weasel, mink, raccoon, skunk, snakes, grey wolf, owls and raven

**Dental Formula:** 1/1, 0/0, 2/1, 3/3 = 22 teeth

The grey squirrel, which is now so common in eastern cities, was once a creature of the virgin hardwood forests of the East. It was most common in large stands along rich river valleys, while its relatives, such as the fox squirrel, were more abundant in upland areas and red squirrels occupied the coniferous forests.

Since it is a tree squirrel, the grey squirrel spends most of its time above ground. It has strong, fixed claws designed for gripping bark and a large, fluffy tail that gives it balance when leaping between branches as well as providing insulation.

Grey squirrels feed primarily on nuts. They eat the large seeds of maples, oaks, hickories and beech trees and cache large numbers of nuts, not in piles but singly, in holes in the ground. They have an amazing ability to relocate these stores, which they disperse throughout their territory. They can smell a nut buried in soil covered by a foot of snow. Yet they miss some 10 to 20 percent of their nuts, and these then grow into trees. Their nut-burying behaviour thus influences the rate and pattern of forest regeneration.

In spring, grey squirrels eat large amounts of tree buds and flowers as well, and in summer, they add leaves, fruit, insects and bird eggs to their diet. They strip the bark off young trees such as the sugar maple and can distinguish which trees have the thickest sap. In some areas, they kill many trees because of their bark stripping. They

*Tall trees in virgin eastern forests are the natural haunt of the grey squirrel.*

eat deer antlers, bones and turtle shells to obtain calcium. In autumn, they eat fungi, including some *Amanita* mushrooms, which are fatal to humans. Presumably, the grey squirrel's liver and digestive system have some unusual detoxifying capabilities.

Tree squirrels have a simple social system. The home range of a male overlaps that of several females. During the mating season, males exclude other males from their territory, and breeding females exclude other squirrels from the vicinity of their nest. Squirrels may also be territorial and aggressive around concentrated food resources, but normally, they are spaced out and have few interactions. As population densities increase, they establish dominance relationships by teeth-chattering threats and chases. Grey squirrels are highly vocal and have a rich repertoire of sounds they use in communication. During winter, territoriality is less intense, and several squirrels may nest in the same den to keep warm.

Grey squirrels use two types of nests. In summer, they build leaf nests in tree crowns. An individual may build several nests at different locations and move to them as food distributions shift. Their winter nests are more protected and are typically found high above ground in a tree hollow, which they line with vegetation.

They favour large, overmature and slightly rotten trees. Foresters and woodlot owners who cut down such trees probably contribute to the over-wintering deaths of grey squirrels and so help to set limits on the overall grey squirrel population. Female grey squirrels also select this sort of den for raising their offspring. Pregnant or nursing females vigorously defend these trees against other squirrels.

This squirrel does not hibernate but remains active during winter. Court-ship begins in the second half of winter. Females make a quacking call to announce that they are in heat. This attracts large numbers of males who then chase them through the trees. Many squirrels are probably killed at this time by such aerial predators as hawks and owls. Females can pro-duce two litters, one at the end of spring and one in late summer — but only 20 percent of the females pro-duce this second litter. Each litter averages two to four young, which are born blind, naked and helpless. The mother may continue to nurse the first litter even while she is pregnant with the second litter. She will also move her young from nest to nest if she is disturbed. The father provides no parental care. Both sexes disperse in the autumn.

A black form of this squirrel is more common in the North. Its darker coat may act as a kind of solar heater on sunny days.

North American hunters shoot more than 40 million grey squirrels a year. Grey squirrel populations fluc-tuate wildly because they depend on the unpredictable fruitings of nut trees. They have also been periodi-cally depleted by mass dispersals, starvation and devastation by mange mites.

### Escape in a Time Warp

*Squirrels have created several kinds of problems for nut growers. The most obvious one is that of sharing the harvest, and it is usually dealt with in a straightforward manner: the squirrels are removed. This does not, however, remove the influence of squirrels. Their impact has been etched deeply into the genetic programmes of the nut trees, and as a result, nut trees have an ingrained tendency toward irregular bearing — a trait that has become*

*the bane of plant breeders. Some years, the trees in a forest or orchard all set a heavy crop; other years, there is nothing.*

*The years in which a heavy crop is set are known as mast years, and these are spaced at irregular intervals, sometimes one, two, three or even seven years apart. In some localities, almost all reproductive trees, regardless of age or location, are synchronized and in phase. The cues that synchronize them are not well known, although weather is important. Low rainfall in early summer stimulates the formation of reproductive buds and controls the*

Grey squirrels are one of the few wild mammals that have thrived in the large cities of eastern North America.

*potential for seed production the next year. This potential can be altered by hard spring frosts. And if the previous year was a heavy mast year, the trees lack the resources to produce a large crop no matter how favourable the environmental cues. The result is a highly erratic pattern that seed-eating squirrels have not yet been able to track closely.*

*Trees bear erratically, not because they are unable to cope with unpredictable weather but to thwart*

Tree squirrels, such as the fox squirrel, **top**, and Douglas' squirrel, **above**, are effective seed predators able to remove 100 percent of the seed crop in some years. Their harvest of nuts and seeds may greatly affect the succession and composition of forests.

*nut-eating squirrels. Trees have evolved to make use of the unpredictable nature of the weather to wipe out the rodents that prey upon their offspring.*

*By interspersing the mast years with barren, nutless years, the trees subject the squirrels to feast-and-famine cycles. Rodent populations decline when there is no nut crop, but when there is a crop, the rodent population is swamped with seeds. There are literally more than they can eat. In mast years, seed predators take only 1 to 10 percent of the nut crop. In off years, rodents harvest almost 100 percent of the crop.*

*Predator swamping, or satiation, is thought to be the explanation of a number of strange animal and plant cycles. Some bamboos fruit together at intervals of more than 100 years and then die off, causing starvation among bamboo-eating pandas. Cicadas tend to emerge en masse every 13 to 17 years, and sea turtles also have massive, unpredictable egg-laying sessions. The mast fruiting of nut trees may be one reason why so many tree squirrels include a wide variety of alternative prey in their diet.*

*The feast-and-famine cycle of nut production no doubt produced the spectacular migrations of grey squirrels in the last century and the first part of this century. The continent then retained more of the grey squirrels' native habitat, and consequently, the squirrels were*

*more abundant. In some years, observers reported thousands of squirrels on the move and many diving into rivers. Ernest Thompson Seton, whose estimates of animal numbers have generally been supported by later observers, calculated that some of these mass movements in the early part of the century involved more than a billion squirrels moving in a wave across the countryside.*

*The most recent documented massive grey squirrel emigration occurred in the southern Appalachians in 1968. Thousands of squirrels moved in the autumn, drowning in reservoirs and being crushed on the highways. The year before had been a mast year, and this had produced an abundance of young squirrels that overwintered with low mortality. The next spring, a frost destroyed the flower and fruit buds of the nut trees. There was no nut crop and the large squirrel population had no food to store for the winter. Chalk one up for the trees.*

# Red Squirrel *Tamiasciurus hudsonicus*

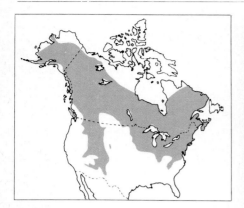

**Mammal:** *Tamiasciurus hudsonicus* — red squirrel, chickaree, fairydiddle, pine squirrel

**Meaning of Name:** *Tamiasciurus* (one who stores, or hoarder + shade tail); *hudsonicus* (refers to Hudson Bay region where type specimen was derived); chickaree is said to be an imitation of its cry

**Description:** soft dense pelage, glossy olive brown dorsally, flecked with black; limbs and backs of ears are cinnamon; winter pelage is thicker, brighter and more reddish; red or black tufts on ears; white eye ring, which, along with the tawny tail, is the only constant coloration

**Total Length:** 11 to 13.4 inches

**Tail:** 3.9 to 5.7 inches

**Weight:** 4.7 to 8.8 ounces

**Gestation:** 35 to 40 days

**Litter Size:** 2 to 7 (usually 4); 1 litter per year (2 in southern Canada)

**Age of Maturity:** 1 year

**Longevity:** probably less than 3 years in the wild; 9 to 12 years in captivity

**Diet:** opportunist; primarily seeds, nuts and cones of conifers; also buds, flowers, fruits, bark, mushrooms and sap; will eat insects, bird eggs, fledglings and mice (more carnivorous than other tree squirrels)

**Habitat:** assorted woody environments from coniferous forests, especially spruce, pine and hemlock, to mixed hardwood deciduous trees (maple and elm in particular); may also be found in swamps

**Predators:** hawks, owls, marten, fisher, badger, bobcat, red fox, wolf and domestic cat

**Dental Formula:** 1/1, 0/0, 1-2/1, 3/3 = 20 or 22 teeth

*The red squirrel's thickly furred tail provides balance as the squirrel races along tree branches.*

Squirrels in this genus are abundant and conspicuous — two characteristics that have earned them many common names such as chickaree and fairydiddle. More often, they are called pine squirrels because they make their home in the northern coniferous forests.

The red squirrel is a small, highly arboreal species that inhabits the northern boreal forest. At the southern edge of their range, particularly in deciduous forest mixed with patches of hemlock and pine, they are found in the same areas as grey squirrels.

Red squirrels are high-energy animals. They are noisy and seem to be constantly active during daylight hours. Where some squirrels are shy and secretive, these are bold and aggressive. They scold intruders, including people, with a vigorous display of foot stamping, tail flicking and chattering. They run through the trees at high speeds, leap into space spread-eagle and drop tens of yards to other trees or to the ground. Even falls from the treetops all the way to the ground do not seem to harm this small squirrel.

Red squirrels have a generalized diet. They will eat insects and can be major predators on bird eggs and nestlings. They heavily crop young conifer sprouts and flowers, eat berries and mushrooms and gnaw holes in bark or use the holes of sapsuckers to lap up tree sap. In short, red squirrels will eat virtually all the items that other tree squirrels eat, aside from low-energy leafy vegetation. Because of their high metabolism, they require a diet high in energy content. While they obtain some of this energy from being more carnivorous than other tree squirrels, they get most of it from their distinctive diet of pine, hemlock and other conifer cones. When the cones bear maturing seeds, these squirrels cut virtually every cone from the branches and let them fall to the ground. They then gather the cones into huge piles. The seed middens may be 3 feet deep and several yards across and contain bushels of cones. They prefer shady and humid sites

*Mating is one of the few occasions when male and female red squirrels,* **top,** *have any social contact. During the rest of the year, neither the male nor the female tolerates other squirrels in its territory. The longest form of social interaction is between mothers and young squirrels,* **above,** *which are born blind and helpless and depend on their mother for food and protection.*

that prevent the cones from drying out and dropping their seeds. These sites and nearby refuse piles of emptied cones are often used year after year and develop into large conspicuous piles. The squirrels also store seeds in tree hollows and hang fungi among the tree branches to dry; later, they cache these in a protected dry spot.

Both sexes are territorial and defend their territories against intruders of their own and other squirrel species. At least four different vocalizations are used during territorial encounters.

Females can have two litters a season but usually have time to rear only one. Females are receptive to males for only a single day. They advertise their receptiveness with an odoriferous vaginal secretion. A group of males collects and the dominant male mates repeatedly with the female. Males must chase and vocalize at other males to keep them away.

The female red squirrels have an unusual coiled vagina that seems to be unique amongst squirrels. This structure is matched by the male's long threadlike penis and loose penis bone. Their reproductive anatomy is so different that it was once suggested that red squirrels be considered a separate family.

They make their nests in tree hollows and also build leaf and twig nests. They may adapt the abandoned nests of large birds, such as crows, hawks and owls, for nesting. Before weaning her young, the mother moves them to a nest at the edge of her territory and begins to exclude them from the rest of it. Daughters are more likely than sons to inherit territory at the edge of their mother's. Territories vary in size according to the abundance of food.

These squirrels do not hibernate, but they spend little time in the trees in winter. Instead, they build an extensive system of runways through the snow.

Red squirrels are eaten by predatory mammals and hawks. The pine marten, a large, fast, arboreal weasel, is one of the few predators that succeeds in pursuing these squirrels through the trees. Before pine martens were depleted by trapping, they may have been the red squirrel's major predator.

Several million red squirrels are trapped each year for the fur trade, making them one of the more economically valuable fur bearers.

# Douglas' Squirrel *Tamiasciurus douglasii*

**Mammal:** *Tamiasciurus douglasii* —
Douglas' squirrel

**Meaning of Name:** *Tamiasciurus* (one
who stores, or hoarder + shade tail);
*douglasii* (named after David Douglas,
botanist and explorer of North
America — same Douglas as Douglas
fir)

**Description:** dark reddish pelage in
summer with blackish ear tufts; black
flank stripe; rust feet, eye ring and
underparts; chestnut-coloured tail with
black subterminal band and prominent
buff white tips; more greyish in winter,
and underparts turn pale yellowish grey

**Total Length:** 11.4 to 12.5 inches

**Tail:** 4.4 to 5.4 inches

**Weight:** 6 to 8.1 ounces

**Gestation:** 35 days

**Litter Size:** 4 to 8 (usually 4); 1 litter per
year

**Age of Maturity:** 1 year; the spring
following birth

**Longevity:** up to 7 years in the wild, but
probably less than 3 years; 10 years in
captivity

**Diet:** more vegetarian than red squirrel;
primarily conifer cones; also fungi,
seeds, nuts, fruits, catkins and ferns

*A Douglas' squirrel harvests tens of
thousands of conifer seeds each year.*

**Habitat:** dense coniferous forests as well
as logged-over areas

**Predators:** pine marten is major
predator; also fisher, lynx, weasel, mink,
bobcat, goshawk, red-shouldered hawk,
sharp-shinned hawk and sparrow hawk

**Dental Formula:** 1/1, 0/0, 2/1, 3/3 = 22
teeth

# Northern Flying Squirrel *Glaucomys sabrinus*

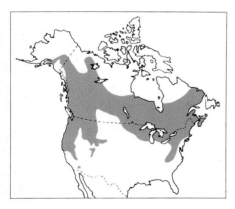

**Mammal:** *Glaucomys sabrinus* —
northern flying squirrel

**Meaning of Name:** *Glaucomys* (grey
mouse); *sabrinus* (river nymph) refers to
Severn River on the west coast of
Hudson Bay where species was first
identified

**Description:** slightly larger than the
southern flying squirrel; back is
cinnamon brown because individual
hairs are slate-coloured and light
yellowish brown at tips; light buff
underparts with hairs lead-coloured at
the base; broad flattened tail, grey
above, paler below and darker toward
the tip

**Total Length:** 9.6 to 14.4 inches

**Tail:** 4.3 to 7.1 inches

**Weight:** 2.5 to 4.9 ounces

**Gestation:** 37 days

**Litter Size:** 2 to 6 (usually 3); 2 litters per
year

**Age of Maturity:** female can give birth at
9 months; the spring following birth

**Longevity:** 3 to 4 years in the wild; 10
years in captivity

**Diet:** prefers seeds; also tree buds, bark,
leaves, lichens, fruits, nuts, fungi, maple
sap, insects, bird eggs and fledglings

**Habitat:** heavily wooded areas primarily
composed of coniferous species and
northern hardwoods, such as spruce and
cedar or hemlock/yellow birch habitats

**Predators:** owls, goshawk, grey fox,
weasel, marten, grey wolf, bobcat, lynx
and domestic cat

**Dental Formula:** 1/1, 0/0, 2/1, 3/3 = 22
teeth

*Even though northern flying squirrels
are common, few people ever see one.
These shy squirrels shun daylight.*

## Southern Flying Squirrel  *Glaucomys volans*

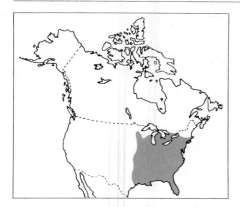

**Mammal:** *Glaucomys volans* — southern flying squirrel
**Meaning of Name:** *Glaucomys* (grey mouse); *volans* (flying)
**Description:** soft silky pelage is pale olive brown, and ventral hairs are white from base to tip (this is different from the northern flying squirrel); tail is grey, ventrally flattened and densely haired; eyes are large, black and luminous; skin of flank extends between wrist and ankle and is supported by cartilaginous spur
**Total Length:** 8.3 to 10.1 inches
**Tail:** 3.1 to 4.7 inches
**Weight:** 1.8 to 2.8 ounces
**Gestation:** 40 days
**Litter Size:** 1 to 6 (usually 2 or 3); 2 litters per year
**Age of Maturity:** usually 1 year; possibly 9 months
**Longevity:** 4 to 5 years in the wild; 8 to 13 years in captivity
**Diet:** omnivore; nuts, acorns, seeds, berries, fruits, moths, Junebugs, trees, buds, bark, eggs and young birds (one of the most carnivorous of sciurids)
**Habitat:** woodlots, prefers seed-producing hardwoods, especially maple/beech stands or poplar stands; also mixed deciduous/coniferous forests
**Predators:** night-flying owls are major predators; also hawks, raccoon, weasel, fox and domestic cat
**Dental Formula:** 1/1, 0/0, 2/1, 3/3 = 22 teeth

Flying squirrels occupy the night-time nut-eating niche in the eastern and northern forests. They are the only nocturnal and gliding North American squirrels. Flying squirrels glide by extending a fold of skin that runs from the wrist of their forearm along the side of their body and out to the ankle of their leg. Their wrist has a cartilage spur that extends outward, further increasing the spread of the membrane. They have flattened tails and a more delicate and lighter body structure than other tree squirrels.

By gliding, they move rapidly from tree to tree, either to forage or to escape predators. A squirrel may start a glide from a running leap, or it may sit motionless on a trunk or limb with its head down in a crouch, then leap outward. They glide at an angle of 30 to 40 degrees and can manoeuvre around tree limbs and other obstacles, even making 90-degree turns. At the end of a glide, they pull up sharply to check their speed and to soften the landing. The length of a glide depends on the height of the launching point. They can glide more than 260 feet — a distance which is not as impressive as the 1,500-foot glides of the larger Asian flying squirrels but which is graceful and beautiful.

Although flying squirrels can soar easily among the trees, they are inept on the ground and are very slow runners. A human can easily run one down. If a flying squirrel is surprised on the ground, it will try to hide if it is not near a tree.

The southern flying squirrel lives in mature hickory, oak and beech forests. They eat the nuts of these trees in addition to bird eggs, nestlings and insects. Their diet is virtually the same as that of *Sciurus* squirrels, but unlike that genus, they cache their nuts above ground in tree hollows.

During the day, flying squirrels den in hollow trees and cavities made by woodpeckers. Sometimes, they use nests of leaves. In winter, as many as 20 squirrels may den together to increase heat retention. Females are territorial during summer and exclude other squirrels of both sexes from their area. Males are less territorial and have broadly overlapping ranges. Females have the potential to breed twice, but whether most females do so is not certain.

*The southern flying squirrel's huge eyes enable it to leap and glide through the forest at night, thereby escaping predators. Some Asian flying squirrels can glide for 1,500 feet, but the two North American species can only glide for 260 feet. Even so, they are capable of manoeuvring around tree trunks and other obstacles and can even execute 90-degree turns.*

## *Eastern Chipmunk* Tamias striatus

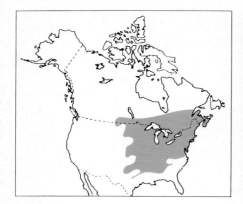

**Mammal:** *Tamias striatus* — eastern chipmunk

**Meaning of Name:** *Tamias* (steward, or one who stores and takes care of provisions); *striatus* (striped)

**Description:** tawny stripes from whiskers to below the ear, which distinguishes it from all other mammals over most of its range; buff cheeks and eye rings; 5 dark brown to black stripes down its back separated by 4 buff lines from shoulders to rump; reddish hips and rump; buff flanks and forefeet; white underparts; openings in sides of mouth lead to pouches for carrying food (each pouch is almost as large as the head when totally filled)

**Total Length:** 9.1 to 11.8 inches

**Tail:** 2.6 to 4.3 inches

**Weight:** 2.3 to 4.5 ounces

**Gestation:** 31 days

**Litter Size:** 1 to 9 (usually 4 or 5); 2 litters per year

**Age of Maturity:** 1 year; occasionally, a female will produce a litter at the age of 3 months

**Longevity:** 2 to 5 years in the wild; 5 to 12 years in captivity

**Diet:** major part of diet consists of reproductive parts of plants (bulbs, seeds, fruits and nuts); also green vegetation, mushrooms, fruits, berries, corn, insects, slugs, worms, frogs, mice, snakes, salamanders and eggs

**Habitat:** deciduous forests with cover and brush; will inhabit more open areas if the earth is porous enough for tunnelling

**Predators:** hawks, fox, raccoon, weasel, domestic cat, snakes, common raven, great blue heron, lynx and coyote

**Dental Formula:** 1/1, 0/0, 1/1, 3/3 = 20 teeth

The eastern chipmunk is one of the most beautifully marked and easily identified squirrels. Many of the rural homes and cottages in eastern North America support a resident population of tame chipmunks, as the species is cute and readily taught to beg for food.

The chipmunk's attractive stripes were not developed with people in mind but are a form of camouflage. Chipmunks are most active during the day when the sun is casting strong shadows; they are thus potential prey for predatory birds. But their striped pattern makes it difficult for aerial predators to isolate them from the shadows cast by tree branches and other plants.

The native habitat of the eastern chipmunk is the deciduous hardwood

*The eastern chipmunk spends most of the daylight hours stuffing its cheek pouches with food. During the summer, chipmunks build up large stores of food to tide them over the winter.*

forest. It is most abundant in mature stands of beech, maple and other trees that produce large nut crops. The chipmunk eats many other foods, however, and can be found in all stages of forest growth including mixed coniferous-deciduous stands. Because they spend most of their time on the ground foraging for nuts and other foods, chipmunks prefer areas with rock piles and other forms of protection where they can easily escape from predators. They rely on vision to detect enemies and so prefer open areas to shade.

*Readily tamed and taught to beg for food, the eastern chipmunk is easily identified by its striped markings, which serve as camouflage from aerial predators.*

Chipmunks have underground nests and only rarely live in tree cavities, even though they are agile climbers. They build a twisting system of burrows, up to 12 feet long, leading to a nest that is about 3 feet below ground. In addition to the nest, the burrow system includes storage tunnels, escape entrances and a work hole. The chipmunk takes care to conceal its burrowing activities, removing the excavated dirt through a work hole (built solely for this purpose) by carrying the soil out in its cheek pouches. It then spreads the soil around the vegetation so there is never a pile of dirt to tell predators where and how fresh the burrow system is. The chipmunk plugs its work hole when not in use and camouflages the regular entrance. It enlarges its tunnel system each year so that by the end of its two-to-five-year life, it has dug an extensive network of side tunnels in addition to the main one. Sometimes, when the original resident of a burrow dies, a new chipmunk takes over and continues to elaborate on the tunnels.

Unlike many other ground-nesting squirrels, the chipmunk does not enter deep hibernation in winter. Instead, it goes into a torpor in which its metabolism is reduced. Periodically, it awakens to eat. In mild weather, it may go above ground to forage, but it usually relies on its large food caches.

The chipmunk devotes much of the summer months to storing food in its burrows, acquiring up to 1 1/2 gallons of tree seeds, nuts and plant tubers that store well. In addition, it eats foliage, buds, many kinds of berries and fruit, insects, mice, frogs, slugs and bird eggs. There are even reports of chipmunks attacking and eating garter and red-bellied snakes.

The social life of the eastern chipmunk is territorial and solitary. Both males and females have their own separate burrow systems that they defend from other chipmunks of either sex. Only in mating season will females tolerate the intrusion of a male into their burrows. Their small home ranges are usually less than 2 1/2 acres in size and sometimes overlap with those of other chipmunks, the size of the home range depends on food availability. They defend their burrow systems vigorously — often with a noisy scolding barrage of chirping and a display of tail jerking — as there is always the risk of having vital food caches robbed.

Male chipmunks remain sexually active from late winter to autumn, which allows females to give birth twice a year, in early spring and again in late summer. The young, which may number up to nine in a litter, are born blind and naked, the usual pattern for underground mammals. They remain with the mother for six weeks before dispersing to establish their own burrows and food stores. This adolescent period is a time of great danger, as a variety of predatory birds, mammals and snakes feed on the young chipmunks while they build new burrows. Even when established in their burrows, chipmunks must watch for weasels and snakes, which enter the tunnels to prey on them.

Eastern chipmunks climb well and are sometimes seen high up in trees, but they are not as adept as tree squirrels in this habitat and thus have trouble competing.

# *Least Chipmunk* Eutamias minimus

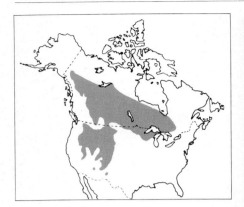

**Mammal:** *Eutamias minimus* — least chipmunk; smallest of chipmunks
**Meaning of Name:** *Eutamias* (true + steward, or one who stores and takes care of provisions); *minimus* (least)
**Description:** small with 3 dark brown stripes crossing the cheeks and 2 white lines between these which terminate at the ears; 5 brown-edged black stripes run across the back to the base of the tail, and the medial ones are mixed with grey; ochraceous shoulders, grey rump and legs and white underparts; buffy orange tail; brown ears with pale grey spots behind them; internal cheek pouches
**Total Length:** male, 8.4 to 12.8 inches; female, 8.9 to 9.4 inches
**Tail:** male, 3.8 to 4.1 inches; female, 3.9 to 4.2 inches
**Weight:** 1.2 to 1.9 ounces
**Gestation:** 28 to 31 days
**Litter Size:** 2 to 7 (usually 5 or 6); 1 litter per year
**Age of Maturity:** the spring following birth
**Longevity:** 6 years in captivity
**Diet:** mostly vegetarian but remains opportunistic and will eat insects and other animal material; seeds, berries, nuts, fruits (except for the pulp)
**Habitat:** alpine tundra; northern mixed hardwood forests and coniferous forests, especially in open jack pine stands and second growth after fires and forestry programmes; shrubby growth, lakeshores, forest edges, brush and log piles
**Predators:** hawks, owls, snakes, ermine, weasel, mink, grizzly bear, red fox and domestic dog and cat
**Dental Formula:** 1/1, 0/0, 2/1, 3/3 = 22 teeth

The least chipmunk is the smallest of the western chipmunks, a group of 19 species that are all very similar in appearance. Accurate identification is difficult, and experts rely on differences in the size, shape and sculpturing of the penis bone to differentiate them. Some biologists consider these chipmunks members of the same genus as the eastern chipmunk.

Unlike most other western chipmunks, the least chipmunk occupies many different kinds of habitats and a broad geographic range. It is found in every habitat from open plains to the edge of the tundra, although its prime habitat is the boreal forest, especially in clearings.

*Being the smallest of all chipmunks enables the least chipmunk to forage on tiny grass seeds, small berries and insects ignored by other squirrels.*

Most of its activities are similar to those of the eastern chipmunk. It tends to eat smaller seeds than eastern chipmunks do, even opting for the tiny seeds of blueberries and many kinds of grasses. It consumes more insects and fewer vertebrates than the eastern chipmunk and normally has only a single litter each year.

## Caching In

*Many small rodents cannot hibernate because their metabolism* is too high and their body too small to put on enough fat for a northern winter without feeding. Caching food has been their solution. The biggest stashes are built by the biggest rodents. Beavers, for example, may cache a mound of tree branches several yards in diameter. The edible part of the cache is bark, which is available all winter long, but by caching it underwater, the beaver minimizes its predation risk. Another winter bark eater — the porcupine — has not evolved caching behaviour, which none of its tropical ancestors needed. Consequently, the porcupine must climb trees to keep feeding all winter and is highly exposed to predators. Fishers can catch large numbers of winter-foraging porcupines, and horned owls will pluck them from the branches. It would seem that porcupines could profit from the use of a cache, even if it were only at the base of a tree with a rock crevice close at hand.

Predator pressure may favour caching in beavers, but most small rodents cache because of energetic necessity. Burrowing root feeders, such as prairie and woodland voles, build large caches of roots and tubers, high-energy foods that store well. One prairie vole cache excavated in Manitoba contained an amazing harvest of 1,176 lily bulbs, 678 onion bulbs, 583 sunflower roots and 417 pasqueflower roots. Such a concentration of resources undoubtedly attracts cache robbers and requires investment in defence. In addition to the depredation by other voles, humans often rob caches. Plains Indians sought prairie vole caches, and the Inuit sought those of yellow-cheeked voles. The natives are reported to have trained dogs to sniff out the licorice root stashed by tundra rodents.

The risk of theft strongly influences the hoarding strategies of squirrels. Sciurus species, like the grey squirrels, hide each acorn and nut separately and thereby decrease the risk of losing an entire stash. Red squirrels that feed on large piles of conifer seeds, on the other hand, build them into vast central middens containing bushels of cones. Red squirrels can afford to concentrate their food stores because they

normally have to defend them only against other red squirrels. Each cone is a small fraction of the total store, and serious losses could not be experienced before being detected by the territorial owner. When their territories overlap those of grey squirrels, the red squirrels must scatter their hoards, for the grey squirrels ignore the red squirrels' threats.

Chipmunks also use scatter hoarding to deal with the problem of theft. The burrow serves as a primary storage site, but nearby chipmunks frequently rob their neighbours' burrows. Large cheek pouches enable a chipmunk thief to run in and quickly carry off prized items such as lily bulbs. Thieving chipmunks will make repeated trips to a neighbour's burrow as long as they can get away with it. The scatter hoards of the chipmunk are smaller and better hidden than the main burrow hoard. When its burrow is robbed, a chipmunk uses the scatter hoards to replace what it lost from the burrow. These scatter hoards are a kind of theft insurance, and when there is no theft, many scatter hoards are left to rot or sprout if they contain seeds. Chipmunks also place the scatter hoards in spots where they can keep an eye on their burrow while they are working and rush back if a thief is spotted.

The scatter hoarding of grey squirrels is less easily explained. Flying squirrels in the same forest

*Harvesting seeds and nuts is only one of the problems a chipmunk must deal with. Theft by neighbouring chipmunks is a constant threat.*

use piles of nuts in tree holes. The strategy may be related to the fact that flying squirrels are much poorer runners on the ground than grey squirrels, and tree holes for caches are limited and must be filled with several nuts. The flying squirrels trade a risk of theft against greater safety from predators. The day-active and visually acute grey squirrel may suffer less predation and be more concerned about minimizing robbery. Storing vegetable food is also done by lagomorphs such as pikas. They use the same haying technique as wood rats, stacking vegetation to dry to prevent it from composting in the cache. This is clearly a case of convergent behavioural evolution, the phenomenon in which two different and unrelated species confronted with the same problem (a long, barren winter) have evolved the same solution.

# Townsend's Chipmunk *Eutamias townsendii*

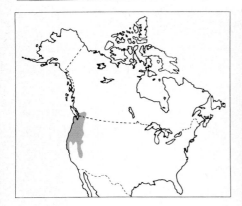

**Mammal:** *Eutamias townsendii* —
Townsend's chipmunk; largest of
western chipmunks

**Meaning of Name:** *Eutamias* (true +
steward, or one who stores and takes
care of provisions); *townsendii*
(named after its discoverer,
J.K. Townsend)

**Description:** dark brown, which offers
little contrast to the dull yellowish or
greyish light stripes along its side and
back, making it difficult to see; 2 brown
stripes cross buff cheeks, tan
underparts; brownish stripe below ear;
reddish tail bordered by subterminal
black band and grey tips

**Total Length:** male, 9.7 to 10.4 inches;
female, 10.4 to 11 inches

**Tail:** male, 4.1 to 4.7 inches; female, 4.7
to 5.1 inches

**Weight:** 2.5 to 4.3 ounces

**Gestation:** 30 days

**Litter Size:** 2 to 7 (usually 5)

**Age of Maturity:** the spring following
birth

**Longevity:** 7 years in the wild

**Diet:** omnivore; diet includes roots,
bulbs, grasses, seeds, berries and nuts
as well as a substantial amount of animal
matter in the form of insects, fledglings
and eggs; also cannibalistic

**Habitat:** dense coniferous forests and
coastal lowlands; often lives in
subclimax brush and log habitat, since
much of its natural habitat has been
logged over

**Predators:** hawks, golden eagle,
badger, marten, fox, skunk, wolverine,
lynx, coyote, fisher and raccoon; weasel
is main predator

**Dental Formula:** 1/1, 0/0, 2/1, 3/3 = 22
teeth

Townsend's chipmunk is the largest species of chipmunk. It favours
thick, tangled vegetation and, when
compared with similar species, is secretive and shy. Its coat is darker than
other chipmunks', a coloration that
may reflect its choice of habitat. It is
found in the wet, humid Pacific coast
forests, which have far less sunlight
than the habitats favoured by light-
coated species. It is more arboreal
than most other chipmunks, climbing
trees and shrubs to forage and building summer tree nests for caching
food. Its diet is typical of chipmunks
and includes a general selection of
plant parts and insects.

*The largest chipmunk, the Townsend's
chipmunk has adapted to life in the tall
forests by becoming a climber.*

# *Yellow Pine Chipmunk* Eutamias amoenus

**Mammal:** *Eutamias amoenus* — yellow pine chipmunk

**Meaning of Name:** *Eutamias* (true + steward, or one who stores and takes care of provisions); *amoenus* (delightful)

**Description:** ochraceous colour with cinnamon flanks and brownish grey rump; ears black dorsally edged with white posteriorly; buff to white underneath; tail rusty above and tawny underneath; cheeks crossed with 3 dark stripes, the middle one running through the eye; 5 dorsal dark stripes with 4 paler stripes in between

**Total Length:** 8.4 to 9.1 inches

**Tail:** 3 to 4.3 inches

**Weight:** 1.6 to 2.2 ounces

**Gestation:** 28 days

**Litter Size:** 5 to 7; 1 litter per year

**Age of Maturity:** the spring following birth

**Longevity:** at least 5 years in the wild

**Diet:** primarily a seed eater; nuts are not as important as they are in other chipmunks' diets; some insects are eaten but less frequently than other chipmunks; fungi

**Habitat:** open coniferous forests, especially burned-over areas with stumps and brush; also brushy zones on the borders of the open alpine tundra

**Predators:** long-tailed weasel is the most dangerous of predators; also pine marten, rattlesnake, pygmy owl and hawks

**Dental Formula:** 1/1, 0/0, 2/1, 3/3 = 22 teeth

*By specializing in dry yellow pine forests, the yellow pine chipmunk has minimized the amount of competition it faces from the many other species of western chipmunk.*

The yellow pine chipmunk is a specialist of the dry, open and rocky habitats found in yellow pine and Douglas fir forests. In mountainous areas, this species ranges from the lowlands all the way to the edge of the tree line.

This species' burrow system is usually less than a yard long and serves as a storehouse for seeds, especially pine seeds. During the summer, the yellow pine chipmunk eats fungi, the needles of coniferous trees and the leaves of herbaceous plants, while in winter it forages more above ground than other chipmunk species. There is a single spring breeding season and a single litter per year.

The ***red-tailed chipmunk***, *E. ruficaudus*, is one of the larger, more arboreal chipmunks, living in dense coniferous forests where it is active among the lower branches. In regions where the yellow pine chipmunk and red-tailed chipmunk are found together, the red-tailed chipmunk usually lives at higher altitudes. Although it sometimes nests in tree cavities, the red-tailed chipmunk usually makes summer nests of balls of grass hidden in the dense foliage of trees 15 feet or more above ground. During winter, it moves to typical chipmunk underground burrows. Its diet is more herbivorous than that of many western chipmunks, consisting mostly of leaves, buds and shoots.

# Pocket Gophers Geomyidae

Pocket gophers are underground specialists. Their short tails, small eyes and reduced flaps are reminiscent of moles' and provide gophers with suitable protection for a life in tunnels. Their eyelids clamp shut so tightly that even the finest dust grains cannot penetrate them, and their ears have valves to close off the outer opening. There are special hairs in the tail and in the loose-fitting skin that are equipped with mechanoreceptors, cells that are sensitive to touch and help gophers orient themselves in the dark. Like moles, they have stout, powerful forelimbs with large scraping claws for digging. Some species, especially those living in hard soil, also appear to use their large projecting incisors in digging. Gophers are small enough to fit in a coat pocket, but their common name actually comes from their fur-lined cheek pouches, which they use to transport food. Presumably, the fur lining is an adaptation to cope with hauling gritty soil-coated roots around in the mouth. Like pants pockets, the gophers' cheek pockets can be turned inside out for food removal and cleaning.

Gophers' teeth and foreclaws grow continuously and rapidly. One study estimates that over the course of a year, their total tooth growth would measure 1 1/2 feet longer than the entire body length of the gopher itself. Of course, this tooth growth is constantly eroded by their digging and gritty diet.

Pocket gophers eat only plant matter, primarily grasses, herbs, limited amounts of shrubbery and great quantities of roots and bulbs, which they drag into their burrows to eat. They build up large caches of roots in autumn for use during winter when the upper soil layers are frozen solid. Pocket gophers are generalists, shifting their diet according to plant availability and their need for water, vitamins and plants to store for winter. Rapidly growing legumes, for example, contain high amounts of protein required by young growing gophers, whereas roots are rich in carbohydrate energy and overwinter well in the storage chambers.

Tunnelling is an energetically costly way to forage. Studies indicate that a gopher's foraging strategy reduces these costs by keeping the tunnel radius to the absolute minimum required for passage. Gophers dispose of excavated soil by piling it in mounds, an activity that attracts predators. Since large mounds must increase mortality rates, smaller gophers that make smaller mounds are more successful. The gopher's size is also influenced by the strength required to excavate soils of different textures. Harder soils demand greater effort, so the gopher is likely to be larger. The combination of predator pressure and soil texture may have led to the evolution of different body sizes in various pocket gopher species and races.

The herbivorous diet of pocket gophers makes them pests in agricultural situations. In addition to the damage they do to root crops, their extensive burrows cause many problems. One gopher built 478 feet of tunnel in five months. It has been estimated that a gopher excavates more than 1 ton of soil every year. Thus in a field occupied by a colony of gophers, as much as 6 tons of earth per acre may be moved yearly. Much of this soil is pushed up to the surface and left in mounds that interfere with the operation of agricultural machinery. As a result of these problems, farmers poison vast numbers of pocket gophers every year.

Gopher mounds can be distinguished from molehills by the fan shape created when the gopher turns around and kicks the dirt out with his hind feet. The soil plug is located to one side rather than in the centre, as in molehills. Gophers also fill in tunnels that have been harvested of roots, whereas moles use them as pitfalls to trap mobile worms and insects.

The tunnel system provides gophers with a stable environment as well as protection from many predators. Gophers have two types of tunnel: a shallow set less than 20 inches below the surface for eating, travelling and collecting roots and a deeper set for breeding and as a refuge from digging predators and excessively hot or cold weather. The nest chamber lies well below the frost line, keeping the gopher warm during harsh winters. Likewise, the nest remains cool and humid during the heat of summer. Pocket gophers, like mountain beavers, have a limited tolerance to high temperatures. A pocket gopher will die within an hour if exposed to temperatures of 100 degrees F. Cold temperatures are less of a problem. Gophers remain active in the winter and extend their burrow system under the snow pack.

Soil characteristics are a large factor in controlling the density and distribution of territories of underground animals. Pocket gophers seal their burrows with a firm plug of soil when they are inside. This keeps out flash-flooding rains, predators and parasitic flies. However, it also makes the gopher dependent on the soil's gas exchange to provide oxygen. Therefore, gophers cannot live in clay or wet

*The northern pocket gopher, like all geomyids, uses its powerful forepaws to excavate tender shoots and plant roots.*

*Spring thaw reveals the extensive labyrinth of pocket gopher burrows built in search of plant roots and tubers.*

soils that have poor gas exchange. They also avoid very shallow soils and excessively rocky or hard soils. Gophers prefer a friable deep loam with good drainage. Wherever such soils occur, pocket gophers of one species or another will be found. They are found in a wide range of habitats in western, north and central North America, except for the northern boreal forest and tundra. Even in porous soils, carbon dioxide concentrations in burrows are high. As a result, pocket gophers have evolved a physiological tolerance for high carbon dioxide and low oxygen. Their metabolism is also lower than expected for animals of that size.

Pocket gophers of different species do not normally live in the same area. The range of one species extends until it abruptly ends and a new species occurs. These contiguous but nonoverlapping distributions suggest that competition between the different species is affected by soil types. It may be that certain species can live only in a particular soil type, thus limiting the range of each species.

Population density is related to the amount of forage available and the size of individual territories. An individual may range over 200 square yards. Pocket gophers, like most burrowing mammals, are intensely territorial. Neither males nor females tolerate intruders, and both sexes will fight fiercely. A burrow is a large time and energy investment and is thus a valuable resource. If a gopher is trapped and removed from its burrow, the burrow is soon reoccupied. During one study on trapping, 18 gophers were consecutively removed from a single burrow. Gophers only cohabit during the mating season. Some species appear to have a social system in which adjacent males and females share a common nesting burrow along with a separate set of shallow tunnels as their territories. Males are polygynous and often have territories that overlap several female territories. Their polygyny is reflected in their size. In some species, the males grow twice as large as the females, suggesting that males are selected for fighting and territorial ability.

Most species of pocket gopher appear to have similar life cycles. Mating takes place in winter or early spring, according to the species and habitat. Northern and high-altitude populations have one litter per year, while southern populations may breed several times in a year, especially if they inhabit rich agricultural areas. Females may mature in their first year, but males mature in their second year. This later maturation is likely part of the successful male reproductive strategy, which requires a large body size for polygynous territorial defence. A large body size may also be necessary because of the costs of finding a mate. Males find their mates by digging underground and constructing long straight-line burrows. This transect approach maximizes the total number of burrows the male may intersect. Straight-line runs of 150 yards have been reported. After mating, females and males reseal and separate their burrows.

Pocket gophers have relatively low litter sizes, often averaging only three offspring. Their closed-burrow system protects their young, so that infant mortality is low. Consequently, they do not need to produce large litters. The young, like most burrowing mammals, are born in a completely helpless altricial state, with their eyes, ears and cheek pouches completely

*An escaping pocket gopher seems to dive literally headfirst into the soil, clearing its way with strong forelimbs.*

closed. They do not open their eyes and ears until they are almost 4 weeks old and are weaned after five to six weeks, which is a long time given the small size and short life span of these animals. When the young gophers are 2 months old, they disperse to set up their own burrow systems. Their chances of success are low. Males have an expected life span of little more than a year, and females of a year and a half. A wide variety of predatory mammals, snakes and birds eat pocket gophers.

Pocket gophers' burrows bring many ecological benefits to natural habitats. They are havens for a wide variety of animals including tiger salamanders, box turtles, burrowing owls, toads, lizards and many mammals such as skunks, weasels and rabbits. One survey of southern pocket gophers revealed that 15 different species of animals were found only in pocket gopher burrows and were highly adapted for a subterranean existence.

In addition, the gopher's digging improves soil aeration and texture and increases the percolation of water into the ground. Their mounds provide germination sites for rare plant species that rely on quick colonization and dispersal to survive competition from larger and longer-lived herbs and shrubs. It has been suggested that the interaction of the great herds of bison — which once grazed western North America — with pocket gophers and prairie dogs helped build the deep grassland soils. The bison created many wallows, trampling and denuding areas that were then colonized by the plants gophers prefer. The plants, in turn, attracted higher populations of gophers, whose deep burrowing brought new mineral soil to the surface where it mixed with plant humus and animal dung to produce the deep loams of the grassland prairies.

Similarly, today's overgrazing by domestic livestock removes vegetative cover and usually results in an increase in pocket gopher populations. The gophers' cropping activities will then keep the area open for decades, even if the livestock is removed.

# Northern Pocket Gopher   Thomomys talpoides

**Mammal:** *Thomomys talpoides* — northern pocket gopher
**Meaning of Name:** *Thomomys* (heap + mouse) refers to the heaps of earth thrown at frequent intervals along the line of the burrows; *talpoides* (molelike), because of its burrowing habits
**Description:** grey colour washed with brown; thick stubby tail that is sparsely covered with short stiff white hairs; soles of feet are naked except for a row of short bristles surrounding them; large fur-lined cheek pouches open on the side of the face; furred lips can close behind projecting incisors, enabling the gopher to cut roots and dig without eating dirt
**Total Length:** male, 7.5 to 10.1 inches; female, 8.7 inches
**Tail:** male, 1.9 to 3 inches; female, 2.6 inches
**Weight:** male, 5.3 ounces; female, 4.5 ounces
**Gestation:** 18 days
**Litter Size:** 1 to 8 (average of 3); 1 or 2 litters per year
**Age of Maturity:** male, in its second year; female, 11 to 12 months
**Longevity:** can live 4 to 5 years in the wild, but most do not live beyond their second year; 6 years in captivity
**Diet:** primarily roots of perennial forbs as well as green parts of plants
**Habitat:** grassy prairies, mountain meadows, fields, brushy areas, riverbanks and open pine forests; broad range of soil tolerance but prefers moist, not wet, soils
**Predators:** owls, badger, weasel, skunk, coyote, fox and snakes
**Dental Formula:** 1/1, 0/0, 1/1, 3/3 = 20 teeth

The northern pocket gopher inhabits the deep soils of the northern prairies and the meadows of the western mountains. It is the northernmost species of pocket gopher. It prefers moist but not wet soils and will tolerate heavy soil. In the summer, these gophers may move from drier soils to damper ones. Also, during the summer nights, they make brief, above-ground foraging trips to cut herbaceous plants, which they drag down into their burrows. Weasels, badgers and gopher snakes are their main predators.

The **plains pocket gopher**, *Geomys bursarius*, is one of the largest pocket gophers. It inhabits sandy soils of the central prairies and avoids clay and gravelly soils.

## The Variable Gopher

*Pocket gophers are an exclusively North American group. They are not particularly old; in fact, modern genera appeared only four million years ago. Yet within that time, the group has diversified into some 35 different species and 300 subspecies.*

*A subspecies is a race or variety of the main species — a group of populations which is physically different and distinct from other populations of the species and which inhabits a distinct geographical area. Nevertheless, there are several difficulties with the basic idea of subspecific description. The description of a subspecies is more arbitrary than that of a true species. Species are usually genetically,*

*The selective grazing of northern pocket gophers influences the composition of plant communities.*

*physically and otherwise distinct entities, but subspecies intergrade. Clear-cut boundaries between subspecies often do not exist, and only sophisticated statistical analyses can distinguish differences between populations.*

*However, members of a species do vary in appearance, and the subspecific category has been a useful way of documenting that variation. The variation is interesting because it suggests how subdivided and plastic some species are.*

*Biologically, a species is defined as a population of individuals that can interbreed. The mixing of genes during sexual reproduction makes every member of the species part of a common gene pool that is distinct and separate from the gene pool of other species. Sometimes, however, members of one population may cross a geographical barrier, such as a river, and interbreed with a different population. Over time, the genetic compositions of the two populations may diverge through mutation or localized selection. A gopher population in a high-altitude region, for example, will be under different environmental pressures than will one living in a low-altitude region. These pressures produce localized differences within the same species, creating subspecies. If the differences and isolation are reinforced, the subspecies may become so different that they are no*

longer capable of interbreeding and thus must be considered separate species.

Pocket gophers represent an extreme case of species subdivision. Because the animals are quite sedentary, rates of interbreeding between various populations may be low. Yet there is great variety within a species, making the taxonomy of pocket gophers exceedingly difficult. Geographically separate populations of some species look as different from each other as do members of other species. Traditional taxonomy relies on physical characteristics to determine to which species an animal belongs. However, this is often not sufficient with gophers, and taxonomists must then use genetic techniques to make an absolute identification. All of this suggests that the speciation process is still active in pocket gophers.

Pocket gophers churn and aerate the layers of soil, improving its texture and ability to hold water.

# *Porcupine* Erethizontidae

## *Porcupine*   Erethizon dorsatum

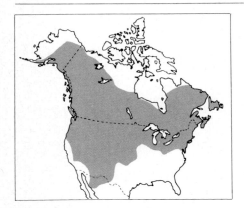

**Mammal:** *Erethizon dorsatum* —
porcupine, the second largest rodent
(next to the beaver)
**Meaning of Name:** *Erethizon* alludes to
the porcupine's ability to excite or
irritate; *dorsatum* (pertaining to the back)
refers to the spines
**Description:** first digit on hind feet is
replaced with a broad movable pad,
allowing a firmer grasp on branches;
adult coat is glossy brown to black
above; individual hairs are often tipped
with white or yellow-white; approximately
30,000 quills with brown tips and hollow
shafts; coarse dark brown hair ventrally
contains no quills
**Total Length:** 25.5 to 35.5 inches
**Tail:** 5.7 to 11.8 inches
**Weight:** 7.3 to 30.2 pounds; large males
may be 39.7 pounds
**Gestation:** 205 to 217 days
**Litter Size:** 1 (twins are rare)
**Age of Maturity:** 1.5 to 2.5 years
**Longevity:** 6 to 11 years
**Diet:** primarily vegetarian; green leaves
of forbs, shrubs and trees; clovers,
alfalfa, corn; cambium layer, inner bark,
needles and barbs of trees (especially
yellow and white pine); in summer and
late winter, they crave sodium and gnaw
on bones and antlers or axe handles,
oars, utensils — anything with salt from
the kitchen or perspiring humans on it .
**Habitat:** forests with mixed deciduous
and coniferous trees but prefers hemlock
and pine habitats; sometimes found on
prairies and in eastern farmland and
aspen swamps; makes use of rocky talus
slopes, quarries and caves
**Predators:** fisher is most successful;
also wolverine, bobcat and occasionally
wolf, coyote, fox and great horned owl
**Dental Formula:** 1/1, 0/0, 1/1, 3/3 = 20
teeth

New World porcupines evolved in
South America as forest animals. Like
many other South American animals,
they are adapted for a life in the trees.
The large pads and claws of their two
hind feet act as clamps when they
climb onto tree trunks. Their stiff belly
hairs give them a further firm grip on
the tree's bark. One South American
genus even has a naked, muscular,
prehensile tail for tree climbing.

The North American porcupine is a
recent offshoot of the South American
stock. Porcupines first moved into
North America when a land bridge
formed, connecting the two previously separate Americas several million years ago. The porcupine found
a ready niche in North American forests, as no large grazer then existed
that could feed on the bark and twigs
of trees as well as on their leaves. Thus
the porcupine became an abundant arboreal animal in North America. It is,
in fact, far more common than South
American porcupines, which face stiff
competition from leaf-eating squirrels, monkeys and other mammals.

The porcupine's most striking feature is its hair, which has been modified into barbed quills. These quills
are designed to penetrate and work
into the skin and flesh of would-be
predators. Each quill has a sharply
pointed end with a series of overlapping shinglelike barbs. When the
quill penetrates skin or flesh, these
shingles expand, and as the muscles
of the victim shift and contract, the
quill is drawn deeper into the flesh.
Porcupines do not throw their quills,
as is commonly believed. They do
have muscles in their skin that cause

the quills to stand erect and detach
easily when the animals are threatened. But it is usually the action of the
attacker or the swinging tail of the porcupine that delivers a load of quills.
Because of their barbs, the quills are
difficult to remove, which often causes
festering and may result in death.
Even if the animal does not die, it has
learned a powerful lesson about porcupines. The lesson may also contribute to the porcupines' continued survival. They are sedentary creatures
and may occupy the same territory for
years. It is likely that raccoons, foxes
and other animals that share their territory only harass a porcupine once.

Porcupines are not, however, invincible. Their large size makes them
a valuable prey item, and there are
animals that have developed techniques for killing them without being
badly quilled. Fishers are the most famous enemies of porcupines. Fast-
moving predators, they can rush in on
the clumsy and myopic porcupine
and bite it in the face until it is dead or
helpless. They then turn the porcupine over, exposing its quill-less
belly, and eat through its gut until
only the outer skin of quills remains.
Great horned owls also kill porcupines by driving a talon through the
eye and into the brain. Various other
large carnivores, such as pumas, also
eat porcupines. The porcupine defends itself from such predators by
climbing a tree and placing its back to
the attacker so that its strong, flailing
tail lies between the two.

*The porcupine is the only animal
adapted for grazing the upper reaches
of northern forests.*

Porcupines are generalized herbivores that eat a wide variety of plants. They feed on almost every kind of tree they encounter. In winter, the bark, sapwood and buds of trees make up the bulk of their diet, especially in areas with severe snow cover. During summer, they feed mainly on the ground, eating shrubs and herbaceous plants. Sometimes, they even wade into ponds to eat water lilies, possibly because of the high sodium content of many aquatic plants. A taste for salt also accounts for the porcupine's habit of eating plywood, outhouses and boat seats, virtually anything that has an elevated salt content. When given a choice, they prefer alkaline food sources to acidic foods.

The porcupine, a powerful gnawing animal, is equipped with large protruding incisors and strong jaw muscles. Its gut, like that of most herbivores, is long, nearly 21 feet in length, and is designed to ferment and extract nutrients from a large volume of plant material. Bacterial fermentation of plant cellulose molecules contributes a third of the porcupine's energy requirements.

The porcupine is usually a solitary animal that feeds by itself. It is not, however, territorial. Often two animals can be seen feeding amicably in the same tree or pasture. During winter, several porcupines may share the same rocky den, hollow tree or cabin crawl space. Each porcupine's home territory shifts with the season. In the winter, they rarely move more than a few hundred yards from their den site. In summer, however, they may range over 250 acres. They also disperse in early and late summer. Some individuals move as far as 20 miles during these times, and a 6-mile dispersal is not uncommon. The reasons for such dispersals are unknown but may be related to the depletion of food resources around their dens, as well as the need to mate with unrelated individuals.

The only intense social interactions seem to occur during the late-summer and autumn breeding season. Females come into heat for only 12 hours, and they mate only once. During the rest of the year, it is thought that a membrane seals the vagina. As a result, there is intense male-male competition for mating opportunities. Males are highly aggressive to other males

and will engage in fierce battles during which they bite and drive hundreds of quills into each other (porcupines are adept at pulling quills out of themselves). They also scream loudly and utter a variety of grunts, whines and screeches while chattering their teeth threateningly. There is usually an excess of females in any porcupine population, indicating that male-male combat may lead to relatively high male mortality rates.

In the mating season, the male searches for females and declares his own presence by urinating in the area. He also searches for female urination sites; these probably contain hormones that indicate the animal's sex and reproductive state. When a male does find a female's urination site, he rubs his genital region over the area, possibly marking it with a glandular signal.

Chemical communication plays a large role in porcupine courtship. Here is one account of the process so many people have wondered about:

*The long fur of the porcupine enables it to forage in the dead of winter.*

"The male usually coaxes the female to the ground, where he will rear on hind legs and tail while emitting low vocal 'grunts.' He then proceeds to spray the female with bursts of urine from a rapidly erecting penis, and after wrestling, chases, vocalization and more urine showers, a coitus is effected. It is performed, as in most mammals, with the male taking the active role and, contrary to folklore, mounting from the rear. The receptive female elevates her hindquarters and arches her tail over her back, providing the male with a platform for his forepaws or chest. The male then permits his forepaws to hang free. Coital contact is brief, with a violent ejaculation, and afterward, the male drops back to groom and clean. Further matings may ensue until one of the pair climbs a tree and ends the contact by hostile screaming. A vaginal plug is formed shortly after mating, and the female is no longer receptive.''

Porcupine males have very large Cowper's and prostate glands, which may produce a secretion that creates the mating plug. The design of their penis is unique. It lies pointing backwards in a sheath, and a complex set of muscles, rather than blood pressure, causes an erection. The reason for this design is unknown, but it may help the porcupine to climb and descend from trees rapidly.

Porcupines invest a great deal of energy in rearing their offspring. The litter size is low, as rodents go — one offspring per year — and the pregnancy period is long, 205 to 217 days. This is as long a gestation period as that of large grazing herbivores, such as moose. The young are born in a den during spring and early summer and are quite precocial. At birth, their eyes are open, their quills are functional, and they are mobile. They are even able to eat vegetation within a week. Nevertheless, the mothers remain close to their young and feed them milk for much of the summer. It is not known why porcupines put such a heavy investment in so few young. It may be that compared with other rodents, porcupines have low mortality rates and stable populations. Their large size may give offspring a competitive advantage and enable them to ward off large predators.

It is difficult to say how long porcupines live, but in captivity, they are known to live more than 10 years. Their longevity means that in spite of their low birth rate, populations can become very dense — and a dense population of porcupines can result in considerable tree mortality. Porcupines are not prudent harvesters. Rather than browsing from tree to tree, a porcupine sits in one mature tree for days. During this time, it will completely girdle the tree, eating the top into a gaunt white skeleton and eventually killing it. As a result, it is necessary to control porcupines, particularly since their natural control, the fisher, has been extinguished by trapping over much of their former range. Ideally, the reintroduction of such natural predators as the fisher should be encouraged, and a moratorium on, or better control of, fisher trapping should be promoted.

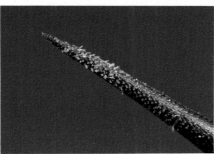

*A threatened porcupine, **top**, erects a set of dense, sharply pointed quills. These specially modified quills have a tip coated with backward-pointing scales, **middle**, that hold the quill firmly in the flesh of an attacker. The powerful claws of the porcupine, **bottom**, are used not defensively but to grip tree trunks and limbs and to press the calloused pad on the palm down to provide firm traction while climbing.*

# Kangaroo Rats & Pocket Mice *Heteromyidae*

## Olive-backed Pocket Mouse *Perognathus fasciatus*

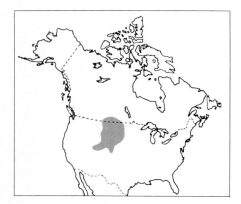

**Mammal:** *Perognathus fasciatus* — olive-backed pocket mouse
**Meaning of Name:** *Perognathus* refers to the fur-lined pockets on the outside of the cheeks where it stores and carries food; *fasciatus* from *fascia* (band, girdle)
**Description:** stiff but silky pelage; external fur-lined cheek pouches can be turned inside out for washing; olive grey dorsally and white underparts bordered by a buffy yellow stripe that runs from the cheek to the thigh
**Total Length:** 4.5 to 5.7 inches
**Tail:** 2.2 to 2.6 inches
**Weight:** 0.25 to 0.35 ounces
**Gestation:** not known (probably 3 to 4 weeks)
**Litter Size:** 4 to 6; 1 litter per year (may have 2)
**Age of Maturity:** if born early in the season, can breed by late summer
**Longevity:** 2 years
**Diet:** major food is weed seed but will also eat insects
**Habitat:** open grasslands with sandy loam; also found on the edge of aspen parklands
**Predators:** rattlesnake, owls, weasel, badger, skunk, fox, coyote and mouse
**Dental Formula:** 1/1, 0/0, 1/1, 3/3 = 20 teeth

Kangaroo rats and pocket mice are close relatives of pocket gophers, but they have evolved in a different direction. While pocket gophers went underground and evolved a long, squat body with powerful forelimbs, kangaroo rats became upright animals with small, weak forelimbs and large hind limbs designed for bouncing across arid open habitats. Like kangaroos, they have a long tail that acts as a balancing organ when they hop. Their hind feet, like those of the kangaroo, are also drawn out to provide a long base. Their neck is short, a design that keeps the head stable when the animal is hopping.

They share with the pocket gophers fur-lined mouth pockets used for transporting large mouthfuls of seeds, and they also have similar teeth.

The heteromyid rodents are delicate mice with thin bones and a narrow mouselike skull that has a huge enlargement at the ear bones, an adaptation used for detecting the sounds of striking predators.

The family is confined to the Americas and contains 75 species.

Pocket mice are bounders. They have enlarged hind feet that propel them along with leaps of a yard or more. But, unlike kangaroo rats, pocket mice stand in a horizontal bipedal posture rather than in an upright position. Their tail is about one body length long, shorter and not as bushy as that of a kangaroo rat.

Only one-quarter to one-third of an ounce, the olive-backed pocket mouse is one of the smallest North American rodents. It is a resident of dry shortgrass prairie, especially where the soil is sandy and there are bare areas. It is a solitary species and makes shallow burrows through the light sand, avoiding heavy and humus-rich soils. The forepaws are used in digging, something that kangaroo rats are unable or unwilling to do. The pocket mouse often takes sand baths, which may reduce its skin-parasite load and help keep it clean. Sand bathing is also thought to be a form of scent-marking that declares territorial presence. The sand piles that result from burrowing and the subsequent use of these piles for bathing may be forms of chemical communication among pocket mice and other heteromyids.

The olive-backed pocket mouse and other pocket mouse species build summer nests roughly 1 to 2 feet below the surface and winter nests 6 feet deep. They go into a torpor during cold weather but are not deep hibernators and rely on caches of stored seeds to get through the winter. They obtain all their water from these seeds.

Owls, snakes and predatory mammals prey on pocket mice.

Pocket mice breed twice a season, in spring and in summer, producing a litter of roughly four.

The **Great Basin pocket mouse**, *P. parvus*, has a similar biology to the olive-backed pocket mouse, except instead of seeds, it eats significant numbers of insects during the summer months. The habitat of this mouse is the shrubby plains of the Great Basin in the western United States.

# *Ord's Kangaroo Rat* Dipodomys ordii

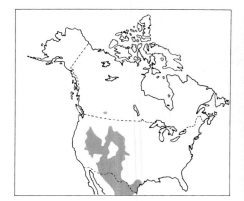

**Mammal:** *Dipodomys ordii* — Ord's kangaroo rat
**Meaning of Name:** *Dipodomys* (two-footed mouse); *ordii* (named after pioneer American zoologist George Ord)
**Description:** upper parts are tawny with a few black hairs along the mid-dorsal line; white underparts; white spot over each eye; white lines across the hips; ventral stripe tapers to a point near the tip of the tail; 2 grey lines above and below tail and grey terminal tuft; furred cheek pouches; large luminous dorsal eyes
**Total Length:** 10.4 to 11.1 inches
**Tail:** 5.6 to 6.2 inches
**Weight:** 1.9 to 3.4 ounces (peaks at breeding season)
**Gestation:** 29 to 30 days
**Litter Size:** 1 to 6; may be 2 litters per year
**Age of Maturity:** may become mature at the age of 2 months
**Longevity:** at least 2 years in the wild
**Diet:** seeds, grasses and forbs form most of the diet; also some fruits, leaves, stems, buds and insects
**Habitat:** sandy soils in open areas with sparse brush or grass
**Predators:** rattlesnake, burrowing short-eared owl, horned owl, badger, black-footed ferret, skunk, fox, coyote and weasel
**Dental Formula:** 1/1, 0/0, 1/1, 3/3 = 20 teeth

Ord's is the most generalized and wide-ranging kangaroo rat. Like all members of the genus, it is a bipedal hopper, living in dry, sandy areas. Its tail and hind legs are large and are used for locomotion, for dodging predators and for communicating and fighting with other kangaroo rats.

This kangaroo rat, like others, is not a strong digger but, instead, builds burrows in the sand where it hides during the day. The burrows run less than 3 feet down to a grass-lined nest. There are side chambers for seed storage and some surface branching tunnels. The nest is usually built into the side of a bank or mound. A series of well-worn trails used in foraging extends from the entrance. This rat also constructs shallow funk holes, which it uses to avoid predators temporarily.

The Ord's kangaroo rat eats most kinds of seeds found in the areas where it lives. It will also eat grasshoppers, moths and other insects along with some roots and green leafy material. It may depend on the presence of succulent legumes with fleshy tubers for much of its water requirement during dry periods.

The breeding system of the Ord's kangaroo rat is tied to the rains. Few females come into oestrus during dry times, whereas rains will stimulate breeding. This corresponds to a similar behaviour on the part of the plants. Many plant species in arid areas adjust their flowering and seed production to the abundance of winter rain. Kangaroo rats can adjust their reproduction to match the expected seed crop. There may be two breeding periods following the winter and summer rainy seasons.

*Heteromyids such as Kangaroo rats can live in the driest habitats, obtaining all their water from dried plant seeds.*

Kangaroo rats are solitary and territorial. Individuals fight by jumping in the air and slashing at each other with their clawed hind legs. They also turn backwards and kick sand at enemies, including rattlesnakes.

Snakes are prominent nocturnal predators in the hot, arid and open habitat of the kangaroo rat, and some of the rat's sensory physiology is designed to match the physical features of this environment. Kangaroo rats have large dorsally placed eyes that give them excellent night vision and a view of aerial predators such as owls and some bats. Their hugely enlarged eardrums are sensitive to very low-frequency sounds, which enables them to hear the wing beat of an approaching owl and to detect the air pressure wave of a striking rattlesnake. Kangaroo rats are often able to leap out of the way of a striking snake because they can hear the strike coming. A kangaroo rat can leap 6 feet in one hop.

Low-frequency sound transmits well in open areas and through the ground. Accordingly, kangaroo rats can pick up the footsteps of approaching predators, and they drum their own feet to communicate with other kangaroo rats. Both the distress call of the young kangaroo rat and the threat growl are sent out at low frequencies. This is at the other end of the spectrum from mice and small insectivores such as shrews, moles and bats, which use high-frequency ultrasound in their communication.

# *Beaver* Castoridae

## *Beaver* Castor canadensis

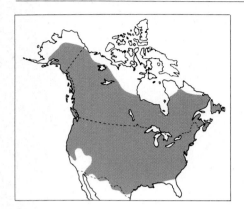

**Mammal:** *Castor canadensis* — beaver; largest rodent in North America

**Meaning of Name:** *Castor* (beaver); *canadensis* (of Canada)

**Description:** unique tail is well furred at the thick base but only sparsely haired on its paddle; rich glossy brown or yellowish brown pelage with chestnut brown to tawny underparts; black tail and feet; horny pads underneath the first 2 claws (claws have serrated edges for combing and grooming); lips meet behind incisors, enabling beaver to cut branches underwater

**Total Length:** male, 39 to 44 inches; female, 37 to 45 inches

**Tail:** male, 15 to 21 inches; female, 16 to 20 inches

**Weight:** 28.7 to 77.1 pounds

**Gestation:** 90 to 110 days

**Litter Size:** 1 to 9 (usually 2 to 4); 1 litter per year

**Age of Maturity:** 1.5 to 3 years (sometimes 4 depending on exploitation and environmental factors)

**Longevity:** 10 to 15 years in the wild; one lived 24 years in captivity

**Diet:** nonwoody vegetation in the summer and woody vegetation in the winter; bark cut from soft cambium layer, leaves, twigs, buds, water vegetation and submerged roots; has been known to exhibit coprophagy

**Habitat:** forested areas (prefers stands in early successional stages) associated with ponds, lakes and slow-flowing rivers and streams; occasionally in streams on the prairies, muskegs, tundra or alpine meadows

**Predators:** coyote, timber wolf, domestic dog, red fox, eagle, black bear, lynx, bobcat, fisher and mink

**Dental Formula:** 1/1, 0/0, 1/1, 3/3 = 20 teeth

Beavers are a declining lineage. They once ranged throughout the northern hemisphere and included terrestrial as well as aquatic species. One extinct group is known for constructing deep spiralling burrows. Another evolved into a gigantic muskratlike animal the size of a black bear that fed on marshy vegetation. The family seems to have originated in North America as a group of digging rodents and eventually spread to Asia. Modern semiaquatic beavers arose in Asia and then emigrated to North America. Now, only a single North American beaver species remains, and the populations of its Eurasian counterpart are reduced to tiny remnants. Nevertheless, the North American beaver is among the most successful of the continent's mammals.

The beaver is not simply a creature of northern forests but ranges from northern Mexico to the southwestern deserts of the United States, from Rocky Mountain meadows to the very edge of the Arctic tundra. Beavers appear to live almost anywhere in the temperate region where there are trees to eat and water to live in. Most of the adaptations of this mammal involve these two necessities.

Physically, the beaver is the second largest rodent in the world. Only the South American capybara, which can weigh up to 150 pounds, surpasses it in size. The beaver has a sturdy skeleton to support the strong muscles it uses when dragging trees and building dams. The skull is massive, to support a bite capable of slicing into large hardwood trees, and its teeth are as wide and stout as wood chisels. The beaver's large hind feet are webbed, making it a powerful swimmer. The beaver has nostrils that can close, valves to shut the ears, lips that seal the mouth while chewing underwater and a membrane to protect the open eye. Its fur is dense and sleek, and the beaver possesses a special split toenail on the hind foot that is used to keep it well groomed. The large flattened tail serves as a rudder, which, among other things, allows the beaver to swim and steer efficiently while towing branches and logs. The tail is muscular and can be used to produce a burst of speed underwater, and on land, it props the beaver into an upright position for cutting trees. The beaver's circulation is adjusted with a well-developed diving reflex that slows the heart, reduces blood circulation to the extremities and conserves enough oxygen to allow beavers to remain submerged for 15 minutes.

The most remarkable adaptations of the beaver are behavioural ones. Beavers build dams, lodges and food caches. When they move into a new area along an unoccupied stream, the first thing they build is a dam. Normally, a dam is placed at a constriction, or narrow place, in the valley. This minimizes the amount of material needed for construction. However, in flat habitats, beaver dams may extend for hundreds of yards. The dam of the beaver is a composite of

*The cutting and building skills of the beaver enable it to alter the landscape.*

*The underwater entrance of the beaver lodge keeps out almost every potential predator.*

logs, sticks, rocks and muck that impedes, rather than halts, the flow of water. Most of the outflow percolates through the dam rather than over the top, so that the current does not continually erode the dam. The dam serves several purposes. It backs up water, giving the beaver easy access to trees and reducing the beaver's need to travel over land, where it is vulnerable to predators. Beavers will also build canals that run for hundreds of feet. They may divert other streams into the canal system and build smaller dams, all to create water access to stands of food. Branches are transported much more easily by towing than they are across land. The dam may be 10 feet high or more, providing adequate water depth to build a secure lodge.

A lodge typically has an underwater entrance close to the pond or stream bottom, making entry difficult for all predators but otters. The interior has a dry raised platform, sometimes created out of the previously emergent stream bank or constructed by layering woody debris and mud to rise above the water level. The roof of the lodge is thickly woven of intermeshed twigs, and before winter, when the lodge is to be occupied, the roof is layered and smeared with muck and mud that freeze into a hard, virtually impenetrable roof. Much of the material used in lodge construction comes from branches that the beavers have already cut and peeled the bark from while eating.

Beavers also build food caches — piles of interwoven branches and sticks placed in the water to which they gain access by swimming under the ice from the lodge. This food caching is an adaptation to the ice cover of northern winters. Southern beaver populations do not cache food.

Beavers will excavate bank burrows for summer use where soil conditions permit. These bank dens may or may not be covered with branches and mud.

Beaver construction requires much of the beavers' time and involves continual maintenance work. The value of the territory created by this work is such that it also requires vigilance against the intrusion of and attempted takeover by other beavers. These two factors have led beavers to develop a territorial and cooperative family unit that maintains its lodges, dams and feeding grounds and excludes nonrelated beavers. All members of the colony scent-mark around the water's edge and along the dam with a musky secretion from the castoreum gland and with urine and possibly oil. Special mounds of vegetation and debris up to a foot high are erected around the colony boundary and marked with these secretions. The castoreum scent gland produces a complex pheromonal mixture of more than 50 different molecules, enough complexity to give every beaver its own unique chemical signature. It is not known how much individual recognition exists in beavers, but it is clear that colony members can smell and distinguish each other's scent from that of outsiders. The dominant male beaver, in particular, becomes highly aggressive if he smells foreign castoreum. The beavers will hiss and slap their tails when they smell the scent and will investigate it. This behaviour is used by trappers who rub beaver castoreum on beaver traps and never fail to attract the resident beaver. Under normal conditions, a foreign beaver thus detected will be attacked and driven out. Beavers can inflict formidable gouges and bites and have been known to kill intruding beavers in territorial disputes.

The social structure of a beaver colony is based on a monogamous pair of mates. They share a lodge and cooperate in building duties and territorial defence. The female normally selects the home site and generates the social stability of the family unit. If her mate dies, she will remain in the territory and accept a new male. However, if the female dies, the territory may be abandoned.

The male and female produce one litter each year and tolerate the presence of previous offspring. How many offspring remain in the colony and for how long apparently varies according to the quality of the habitat. Typically, the male and female pair is accompanied by the immature young of the year and several other juveniles that may be as old as 2 1/2 years. The presence of an extended family of closely related kin explains the use of the tail slap on the water as a warning signal. Even though the slapping draws a predator's attention to the beaver issuing the warning, the beneficiaries of this warning in most cases will be close relatives.

Most colonies contain five to six individuals, with 12 being a reported maximum. Twelve adult beavers would weigh close to half a ton and would place severe grazing pressure on the surrounding trees. Pressure on the local food resource seems to select for juvenile dispersal, which appears to be instinctive in 2-year-old beavers and is not necessarily the result of eviction by the parents. Low-quality habitats have the highest rate of juvenile dispersal. Most beavers move only a few miles during this dispersal phase, but one tagged beaver has been recorded moving 150 miles. It is also possible that one of the juvenile beavers may ultimately inherit the lodge

*The loud tail slap of a diving beaver alerts family members to the approach of a predator.*

and territory of its parents.

In any case, all juveniles inherit considerable amounts of learning experience from their residency within the parental colony. Young beavers are born in spring in the lodge, usually in a clutch of two to four. They are furred but remain in the lodge breastfeeding for a full month or more before they are weaned. All members of the colony cooperate in bringing food to the young, but the parental male does most of this work, a highly unusual pattern in mammals. The year or more that young beavers spend as members of the parental colony is devoted not just to growth but to learning and polishing the techniques of construction and tree felling. Experience and strength appear to be necessary for a beaver to be successful. Reproduction is usually physiologically impossible until the animal is 2 years old, an old age as rodents go. Beavers continue to grow for four to five years in the extreme parts of their range and for as long as nine years in more central regions.

Beavers eat shrubs and weedy vegetation during summer months, but their tree cutting gives them a unique resource base. Beavers have felled trees close to 4 feet in diameter. Cutting and harvesting a tree this size requires some special techniques. Beavers are not able to fell trees with any great directional precision, but they may not need to. The direction in which a tree falls depends on its lean, the wind and the presence of obstruc-

tions. However, since trees are cut near the pond edge, they will naturally tend to lean toward the open area above the pond or stream surface and usually away from a downhill slope. Thus, on average, trees fall toward the water. Beavers trim smaller limbs for transport and normally leave the heavy trunk. Although considerable quantities of wood are left behind, most of the nutrients are contained in the young bark and leaves. This felling of large trees allows sun-loving pioneer trees, such as willow and aspen, to sprout. These trees become coppice easily, and many generations of quickly harvested stump sprouts must be taken before the tree dies. Thus the beaver often modifies mature stands of unpalatable hardwoods and conifers to create faster-growing stands of palatable species that are easily harvested.

Few other wild animals, except possibly elephants, modify the landscape as much as beavers do. Prior to the European colonization of North America, an estimated 60 million beavers existed. Colonies require from about 1/2 to 1 1/2 miles of stream or pond shoreline, so the result must have been many millions of acres of forest and wetland wildlife under the considerable influence of beavers. Although beavers were decimated and

*The beaver is a selective forager, eating only specific sizes and species of trees.*

entirely trapped out in many regions, they have been restored to most of their former range. However, much of the habitat previously dominated by beavers is now subject to human occupation. At the same time, humans have eliminated many of the large carnivores that once preyed on beavers, and as a result, beavers frequently come into conflict with farmers and other landowners.

Beavers are still heavily trapped in many areas, but in semi-urban and farming areas, trapping is often economically and aesthetically unattractive, and beavers may become a problem, flooding land, plugging culverts and irrigation canals and cutting valuable trees. Without some form of regulation, populations grow until the beavers deplete their food resources and then become subject to epidemic diseases such as tularemia. However, where beaver populations are regulated by natural predation and management plans, they provide innumerable benefits.

In addition to their high-quality fur, beavers provide significant ecological benefits. The wetlands they create provide breeding and feeding habitats for waterfowl, frogs, salamanders, fish and mammals such as otter, muskrat and water shrews. Their dams provide erosion control, con-

serve water and increase the water quality of large rivers by reducing the amount of silt introduced. The open areas that beavers create and then abandon support a distinctive set of plants that depend on disturbance for their continued existence.

The impact of the beaver is so great that many of the ecological dependencies that have developed in concert with the presence of beavers remain to be discovered. A recent example concerns a group of fruit flies that have been found to be heavily dependent on the presence of beavers. These fruit flies breed under the rotting bark and sapwood of cut willows and aspens. They are never found more than a few dozen yards from water, except during very wet periods. It is most likely that these flies are strongly dependent on beavers to provide them with breeding sites and that when the beavers were threatened with extinction by overtrapping, these flies were equally threatened. This may seem insignificant, but it is worthwhile recalling that fruit flies, including those associated with beavers, have been the laboratory organism and tools with which major insights into the genetic basis of life have been so recently achieved.

## The Juggling Beaver: The Tactics of Optimal Foraging

*A beaver is confronted with a complicated foraging problem. It eats plants, usually trees that grow on land, but its home and refuge is in the water. It is well adapted for tree cutting but poorly adapted for moving trees across the land and for escaping land predators. It must assess whether it is more profitable to expend the time cutting through a large tree with a huge crown of branches or to move from small tree to small tree cutting quickly but getting little yield per tree and spending more time waddling along the ground. How far should it go away from the safety of the water to get how large a tree? Some trees are more nutritious, some are hard to cut, some are better for storage, while others make better building material. Should the beaver cut in the day, when it is hotter and more costly, or at night, when it is cooler but when predators, such as bears and wolves, are active?*

*These are some of the difficult trade-offs that the foraging beaver faces. This kind of problem is one of optimal foraging, a branch of ecological study that addresses how animals solve these complicated questions and what constraints have influenced the design of foraging behaviour by natural selection. No one believes that an individual beaver consciously assesses the pros and cons of foraging. However, the way in which its behaviour has evolved should reflect the relative intensities of the different constraints. For example, beavers that spend long periods of time away from water would suggest that predation pressure is relatively insignificant. On the other hand, if many animals are known to attack beavers, biologists might expect to see beavers restrict the distance they move from the water and to venture far away only for particularly valuable food items. In the end, the best foraging strategy will not be the one that yields the most food but will be the one that yields the most descendants. Several studies have looked at how beavers solve their foraging problems.*

*The most obvious relationship is between the size of the tree and how far a beaver will go to cut it. One might think that beavers would be willing to walk a long way to cut a large tree with many leaves and branches. But the reverse is true. The*

larger the tree cut, the closer it must be to the edge of the pond. Beavers will usually go only 40 to 50 yards from water to cut, and the farther they go, the smaller the tree they cut. This reflects the inefficiency of a beaver on land and the high cost of dragging logs across the ground. Small trees that can be quickly cut and dragged are taken far from water. Beavers are formidable opponents of most animals, but wolves and bears often kill them. However, the evidence indicates that the foraging beaver is not trying to minimize time and exposure to predators, but rather, it is trying to maximize energy by reducing the cost of the harvest.

Tree type has also been found to affect the distance and size of trees beavers cut. For example, in a comparison of ash and aspen cutting, beavers would cut aspen, peel it to eat the bark or store it in a food cache and then use the remaining branches in construction. Ash was used only in construction. Accordingly, beavers would travel

farther to cut an aspen than an ash. Size selectivity was influenced by distance. Beyond 40 yards from the water's edge, the beavers became significantly more selective about the size of the tree they cut. Since aspen is softer and more valuable than ash, the aspens cut were bigger than the ashes cut at the same distance from the pond. These relationships indicate that the foraging strategy of the beaver is indeed a sophisticated juggling act.

*The low energy cost and high safety of water transport is one reason why the beaver builds dams and canals.*

# *Jumping Mice* Zapodidae

## *Meadow Jumping Mouse* Zapus hudsonius

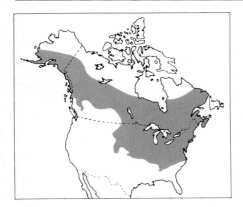

**Mammal:** *Zapus hudsonius* — meadow jumping mouse
**Meaning of Name:** *Zapus* (strong or big feet); *hudsonius* refers to Hudson Bay area, from which the specimen used in the original description was obtained
**Description:** coarse wiry pelage; back is olive brown, caused by a mixture of black and buff hairs; flanks are paler and underparts are buffy white; belly and back are distinctly separated by clear pale yellow stripes; sharply bicoloured tail (brown above and white below)
**Total Length:** 7.1 to 9.3 inches
**Tail:** 4.3 to 5.5 inches
**Weight:** 0.42 to 0.53 ounces in spring and early summer; 0.99 ounces prior to hibernation
**Gestation:** 17 to 21 days
**Litter Size:** 2 to 8 (usually 4 to 6); 2 or 3 litters per year
**Age of Maturity:** male, if born early in season may breed the same year; female, 2 months
**Longevity:** 1 to 2 years in the wild; 5 years in captivity
**Diet:** omnivore, but primarily seed eater; also fruit, insects and their larvae
**Habitat:** various habitats including grassland, low meadows, edges of forests and fencerows; also along grassy stream banks
**Predators:** owls, hawks, raven, red fox, grey fox, wolf, mink, long-tailed weasel, domestic cat, snakes, frogs and pika
**Dental Formula:** 1/1, 0/0, 1/0, 3/3 = 18 teeth

This small Zapodidae family contains only four species in North America. They are specialized for jumping and, like kangaroo rats, have large hind limbs and long tails. Jumps are usually not more than a yard and are normally much less. When the animal is startled, it makes a large jump first, then rapidly hops away using jumps only a foot long. The forelimbs are short and are used in holding and manipulating the food as the mouse feeds in an upright position. Unlike kangaroo rats, jumping mice prefer wet areas and are adept at swimming and even diving. They are capable of hibernation for seven to eight months of the year, and they store large quantities of fat. They do not build up winter food caches, and they lack cheek pouches. They include insects and spiders in their diet, as well as seeds. They are most active at night.

Nests are built in fallen rotted logs and grass clumps. Pregnancy takes close to three weeks, and the young are born helpless and are weaned at 4 weeks. Females may breed three times during the spring-to-late-summer breeding season. All species appear to have similar natural histories and differ primarily in geographic range and habitat.

The meadow jumping mouse is found in damp meadows across the continent. Its range includes northern hardwood forests in the east and coniferous forests in the north and west. The ***Pacific jumping mouse***, *Z. trinotatus*, is a resident of moist habitats along the west coast. The **western jumping mouse**, *Z. princeps*, lives in the western mountain region. The **woodland jumping mouse**, *Napaeozapus insignis*, is an eastern species that overlaps the eastern range of the meadow jumping mouse. As their common names imply, these species are separated by different habitats.

*The meadow jumping mouse uses its large hind feet to propel it with kangaroo-style hops through the wet meadows and woodlands it inhabits.*

# *New World Mice* Cricetidae

The Cricetidae family is a confusing one, as mammalogists cannot decide how to group the various rodents that look like mice, voles and hamsters. One system separates the Old World rats and mice, the Muridae, from the New World rats and mice, the Cricetidae. Another system lumps them together and divides them into subfamilies. Everyone does agree, however, that the New World and Old World mouselike rodents are closely related, and because they have radiated into such different forms, splitting the group makes them somewhat more manageable. As it now stands, the Cricetidae is the largest mammal family in North America, with 70 species.

If all lumped together, the family Muridae, including both New and Old World forms, contains well in excess of 1,000 species divided into 15 subfamilies. These subfamilies, in North America at least, separate into rather distinct groups. Voles, lemmings and the muskrat form a group known as the subfamily Microtinae, while the deer mice, harvest mice and wood rats fall into another subfamily, the Cricitinae. Some taxonomists recognize these as distinctive enough to deserve status as truly separate families. The Cricitinae tend to be mouselike with a pointed muzzle and a long, naked tail. Their natural history and generic classification are diverse, as are their habits, and these are discussed separately in the species accounts.

The microtines — voles and lemmings — are compact with a shortened tail and a rounded muzzle and head. Both groups originated during the Tertiary period (70 million years ago), but it was only more recently, especially in the Pleistocene epoch (1 million years ago), that their explo-

sive and rich speciation took place. The entire Cricetidae family is usually nocturnal and omnivorous, having multiple litters, and its members do not hibernate.

Voles and lemmings are the dominant small mammals of the Far North and are an important source of food to predatory mammals and raptors. There is little physical variation between the microtine species. They are all stocky with blunt noses, small eyes and ears and short tails, and they run low to the ground with the legs almost hidden below the body. The largest species, such as Richardson's water vole or the yellow-cheeked vole, weigh about 4 ounces and the smallest, the creeping vole, weighs less than 1 ounce.

All of the species are herbivores with teeth adapted for grinding vegetation very finely, and there is an enlarged intestinal chamber for fermentation of the ground plant material. Some species cache food stores, and others do not. Most of them, however, eat a significant proportion of their feces in the same manner as rabbits. Voles and lemmings depend on plant material to supply their water, and as their kidneys are not efficient in water conservation, only a few species are found in arid habitats.

Voles and lemmings have a high reproductive rate. Males become reproductive two months after birth, but females may mature at only three weeks. Pregnancy is short, usually less than three weeks.

Most species have eight mammary glands and can feed that many young when there is adequate food. The young are born in a well-insulated nest and are naked, blind and helpless. They develop rapidly and are weaned within three weeks. Mothers can become pregnant immediately

after giving birth and while they are still lactating. This gives them a phenomenal reproductive potential — in captivity, one meadow vole female produced 17 consecutive litters within a year, resulting in 83 offspring and 78 grandchildren before she reached her first birthday.

This high birth rate is accompanied by a high mortality rate. Average life expectancy in the field is often only a month; under ideal conditions, they may live roughly a year and a rare few live two years. Three-to-four-year population cycles fluctuate wildly from less than one animal to thousands per acre, and at population peaks, many mammals and bird predators eat nothing but voles and lemmings.

Most species have aggressive, territorial females, and males may sometimes be territorial and fight for access to females. Females take an active role in courtship, following the male and investigating his scent, sometimes attacking and killing strange males. Males taking over territory may kill the offspring of a female and, when mating, produce a mating plug to seal the female from other males. Home ranges of polygynous males tend to be larger than those of females, taking in several burrows. Mature males use scent glands along the sides of their bodies to mark their territories. The marked area changes radically with population density but usually measures a little over an acre. An acre will normally accommodate dozens of voles or lemmings.

*The New World mice and voles, such as this meadow vole, may look unassuming, but they are among the most successful of all the mammals, comprising dozens of species.*

# *Bushy-tailed Wood Rat* Neotoma cinerea

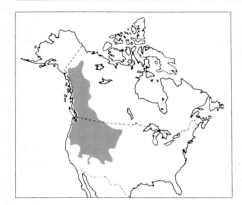

**Mammal:** *Neotoma cinerea* — bushy-tailed wood rat, packrat
**Meaning of Name:** *Neotoma* (new + sharp, cutting), an allusion to the teeth indicating a new genus of rodent; *cinerea* refers to ash colour
**Description:** squirrel-like tail covered with long fur; soft dense pelage; varies in colour from pale grey washed with tawny to black; greyish white ventrally stained with creamy patches; tail is dark grey above and white below
**Total Length:** 15 to 17 inches
**Tail:** 5.2 to 8.7 inches
**Weight:** 7.5 to 20.5 ounces
**Gestation:** 27 to 32 days
**Litter Size:** 1 to 6 (usually 2 to 4); 1 litter per year
**Age of Maturity:** 11 months
**Longevity:** at least 4 years
**Diet:** roots, stems, leaves and seeds of trees, shrubs and forbs; needles of conifers and berries; does not eat grass
**Habitat:** Arctic alpine to desert areas, prefers transitional zones; found on cliffs, rock slides, caves, river canyons and rock outcrops in pine forests
**Predators:** great horned owl, rattlesnake, weasel, skunk, marten, wolverine, fox, coyote and wolf
**Dental Formula:** 1/1, 0/0, 0/0, 3/3 = 16 teeth

The bushy-tailed wood rat is also known as the packrat, a name it earned for its habit of carrying shiny objects such as spoons, cigarette lighters, matches and other human debris away from cabins and campsites. It incorporates these into its jumbled nest of sticks, bones and foliage. The tangled pile of debris may be 3 feet in circumference and is built in a rock crevice or other protected spot. In forested areas without rocky outcrops, the nest may be located high in the branches of a large coniferous tree. Inside a coarse outer debris pile is a compact inner nest of fine, dry, shredded plant material. The coarse outer pile is a form of protection from predators and is also used as a spot to dry food caches and to sit and eat. Sometimes, a packrat will build a debris nest only for use as a food cache and will use a rock crevice for its resting nest. A wood rat finds a cabin a convenient den spot. Left for a few days, it will coat it with urine and musk and will shred and disturb the entire contents.

The bushy-tailed wood rat is a herbivore of the western mountain conif-

*The bushy-tailed wood rat uses twigs and debris of all sorts, including human litter, to weave its large nests.*

erous forest and grazes on the leaves of shrubs and conifers. In the autumn, it caches large piles of twigs and dried vegetation, a behaviour similar to that of pikas, which also live in mountainous talus areas, except the wood rat is able to use coarser woody vegetation in its caches.

Wood rats of both sexes are territorial. Males fight for access to female territories and spend much effort scent-marking with musk glands and urine.

# *Ungava Lemming* Dicrostonyx hudsonius

**Mammal:** *Dicrostonyx hudsonius* — Ungava lemming, Hudson Bay collared lemming, Labrador collared lemming
**Meaning of Name:** *Dicrostonyx* (forked + a sharp point + a claw) refers to the 2 claws on forefeet that become enlarged and prominent in the winter; *hudsonius* (of Hudson), from Hudson Bay
**Description:** grizzled grey with dark stripe running along middle of back; tawny ear spots and pale collar; tawny flanks and tawny band runs across the throat in summer; white in winter; develops characteristic winter claws on the third and fourth digits
**Total Length:** 5.3 to 6.6 inches

**Tail:** 0.4 to 0.9 inches
**Weight:** 1.6 to 2.4 ounces
**Gestation:** 19 to 21 days (longer if female is still nursing a litter)
**Litter Size:** 1 to 11 (usually 3 or 4); 1 or 2 litters per year
**Age of Maturity:** not known
**Longevity:** some have lived longer than 2 years in captivity
**Diet:** any available vegetation
**Habitat:** tundra of Ungava and islands in

*The female Ungava lemming is able to give birth to naked, helpless young in the cold of the Arctic by heating the grassy nest with her body.*

Hudson Bay
**Predators:** not recorded, but probably include owls, hawks and carnivores such as fox, weasel and wolf
**Dental Formula:** 1/1, 0/0, 0/0, 3/3 = 16 teeth

# *Greenland Collared Lemming* Dicrostonyx groenlandicus

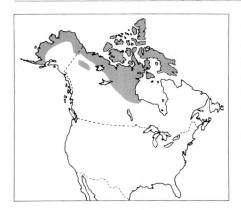

**Mammal:** *Dicrostonyx groenlandicus* — Greenland collared lemming
**Meaning of Name:** *Dicrostonyx* (forked + a sharp point + a claw) refers to the 2 claws on forefeet; *groenlandicus* (of Greenland)
**Description:** the only rodent that turns white in winter; feet are broad and heavily furred on the soles for life in the Arctic; shoulders, chest and flanks are tawny to chestnut; grey back with black median stripe running down it; tawny flanks and belly; tawny or chestnut ear spots with grey crescent behind
**Total Length:** 5.2 to 6.4 inches
**Tail:** 0.4 to 0.8 inches

**Weight:** 1.6 to 4 ounces
**Gestation:** 19 to 21 days (may extend from 22 to 26 days because of delayed implantation as a result of lactation)
**Litter Size:** 1 to 7 (usually 5); 2 or 3 litters per year
**Age of Maturity:** male, 46 days; female, 27 to 30 days
**Longevity:** few live beyond 1 year in the wild; just over 3 years in captivity (maximum)
**Diet:** primarily willow leaves and forbs;

*As winter approaches, the Greenland collared lemming turns white, which allows it to forage above the snow without being conspicuous.*

also sedges, cottongrass, grasses, bearberries, buds and twigs
**Habitat:** Arctic tundra zone
**Predators:** raptors and carnivores
**Dental Formula:** 1/1, 0/0, 0/0, 3/3 = 16 teeth

# *Brown Lemming* Lemmus sibiricus

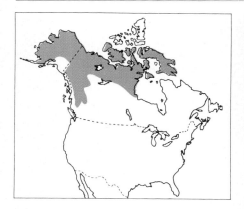

**Mammal:** *Lemmus sibiricus* — brown lemming

**Meaning of Name:** *Lemmus* (lemming), derived from the Norwegian lemming; *sibiricus* (of Siberia)

**Description:** large head with no apparent neck, fat body, short furry feet, stubby tail; claws are specialized for digging, and soles and toes are covered with long, stiff bristles; reddish brown back and rump; greyish head and shoulders; winter coat is longer and greyer

**Total Length:** male, 5.2 to 6.6 inches; female, 5.2 to 6.3 inches

**Tail:** male, 0.6 to 1 inch; female, 0.7 to 1 inch

**Weight:** male, 1.7 to 4 ounces; female, 1.4 to 3.7 ounces

**Gestation:** 16 to 23 days

**Litter Size:** 1 to 13 (usually 4 to 8); 1 to 3 litters per year

**Age of Maturity:** male, 4 to 5 weeks; female, 3 to 4 weeks (delayed until 6 to 9 months if population is too high)

**Longevity:** 1 or 2 years in the wild; up to 3 years in captivity

**Diet:** primarily grasses and sedges; monocotyledons; tundra grass and cottongrass sedge are among the most important; also mosses, bark and twigs of willows and dwarf birch, berries, lichens and roots

**Habitat:** wet tundra areas covered with grasses and sedges, stream banks, lakeshores, grassy slopes, alpine meadows and rock talus

**Predators:** owls, glaucous gull, raven, gyrfalcon, hawks, jaeger, least weasel, ermine, Arctic fox, wolf, wolverine, grizzly bear and even caribou

**Dental Formula:** 1/1, 0/0, 0/0, 3/3 = 16 teeth

The brown lemming is a tundra species that favours damp meadows and the edges of watercourses and lakes. Although its major food source is the shoots of grasses and sedges, it will browse in winter on shrubs, such as dwarf willow, that lie under the snow cover. Lemmings often cluster in suitable habitats and build extensive networks of runways just under the surface and through the tangled vegetation. Nests are balls of grass built on the soil surface.

Although lemmings are densely packed, they are far from being amicable and sociable. They fight often with one another during breeding season and as populations become dense. The Arctic lemmings follow a three-to-four-year cycle. Because they can become so abundant, they are an important food item for many Arctic mammals. The breeding success of predatory birds, such as jaegers and snowy owls, is closely tied to the lemming population.

Lemming populations may exhaust their food resources and remove 95 percent of the vegetation cover in peak years. Dense populations result in reduced reproduction and cause mass lemming migrations that allow predators to eat large numbers and lead

*Brown lemmings undergo population explosions that subside only after they have grazed away large portions of the tundra vegetation.*

to the death of many lemmings by drowning and starvation.

Brown lemmings occur in the same geographic area as Greenland collared lemmings. The two species differ in the plants they eat. Brown lemmings eat grasses, sedges and mosses; collared lemmings feed primarily on willow leaves and forbs.

Both the **southern bog lemming**, *Synaptomys cooperi*, and the **northern bog lemming**, *S. borealis*, are found in eastern forest areas where marshes and other wet habitats such as sphagnum bogs occur. They are similar in appearance to the common meadow vole but have long shaggy fur and a delicate skull. They have a more specialized diet than the vole, feeding mainly on grass and sedges. Southern bog lemmings build shallow runways, while nests of northern bog lemmings are underground in summer and above ground in winter. This may be an attempt to take advantage of the insulating value of snow in areas where the soil is wet and freezes solid.

# Heather Vole *Phenacomys intermedius*

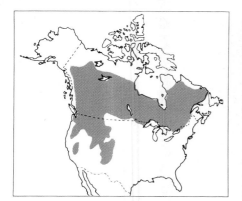

**Mammal:** *Phenacomys intermedius* — heather vole

**Meaning of Name:** *Phenacomys* (cheat or deceiver mouse) refers to the fact that the external appearance gives no clue to its real affinities; *intermedius* (between, intermediate) probably refers to medium-length tail

**Description:** fairly loose, thin skin; long, fine-textured pelage; varies from greyish brown to dark brown; nose also varies from yellowish to orange-brown to grey; bicoloured tail; silvery grey underparts; white feet

**Total Length:** 4.8 to 6.1 inches

**Tail:** 1 to 1.6 inches

**Weight:** 0.9 to 1.4 ounces

**Gestation:** 19 to 24 days

**Litter Size:** 2 to 8 (average of 5); 2 or more litters per season

**Age of Maturity:** female, 4 to 6 weeks; male, not until the following spring

**Longevity:** not known (probably 1 to 2 years)

**Diet:** bark and buds of shrubs and heaths; forbs, berries, seeds and lichens

**Habitat:** dry open stands of pine or spruce; usually near water; also near forest edges in shrubby vegetation; open moist grassy areas near mountaintops and rocky slopes

**Predators:** hawks, owls, weasel and marten

**Dental Formula:** 1/1, 0/0, 0/0, 3/3 = 16 teeth

The heather vole is a vole of the boreal forest, a habitat it shares with the red-backed vole. Red-backed voles are often day-active, whereas heather voles are mainly nocturnal. Heather voles store food in caches. In summer, they browse the foliage of shrubs and herbs, and in winter, they eat twig buds and bark. The heather vole does not eat the grasses and sedges that some voles and lemmings specialize in. It is a completely docile animal and does well in captivity. It follows the same pattern of nesting below ground in winter, above ground in summer, and it uses runways through the litter and snow.

One interesting aspect of this vole's reproductive biology is that females mature within four to six weeks of birth and breed in the same summer they are born, but males do not mature until the following year.

*For the sake of warmth, heather voles raise their young in well-insulated nests of dried grasses and moss.*

# Southern Red-backed Vole *Clethrionomys gapperi*

**Mammal:** *Clethrionomys gapperi* — southern red-backed vole, boreal redback vole, Gapper's redback vole
**Meaning of Name:** *Clethrionomys* (bolt-toothed mouse) refers to rounded enamel ridges on teeth or to the fact that molars are rooted; could also be translated as alder-grove mouse, in reference to its habitat; *gapperi* (named after naturalist W. Gapper, who trapped specimens in the Ontario area about 1830)
**Description:** bright reddish dorsal stripe runs from forehead to base of tail; grey face, flanks and rump; whitish or buff feet and underparts; brown ears; bicoloured tail; during a grey phase, a sooty dorsal stripe replaces the reddish one
**Total Length:** 4.7 to 6.5 inches
**Tail:** 1.2 to 2.3 inches
**Weight:** 0.5 to 1.4 ounces
**Gestation:** 17 to 19 days
**Litter Size:** 2 to 8 (usually 4 to 6, but size increases with latitude); 3 or 4 litters per year
**Age of Maturity:** female has first litter at 4 months
**Longevity:** usually 1 year in the wild, but some have lived 20 to 36 months
**Diet:** omnivore; prefers petioles of broad-leaved forbs and shrubs and other growing vegetative parts of weeds and some grasses; also large quantities of conifer seeds, nuts, bark, roots, insects, centipedes, spiders and snails as well as fungal materials
**Habitat:** both coniferous and mixed-hardwood forests close to springs, brooks or bogs; around mossy decaying stumps, scattered shrubs, leaf litter and exposed tree roots
**Predators:** hawks, owls, raccoon, weasel, red fox, coyote, skunk, marten, mink, short-tailed shrew, red squirrel and domestic cat
**Dental Formula:** 1/1, 0/0, 0/0, 3/3 = 16 teeth

The southern red-backed vole is a hyperactive, nervous animal found in a variety of forested and shrubby habitats. It uses the runways of other small mammals in its excursions across the forest floor. It will also climb and forage in shrubbery and in trees. During winter, red-backs build tunnels through the snow.

This species has sometimes been found nesting in tree hollows, but normally, it builds a round ball of shredded plants under a stump or fallen log. Females are aggressively territorial, more so than males, whose ranges often overlap. Its diet is a mixture of leaf stems, berries, nuts, tree sprouts, bark and any young mouse nestlings it happens to find. Red-backed voles grind their food very finely and probably digest it more efficiently than the deer mice that share the same habitats.

Females have multiple litters from spring through autumn. The young are born helpless after a three-week pregnancy. Weaning and dispersal occur after another three weeks.

Closely related species are the ***western red-backed vole***, *C. occidentalis*,

*Red-backed voles are forest creatures sensitive to logging and development.*

and the ***northern red-backed vole***, *C. rutilus*. The former species is found in the thick damp West Coast forest and the latter is a tundra species.

Red-backed voles are a good indicator of environmental disturbance. Clear-cut logging and land development normally cause them to become extinct locally. The reason for this may be a high food dependence on fungi, such as bolete mushrooms, that live in symbiosis with tree roots. When the trees disappear, so do the mushrooms and the voles. These voles also eat lichens that grow on trees and may depend on them. Deer mice, which do not feed heavily on these items, often increase when logging and development occur.

All voles are eaten by predatory birds and mammals.

## *Singing Vole* Microtus miurus

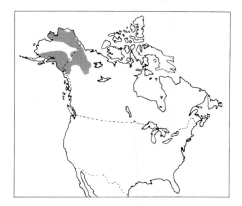

**Mammal:** *Microtus miurus* — singing vole, Alaska vole,

**Meaning of Name:** *Microtus* (small ears); *miurus* (small + wild ox) or could be derived from Latin word *mirus*, meaning wonderful; also called singing vole because of its habit of coming to the entrance of its burrow and uttering a high-pitched trill

**Description:** small vole with short tail; colour varies with range; buff or tawny ear spot; bicoloured tail tipped with stiff buff or tawny hairs; greyish flanks and feet; grey underparts with an ochraceous tint; may have buff patch at base of whiskers

**Total Length:** male, 5.8 to 6.3 inches; female, 5.3 to 6.3 inches

**Tail:** male, 0.8 to 1.4 inches; female, 1 to 1.3 inches

**Weight:** male, 1.4 to 2.1 ounces; female, 1.1 to 1.8 ounces

**Gestation:** not known (probably 20 or 21 days)

**Litter Size:** 4 to 12; up to 3 litters per year

**Age of Maturity:** not known (probably 25 to 45 days)

**Longevity:** not known (probably less than 1 year)

**Diet:** Arctic forbs and leaves and twigs of dwarf Arctic willows

**Habitat:** alpine tundra, willow thickets; along riverbanks, lakeshores and gravel beds; high well-drained slopes

**Predators:** gull, grey jay, jaeger, short-eared owl, grizzly bear, wolf, red fox, Arctic fox, ermine and least weasel

**Dental Formula:** 1/1, 0/0, 0/0, 3/3 = 16 teeth

The song of the singing vole is a high-pitched trill that may act as an alarm call. The species is colonial and exhibits some of the same communal warning systems as ground squirrels. The song may also be a territorial call uttered to discourage intruders. This species inhabits the tundra of the west, and like pikas, it collects huge hay piles for winter, up to half a bushel in a pile. It also caches large stores of tubers, valuable resources which Indians and Inuit used to rob and which other voles, no doubt, still do. The singing vole makes an underground nest and storage chamber, is active climbing in shrubbery and swims well.

## *Richardson's Water Vole* Arvicola richardsoni

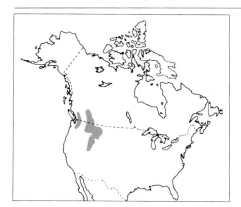

**Mammal:** *Arvicola richardsoni* — Richardson's water vole

**Meaning of Name:** *Arvicola* (ploughed land, a field + till, cultivate or inhabit), probably translates as "inhabits a field"; *richardsoni*, likely after discoverer of species

**Description:** largest vole within its range; amphibious adaptations include a fusiform body, dense underfur and fringes of stiff hairs on the edges of the hind feet; combination of reddish brown and black-tipped hairs dorsally; smoky to pale grey ventrally; bicoloured tail is brown above and light grey beneath

**Total Length:** 9.2 to 10.8 inches

**Tail:** 2.6 to 3.9 inches

**Weight:** 2.5 to 3.5 ounces

**Gestation:** not known

**Litter Size:** 2 to 8 (average of 5); 2 litters per year

**Age of Maturity:** female can mature in 5 weeks (has smaller litters)

**Longevity:** not known (probably 1 or 2 years)

**Diet:** herbs, twigs and buds of willows

**Habitat:** alpine meadows; along mountain streams, creek banks and marshes; occasionally found along stream banks in alpine forests or in forest glades

**Predators:** probably hawks, owls, gulls, small carnivores and possibly large fish

**Dental Formula:** 1/1, 0/0, 0/0, 3/3 = 16 teeth

The water vole has a tiny geographic distribution and a specific habitat. It is found in Rocky Mountain meadows and alongside mountain streams and ponds, where it builds extensive burrow systems. One of the largest of North American voles, it has large feet that are relatively powerful and adapted for digging. Most of its food is herbaceous vegetation gathered above ground. It dives and swims well and takes to water when pursued.

## Root Vole  *Microtus oeconomus*

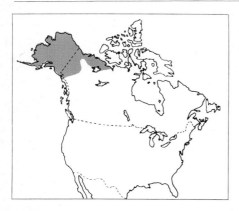

**Mammal:** *Microtus oeconomus* — root vole, tundra vole
**Meaning of Name:** *Microtus* (small ears); *oeconomus* (economic) refers to its habit of storing grass seeds and forb rhizomes in its burrow in the fall
**Description:** grizzled brown washed with buff or fulvous; grey feet; heels and wrists are well covered with stiff silvery hairs in winter; bicoloured tail
**Total Length:** 6 to 7.4 inches
**Tail:** 1.4 to 2.1 inches
**Weight:** male, 1.2 to 1.6 ounces; female, 0.9 to 2.8 ounces

**Gestation:** not known (probably 20 to 21 days)
**Litter Size:** 5 to 11
**Age of Maturity:** not known (probably 25 to 45 days)
**Longevity:** not known (probably less than 1 year)
**Diet:** sedges, grasses, seeds and rhizomes
**Habitat:** tundra in close association with water; sedge and cottongrass marshes
**Predators:** owls, hawks, gyrfalcon, jaeger, gull, shrike, ermine, Arctic fox, wolverine and even lake trout
**Dental Formula:** 1/1, 0/0, 0/0, 3/3 = 16 teeth

The root vole is found in the tundra of the far northwestern Arctic and in northern Russia and Scandinavia. It often builds shallow burrows in moist habitats, feeds heavily on grasses and sedges and caches roots, seeds and grass for winter use.

## Yellow-cheeked Vole  *Microtus xanthognathus*

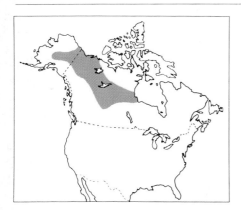

**Mammal:** *Microtus xanthognathus* — yellow-cheeked vole, taiga vole, chestnut-cheeked vole
**Meaning of Name:** *Microtus* (small ears); *xanthognathus* refers to yellow cheek patch
**Description:** dull brown above, grey below; ears have rusty edges; prominent chestnut to rusty yellow cheek patch
**Total Length:** 7.3 to 8.9 inches
**Tail:** 1.8 to 2.1 inches
**Weight:** 4 to 6 ounces
**Gestation:** not known (probably 20 or 21 days)
**Litter Size:** 7 to 11
**Age of Maturity:** the year following birth

**Longevity:** not past second winter
**Diet:** opportunistic feeder, with horsetails, grasses and berries predominating diet in summer and stored rhizomes in winter
**Habitat:** riparian forest edge; lightly burned forest; bordering tundra and sphagnum bogs
**Predators:** marten, great grey owl
**Dental Formula:** 1/1, 0/0, 0/0, 3/3 = 16 teeth

The yellow-cheeked vole is found in western boreal forests, often near bogs and other wet areas. It constructs runways through the litter on the forest floor. The runways are relatively deep and marked by dirt piles that suggest the activity of moles rather than voles. The yellow-cheeked vole is colonial in distribution. It eats large quantities of lichen and horsetail, foods favoured by few other species.

# *Meadow Vole* Microtus pennsylvanicus

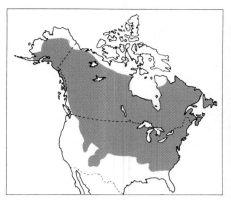

**Mammal:** *Microtus pennsylvanicus* — meadow vole

**Meaning of Name:** *Microtus* (small ears); *pennsylvanicus* (of Pennsylvania)

**Description:** long, soft, dense fur; coat varies from grizzled rusty brown to dark brown above and dusky grey below; winter coat is longer and greyer

**Total Length:** male, 5.9 to 7.8 inches; female, 5.7 to 7 inches

**Tail:** male, 1.6 to 1.8 inches; female, 1.6 to 2 inches

**Weight:** male, 1.1 to 1.6 ounces; female, 1.1 to 1.8 ounces (maximum 2.5 ounces)

**Gestation:** 20 to 21 days

**Litter Size:** 1 to 11 (usually 3 to 5); average of 4 litters per year (17 litters were born to one animal in captivity)

**Age of Maturity:** male, 45 days (if born in midsummer, probably not until the following season); female, 25 days

**Longevity:** usually less than 1 year in the wild; can survive several years in captivity

**Diet:** primarily herbaceous vegetation; seeds, grain, bark, fruits, insects, snails and other invertebrates and small

*Meadow voles are highly prolific, ready to breed at the age of 3 weeks.*

vertebrates

**Habitat:** wet meadows and open grassland; near water; overhead grass cover is essential

**Predators:** owls, snakes, fish, carnivores and birds

**Dental Formula:** 1/1, 0/0, 0/0, 3/3 = 16 teeth

# *Prairie Vole* Microtus ochrogaster

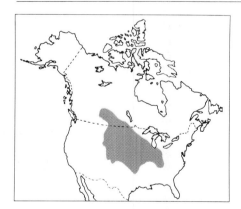

**Mammal:** *Microtus ochrogaster* — prairie vole

**Meaning of Name:** *Microtus* (small ears); *ochrogaster* (yellow belly)

**Description:** greyish to dark brown with a mixture of buff and black hairs; buffy grey underparts tipped with light cinnamon to buff; tail is dark brown above and light grey beneath

**Total Length:** male, 4.8 to 6.6 inches; female, 5.2 to 6.7 inches

**Tail:** male, 1 to 1.7 inches; female, 1.2 to 1.6 inches

**Weight:** male, 1.3 to 1.9 ounces; female, 1.3 to 2 ounces

**Gestation:** 21 days

**Litter Size:** 2 to 6 (usually 3 or 4); up to 5 litters per year

**Age of Maturity:** female, 35 to 40 days

**Longevity:** less than 1 year in the wild (can live up to 22 months); approximately 35 months in captivity

**Diet:** varies with season; green forbs, grasses, bulbs, rhizomes, seeds, acorns, grains, fruits, tree bark, insects, invertebrates, small vertebrates and each other

**Habitat:** open habitats (grassland plains, fencerows and prairies) with lots of vegetation for cover; not usually found in wooded or damp areas but does occur in hayfields and along field borders

**Predators:** diurnal and nocturnal predators; fish, frog, snakes, owls, hawks, opossum, short-tailed shrew, coyote, fox, mink, least weasel, domestic cat

**Dental Formula:** 1/1, 0/0, 0/0, 3/3 = 16 teeth

Prairie voles live in grassland areas with light soils and have one of the most interesting social biologies of all voles. Both sexes cooperate in caring for the young, and families may remain together after the young mature. They share the same burrow and food caches. The burrow systems are shallow but extensive — some runs extend more than 325 feet — and these voles will also use the tunnels of moles. The food caches contain up to 7 pounds of plant roots for winter provisions.

## Yellownose Vole Microtus chrotorrhinus

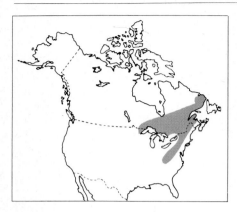

**Mammal:** *Microtus chrotorrhinus* — yellownose vole, rock vole; one of the rarer Canadian small mammals
**Meaning of Name:** *Microtus* (small ears); *chrotorrhinus* (colour + nose) refers to yellow nose
**Description:** greyish brown back and dull to silvery grey ventrally; orange or rufous face with rich yellow around the nose spreading backwards to include the ears; winter coat is longer and glossier
**Total Length:** 6 to 7.3 inches
**Tail:** 1.7 to 2.1 inches
**Weight:** 1 to 2 ounces
**Gestation:** not known (probably 20 or 21 days)
**Litter Size:** 2 to 5; 2 or more litters per year
**Age of Maturity:** not known (probably 25 to 45 days)
**Longevity:** not known (probably less than 1 year)
**Diet:** stems and leaves of forbs and other green plants (false mitrewort, violet, bunchberry and mayflower)
**Habitat:** cool, moist, rocky woodlands under cliffs or rock outcrops; usually found near forest springs or among the bracken in small clearings in spruce/birch/balsam fir forests
**Predators:** hawks, owls, gull, snakes and small carnivores
**Dental Formula:** 1/1, 0/0, 0/0, 3/3 = 16 teeth

The yellownose vole occurs in colonies associated with rocky talus areas in the eastern coniferous forests of Canada and the upper elevations of the northern Appalachians. It is a shy, secretive species that is day-active but rarely seen. Colonies seem to be associated with small clearings in moist forested areas with water nearby.

## Oregon Vole Microtus oregoni

**Mammal:** *Microtus oregoni* — Oregon vole, creeping vole; the smallest species of the genus
**Meaning of Name:** *Microtus* (small ears); *oregoni* (of Oregon)
**Description:** dusky brown above, silvery ventrally; black-tipped ears; grey feet; bicoloured tail, darker below
**Total Length:** 4.9 to 6 inches
**Tail:** 1.1 to 1.5 inches
**Weight:** 0.6 to 0.7 ounces
**Gestation:** 23 or 24 days
**Litter Size:** 1 to 5; usually 3 litters per year (maximum of 5 or 6)
**Age of Maturity:** male, 40 to 50 days; female, 22 to 27 days
**Longevity:** 320 days in captivity
**Diet:** underground rootstocks and green forage
**Habitat:** coniferous forest edges or bushy grassy areas; prefers relatively dry conditions
**Predators:** hawks, owls, snakes and small carnivores
**Dental Formula:** 1/1, 0/0, 0/0, 3/3 = 16 teeth

The Oregon vole has a narrow distribution along the west coast. It inhabits most coniferous forests but favours forest-edge situations and locally dry conditions where it burrows extensively just below the surface. It feeds generally on leaves and berries of shrubs and herbs but derives most of its food from underground roots and tubers. The mild coastal climate allows Oregon voles to reproduce year-round.

## *Sagebrush Vole* Lagurus curtatus

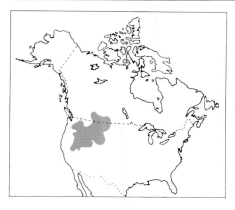

**Mammal:** *Lagurus curtatus* — sagebrush vole

**Meaning of Name:** *Lagurus* (hare + tail) because it has a short tail similar to a hare's; *curtatus* (shortened) probably refers to short legs and tail

**Description:** has modifications for burrowing in sand, including small ears, short tail, stout claws and haired palms and soles; palest of voles, with buffy or ash-grey back, paler sides, soiled white underparts and whitish feet; clear buffy areas on nose, ears and flanks; whitish tail with a dark grey dorsal stripe and terminal "pencil" of hairs

**Total Length:** 4.4 to 5.1 inches
**Tail:** 0.7 to 0.8 inches
**Weight:** 0.8 to 1.3 ounces
**Gestation:** 24 or 25 days
**Litter Size:** 1 to 13 (usually 5); more than 1 litter per year (14 litters per year in captivity)
**Age of Maturity:** male, 60 to 75 days; female, 60 days
**Longevity:** not known (probably 1 or 2 years)
**Diet:** green vegetation, rather than seeds, especially sagebrush
**Habitat:** high, dry sagebrush steppes; semiarid prairies; rolling hills or brushy canyons; prefers loose soil (found in driest places of all voles)
**Predators:** short-eared owl, snakes, hawks, weasel, ferret, badger, fox and coyote
**Dental Formula:** 1/1, 0/0, 0/0, 3/3 = 16 teeth

The sagebrush vole specializes in dry habitats with open areas and scattered shrubbery. It builds underground nests at the base of shrubs and constructs shallow runways to adjacent shrubs. It is active during the day as well as the night and forages on a mixture of plant leaves in summer, seeds in autumn and bark and twigs during winter.

## *Long-tailed Vole* Microtus longicaudus

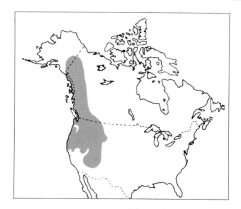

**Mammal:** *Microtus longicaudus* — long-tailed vole

**Meaning of Name:** *Microtus* (small ears); *longicaudus* refers to long tail

**Description:** large vole; dark grey with brown or blackish overtones; grey underparts and soiled whitish feet; bicoloured tail, slightly paler underneath; relatively long tail for a vole; winter pelage is longer and greyer

**Total Length:** 6.6 to 7.6 inches
**Tail:** 2 to 3.5 inches
**Weight:** male, 1.4 to 2.1 ounces; female, 1.3 to 2 ounces
**Gestation:** not known (probably 20 or 21 days)
**Litter Size:** 2 to 8; more than 1 litter per year

*The long-tailed vole, like all voles, is one of the most important foods for owls, hawks and weasels.*

**Age of Maturity:** not known (probably 25 to 45 days)
**Longevity:** not known (probably less than 1 year)
**Diet:** grasses, bulbs, bark of small twigs
**Habitat:** grassy areas in forests, alpine stream banks and meadows, marshes, grasslands and sagebrush plains; brushy areas in winter
**Predators:** hawks, owls, gulls, snakes and small carnivores
**Dental Formula:** 1/1, 0/0, 0/0, 3/3 = 16 teeth

## *Woodland Vole* Microtus pinetorum

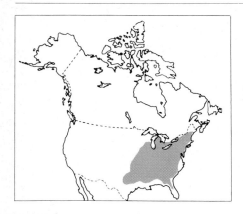

**Mammal:** *Microtus pinetorum* — woodland vole, pine vole

**Meaning of Name:** *Microtus* (small ears); *pinetorum* (of the pines); the name pine vole is misleading since the species actually prefers areas of deciduous woods

**Description:** very small eyes and ears; dull, reddish brown, plush, thick "molelike" fur; soft individual hairs; no scattered long guard hairs as found in most other voles; silvery or buffy grey ventrally; bicoloured tail, brown above and grey below

**Total Length:** 4.3 to 5.2 inches

**Tail:** 0.7 to 0.9 inches

**Weight:** 0.7 to 1.3 ounces

**Gestation:** 20 to 24 days

**Litter Size:** 2 to 7; perhaps 4 to 6 litters per year

**Age of Maturity:** male, 48 to 56 days; female, 70 to 84 days

**Longevity:** 1 year in the wild, but usually less than a few months

**Diet:** nuts, seeds, bark from roots, bulbs, tubers, rhizomes and green leaves; also a variety of ground-living insects, their larvae and other invertebrates; can be cannibalistic

**Habitat:** deciduous forests with loose sandy soils and a thick layer of humus for burrowing; occasionally found in grassy areas in orchards, sand dunes, hillsides and along fence rows

**Predators:** snakes and short-tailed shrew are main enemies; also fox, raccoon, opossum, skunk, mink, weasel, coyote, domestic dog and cat

**Dental Formula:** 1/1, 0/0, 0/0, 3/3 = 16 teeth

Woodland voles live in deciduous eastern forests. They are subterranean and usually do not come above ground, except for brief periods at night. Their eyes and ears are reduced. Tunnels of the woodland vole are shallow and run through the leaf litter, so this vole favours well-drained mature forests with light soils and a thick leaf mulch. It feeds heavily on the roots and underground tubers of perennial wildflowers, which are cached in underground storage chambers. Leafy material and seeds are also eaten. Females aggressively defend their nests.

## *Townsend's Vole* Microtus townsendii

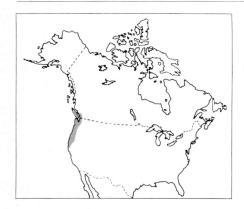

**Mammal:** *Microtus townsendii* — Townsend's vole

**Meaning of Name:** *Microtus* (small ears); *townsendii* (Latinized surname of its discoverer, J.K. Townsend)

**Description:** blackish brown dorsum, greyish underneath; black tail; winter coat is longer with more silvery grey underparts

**Total Length:** 6.7 to 8.7 inches

**Tail:** 1.9 to 2.8 inches

**Weight:** approximately 0.6 to 0.7 ounces

**Gestation:** 21 to 24 days

**Litter Size:** 1 to 9 (usually 4 or 5)

**Age of Maturity:** not known (probably 25 to 45 days)

**Longevity:** not known (probably less than 1 year)

**Diet:** underground rootstocks

**Habitat:** moist fields and meadows; marshes and mountain slopes; usually near water

**Predators:** hawks, owls, gulls, snakes and small carnivores such as the short-tailed shrew, badger, coyote, fox, skunk and weasel

**Dental Formula:** 1/1, 0/0, 0/0, 3/3 = 16 teeth

Townsend's vole is a large west coast vole and is a good swimmer, often associated with water during summer. It digs long shallow runways in light soil and may place the entrance to its nest underwater. Its winter nest is located on drier ground, where soil freezing is less of a problem. It cuts a variety of green vegetation and tubers as food.

### Voles as Vectors

*Plagues such as the black death and typhus epidemics that have periodically decimated the human inhabitants of Asia and Europe have relied on rodents to carry them: mice and rats that have adapted to human environments have proved convenient vectors for the bacteria involved. They do a good job of spreading the bacteria, introducing them to new hosts, such as urban humans, mammals whose bodies have not evolved the biochemistry nor developed the immune reactions needed to fight off the disease.*

*In the New World, lemmings and voles are also convenient hosts for many parasites of mammals. Fortunately, voles and lemmings have remained creatures of the wild and do not pose a threat to urban North Americans. Nevertheless, every year, humans contact some of the pathogens carried by wild voles and lemmings. A common affliction known as "backpacker's disease" — a kind of intestinal diarrhea caused by the protozoan Giardia lamblia — infects the gastrointestinal tract and can be severe if not treated. Normally, Giardia is thought of as a disease of polluted Third World cities with poor sanitation. However, backpackers who drink from crystal-clear mountain streams and seemingly pure Arctic lakes hundreds of miles from the nearest city can pick up Giardia. The protozoan is found in several species of voles. Their feces' washing into a water supply can infect humans.*

In the Far North and in the West, voles are implicated as vectors of tularemia, a bacterial disease that can be fatal to humans. It causes a severe inflammation of the lymphatic system. Voles may introduce tularemia into water sources used by humans. The voles may spread the disease among themselves through cannibalism at high population densities. In Asia, the clearing of forests and the subsequent rise in the vole population is credited with increasing human tularemia infections. Trappers who handle wild animals are constantly at risk of contracting tularemia.

Voles are strongly implicated as reservoirs of Babesia microti, a parasite of the mammalian bloodstream. It is transmitted by tick bites among animals such as voles. A recent survey of New Englanders bitten by ticks or suffering from a fever showed that 7.5 percent had contact with Babesia. This disease can kill people who have had their spleen removed or who are using chemotherapeutic drugs that depress the immune response of the body.

Voles are also vectors for many kinds of parasitic worms that complete their final stages of development in large mammalian carnivores and predatory birds. There is a cestode worm parasite transmitted from voles to Arctic foxes that also finds its way into human populations in Siberia and Alaska. This worm can destroy the liver and cause death if not treated.

The catalogue of vole pathogens is a long one and includes many species that are not human health threats. They are a clear reminder of the benefits that humans acquired when they began to associate disease with biological vectors, rather than with supernatural causes, and learned to wash, to disinfect with soap and to cook their meat.

Even though voles, such as this red-backed vole, are found in the most pristine wilderness habitats, they can still transmit serious bacterial diseases to backpackers and trappers who come in contact with them.

# *Muskrat* Ondatra zibethicus

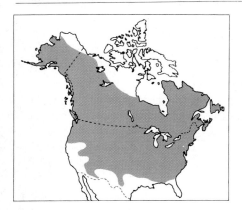

**Mammal:** *Ondatra zibethicus* — muskrat; the largest of North American cricetids

**Meaning of Name:** *Ondatra* is the Iroquois Indian name for this animal; *zibethicus* refers to the fact that there are 2 anal glands found beneath the skin that enlarge during the breeding season and produce a musky-smelling substance

**Description:** waterproof fur is composed of dense, soft underfur and long, coarser, shiny guard hairs; pelage is silvery brown to glossy dark brown with chestnut- to hazel-coloured flanks; grey underparts are paler; scaly, black, naked tail is flattened from side to side; small spot on chin; blackish nasal pads and soles of feet; some modifications for aquatic life include partially webbed toes, strong claws, large hind feet that are slightly rotated

**Total Length:** male, 19.3 to 24.3 inches; female, 20.2 to 23.5 inches

**Tail:** male, 8.7 to 11.1 inches; female, 7.6 to 10.9 inches

**Weight:** male, 1.7 to 2.6 pounds; female, 1.8 to 3 pounds

**Gestation:** 22 to 30 days

**Litter Size:** 1 to 12 (usually 6 to 8); 2 or 3 litters per year

**Age of Maturity:** 6 months in the south; 1 year in the north

**Longevity:** 3 or 4 years in the wild; 10 years in captivity

**Diet:** primarily a herbivore eating aquatic vegetation; cattail is one of the most important plant foods; also eats frogs, clams, crayfish, mussels, small turtles and young water birds

**Habitat:** ponds, lakes, streams, canals and reservoirs (deep enough so that water will not freeze); freshwater marshes, marshy areas of lakes and slow-moving streams

**Predators:** mink is the most serious; also preyed upon by fox, coyote, wolf, weasel, raccoon, black bear, lynx, bobcat, otter, owls, hawks, raven, pike and snapping turtle (preys on young)

**Dental Formula:** 1/1, 0/0, 0/0, 3/3 = 16 teeth

The muskrat is a giant among microtines, the largest of the North American species. It has an extensive range, from the north of Mexico to the very northern edge of the Canadian mainland, far above the tree line. It is also the most valuable North American species in the modern fur trade. There is an annual harvest of 4 to 8 million muskrats, worth many millions of dollars.

The tremendous value of muskrats results from their wide distribution and the fact that they are adapted to highly productive aquatic habitats. They share many similarities with the beaver: their coat is designed for activity in the water and consists of a thick, waterproof underfur overlaid with long, glossy guard hairs; their hind feet are partially webbed and sport large claws; their long tail is flattened vertically and used in swimming. And, like the beaver, the muskrat has a high tolerance for carbon dioxide in its blood, being able to swim at least 100 yards underwater and to stay submerged for as long as 17 minutes.

Another similarity between muskrats and beavers is their ability to build houses and canals. Muskrats nest in a wide variety of habitats, from large lakes and rivers to small ponds and marshes. Where a solid bank is available, they will build burrows with an underwater entrance that runs toward a nesting chamber that sits above the water level and usually has more than one exit tunnel. During dry spells, when water levels decline, muskrats will extend their entrance tunnel to deeper water. In areas without raised banks, muskrats will build lodges out of vegetation, such as cattails and bullrushes, piled into a mound roughly 3 feet above water level and plastered with mud and muck. Inside, they construct a dry, grass-lined nest. These huts are normally built in autumn and are designed to last only through the winter.

In open water, muskrats will also build feeding platforms of organic debris and vegetation, allowing the animal to bring its food up onto the platform and out of the water to prevent the loss of body heat. The muskrat is a small mammal with naked feet and tail, and it loses considerable heat when in the water.

During winter, in areas where the water surface freezes, muskrats build "push-ups," a dome of roots and vegetation over a hole in the ice where they can emerge to breathe and feed. The insulating quality of the push-up, especially when it is snow-covered, prevents a thick ice cover from forming and enables the muskrat to keep its breathing holes open all winter.

The construction and feeding activity of muskrats has considerable ecological impact on marshes. They are credited with creating the large open-water areas needed to attract water fowl. Their lodges, abandoned in summer, provide nesting sites for water birds, and they support rare and diverse miniature plant communities of marsh plants that do not occur in thick stands of cattail and bullrushes.

Muskrats are mostly herbivorous, eating the roots, tubers, stems and leaves of many aquatic and terrestrial plants. Like the beaver, they are able to pull their lips in behind their incisors to gnaw underwater. When they have the opportunity, muskrats will eat frogs, crayfish, clams and young waterbirds. During times of abundant food, muskrat populations can soar to densities of 12 to 36 per acre of marsh.

The density of muskrat populations fluctuates cyclically in some areas. In northern Canada, it sometimes appears to follow a 6-year cycle and, in other areas, a 10-year cycle. The factors driving the cycle are unknown, but it is known that food depletion can occur and water fluctuations also seem to affect populations significantly. The highest populations usually occur after wet years, while droughts cause high dispersal and mortality. Wildlife managers sometimes encourage muskrat populations to explode by reducing trapping in densely vegetated marshes. Eventually, this results in an "eat out" in which almost all the vegetation is consumed. The large areas of open water that result make perfect waterfowl habitats.

Many animals prey regularly on muskrats. Large raptors such as

*Well adapted for wetland living, muskrats are able swimmers and eat both land and aquatic plants. To preserve body heat, they prefer to eat out of the water.*

*While really a giant vole modified for aquatic life, the muskrat has many similarities to the beaver, including webbed hind feet and a flattened tail.*

horned owls and marsh hawk and mammals such as foxes, raccoons, weasels, otter, mink and coyotes all eat muskrat. Mink, with their aquatic ability and streamlined shape, are able to catch muskrats in their burrows. However, none of these predators appears to cause the decline of muskrat populations. It may be that changes in breeding biology and aggression between muskrats have the same influence on cycles that they are thought to exert on voles and lemmings. The fact that their cycles are longer may be due to their lower reproductive rate, which increases the time that the population needs to reach peak densities. The longer 10-year cycle occurs farther north, suggesting that the shorter breeding season and slower growth rates influence the length of the cycle.

Muskrats are territorial. Females will kill other females and their offspring to gain control of a burrow, and there is considerable fighting among muskrats at high population densities. A monogamous pair bond appears to exist during the breeding season, with females aggressively defending their nest against other females and males fighting with other males. Males, however, do not seem to offer much, if any, parental care.

Young muskrats are altricial, born blind and virtually naked. They are usually weaned after a month, and the female will then breed again. Litters are larger in the north than in the south, and large females may bear up to 12 young per litter. Compared with other microtines, the muskrat has delayed maturity, something to be expected because of its large size and territorial nature. In northern areas, muskrats seem to take a full year to reach maturity.

Males advertise their maturity and territorial status by excretions from a pair of glands in the anal region. Females have a less-developed set. During the mating season, these glands enlarge and leak an oily, musky secretion through pores in the male's foreskin. The secretion mixes with the urine, to be deposited around the territory. It is this musky advertisement that gives the muskrat its name.

# Western Harvest Mouse *Reithrodontomys megalotis*

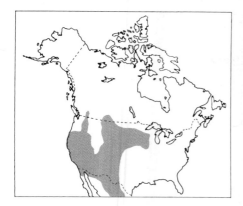

**Mammal:** *Reithrodontomys megalotis* — western harvest mouse

**Meaning of Name:** *Reithrodontomys* (groove-toothed mouse) refers to grooves on upper incisor teeth; *megalotis* (large + ear)

**Description:** pale grey to brown above; dark mid-dorsal stripe runs from forehead to tail; brown flanks and cheeks; underparts and feet vary from white to deep grey

**Total Length:** 4.7 to 6 inches

**Tail:** 2.3 to 3.2 inches

**Weight:** 0.32 to 0.60 ounces

**Gestation:** 23 to 24 days

**Litter Size:** 1 to 9 (usually 2 to 4); several litters per year (up to 14 in captivity)

**Age of Maturity:** 4.5 months

**Longevity:** few live more than 1 year in the wild (18 months is the maximum)

**Diet:** primarily seeds of grasses and forbs as well as green shoots of vegetation; insects (moths and grasshoppers)

**Habitat:** stands of shortgrass with clumps of forbs and small shrubs scattered throughout; dense vegetation near water

**Predators:** snakes, squirrel, owls, shrike, weasel, skunk, fox and larger shrews and mice

**Dental Formula:** 1/1, 0/0, 0/0, 3/3 = 16 teeth

The western harvest mouse is one of the tiniest mice in North America, weighing roughly four-tenths of an ounce. It is a grassland species using areas with a mixture of open and shrubby vegetation. It is mainly a herbivore that feeds during summer on leaves, grass and herbs and later switches to seeds in autumn and winter. It will cache both leaves and seeds. Western harvest mice will also eat insects. Grasshoppers are a common prey species. The western harvest mouse often uses the runways of other rodents, especially those of meadow voles. It builds fist-sized grass nests in vegetation clumps and other protected spots and rests in these during daylight hours. A harvest mouse's light weight enables it to climb around shrubbery and other

*For the western harvest mouse, the advantages of being light and small include the ability to climb small plants to hunt for grasshoppers and other insects.*

vegetation in search of food. These mice seem to be continually reproductive, except for the winter months, with females producing several litters of between one and nine offspring a year. Harvest mice live only one year.

# Deer Mouse  *Peromyscus maniculatus*

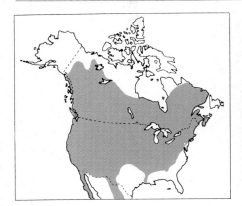

**Mammal:** *Peromyscus maniculatus* — deer mouse

**Meaning of Name:** *Peromyscus* (little pouched mouse); may also be from Latin *pero* (pointed), which refers to the characteristic pointed nose; *maniculatus* (small-handed)

**Description:** pale greyish buff to deep reddish brown dorsally with white flanks and underparts; tail is always sharply bicoloured, black above and white below; ears are covered in fine grey hair with tufts of whitish hair at the anterior base of each

**Total Length:** 4.8 inches

**Tail:** 1.8 to 5 inches

**Weight:** 0.42 to 1.2 ounces

**Gestation:** 22 to 35 days

**Litter Size:** 1 to 11 (usually 4 to 6); 2 to 4 litters per year (can have up to 14)

**Age of Maturity:** male, 40 to 45 days; female, 32 to 35 days

**Longevity:** few survive past 1 year in the wild (32 months is maximum); have lived as long as 8 years in captivity

**Diet:** primarily a seed eater; also nuts, acorns, fruits, mushrooms, flowers and berries as well as insects and their eggs and larvae, caterpillars and spiders

**Habitat:** broad tolerance; occurs in almost every dryland habitat within its range (not found in moist areas); alpine areas, boreal forests, woodlands, grasslands, brushlands, meadowlands and cultivated fields

**Predators:** owls, weasel and fox are probably its most important predators; also snakes, short-tailed shrew, squirrel, skunk, mink, raccoon, bear, coyote, wolf and large fish

**Dental Formula:** 1/1, 0/0, 0/0, 3/3 = 16 teeth

The deer mouse is extremely common and extremely widespread. It is a habitat generalist, ranging from mature deciduous and boreal forests to dry grasslands, and in rural areas, it is often a common resident of human habitations. The deer mouse is the only native rodent that seems to prefer houses as a place to live. Of all the noncommercial mammals, this species is the best studied. Almost any North American mammalogist can find a nearby population to observe.

The diet of deer mice is as general as its choice of habitat. It eats and stores many kinds of seeds, flowers, berries and insects, and it will even eat salamanders and bird eggs when given the chance. Deer mice cache large volumes of seeds for winter use, up to almost a gallon in each cache. Generally, these seeds are smaller than those selected by squirrels and include species such as ragweed, ticktrefoil and grasses. Seed abundance is the most critical part of the deer mouse's feeding requirements.

Deer mice are sedentary with well-defined home ranges 3 acres or less in size. They use clearly defined trails

*Life in the wild for the deer mouse is difficult. While it can live for eight years in captivity, 95 percent of wild mice do not survive their first year.*

and build well-insulated nests of fine, dry vegetation in protected spots such as hollow logs and under rocks. They have a strong homing tendency and will return to the home range even after being moved 2 miles. Home ranges overlap, and there is little aggressive territoriality except for breeding purposes. A female will repel intruders from the vicinity of her breeding nest.

Females can breed several times in a season. They usually mate and give birth in spring to a litter of one to eleven and mate and become pregnant almost immediately afterward. Gestation lasts three weeks to a month, depending on whether or not the female is breast-feeding another litter. The young are born helpless and take roughly a month to be weaned. As weaning approaches, the pregnant mother will usually move to a new nest to give birth.

One important aspect of the breeding biology of the deer mouse may be male parental care. Few mammals have male parental care, but deer mice do. The female excludes the male from the nest at birth but later accepts his presence. He assists in grooming the young, maintaining the nest and accompanying the young weaned mice on foraging trips. When juveniles mature, the adult male is thought to expel them aggressively from his territory. Whether males help or not may depend on the density of females. Males can sometimes exclude other males and mate with several different females. This may reduce the opportunity and value of parental care for the male. On the other hand, if male parental care increases the female reproductive rate and juvenile survival, it might pay females to tolerate the presence of other females. There are some reports of communal broods of two females.

Deer mouse densities vary greatly from season to season and from year to year. The abundance of the year's seed crop may greatly affect overwintering mortality. Captive deer mice

live as long as eight years, but in the wild, few of them ever see their first birthday. Densities at the start of spring are often one-tenth as high as they were the previous autumn. Population turnover — the replacement of older individuals by new individuals — has been measured at 95 percent per year. In other words, only 5 percent of deer mice survive for more than a year.

To conserve heat during winter, deer mice may huddle in groups. They enter a daily torpor, allowing their body temperatures to drop and then heat up again for their active feeding and foraging period during the evening.

Owls and carnivorous mammals feed heavily on deer mice, especially during winter when the mice travel over snow fields and there is little protective cover. Deer mice wisely avoid travel on moonlit nights. It has been shown that the success of short-eared owls hunting for deer mice increases as the moon waxes.

The ***cascade deer mouse***, P. *oreas*, is so closely related to the deer mouse that it was formerly thought of as a subspecies. It inhabits the damp West Coast forests of Englemann spruce and other conifers. It is not known how different this species' life history might be from that of the more common deer mouse.

The ***Sitka mouse***, P. *sitkensis*, is a close relative of the deer mouse. The species probably arose as an isolated population in a coastal area that was not glaciated during the last Ice Age. Cut off by the ice sheets from the central population of deer mice, Sitka mice evolved into a genetically separated group. They are restricted to coastal islands of British Columbia. Where the deer mouse is found, Sitka mice seem to disappear, even though they are larger. The more generalized deer mouse probably outcompetes the Sitka. The Sitka mouse will face extinction if deer mice are introduced to the islands that are its home.

## White-footed Mouse *Peromyscus leucopus*

**Mammal:** *Peromyscus leucopus* — white-footed mouse

**Meaning of Name:** *Peromyscus* (little pouched mouse); *leucopus* (white foot)

**Description:** short, soft, dense pelage; light brown in colour with dark dorsal stripe; white underparts with grey base; white throat; black spot at base of whiskers; ears outlined in white but no preorbital tuft of white hair; indistinctly bicoloured tail is paler below

**Total Length:** 5.7 to 7.7 inches
**Tail:** 2.4 to 3.7 inches
**Weight:** 0.53 to 1.1 ounces
**Gestation:** 22 to 25 days
**Litter Size:** 1 to 9 (usually 4); 2 to 4

litters per year
**Age of Maturity:** 7 to 11 weeks (as early as 4 weeks for females)
**Longevity:** usually do not survive into second year in the wild; can survive 5 years or more in captivity
**Diet:** primarily seeds of grasses, weeds, clover, fungi, fruits and nuts; also larvae and cocoons of beetles, moths, butterflies and other invertebrates
**Habitat:** primarily associated with

*While the white-footed mouse looks like the deer mouse and shares the same habitat, it is more of a tree climber than its ground-bound counterpart.*

deciduous woodland and shrubby habitat; sometimes occurs in open areas
**Predators:** snakes, owls, weasel, mink, fox, skunk, raccoon and domestic cat
**Dental Formula:** 1/1, 0/0, 0/0, 3/3 = 16 teeth

## Northern Grasshopper Mouse  Onychomys leucogaster

**Mammal:** *Onychomys leucogaster* — northern grasshopper mouse
**Meaning of Name:** *Onychomys* (claw-mouse), due to its large claws; *leucogaster* (white belly)
**Description:** short, fleshy tapering tail; stomach has specialized brown glandular swelling midway along the greater curvature; no cheek pouches; ruffled-looking pelage is long, fine and oily; brownish grey to pinkish cinnamon or buff upperparts; greyish white cheeks, nose, feet; underparts are pure white; tail is greyish white below and grey above and has white tip; whitish tufts around ears
**Total Length:** 5.6 to 6.3 inches
**Tail:** 1 to 2.4 inches
**Weight:** 0.9 to 1.8 ounces
**Gestation:** 26 to 37 days for nonlactating females; 32 to 47 days for lactating females
**Litter Size:** 1 to 6 (average of 4); several litters per year (up to 12 in captivity)
**Age of Maturity:** 2 to 5 months
**Longevity:** not known (probably 1 year in the wild)
**Diet:** primarily an insectivore (grasshoppers, beetles, caterpillars, moths, ants, flies); also other invertebrates such as spiders and small vertebrates (mice and voles); plant seeds and seeds of wild forbs in summer
**Habitat:** shortgrass prairies and desert scrub
**Predators:** rattlesnake, ground squirrel, weasel, ferret, badger, fox, coyote and owls
**Dental Formula:** 1/1, 0/0, 0/0, 3/3 = 16 teeth

Although most mice feed primarily on plants, the grasshopper mouse thrives on meat. It has a stout body, large claws, heavy forepaws, a strong set of jaws, a sturdy head and no cheek pouches, all of which are related to its diet. Grasshopper mice do, in fact, eat grasshoppers and many other invertebrates, including scorpions, caterpillars and even groups with hard bodies, such as dung beetles. Grasshopper mice will corner and kill other species of mice with a bite to the base of the skull, the same technique used by carnivores such as weasels and cats.

The grasshopper mouse is a slow runner. Its short, stubby limbs seem more designed for digging. In its native desert and grassland habitat, the grasshopper mouse builds an extensive system of burrows at the soil surface and will use the runways of other small mammals. The burrows have sections for food caches, an underground nest to retreat to during the day, sanitation burrows and short segments at the edge of the territory that are scent-marked and used to declare territorial perimeters. Like other carnivores, this mouse has a relatively large home range and is intensely territorial. The grasshopper mouse emits a loud wolf-style "howl." It rears up on its hind legs with its head back and utters a high-pitched shriek that sounds like a whistle. The howl is thought to be a declaration of territoriality. Grasshopper mice also use other vocal calls, including a repeated barking squeak.

During winter, when insect abundance is reduced, the grasshopper mouse relies on seeds for food. It is possible that this mouse competes more with shrews than with other species of mice.

## Sex-Ratio Manipulation

*Most mammals have close to a 1-to-1 sex ratio at birth. Such a ratio will maximize the reproductive success of the average mother. Since every individual is derived from a male and a female parent, the average genetic value of a son will equal that of a daughter. They both have the same opportunity to contribute genes to the next generation. That is what a mother is selected to do — to maximize the number of genes that her sons and daughters will contribute to future generations. What happens if she produces only sons or only daughters instead of a 1-to-1 mixture?*

*When a population produces an excess of females, selection will favour the female that produces plenty of sons, since their mating success will be higher than that of daughters. There will be a large number of females to mate and few male competitors, and therefore, the sons will produce more offspring than the average daughter. The reverse situation also holds: when there is an excess of males, producing daughters is the best strategy. Thus the population converges to the 1-to-1 sex-ratio strategy.*

*The best strategy is for females to produce a litter of half males and half females. Nature, however, is more complicated than this. Sons and daughters are not equally valuable. Their value — measured as the benefits they will yield in grandchildren minus the costs of producing them — ought to influence the parent. Normally, parents give birth to equal numbers of males and females. If one sex costs more than the other to produce, then comparatively few of the costly sex will be produced, so that on average, the total amount of resources invested in males will equal the amount invested in females.*

*A further complication is that the reproductive success of sons and daughters depends on the breeding system of the population, on whether the population is growing, stable or declining and on the condition of the mother and how that affects the condition of her offspring. If the mating system is a harem system, where only a few males control access to the females, there may be intense selection for producing large high-quality sons. A large, competitive son may mate with many females, and a low-quality son will have almost no chance to fight for and to obtain a harem.*

*By contrast, virtually all daughters, fit or not, will be mated and included in a harem. In this situation, a mother in less than prime physiological condition ought to produce more*

daughters than sons. Her daughters might be somewhat less than prime, but they will all get mated, whereas less-than-prime sons have almost no chance of breeding. The reverse strategy ought to hold for females in excellent condition. They can get the most return by producing sons whose prime condition ensures that they will gain a harem and will sire many offspring.

This pattern might also operate within the lifetime of a single female. When a female is young and has few resources to invest, she might produce more daughters and shift toward producing sons as she grows older and acquires more resources for rearing better-quality offspring. When mice are fed a deficient diet, for instance, they produce smaller litters than adequately fed mice, and this reduction in litter size is due

almost entirely to the selective reabsorption of male embryos by the mother. The hungry mother diverts investment away from her embryonic sons and shunts it into producing daughters. Similarly, in wood rats, mothers that had a deficient diet selectively starved their sons and concentrated on feeding their daughters. In all of these cases, the results depend on the mating system. If the mating system is polygynous, with intense competition and selection for high-quality males, biologists expect this pattern. But in a monogamous system, with low male-male competition, biologists would not expect it.

A different social and mating system may favour a different strategy of sex-ratio manipulation. If, for example, most of the social

Deer mice are just one species whose females are able to aid the future breeding success of their young by choosing the sex ratio of their litters.

competition is between females, not males, biologists might expect the reverse pattern. In rhesus monkeys, where females compete for dominance status, a mother's rank will influence a daughter's rank. Dominant females suppress the reproduction of subdominants, and their daughters are more likely to become dominant breeders. Accordingly, it has been found that dominant females produce an excess of daughters. By contrast, the success of a son is not influenced by the rank of a mother, so subdominant females may increase their chances by producing sons, rather than daughters.

To understand the pattern of sex ratio in a population, one must know the costs of producing sons and daughters. Even though one might expect females to bias their investment toward males or females according to their age, status or health, one still expects to see the population exhibit a 1-to-1 ratio of investment in the two sexes. For every female that overproduces sons, there will be a corresponding advantage for a female that is able to produce more daughters. To know whether this argument holds, it is necessary to count the number of sons produced and the cost of producing them, total it and compare it with the number of daughters and the cost per daughter. If the theory holds, biologists expect that the most costly sex will be less common.

Red deer, which are close relatives of North American elk, provide a bizarre variation on this theme. Male red deer would seem to cost more to produce than female red deer. A mother's sons suckle more than daughters, and the sons are weaned at a heavier weight. This makes sense, since red deer are a harem-breeding species with intense male-male competition and a selective demand for large, fit sons. If a female produces a son, the high cost of rearing him apparently so depletes the mother that she is much more likely not to breed the next season than if she had reared a daughter. Given that males cost much more to produce, the population should contain more females than males. It does not. This points out the difficulty of measuring costs. It turns out that part of the cost of a daughter is in sharing the foraging range with her. Males move away from the area where they were born; females tend to stay and forage in their mother's home range. Evidence indicates that they compete with her and with each other for food, and the more daughters a female has near her, the lower is her reproductive rate.

In this sense, red deer are like honeybees. A queen produces only a few daughters and thousands of sons, yet daughters and sons are roughly the same size. However, a daughter will assume control of her mother's hive and the mother will leave, thus the cost of each daughter

is high compared with the cost of a son. Those thousands of sons probably cost only as much as one daughter.

## Infanticide

Rodents have a habit of committing infanticide, killing both their own offspring and those of other members of their species. Biologists have known about this for at least two centuries, but until recently, they gave it little attention. Darwin, for instance, noted that in our species, abortion and infanticide have traditionally been the most widespread form of birth and population control. "But," he

To a subordinate western harvest mouse, the birth of a daughter may be preferred to a weak son — as a daughter will not have to compete with other females to mate.

claimed, "the instincts of the lower animals are never so perverted as to lead them regularly to destroy their own offspring." In this case, Darwin was wrong. Biologists are discovering that infanticide is a conspicuous part of the biology of rodents and other mammals and that it is not perverted but makes sense as a reproductive strategy.

It is hard to imagine how killing one's own offspring could be favoured by natural selection, and perhaps that is the reason why infanticide was long considered merely an expression of social pathology. Overcrowding, stress and hunger were thought to lead to cannibalism, abortion and infanticide, as indeed they do, but it may be that the individuals who commit infanticide are actually increasing their reproductive success.

There are several distinct forms of infanticide. A female may kill some of her own offspring as a means of adjusting her litter size to match her resources. Experimental manipulations in which mouse pups are added to the litter of a mother mouse show that a female with a limited amount of food and teats will eat some of the offspring, reducing the clutch size to a normal level. Under conditions of food stress, it has been shown, for example, that a female who raises seven offspring will actually have an overall higher reproductive success than a female who attempts to rear eight. The offspring from the smaller clutch are larger and have a higher survival rate, and the mother may have increased her chances to rear another litter in the future. This form of infanticide regulates the quality of surviving offspring and increases the total lifetime production of the female.

A different form of infanticide is directed against the offspring of other mothers and fathers. Both males and females may practise this, the most overt expression of reproductive competition. Since natural selection favours individuals who leave the most descendants, killing the offspring of a competitor is one of the most direct ways of raising one's reproductive success. This practice is carried on by several rodents. Female muskrats apparently kill the offspring of other females while taking over their burrows. This has also been documented in Belding's and Arctic ground squirrels. So intense is this competition for burrows that many students of colonial squirrels and rodents believe that female infanticide and competition for burrows is a driving force favouring social groupings and extended families. The closely related females of the extended families cooperate to repel intruders.

Deer mice may kill some offspring to raise the quality of the survivors.

Another form of genetic competition appears to influence male infanticide. Male rodents and several kinds of monkeys, lions, horses and other mammals often kill the offspring of a female after they have taken control of a territory or harem and evicted the previous resident male. They are disposing of offspring with whom they have no close genetic relationship, and in so doing, they return the female to reproductive readiness sooner. If a nursing female kept her offspring, the intruding male would ordinarily have to wait until the litter was weaned before he could father his own. Without her young, the female is ready to breed within days — increasing the number of offspring the new male can sire within his lifetime. At the same time, he disposes of individuals that will be the competitors of his own heirs.

Some females probably have evolved ways of countering the infanticidal male. Pregnant females may enter into a fake oestrus, copulate with the new resident male and deceive him into believing that her offspring resulted from that copulation. Males must have some mechanisms designed to prevent them from committing infanticide on their own offspring. Copulation with the mother may be the best means they have of assessing their paternity. Females may also simply be more aggressive. Lactating female microtine rodents are more aggressive than males or nonbreeding females and will physically drive intruders away.

If a female has little opportunity for preventing male infanticide, she may evolve a physiology that minimizes her losses — the strange Bruce effect. A pregnant mouse female may spontaneously abort her embryos if she is exposed to the urine of a strange male. The new smell may signal to her that her mate has been displaced, and if the new male is likely to kill her newborn pups, she would be better off aborting them as soon as possible and starting over.

Infanticide studies are difficult to conduct. Laboratory work is full of artificialities, and field observations are hard to come by. However, the patterns of infanticide that have been recorded suggest that the behaviour is not simply social pathology with individuals too stressed and starved to behave in a biologically adaptive manner, but rather, it is a behaviour moulded by natural selection.

# RABBITS, HARES & PIKAS
## Lagomorpha

Lagomorphs have suffered from a case of mistaken identity. Biologists once lumped them together with the rodents, but now lagomorphs are recognized as a separate order.

The Lagomorpha is a small order of two families: one includes rabbits, the other contains only pikas. Neither family is very diverse, but in many places, the animals are the dominant small herbivore. Like rodents, lagomorphs have chisel-shaped front incisors for chewing leafy vegetation and shrubbery. There are many morphological and behavioural differences between lagomorphs and rodents. For example, lagomorphs have two sets of upper incisors: a long front pair and a rear pair shaped like small pegs. Rodents, on the other hand, have just one set of upper incisors. Lagomorphs are strictly herbivores, whereas rodents have a highly diverse diet.

Lagomorphs evolved more than 50 million years ago in Asia, probably in large grassland and meadow areas. The greatest radiation of rabbits and hares has occurred in North America. Pikas were more diverse at one time and were even found in Africa. In North America, pikas have never diversified, either taxonomically or ecologically, to the extent that rabbits and hares have.

Many of the lagomorphs' physical characteristics reflect their grazing habits, grassland origins and appeal to predators. Thus their wide-set eyes and erect heads give them a wide field of vision. Their long necks are easily swivelled, enabling them to look behind themselves; and their large ears help them to detect the stealthy sounds of predators. These features are most developed in hares that live in open areas and least developed in pikas, whose homes are in rockier regions that offer more shelter.

The digestive system of lagomorphs reflects their herbivorous specialization and is similar to that of other grazing ruminant mammals, such as deer. Both lagomorphs and ruminants have a large baglike digestive chamber. Chewed and semidigested food is collected in this chamber, where various microorganisms subject it to fermentation. Because the fermentation system in lagomorphs is not as extensive as that of large grazing ruminants, they must pass some of their nutrients through their system twice. They do this by eating some of their dung, a behaviour called refection.

Lagomorphs produce two kinds of dung pellets: a soft kind that they eat and a hard, fully processed pellet that is not eaten. They excrete the soft pellets when they are inactive and eat them as they emerge from the anus. These pellets are then stored in the stomach where they are mixed with a new load of vegetation and subjected to fermentation again. Refection increases digestive efficiency and enables the lagomorph to recapture nutrients, particularly vitamin $B_{12}$, which the gut bacteria produce. These go back to be stored in the stomach where they will be mixed with new vegetation that the animal will harvest when it becomes active.

*Lagomorphs such as the pika are often the most abundant grazers and browsers in grassland, forest and tundra habitats.*

# *Pikas* Ochotonidae

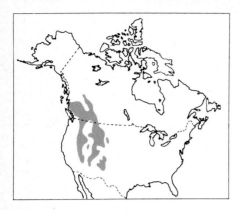

**Mammal:** *Ochotona princeps —* American pika
**Meaning of Name:** *Ochotona,* derived from *ochodona,* a Mongolian name for the pika; *princeps* (chief) refers to an Amerindian name translated as little chief hare
**Description:** small, stocky, tailless mammal with dense, long, fine pelage; greyish buff or brownish with a mixture of black resulting in a salt-and-pepper look dorsally; greyish underneath; dusky ears are edged with white; small harelipped mouth
**Total Length:** 7.1 to 8 inches
**Weight:** 0.25 to 0.5 pounds (4 to 8.2 ounces)
**Gestation:** 30 days
**Litter Size:** 2 to 5 (average 3); 2 litters per year
**Age of Maturity:** the year following birth
**Longevity:** few live for more than 5 years; maximum is 7
**Diet:** grasses, sedges, herbs and tender flowering plants; engages in reingestion
**Habitat:** talus, broken rock, rock slides; usually above the tree line; sometimes in rock piles and on lakeshores on the coast of British Columbia
**Predators:** eagle, buteo hawks, fox, marten, fisher, wolverine, lynx, bear and especially ermine, which follow it through its maze of rock tunnels
**Dental Formula:** 2/1, 0/0, 3/2, 2/3 = 26 teeth

The heyday of pikas has come and gone. Pikas arose in Eurasia and spread to Africa and North America. They are now confined primarily to Asia, where 16 of the 18 surviving species live. Only two species survive in North America, where they inhabit the high mountains of the West.

Pikas have a peculiarly narrow range of temperature tolerances. They can survive long frigid mountain winters but will die from heat stress at only a couple of degrees above their body temperature. This has limited them to the type of habitat in which they probably evolved: high-altitude rock slopes and grasslands.

Some Asian pikas burrow in grassland areas, but in North America, pikas occupy a single highly specific habitat: the rocky talus slopes next to mountain meadows. The rocks and boulders provide protected nest sites for the pika, while the meadow provides their food. Unlike rabbits, pikas are diurnal, relatively sedentary creatures that scuttle into the rocks when threatened. Accordingly, they differ radically from rabbits and hares in body plan. Their legs are short, their eyes comparatively small and their bodies compact like those of rodents.

The habitat required by the North American pikas is extremely small in size. Talus with good forage nearby is limited, and as a result, pikas live in concentrated populations. Both males and females defend territories that cover several hundred square yards. Usually, a male's territory is adjacent to a female's, with the two sexes alternating along the rocky slope. During the mating season, a male's territory may overlap that of the adjacent female. Females repel other females during this time but are less aggressive toward males and vice versa. However, once the young are born, females vigorously exclude males from their territories.

There are two reasons for pika territoriality: a limited number of good nesting sites and the need to stock up a winter food supply. Pikas live up to six years and remain on the same territory during this time. The offspring of a pair will thus face limited prospects of finding their own territory, but if the parents aggressively exclude immigrants, the chances that their offspring may occupy adjacent vacancies will be increased. Females are aggressive toward males after the arrival of their young because of the limited food supply. Males provide no parental care, and they deplete the meadows closest to the talus slope.

Pikas cannot save fuel by hibernating and so remain active throughout the long mountain winter. To have enough food for this time, they cut, dry and store large piles of hay. This hay is cut in the meadow and dried on rocks within the pikas' territory. Vigilance and territoriality are probably required to keep others from stealing already processed hay.

Female territoriality forces the male pikas to be monogamous. Males cannot control access to a group of females because the females are dispersed along the slope and are aggressive toward other females.

The **American pika**, *Ochotona princeps*, is the most common and widely distributed of the two North American species. It is greyish to cinnamon on its upperparts and buff underneath, whereas the **collared pika**, *O. collaris*, is more drab, with greyish patches on the cheeks and around the neck and whitish underparts.

*Pikas are one of the few mammals that cut, dry and stack hay in preparation for winter.*

# Rabbits & Hares *Leporidae*

"Rabbit" and "hare" are categories that connote two different behavioural and ecological patterns within the family Leporidae. Hares and jackrabbits all belong to the same genus, *Lepus*. They are creatures of exposed habitats and are specialized for running. They rarely form burrows except to escape extreme cold or heat. Their young are born fully furred with open eyes and a readiness for activity at birth. By contrast, rabbits are divided into several genera. With their shorter hind limbs, they are not as adept at running. They occupy a variety of habitats from marshy areas to heavy forest, where they often build burrows for nesting and give birth to almost naked helpless young that are nursed by their mother.

All rabbits and hares are runners, and their bodies reflect their dependence on high speed, leaps and bounds to escape predators. Their limbs are elongated, with the hind feet and hind legs much longer than the front, giving them a jacked-up race car build. Some of their hind leg bones are also fused together, allowing them to push off with great force. Their skull is fenestrated; that is, the bones are pitted with cavities, which make them lighter, so the rabbit has less weight to carry. The collarbone is also reduced in size and weight as it is in other bounding, running mammals. All these characteristics adapt the rabbit to its special style of movement. It jumps, leaps and spurts, often from side to side. The combination of high acceleration and speed makes pursuit on the ground difficult for most predators.

The extent to which this ability is developed varies with the rabbit species and the habitat it prefers. Rabbits that rely on extensive burrow systems and brushy vegetation for protection have comparatively shorter hind legs and less running ability than jackrabbits. Jackrabbits live in open habitats where protective cover is often widely dispersed, increasing their dependence on running to escape predators. Consequently, of all the rabbits, jackrabbits have the greatest hind-limb development and are capable of bounding across the terrain at 40 miles per hour.

Most rabbits and hares are active at dusk and during the night, a behavioural pattern that reduces their detection by predators. Like other nocturnal mammals, they have relatively large eyes and ears and a good sense of smell. The social behaviour of rabbits and hares depends on whether the species lives in burrows and, if it does, how closely the burrows are clustered. Some rabbits, such as the European rabbit, live semicommunally in warrens of many burrows. These burrows are used for generations and are thus an important factor in evolutionary success. Both males and females defend their own burrows. In areas where soils suitable for burrow construction are limited, burrows are a valuable resource, and females may fight to the death for possession of one.

The concentration of many individuals in an area ultimately places some stress on local food resources. Thus, as in other social mammals with clumped breeding sites, such as ground squirrels, female rabbits form dominance hierarchies. The dominant females suppress the reproduction of subdominant females by denying them access to nest sites and by physical intimidation. Fighting for burrows is less intense in regions where good soil is dispersed and burrows can be made easily. Such fighting for burrows is not reported among cottontail rabbits, perhaps because the females do not dig clustered burrows. Similarly, this sort of interaction is unknown for female hares because they do not dig extensive burrows.

Like the females, male European rabbits can be intensely territorial when burrows are clumped. In such situations, the females constitute a large defensible resource to which a male can gain exclusive access by fighting and with other forms of dominance signalling. Males of this species pile up their dung pellets to form territorial markers. They also have a chin gland that produces an odorous secretion which they rub around the warren and onto the fur of females within their territory. In rabbit and hare species where females are dispersed, males use a different strategy. They also scent-mark a territory, but then they must search for females within it as well as repel other males they encounter.

Most people have heard the phrase "as mad as a March hare," which comes from the springtime mating antics of hares and rabbits. This behaviour often involves boxing: individuals stand up on their hind legs and cuff each other in the face and ears. It was once thought that this was a case of male-male competition. However, careful videotaping has revealed that females do most of the cuffing, and the individuals they cuff are courting males. Females appear to be testing male status. In some species, such as the black-tailed jackrabbit, females attack hesitant males,

*As creatures of exposed habitats, rabbits have large eyes and ears to enable them to detect predators.*

*Rabbits, such as the cottontail, build a well-insulated nest that keeps the young warm while the mother is away foraging.*

leaping and pawing at them until they are driven off. Females subject persistent males to further tests, leading them on a series of runs and sparring matches.

Female hares and rabbits are usually larger than males, and this form of sexual dimorphism may indicate a history of selection for combative females.

This story is reported of the courtship behaviour of the snowshoe hare: "The male snowshoe approached the female, sniffed her and jumped into the air. After landing, the male urinated on the female and left. The male reapproached the female, and the female jumped into the air twice, after which the male left. The male returned, jumped into the air and urinated on the female. Both snowshoes then went into the bushes where more jumping occurred." Males of other species also run or leap past the fe-

male, urinating as they go. This behaviour, which is developed in some rodents, such as guinea pigs, may provide the female with pheromonal cues about the physiological and hormonal state of the male. Many mammals assess reproductive maturity and territorial signals from the odour of each other's urine.

Copulation is generally brief and may be accompanied by squeaks and squeals by either sex. After copulation, contact and communication between the male and female generally cease, although males may follow a female around and defend her from other males. Males, however, offer no parental care.

Female rabbits become pregnant by induced ovulation; that is, courtship and copulation stimulate the release of eggs for fertilization. Females produce more eggs and implant more embryos than they rear. As pregnancy proceeds, they digest and reabsorb some of the embryos, usually 6 to 30 percent of the fetuses. This may be one means of adjusting the litter size to the amount of food resources

available and the amount of food the female requires for pregnancy and nursing.

Rabbits and hares have a high reproductive rate. Many species are sexually mature when they are just 3 months old. Females may produce several litters per year of 2 to 12 young per litter, giving a total of 12 to 40 young per year. The number of young produced depends on the species, locality and local conditions. Throughout the animal kingdom, fecundity and mortality generally balance each other, and rabbits are no exception. They are subject to intense predation and low survival rates. The prolific cottontail has a life expectancy of six months. Only a quarter of these rabbits survive for more than a year, and few see their fourth birthday. Hares and rabbits are the major food resource for several large carnivores, including lynx, bobcats, Arctic foxes and golden eagles.

## Precocial and Altricial Young

*Large, long-lived mammals generally produce precocial young;*

that is, young that are born already alert, with their eyes open, well-developed muscles and a coat of fur. Small mammals, on the other hand, give birth to altricial young — nearly naked babies that have closed eyes and weak muscles. Both strategies have advantages and disadvantages and seem to reflect the animals' differing responses to environmental fluctuations.

Small mammals have high metabolisms and so grow faster than large mammals. They are also better able to take advantage of sudden increases in food resources. On the other hand, they are more affected by unpredictable environmental changes, such as bad weather, and so hedge their bets against infant mortality by having larger litters, shorter pregnancies and altricial young. The advantage of this system is that the mother can adjust her parental care according to changes in available resources. If food is unavailable, for example, she can abandon her young, and if they are very young, her losses will be slight. If they are large and she is omnivorous or carnivorous, she can eat them, as certain rodents do.

By contrast, a mother that produces a single large precocial offspring has put all her eggs into one basket. If the mother is a large grazer, she cannot recoup her investment in offspring by eating it, even if it is starving. Thus the mother's reproductive success depends heavily on the survival of that one offspring. Such a strategy implies a high survival rate for the young. The precocial system also assures that the offspring will soon be ready to fend for itself, giving both parent and young greater mobility. In addition, a pregnant adult female is far more mobile than a nest of altricial young — she can run from predators, while the mother of altricial young must hide her family. Competition among juveniles for food resources may also tip the balance toward the precocial strategy. Fewer but larger and more developed young have a greater chance of survival where food is scarce.

Hares always have precocial young, whereas rabbits are more altricial, especially those species found in northern climates where the

weather is unpredictable. Tropical rabbits, however, are more like hares, having smaller litter sizes and precocial young, a pattern that suggests greater predation and more competition among the young. However, lower mortality rates from environmental changes favour the precocial strategy.

Hares, which have no well-developed burrow system for protecting their young and which live in exposed habitats, are like the large grazing mammals, such as pronghorn antelope, whose habitat they share. The mother hare is usually pregnant for six weeks (cottontail rabbits are pregnant for only four), gives birth in the open, perhaps in a shallow depression, and visits her babies for nursing only once a day for 10 minutes. Her young are soon able to run from predators and to move in search of new and shifting food supplies. The mother cottontail, on the other hand, must spend more time and energy nursing her babies, and they are usually not ready to move about and leave the nest until 16 days after their birth.

These different patterns suggest that parental care evolved in response to varying combinations of ecological pressures: predation, competition and unpredictable weather.

Cottontail rabbits, like all rabbits, are born relatively helpless in comparison with the more advanced offspring of hares.

# *Eastern Cottontail* Sylvilagus floridanus

**Mammal:** *Sylvilagus floridanus* — eastern cottontail

**Meaning of Name:** *Sylvilagus* (wood hare); *floridanus* (of Florida) refers to Florida, where it was first recognized and named

**Description:** brownish to grey pelage; prominent rusty patch on nape; legs and throat are buff with dark brown anterior borders and grey posterior borders; tail is brown above and white below

**Total Length:** 17.5 inches

**Tail:** 2.4 inches

**Weight:** 1.8 to 3.3 pounds

**Gestation:** 25 to 35 days

**Litter Size:** 2 to 12; 3 to 7 litters per year

**Age of Maturity:** 2 or 3 months

**Longevity:** approximately 6 to 15 months in the wild to a maximum of 3 years (due to large number of predators); one lived more than 9 years in captivity

**Diet:** green vegetation (tender green grasses and herbs) in summer and bark and twigs in winter

**Habitat:** great diversity of habitats (meadows, orchards, fence rows, edges of swamps and woodlots); also heavy brush and grassland pasture with dense clumps of shrubs and trees

**Predators:** hawks, owls, red fox, Arctic fox, grey fox, long-tailed weasel, marten, raccoon, fisher and coyote; bobcat, lynx, snakes, shrike, golden eagle and crow take the younger ones

**Dental Formula:** 2/1, 0/0, 3/2, 3/3 = 28 teeth

*Cottontail rabbits have thrived in the open-meadow habitats created by the cutting of eastern forests.*

The eastern cottontail is actually a southern rabbit. Now one of the most common of eastern mammals, it was once a rare beast. It has probably spread north and increased in abundance because of the destruction of mature hardwood forests. It did not get as far as southern Ontario until the second half of the 19th century, and it did not get up to the Ottawa Valley until 1931.

The cottontail prefers second-growth areas with adjacent meadows. It probably became locally common after severe forest fires cleared mature forests and dense scrub, allowing meadows to grow up. It has the characteristics of a typical "fugitive" species that specializes in short-lived productive habitats, dispersing in search of new areas as older ones decline.

Of the many species of cottontails, the eastern cottontail has the highest reproductive rate. Litter size may be as high as 12, and up to seven litters a year may be born. A female may produce 35 to 38 young per season. More importantly, cottontails reach reproductive maturity at a young age. Some may breed within two or three months of birth.

Like other rabbits, cottontails give birth to helpless young, born almost naked and blind in a well-constructed nest. The female builds a shallow nest hole into the ground and lines the outside with vegetation and the inside with soft fur that she plucks from her belly. The investment in each off-spring is relatively low. The pregnancy is short, only 28 days versus 40 or more days in hares, yet the young are free-living in two weeks, and a new litter is already on the way. Few cottontails live more than one or two years.

All of these life-history traits suggest that the eastern cottontail is a rabbit that invests heavily in reproduction and more lightly in competitive ability and predator avoidance. Virtually every raptor and carnivorous mammal will eat cottontails, but there is no evidence that they regulate cottontail density. Before human disturbance, cottontails were probably regulated by the successional loss of habitat and competition for food.

The destruction of forest and predator populations in eastern North America has made the cottontail an extremely abundant animal. It feeds on a tremendous variety of weeds, herbs and shrubs, and its populations now seem limited primarily by human-induced mortality. Road kills and hunting are major controls on cottontails. Indeed, the cottontail is considered the most important game animal in North America.

Little is known about the **Nuttall's cottontail**, *S. nuttallii*, found in the West, but biologists suspect its natural history is similar to that of the eastern cottontail.

## *Arctic Hare* Lepus arcticus

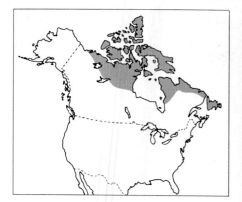

**Mammal:** *Lepus arcticus* — Arctic hare
**Meaning of Name:** *Lepus* (hare); *arcticus* (of the Arctic)
**Description:** pure white in winter with moderately long black-tipped ears; summer coat, which is carried for only a short time, varies depending on latitude — can be bluish grey with a frosting of white, white with a cinnamon or grey wash, or cinnamon with pinkish buff mottling; tail remains white; feet are covered with a yellowish brush and have long, strong curved claws
**Total Length:** male, 23.5 to 31.5 inches; female, 23.8 to 28 inches (female averages slightly larger than the male)
**Tail:** male, 1.6 to 4 inches; female, 1.9 to 2.9 inches
**Weight:** 6 to 12 pounds
**Gestation:** 50 days
**Litter Size:** 2 to 8 (average 5); 1 litter per year
**Age of Maturity:** not first year
**Longevity:** not known (probably up to 5 years)
**Diet:** low-growing tundra plants, twigs and roots of Arctic willows and crowberry; meat and seaweed
**Habitat:** only tundra, beyond the tree line
**Predators:** Arctic fox, wolf, ermine, snowy owl, rough-legged hawk
**Dental Formula:** 2/1, 0/0, 3/2, 3/3 = 28 teeth

The Arctic hare is a more northern version of the snowshoe hare. It is the most northern of all lagomorphs, extending high into the Arctic archipelago. Accordingly, this species is much larger and more thickset than most other hares. Its fur is longer and finer, and its ears are relatively short compared with those of temperate hares. It lives and feeds on the tundra, which is frozen for much of the year, and it has some adaptations for extracting plants from the hard dense crust of ice that can cover the low-growing flora. Its incisors are long and differently shaped than those of other hares, and it has large claws on all four feet that enable it to scrape and chisel away snow and ice to expose its food.

Arctic hares eat a wide variety of plants — herbs in the summer and the more exposed twigs of shrubs in winter. They will also eat meat when they get the opportunity. Fox trappers who bait their sets with meat often trap hares instead of foxes.

Arctic predators such as wolves and Arctic foxes and such raptors as hawks and snowy owls all feed on Arctic hare. This makes the hare's tame behaviour seem rather strange: they show little reaction to humans,

*Arctic hares change their white winter coat to grey-blue for summer.*

although they will hop away to maintain some distance. Dogs and wolves also produce the expected flight, which may involve a strange kangaroo-style hopping on the hind legs. This presumably allows the hare to scan the terrain and watch for lurking wolves that have circled for ambush. Use of the kangaroo hop is apparently correlated with how open the terrain is. Arctic hares show the typical sedentary behaviour of hares, which allows them to build up a series of runways and escape routes.

The short summer season of the high Arctic appears to restrict this species to a single clutch of up to eight offspring. These grow extremely quickly, at twice the rate of other hare species, and they may reach 8 1/2 pounds by summer's end.

Arctic hares also undergo population cycles, but these cycles are less well studied. High populations may account for the observations of more than a hundred hares feeding together — the hares may sometimes act like mildly gregarious grazers akin to other herbivores that herd together.

# Snowshoe Hare *Lepus americanus*

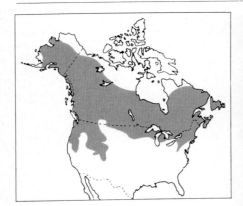

**Mammal:** *Lepus americanus* —
snowshoe hare, varying hare
**Meaning of Name:** *Lepus* (hare);
*americanus* (of America)
**Description:** very broad hind feet; in
summer, pelage has 3 different coloured
layers that distinguish it from the other 2
*Lepus* species; rusty or dark brown
pelage, with a blackish mid-dorsal line
and grey flanks; ventrally, it is white;
cinnamon-brown face, legs and throat,
brown ears with black tip behind and
edged with creamy white; tail is black on
top and white below; the soles of the feet
are densely furred and the hind feet are
padded with stiff hairs (hence snowshoe
hare); in winter, pelage is white and tips
of ears are black
**Total Length:** 14.3 to 20.5 inches
**Tail:** 0.9 to 2.2 inches
**Weight:** male, 3.2 pounds (November);
female, 3.4 pounds (November); weight
fluctuates, with peaks in December and
June
**Gestation:** 34 to 40 days
**Litter Size:** 1 to 8 (usually 2 to 4); as
many as 4 litters per year (first litter is the
smallest)
**Age of Maturity:** the spring following
birth
**Longevity:** 3 to 5 years in the wild; up to
8 years in captivity
**Diet:** green succulent vegetation (usually
clovers, grasses, sedges, ferns and
forbs); in winter, buds, twigs, bark and
evergreen leaves of woody plants; also
frozen meat; can be cannibalistic;
coprophagous
**Habitat:** dense second-growth-type
forests, swamps and thickets
**Predators:** great horned owl, great grey
owl, barred owl, goshawk, lynx, bobcat,
red fox, coyote, wolf, black bear, mink
and weasel
**Dental Formula:** 2/1, 0/0, 3/2, 3/3 = 28
teeth

The snowshoe hare gets its name from its large hind feet, which are thickly padded with coarse hairs and do indeed have the same effect as snowshoes: they distribute the hare's weight over a large surface area, enabling it to run through deep snow. Much of the life of this hare depends on snow. It is a resident of north temperate forests with long winters and heavy snowfalls. As one of the most abundant of all small-game animals, it is sought by a great variety of predators. Its status as a preferred prey item also accounts for another one of its common names, the varying hare.

The snowshoe varies its colour as a camouflage strategy to conceal itself

*Snowshoe hares have strongly cyclical populations that go through boom-and-bust periods every 6 to 10 years.*

from predators. In winter, it is snow-white, all except its black-tipped ears, and in spring, it turns rusty brown, a pattern that increases its camouflage. The moult follows the normal pattern for temperate mammals. It is triggered in autumn by decreasing day length and in spring by increasing day length. The autumn moult results in the growth of a distinct set of white guard hairs that replace the brown guard hairs. In spring, the process is reversed. In both seasons, the snowshoe retains a brownish grey underfur that is absent in Arctic hares and white-tailed jackrabbits. The white winter coat is also designed to meet winter cold stress and has 27 percent more insulating effect than the summer coat.

Snowshoes tolerate others of their own species, and several can often be seen feeding in the same clearing. At mating time, males become more aggressive and may fight over access to a female, wounding each other with their teeth. The male territory typically overlaps that of several females, and at any one time, a receptive female may be courted by several males. Females are sometimes seen with a train of several males following behind, jumping and drumming with their hind legs. Courtship involves much leaping and urination, as with other rabbits and hares. The female rears her young without male assistance. She gives birth in a protected spot in brush or grass, stomping the vegetation into a crude nest. The young are well furred, born alert and with eyes open, and after a week, they are actively feeding and moving around. Within three weeks, they are ready to leave the nest area, freeing the mother to have three or four litters in a season.

The fecundity of snowshoe hares is greater in the northern part of their range, where litter size averages four. In southern areas, such as Colorado, it is half as high. As well, northern hares reproduce often enough that their seasonal total of individual young is also higher. They produce 10 to 12 offspring per female each year, whereas southern populations, such as those in southern Ontario and in Michigan, produce half as many. Even though the northern spring and summer are shorter, it is thought that the longer daylight hours affect the hare's reproductive hormones. While this accounts for the physiological mechanism, the ecological reasons behind the trend may be that competition is more severe in southern populations and that weather-influenced mortality of the young is more severe in the north, favouring larger clutches but smaller offspring. This clutch size also increases and decreases according to how dense populations are.

The young hares have an interesting behaviour designed to reduce predation. Each day, they separate and

*The large feet of the snowshoe hare enable it to bound across the deep snow of the boreal forest.*

move to a sheltered spot by themselves. At feeding time, they return to a central location, where their mother suckles each of them for 5 to 10 minutes. After feeding, they again disperse. This continues until they are all fully weaned. The juvenile hares will not breed until the following spring and summer.

Snowshoe hares are sedentary animals that live in a limited home range with an area that depends on food availability. It is normally less than 25 acres. A limited range enables the animal to become intimately acquainted with its terrain. The territory of a snowshoe hare is crisscrossed with runways leading between open areas and those with brushy cover. The trails are put to use when the hare is pursued by predators. The hares even spend time grooming the trails, clipping away twigs that could impede their movement. In winter, the trails become snow-packed, allowing the hare to use its explosive speed, which may be as fast as 32 miles an hour.

Many raptors catch these hares by surprise attack, as do various mammals including mink, foxes, coyotes, bobcats and lynx — virtually all of the larger predatory mammals.

The incidence of predation can be extremely high — up to 40 percent of a hare population is eaten by predators during the winter. This explains why the hare spends large amounts of time motionless and quiet. It is also nocturnal, and because its zigzagging trails run through brushy cover, it is

likely to escape pursuit if it has advance warning. Much of the time, it simply relies on camouflage, remaining motionless until the danger has passed and breaking into a run only if the predator comes too close. These hares are good swimmers and will plunge into ponds or rivers to escape a predator.

Their preferred habitat is a mixture of dense brushy cover interspersed with forest, especially conifer and the cedar-alder stands associated with wet soils. During the day, the hares remain in the thickets resting, and at night, they forage along thicket and forest edges. They do not favour mature hardwood forests. Their food is extremely generalized. They eat dozens of different herbs and tender twigs during summer and switch to bark, buds and twigs during winter. Fast-growing trees, such as willow, poplar, alder and young conifers, are preferred.

Hares can be tremendously abundant, which affects virtually every major predator and many herbivores in the north temperate forest community. They may compete with moose and deer for browse. They play a role in thinning naturally dense stands of forest, especially after forest fires, and they profoundly affect the density and abundance of some predators, such as lynx.

# White-tailed Jackrabbit  *Lepus townsendii*

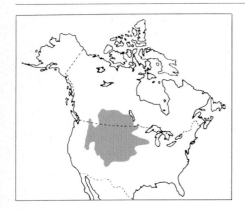

**Mammal:** *Lepus townsendii* — white-tailed jackrabbit

**Meaning of Name:** *Lepus* (hare); *townsendii* (named after J.K. Townsend, an ornithologist and author who explored the Rockies in 1834)

**Description:** uniformly browny grey with a "hoary" face; grey ears are rimmed with white and have prominent black tips; grey throat; white underparts and hind feet; buffy forelegs; tail is white above and below; in the southern part of its range, it is more buffy and winter coat is white with black-tipped ears

**Total Length:** 19.5 to 27.5 inches

**Tail:** 2.5 to 4.4 inches

**Weight:** 4.9 to 9.9 pounds

**Gestation:** 42 days

**Litter Size:** 3 to 6 (usually 4); 1 or possibly 2 litters per year

**Age of Maturity:** the spring following birth

**Longevity:** not known (probably up to 5 years)

**Diet:** grasses, clovers, cultivated grains and alfalfa; in winter, twigs, buds, haystacks and bark of shrubs and trees

**Habitat:** open grassland habitat, pastures, cultivated grainfields, sagebrush plains

**Predators:** coyote, wolf, fox, large hawks and owls, bobcat and eagle

**Dental Formula:** 2/1, 0/0, 3/2, 3/3 = 28 teeth

*With big, long ears for predator detection and huge hind legs for high-speed running, the white-tailed jackrabbit is designed for open spaces.*

The white-tailed jackrabbit is a creature of the great plains and prairies. The adaptations that characterize hares are all highly developed in this species. It has powerful hind legs capable of sprinting at speeds of up to 40 miles an hour and of making great 5-yard leaps. This hare's extremely large ears are used in predator detection; when the hare hears something suspicious, the ears are raised and swivelled to triangulate and pinpoint the source of the sound.

The ears also serve as heat radiators. During the heat of the prairie summer, jackrabbits can erect their ears and dilate the blood capillaries in them to give off excess body heat. This reduces some of the need for cooling via evaporation of perspiration.

Jackrabbits often live in areas where water is usually in short supply. To reduce the amount of water lost by sweating, jackrabbits can let their body temperature rise. Normally, they have a body temperature of 98.6 to 100.4 degrees F, but during the hot noontime part of the day, they may allow their temperature to rise to 105.8 degrees. They are also able to concentrate urine and feces and to reduce water loss through excretion.

Jackrabbits follow the typical grassland pattern of having larger home ranges than forest animals. The home range of a jackrabbit has been measured at 220 acres — on average, many times larger than that of a snowshoe hare. They show none of the tendency toward gregariousness known in other hares.

## The 10-Year Cycle

*In 1865, the Hudson's Bay Company was flooded with snowshoe hare pelts. By 1870, only a trickle was being offered by trappers. In 1875, snowshoe pelts poured in again in tremendous numbers, hundreds of thousands, and again in 1885, 1895, 1905, 1915 . . . every 10 years, the fur returns peaked and then declined sharply. They stayed low, almost zero, for a couple of years and then grew explosively. These fur returns had nothing to do with fur prices; they reflected tremendous changes in the density of snowshoe hares, estimated to peak in some areas at 10,000 per square mile and then to decline to 1 per square mile.*

*The snowshoe is an important element in the northern-coniferous-forest food web, and the cycle has an impact on the populations of lynx, coyote, fox, mink, marten and fisher. The most dramatic effect is on the lynx, which shows that same cyclical change in abundance, slightly out of phase with the hare population.*

*The fact that both lynx and snowshoe hares show the same periodicity in their cycles and the observation that lynx feed heavily on snowshoe hares gave rise to the suggestion that predation by lynx was responsible for generating the cycle. The idea was that the lynx are always slightly behind the hare in population growth because they reproduce more slowly and it takes time to convert hares into new lynx. The hare population would peak ahead of the lynx, and then the next generation of lynx would send the hare population crashing down. This has not proved to be the case. The growth of the lynx population and the subsequent decline seems to be a product of the hare cycle and not the cause of it.*

*Snowshoe hares reach the carrying capacity of the environment and are limited by food before lynx populations are ever large enough to control or overharvest them. The hare population crashes because of a lack of food and because of diseases that ravage the weakened and overcrowded animals. Aggression among crowded animals lowers the reproductive rate. The lynx and other predators appear to hasten the drop and to keep the population at a low ebb for longer. When the hare population declines and remains at very low densities, other predator populations drop, the thick brushy and herbaceous vegetation rebounds and the hares can then begin an explosive growth phase.*

*The length of the cycle is not uniform across the entire range of the snowshoe hare, and it is not perfectly*

*regular. Some areas appear to have a 6-year cycle, others a 12-year cycle, which is what one would expect since food, winter mortality, diseases and a variety of predator populations are all involved. Nevertheless, it is remarkable that the cycle is synchronized over such huge areas involving thousands of square miles. One explanation for this is that as populations grow, immigration from the choicest dense habitats quickly distributes both hares and predators over a wide area so that a few small local populations are soon converted into a large continuous and synchronous population.*

The snowshoe hare, with its great population fluctuations, affects the fortunes of most of the carnivores in the boreal forest.

# *BATS* Chiroptera

Few mammals have been more successful than bats. There are close to 1,000 bat species, a richness that only rodents exceed. The good fortune of bats has its origin in an event that took place millions of years before mammals existed, the moment when insects began to fly. The entry of insects into the air to escape predators, to mate and to disperse opened up a resource that remained unexploited until birds evolved into efficient fliers. Birds, however, remained primarily a day-active group. Accordingly, many insects evolved to become night fliers. The success of bats seems largely attributable to the night-flying insect resource. Most bats are night-active and eat insects that they catch on the fly.

Bats are thought to have originated from the same insectivore stock that gave rise to shrews and moles. The ancestors of bats were probably nocturnal and perhaps already possessed the ability to echolocate, as do shrews and perhaps moles, an ability that pre-adapted them for night flight. How they went from being a small mammal running on the ground to one that flies is unknown. One idea is that the ancestral bat pursued prey by leaping and used its large webbed forefeet to catch its quarry. Using the webbed forefeet as a gliding device may then have led to a greater and greater dependence on movement through the air. No one has found any fossils to disprove or support this notion. There is so little fossil record for bats that some scientists disagree about a common ancestry for all bats. Some believe that the fruit-eating bats evolved from mammals unrelated to those that gave rise to insectivorous bats.

Bats' mammalian body plan is substantially different from that of birds. Bats have strong jaws and teeth, making them nose-heavy. As a result, they have had to shorten their necks to shift the weight back more toward their wings and therefore lack the abilities that come with the long flexible neck of many birds. Birds have specialized their forelimbs for flight, but bats have pursued a mixed strategy. Their forelimbs not only act as wings but are used for crawling, prey capture and grooming, while their hind limbs are used for perching, hanging and, in some species, for prey capture. The hind limbs also form part of the bat's wing, so they are less suited for terrestrial locomotion than bird legs.

Bats have not developed the large and powerful breast muscles and bones of birds. Bats roost in rock crevices, hollow trees, curled-up leaves and in areas where a slender body is advantageous. The resulting wide, thin body of bats is less aerodynamically efficient than the deep, rounded form of birds. The large ears and facial protuberance used in bats' echolocation must also cause considerably more aerodynamic drag than the smooth head of a bird would. Mammalian fur lacks the lift-giving abilities of feathers. The membrane that gives lift to the bat wing is efficient at low flight speeds but offers more drag than a feathered wing at high speeds. Consequently, bats are less efficient at long-distance flight. However, they are superb at manoeuvring and flying in total darkness.

Some other mammal groups, such as flying squirrels, can glide, but bats are the only mammals that can actually fly by flapping their "wings" and lifting themselves by the power of their own muscles. Most of a bat wing

*A* Myotis *bat displays the fiercely efficient jaws that make the* Chiroptera *order the most important predators of night-flying insects.*

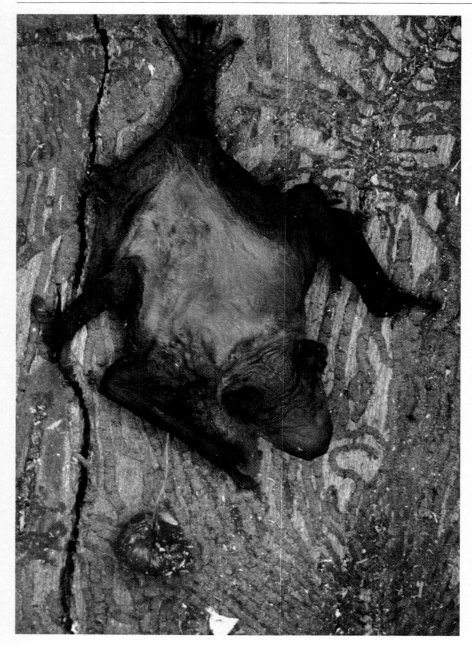

*Blind and virtually naked, a newborn little brown bat awaits food from its mother in the safety of its roost.*

The large flap of skin running from the body to roughly midwing provides lift while the movement of the wing-tip area generates propulsive power. Altering the shape of the outer wing and use of the tail-membrane area (some species lack a tail membrane) affects manoeuvrability.

Species of bats that forage for insects such as moths and beetles by active pursuit are often small with relatively broad wings. These wide wings provide a large lift, enabling the bat to decelerate and turn at slow speeds without stalling, an adaptation useful for the pursuit of insects such as moths, which may take evasive dives and turns when they hear the sound of an approaching bat. Bats that are fast long-distance fliers have long, narrow wings that trade manoeuvrability and lift for greater propulsive power and efficiency. The Mexican free-tailed bat, which nests in dense colonies in the southwestern United States, is an example of this design. These bats may fly 60 miles each night to foraging sites. One observer, using radar and a helicopter, recorded free-tailed bats flying 2 miles high and travelling at 65 miles an hour.

Bats have at least five patterns of wing design, each adapted to a different method of obtaining food. Specialized wings allow some bats to grab lone insects while flying. Other bats wait on perches and leap out after passing insects. One pattern of bat wing allows the bat to travel to, and feed in, fruit trees; another is designed specifically for flying long distances to feed on swarming insects. Bats are able to snag fish from the surfaces of ponds, rivers and other bodies of water. They can forage on the ground, pick frogs or roosting birds out of the vegetation or lap the blood of large mammals, activities that demand some modification in the wing. The bat wing, awkward though it may seem, has allowed bats to forage in ways that no bird can. Insectivorous bats are capable of continuous flight through a tree canopy in pursuit of flying insects, an unrivalled feat of slow, manoeuvrable flight. However, what truly separates bats from birds is bats' ability to echolocate and forage effectively at night. Bats that do not hunt by echolocation and birds that echolocate and forage primarily at night are minor exceptions.

is hand. The fingers of the hand have become tremendously elongated to serve as a support for the wing membrane. The thumb has remained as a small and usually sharply clawed hook near the midwing. The wing membrane is a large flap of skin reinforced with muscles and cartilage that extends from the body along the forearm and hand back over the hind-leg bones. The resulting wing shape varies according to the bat's particular style of flight, which in turn reflects the forage strategies and foods preferred by each species.

The wing must be designed both to lift the bat and to propel it forward.

In the northern temperate regions, all bats eat insects, but there seems to be a division based on whether hard insects such as beetles or soft insects such as moths are most important. The two different classes require different types of jaws and teeth. However, within each species, there is considerable variation among prey types according to the time of year. Some habitat specialization also occurs, some bats preferring to forage mainly above water, where there are large emergences of soft-bodied aquatic insects, and others foraging above the land. Bats are also separated ecologically according to the type of roosts and hibernation sites they select. Big brown bats, for example, will tolerate drier hibernation sites than little brown bats. Some species will roost in rock crevices, others in trees, and yet others in caves or house attics. The rate at which nest boxes and roosts created by human architecture are occupied suggests that roost type and availability play a major ecological role in bat populations. However, there has been little study on how, or even if, bats compete with each other.

Bats are able to use senses other than echolocation. All bats can see. Their eyes are normally adapted for use under low-light conditions, which is why they appear disoriented and blind if disturbed during the day in bright light. Little is known about how important vision is to bats. Some species use visual cues to navigate over long distances. Bats also have functional noses capable of sophisticated discrimination. Mothers can sniff out their own infant from among thousands of others, and they rarely suckle the wrong one. Bats probably also use odour to identify their food, being drawn to fruits and flowers and avoiding distasteful insects. However, in comparison with echolocation, little is known about bat sight or smell.

Bats are small mammals, and one might expect them to have a high energy consumption. They do, in fact, burn energy at a rate comparable to that of shrews. During flight, a bat's heart may reach 1,300 beats per minute. Thus, like other insectivores, bats must eat large amounts of food and process it quickly. Bats usually eat one-third to one-half their body weight each night. This is clearly less than

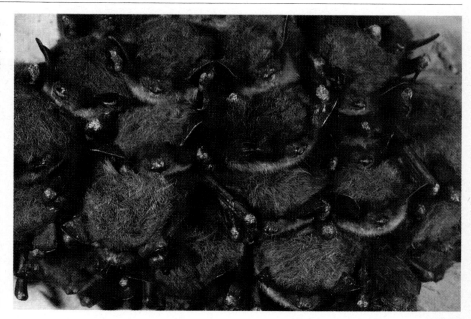

shrews, which consume more than their body weight each day. Bats may be more efficient at energy conservation than shrews and moles because they are active during the night and torporous during the day. It used to be thought that bats were poor thermoregulators, not always able to keep a constant body temperature, but daily torpor is clearly an energy conservation device. By dropping its body temperature from near 100 degrees F to the temperature of its roost, say, 75 degrees, a bat saves huge amounts of energy. Bats may also alter their energy costs by choosing particular kinds of roosts. Warm roosts, like the tops of buildings, may speed up digestion and reduce heating costs. On the other hand, during summer, bats that roost in attics may expend large amounts of energy staying cool. Hot bats will extend and slowly flap their wings to radiate body heat. In addition to sweating, they may urinate on their fur or lick it to increase evaporative cooling.

Shrews and moles have access to soil insects all winter, but bats' favoured food, aerial insects, vanishes during winter in temperate areas. Thus many temperate species of bats have made use of body temperature control and have developed true hibernation. They lower their body temperature to a few degrees above freezing, or even below freezing, and their heartbeat drops by a factor of 10 to 24 — to 82 beats a minute. They stay in this dormant state for most of the

*Hibernating little brown bats cluster in caves and mine tunnels where high humidity protects them from water loss.*

winter, waking only occasionally to urinate or to shift position. Crucial to the success of this strategy is finding suitable hibernating sites. For many species, the ideal hibernation site is an abandoned mine or cave. Underground cavities are usually humid, as water loss is a major stress on hibernating bats. Because these sites are limited in nature, many bats migrate considerable distances between their summer roosting and feeding areas and their winter hibernacula. Little brown bats, for example, may fly as far as 500 miles to reach an overwintering site. Banding studies show that individuals of many temperate bat species learn the location of caves and return to them year after year.

The reproductive biology of temperate-zone bats has also been modified according to the need for a long winter's dormancy followed by a summer of intense insect feeding and growth. Mating takes place in autumn, but surprisingly, the females do not ovulate until the spring. After mating, the male sperm are stored but not immediately used in fertilization. For as long as seven months, the sperm lie dormant, lined up along the uterine wall where they may absorb nutrients and wait for spring and ovulation. Presumably, the female hormone system provides a cue to awaken the

*The wing of a bat is actually a hand modified by natural selection for flying.*

sperm so they can begin their competitive swim toward the eggs.

One advantage to this system is that it enables the female to time her pregnancy independently of male courtship. The northern spring comes at variable dates according to the weather. The already-bred female can wake from hibernation and become active and ovulate according to how she perceives conditions. Thus if spring comes early, she does not have to wait for courtship and mating to proceed. She can, instead, ovulate and become pregnant, taking advantage of the early spring. Perhaps the best evidence that this is an important consideration is the convergence in the reproductive time of temperate bats. Virtually all species give birth at roughly the same time in late spring and early summer. Pregnancy is normally short, between two and three months depending on the species, and the young bats are weaned by midsummer.

Bats have a low reproductive rate, normally a single offspring per female annually. The largest litter size is only four offspring. This small annual rate is compensated for by a long reproductive career, which may span

two decades or more. The small litter size no doubt reflects the constraints imposed by flight. A female must still fly and feed while she is pregnant and lactating. Males provide no parental care. Temperate bat females usually congregate at specific nursery sites where they give birth and rear their young. The infant bats cluster together while their mothers are out feeding.

Once the initial stage of juvenile mortality is past, a temperate-zone bat can expect a surprisingly long life. Some little brown bats have lived as long as 30 years. Few animals prey on bats, and no temperate-zone vertebrates are specialized as bat predators (in the tropics, some birds and some bats specialize in eating bats). Bats are host to a wide array of insect and microscopic parasites, but their impact is not enough to induce high adult mortality. The vulnerability of bat populations comes from their low reproductive rate, their dependency on traditional roost and hibernating sites, pesticides and public apprehension about bats as vectors of rabies. When hibernating bats are disturbed, many die as a result. Many more are gassed or poisoned by exterminators or killed by accumulated pesticides from the insects they eat. Several North American bats have declined to the point

of being considered endangered species. These declines are undesirable, since bats are important insect predators. The risk of contracting rabies from them is minimal.

## Echolocation

*Echolocation is the term for the sonarlike method bats use to determine how large and how far away objects are. The process requires sending a sound that travels as a pressure wave through the air. When the sound wave hits an object, part of it is reflected back toward the sender.*

*Sound waves have various features that convey information to ears and brains designed to read them. Each wave has a given frequency, measured in hertz, the number of vibrations per second. High-frequency sounds have short wavelengths and different transmission characteristics than low-frequency sounds.*

*Bats often use high-frequency sounds. While humans can hear from about 20 hertz to 20,000 hertz, bats can hear sounds from roughly 100 hertz to 200,000 hertz. The high-frequency sound is like a dog whistle. It can be blown with great energy right beside a human's ear, but our nerves will neither register nor transmit it. The tendency of most bats to use ultrasound is why bat navigation and echolocation remained a mystery for many hundreds of years.*

*The advantage of these high-frequency sounds is that they produce precise information about small objects. The best echo reflection occurs when the object being hit has roughly the same size as the wavelength. When the wavelength is larger than the target object, much of the sound wave will not be reflected as an echo. However, high-frequency sound travels a shorter distance than low-frequency sound. For example, one feels the low-frequency rumble of an earthquake or train many miles away, but the high-pitched squeak of a mouse travels only a few feet before its energy is dissipated. The cost of precision is a loss of range. Range is also affected by how many decibels of sound energy the bat produces. Some bats produce a sound comparable in intensity to a jet engine, although humans can never hear it. Bats can also focus the sound beam they send out by means of membranes and muscles of the nose and mouth.*

*The simplest sound a bat produces is a constant frequency tone. The echoes returning from this enable the bat to estimate its velocity in relation to a target. Some bats can detect velocities as low as 1½ inches a second, about the speed of a caterpillar crawling. But a constant frequency cannot give much information about the texture of a target — whether it is hairy or smooth, for example.*

*To compensate, many bats use a technique identical to that used in FM broadcasting. They vary the sound by frequency modulation (FM). This also helps bats make use of the Doppler effect, a sound familiar to anyone who has heard the wail of a train whistle. As a train approaches then passes a listener, the sound of its whistle seems to change in pitch. As the train rushes away, the number of waves reaching the listener per second decreases, and the note is perceived as being lowered. This is especially true if the whistle is a tone of just one frequency. When a bat is stationary or moving at a constant speed in one direction, the Doppler effect from a constant-frequency signal can be used to calculate an object's speed, but it may also confuse the bat when it is flying complicated manoeuvres. A bat can compensate for the Doppler effect by sweeping down a scale of frequency. Then it gets a variety of echo ranges and varying precision.*

*All of this happens extremely quickly over short distances, with the bat processing and reacting to sounds at a mind-boggling speed. A bat that sends out a sound to strike an object 3 feet away is hit by the echo in 6 milliseconds. Bats may be able to detect objects as far as 50 feet away, but most echolocation takes place at closer distances. Big brown bats are reported to detect a ¾-inch sphere 15 feet away from them. At closer distances, bats are able to read fine details in the echo. They can detect an insect sitting on a*

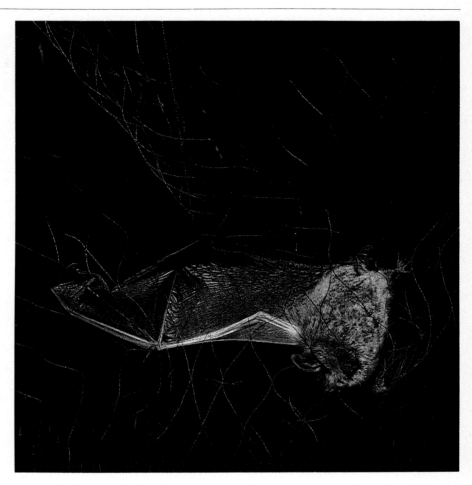

*leaf or a crevice in a cliff face. Some can detect a wire only 3/1,000 inch thick. These judgments are based on echoes that must be interpreted by the brain. To make sense of the echoes, especially FM echoes, there must be some space between the signals. Thus bats send their sounds out as pulses. It may also be energetically costly to produce these sounds, as exhausting as singing at full voice, so when bats are navigating, they may simply emit constant-frequency tones at a slow pulse rate, then pick up the pulse rate if a possible prey item is detected, adding FM to identify the item. As the bat zeroes in on the prey, the pulse rate may accelerate up to 200 times per second, 40 times higher than when navigating.*

*In spite of the sophistication of their echolocation system, bats are not invincible predators of night insects. Various moths have ears capable of detecting the ultrasonic waves of an approaching bat and can hear a bat as far away as 100 feet, beyond the range at which the*

Normally, the bat's sonarlike echolocation warns it of obstacles in its path, so researchers must use finely woven mist nets to capture specimens.

*bat can detect the echo from the moth. This enables the moth to fly away from the bat, a reason for a bat to stay silent for brief intervals. If a bat does get close to a moth with ultrasonic hearing, the moth may dive, turn and plummet to the ground. However, diving does not make a moth invulnerable. A little brown bat foraging for moths around a streetlight, for example, is capable of sharp diving turns. To compensate, some moths have evolved a series of grooves on their thorax that they can scrape together to produce ultrasound. As the bat dives in on the moths, they produce a burst of sound that jams the bat's navigation system with noise. In response, some bats have switched to frequencies higher than those the moths are capable of producing, and the coevolutionary battle between the hunters and the hunted continues.*

# *Smooth-faced Bats* Vespertilionidae

With 315 species distributed on every continent other than Antarctica, the smooth-faced bats are the most widespread family of bats. Many smooth-faced species are tropical, but some range into the north, and the majority of temperate bats are members of this family. Females are slightly larger than males, which is in keeping with what is known about their mating biology. Little male-male combat or highly demonstrative courtship occurs, and some species appear to be relatively promiscuous. True to their name, the smooth-faced bats lack the facial protuberances of many other bat groups. Except for a few tropical species that eat fish, smooth-faced bats are all insectivores and show the modification on their wings for highly manoeuvrable flight: the joint at the arm and shoulder blade is reinforced; the tail has a large membrane; the forelimbs are strong; and the wing is broad with a high lift at low speed — all modifications that suit these bats for sudden, sharp turns in pursuit of insects. All species have retained the ability to walk relatively well and have long legs.

## Home Is Where You Hang Yourself

*Finding appropriate summer and winter roosting spots is a major concern for temperate and northern bats. In temperate climates, bats are vulnerable to cold. They also sleep and rest much of the time, which means they need a protected spot. Half of a bat's life is spent dormant in a winter roost, and half of its more active summer life is spent in the summer roost.*

*The size and the availability of roosts determine how far bats must migrate, how far they must commute to water and foraging grounds and how many potential mates they have to choose from. The shape of the roost and its accessibility have determined how different bats have evolved in body size, shape and posture and how exposed they are to predators and physical stresses.*

*There are several distinct kinds of roosts, and different syndromes of behaviour, morphology and physiology are associated with each. Although there are as many roosts as there are cavities — from curled leaves to gigantic caverns — for convenience, bat biologists classify roosts into three types: foliage, crevices and hollows. Each of these has a different set of costs and benefits.*

*Foliage roosts, in summer at least, are virtually unlimited, and foliage roosters, such as red bats, can hang themselves up almost anywhere. One disadvantage is that such a roost undergoes wild temperature and humidity fluctuations. Bats of this type can choose a sunny south exposure when the weather is cold, but other than that, they are at the mercy of the weather. To compensate, foliage roosters typically have thick fur coats, which cause some drag during flight.*

*These bats are also exposed to predators, such as opossums and even blue jays, which will eat or otherwise molest bats. Accordingly, many of the tree-roosting bats are cryptically coloured. Tree-roosting hoary bats select roosts that are dark, have a minimum of reflected light from the ground and provide difficult access for arboreal predators. In the tropics, many foliage-roosting bats fold their wings about themselves for protection, using a special see-through part in the wing membrane to spot the arrival of a predator.*

*Crevice roosters are more concealed, but they pay a morphological and anatomical price. Their body and head must be thin. This means that developing large chest muscles, or in fact a large body size, is prevented. By contrast, bats that hang from either tree limbs or cave ceilings have large pectoral muscles and deep chests.*

*Rock crevices are cool and well protected but in limited supply, and they may be physically difficult to occupy. Many rock-crevice-dwelling bats have special pads on their feet and thumbs for gripping the substrate. Crevices under the bark of trees such as shagbark hickory are more common and offer some insulation and concealment, but the residents are still exposed to climbing snakes and mammalian predators.*

*Hollows are the most protected sites. While they offer moderated temperature and humidity, natural cavities such as caves are scarce, and they are not evenly dispersed. This has the effect of crowding hundreds of thousands of bats into an area. Populations of fleas and other parasites increase. Competition for local food resources and travel time to foraging areas must increase. Some free-tailed bats, which congregate by the millions in the huge caverns of the southwest United States, fly hundreds of miles in search of food each night. The bat dung, or guano, they excrete into the cavern gives off large quantities of ammonia, which some species of bat find toxic.*

*A Keen's bat hangs safely from its secure daytime roost — a primary criterion for any bat's survival.*

# Little Brown Bat *Myotis lucifugus*

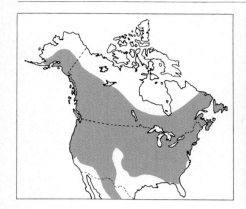

**Mammal:** *Myotis lucifugus* — little brown bat

**Meaning of Name:** *Myotis* (mouse + ear) alludes to large ears; *lucifugus* (shunning the light)

**Description:** brown pelage; hairs on back are long and have coppery, glossy tips; buffy grey underneath; dark shoulder spot

**Total Length:** 3.1 to 3.7 inches

**Tail:** 1.2 to 1.6 inches

**Forearm:** 1.3 to 1.6 inches

**Weight:** 0.19 to 0.42 ounces

**Gestation:** 50 to 60 days

**Litter Size:** 1 (sometimes 2)

**Age of Maturity:** male, 14 months; female, 1 year

**Longevity:** 24 to 30 years in the wild

**Diet:** primarily soft-bodied flying insects, especially flies and moths; some hard beetles

**Habitat:** caves, mine tunnels, hollow trees; has adapted to urban life during summer months and uses buildings as roosting sites

**Predators:** domestic cat, raccoon, weasel, snakes, owls, hawks and bobcat

**Dental Formula:** 2/3, 1/1, 3/3, 3/3 = 38 teeth

*The little brown bat, a member of an extremely abundant species, consumes billions of insects over the course of a summer season.*

The little brown bat is the most common and best known bat of the north temperate zone. Its natural habitat is forest areas with winter and summer roosts. Often, winter-roost sites are more limited, and this bat may migrate several hundred miles between its winter and summer sites.

Overwintering takes place in caves and abandoned mines. Sometimes, tremendous densities of up to 300,000 little brown bats cluster in a single cave. Large cavities that remain a few degrees above freezing and maintain a humidity close to 80 percent are preferred. Individuals show great fidelity to a wintering site and return to the same cave year after year.

In spring, groups of 50 to several hundred females move to summer roosts to give birth. Little brown bats often use human constructions, such as cottage attics. In large structures such as barns, thousands may roost together. Males are usually solitary and have a daytime roost and a night-time roost in various cavities, but good data on their locations and densities are scant.

Little brown bats are tolerant of high temperatures; they have been heated to 130 degrees F and have survived, which makes summer roost sites, such as hot attics, available to them more than to other bats. Normally, roost locations are within a short flight of water.

Little brown bats pursue and eat a wide variety of soft-bodied insects as well as some hard beetles. They feed at a rate of some seven to eight insects per minute. They often feed on aquatic insects emerging from ponds and rivers and are able to skim insects from the water surface. If they crash into the water, little brown bats can swim. Like other small insectivores, the little brown bat has a large appetite and a high rate of digestion. It can fill its stomach in 15 minutes and empty its digestive system several times an evening.

Mating takes place in autumn and appears to be highly promiscuous. Males perch in caves and mine shafts and produce echolocation calls —

apparently to court females. Females fly around and eventually land next to a male and mate. Both males and females may copulate with more than one partner, and mating takes place over an extended period of time. Gradually, torpor engulfs the bats, and they huddle together in the typical winter-hibernation group. Some males remain sexually active and crawl about attempting to inseminate dormant females.

Females ovulate in spring and give birth to a single offspring, which travels with its mother on her nightly foraging trips by clinging sideways across her chest, providing a balanced, symmetrical load. After a few days, the young bat is competent enough to be left hanging in the nursery and is flying by itself after three weeks. Little brown bat mothers scent-mark trees outside nursery roosts with a glandular excretion. It is possible that scent-marked trees help young, inexperienced bats find their way back to the roost during their first excursions.

Females also communicate with their young through "isolation calls." A young bat that falls will call, and its mother will recognize and distinguish its call from that of other young, unrelated bats. Mothers also use a two-note signal directed toward their nursing infant.

Little brown bats may live 30 years.

*Little brown bats communicate by producing ultrasonic squeals that are readily picked up by the large and precisely tuned ears of other bats.*

---

## *Yuma Bat* Myotis yumanensis

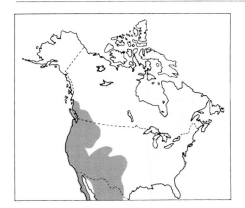

**Mammal:** *Myotis yumanensis* — Yuma myotis

**Meaning of Name:** *Myotis* (mouse + ear) alludes to large ears; *yumanensis* (of Yuma) refers to the fact that the type specimen was described in Yuma, Arizona

**Description:** dull brown upper parts; buffy grey below; similar to little brown bat but smaller; interfemoral membrane is haired nearly to the knee

**Total Length:** 3 to 3.6 inches

**Tail:** 1.3 to 1.7 inches

**Forearm:** 1.3 to 1.5 inches

**Weight:** 0.21 to 0.25 ounces

**Gestation:** not known (probably about 40 days)

**Litter Size:** 1

**Age of Maturity:** 1 to 3 years

**Longevity:** not known

**Diet:** flying insects; opportunistic and selective feeder

**Habitat:** open arid areas preferred over forests; found in caves, tunnels or buildings

**Predators:** weasel, domestic cat, raccoon, skunk, rat, snakes, hawks and owls

**Dental Formula:** 2/3, 1/1, 3/3, 3/3 = 38 teeth

*A southwestern version of the little brown bat, the Yuma bat specializes in dry, open habitats rather than the forested regions that are preferred by other small Myotis species.*

## Keen's Bat *Myotis keenii*

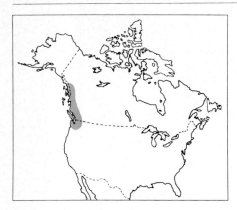

**Mammal:** *Myotis keenii* — Keen's bat
**Meaning of Name:** *Myotis* (mouse + ear) alludes to large ears; *keenii* (named after Reverend J.H. Keen, who collected the type specimen in 1894)
**Description:** similar to little brown bat but sheen is brassier; dark brown above, buffy grey below; dull brown shoulder spot; long, round ears; tragus is long
**Total Length:** 3.1 to 3.5 inches
**Tail:** 1.4 to 1.7 inches
**Forearm:** 1.4 to 1.6 inches
**Weight:** 0.25 to 0.32 ounces
**Gestation:** not known (probably about 40 days)

**Litter Size:** 1
**Age of Maturity:** 1 to 3 years
**Longevity:** 18 years
**Diet:** caddisfly adults, small moths, mosquitoes
**Habitat:** forested areas near glades and rivers; also in mine tunnels, caves, buildings, storm sewers
**Predators:** owl is major predator
**Dental Formula:** 2/3, 1/1, 3/3, 3/3 = 38 teeth

*Keen's bat populations are restricted to the heavy forest regions of the Pacific coast.*

## Long-eared Bat *Myotis evotis*

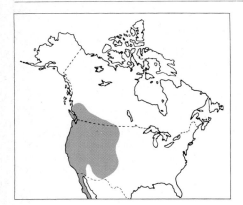

**Mammal:** *Myotis evotis* — long-eared bat
**Meaning of Name:** *Myotis* (mouse + ear) alludes to large ears; *evotis* (good, well + ear)
**Description:** pale brown; large rounded black ears; long slender tragus
**Total Length:** 3.6 to 4.1 inches
**Tail:** 1.7 to 1.9 inches
**Forearm:** 1.4 to 1.6 inches
**Weight:** 0.35 ounces
**Gestation:** not known (probably about 40 days)
**Litter Size:** 1
**Age of Maturity:** 1 to 3 years
**Longevity:** up to 22 years

**Diet:** small moths, flies, beetles and other insects
**Habitat:** forested areas; in crevices around buildings or trees; found on rocky habitats of the coast of British Columbia as well as on open Alberta plains
**Predators:** raptors, weasel, domestic cat, raccoon, skunk, rat and snakes
**Dental Formula:** 2/3, 1/1, 3/3, 3/3 = 38 teeth

*Researchers theorize that the large ears of the long-eared bat have evolved as an efficient tracking device, enabling it to find the beetles it preys on.*

## *Long-legged Bat* Myotis volans

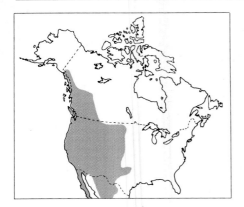

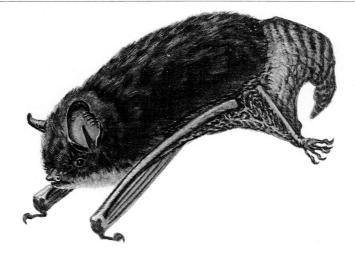

**Mammal:** *Myotis volans* — long-legged bat
**Meaning of Name:** *Myotis* (mouse + ear) alludes to large ears; *volans* (flying)
**Description:** large; dark brown above, smoky brown underneath; short round ears; keeled calcar; sparse fur on wing membrane; fur on underside of interfemoral membrane goes as far out as the elbow and knee
**Total Length:** 3.5 to 3.9 inches
**Tail:** 1.5 to 2.1 inches
**Forearm:** 1.5 to 1.6 inches
**Weight:** female, 0.30 to 0.38 ounces
**Gestation:** not known (probably about 40 days)
**Litter Size:** 1
**Age of Maturity:** 1 to 3 years
**Longevity:** not known
**Diet:** insects (especially small moths)
**Habitat:** wooded areas and open scrub; found in buildings, small pockets and crevices in rock ledges
**Predators:** weasel, domestic cat, raccoon, skunk, rat, snakes, hawks and owls

*Long-legged bats are specialists in catching small night-flying moths.*

**Dental Formula:** 2/3, 1/1, 3/3, 3/3 = 38 teeth

## *California Bat* Myotis californicus

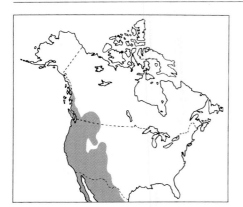

**Mammal:** *Myotis californicus* — California bat
**Meaning of Name:** *Myotis* (mouse + ear) alludes to large ears; *californicus* (of California)
**Description:** rich reddish brown dorsally and buffy brown ventrally; keeled calcar; dorsal base of interfemoral membrane is covered with fine hairs to approximately one-third of the way down the tibia
**Total Length:** 3.1 to 3.3 inches
**Tail:** 1.2 to 1.6 inches
**Forearm:** 1.2 to 1.4 inches
**Weight:** approximately 0.20 to 0.33 ounces
**Gestation:** not known (probably about 40 days)
**Litter Size:** 1
**Age of Maturity:** 1 to 3 years
**Longevity:** not known
**Diet:** insects
**Habitat:** both forested areas and semi-arid areas (in southwest); mainly found in crevices such as tunnels, hollow trees, buildings and bridges
**Predators:** lesser carnivores, snakes, hawks and owls

*A highly manoeuvrable flier, the California bat flies in close to its insect prey before detecting it and then makes sharp swerves to grab its victim.*

**Dental Formula:** 2/3, 1/1, 3/3, 3/3 = 38 teeth

## *Fringed Bat*  Myotis thysanodes

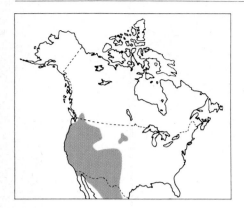

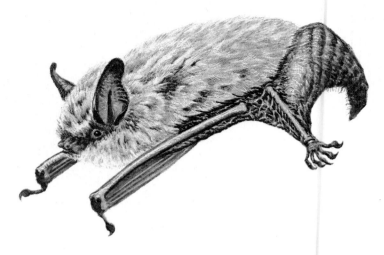

**Mammal:** *Myotis thysanodes* — fringed bat

**Meaning of Name:** *Myotis* (mouse + ear) alludes to large ears; *thysanodes* (fringelike) refers to short, stiff hairs along the posterior border of the tail membrane

**Description:** medium-sized buffy brown bat; fringe of short stiff brown hairs on free edge of interfemoral membrane

**Total Length:** 3.4 to 3.7 inches

**Tail:** 1.4 to 1.6 inches

**Forearm:** 1.6 to 1.8 inches

**Weight:** 0.19 to 0.30 ounces

**Gestation:** not known (probably about 40 days)

**Litter Size:** 1

**Age of Maturity:** 1 to 3 years

**Longevity:** one lived at least 11 years

**Diet:** insects

**Habitat:** arid yellow pine zone of Pacific Northwest in caves and attics of old buildings

**Predators:** weasel, domestic cat, raccoon, skunk, rat, snakes, hawks and owls

**Dental Formula:** 2/3, 1/1, 3/3, 3/3 = 38 teeth

*The fringed bat has such precise echolocation and flight abilities that it can hover in front of leaves to search for insects before darting forward to capture them.*

## *Eastern Small-footed Bat*  Myotis leibii

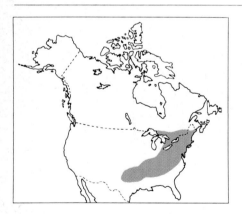

**Mammal:** *Myotis leibii* — eastern small-footed bat; also known as *Myotis subulatus*

**Meaning of Name:** *Myotis* (mouse + ear) alludes to large ears; *leibii* (named after Dr. G.C. Leib, collector of the type specimen)

**Description:** varies from yellowish to copper brown to buffy grey dorsally; ears and wing membrane are dark brown to black; calcar has pronounced keel; external distinguishing mark is black facial mask

**Total Length:** 2.8 to 3.3 inches

**Tail:** 1.2 to 1.5 inches

**Forearm:** 1.2 to 1.4 inches

**Weight:** 0.21 to 0.32 ounces

**Gestation:** not known (probably about 40 days)

**Litter Size:** 1

**Age of Maturity:** second year

**Longevity:** 9 years in the wild

**Diet:** soft-bodied insects; beetles are a predominant food source

**Habitat:** eastern range, hills covered with coniferous forests; western range, arid sites

**Predators:** hawks, owls, snakes, weasel, domestic cat, raccoon, skunk and rat

*At less than 3 inches in length and 0.3 ounces, the eastern small-footed bat is the smallest of all the northern bat species. Because of its small size, it has a high metabolism and little ability to store fat for a long hibernation. As a result, it is often active while other bats are dormant.*

**Dental Formula:** 2/3, 1/1, 3/3, 3/3 = 38 teeth

## *Northern Long-eared Bat* Myotis septentrionalis

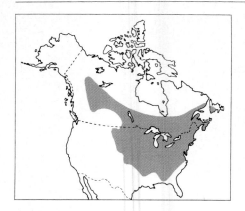

**Mammal:** *Myotis septentrionalis* — northern long-eared bat
**Meaning of Name:** *Myotis* (mouse + ear) alludes to large ears; *septentrionalis* probably refers to northern distribution
**Description:** long, narrow tragus; light reddish brown above and buffy grey below
**Total Length:** 3 to 3.5 inches
**Tail:** 1.4 to 1.6 inches
**Forearm:** 1.3 to 1.5 inches
**Weight:** 0.10 to 0.20 ounces
**Gestation:** not known (probably about 40 days)
**Litter Size:** 1 or 2
**Age of Maturity:** 1 to 3 years

**Longevity:** up to 18 years
**Diet:** flying insects
**Habitat:** dry forests, coniferous boreal forests
**Predators:** weasel, domestic cat, raccoon, skunk, rat, snakes, hawks and owls
**Dental Formula:** 2/3, 1/1, 3/3, 3/3 = 38 teeth

*Northern long-eared bats inhabit dry forests where females often roost by the dozen under loose sheets of tree bark, as well as house window shutters and open wall cavities. Males tend to roost singly or with a few other males.*

## *Western Small-footed Bat* Myotis ciliolabrum

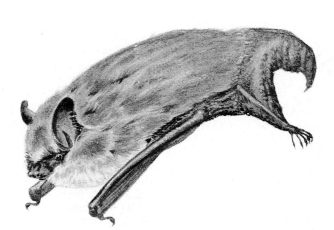

**Mammal:** *Myotis ciliolabrum* — western small-footed bat
**Meaning of Name:** *Myotis* (mouse + ear); *ciliolabrum* (eyelid + lip) refers to its whiskered lip
**Description:** small; dense, long fur varies from pale yellow-brown to flaxen dorsally and from buff to white ventrally; black flight membranes, ears and face
**Total Length:** 3.34 inches
**Tail:** 1.5 inches
**Forearm:** 1.27 inches
**Weight:** 0.17 ounces
**Gestation:** probably 40 days
**Litter Size:** probably 1

**Age of Maturity:** 1 to 3 years
**Longevity:** not known
**Diet:** a variety of small insects
**Habitat:** arid habitats; cliffs, talus, clay buttes and steep riverbanks
**Predators:** owls, hawks, snakes, domestic cat and other carnivores
**Dental Formula:** 2/3, 1/1, 3/3, 3/3 = 38 teeth

*The western small-footed bat prefers to roost along the cliffs and steep banks of the badlands and the riverbanks of the prairies, where it forages for desert insects.*

# Big Brown Bat *Eptesicus fuscus*

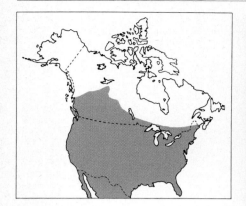

**Mammal:** *Eptesicus fuscus* — big brown bat

**Meaning of Name:** *Eptesicus* (house flyer) refers to the fact that it is often seen flying near houses and roosting under eaves; *fuscus* (dark coloured)

**Description:** glossy dark brown fur with reddish tips and greyish brown underparts; leathery black wing and tail membranes; calcar has pronounced keel; broad blunt tragus; face is almost naked except for forehead; black skin and fleshy lips

**Total Length:** 4.5 to 5.2 inches

**Tail:** 1.7 to 2.1 inches

**Forearm:** 1.7 to 2 inches

**Weight:** 0.49 to 1.1 ounces (varies with season and hibernation)

**Gestation:** not known (probably about 40 days)

**Litter Size:** western females, 1; eastern females, 2

**Age of Maturity:** usually first year; however, one-quarter of females do not mature early enough to bear young the first year

**Longevity:** 7 to 9 years in the wild

**Diet:** beetles are main food; also other flying insects

**Habitat:** urbanized areas and around farm buildings, pastures, meadows, creeks, ponds and wooded areas; suburban vegetation and city streets

**Predators:** owls; grounded bat may fall prey to skunk, opossum and snakes

**Dental Formula:** 2/3, 1/1, 1/2, 3/3 = 32 teeth

The big brown bat, like its small cousin the little brown bat, is quite common and uses the houses and other cavities created by humans. It is a strong flier and, unlike the small *Myotis*, includes many hard-bodied beetles in its diet. Accordingly, the big brown bat's jaws and teeth are well developed and capable of a strong bite. Big brown bats can detect beetle-sized objects as far away as 15 feet. The low-frequency echo of a swarm of insects may be read from a remarkable range of 600 yards. Big brown bats can fly at 25 miles an hour.

The big brown bat has a remarkable tolerance for cold temperatures. It enters hibernation cavities just before the start of severely cold and insect-free winter weather. It uses cold, drafty cavities, such as abandoned buildings, that other bats avoid. Its broader tolerance means that the big brown bat has to migrate comparatively short distances between its summer foraging and breeding grounds and its hibernation sites, but when it has to, the big brown bat can travel great distances — some banded big brown bats displaced by researchers travelled 450 miles back to their home

*With its large powerful jaws and strong teeth, the big brown bat specializes in preying on hard-bodied beetles that other bats ignore.*

territory, probably by using celestial orientation.

Maternity colonies can number as high as 200 females but are usually half that size or smaller. Although eastern big brown bats frequently give birth to two young, the western big browns have only one offspring per year. Populations grow so large in some areas that the reproductive rate is depressed, which suggests that food availability is more important to the control of big brown bat populations than other factors, such as the availability of roost and hibernation sites, predation and winter mortality.

## *Pallid Bat* Antrozous pallidus

**Mammal:** *Antrozous pallidus* — pallid bat

**Meaning of Name:** *Antrozous* refers to the fact that it usually roosts in caves; *pallidus* (pale)

**Description:** creamy yellowish on upper parts; ventral surface is almost white; blunt bare pad at end of muzzle; scroll-shaped nostrils; two glandular swellings on each side of muzzle (behind nostrils) emit strong odour; large interfemoral membrane; weakly keeled calcar

**Total Length:** male, 4.4 to 4.9 inches; female, 4.2 to 5.1 inches

**Tail:** male, 1.4 to 1.7 inches; female, 1.5 to 1.9 inches

**Forearm:** 2 to 2.6 inches

**Weight:** male, 0.74 to 1 ounce; female, 0.84 to 1.2 ounces

**Gestation:** 53 to 71 days

**Litter Size:** 1 to 3 (since there are only two teats, just 2 survive)

**Age of Maturity:** 1 to 3 years

**Longevity:** 9 years

**Diet:** moths, orthopterans (grasshoppers, crickets, etc.), beetles, neuropterans (fishflies, snakeflies), chilopods (centipedes), scorpions, mice and lizards

**Habitat:** rocky outcrops, open arid plains or cultivated areas; sometimes forested areas or open brushland; requires water surfaces nearby from which to drink

**Predators:** owls, hawks and snakes

**Dental Formula:** 1/2, 1/1, 1/2, 3/3 = 28 teeth

The pallid bat is a large, big-eared bat of the southwestern United States that is sometimes caught in the north. Most information on its biology comes from populations of the arid southwestern United States.

Pallid bats inhabit dry areas with low shrubbery and rocky outcrops, but they also occur in dry forests, such as ponderosa pine, and along the riparian forest of desert streams. Pallid bats use rock crevices and cavities for day roosts and large cavities, such as cave entrances, for night roosts.

Pallid bats' distinctive appearance is matched by a unique foraging technique. They fly low and slowly and are capable of hovering but are not highly manoeuvrable. Instead, they spend much of their time picking larger prey species off foliage and off the ground. Prey items are located not by echolocation but by listening to the rustling sounds insects make as they crawl. Pallid bats crawl efficiently, compared with other bats, and will alight on the ground and pursue their prey on foot. They eat large katydids, crickets and even scorpions, mice and horned toad lizards. Small items are eaten on the spot, but larger items are taken to the night roost for consumption. Maternity colonies are formed in

*While less manoeuvrable than other species, pallid bats can land near insect prey and give chase by crawling.*

spring and may contain several hundred individuals of both sexes. Females give birth to one, two and even three young, born after a pregnancy of 7 to 10 weeks and weaned in a comparable time. Year-old females give birth to single offspring.

Hibernation takes place in caves and mines near the summering areas.

Pallid bats are gregarious, and they communicate vocally. Four calls are recognized, three of which can be heard by humans: directive calls communicate the location of individuals and of roosting sites; squabble calls communicate positions and may keep the bats spaced within the roost; buzzing calls indicate aggressive intentions. The fourth call, an echolocation FM call in ultrasound cannot be heard by humans but is used by pallid bats for orientation at night. Young bats call to their mothers, and the mothers can distinguish the individual calls and smells of their own offspring.

Pallid bats have a series of glands that exude a skunky odour when the animals are molested.

# Hoary Bat *Lasiurus cinereus*

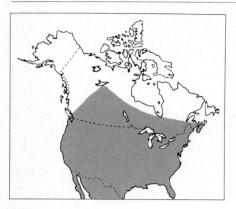

**Weight:** 1 ± ounce
**Gestation:** not known (probably about 40 days)
**Litter Size:** 1 to 4 (usually 2)
**Age of Maturity:** 1 to 3 years
**Longevity:** not known
**Diet:** primarily a moth feeder; also dragonflies
**Habitat:** wooded areas, especially coniferous regions
**Predators:** weasel, domestic cat, raccoon, skunk, rat, snakes, hawks and owls
**Dental Formula:** 1/3, 1/1, 2/2, 3/3 = 32 teeth

**Mammal:** *Lasiurus cinereus* — hoary bat
**Meaning of Name:** *Lasiurus* (hairy-tailed bat); *cinereus* (ash-coloured); hoary can mean white or greyish white
**Description:** dark brown with a silver frosting; ventral surface covered with tawny woolly hair; buffy patch at base of thumb and on throat; bases of wing membrane and dorsal surface of interfemoral membrane are covered with fur
**Total Length:** 5.1 to 5.7 inches
**Tail:** 2.2 to 2.6 inches
**Forearm:** 2+ inches

*The hoary bat prefers wooded habitats and roosts in trees in the open, wrapping its wings around itself to conserve body heat.*

# Townsend's Big-eared Bat *Plecotus townsendii*

**Tail:** male, 1.7 to 2 inches; female, 1.8 to 2.1 inches
**Forearm:** 1.6 to 1.8 inches
**Weight:** 0.32 to 0.39 ounces
**Gestation:** 56 to 100 days (depends on body temperature and on period in which the female was lethargic after ovulation)
**Litter Size:** 1
**Age of Maturity:** female, in first autumn; male, probably not until the year after its birth
**Longevity:** average is about 5 years; 16.5 years is the record
**Diet:** moths
**Habitat:** cultivated valleys bordered by deciduous forests, brush, junipers or pine forest
**Predators:** weasel, domestic cat, raccoon, skunk, rat, snakes, hawks and owls
**Dental Formula:** 2/3, 1/1, 2/3, 3/3 = 36 teeth

**Mammal:** *Plecotus townsendii* — Townsend's big-eared bat, western big-eared bat
**Meaning of Name:** *Plecotus* (twisted ear) may refer to its habit of coiling the ears back against the body during hibernation; *townsendii* (named after J.K. Townsend, an ornithologist and author)
**Description:** very long ears that are joined across the forehead; crescent-shaped nostrils are covered posteriorly by a pair of lumps made of sebaceous glandular tissue; dark and naked wing membrane; prominent calcar; greyish brown above, tan underneath
**Total Length:** male, 3.8 to 4.1 inches; female, 3.9 to 4.4 inches

*The huge ears of the Townsend's big-eared bat are indispensable for reading soft and low-frequency echoes and for detecting moths at a great distance.*

## *Spotted Bat* Euderma maculatum

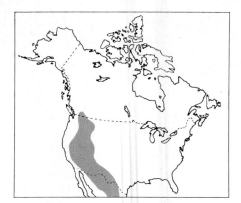

**Mammal:** *Euderma maculatum* —
spotted bat, death's head bat
**Meaning of Name:** *Euderma* (nicely
coloured skin); *maculatum* refers to
unique colour pattern with white spots
**Description:** dark reddish brown to
black; white spot on rump and on each
shoulder; greyish ears and membranes
**Total Length:** 4.2 to 4.5 inches
**Tail:** 1.9 to 2 inches
**Forearm:** 1.9 to 2 inches
**Weight:** 0.54 to 0.60 ounces
**Gestation:** not known (probably about
40 days)
**Litter Size:** 1
**Age of Maturity:** 1 to 3 years
**Longevity:** not known
**Diet:** moths and other insects caught in
flight
**Habitat:** variety of habitats, but usually
dry, arid, rough desert country
**Predators:** hawks, owls and snakes
**Dental Formula:** 2/3, 1/1, 2/2, 3/3 = 34
teeth

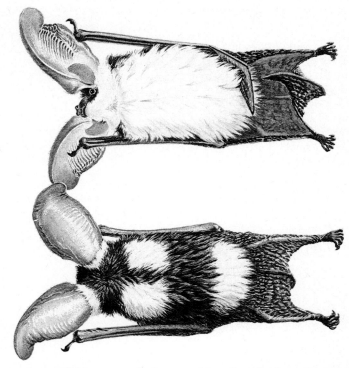

The most beautiful bat recorded in North America, the spotted bat is also one of the continent's rarest bats. This species is a resident of the arid west, ranging from open desert to ponderosa pine forest. It occasionally flies into Canada during the summer. Spotted bats roost in rock crevices in summer, but their winter habits are unknown.

They are moth specialists that fly a regular circuit through clearings and may defend these circuits from other spotted bats, avoiding echolocating foragers. Their echolocation call can be heard by humans as a high-pitched cry. The call's frequency means that the spotted bat has a long range, which may help it to detect moths at a great distance. Humans can hear the sound from 250 yards, but moths probably find it hard to detect since most of the moths that have ears hear only higher-frequency sounds.

Almost nothing is known about the reproduction of the spotted bat, nor have researchers explained why it is so beautifully marked.

### Rabies

*Rabies, a virus that feeds on mammals and subjects many of them, including humans, to a gruesome death, is both horrible and fascinating. Its manner of*

*Although its high-pitched cry is audible to human ears, the spotted bat is one of the rarest and least known bats in North America.*

*transmission is a marvel of evolutionary ingenuity. Rabies is transmitted in the saliva of its carrier. When the rabies virus contacts the victim's nerve tissue, it travels along the nerve until it reaches the brain and spinal stem, where it produces inflammation and, usually, death. However, before the affected animal dies, the virus manipulates the brain, changing the animal's behaviour in a way that helps spread the virus.*

*There are two forms of rabies syndrome, the furious and the dumb. In the furious form of rabies, victims become prone to attack and bite other animals. Often, the throat is paralyzed so that swallowing is impossible and saliva accumulates in the mouth. The mad dog "foaming at the mouth" is the virus's way of transporting and perpetuating itself. The dumb form may spread itself by exposing the carrier to attack by predators. In either case, once the rabies virus enters the bloodstream, it usually results in the death of the carrier. All mammals are susceptible.*

*Dog bites inflict most cases of rabies in humans. In India alone, there are tens of thousands of cases of human rabies each year, primarily*

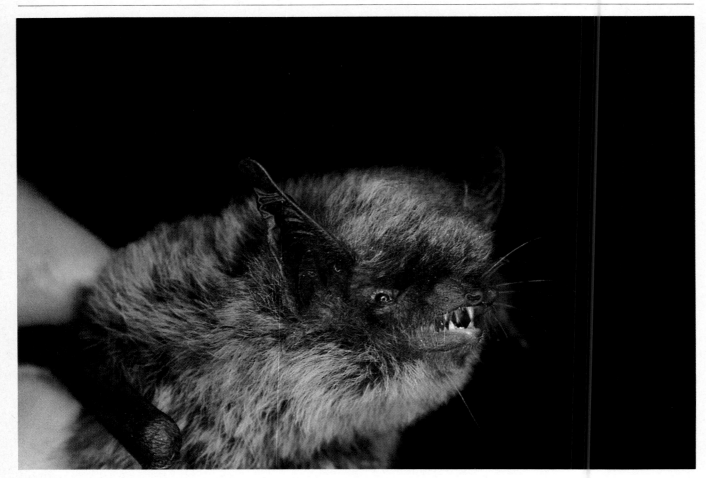

*from this source. In North America, the vaccination of dogs has made rabies largely a disease of wildlife. In the eastern region of North America, red foxes are among the most infected of animals, while in the west, skunks and ground squirrels are most infected. This reservoir of rabies rarely affects humans directly, but it does represent a source of infection of animals such as dogs and livestock, which have close contact with humans. In the tropics, vampire bats, which feed directly on the blood of livestock, are important agents of rabies transmission. However, in the temperate zone, most evidence suggests that bats are a minor source of rabies. Only one case of rabies transmitted by a bat bite is known in Canada, while in the United States, bat bites transmit less than one case every three years.*

*Since dogs, cats and livestock can be vaccinated, rabies is a highly avoidable disease. If the public would avoid handling obviously sick or strange-acting wildlife and vaccinate their pets, the risk of*

*exposure to rabies would be trivially small. Nevertheless, public fear of rabies has led to some excessive campaigns designed to stop the spread of rabies by means of wildlife eradication. In 1952, Alberta embarked on a famous poisoning campaign in which trappers were given cyanide and strychnine poison to set out for wildlife. In an 18-month period, the minimal estimate of wildlife destroyed by this unselective poisoning amounted to 50,000 foxes, 35,000 coyotes, 7,500 lynxes, 4,300 wolves, 1,850 bears, 500 skunks, 64 pumas, 4 badgers and 1 wolverine. Farmers were also given poison to use and may have killed comparable numbers of animals. Such programmes did little except decimate wildlife populations. Fortunately, animals such as red foxes can now be vaccinated by broadcasting vaccine in meatballs dropped from airplanes.*

*The fear of rabies has allowed pest exterminators to sell bat-extermination services that needlessly destroy bats and actually*

Bats such as the California bat bite only when molested and are thus unlikely sources of rabies for humans.

*increase the public's health risk. It is estimated that less than one half of one percent of North American bats carry rabies. Bats that do become rabid rarely attack people. If sick bats are not handled, they present a minimal health risk. The best measure is simply for people to exclude bats from their dwellings — by screening and sealing attic vents, for example. Extermination programmes that poison bats use toxins that are directly hazardous to other mammals, including humans, and the poisoned bats end up flapping around on lawns and in the street where they are more likely to be handled by children and pets. The best solution to bats living inside a dwelling or building is to make it unattractive and inaccessible to the bats. Leave bright lights burning 24 hours a day to drive the bats out, and then screen or otherwise seal all entrances wider than 1/5 inch.*

## Red Bat *Lasiurus borealis*

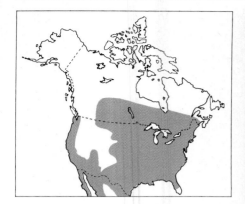

**Mammal:** *Lasiurus borealis* — red bat
**Meaning of Name:** *Lasiurus* (hairy-tailed bat); *borealis* (of the north)
**Description:** male is bright brick-red above and paler below; frosting around neck area and pair of creamy shoulder flashes; dorsal surface of interfemoral membrane, hind legs and bases of the wing membrane are all heavily furred; orange fur covers face and back of ears; females are paler and have frosted appearance due to cream-coloured tips of dorsal hairs
**Total Length:** 3.7 to 4.4 inches
**Tail:** 1.8 to 2.4 inches
**Forearm:** 1.4 to 1.8 inches
**Weight:** 0.25 to 0.53 ounces
**Gestation:** not known (may be up to 90 days)
**Litter Size:** 1 to 4 (only genus of bat in which there are commonly more than 2 young per birth)
**Age of Maturity:** 1 to 3 years (probably not during first summer)
**Longevity:** not known
**Diet:** variety of hard and soft flying insects, including moths, beetles, crickets, flies and cicadas
**Habitat:** wooded areas; has also adapted to villages and towns
**Predators:** hawks, owls, opossum, blue jay and crow
**Dental Formula:** 1/3, 1/1, 2/2, 3/3 = 32 teeth

The red bat has long, narrow wings, and it may be one of the faster northern fliers, reaching speeds of up to 40 miles per hour. This probably enables red bats to pursue prey that the broad-winged and flutter-style fliers cannot catch. Red bats are high fliers, capable of foraging at heights of 200 yards. After dark, they may lower their foraging and work close to the ground and over water, but they continue to fly quickly. Their prey includes a mixture of hard-bodied beetles and soft-bodied insects such as moths.

Red bats also have distinctive roosting methods. During summer, they often hang up alone in a sheltered part of a tree, shrub or vine. This gives them freedom to range over a wide area but also exposes them to arboreal predators such as the opossum and

*The red bat's habit of roosting in open areas during the day leaves it vulnerable to attack by opossums and aggressive birds like crows.*

some large aggressive birds such as blue jays and crows. Roost sites may be almost anywhere in the tree from top to bottom, but they are generally above an opening that allows the bat to drop freely.

The red bat has the highest fecundity of any northern temperate bat, giving birth to one to four young at a time. Unlike other bats, the red bat has four nipples, not two. The young of a red bat are accordingly less precocial and developed at birth than those of other bats, and the mother must carry and feed them for a longer period of time. Pregnancy may last as long as 90 days, much longer than in *Myotis* bats, which produce only one infant after a pregnancy of roughly two months. Many *Myotis* can fly and forage effectively at the age of 3 weeks, but red bats take twice as long to reach the same level of competence. Care of the young takes place in the tree roost.

Red bats' high fecundity may be an adaptation to high mortality resulting from roosting in trees and being exposed to predators such as hawks and owls during migration. The red bat has a tremendous geographic range, from northern Saskatchewan all the way south to Argentina and Chile. This may reflect an opportunistic character, which trades mobility and the opportunity to migrate to rich feeding areas against the higher probability of offspring failing to survive the autumn migration and first winter.

Red bats have an unusual courtship system. There is a sexual dimorphism in colour, with males being brighter red than females. Courtship in the air at dusk has been observed, with the pair descending to the ground to mate.

*While the metabolisms of most temperate bats are reduced in winter, the red bat's increases, producing enough heat to keep it from freezing.*

## *Eastern Pipistrelle* Pipistrellus subflavus

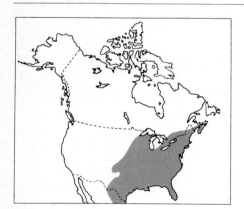

**Mammal:** *Pipistrellus subflavus* — eastern pipistrelle
**Meaning of Name:** *Pipistrellus* from Italian word meaning bat; *subflavus* (yellow beneath) refers to pale underparts
**Description:** yellowish brown woolly pelage; paler buffy brown underneath; short ears with tapered round tips; short blunt tragus; calcar is prominent and unkeeled
**Total Length:** male, 2.9 to 3.5 inches; female, 3.5 inches
**Tail:** male, 1.4 to 1.8 inches; female, 1.6 inches
**Forearm:** 1.2 ± inches

**Weight:** 0.12 to 0.21 ounces (depending on sex and season)
**Gestation:** not known (probably about 40 days)
**Litter Size:** 2 (rarely 1 or 3)
**Age of Maturity:** over 1 year
**Longevity:** 7 to 10 years in the wild (15 years maximum)
**Diet:** flying insects
**Habitat:** wooded areas along slow-moving streams or rivers; near water
**Predators:** weasel, domestic cat, raccoon, skunk, rat, snakes, hawks and owls
**Dental Formula:** 2/3, 1/1, 2/2, 3/3 = 34 teeth

*The eastern pipistrelle is a slow flier with a fluttering erratic flight similar to that of a large moth. It is unusual because it is one of the few bats that give birth to more than one offspring at a time.*

## *Silver-haired Bat* Lasionycteris noctivagans

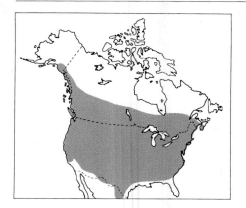

*While most bats seek shelter in cool weather, the silver-haired bat continues to forage in below-freezing temperatures.*

**Mammal:** *Lasionycteris noctivagans* — silver-haired bat; the slowest-flying bat

**Meaning of Name:** *Lasionycteris* probably translates as "playful at dusk"; *noctivagans* (wandering by night)

**Description:** blackish brown; silver-tipped hairs of back and belly give the appearance of a silver-frosted cape since head and neck lack silver tips; short rounded ears; blunt tragus; dark brown wing membrane; interfemoral membrane is covered with fine frosted hairs three-quarters of the way down

**Total Length:** 3.6 to 4.3 inches

**Tail:** 1.5 to 2 inches
**Forearm:** 1.5 to 1.7 inches
**Weight:** 0.21 to 0.49 ounces
**Gestation:** not known (probably about 40 days)
**Litter Size:** 1 or 2
**Age of Maturity:** 1 to 3 years
**Longevity:** 12 years

**Diet:** insects; possibly prefers emerging aquatic insects
**Habitat:** flies along streams, rivers and lakes in forested areas
**Predators:** weasel, domestic cat, raccoon, skunk, rat, snakes, hawks and owls
**Dental Formula:** 2/3, 1/1, 2/3, 3/3 = 36 teeth

## *Evening Bat* Nycticeius humeralis

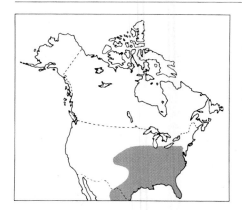

**Mammal:** *Nycticeius humeralis* — evening bat

**Meaning of Name:** *Nycticeius* (belonging to the night); *humeralis* pertains to the humerus, a bone of the upper arm

**Description:** smaller version of big brown bat; pelage dark brown above, paler below; ears and wing membrane are black, hairless and leathery; blunt tragus

**Total Length:** 3.3 to 3.7 inches
**Tail:** 1.5 inches
**Forearm:** 1.4 to 1.5 inches
**Weight:** 0.21 to 0.42 ounces
**Gestation:** not known (probably about 40 days)
**Litter Size:** 2 (sometimes 1)
**Age of Maturity:** 1 to 3 years
**Longevity:** usually 2 years; a few have survived for over 5 years
**Diet:** insects, probably small soft-bodied forms
**Habitat:** found in cultivated and natural clearings in hardwood forests
**Predators:** weasel, domestic cat, raccoon, skunk, rat, snakes, hawks and owls
**Dental Formula:** 1/3, 1/1, 1/2, 3/3 = 30 teeth

The evening bat is a medium-sized bat with dull brown fur and blackish ears. It lives in the southeastern United States and sometimes migrates to the north. Only one specimen has been collected in Canada, at Point Pelee on Lake Erie. It forages above the treetops early in the evening and then moves low to the ground later at night. The diet of the evening bat is generalized to include most kinds of insects. Females form small nursery colonies in hollow trees and buildings and migrate south in the winter. In buildings, these maternity colonies may be much larger, with several hundred individuals. No large winter aggregations are reported, and these bats probably roost in small tree cavities.

The litter size is two and the young are born in June in the northern part of the evening bat's range. The young bats are weaned at about four weeks and start foraging for themselves at that time.

# *Free-tailed Bats* Molossidae

## *Big Free-tailed Bat* Tadarida macrotis

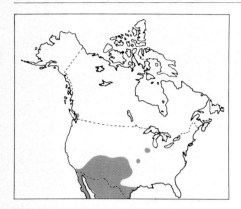

**Mammal:** *Tadarida macrotis* — big free-tailed bat
**Meaning of Name:** *Tadarida* may come from the Greek *ta darida*, meaning long ones, or it may mean withered toad; *macrotis* (large, long + ears); free-tailed refers to the tail being independent of the posterior portion of the flight membrane
**Description:** brown fur, paler beneath; dorsal hairs have whitish base; half of tail extends beyond the interfemoral skin; ears attach to forehead between the eyes; stiff hairs as long as the foot extend from toes
**Total Length:** 5.1 to 5.4 inches
**Tail:** 1.9 to 2.1 inches
**Forearm:** 1.4 to 1.8 inches
**Weight:** approximately 0.25 to 0.50 ounces
**Gestation:** 77 to 90 days
**Litter Size:** 1
**Age of Maturity:** 9 to 12 months
**Longevity:** not known
**Diet:** moths, beetles, ants, midges and other kinds of insects
**Habitat:** rugged, rocky country; deserts and steppes
**Predators:** barn owl, great horned owl, red-tailed hawk, rat, raccoon, opossum and snakes
**Dental Formula:** 1/2-3, 1/1, 2/2, 3/3 = 30 or 32 teeth

The 86 species of free-tailed bats form a family of large fast-flying bats that live mainly in the tropics. Their wings are long and narrow, adapted for high-speed flight. Instead of a large tail membrane used by many bats for sharp manoeuvring, they have a free tail that is thick and ratlike. They typically have a very short velvety fur, which, because it reduces air resistance, may be another adaptation for high-speed flight. Their large ears are positioned sideways so that they act like wings, rather than facing forward and catching the airstream.

The big free-tailed bat is a large bat with the typical molossid appearance. It is normally a resident of the arid southwestern United States, but its tremendous flight abilities sometimes carry it to Canada. Virtually nothing is known of its life history, but it is probably a resident of high cliffs, where it roosts in crevices. It forages at night and appears to specialize in capturing high-flying moths. Northern populations are probably migratory. The litter size is one.

### A Communal Cost

*Many bats are gregarious, roosting together in large numbers. There are some benefits to communal roosting. Wintering bats stay warmer and more humid when clustered. If a predator finds the roost, a member of a large cluster is probably less likely to be eaten than one that is in a small cluster. Sometimes, females help other females guard and retrieve young that fall to the ground. Young, inexperienced bats may learn about foraging opportunities by tracking older, more experienced bats.*

*But communal roosting also carries costs. Because bats roost in tight packs and use the same small sites year after year, they are perfect hosts for a variety of parasites that flourish on social mammals. Bats rarely groom each other in the way that monkeys do. This makes communal bats vulnerable to an itchy version of a social disease: ectoparasitism. Bats are host to large numbers of external parasites, such as fleas and bedbugs. Other mammals harbour fleas, chiggers, ticks and mites, but bats, in addition to hosting these pests, also have a unique range of parasites. Six entire insect families are found only on bats, and another, the bedbug family, has developed extensively on bats. Indeed, the bedbug that plagues humans probably first evolved on cave-roosting bats, gravitated to cave-dwelling humans and eventually moved with humans into their hovels.*

*Close to 700 species of insects live exclusively on the bodies of bats, and it is tempting to believe that this is because their gregarious roosting habits favour the life styles of parasites. Most families of bat insects spend part of their lives either living in the roost and feeding on bats that visit or living directly on a bat and using the roost mainly as a place to disperse offspring to new bat hosts.*

*Life on a bat that flies through the air at high speed and allows its body*

temperature to drop nearly to freezing during hibernation has led to some unique adaptations in certain bat insects. One group of flies, the streblids, or bat lice, hatch looking like most flies, with wings and legs. But in some species, as soon as the female finds the appropriate spot on a bat, her wings and legs fall off. She embeds herself in the bat skin, and her abdomen swells up like a balloon, completely enclosing her head and thorax. Mobility is traded for security.

The lack of mobility of bat lice means that they must be concerned with selecting bats that will be close enough to other bats for their offspring to find new hosts. This requires some sexual discrimination. The streblids that live on Townsend's big-eared bat can distinguish male bats from females. They prefer females as hosts. This seems logical. Females form dense nursery roosts in summer, so the streblid and its progeny have a large food resource. Male big ears are solitary, thus a streblid on a summer male would have a dim future.

Streblids are also among the most devoted mothers in the insect world. Rather than simply laying eggs on the host or food source, as most flies do, the female streblid hatches a single egg at a time inside her body and feeds it internally with special "milk" glands. When the fly emerges, it is almost adult size, and it pupates instantly, ready to become an adult. This would be comparable to a human female carrying on her pregnancy until the fetus was 18 years old. The reason why these flies find such a high degree of parental care adaptive is clear: the adult female is much better at extracting resources from the host than a fly maggot could ever be, and the host's body is a better resource base than the detritus in the bat roost. A fly on a bat has an almost infinite supply of high-quality food, and since the bat roost is a predictable source of new hosts, there is no need to produce large numbers of young.

These parasites do not appear to harm bats seriously, but they are undoubtedly irritating, and the bats expend large amounts of energy

Clustering reduces the heating costs for these little brown bats but at the same time makes it possible for parasites to crawl from one bat to another.

---

grooming themselves. Mammalogists, at least, are happy they exist. Most bat parasites are found on only one or a few closely related bat species, and by comparing the parasites of different bats, biologists gain insights into how various groups of bats are related.

# INSECTIVORES *Insectivora*

One of the first things a mammalogist who sets out to livetrap animals must learn is that shrews and moles starve to death within hours if not supplied with large quantities of food. These animals are tiny. Some species would fit comfortably in an egg cup or even a thimble, but they have huge appetites, completely out of proportion to their size. The famous Canadian mammalogist Randolph Peterson once recorded what a single tiny pygmy shrew ate during 10 days of captivity: "the carcasses of 20 *cinereus* shrews, 1 white-footed mouse and 1 pygmy shrew, 20 houseflies, 22 grasshoppers, 2 craneflies, 1 beetle and the liver of a meadow mouse." In spite of this huge intake of food, the captive shrew did not get fat. A captive short-tailed shrew ate 20 crickets, 4 carabid beetles, a centipede and a beetle larva in a morning and was still hungry. Life for a shrew is one of seemingly perpetual hunger.

Living insectivores are a complicated blend of ancient primitive characteristics and highly evolved specialized traits. On one hand, insectivores are considered to be the most primitive placental mammals. Among the primitive features that many insectivores exhibit are the structure of the ears, the small brain, primitive teeth, testes that are usually inside the abdomen, rather than in a scrotum, and the joining of the urinary and reproductive tract and the intestine into a common channel called a cloaca. At the same time, the different families have developed highly specialized adaptations, such as the mole's digging apparatus and the ultrasonic communication system of shrews, which are specific to particular groups and which are of recent evolutionary origin.

Each family of insectivores has specialized abilities: hedgehogs have evolved a unique prickly coat of quills along with the strange behaviour of coating these spines with saliva and poison collected from toads. The Solenodons, rat-sized predators of insects and other small animals on the isolated islands of Cuba and Hispaniola, have developed a potent venomous saliva that enables them to subdue lizards, frogs and birds. Moles have evolved into underground specialists. Each insectivore family has become substantially different from other families in the order as well as from their common ancestor.

North America has only two insectivore families: the shrews and the moles. All species in this order tend to be small. They have reduced eyes and ears and their feet have five clawed toes, which distinguish insectivores from other small mammals such as mice, which have four clawed toes on their forefeet.

*Insectivores, such as this masked shrew eating a grasshopper, will starve to death in a few hours without food.*

# *Shrews* Soricidae

The pygmy white-toothed shrew of Africa is the world's smallest mammal. The next smallest mammal, the pygmy shrew, is a resident of North America and is scarcely larger than its African counterpart. Two hundred adult pygmy shrews would weigh one pound. The small size of shrews dominates their life history and behaviour.

With small, hot bodies, shrews radiate a tremendous amount of heat energy. They have the highest surface area relative to their body mass of all mammals, which means the heat they generate metabolically to maintain their body temperature soon dissipates into the air. The calories needed to maintain their body temperature are acquired with the aid of a gargantuan appetite.

Shrews' high metabolic rate and large appetite means they will attack almost any prey item they can subdue. They eat far more than just insects. They will prey on earthworms, seeds, fish, frogs and carrion, indeed almost any food with a high protein and calorie content that can easily be digested.

One North American shrew has even evolved a poisonous venom to increase the size and type of prey it can immobilize. The salivary glands of the short-tailed shrew contain a neurotoxin that quickly paralyzes and will kill other small mammals and even larger prey, such as frogs. The venom is delivered along a special groove between the front lower incisor teeth. The poison is a water-soluble compound similar to cobra venom. A short-tailed shrew does not contain enough venom to kill a human, but a bite can cause swelling and a bad local reaction. Short-tailed shrew poison can kill mice within minutes and,

over time, can be lethal for animals as big as cottontail rabbits.

Shrews possess many other adaptations related to their need for a continuous supply of food. The front incisor teeth of all shrews are enlarged to form a shearing and pinching apparatus. The upper incisors are double-pronged and hooklike and cut against the long horizontal lower incisors, which have a set of cusps. The resulting apparatus can grasp and slice up prey. Shrews do not have time to shed a set of milk teeth — they might starve in the process — so they are born with a single set of permanent teeth. This enables mammalogists to calculate the age of a shrew from its tooth wear. Shrews rarely live more than a year and a half, and even in that brief time, older shrews sometimes wear their teeth down completely.

The stomach and digestive tract of shrews is simple and short, designed to move, process and evacuate food at a high rate. If shrews kill more than they can eat immediately, they will cache the surplus. Shrews can immobilize grasshoppers with a specialized bite at a main nerve centre that paralyzes but does not kill them, and a stack of grasshoppers can be built up for later consumption.

Shrews usually work at night or underground along a series of runways and burrows (often those of other animals such as moles), so their eyes, of little use in prey capture, are reduced in size. To compensate, shrews have a well-developed sense of smell. Their pointed snouts always seem to be twitching and moving, reading the scents in the air. Some shrews use ultrasound to locate prey.

Small size opens foraging opportunities to shrews — they can profitably handle small prey items that are

uneconomical for larger animals. For example, shrews will eat ants, fly larvae and even mites and nematode worms that are scarcely more than a fraction of an inch long. Shrews can run through leaf litter and slip under logs and stones, where insects and worms hide, unavailable to predators such as birds or larger mammals. Because they exploit such a huge resource base, shrews can be exceedingly abundant in spite of their demand for food.

During winter, most shrew activity takes place beneath the insulating blanket of snow. Their fine fur is effective insulation. Unlike other northern mammals such as ground squirrels, shrews are too small to hibernate. They would lose heat and burn body fat at too high a rate even if they reduced their body temperature like true hibernators. Instead, shrews respond to low temperatures in the environment by turning up their bodies' metabolism and generating even more heat. This is especially true of temperate zone and northern shrews, known as "hot" shrews. Their metabolism is considerably faster than that of tropical and desert shrews, which are known as "cool" shrews. The high metabolic rate of northern shrews may be an adaptation that permits them to exploit the tremendous spring and summer surge of insect food in the North.

Overwintering is a challenge for shrews, and many starve to death. The successful ones, however, are able to feed on the many dormant insect larvae and pupae and other small mammals, such as voles, available along the soil surface.

*The northern water shrew is one of the largest of all shrews, but it would take 30 of them to weigh a pound.*

*Shrews have poor eyesight, but they can use ultrasonic waves and their long, pointed snout to communicate and to find prey.*

The success of these adaptations is made clear by the evolutionary history of shrews. Fossil shrews go back as far as 50 million years, and in overall body plan, they have changed little. They have spread from an apparently European origin through Africa, Asia and North America. In South America, they have penetrated only the north of the continent, and they never reached Australia because of its isolation. Shrews have radiated into a vast array of habitats from tropical rain forests to deserts, grasslands and high Arctic tundra.

In spite of their ubiquity, little is known about the social life of shrews. They are difficult to study under natural conditions, so what is known about their behaviour is largely derived from captive animals. Studies of acoustic communication in shrews have recently revealed an unsuspected richness of signals. Shrews such as the short-tailed shrew and the least

shrew have a vocal repertoire that includes chirps, clicks, twitters and buzzes. These sounds carry different meanings. Cheeping by young, for instance, can trigger a search-and-rescue response by mother and father short-tailed shrews. Male short-tailed shrews in pursuit of oestrous females produce a stream of dry unmusical clicks, similar to the sounds of a twig brushing against bicycle spokes.

Acoustic signals play an important role in fights between male shrews. Territorial male common shrews confront adversaries with screaming and staccato squeaking. These sounds are also used in echolocating objects and other shrews. In a manner similar to the system used by bats, shrews can read the distortion and other features of the echo to assess the size and location of an object.

Shrews also communicate chemically. The male short-tailed shrew uses a large belly gland together with sounds to communicate with the female during courtship. In the words of one researcher: ''The male appears to play a passive role — approaching the female, rubbing the substrate, tol-

erating bites from the female without biting her — while rubbing and exuding odour in new areas and gradually increasing the receptivity of the female. The female repels the male with high-intensity chirps and buzzes; the male is easily repelled by the female's loud vocalizations. The male responds to bites and loud chirps by closing his eyes and ears and exposing his gland-covered neck. The male rubs his venter over the substrate and simultaneously over his body. His glandular odour, immediately detectable by the observer, is emitted after two or three minutes.'' Shrews also have conspicuous glands along their sides, but their function has yet to be established. They may act to deter predators. A single short-tailed shrew gives off enough scent to fill a room with a rank, repulsive smell.

Shrews have limited opportunity to communicate with each other. Females and males are normally hostile to each other and to members of their own sex during all but breeding season, when females may tolerate the presence of males. The only other well-developed communication is between the young and their mother.

There is, however, one North American shrew that has a greater propensity for social life — the least shrew. Adult least shrews often nest together, perhaps to increase heat retention, and both sexes reportedly care for their young. Short-tailed shrews also exhibit this behavioural pattern, but no detailed studies of their social behaviour under natural conditions have been conducted.

Reproduction in shrews is as hurried as the rest of their lives. Copulation usually lasts only 10 seconds. Their gestation period is three weeks or less. Litters of 2 to 10 young are born naked and helpless in a well-insulated nest of grass and other materials. They grow rapidly. Some species are ready to leave the nest within three weeks. This rapid development enables an adult female to breed several times during a season, which normally begins in early spring and continues during summer months.

# *Saddlebacked Shrew* Sorex arcticus

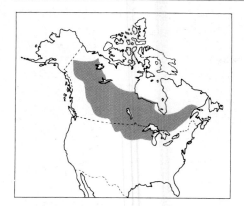

**Mammal:** *Sorex arcticus —* saddlebacked shrew, Arctic shrew, black-backed shrew

**Meaning of Name:** *Sorex* (the shrew mouse); *arcticus* (land of the bear) refers to constellations of greater and lesser bear (i.e., the north)

**Description:** the most brilliantly coloured shrew; tricoloured with dorsal region the darkest (brown to black); lighter brown flanks and paler greyish brown underparts

**Total Length:** 3.8 to 5 inches

**Tail:** 1.2 to 1.9 inches

**Weight:** 0.18 to 0.5 ounces

**Gestation:** probably 21 to 25 days (possibly delayed implantation or ovulation)

**Litter Size:** 5 to 9; 3 litters per year

**Age of Maturity:** female, rarely breeds during first summer; varies with localities, depending on quantity and quality of available food

**Longevity:** 12 to 18 months

**Diet:** almost exclusively insects; caterpillars, centipedes, beetles and their larvae, sawfly cocoons

**Habitat:** nonforested areas; swamps, bogs, grass/sedge marshes, edges of willow-alder zone, meadows or grassy clearings within forests

**Predators:** hawks, owls and lesser carnivores

**Dental Formula:** 3/1, 1/1, 3/1, 3/3 = 32 teeth

A dark brown to black back, reddish sides and greyish belly distinguish the saddlebacked shrew from most other shrews, which tend toward drab grey or black coloration. Despite its Latin name, *arcticus*, this shrew lives in boreal coniferous forests, especially in damp areas. In prairie regions, it is confined to moist shrub and forest edges. Where the saddleback occurs with the common shrew, *Sorex cinereus*, it uses the drier parts of the habitat.

Saddlebacked shrews also climb trees. Studies have found that the saddleback feeds heavily on sawflies found on larches and other coniferous trees. One shrew may require 123 of these sawflies per day, and at densities peaking at five individuals per acre, these shrews may have a major impact on the sawflies that sometimes invade northern forests. This shrew has also been seen climbing shrubs and jumping on grasshoppers. It will build runways and use those of other small mammals. Most of its foraging takes place in bursts of only a few minutes, followed by resting. This continues day and night, with somewhat more activity during the night.

Two generations may be produced in a season. Saddlebacks born in late summer begin to reproduce the following spring and die by fall. Spring-born saddlebacks may produce the late-summer and autumn generation, but this is not definitively known.

In captivity, the saddleback is docile and can be held in the hand.

*Saddlebacked shrews are one of the few species of shrew that have a colour pattern in their fur.*

# *Least Shrew* Cryptotis parva

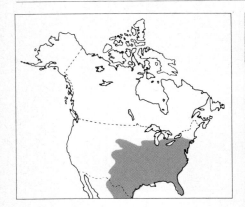

**Mammal:** *Cryptotis parva* — least shrew
**Meaning of Name:** *Cryptotis* refers to the fact that the ears are small and hidden under the fur; *parva* (small)
**Description:** small size and short tail distinguish it from other species; greyish brown above and silver grey to white below; winter pelage is darker
**Total Length:** 2.7 to 4.1 inches
**Tail:** 0.5 to 0.9 inches
**Weight:** 0.16 to 0.2 ounces
**Gestation:** 21 to 23 days
**Litter Size:** 1 to 9 (usually 3 to 6); 2 or 3 litters per summer
**Age of Maturity:** before the age of 40 days for both sexes
**Longevity:** 18 months in the wild; 20 months in captivity
**Diet:** insects, earthworms, centipedes, mollusks, amphibians, lizards and small mammals; also some fruit and plant material
**Habitat:** open grassy fields with scattered weedy or brushy vegetation; the only Canadian locality is a grassy sand area
**Predators:** owls, hawks, snakes, weasel, domestic cat and short-tailed shrew
**Dental Formula:** 3/1, 1/1, 2/1, 3/3 = 30 teeth

Not much larger than a pygmy shrew, the least shrew looks like the bigger short-tailed shrew, but it is a surface dweller and does not burrow extensively. Least shrews are found in habitats ranging from open grasslands and salt marshes to forested areas.

Leasts may have the most interesting social lives of all shrews. Like the short-tailed shrew, the least shrew has a well-developed vocal repertoire, communicating with a variety of clicks and chirping sounds. Up to 31 individuals have been found in the same nest. In captivity, they do not fight. There is also an interesting observation of parental behaviour: when a nest containing young was opened and the immature shrews were scattered, all of the adults helped in retrieving the young. It is possible that these shrews live in large cooperative groups, which would make them completely unlike any other North American shrew species.

## Small Is Costly

*When an animal is warmer than its environment, it loses heat; when it is cooler than the environment, it gains heat. Any mammal generates heat because all the chemical reactions of the body create waste heat energy. The rate at which this heat is radiated and lost depends on the surface area of the mammal's body, how well it is insulated and other factors, such as how windy and humid the weather is and what the temperature difference is between the animal and the*

*Least shrews seem to be the most social of all shrews, with as many as 31 huddling together.*

*environment. Mammals differ vastly in size, from tiny shrews to monstrous whales. Consequently, the rate at which they lose heat energy varies tremendously.*

*Small mammals, such as shrews, moles and mice, must be capable of producing large amounts of heat. Their relatively large surface-to-volume ratio means that they lose heat at a high rate. Thus they must be able to generate heat at a high rate. Shrews have the smallest bodies and the fastest metabolisms of any mammals. A shrew must eat several times its body weight each day to produce the calories needed to maintain its constant and high body temperature. By contrast, a large mammal such as a moose or whale needs to eat only a small fraction of its body weight to maintain its body temperature.*

*The difference in metabolism between shrews and larger mammals is reflected in the rate at which they absorb and pump oxygen around their bodies to fuel their metabolic fire. A shrew's heart is capable of beating more than 1,000 times a minute when the shrew is active. A large mammal may have a heart rate of only 10 beats per minute. If the metabolic fire of the shrew goes out, it cools quickly.*

When a shrew dies, it is at the temperature of the environment within a few minutes. By contrast, a large whale that had been killed showed a drop in body temperature of only 2 Fahrenheit degrees in 28 hours.

An ounce of shrew or mouse biomass burns far more food and oxygen than an ounce of moose flesh, for example. One biologist has calculated that the plant food which would support a half-ton moose would only support about 90 pounds of mice and probably less than 40 pounds of shrew biomass. This has some interesting behavioural and ecological consequences. It means that a larger animal will be able to survive longer than a smaller one on its energy stores, assuming both store the same proportion of their body weight. Some whales, for example, spend the better part of the winter migrating to tropical breeding sites and eat almost nothing. Large male seals and walruses may spend their two-month breeding season without eating, but a shrew or mole starves to death after only a few

hours without food. A large mammal can afford to eat low-energy foods such as twigs and shrubbery and to spend much of its life sleeping and digesting. Shrews must spend most of their lives foraging and can eat only high-quality, easily digested items.

Since oxygen consumption is proportional to metabolic rate, it is easy to see why there are no deep-diving small mammals, only relatively large mammals such as seals and whales. A shrew or mole will burn up all its oxygen in a matter of minutes.

There are also some interesting life-history patterns associated with body-size variation. In general, small mammals are more fecund; that is, they breed more often and have more offspring than large mammals do, and their populations can grow faster than those of large mammals. But small mammals mature and die earlier than large mammals. Whales may live for a century, while many small mammals live at most a year or two, no matter how well they are fed and protected. Early death, a kind of planned obsolescence, seems

These water shrews, like other small mammals, must feed heavily to make up for a high rate of heat loss.

designed into their bodies. The reason for this remains unexplained and is one of the most challenging problems of ecology and evolution.

# Smoky Shrew *Sorex fumeus*

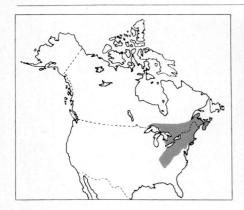

**Mammal:** *Sorex fumeus* — smoky shrew
**Meaning of Name:** *Sorex* (shrew mouse); *fumeus* (smoky) refers to greyish brown colour on back
**Description:** well-developed flank glands in both sexes; grizzled brown dorsally, slightly lighter underneath; tail is bicoloured, yellow below and brown above; winter pelage is slate-grey to blackish
**Total Length:** 4.1 to 5 inches
**Tail:** 1.6 to 2.1 inches
**Weight:** 0.2 to 0.39 ounces
**Gestation:** less than 2 weeks
**Litter Size:** 5 or 6; 2 or 3 litters per year
**Age of Maturity:** year after birth; does not breed in year of birth
**Longevity:** 12 to 18 months; few live more than 1 year in the wild
**Diet:** insects, insect larvae, earthworms, moths, centipedes, snails, spiders, sow bugs, some mammals, salamanders and birds; also vegetable matter
**Habitat:** moist leaf mould, leaf litter, rotten logs in mature deciduous or mixed woods (uses tunnels in the leaf mould made by other small mammals)
**Predators:** owls and small predators such as short-tailed shrew
**Dental Formula:** 3/1, 1/1, 3/1, 3/3 = 32 teeth

The habitat of the smoky shrew is the mixed deciduous forest of the northeastern United States and eastern Canada. It builds nests of shredded leaves under stumps and logs and forages along the forest floor. Most of the time, the smoky shrew uses the runways of other small mammals, but it may make its own tunnels through loose leaf litter. It also modifies abandoned burrow systems of other small mammals. These burrows have openings scarcely larger than a dime and are easy to miss even when they are common. The smoky shrew's habit of rummaging through leaf litter may account for its preference for mature deciduous forests. Areas with rich loose soils such as stream and marsh edges are also suitable for this shrew. Like other shrews, the smoky feeds mainly on insects, but its use of mole runways may enable it to capture a large number of earthworms that other shrews, except for short-tailed shrews, do not encounter or are too small to subdue.

When captured or harassed, a smoky shrew shrieks loudly. It is possible that screaming may startle small predators such as the short-tailed shrews and give the screaming animal an opportunity to escape.

The ***wandering shrew***, S. *vagrans*, seems to be a western version of the smoky shrew, and like that species, it patrols the runways of other small mammals. It eats organisms associated with the damp soil litter, including slugs, snails, insect larvae and

*Smoky shrews root through the upper soil and leaf litter to capture more earthworms than other shrews.*

even the underground fruiting bodies of truffles, a fungus in the genus *Endogone*.

## *Water Shrew* Sorex palustris

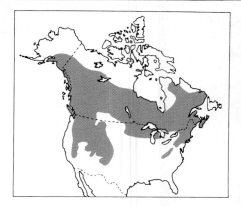

**Mammal:** *Sorex palustris* — water shrew, northern water shrew
**Meaning of Name:** *Sorex* (shrew mouse); *palustris* (dwelling in marshes or bogs)
**Description:** large; big hind feet bear a row of stiff hairs along outer and inner margins of feet and toes; middle toes are partially webbed; soft velvety fur is grey to black above and white or greyish underneath; distinctly bicoloured tail
**Total Length:** 5.1 to 6.4 inches
**Tail:** 2.4 to 3.5 inches
**Weight:** 0.3 to 0.63 ounces
**Gestation:** not known (probably 13 to 28 days)
**Litter Size:** 4 to 8 (average 6); 2 or 3 litters per year
**Age of Maturity:** male, winter of first year; female may breed when slightly more than 3 months
**Longevity:** 12 to 18 months; dies after its second summer
**Diet:** primarily insects, insect larvae and nymphs of aquatic insects, planarians, small fish, spiders, slugs, snails, other invertebrates and larval amphibians
**Habitat:** streams, lakes and ponds if adequate cover is available along banks or on shores; can also adapt to habitats with little water
**Predators:** hawks, owls, snakes, weasel and mink
**Dental Formula:** 3/1, 1/1, 3/1, 3/3 = 32 teeth

This large shrew has radiated into a niche unoccupied by other shrews and has therefore achieved a wide geographic range. It occurs along lakes, ponds, streams and rivers, any wet habitat where sheltering banks, tree roots or rocky debris offer seclusion. It is most abundant along fast-flowing streams with well-vegetated shorelines.

True to its name, the water shrew dives and swims well and is able to catch much of its diet underwater. It eats aquatic insects, fish and tadpoles. The water shrew makes very brief dives, usually lasting less than a minute. Longer immersion risks wetting the coat, which would cause the shrew to lose large amounts of heat. Even half a minute underwater produces a drop in body temperature.

The water shrew is protected to some extent against heat loss by its coat, which traps air between the hairs. Underwater, the shrew looks silvery, an effect produced by the air bubbles trapped in the coat. This air makes the water shrew very buoyant. It paddles vigorously to submerge itself; when it stops swimming, it

*Water shrews are able to kill frogs and fish larger than themselves.*

shoots up to the surface and floats well out of the water. The water shrew is so buoyant that it seems to run across the surface of ponds.

Immediately after a dive, this shrew leaves the water and grooms and dries itself, allowing its body temperature to return to normal.

Trout and other fish eat the water shrew, another reason for it to minimize its time in the water.

The ***Pacific water shrew***, S. bendirii, the largest of the northern long-tailed shrews, is highly aquatic. It also occupies wood habitats, making it less restricted to water than the water shrew. During wet weather, it may forage far from water.

## Dusky Shrew *Sorex monticolus*

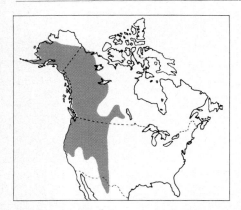

**Mammal:** *Sorex monticolus* — dusky shrew

**Meaning of Name:** *Sorex* (shrew mouse); *monticolus* (mountain-dweller)

**Description:** larger and paler than *Sorex vagrans*, the other family stock; short rust-brown fur above in summer, with brownish to silver-grey underparts; tail indistinctly bicoloured; winter pelage is darker above and below

**Total Length:** 3.7 to 5.5 inches

**Tail:** 1.2 to 2.4 inches

**Weight:** 0.16 to 0.36 ounces

**Gestation:** not known (probably 13 to 28 days)

**Litter Size:** 4 to 7

**Age of Maturity:** not known (probably the spring following birth)

**Longevity:** 12 to 18 months

**Diet:** insects and their larvae, earthworms, spiders, snails and other invertebrates

**Habitat:** many different habitats subject to a wide range of climatic conditions; prefers wet meadows, grass/sedge marshes and coniferous forests near streams

*The dusky shrew occupies the full spectrum of western habitats: tundra, alpine meadows, forests and prairies.*

**Predators:** hawks, owls, snakes and carnivores

**Dental Formula:** 3/1, 1/1, 3/1, 3/3 = 32 teeth

## Trowbridge Shrew *Sorex trowbridgii*

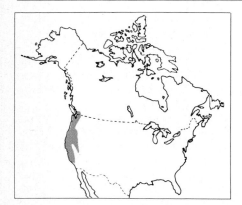

**Mammal:** *Sorex trowbridgii* — Trowbridge shrew

**Meaning of Name:** *Sorex* (shrew mouse); *trowbridgii* (named after W.P. Trowbridge)

**Description:** dark grey or blackish with brownish hue; lighter underparts; brownish in summer; strikingly bicoloured tail; dark dorsally and white below

**Total Length:** 4.1 to 4.9 inches

**Tail:** 1.9 to 2.3 inches

**Weight:** 0.43 to 0.53 ounces

**Gestation:** not known (probably 13 to 28 days)

**Litter Size:** 3 to 6; 1 or possibly 2 litters per year

**Age of Maturity:** not known (probably the spring following birth)

**Longevity:** 12 to 18 months

**Diet:** insects, spiders, centipedes, isopods and some other invertebrates; in winter, conifer seeds and vegetable matter

**Habitat:** prefers moist ground litter of well-drained coniferous forests, where it finds shelter among logs, stumps and decaying vegetation; also found in brushlands and cutover areas

**Predators:** hawks, owls, snakes and carnivores

**Dental Formula:** 3/1, 1/1, 3/1, 3/3 = 32 teeth

*Because of its massive appetite for seeds, the Trowbridge shrew can affect the rate of reseeding of a cleared Douglas fir forest.*

# Short-tailed Shrew *Blarina brevicauda*

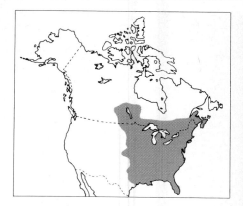

**Mammal:** *Blarina brevicauda* — short-tailed shrew

**Meaning of Name:** *Blarina* is a coined name for certain shrews — the actual meaning is unknown; *brevicauda* (short tail)

**Description:** large with a short tail and blunt nose; glandular hairless area on the mid-ventral region; eyes are so small that they are barely apparent; slate-coloured fur; paler underparts

**Total Length:** 3.5 to 5.7 inches

**Tail:** 0.7 to 1.4 inches

**Weight:** 0.53 to 1.2 ounces

**Gestation:** 21 or 22 days

**Litter Size:** 3 to 10 (usually 5 to 7); 2 or 3 litters per year

**Age of Maturity:** male, 12 weeks; female, 6 weeks

**Longevity:** 1 to 2 years (a potentially greater longevity than long-tailed species)

**Diet:** insects, insect larvae, earthworms, snails, some vegetable matter and small vertebrates (young mice, meadow voles)

**Habitat:** hardwood forests with high humidity and loose humus; also coniferous forests, bogs, marshes, fields and grasslands if there is a lot of moisture

**Predators:** hawks, owls, shrike, weasel, skunk, fox, bobcat and coyote; domestic dog and cat may worry them to death

**Dental Formula:** 3/1, 1/1, 3/1, 3/3 = 32 teeth

*Neurotoxic saliva similar to a cobra's allows the short-tailed shrew to kill lizards and prey larger than itself.*

The short-tailed shrew can be one of the most abundant of mammals, with up to 80 animals per acre. It is tempting to attribute this to the range of food available. Its neurotoxic saliva enables it to kill animals such as garter snakes and young rabbits, prey much larger than itself and unavailable to other shrews and similar-sized rodents. These shrews also use their venom to paralyze victims such as earthworms and then store them in caches, alive but immobile. Short-tailed shrews also cache large quantities of snails and sawfly pupae.

During some periods, half of this shrew's diet may consist of meadow voles. It is credited with controlling and depressing meadow vole population explosions, and huge increases in vole numbers are responsible for the extreme densities of short-tailed shrews in some years. Short-tails and voles may cycle together in the same way that lynx and snowshoe hares do.

Despite the short-tailed shrew's venom, the voles and mice fight back. Although the venom slows and weakens the victim, reducing its respiration rate and reaction time, it can take between 10 and 30 minutes before the short-tailed shrew can deliver its *coup de grâce*: a bite to the base of the skull. Voles have evolved the ability to recognize and avoid the smell of the short-tailed shrew. Mammalogists trying to trap voles in devices that previously held short-tailed shrews have found that the voles avoid them.

Shrew venom is also reported to contain an enzyme, glycosidase chitinase, which may improve the digestive efficiency of this species. Insect skin and skeletons are built of chitin, a compound that most mammals cannot digest. The feces of other shrews often contain large quantities of undigested insect exoskeleton and chitin, recognizable as poorly digested legs and other body parts. The feces of the short-tailed shrew, however, are mushy and well digested.

There is also a suggestion that the side glands of this shrew produce such an unpalatable odour and taste that mammalian and bird predators

*Normally a resident of deciduous forests, where it feeds mainly on earthworms, the short-tailed shrew also lives in open and wet areas, preying on frogs and other aquatic creatures.*

avoid it, thereby allowing populations to reach great densities.

The short-tailed shrew is the most underground North American shrew and is a competent digger. Its short tail, slit-like ears and short, stout limbs all reflect its adaptation for life underground. The short-tailed shrew eats more earthworms than any other shrew, and moles could be its main competitors for food. It builds its own runways and constructs a nest that is well underground, often a foot below the surface.

This shrew is most common in rich deciduous forests but is found in a variety of other habitats, including coniferous forests and, to a lesser extent, in open and wet areas.

The short-tailed shrew has one of the most interesting and best-studied social behaviours of all shrews. Unlike most shrew species, the short-tailed shrew can be kept in captivity with other members of its species. They are antagonistic toward each other at times but will also sleep together and adjust to each other's presence.

These shrews are reproductively active for a large portion of the year, from early spring through to autumn. Females may breed two to three times in a season. They have the typically short shrew pregnancy of three weeks and a similar period passes before weaning.

## A Test of the Male

*Dogs, wolves and coyotes are well known for the "copulatory tie" in which two mating individuals seem stuck together for as long as an hour. In fact, the male is held in place and cannot easily separate from the female. This same situation is found in the short-tailed shrew. Most shrews copulate for only a few seconds, but in this species, the male and female remain stuck together for almost half an hour. When the male short-tailed shrew mates, his erect and inserted penis bends with an S-shaped curve, following a similar shape in the female's vagina. This lock-and-key mechanism holds the male in place. The tip of the penis also has a series of pointed hooking structures that* further secure it. Even after he dismounts, the male remains attached to the female. She may drag him around backward for as long as 25 minutes.

The adaptive significance of this is unclear. It may prevent a male from being displaced by another male, and it may provide the female with some information about the status and competence of the male, as subdominant males thus engaged would be extremely vulnerable to attack and unlikely to attempt copulation.

Another curious feature about the male short-tailed shrew's penis is that it can only be retracted into its storage sheath with the aid of the mouth. This seems a somewhat cumbersome arrangement, especially since a pair may mate as often as 20 times a day. Short-tailed shrews run down burrows much of the time, and like moles, they have grain-free fur and reduced external extremities, such as ears, that might be snagged by obstructions. An unretracted penis would seem to be a definite liability. This suggests that some form of female choice of male quality may be operating to produce a male reproductive morphology that inconveniences the male in some way but acts to give the female information on the fitness of the male.

## Why There Are So Many Shrews

One of the basic questions of ecology is: How do so many species coexist? If two species require the same resources to live, the species that is better at acquiring or controlling resources will outcompete and eventually displace the less efficient species.

How, then, do so many species of shrews coexist? Shrews seem similar. They are all small, hungry insectivores with a catholic diet. Shrews have to be voracious. Their high metabolism means they often must eat more than their own body weight each day, so one would expect shrews to compete strongly with each other for food. Yet one study found six species of shrews living in the same area.

There are two kinds of competition that confront an individual: competition from members of the

same species (intraspecific competition) and competition from members of different species (interspecific competition). Normally, intraspecific competition will be most intense because the more similarities there are among individuals in a population, the more likely they are to need exactly the same kinds of resources. Under the pressure of intraspecific competition, evolution will favour the individuals who use resources that are less used by other members of the species. If every short-tailed shrew is searching for sawflies, the individual who is able to eat earthworms may enjoy a great competitive advantage. The long-term evolutionary effect of intraspecific competition is a broadening of the resources that a species will use. The resource base will grow until it is checked by inefficiency (a jack-of-all-trades is master of none) or is opposed by interspecific competition.

Interspecific competition is hard to demonstrate experimentally under natural conditions, but there is evidence that it is important. Rarely have two different species ever been found to use exactly the same set of resources. One community of six shrews, each of a different species, living on Sagamook Mountain in New Brunswick, showed important differences in diets and habitat choices. All six species shared the same kinds of foods, eating dozens of different invertebrates, but each

*Small, even by the diminutive standards of shrews, this least shrew is able to exploit food items unavailable to its larger relatives.*

species ate different proportions. The short-tailed shrew, a strong burrower, ate more earthworms and snails than the others; the water shrew ate more aquatic organisms; the Gaspé shrew, more spiders; the smoky shrew, earthworms and a mix of insects, including a high proportion of moths. The common shrew favoured insects, especially beetle larvae, while the pygmy shrew ate insect larvae and caterpillars.

Each shrew has access to a different microhabitat. The short-tailed shrew can reach earthworms by burrowing, but it cannot reach the items available to the Gaspé shrew, whose small body and flattened head enable it to reach into tight rock crevices. The tiny pygmy shrew might be a strong competitor of the Gaspé shrew, but it avoids rocky areas and prefers the understorey of forested stream areas. When two shrew species share the same microhabitat, they will differ greatly in body size and will take different-sized prey. If two similar-sized shrews occur in an area, they will tend to prefer different microhabitats.

## *Common Shrew* Sorex cinereus

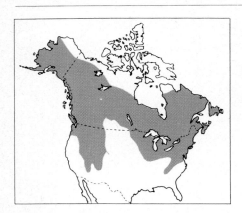

**Mammal:** *Sorex cinereus* — common shrew, masked shrew

**Meaning of Name:** *Sorex* (shrew mouse); *cinereus* (ash-coloured)

**Description:** slender body; long, slender snout that is always moving; brownish back and silvery or greyish white underneath; bicoloured tail, brown above, paler below, with a black tip

**Total Length:** 2.8 to 4.9 inches

**Tail:** 0.98 to 2 inches

**Weight:** 0.09 to 0.28 ounces

**Gestation:** 17 to 28 days

**Litter Size:** 2 to 10; 1 or sometimes 2 litters per year

**Age of Maturity:** female, some at 4 to 5 months, but most breed for the first time in the spring following birth; male, some individuals can breed at 2 months

**Longevity:** 12 to 18 months

**Diet:** mostly insects but also many small mammals; some seeds, moth and beetle larvae, slugs, mollusks, spiders, young mice and salamanders

**Habitat:** along margins of moist fields, bogs, marshes, moist or dry woods, willow/alder thickets and brushland

**Predators:** various small predators; larger shrews, hawks, owls, snakes, shrike, heron, merganser, fox, weasel and fish

**Dental Formula:** 3/1, 1/1, 3/1, 3/3 = 32 teeth

As its name implies, the common shrew is more widely distributed than any other shrew. It lives in forests and open meadows, in drylands and marshes. In off years, populations may number only one per acre, but in peak years, common shrew populations can climb as high as 13 per acre. But for all its ubiquity, it is a relatively unknown mammal.

It is known that common shrews are voracious hunters. One researcher observed a common shrew stalking butterflies, which it could detect visually as far away as 25 feet. The common shrew can also detect prey by smell. In an attempt to control sawfly pests in Newfoundland, the common shrew was introduced to that province. The introduction was successful, and the shrew apparently does provide some biological control of those pests. It also may be able to kill young mice and salamanders. During winter, the common shrew will also eat significant quantities of tree seeds, especially those of conifers.

Common shrews do not build runways but will use those of other animals. They do, however, build grassy nests, which they defend from other shrews.

In the northern part of their range, common shrews appear to breed only once a year, in spring. The young mature one year after birth. In the southern area of their range, common shrews may breed several times in a season. The young show caravan behaviour, following single file behind an adult. This may be of use if the female's nest is destroyed before the young shrews are fully mature.

The ***prairie shrew***, S. *haydeni*, once thought to be a race of common shrew, is now recognized as a distinct species. It is similiar to the common shrew, except it specializes in prairie

*Keen hunters, common shrews have been observed stalking butterflies they have detected 25 feet away.*

and parkland habitats. No study of the behaviour or ecology of this shrew exists.

The ***barren-ground shrew***, S. *ugyunak*, is another close relative of the common shrew, specialized to survive on the barren-ground habitat of the Northwest Territories. It is found in wet sedge-grass meadows and dwarf-willow and birch clumps.

# Gaspé Shrew  *Sorex gaspensis*

**Mammal:** *Sorex gaspensis* — Gaspé shrew, the least-known and rarest shrew
**Meaning of Name:** *Sorex* (shrew mouse); *gaspensis* (of Gaspé Peninsula)
**Description:** small with long tail; long whiskers; greyish; underparts are lighter than dorsum; bicoloured tail
**Total Length:** 3.7 to 4.7 inches
**Tail:** 1.6 to 2.2 inches
**Weight:** 0.08 to 0.18 ounces
**Gestation:** not known (probably 13 to 28 days)
**Litter Size:** possibly 5 or 6
**Age of Maturity:** not known (probably the spring following birth)
**Longevity:** 12 to 18 months
**Diet:** spiders, flies, beetles, insect larvae and plant matter
**Habitat:** coniferous and mixed forests; restricted to rocky-hilly terrain with a substrate of boulders; along small swift-flowing streams
**Predators:** hawks, owls, snakes and carnivores
**Dental Formula:** 3/1, 1/1, 3/1, 3/3 = 32 teeth

Gaspé shrews are extremely rare and poorly understood. The species seems restricted to habitats along streams in the rocky and hilly areas of the Gaspé region of Quebec and in New Brunswick. There is some dispute over whether this is a distinct species or merely a geographic race of the more southern and somewhat larger long-tailed shrew. It has a flattened skull, small body, long snout and long tail, all adaptations to moving through and hunting in rock crevices.

The ***long-tailed shrew***, S. *dispar*, is similar in appearance to the Gaspé shrew, although it is somewhat heavier and its fur is darker and less grey. The long-tailed shrew lives in mountainous regions in rocky talus slopes and areas with plenty of cracks and crevices among boulders, taking advantage of cover provided by moss and leaf mould and the roots of trees. The cool, moist habitat has resulted in a specialized diet: a high proportion of crevice-dwelling arthropods, especially the flat crack-dwelling centipedes, as well as spiders and insects.

Little is known of the long-tailed shrew, and there have been less than 10 recorded sightings of it in Canada. Experts assume that there is a substantial population near the Quebec/Maine border and throughout the Maritime Provinces, but study is nearly impossible given the species' subterranean life. Certainly, its predominant range is in the eastern mountains from Maine through to West Virginia and eastern Tennessee.

The primary predators of long-tailed shrews are the hawks, owls, snakes and carnivores with which it shares the talus mountain terrain. Long-tails are not considered territorial, as they are usually found within close proximity to red-backed voles and the common shrew. It is likely

*Restricted to the rocky hills of Quebec's Gaspé region and New Brunswick, the Gaspé shrew has a flat skull, enabling it to move through rock crevices.*

that they avoid confrontation by concentrating on different sources of food.

Life expectancy is probably 12 to 18 months, and females average one litter of five young after maturity.

## *Pygmy Shrew* Sorex hoyi

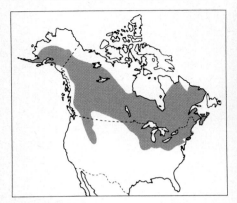

**Mammal:** *Sorex hoyi* — pygmy shrew; averages less in weight than any Canadian mammal
**Meaning of Name:** *Sorex* (shrew mouse); *hoyi* (named after Philip Hoy)
**Description:** sepia brown above with paler greyish or brownish underparts; winter pelage is greyer and longer
**Total Length:** 2.8 to 4.1 inches
**Tail:** 0.9 to 1.4 inches
**Weight:** 0.07 to 0.22 ounces
**Gestation:** 13 to 24 days
**Litter Size:** 3 to 8; 1 litter per year
**Age of Maturity:** not known (probably the spring following birth)

**Longevity:** 12 to 18 months
**Diet:** insect larvae, insects, beetles, spiders, invertebrates and carrion
**Habitat:** wooded areas (coniferous and deciduous); bogs, wet meadows
**Predators:** hawks, owls, snakes and carnivores

*This dead mouse dwarfs the pygmy shrew beside it, but the shrew will eat and digest the mouse within hours.*

**Dental Formula:** 3/1, 1/1, 3/1, 3/3 = 32 teeth

## *Tundra Shrew* Sorex tundrensis

**Mammal:** *Sorex tundrensis* — tundra shrew
**Meaning of Name:** *Sorex* (shrew mouse); *tundrensis* (of the tundra)
**Description:** in summer, pelage is tricoloured (brown back, pale greyish underparts and lighter sides); in winter, pelage is bicoloured (sides and underparts greyish, back brown)
**Total Length:** 3.3 to 4.7 inches
**Tail:** 0.9 to 1.4 inches
**Weight:** 0.18 to 0.35 ounces
**Gestation:** not known (probably 13 to 28 days)
**Litter Size:** 8 to 12; several litters in quick succession

**Age of Maturity:** not known (probably the spring following birth)
**Longevity:** 12 to 18 months
**Diet:** insects, earthworms, floral parts of small grass
**Habitat:** well-drained habitats with dense vegetation; along northern border of boreal forest; dry tundra ridges
**Predators:** hawks, owls, snakes and carnivores
**Dental Formula:** 3/1, 1/1, 3/1, 3/3 = 32 teeth

*Although tundra shrews are restricted to the extreme north, females are still able to raise three litters of up to 12 young each year.*

## The Splitting of the Shrews

*No one is certain how many shrews there are. This is surprising because the taxonomy of most temperate mammals was worked out long ago. But new species of shrews continue to be recognized. In North America, more than 30 different shrew species have been described, many of them only in the last few years. One reason is that shrews are small and difficult to handle and study. The differences used to separate these newer species are subtle, requiring the precise measurement and study of hundreds of specimens and sophisticated statistical analysis. The fact that many of our shrew species are so similar suggests that these species are newly formed and have not followed different evolutionary pathways for long.*

*The geographic range of closely related and newly formed species may give biologists insight into what causes speciation. Normally, species are created by geographic isolation. A large population gets split into two or more populations isolated from each other by a geographic barrier such as a mountain range or large body of water. The split populations no longer mate and mix their genes. Because geographically separated populations live in different environments, they are subject to different forms of selection. Gradually, different genes and gene combinations develop in the populations until they become so distinct that they may be called separate species. This is especially true if the groups later come into contact but maintain their identity and do not interbreed.*

*There are good reasons why genetically different individuals ought not to interbreed. When a female and male mix their genes to produce offspring, each contributes a similar set of genes arranged in structures called chromosomes. During the fertilization of the egg and its division into cells, the male and female pairs of chromosomes must match reasonably well, or the resulting offspring will be genetically defective. Selection will favour individuals that choose not to mate with individuals who are too different from*

*themselves because of the risk that their hybrid offspring will be defective. This reinforces the genetic separation of the two different populations, a process most biologists agree creates two or more new species out of one ancestral species.*

*It is more difficult to discover how populations become isolated, particularly for species that are millions of years old. But for some shrews, the isolation events may have been much more recent. It is quite possible that the waves of glaciation, which saw ice sheets march south during cool times and then retreat north during hot times, played a major role in isolating populations and fostering the speciation process.*

*In the case of the Gaspé shrew and the related long-tailed shrew, a single ancestral species was probably distributed along the upper forest regions of the eastern mountain ranges running from the Gaspé through the southern Appalachian mountains. During the peak of glaciation, the forested region moved to the south. There was a narrow strip of tundra in front of the glaciers. The northern forests spread out in a wide band, and populations of forest animals remained continuous for the most part. Some populations were isolated. Certain islands off the coasts remained unglaciated, and the animals were cut off from populations that had been pushed south.*

*When glaciers retreated, there were often pronounced hot and dry spells. During such spells, the northern forest home of the long-tailed and Gaspé shrew stock must have retreated up mountainous areas higher and higher, until the two*

Once thought of as the same species as the common shrew, the barren-ground shrew, **above**, is now recognized as a separate, newly evolved species that arose during the last Ice Age.

*species were confined to strips and circles around mountaintops, separated from other similar forest pockets by grasslands and oak scrub. During one of these isolating episodes, the Gaspé shrew became separated and differentiated from the long-tailed shrew.*

*The same recent fragmentation appears to have happened to the common shrew. The prairie shrew, the barren-ground shrew, the Mount Lyell shrew and Preble's shrew have all recently been separated from the common shrew by taxonomists. The Mount Lyell's shrew is found only in two counties in California, and it is probably a species formed from an isolated remnant population created when the common shrew was forced south by the ice sheets. It was left behind in an ecological island when the flora and fauna moved north with the retreat of the glaciers.*

*Many large mammals disappeared during the Pleistocene for mysterious reasons. But at the same time, the divisive influence of the ice sheets' waxing and waning across the continent had a creative effect and probably generated many of our most recent species of shrews and made the shrew family one of the most diverse groups of northern mammals.*

# *Moles* Talpidae

Moles have been called the least understood major component of our mammalian fauna. The reason for this seems clear: moles live mostly out of sight underground in conditions hard to simulate in captivity. Most of what is known about moles is related to the sophisticated adaptations they have made to a subterranean life.

Like shrews and voles, which also spend much time in tunnels and under leaf litter, moles have a compact, elongate body. There are no awkward protruding limbs to snag on roots. Moles dig their own tunnel systems, and many features of their body reflect a design for digging. The evolutionary success of moles is tied to digging. The most primitive surviving mole, *Uropsilus*, looks much like a shrew and has no special adaptations for digging. The more modern moles have evolved a unique digging apparatus that enables them to occupy niches unexploited by primitive moles and other insectivores such as shrews.

The shovels of a mole are in its forelegs and feet. Other digging mammals, such as squirrels, badgers and occasional excavators such as coyotes, have their limbs placed under the body, and they scrape and throw the soil under and behind them. Moles have developed a lateral-stroke digging technique, one that is unique among mammals. This special method has involved a radical redesign of their forelimbs. The shoulder and collarbone of the mole are joined in a different way than those of other mammals. Moles' shoulder blades are large, and their forepaws have grown into huge, flat paddles with stout claws. The fingers have flat ridges of skin along their sides, increasing their surface area. The breastbone is deeply ridged to allow the attachment of powerful chest muscles.

A mole digging in its tunnel braces its hind feet against the tunnel walls and then shoves its forepaws forward one at a time, scraping backward as if rowing. When placed on the soil surface, a mole can disappear in about five seconds. After two seconds, by pulling on the mole's tail, a person might be able to retrieve it, but when it has all four feet firmly implanted, it is almost impossible to drag it back onto the surface.

Eyes are all but useless in a dark tunnel, so the size of moles' eyes has been greatly reduced. Some moles are blind, and the eyes are completely grown over with skin, while others are able to distinguish light from dark and, possibly, to perceive objects. Visual abilities are useful when moles are forced out of their burrows by flooding, fighting with territorial rivals, predators or lack of food, and there are some species that forage mainly above ground. It is not known how well moles smell; they may rely more on taste after touching objects, but they are apparently able to smell the slime of a worm several inches away. Some moles hear well. Evidence suggests that they may use ultrasonic echolocation as their shrew relatives do. They also produce sound audible to the human ear and can hear sounds useful in detecting both prey and predators. However, the mole perceives its environment largely through touch.

The snout of the mole is extremely sensitive and covered with a dense array of nervous receptors. The complexity of these nervous receptors, a tangle of various nerve cells including bare nerve endings and a rich supply of blood vessels, is unmatched in the animal kingdom. The nerves are organized into structures known as Eimer's organs, thought to be sensitive to touch, vibration, pressure changes, chemical sensation and, possibly, heat. The snout, paws, tail and the back of the head also have sets of sensitive bristles, like a cat's whiskers, that enable the mole to detect objects in advance of a collision.

Streamlined body features assist moles in their movement through the soil. The most notable adaptation is in the fur. There was once a booming business in moleskins in both the United States and Europe, as they were used for various garments, gloves and purses. The demand for moleskin was so high that legal attempts were made to protect moles in countries such as Germany, because overtrapping threatened them with extinction. Moles are still trapped in England, but most moleskins now come from Russia. The appeal of moleskin is unexpected, since mole pelts are small and difficult to assemble into large items such as coats. Nevertheless, mole fur is of extremely high quality. It is shiny and dense and has no grain, which means it can be rubbed in any direction and still lie sleek and unruffled. This is because of a unique design in the hair itself. Moles have hinged hair. Each hair is built from alternating sections: cylindrical and strong pigment sections joined by flat, flexible sections. The flat sections act as hinges, allowing the hair to bend easily in any direction. The adaptive significance of this design is that it allows the mole to run both backward and forward in its tunnels unimpeded by fur friction against the walls.

*Members of the Talpidae family, such as this star-nosed mole, are well adapted for life underground. Sensitive nerve receptors on their noses lead them to worms and other food sources.*

Mole tunnels often form intricate networks. Different kinds of moles build different kinds of tunnels, but in general, two types of tunnel can be recognized for each species. The first are deep permanent tunnels that may go down 3 yards. These are used for sleeping, escaping from most predators and avoiding the cold of winter. They may have nesting and resting chambers attached to them. The second type of tunnel is a shallow network just below the soil surface. Familiar to anyone who has ever had moles in his yard, these tunnels can often be recognized as raised meandering ridges in the ground surface. When a mole digs one of these shallow tunnels, it does not remove and pile the soil. Instead, it turns its body at a 45-degree angle and pushes the soil upward. These tunnels meander according to the texture of the soil and the ease of digging — hard and excessively wet soils are avoided. The energetic cost of digging is high, and ac-

cordingly, some mole tunnels are used for up to eight years.

It was once believed that moles spent most of their time digging in pursuit of prey such as worms and grubs buried in the soil. But it is now believed that moles spend little time searching for food in this way. No doubt, they will eat almost any food they encounter while excavating, but the burrows and tunnels of moles are relatively permanent. Moles spend much of their time patrolling the system of runways and eating food that has crawled and fallen into the passageways. This is probably especially true in areas with hard-to-work soils, like clay, which have a high density of worms and soil animals. The burrow network acts as a giant pitfall trap. In loose soils and especially acid peaty ones that are poor in food, moles probably spend more time searching for food by digging shallow tunnels.

Usually, the only evidence of these tunnels is the piles of excavated dirt,

*The shallow tunnel network of a mole acts as a pitfall trap for the digger's underground prey.*

molehills, that moles bring to the surface. Otherwise, moles keep their burrows closed and inconspicuous as protection against predators.

The social life of moles is poorly known. Trapping evidence suggests that most species are solitary for much of the year. However, many species appear to share certain tunnel sections as access routes to water, for example. Some species, such as the star-nosed mole, may live as male-female pairs during winter, and shrew moles, which forage much of the time above ground, are sometimes seen in small groups. But other species are socially intolerant. Male moles fight violently with, and even kill, intruders.

According to one mole biologist, "The courtship of the mole has only been described in highly fanciful terms by early French writers who were obviously well accustomed to describing certain aspects of social activity for which their royal courts were renowned.'' Mole courtship presumably involves some fighting between males for access to receptive females. Male moles of all species, except the star-nosed mole, are considerably larger than females, which is usually a clear sign that male-male combat is well developed. Some male moles also employ another strategy to gain exclusive access to a female. A mixture of compounds from the prostate glands and Cowper's glands in the male's reproductive tract are secreted into the female's vagina after mating. These compounds then solidify into a mating plug, a kind of chastity belt that prevents other males from mating with the plugged-up female. This is exactly the kind of male-mating tactic to be expected in mammals in which the females are themselves territorial and highly dispersed. A male can increase his reproductive success by mating with a female, then leaving to search for another mate while the mat-

ing plug guards his paternity. Without the plug, the male would risk being cuckolded, thereby lowering his reproductive success. Males who use the plugging tactic also have reproductive systems where testes and other glands swell to 14 percent of body weight during mating season. Human testes weigh less than 1 percent of body weight. So for moles, the investment in mating is considerable.

Outside of the reproductive period, females are unreceptive to the extent that a membrane grows over and seals off the vagina. They are receptive only once a year, usually in early spring. Southern populations may start reproduction several months ahead of northern populations. Pregnancy is thought to last four to six weeks and gives rise to between one and nine young, depending on the species. Females give birth inside a nest, which is usually lined with leaves and grass.

North American mole species vary in size, but all are small mammals, and like shrews and mice, they have a high metabolic rate. Moles are active

day and night year-round and are incapable of hibernating. Consequently, they consume and burn large quantities of food. The larger species may eat one-half to one-third of their body weight per day, while smaller species can eat one or two times their body weight, making them comparable to shrews in food consumption. Earthworms form most of the mole's diet, with the rest being taken up by soil insects. Some moles even attack the underground nests of hornets. On occasion, they will eat roots and bulbs and become pests in gardens and vegetable fields. The star-nosed mole is semiaquatic and eats many pond- and stream-dwellers, including fish. Like shrews, moles will cache an abundance of items, such as earthworms, which the mole immobilizes by biting off their digging end. The appetite of moles translates into a considerable ecological impact. A single mole may consume up to 80 pounds of food yearly, or roughly 8,000 earthworms, and moles' digging results in significant soil aeration and mixing.

## *Hairy-tailed Mole* Parascalops breweri

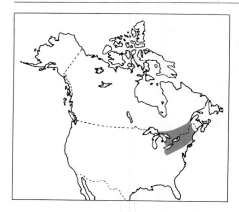

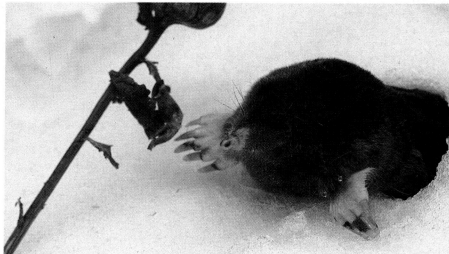

**Mammal:** *Parascalops breweri* — hairy-tailed mole, the smallest of eastern moles

**Meaning of Name:** *Parascalops* (resembles the digger, or mole); *breweri* (named after Dr. T.M. Brewer, a zoologist and author)

**Description:** tail distinctly covered with long stiff black hair; snout is conical and mobile; dense, velvety pelage; greyish black with metallic sheen; often a creamy irregularly shaped spot on the breast or abdomen; light brownish secretions stain the fur of both sexes during breeding season

**Total Length:** 5.4 to 6.7 inches
**Tail:** 0.9 to 1.5 inches
**Weight:** 1.4 to 2.3 ounces
**Gestation:** 4 to 6 weeks
**Litter Size:** 4 or 5; 1 litter per year
**Age of Maturity:** 10 months
**Longevity:** 4 to 5 years
**Diet:** earthworms, insects, soil invertebrates
**Habitat:** hardwood forests and fields

*A denizen of the eastern forests, the hairy-tailed mole lives for up to five years, twice as long as most moles.*

near hardwood stands; prefers light, loose, moist but well-drained soils with well-mixed organic matter and minerals
**Predators:** fox, owls, snakes, bullfrog and opossum
**Dental Formula:** 3/3, 1/1, 4/4, 3/3 = 44 teeth

## *Shrew Mole* Neurotrichus gibbsii

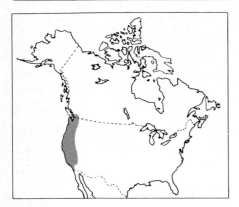

**Mammal:** *Neurotrichus gibbsii* — shrew mole, the smallest of American moles
**Meaning of Name:** *Neurotrichus* (new + tail + hairy); *gibbsii* (named after collector G. Gibbs)
**Description:** small and shrewlike; tail has sparse coarse hairs projecting between annular scales and stiff brush of hairs at the tip; elongated flexible snout terminates in a naked pink nose pad; small eyes; feet are less modified for digging than other North American talpids; colour is sooty blue to black with a slightly metallic gloss
**Total Length:** 3.9 to 4.9 inches
**Tail:** 1.2 to 1.8 inches
**Weight:** 0.32 to 0.39 ounces
**Gestation:** not known (probably 4 to 6 weeks)
**Litter Size:** 1 to 4
**Age of Maturity:** breeding season following birth
**Longevity:** not known
**Diet:** earthworms, isopods, sowbugs, insects and their larvae and pupae; some plant seeds and vegetable matter
**Habitat:** shady ravines; stream banks and riverbanks; forested hillsides and valley bottoms where there is moist loose soil with high humus content, lots of leaf litter and no thick sod or turf
**Predators:** small predators such as snakes, hawks, owls and raccoon
**Dental Formula:** 3/3, 1/1, 2/2, 3/3 = 36 teeth

The shrew mole, as its name implies, has a life history that is similar to a shrew's in several respects. It is found on the Pacific slope of extreme southern Canada and the northwestern United States in areas where there is heavy forest along valley bottoms and hillsides. This habitat contains a rich and abundant leaf litter layer, and the shrew mole is specialized in harvesting the small residents in the litter and on the surface. This mole is a habitat specialist associated with loose and productive soils in deciduous forest. It is rare in open habitats or areas with heavy and wet soils.

Shrew moles do less digging than other North American moles and, accordingly, are different structurally and behaviourally. The shrew mole's hind feet are relatively large and so is its tail, which enables it to rear up, a difficult act for other moles. It is the only mole that can turn its front paws flat on the ground underneath it, and it can run on the backs of its claws. Unlike those of other moles, the front feet of a shrew mole are longer than they are wide, making it more efficient at locomotion than at shovelling. It is even able to climb around low shrubbery. But the shrew mole is less efficient as a digger. A powerful digger such as the eastern mole can move 35 times its own weight, but the shrew mole can only move 20 times its own weight. Most shrew mole tunnels are shallow, running just below the leafy humus layer. They have many openings, which the shrew mole uses as entrances and exits.

Although it forages extensively on the surface, the shrew mole has weak

*Less adapted for life underground than most moles, the shrew mole forages extensively on the surface and can even climb small bushes.*

eyesight. To compensate, its snout is elongated and ends in a pink pad with the nostrils on the side. This snout and its tip are thought to be highly sensitive, and they are used like a blind person's cane. As the shrew walks or runs, it taps its snout ahead and from side to side, reading tastes and textures as it goes. As a further aid to navigation, the shrew mole hears ultrasound and can echolocate.

The advantage of a mole being more shrewlike is that it can exploit the rich fauna of the upper soil area, the surface and even low herb layers, a resource that is unavailable to conventional moles. Earthworms are a prominent element of its diet as they are for other mole species, but the shrew mole also eats many litter arthropods, especially sowbugs, and an assortment of insects, mushrooms, seeds and other surface items. A disadvantage to its aboveground feeding is that the shrew mole suffers heavy predation by owls, hawks, snakes and other carnivorous mammals.

The behaviour of this mole is poorly known. Several individuals have been trapped in a single set of runways, suggesting that the shrew mole may be more gregarious than other moles. It has an extended breeding season, from February to September, which may reflect the mild and damp climate where it occurs. This mole has a pronounced musky smell that is most noticeable in reproductively active males.

# *Star-nosed Mole* Condylura cristata

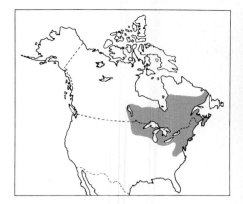

**Mammal:** *Condylura cristata* — star-nosed mole

**Meaning of Name:** *Condylura* (knuckle + the tail) refers to the knotty appearance of the tail in dried specimens; *cristata* (crested) refers to the star, or crest, of 22 pink fleshy fingers growing on the snout

**Description:** blackish brown; dense, long, soft pelage is waterproof; naked pink disk at tip of snout with 22 radially symmetrical tentacles; long fleshy tail thickens in winter with stored fat; large scaled feet are thinly furred on top and naked below

**Total Length:** 6.4 to 9.4 inches

**Tail:** 2.2 to 3.6 inches

**Weight:** 1.1 to 2.8 ounces

**Gestation:** 45 days

**Litter Size:** 2 to 7 (usually 5); 1 litter per year

**Age of Maturity:** 10 months (the spring following birth)

**Longevity:** not known

**Diet:** aquatic insects, worms, crustaceans, mollusks and small fish; may be entirely dependent on benthic prey in winter

**Habitat:** prefers low wet habitats near lakes and streams; woods, marshes and meadows; soils ranging from clay loam to sand or muck

**Predators:** few enemies due to odour and protective habitat; red-tailed hawk, great-horned owl, skunk, weasel, chipmunk and perhaps large fish such as pike and bass

**Dental Formula:** 3/3, 1/1, 4/4, 3/3 = 44 teeth

Outside of sea anemones, few animals have stranger appendages than the star-nosed mole with its ring of tentacle-like Eimer's organs surrounding its snout. The star-nosed mole is semiaquatic and adapted for a life in wet soils and shallow bodies of water. Its water-shedding fur is longer and coarser than that of other moles, its hind feet flat and wide and its tail long, all adaptations that suit it for swimming. The star-nose can stay underwater for about 3 minutes and dive about 3 feet deep. It is often seen swimming beneath the ice of ponds in winter and is caught in minnow nets and muskrat traps. In marshy areas, the star-nosed mole is often the only mole present. The strange nose organs may be of most use when the mole forages in the bottom muck of streams and ponds. During tunnel digging, the tentacles lie folded together and are kept protected, but underwater, they are fully expanded and presumably used to identify prey items. Much of its diet consists of aquatic insect lar-

*Eimer's organs, which surround the star-nosed mole's snout, are useful when it forages in the muck.*

vae but includes tadpoles, minnows, snails and leeches.

The star-nosed mole also builds the usual shallow and deep burrow systems, the former for foraging and the latter for reproduction and overwintering. The deep burrow system, by necessity, must be placed in solid ground above the waterline, a factor that may limit the abundance and distribution of these animals. The shallow system often has entrance openings right at the waterline and even underwater. During the winter, these moles also make a tunnel system through the snow. Several animals may use the same system of runways, and there is a possibility that this mole is more social than other mole species.

Because it forages in exposed conditions, the star-nosed mole is eaten by many raptors, carnivorous mammals and large fish.

# *Eastern Mole* Scalopus aquaticus

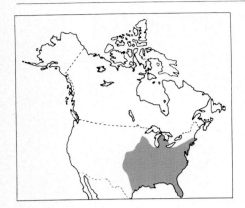

**Mammal:** *Scalopus aquaticus* — eastern mole

**Meaning of Name:** *Scalopus* (a foot for digging); *aquaticus* (living in the water); this animal is not aquatic, however, even though it is a good swimmer and has webbed toes

**Description:** stocky; feet and snout are almost naked; webbed toes; small eyes are hidden in fur; wrists are lined with a row of short stiff hairs; velvety dense slate-coloured fur

**Total Length:** 6.8 to 8.3 inches

**Tail:** 1.1 to 1.6 inches

**Weight:** 2.5 to 4.9 ounces

**Gestation:** approximately 4 weeks

**Litter Size:** 2 to 5 (usually 4); 1 litter per year

**Age of Maturity:** 1 year (breeding season following birth)

**Longevity:** not known

**Diet:** primarily earthworms, insects and their larvae, as well as a small amount of vegetable matter

**Habitat:** moist, friable humus in open woodlands, fields, meadows or pastures

**Predators:** hawks, owls, snakes, shrew, skunk, coyote, fox and weasel

**Dental Formula:** 3/2(3), 1/0(1), 3/3, 3/3 = 36 or 38 teeth

A heavyset generalized mole, the eastern mole is found in a wide range of forested and open habitats. It is most common in rich, loose forest soils, avoiding stony soils but tolerating harder clay soils that some mole species avoid. This may reflect the digging power of the eastern mole. It is one of the largest and strongest of moles and possibly the species most adapted for life underground. Its eyes are completely overgrown with skin. It is a prolific tunneller, able to construct its near-surface tunnels at a rate of nearly 13 feet per hour. One of these tunnels was traced along a fenceline for 3,300 feet.

During dry and cold periods, eastern moles use their deep tunnel and nest system, which may run 18 inches or more underground. They are active all winter but may spend periods in a semidormant state. Each mole defends its own exclusive burrow system, occupying from one-half to two acres.

The near-surface tunnels of the eastern mole are built and used during warm weather to gain access to the concentrations of earthworms and insects in the rich upper organic layer of the soil. Most of the eastern's diet is earthworms, but it will eat a great variety of soil insects and a limited amount of plant material. Eastern moles also attack hornets, many of which nest underground. One mole was even observed extending one of its molehills up to reach an aerial nest of bald-faced hornets. Hornet nests are usually full of fat, helpless larvae.

During breeding season, males enter the burrow system of receptive females. They show the typical mole pattern of tremendous enlargement of the reproductive organs, 10 times what they are during the nonreproductive season, and it is likely that these moles use mating plugs.

*A prolific tunneller, the eastern mole can dig at a rate of 13 feet per hour, and some single tunnels have extended as far as 3,300 feet.*

Females breed at age 1 and normally produce a litter of four in late spring. After four weeks, the helpless young are weaned.

## Adaptation: Nobody's Perfect

*Hardly an evening goes by without some gravelly voiced television narrator explaining how perfectly adapted this or that animal is to its environment. In truth, no animal is perfectly adapted. Strictly speaking, adaptation can be defined as a characteristic that increases an individual's chances of leaving descendants. An adaptation increases the reproductive success of individuals possessing it in comparison with the success of individuals who lack the adaptation. But more generally, nonbiologists think of adaptations as structures or behaviours that match the environment and tasks that confront an animal. The digging apparatus of a mole is highly, even beautifully, adapted for tunnelling in soil. However, it is misleading to say that the mole is perfectly adapted for its environment. It is more profitable to think of organisms and their evolutionary adaptations as compromises.*

*Everything an animal does and every part of its design by natural selection is the result of a series of cost-and-benefit trade-offs. For example, moles have degenerate eyes, which, in some species, are completely covered by skin. Yet moles do occasionally have to run across the ground's surface. At these times, moles could no doubt profit by having well-developed eyes. But the*

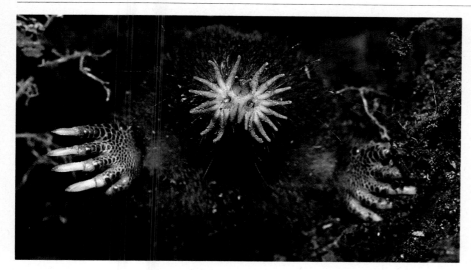

*Every adaptation has limits and virtues, and the discovery of these and the unravelling of the ecological and evolutionary forces that create them are a continual challenge for biologists. Perfection would be beautiful, but boring.*

Designed for a life underground, a star-nosed mole, like other members of its family, is at a disadvantage on open ground.

cost of having a conventional mammalian eye would be that during tunnelling and fighting with worms and noxious insects, the mole eye would be continually assailed by dirt and organic debris and would

probably be a vulnerable site for bacterial infections. Shrinking and covering the eye has the benefit of reducing that risk, but it is a compromise. So, too, with the forelimb structure of moles. It is a superb digging device, but for species such as the shrew mole, which obtains much of its food on the surface, the limb design is clumsy compared with that of true shrews.

## Townsend's Mole  Scapanus townsendii

**Mammal:** *Scapanus townsendii* — Townsend's mole; largest North American mole

**Meaning of Name:** *Scapanus* (a spade or hoe) refers to claws, which are specially adapted for digging; *townsendii* (named after J.K. Townsend, 1809-51, an author)

**Description:** stocky and robust; slate black fur with velvety sheen; darker in winter; pink snout is covered with sparse fine white hairs; tail is nearly hairless as are front feet, which are whitish
**Total Length:** 7 to 9.3 inches
**Tail:** 1.3 to 2.2 inches

**Weight:** male, 5.2 ounces; female, 4.1 ounces
**Gestation:** 1 month
**Litter Size:** 1 to 6; 1 litter per year
**Age of Maturity:** breeding season following birth
**Longevity:** not known
**Diet:** earthworms, insects and their larvae and pupae, centipedes, grubs and some vegetable matter, including bulbs of plants, wheat, corn and oats
**Habitat:** moist, loose soil of cultivated

*The largest North American mole, the west coast Townsend's will eat crops such as potatoes and carrots.*

fields, meadows, open forests and valley bottoms
**Predators:** only a few natural predators but may be taken by weasel, snakes or owls
**Dental Formula:** 3/3, 1/1, 4/4, 3/3 = 44 teeth

# *MARSUPIALS* Marsupialia

All North American mammals except the opossum are placentals, which means that the female raises her immature young by feeding them through the placental membrane in the uterus. Marsupials, such as the opossum, have a different reproductive system and strategy. Most mother marsupials have a pouch, a fold of skin over the teats where the young marsupials feed and undergo much of their growth.

Marsupials differ from placentals in many other aspects of their body plan. These differences arose early in mammalian history, as far back as the Cretaceous era between 75 and 100 million years ago. Marsupials are called "primitive" because of their ancient origin and for two other reasons: first, their skeletal system is closer to that of the reptiles from which mammals evolved; second, placental mammals appear to have outcompeted and replaced their marsupial competitors in many parts of the world.

Among the primitive features that marsupials exhibit are a narrow brain case, a small brain and more teeth. The common opossum, for example, has 50 teeth, whereas many placentals have only 44 at most. A marsupial's inner ear is built from different bones than that of a placental. But it is the evolutionary history of marsupials more than anything else that suggests they are less advanced than placental mammals.

At the time that the earliest marsupials began evolving, the three southern continents — Australia, Africa and South America — were still joined in one large landmass known as Gondwanaland. When this landmass began breaking apart, Australia and South America became isolated from the rest of the continents. In North America, Asia, Africa and Europe, the placental mammals began to diversify and increase. Marsupials declined until, by 15 to 25 million years ago, they were surviving only in Australia and South America. In Australia, where there was no competition from placental mammals, the marsupials diversified into a great variety of life forms, such as the large grazing kangaroos, the digging rodentlike wombats, koala bears, marsupial lions and other carnivores like the Tasmanian devil.

The reconnection of South America and North America suggests that competitive extinctions were important in the decline of many marsupial groups. For some 60 million years, South America had been separated from North America. During that interval, the South American marsupials had diversified into forms that resembled giant hyenas and sabre-toothed tigers. But when the land bridge linking the Americas rose some two to five million years ago, large placental carnivores, such as jaguars and pumas, began invading South America. The fossil record shows that this corresponds with the extinction of their marsupial counterparts.

Marsupials, however, are not simply "living fossils" that survived just because continental drift kept them isolated from competition by placental mammals. In spite of a long history of contact with placental mammals, marsupial opossums have survived, and indeed, they have moved north out of South America and well into Canada.

*North America's only marsupial, the opossum evolved in South America at a time when that continent supported a wide variety of now-extinct pouched mammals, including some that resembled giant hyenas and sabre-toothed tigers.*

# New World Opossums Didelphidae

The Didelphidae is primarily a South American family. Many mammalogists consider it to be the most primitive surviving marsupial family, from which all other marsupials have evolved. Opossums never get very large, no bigger than a small dog, and many are much smaller. There are 75 species in the family. The most diverse and widespread group is the mouse opossums in the genus *Marmosa*, which contains 47 species widely distributed over Central and South America.

In South and Central America, some sort of opossum can be found in almost any habitat, from wet marshy areas to dry savanna to the edge of the tree line high in the mountains. Opossums are omnivores — generalized feeders. Their adaptive radiation seems to be based more on adaptations to different ecological habitats than on food preferences. Nevertheless, there are groups within the family that are relatively specialized in their habits in ways comparable to some North American placental mammals. Shrew opossums are indeed shrewlike in several respects, having reduced eyes, short tails adapted to a more terrestrial life, a small body size and an appetite for insects and small mammals. The water opossum is similarly specialized, having webbed hind feet and pouches with watertight seals.

As a group, opossums are somewhat arboreal; that is, they are adept at climbing and living in trees. This is reflected in the design of their feet, which are narrow and have an opposable big toe and an enlarged fourth toe that are used to grip branches. The naked, muscular and prehensile tail is also used in hanging onto branches. Some opossums, such as the woolly opossums, are almost completely arboreal, feeding on fruits and flowers in the canopy of tropical forests.

One of the most diverse groups of opossums is that of the mouse opossum, which fills many of the ecological niches occupied by mice in temperate and northern habitats. These animals seem to be generalized feeders, eating a wide variety of plant and animal matter. They differ in their use of habitats. Many species are highly arboreal and spend most of their time climbing trees. Other species spend more of their time on the ground, but in any case, virtually all mouse opossums have long, naked prehensile tails that act like a fifth limb. This not only makes climbing easier but enables them to dangle from branches to reach fruits and berries hanging from slender twigs. Thus, at night, these creatures can harvest foods which are accessible only to day-flying birds and which may be beyond the reach of heavier animals such as squirrels and monkeys.

In some species of opossum, such as the Patagonian opossum, the tail can act as a fat storage organ, swelling and thickening when feeding is good. This may enable opossums to occupy seasonal habitats where the temperature or rainfall differs between winter and summer.

In spite of its success in Latin America, only a single species of this family has penetrated north of Texas. That species is the Virginia opossum, a highly generalized mammal that has extended its range into Canada.

*Thought to be the most primitive surviving marsupial family, the Didelphidae includes 75 species that range from small mouse-sized shrew opossums to the omnivorous Virginia opossum,* **right**, *which has extended its range as far north as Canada.*

# *Virginia Opossum* Didelphis virginiana

**Mammal:** *Didelphis virginiana* — Virginia opossum

**Meaning of Name:** *Didelphis* (double womb) refers to the pouch as a secondary womb in which the young develop after birth; *virginiana* (of Virginia)

**Description:** domestic cat size; female has fur-lined abdominal pouch; naked prehensile tail; large, naked, paper-thin ears tipped with pink; male has gland on throat that stains the fur yellow; grey is most common colour pattern; white face

**Total Length:** 25.4 to 32.9 inches

**Tail:** 9.1 to 21.3 inches

**Weight:** 4.4 to 13 pounds

**Gestation:** 12 to 13 days

**Litter Size:** 1 to 14; 1 or 2 litters per year

**Age of Maturity:** male, 8 months; female, 6 months

**Longevity:** 7 years

**Diet:** omnivore; unselective; will use most abundant foods; carrion forms a large part of diet along with mammals, insects, lizards, frogs, birds, eggs, fruits and vegetables

**Habitat:** open woodlands in association with streams; farming areas with sufficient cover

**Predators:** domestic dog, coyote, bobcat, fox, raccoon, raptors and large snakes

**Dental Formula:** 5/4, 1/1, 3/3, 4/4 = 50 teeth

As one of the first white men to see a live opossum in its native haunts, Captain John Smith, who settled Virginia in the early 1600s, remarked: "An Opossum hath a head like a Swine, & a taile like a Rat, and is of the Bignes of a Cat. Under her belly, she hath a bagge, wherein she lodgeth, carrieth and sucketh her young."

It is often claimed that the Virginia opossum is a living fossil, a survivor in North America for the last 75 or 100 million years. But in truth, this species is one of our newest arrivals from South America. Both genetic and geological evidence indicate that this species has evolved only since the last Pleistocene glaciations, and its arrival in North America is even more recent.

The Virginia opossum is a relatively recent immigrant to Canada. Prior to the European colonization of North America, the northern limit of this opossum was Virginia and Ohio. The opossum is one of the few animals that benefited from the changes wrought by the agricultural transformation of North America. The extermination of large predators, such as pumas, wolves and fishers, in the eastern United States and in southeastern Canada allowed the opossum to multiply and extend its range. Opossums will eat almost anything, and it is safe to say that the garbage generated by human settlements, a share of vegetable and fruit crops and a rise in various small-mammal populations associated with land clearing all increased their food availability.

*One of the few wild mammals to have benefited from changes brought about by land clearing, the opossum feeds on a variety of fruit and vegetable crops as well as human garbage.*

In any case, the opossum has experienced a kind of ecological release, allowing it to increase its range both north and south. The invasion into Canada appears to have come in pulses, the first immigrants reaching southern Ontario around 1850 to 1860, followed by other colonizations near the turn of the century, in the 1930s and following World War II. In British Columbia, the opossum is present because it was introduced on purpose by humans. Its present northern limits seem to be set mainly by its ability to withstand the Canadian winter. The opossum has a naked tail, which is vulnerable to frostbite, and as an animal with recent origins in the tropics, it lacks adaptations such as the ability to store food or to hibernate to help cope with the lack of food and warmth in the north in winter.

The opossum does have the capability of putting on a huge quantity of body fat, which is one reason why it can survive in southern Canada. Opossums can put on more than 30 percent of their body weight as fat, and they can lose as much as 45 percent of their body weight and still survive the overwintering period. This ability of opossums to get very fat in autumn is, no doubt, why residents of some areas, such as the southern United States, once prized opossum as a food — in

spite of its rank odour and pronounced taste for garbage and carrion. ''Possum and taters'' (sweet potatoes) is one of the traditional dishes of the southern United States.

As the only North American marsupial, the opossum seems anatomically bizarre, and many misconceptions about its reproductive biology exist. Folklore often has it that male opossums copulate with the female's nose. There is a logical origin of this belief: males do have a forked, two-pronged penis. But the supposition is incorrect, since females have a forked vagina and two uteri.

Less obvious but equally unusual is the fact that opossums produce paired sperm. Together, the sperm pairs swim in a straight line, but if they are separated, they swim in circles.

The opossum's courtship and mating procedure exhibits similar oddities. As with many kinds of mammals, male opossums will fight savagely for access to sexually receptive females, slashing at each other with their enlarged canine teeth and occasionally

killing or maiming one another. Part of the threat display used in aggressive encounters is a clicking noise, probably produced with the canine teeth. When a male is courting a female, he shuffles after her, making this clicking noise continuously. If she is receptive, he will climb onto her back, grasp her neck in his mouth, grip her hind legs with his feet and proceed to mate, none of which is particularly unusual. What is unusual is that the pair of mating opossums almost invariably flop over so that the female is lying on her right side. Examinations of females from pairs that stayed upright or flopped to the left instead of the right revealed that they were not successfully inseminated.

The female's reproductive biology is as curious as that of the male. Females become reproductively mature as early as 6 months old, and the breeding season begins in January in the southern United States and in early spring in Canada. The female is in heat for less than two days, and her pregnancy is likewise quickly completed, with the young being born on

*After weaning, young opossums ride with their mother for two or three months until they have mastered foraging techniques.*

the thirteenth day of pregnancy. At birth, opossums are very poorly developed, compared with placental mammals. They are naked, only one-half inch long, and it would take 3,500 to weigh a pound. Their organs are still forming, the chambers of the heart have not been separated, the kidney does not work, there are no pigments in the eyes, and the hind limbs and tail are almost nonexistent. All the young opossum is equipped with are the tools needed to crawl up the furry belly of the mother and into her pouch: well-developed forearms and fingers with claws that are able to grab hair and pull the newborn opossum upward, hand-over-hand, to the fur-lined pouch that offers warmth and milk.

The newborn's mouth muscles that attach it to the mother's nipple are also functional at birth. The nipple swells within the infant opossum's

*Neither territorial nor possessing a well-defined home range, the opossum can cover several miles per night on foraging outings.*

mouth, holding it firmly attached. As it swells, the nipple lengthens, until it is about 1 1/2 inches long, a cordlike lifeline that enables the developing opossums to move about in the pouch and strengthen limb muscles and co-ordination. Once attached, the young feed on milk for roughly 60 days and complete the developmental changes that in other placental mammals, such as ourselves, take place inside the mother's uterus. At the end of 60 days, the young opossums have developed fur and will venture outside the pouch. The elongated nipples enable them to lie outside the pouch and still continue suckling. After 30 to 40 more days, the young are ready to be weaned and to eat solid food.

During their early life after weaning, the young opossums ride with their mother, clinging to the hair on her back, a period during which they are probably learning much about food and foraging. However, once they are able to forage independently, the young become unsociable. Normally, within two to three months of weaning, all of the offspring have dispersed. From then on, they remain as solitary animals, the only contact with other opossums coming during mating periods and during the raising of litters of young.

The opossum's ecological strategy is best described as opportunistic or generalized. Originally, opossums were found primarily in deciduous woodlands, but they now occupy many habitats including agricultural areas, marshland and even canyons in dry grassland areas. They depend on ready access to water, and because they do not excavate, they rely on burrowing mammals, rock cavities and hollow trees for their dens.

However, although they depend on dens for reproduction and overwintering, opossums do not defend a specific foraging area or even possess a well-defined home range. Many of them seem to wander.

During the foraging season, most dens are used for only a single night. The opossums may cover several miles a night during foraging outings and move regularly to a new den site several hundred yards away. During any given night, the opossum makes many trips, usually only a few hundred yards or less, between the denning site and some food source. When the number of different den sites, the number of moves and the foraging distances are taken into account, it appears that opossums have a foraging range of roughly 50 to 500 acres. The home ranges of several resident opossums overlap, and opossum densities can range from one opossum per 2 acres to one opossum per 10 acres.

The abundance of opossums and their wide distribution is made possible by their broad diet. They are nocturnal foragers that will eat carrion, mushrooms, grass and other green vegetation, fruits, acorns, nuts, lizards, frogs, toads, many kinds of insect grubs, stinkbugs, hornets, worms and millipedes. Opossums can kill animals, such as rabbits, as well as small livestock, such as chickens. They are one of the few predators that catch large numbers of shrews and moles.

One of the most interesting foods available to opossums are poisonous snakes in the family Crotalidae, which includes rattlesnakes, water moccasins and copperheads. Opossums, which evolved in the snake-rich regions of the south, are virtually immune to the venoms of these snakes. Researchers have injected opossums with as much as 60 times the dose that is lethal to other mammals. The opossums respond with only a mild increase in heartbeat and blood pressure and none of the massive bleeding and allergic and tissue-damaging reactions that mammals normally suffer. Treating human cases of snakebite still relies on the production of antivenoms made from horse or sheep serum, which often produce violent allergic side effects. Somehow, opossums have evolved a biochemical alternative, and perhaps a study of their solution will lead medicine to a better form of snakebite therapy.

Many people have heard that opossums feign death when they are threatened, hence the phrase "to play possum." An opossum will, in fact, do this, a behaviour that involves lying on its side with its mouth open, drooling saliva and often defecating and oozing a noxious stink from its anal glands, which must make the inert opossum uninteresting to all but the most avid predator. However, not all opossums play possum. Humans who harass them are surprised to find that they will growl and attack aggressively with a formidable bite that can easily become seriously infected because of the carrion- and garbage-eating habits of the opossum.

No predators appear to specialize on opossums. They are eaten by coyotes, bobcats, foxes, raccoons and some large birds such as eagles and the great horned owl.

## The Pouch Strategy

*Abortion and infanticide are methods of limiting the progeny of any given species. A curious feature of marsupial biology is that in many*

Born naked and poorly developed, only the most vigorous of the two dozen half-inch-long young that a mother opossum gives birth to will be able to crawl into her pouch and affix themselves to her 13 nipples.

species, abortion and infanticide seem to be designed into the reproductive system. Some ecologists argue that this represents an important marsupial adaptation to unpredictable environments.

There are two ways in which the reproductive biology of marsupials results in the destruction of offspring. In species such as the Virginia opossum, Canada's only marsupial, it is almost inevitable that some of the young opossums are doomed. A female opossum will often give birth to two dozen infants, but normally, her pouch, or marsupium, contains only 13 nipples. This means that up to half of the young will starve to death because each successful individual attaches to and gains exclusive access to one nipple.

What sense does this overproduction make? One

possibility is that slight overproduction is a bet-hedging strategy that allows for the possibility that not all of the young will find their way to the pouch. However, there is an alternative. It may be that overproduction is a culling mechanism. Only the most vigorous young will be able to crawl rapidly up into the pouch, and thus defective offspring are weeded out. This makes sense in light of the parental-care costs involved. Pregnancy in the opossum is only two weeks long, and the resulting offspring are tiny. Therefore, the physiological and energetic cost of pregnancy is small compared with the cost of feeding and carrying a growing infant for several months. Culling early will cut the costs and losses that would result from rearing any defective offspring. In placental mammals, the uterus is able to reject some genetically defective embryos and to abort them spontaneously, but this is more complicated than the marsupial procedure.

This latter argument has led some mammalogists to reinterpret the

entire marsupial reproductive method. Formerly, the marsupial life style was explained as a primitive artifact that was a poor design compared with that of placental mammals. In placental mammals, the close ties between the offspring and the mother's placenta and circulatory system, combined with a long pregnancy, produce offspring that generally have fully formed organs and are more capable at birth than marsupials. The defenders of the marsupial life history point out that it is relatively easy for a mother marsupial to get rid of her offspring if the environment or her health and food resources suddenly change so that she is no longer able to feed her offspring. The advantage of a mother cutting her losses early would be that it might increase her chances of survival until a time when conditions for reproduction were improved. Marsupiality, according to this school of thought, enables a female to adjust her reproductive episodes in an unpredictable environment and, in the long term, to maximize her total lifetime output of offspring.

# GLOSSARY

Adaptation: traits an animal develops in the face of environmental and biological challenges

Adaptive Radiation: the evolution, from a common ancestor, of many different descendant species, each adapted to a diverse life style

Altricial: young that are helpless at birth and require intensive parental care

Ambergris: a substance, composed of various products of digestion, found in the large intestine and rectum of sperm whales; commercially used as a fixative in perfume

Ambient Temperature: temperature of the surrounding environment

Amphipod: a crustacean; includes many freshwater and shrimplike animals

Anaerobic: living in absence of free oxygen; anaerobic respiration is the derivation of energy by breakdown of substances in the absence of oxygen

Anal Gland (sac): a gland located near the anus that opens into the rectum of many vertebrates such as skunks

Ancestral Stock: a group of primitive animals from which later, more specialized animals are thought to have arisen

Annulation: the formation of rings, such as those found on the horns of bighorn sheep or on the teeth of seals

Antlers: branched, and usually bony, outgrowths found on deer; they are shed annually

Aquatic: living primarily in water

Arboreal: living in trees

Arthropoda: phylum of the animal kingdom characterized by a hard jointed exoskeleton and jointed appendages; includes insects, spiders, crabs, etc.

Baculum: bone found in the penis of some male mammals

Baleen: fibrous plates found in the mouth of certain whales and used to filter food

Bends: a painful and potentially fatal condition brought about by a rapid reduction in atmospheric pressure from high to normal, causing nitrogen bubbles to form in the blood and body tissues; commonly the result of a too rapid ascent from deep water

Benthic: pertaining to the bottom layer of freshwater and marine habitats

Bergmann's Rule: the principle that geographically variable species tend to be larger in the colder parts of their range than in the warmer parts

Binomial: a two-part name in biology (often Latin) consisting of a genus name, followed by a species name (e.g., *Canis lupus*, the wolf)

Bipedal: walking on two feet

Birth Synchrony: the timing of births within a population so that they occur at the same time in the season

Blowhole: the nostril on top of the head of whales and dolphins through which they exhale

Blubber: a thick insulating layer of fat beneath the skin of whales and other marine mammals

Boreal Forest Zone: a geographic zone consisting primarily of coniferous forest that extends from Newfoundland and Labrador to the Rocky Mountains and Alaska

Bovid: a member of the artiodactyl family Bovidae, which includes cattle, bison and their relatives

Breaching: leaping clear of the water, a behaviour common to whales and dolphins

Browser: a herbivore that feeds on shoots, twigs and leaves of trees, shrubs, etc., rather than grasses

Cache: a hidden food store or the act of hiding food for future use

Calcar: a spurred prominence on the heel bone of bats that supports the tail membrane (uropatagium) between the foot and the tail

Callosity: a hard or thickened area or protuberance on the skin of some whale species

Canid: a member of the carnivorous Canidae mammal family, which includes dogs, wolves and jackals

Canine: one of four basic kinds of mammalian teeth; a unicuspid tooth located immediately behind the incisors; often has a prominent conical crown; also a term pertaining to dogs

Carnassial: pair of large opposing teeth that act as scissors to shear meat and tendons and to crack bones

Carnivore: flesh eater (meat is the primary component of its diet); member of the mammalian order Carnivora

Castoreum Gland: anal gland of the beaver that secretes a waxy substance called castoreum, which was once used in the production of perfume

Cecum: a blind pouch of the digestive tract; often very large in herbivorous mammals, it is the site of bacterial action on the cellulose

Cervid: a member of the artiodactyl ruminant family Cervidae, the deer family, that is distinguished from all other ruminants by the possession of antlers

Cetacean: whale; member of the mammalian order Cetacea

Cheek Teeth: collectively refers to the molar and premolar teeth situated behind the canines

Chevron: two diagonal stripes meeting at an angle like a V or an inverted V as in the colour pattern of the finback whale

Chordata: the highest phylum in the animal kingdom; all vertebrates are members of this phylum

Chromosome: a complex threadlike nuclear body composed primarily of DNA and protein; carries the linearly arranged genetic units

Class: a taxonomic category that is a division of a phylum and is separated into orders

Clavicle: collarbone

Climax: a more or less stable biotic community which is in an equilibrium with the surrounding environmental conditions and which represents the terminal stage of an ecological succession

Cloaca: a common chamber into which the intestinal tract and reproductive and urinary ducts open; the cloacal opening is the only opening in amphibians, birds, reptiles, some fish and some mammals

Competition: a relationship in which the use of resources by one organism reduces the amount available to other organisms

Convergence, Convergent Evolution: development of similarities between animals or plants that are distantly related, resulting from adaptation to similar habitats, as opposed to possession of similarities due to descent from a common ancestor

Coprophagy: feeding on excrement

Copulatory Plug: see Mating Plug

Coterie: a social group of animals that defends a common territory against members of other coteries (e.g., prairie dog coteries)

Cowper's Glands: compound tubular glands in front of a male's prostate gland that discharge into the urethra; also known as the bulbourethral glands

Crepuscular: active during the periods of half-light at dawn and dusk

Cricetid: a member of the rodent family Cricetidae, including rats, some mice, hamsters and voles

Crustacean: animal belonging to the class Crustacea (part of the phylum Arthropoda); includes crabs, lobsters, shrimp, sow bugs and water fleas

Cursorial: adapted for running

Delayed Implantation: the process whereby the early embryo remains dormant in the uterus, resulting in the period of pregnancy being longer than the period during which the embryo is actually developing

Deleterious Recessive Genes: defective genes that are not expressed when a functional copy of the gene exists in the same body

Den Up: to retire into a den for a long period of sleep in winter but without the same internal temperature drop that "true hibernators" experience

Dental Formula: a simple method for expressing the number and kind of teeth in mammals; the number of teeth in each jaw is expressed like a fraction, the first figure showing the number in the upper jaw and the second figure the number in the lower jaw; the first fraction indicates incisors, followed by canines, premolars and molars

Dentition: the collective arrangement of teeth, used to characterize particular species

Dew Claw: a vestigial digit on the foot of a mammal; it does not reach the ground

Dimorphism: existing in 2 separate forms (different from polymorphism, which means several distinct forms)

Dispersal: outward spreading of animals from their previous home range or birthplace, often as they reach maturity

Display: a behaviour pattern or signal that conveys information to others, usually to members of the same species (e.g., threat, courtship or greeting displays)

Diurnal: active during day

Dominance Order: dominance hierarchy; a social order of dominance sustained by aggression or other behaviour patterns

Dominant: the highest-ranking individual in a dominance hierarchy

Dormancy: a state of relative metabolic slowdown, such as hibernation

Dorsal: located near or on the back of an animal

Dorsum: the entire dorsal surface of an animal's body

Echolocation: a process in which echoes are used to locate objects; highly developed in most bats and whales

Ecology: the study of the relationships between living things, with each other and with their environment

Ecosystem: a community of organisms and their physical environment

Ectoparasitism: a parasite that lives on the outside surface of its host

Ectotrophic: obtaining nourishment externally without marked penetration into the food source

Eimer's Organs: projections on the muzzles of moles, which are sensitive to touch

**Enaliarctids:** members of the extinct family Enaliarctidae, which evolved 22 million years ago from a group of terrestrial ursid carnivores; they lived in the North Pacific seas and evolved into walruses, fur seals and sea lions

**Epidermis:** outermost layer of cells of a plant or animal

**Epoch:** a major interval of geological time; a subdivision of a period

**Facultative:** assuming a particular role or mode of life but not restricted to that condition

**Falcate:** sickle-shaped

**Fast Ice:** coastal sea ice that is attached to the shore, an ice wall or an ice front and therefore remains fast

**Fecundity:** the capacity for producing young

**Fenestrate:** having openings

**Flehmen:** a German word used to describe a facial expression often associated with animals sniffing out scent marks or olfactory cues; the lips are pulled back, the head is lifted, the nose is wrinkled, and the teeth may chatter

**Flukes:** the rear extremities, or caudal fin, of a whale

**Food Chain:** a sequence of organisms on successive trophic levels within a community through which energy is transferred by feeding; energy enters the food chain by primary producers (green plants) and passes to primary consumers (herbivores) and then to the secondary and tertiary consumers (carnivores)

**Forb:** a broad-leaved herb

**Form:** a depression in the ground or ground vegetation used as a nest or shelter (usually by a rabbit or a hare)

**Fossorial:** adapted for burrowing and life underground

**Fulvous:** tawny coloured

**Funk Hole:** a shallow hole in which an animal hides when frightened, like those on the border of the home range of the Ord's kangaroo rat

**Fusiform:** compact and tapered; refers to body forms with shortened projections and no abrupt constrictions

**Gene Pool:** the total genetic information of a population

**Genus:** a taxonomic category that includes groups of closely related species; the principal subdivision of a family

**Gestation:** the period of development between fertilization of egg and birth

**Gestation Period:** the time between fertilization of egg and birth

**Grazer:** a herbivore that feeds on grass

**Gregarious:** tending to socialize and to form social groups

**Guano:** an accumulation of seabird or bat droppings rich in phosphates and nitrates; sometimes sold commercially as fertilizer

**Guard Hairs:** long, relatively coarse hairs that project beyond and therefore lie over the underfur

**Habitat:** a particular area in which a species lives

**Harem Group:** a group of females associated with a single male that tries to prevent other males from mating with them

**Haul-Out:** the action of seals and walruses pulling themselves out of the water; haul-out site is the actual location at which pinnipeds leave the water

**Haemoglobin:** the iron-containing oxygen-carrying protein molecule in the red blood cells of vertebrates

**Herb:** any green flowering plant, not a shrub or tree

**Herbivore:** an animal that eats only vegetation

**Heteromyid:** a member of the family Heteromyidae, which belongs to the order Rodentia; includes the North American kangaroo mice and pocket mice

**Hibernaculum:** winter quarters; applied to any structure that helps organisms to withstand cold weather

**Hibernation:** the condition of decreased physical and metabolic activity in which some organisms pass the winter, thereby lowering their energy requirements

**Hierarchy (social or dominance):** a system whereby a society is comprised of two or more levels; based on the outcome of interactions that show some individuals to be dominant

**Hindgut Fermenter:** herbivores in which the bacterial breakdown of swallowed plant tissue occurs in the cecum and not in the rumen, or foregut

**Hock:** the tarsal joint of the hind limb of perissodactyl and artiodactyl mammals

**Home Range:** the entire area in which an individual moves around (generally excluding migrations), irrespective of whether or not the area is defended from other animals, as in a territory

**Honest Advertisement:** a display, behaviour or morphology that cannot be easily faked by an animal and is therefore a reliable indicator to other individuals of the animal's fitness

**Hybrids:** offspring of parents of different species

Implantation: the fertilized egg attaching itself to the wall of the uterus

Incest: interbreeding between closely related animals

Incisor: the tooth in front of the canine tooth, often chisel-like

Induced Ovulation: ovulation that is triggered by copulation, rather than occurring spontaneously

Infanticide: the killing of infants

Insectivore: an animal that eats insects and small terrestrial or aquatic arthropods or other invertebrates; a member of the mammalian order Insectivora

Interfemoral Membrane: web of skin between the hind legs of bats, which frequently encloses the tail; also called the uropatagium

Interspecific: between two or more distinct species (e.g., interspecific competition)

Intraspecific: between individuals or populations of the same species (e.g., intraspecific competition)

Invertebrate: an animal lacking a backbone and internal skeleton

Jacobson's Organ: an olfactory canal in the palate of many vertebrates that ends in a blind pouch; it is highly developed in reptiles and is vestigial in humans

Keratin: a tough protein with a high sulphur content occurring in the epidermis of vertebrates; forms hair, feathers, horny scales, nails, claws, hooves and the resistant outermost layer of skin

Kin Selection: natural selection acting on one or more individuals and favouring or disfavouring the survival and reproduction of relatives (other than offspring) that possess the same genes by common descent

Krill: a name applied to the shrimplike crustaceans that constitute the diet of many baleen whales

Lactation: secretion of milk by the mammary glands

Lagomorph: a member of the mammalian order Lagomorpha; includes rabbits, hares and pikas

Laminar Flow: the streamlined movement of water in which water particles appear to move in smooth paths and one layer of water slides over another; the flow of water over the surface of a whale is laminar

Leporid: a member of the Leporidae family in the order Lagomorpha; includes rabbits and hares

Lobtailing: the action of a whale beating the surface of the water with its flukes, possibly to communicate

Mammal: a member of the vertebrate class Mammalia, characterized by mammary glands and a body covering of hair

Mammary Glands: milk-secreting organs

Mammilla: the nipple on the mammary gland of a female mammal through which milk is passed from the mother to her young

Marsupial: having a pouch; a member of the order Marsupialia

Marsupium: a fold of skin that forms a pouch enclosing the mammary glands on the abdomen of most female marsupials; the young are housed and fed in this pouch for a considerable time after birth

Masseter Muscle: a large cheek muscle that inserts into the lower jaw

Mast: nuts that are used as forage

Mast Year: a year in which seed production is exceptionally high (usually followed by a longer period during which few seeds are produced)

Mating Plug (also known as copulatory plug): a plug formed by male glandular secretions in the vagina of some female mammals

Matriarchy: a system of social organization in which descent is traced primarily through the female line

Mechanoreceptor: a receptor that provides the organism with information about mechanical changes, such as movement, tension and pressure

Microhabitat: a small specialized habitat; microenvironment

Midden: piles of fodder or conifer cones that rodents collect and store for use in winter; also a site for regular deposition of feces by mammals

Migration: periodic movement of animals to new climatic areas or habitats for breeding or feeding purposes

Monoestrous: having one oestrus, or heat period, in a breeding season

Monogamy: a mating system in which individuals have only one mate per breeding season

Monotremes: a member of the mammalian order Monotremata; represented today by the duck-billed platypus and the spiny anteater; reproduces by means of eggs, and mammary glands are reduced to enlarged sweat glands

Morphology: the structure and form of an organism

Mortality: death rate as a proportion of the population; expressed as a percentage or as a fraction

Musk Gland: a large scent gland of mammals such as the skunk and muskox that produces secretions which have a musky odour

Mycorrhizal: a mutual association between a fungus and the root system of a plant

Myoglobin: an iron-containing protein pigment (a variation of haemoglobin) occurring in muscle fibre

Mystacial Vibrissae: bristly hairs (whiskers) found on the snout of a mammal

Nape: the back part of the neck

Nares: the openings of the nose

Natural Selection: the principal mechanism of evolutionary change by which some individuals contribute more offspring to the succeeding generations than other individuals; if the traits influencing the genetic contribution of individuals have an inherited basis, they will spread in a population and thereby change the composition of the population

Nepotism: showing favouritism to a relative

Nocturnal: active at night

Nuchal: pertaining to the dorsal area immediately behind the head or back of the neck of mammals

Obligate: binding, necessary or essential

Ochraceous: a brownish yellow or rusty yellow colour

Odontocete: a member of the suborder Odontoceti, the toothed whales

Oestrous Cycle: the physiological changes that take place between periods of oestrus

Oestrus: the period in female mammals during which ovulation occurs and the animal is receptive to mating

Olfactory: pertaining to the sense of smell

Omnivore: an animal that feeds on both plants and animals

Otariid: a member of the pinniped family Otariidae, which contains the sea lions

Ovulation: the shedding of a ripe egg from the ovary, where it is produced, to the fallopian tubes

Pack Ice: sea ice formed into a mass by the crushing together of ice floes that have been broken up by wind and waves

Palmate: shovel-shaped; a good example is the massive antlers of male moose

Pelage: the covering or coat of a mammal, such as hair, fur or wool

Pelagic: pertaining to the upper layer of water in the open ocean

Perissodactyl: a member of the order Perissodactyla, odd-toed herbivorous ungulates; includes horses, tapirs and rhinoceroses

Pheromones: chemical substances secreted by an animal that influence the behaviour or development of other animals

Phocid: a member of the family Phocidae, which contains the true seals

Phylogeny: the evolutionary or ancestral history of organisms

Phylum: a major taxonomic category used in classifying animals

Physiology: study of the activities that occur in the cells and tissues of living organisms

Pinniped: a member of the order Pinnipedia; includes true seals, eared seals and walruses

Placenta: a structure composed of maternal and fetal tissues that ensures a supply of nutrients to the fetus and allows for the elimination of its waste products by interchange

through the membrane of the uterus of the mother; in all mammals except the monotremes, which lay eggs, and the marsupials, which have a rudimentary placenta

Plantigrade: walking with the whole sole of the foot touching the ground (as in humans and bears)

Pleistocene: a geological epoch of the Quaternary period, originating about 1 million years ago and characterized by Ice Ages

Pod: a cohesive social group of whales

Polyandrous: a mating system in which a female mates with several males during a breeding season

Polygamous: a mating system in which an individual has more than one mate during a breeding season

Polygynous: a mating system in which a single male mates with several females during a breeding season

Polymorphism: the co-occurrence of several different morphological forms in a population

Pouch: a flap of skin found on the belly of female marsupials that covers the mammillae

Precocial: young born relatively mature at birth, requiring only a short period of parental care

Predator: an organism that forages for live organisms (prey), killing them for food

Prehensile: adapted for gripping

Premolar: a tooth in front of the true molars (a maximum of 4 on each side of the upper and lower jaws of placental mammals, 16 in all)

Proboscis: the flexible elongated snout of certain mammals

Procyonid: a member of the family Procyonidae, which contains raccoons

Promiscuous: a mating system in

which an individual mates more or less indiscriminately with no subsequent pair bond

Prostate: a gland of the male reproductive system of mammals that surrounds the urethra and contributes substances to semen

Quaternary: relating to the geological period from the end of the Tertiary to the present time, about 1 1/2 million years

Rabies: viral disease affecting the nervous system; usually fatal; most commonly transmitted to humans and other animals by the bite of a rabid animal

Race: subspecies or microspecies; a taxonomic division linking populations with similar distinct characteristics

Radio-Tracking: a method used to study an animal's movements and current location in which a radio transmitter, attached to the animal, sends out signals that are picked up by a directional antenna

Raptor: bird of prey

Refection: eating incompletely digested fecal pellets to ensure complete digestion; used by hares, rabbits and the common shrew

Retractile: capable of being drawn back into a protective sheath, like the claws of cats

Rhizome: an underground horizontal stem

Rorqual: family of whales; derived from the old Norwegian words *ror hval*, referring to the grooves that run from just behind the lower lip to the chest; includes blue, fin, sei, humpback and minke species

Rostrum: a beak or a beaklike projection

Rufous: reddish brown colour

Rumen: the first of four large digestive chambers of the ruminant mammal's stomach

Ruminant: a herbivorous mammal with a specialized digestive tract that allows it to regurgitate and chew cud to macerate vegetation, which is then swallowed and broken down by symbiotic bacteria in the stomach

Rut: breeding or mating season, usually in reference to male hoofed animals

Scatter Hoard: to store items individually over a wide area

Scent Mark: a site where scent-gland secretions, urine or feces are deposited; can refer to the actual secretions or the action of leaving such secretions

Scrotum: the pouch that contains the testes

Sedentary: applies to mammals that tend to occupy a small home range and do not migrate or disperse very far, if at all

Selective Pressure: environmental factor that results in natural selection and therefore affects the reproductive success of individuals

Seral Stages: the developmental stages of an ecological succession

Sexual Dimorphism: differences in shape, size, coloration and armament between the sexes of a species

Siblings: brothers and/or sisters

Specialist: an animal that has special adaptations to a life style

Spermaceti: whitish fatty substance in the head cavity, or melon, of sperm whales

Springing, or Nuchal, Ligament: an elastic ligament reaching from the nape area to the seventh cervical vertebra

Spy Hopping: a behaviour used by some cetaceans to look for landmarks or a coastline when migrating; the whale rises vertically from the surface of the water until its head is clear and stays like this for several seconds, sometimes turning on its axis

Subfamily: a division of a family

Suborder: a division of an order

Subterranean: living or occurring underground

Successional: the geological, ecological or seasonal sequence of species within a habitat or community

Symbiosis: an interrelationship between two different species or organisms that is to the mutual advantage of both

Taiga: northernmost coniferous forest, characterized by long, cold winters, relatively cool summers and moderate to high annual precipitation; in North America, it occurs generally south of the permafrost line

Talus: a sloping mass of rock fragments, usually at the base of a cliff

Tapetum Lucidum: a reflecting layer behind the retina of the eye; chiefly in nocturnal mammals

Tarsal: pertaining to the terminal joints of a limb

Tarsal Bone: a bone in the vertebrate leg commonly called the ankle bone

Taxonomy: the science of classifying organisms in a way that best reflects similarities and differences; as a result, each organism is a member of the seven major taxonomic categories — kingdom, phylum, class, order, family, genus, species

Temporalis: a muscle used for chewing

Territory: the portion of an animal's home range that it actively defends

Tertiary: a geological period; from approximately 65 million to 1 1/2 million years ago

Thermoregulation: regulation of an animal's body temperature

Tine: the terminal pointed subbranches of an antler

Torpor: a temporary sluggish condition in some mammals to reduce energy expenditure in periods of cold or food shortage; akin to short-term hibernation

Tragus: a small projection in front of a bat's ear

Trophic: of or relating to nutrition

Tubercule: a small knoblike prominence

Tundra: a barren, treeless area supporting Arctic or alpine vegetation composed of low shrubs, herbs, grasses, mosses, lichens, etc.; between the northern upper tree limit and the lower limit of perennial snow on mountains

Underfur: the thick soft fur lying beneath the longer and coarser guard hairs of a mammal

Uterus: the organ of gestation in mammals in which the fertilized egg is retained and fetal development occurs

Vector: an individual or species that transmits diseases

Velus: extremely fine, downy hairs covering the body of some mammals

Venter: belly or abdomen

Ventral: on or near the lower or anterior surface of an animal

Vibrissae: stiff tactile hairs on the wrist or face of a mammal

Warren: an area of uncultivated ground where many rabbits breed

Zooplankton: microscopic animals that move passively near the surface of the sea

# BIBLIOGRAPHY

The literature on mammals is vast, and there would be little point in listing even a fraction of it. Instead, this bibliography will suggest some books that are available to the average reader who wishes to know more about animal ecology and behaviour. Many of the sources can be found in public libraries, and virtually all of them are included in university library collections. Some of the books are simply references for identifying or finding out more about the range of an animal, but most of them are well-written books about mammals and animal behaviour, ecology and evolution.

## ANIMAL BEHAVIOUR, ECOLOGY AND EVOLUTION

The first book in this section, *Animal Behaviour: An Evolutionary Approach* by John Alcock, is highly recommended. It assumes relatively little background knowledge of biology and is clearly and elegantly written. It should be read before all the others. A good follow-up would be the books of Richard Dawkins, starting with *The Selfish Gene*. S.J. Gould's *Ethology* is a more mechanistic account of behaviour.

For an overview of the basic principles of evolutionary ecology and behaviour, few books surpass E.O. Wilson's *Sociobiology*. A more specialized and sophisticated treatment is found in Krebs and Davies' *Behavioural Ecology*, which gives a good impression of the kinds of problems that behavioural ecologists study. In order to understand how this sort of biology developed, Sparks' *The Discovery of Animal Behaviour* is a highly readable account. Sebeok's *How Animals Communicate* is a good reference book that indicates some of the range of animal-communication abilities and some problems for study.

For those who would enjoy making a contribution to the field of animal behavioural ecology, there are two good how-to books listing techniques and methods of observation, one by P.N. Lehner and one edited by D. McFarland.

The books by Stephen J. Gould are recommended because they are so well written and because Gould stresses the historical development of science and the pitfalls and problems of doing science. These essays, although highly personal and often opinionated, are also a good introduction to some of the larger questions in evolution.

**Alcock, J.** *Animal Behaviour: An Evolutionary Approach*, 3rd Edition. Sinauer Associates Inc. Publishers, Sunderland, Massachusetts, 1984.

**Darwin, C.** *On the Origin of Species by Means of Natural Selection.* John Murray, London, 1859.

**Darwin, C.** *The Descent of Man and Selection in Relation to Sex*, 2 Volumes. Appleton, New York, 1871.

**Dawkins, R.** *The Selfish Gene.* Oxford University Press, New York, 1978.

**Dawkins, R.** *The Extended Phenotype: The Gene as the Unit of Selection.* W.H. Freeman and Company, Oxford, 1982.

**Fagen, R.** *Animal Play Behaviour.* Oxford University Press, New York, 1981.

**Gould, J.L.** *Ethology: The Mechanisms and Evolution of Behaviour.* W.W. Norton & Company, New York, 1982.

**Gould, S.J.** *Ever Since Darwin.* W.W. Norton & Company, New York, 1977.

**Gould, S.J.** *The Panda's Thumb.* W.W. Norton & Company, New York, 1980.

**Gould, S.J.** *Hen's Teeth and Horse's Toes.* W.W. Norton & Company, New York, 1983.

**Krebs, J.R. and N.B. Davies** (eds.). *Behavioural Ecology: An Evolutionary Approach.* Sinauer Associates Inc. Publishers, Sunderland, Massachusetts, 1978.

**Lehner, P.N.** *Handbook of Ethological Methods.* Garland STPM Press, New York, 1979.

**McFarland, D.** (ed.). *The Oxford Companion to Animal Behaviour.* Oxford University Press, New York, 1981.

**Sebeok, T.A.** (ed.). *How Animals Communicate.* Indiana University Press, Bloomington, 1977.

**Sparks, J.** *The Discovery of Animal Behaviour.* Little Brown and Company, Boston, 1982.

**Wilson, E.O.** *Sociobiology.* The Belknap Press of Harvard University Press, Cambridge, Massachusetts, 1975.

## GENERAL MAMMALOGY REFERENCE BOOKS

Most libraries will have some or all of these books, which are useful for looking up more facts and figures on mammals. A book I highly recommend for the average reader is David Macdonald's *The Encyclopedia of Mammals* — a beautiful overview of mammals around the world.

**Anderson, S. and J. Knox Jones Jr.** (eds.). *Orders and Families of Recent Mammals of the World.* John Wiley & Sons, Inc., New York, 1984.

**Chapman, J.A. and G.A. Feldhamer.** *Wild Mammals of North America: Biology, Management and Economics.* The Johns Hopkins University Press, Baltimore, Maryland, 1982.

**Gotch, A.F.** *Mammals — Their Latin Names Explained: A Guide to Animal Classification.* Blandfield Press, Poole, England, 1979.

**Macdonald, D.** (ed.). *The Encyclopedia of Mammals.* Facts on File Publications, New York, 1984.

**Matthews, L.H.** *The Life of Mammals*, Volume 1. Weidenfeld and Nicolson, London, 1969.

**Matthews, L.H.** *The Life of Mammals*, Volume 2. Weidenfeld and Nicolson, London, 1971.

**Nowak, R.M. and J.L. Paradiso** (eds.). *Walker's Mammals of the World*, 4th Edition. Volumes 1 & 2. The Johns Hopkins University Press, Baltimore, Maryland, 1983.

**Savage, A. and C. Savage.** *Wild Mammals of Western Canada.* Western Producer Prairie Books, Saskatoon, Saskatchewan, 1981.

**Seton, E.T.** *Life-histories of Northern Animals.* Charles Scribner's Sons, New York, 1909.

**Stoddart, D.M.** (ed.). *Ecology of Small Mammals.* John Wiley & Sons, Inc., New York, 1979.

**Vaughan, T.A.** *Mammalogy.* W.B. Saunders Company, Philadelphia, 1972.

## SPECIFIC TOPICS

These books will be useful for those who wish to delve further into some of the topics discussed in the small essays in this book. Many of them are rather technical, but *How Animals Work* by K. Schmidt-Nielsen is a book that most naturalists will find worthwhile.

**Albone, E.S.** *Mammalian Semiochemistry: The Investigation of Chemical Signals Between Mammals.* John Wiley & Sons Limited, Chichester, 1984.

**Finerty, J.P.** *The Population Ecology of Cycles in Small Mammals: Mathematical Theory and Biological Fact.* Yale University Press, New Haven, Connecticut, 1980.

**Kurten, B. and E. Anderson.** *Pleistocene Mammals of North America.* Columbia University Press, New York, 1980.

**Lyman, C.P., J.S. Willis, A. Malan and L.C.H. Wang.** *Hibernation and Torpor in Mammals and Birds.* Academic Press, Inc., New York, 1982.

**Martin, P.S. and H.E. Wright Jr.** (eds.). *Pleistocene Extinctions: The Search for a Cause.* Yale University Press, New Haven, Connecticut, 1967.

**Peters, R.H.** *The Ecological Implications of Body Size.* Cambridge University Press, Cambridge, Massachusetts, 1983.

**Purves, P.E. and G.E. Pilleri.** *Echolocation in Whales and Dolphins.* Academic Press, Inc., New York, 1983.

**Schmidt-Nielsen, K.** *How Animals Work.* Cambridge University Press, Cambridge, Massachusetts, 1972.

## RECOMMENDED GENERAL ACCOUNTS OF MAMMALS

All of the books listed in this section are worth reading at least in part. They are a tiny fraction of what is available. Some are included for specific reasons. Erich Hoyt's *Orca: The Whale Called Killer* not only is highly enjoyable to read, for instance, but is a perfect example of the valuable contribution that can be made by people who are not professional academics but are simply interested in observing and thinking about nature.

Some books are listed for contrast. For example, if one compares Peterson's respected book on moose — state of the art when it was published in 1955 — with the books by Valerius Geist or Clutton-Brock and his collaborators, one can see how rapidly the science of mammalogy and related disciplines are progressing.

*Chiroptera*
**Fenton, M.B.** *Just Bats.* University of Toronto Press, Toronto, 1983.

**Hill, J.E. and J.P. Smith.** *Bats: A Natural History.* University of Texas Press, Austin, 1984.

**Kunz, T.H.** (ed.). *Ecology of Bats.* Plenum Press, New York, 1982.

*Rodentia*
**Woods, S.E. Jr.** *The Squirrels of Canada.* National Museums of Canada, Ottawa, 1980.

*Carnivora*
**Craighead, F.C. Jr.** *Track of the Grizzly.* Sierra Club Books, San Francisco, 1979.

**Fox, M.W.** (ed.). *The Wild Canids: Their Systematics, Behavioral Ecology and Evolution.* Van Nostrand Reinhold Company, New York, 1975.

**Harrington, F.H. and P.C. Paquet** (eds.). *Wolves of the World: Perspectives of Behavior, Ecology and Conservation.* Noyes, Park Ridge, New Jersey, 1982.

**Klinghammer, E.** *The Behavior and Ecology of Wolves.* Garland, New York, 1978.

**Koch, T.J.** *The Year of the Polar Bear.* Bobbs and Merrill, New York, 1975.

**Lawrence, R.D.** *The Ghost Walker.* McClelland and Stewart, Toronto, 1983.

**Mech, L.D.** *The Wolf: The Ecology and Behavior of an Endangered Species.* University of Minnesota Press, Minneapolis, 1970.

**Powell, R.A.** *The Fisher: Life History, Ecology and Behavior.* University of Minnesota Press, Minneapolis, 1982.

**Wayre, P.** *The Private Life of the Otter.* B.T. Batsford Ltd., London, 1979.

*Pinnipedia*
**King, J.E.** *Seals of the World,* 2nd Edition. British Museum (Natural History), London, 1983.

**Peterson, R.S. and G.A. Bartholomew.** *The Natural History and Behavior of the California Sea Lion.* Special Publication No. 1. The American Society of Mammalogists, 1967.

**Ridgway, D.H. and R.J. Harrison** (eds.). *Handbook of Marine Mammals;* Volume 1: The Walrus, Sea Lions, Fur Seals and Sea Otter; Volume 2: Seals. Academic Press, London, 1981.

*Cetacea*
**Gaskin, D.E.** *The Ecology of Whales and Dolphins.* Heinemann Educational Books Ltd., London, 1982.

**Herman, L.M.** (ed.). *Cetacean Behavior: Mechanisms and Functions.* John Wiley & Sons, Inc., New York, 1980.

**Hoyt, E.** *Orca: The Whale Called Killer.* Camden House Publishing Ltd., Camden East, Ontario, 1981.

*Artiodactyla*
**Calef, G.** *Caribou and the Barren-Lands.* Canadian Arctic Resources Committee, Ottawa, 1981.

**Chadwick, D.H.** *A Beast the Colour of Winter: The Mountain Goat Observed.* Sierra Club Books, San Francisco, 1983.

**Clutton-Brock, T.H., F.E. Guinness and S.D. Albon.** *Red Deer: Behavior and Ecology of Two Sexes.* University of Chicago Press, Chicago, 1982.

**Geist, V.** *Mountain Sheep: A Study in Behavior and Evolution.* University of Chicago Press, Chicago, 1971.

**Peterson, R.L.** *North America Moose.* University of Toronto Press, Toronto, 1955.

## SCIENTIFIC JOURNALS

There is no reason why scientific journals should be read only by professional scientists. Once one learns the jargon, many papers can be of interest to the average nature lover. And in some journals, amateur naturalists make a significant contribution to every issue. This is true of the *Canadian Field Naturalist*, which is relatively easy to read. The other journals often are more theoretical and more mathematical. However, if one reads them after digesting the books listed in the animal behaviour section, then much more of it will be comprehensible.

Don't try to read an entire issue. The important point is to pick and choose. If a special animal or topic is of interest, it may be more profitable to search out specific papers listed in reference sources, such as *Biological Abstracts* or *Zoological Record*, that are available at most larger libraries.

*The American Naturalist.* The American Society of Naturalists, University of Chicago Press, 5801 Ellis Avenue, Chicago, Illinois 60637; monthly

*Animal Behaviour.* Bailliere Tindall, 1 Vincent Square, London SW1P 2PN, U.K.; quarterly

*Behavioral Ecology and Sociobiology.* Springer Verlag, 175 Fifth Avenue, New York, New York 10010; 2 volumes per year, 4 numbers per volume

*The Canadian Field-Naturalist.* Ottawa Field-Naturalists' Club, Box 3264, Station C, Ottawa, Ontario K1Y 4J5; quarterly

*Canadian Journal of Zoology.* National Research Council of Canada, Research Journals, Ottawa, Ontario K1A 0R6; monthly

*Ecology.* The Ecological Society of America, Arizona State University, Tempe, Arizona 85287; bimonthly

*Evolution.* The Society for the Study of Evolution, Dr. R.E. Beer, University of Kansas, Entomology Department, Lawrence, Kansas 66045; quarterly

*Journal of Wildlife Management.* Wildlife Society, 5410 Grosvenor Lane, Bethesda, Maryland 20814; quarterly

*Journal of Mammalogy.* American Society of Mammalogists, c/o Dr. Gordon L. Kirkland Jr., Vertebrate Museum, Shippensburg, Pennsylvania 17257; quarterly

*Oecologia.* International Association for Ecology, Springer Verlag, 175 Fifth Avenue, New York, New York 10010; 4 volumes per year, 3 numbers per volume

## IDENTIFICATION AND LIFE-HISTORY GUIDES

*The Audubon Society Field Guide to North American Fishes, Whales and Dolphins.* Alfred A. Knopf, Inc., New York.

*The Audubon Society Field Guide to North American Mammals.* John O. Whitaker Jr., Alfred A. Knopf, Inc., New York, 1980.

**Baker, R.H.** *Michigan Mammals.* Michigan State University Press, Detroit, 1983.

**Banfield, A.W.F.** *The Mammals of Canada.* University of Toronto Press, Toronto, 1974.

**Burt, W.H. and R. P. Grossenheider.** *A Field Guide to the Mammals of America North of Mexico.* The Peterson Field Guide Series. Houghton Mifflin Company, Boston, 1952.

**Hoyt, E.** *The Whales of Canada.* Camden House Publishing Ltd., Camden East, Ontario, 1984.

**Hoyt, E.** *The Whale Watcher's Handbook.* Penguin/Madison Press, Toronto, 1984.

**Jones, J.K. Jr., D.M. Armstrong, R.S. Hoffmann and C. Jones.** *Mammals of the Northern Great Plains.* University of Nebraska Press, Lincoln, Nebraska, 1983.

**Katona, S.K.V., V. Rough and D.T. Richardson.** *A Field Guide to the Whales, Porpoises and Seals of the Gulf of Maine and Eastern Canada: Cape Cod to Newfoundland.* Charles Scribner's Sons, New York, 1983.

**van Zyll de Jong, C.G.** *Handbook of Canadian Mammals;* Volume 1: Marsupials and Insectivores. National Museums of Canada, Ottawa, 1983.

**van Zyll de Jong, C.G.** *Handbook of Canadian Mammals;* Volume 2: Bats. National Museums of Canada, Ottawa, 1985.

## CONSERVATION

**Bush, B.C.** *The War Against the Seals: A History of the North American Seal Fishery.* McGill-Queen's University Press, Montreal, 1985.

**Lopez, B.H.** *Of Wolves and Men.* Charles Scribner's Sons, New York, 1979.

**Mowat, F.** *Sea of Slaughter.* McClelland and Stewart, Toronto, 1984.

**Roe, F.G.** *North American Buffalo: A Critical Study of the Species in Its Wild State,* 2nd Edition. University of Toronto Press, Toronto, 1970.

**Small, G.L.** *The Blue Whale.* Columbia University Press, New York, 1971.

# INDEX

# ACKNOWLEDGMENTS

**CONTENTS**
3 Michael H. Francis

**INTRODUCTION**
5 Erich Hoyt; 7 Jerry Pavia

**CLOVEN-HOOFED MAMMALS**
8-9 Michael H. Francis; 11 Lewis Bevan; 12-13 George Calef; 14 Rick McIntyre/Tom Stack & Associates; 15 Ronald M. Curtis/The Stock Market Inc.; 16 Tim Fitzharris; 17 Alan G. Nelson/Tom Stack & Associates; 18 Wayne Lynch/Masterfile; 19 Tom W. Hall; 20 Murray O'Neill; 21 W. Perry Conway/Tom Stack & Associates; 22 Brian Milne/Animals Animals; 23 Jacob Formsma/Network Stock Photo File; 24 Jeff Foott; 25 Tom W. Hall; 26 Patrick McGinley; 27 Michael H. Francis; 29 Mark Newman/Tom Stack & Associates; 30 Wilf Schurig; 31 Michael H. Francis; 32 Jeff Foott; 33 Michael H. Francis; 34-36 Jeff Foott; 37 Tom W. Hall; 38 Mike Pirnke; 39 Jeff Foott; 40 Wilf Schurig; 41 Brian Milne/Animals Animals; 42 Tom W. Hall; 43 Patrick Morrow; 44 Mike Pirnke; 45 Bill McRae; 46 Karvonen Films Ltd.; 47 Fred Bruemmer

**WHALES, DOLPHINS & PORPOISES**
49 G. Williamson/Bruce Coleman, Inc.; 50 Richard Sears/MICS Photo; 51 Jeff Foott; 52 M. A. Hobson; 53-54 Larry Foster*; 55 C.C. Lockwood/Animals Animals; 56 Fred Bruemmer; 57 Russ Kinne, The National Audubon Society Collection/Photo Researchers, Inc.; 58 Larry Foster*; 59 Fred Bruemmer; 61 Erich Hoyt; 62-63 Jeff Foott; 64 Erich Hoyt; 65 top Jeff Foott, bottom Maurice Lafreniere/Corbima; 66 Larry Foster*; 67 Alan D. Briere/Tom Stack & Associates; 68 Larry Foster*; 69 top Jeff Foott; bottom Larry Foster*; 70-72 Larry Foster*; 73 Jeff Foott/Tom Stack & Associates; 75 Richard Sears/MICS Photo; 76-80 Larry Foster*; 81 Jeff Goodyear/The Stock Market Inc.; 82 Richard Sears/MICS Photo; 85 Dotte Larsen/Bruce Coleman, Inc.; 86 Larry Foster*; 87 Dotte Larsen/Bruce Coleman, Inc.; 88 Larry Foster*; 89 Dotte Larsen/Bruce Coleman, Inc.

**SEALS & SEA LIONS**
90-91 Jeff Foott; 93 Wayne Lynch; 94 Tim Fitzharris; 95 Jeff Foott; 97 Karvonen Films Ltd.; 98-99 Mark Newman/Tom Stack & Associates; 101 Dykstra Photo/The Stock Market Inc.; 102 Jeff Foott; 103 Robert McCaw; 104 George Halton, The National Audubon Society Collection/Photo Researchers, Inc.; 105 Jeff Foott; 106 Norman R. Lightfoot; 107 Rod Allin/Tom Stack & Associates; 108 Norman R. Lightfoot; 109 C. Ray, The National Audubon Society Collection/Photo Researchers, Inc.; 110 Norman R. Lightfoot; 111-113 Jeff Foott

**MEAT EATERS**
114-115 Wilf Schurig; 117 Alan Carey; 118 Tom W. Hall; 119 Richard P. Smith/Tom Stack & Associates; 120 Alan Carey; 121 Wolfgang Bayer/Bruce Coleman, Inc.; 122 Jeff Foott; 123 Tom W. Hall; 124 Stephen J. Krasemann/DRK Photo; 125 Leonard Lee Rue III; 126 D. Horwood; 127 top Tom W. Hall, bottom Bruno Massenet/Corbima; 128 Gary R. Jones; 129-130 Jeff Foott; 131 Jim Brandenburg/The Stock Market Inc.; 133 Alan Carey; 134 Jeff Foott; 135 Rick McIntyre/Tom Stack & Associates; 136 Alan Carey; 137 top Bill Everitt/Tom Stack & Associates, bottom Tim Fitzharris; 138 George Calef; 139 Fred Bruemmer; 140 Larry Halverson; 141 Wayne Lankinen/Bruce Coleman, Inc.; 143 Tim Fitzharris; 144 Rod Allin/Tom Stack & Associates; 145 Arnold Zageris; 147 Jeff Foott; 148 John Eastcott/Yva Momatiuk/DRK Photo; 149 Gary Milburn/Tom Stack & Associates; 150 Alan Carey; 151 Leonard Lee Rue III; 152 Alan Carey; 153 Patrick Morrow; 154 Nadine Orabona/Tom Stack & Associates; 155 Thomas W. Kitchin; 156 Wilf Schurig; 157 top Jeff Foott, bottom Gary Milburn/Tom Stack & Associates; 158 Wayne Lynch/Masterfile; 159 Leonard Lee Rue III; 160 Tim Fitzharris; 161 Jeff Foott; 162 Leonard Lee Rue III; 163 Alan Carey; 164 Leonard Lee Rue III; 165 Chuck Gordon; 166 Leonard Lee Rue IV/Leonard Lee Rue Enterprises; 167 Stephen J. Krasemann/DRK Photo; 168 E.P.I. Nancy Adams/Tom Stack & Associates; 169 top Tim Fitzharris, bottom Tom Cajacob/Mn. Zoo; 170 Jeff Foott; 171 M.A. Hobson; 173 Tim Fitzharris; 174 Alan Carey; 175 Leonard Lee Rue III; 176 Larry Halverson; 177 Alan Carey; 178 Wayne Lynch/Masterfile; 179 Alan Carey

**RODENTS**
180-181 Alan Carey; 183 Joseph Van Wormer/Bruce Coleman, Inc.; 185 Erika Thimm/The Stock Market Inc.; 186 Robert McCaw; 187 Leonard Lee Rue III; 188 top Thomas W. Kitchin, bottom Roger Hostin; 189 Thomas W. Kitchin; 190 Tom W. Hall; 191 Tim Fitzharris; 192 Tom Cajacob/Mn. Zoo; 193 Rod Planck/Tom Stack & Associates; 194 Jeff Foott; 195 Wilf Schurig; 196 Chuck Gordon; 197 Robert McCaw; 198 Tim Fitzharris; 199 top and middle Tom W. Hall, bottom Wayne Shiels/Four Winds Prairie Photography; 200 top Cris Crowley/Tom Stack & Associates, bottom John Gerlach/Tom Stack & Associates; 201 V. Clarehout; 202 Leonard Lee Rue III; 203 Jeff Foott; 204 John Shaw/Tom Stack & Associates; 205 B.T. Aniskowicz; 206 Bill Ivy; 207 top Wilf Schurig, bottom Thomas W. Kitchin; 208 Bob Breler/Corbima; 209 top M.A. Hobson, bottom Leonard Lee Rue III; 210 top Thomas W. Kitchin, bottom Bristol Foster; 211 Gary Milburn/Tom Stack & Associates; 212 Tim Fitzharris; 213 Rod Planck/Tom Stack & Associates; 214 Chuck Gordon; 215 Tim Fitzharris; 216 Thomas W. Kitchin; 217 Mike Pirnke; 219-223 Jeff Foott; 225 Stephen J. Krasemann/DRK Photo; 226 Alan Carey; 227 top Stephen Krasemann/DRK Photo, middle Wilf Schurig, bottom Tom W. Parkin; 229 Larry Brock/Tom Stack & Associates; 231 Alan Carey; 232 Tom Cajacob/Mn. Zoo; 233 Tom W. Hall; 234 Tom Cajacob/Mn. Zoo; 235 G.C. Kelley/Tom Stack & Associates; 237 John Gerlach/Tom Stack & Associates; 239 R.C. Simpson/Tom Stack & Associates; 240 Halle Flygare; 241 top Bristol Foster, bottom Karvonen Films Ltd.; 242 Edgar T. Jones; 243 Bristol Foster; 244 Rod Planck/Tom Stack & Associates; 247 Duane Sept; 249 M.A. Hobson; 251 Dave Elphinstone; 253 Thomas W. Kitchin; 254 Leonard Lee Rue III; 255 E.P.I. Nancy Adams/Tom Stack & Associates; 256 Rod Planck/Tom Stack & Associates; 257 Leonard Lee Rue III; 259 Dwight Kuhn; 260 E.P.I. Nancy Adams/Tom Stack & Associates; 261 Jeff Foott

**RABBITS, HARES & PIKAS**
262-263 Pat Halligan; 265 Jackie Gilmore; 267 Robert McCaw; 268 Leonard Lee Rue III; 269 Bill Ivy; 270 Leonard Lee Rue III; 271 R. Hamaguchi; 272 Alan Carey; 273 Michael H. Francis; 274 Douglas F. MacDonald; 275 C.W. Perkins

**BATS**
276-277 Jeff Foott; 278 Brock Fenton; 279 Kerry T. Givens/Tom Stack & Associates; 280 Jeff Foott; 281 J. Woods; 283 R.C. Simpson/Valan Photo; 284 David M. Dennis/Tom Stack & Associates; 285 top Brock Fenton, bottom Paul Geraghty/National Museum of Natural Sciences**; 286-289 Paul Geraghty/National Museum of Natural Sciences**; 290 Wayne Lankinen/DRK Photo; 291 Brock Fenton; 292 top John Gerlach/DRK Photo, bottom Brock Fenton; 293 Paul Geraghty/National Museum of Natural Sciences**; 294 Brock Fenton; 295 Herman H. Giethoorn/Valan Photo; 296-297 Paul Geraghty/National Museum of Natural Sciences**; 299 Wayne Lankinen/DRK Photo

**INSECTIVORES**
300-301 Jeff Foott; 303 Stouffer Productions Ltd./Animals Animals; 304 Norman Lightfoot/Miller Services; 305 Brenda Carter/National Museum of Natural Sciences***; 306 Don & Pat Valenti/DRK Photo; 307 Stouffer Productions Ltd./Animals Animals; 308 Breck Kent/Animals Animals; 309 Dwight Kuhn; 310 Brenda Carter/National Museum of Natural Sciences***; 311 John Gerlach/DRK Photo; 312 Dwight Kuhn; 313 Don & Pat Valenti/DRK Photo; 314-315 Brenda Carter/National Museum of Natural Sciences***; 316 top R.C. Simpson/Tom Stack & Associates, bottom Brenda Carter/National Museum of Natural Sciences***; 317 Brenda Carter/National Museum of Natural Sciences***; 319 Dwight Kuhn; 320 D. Cavagnaro/DRK Photo; 321 Ted Levin/Animals Animals; 322 Brenda Carter/National Museum of Natural Sciences***; 323 Dwight Kuhn; 324 Brenda Carter/National Museum of Natural Sciences***; 325 top Rod Planck/Tom Stack & Associates, bottom Bruce A. Macdonald/Animals Animals

**MARSUPIALS**
326-327 Wayne Lynch/Masterfile; 329 R.C. Simpson/Valan Photo; 330 Stephen J. Krasemann/Valan Photo; 331 Jack Dermid/Bruce Coleman, Inc.; 332 R.C. Simpson/Valan Photo; 333 Wayne Lynch/Masterfile

*Whale illustrations courtesy of the Sierra Club. Excerpted from *The Sierra Club Handbook of Whales and Dolphins* by Stephen Leatherwood and Randall R. Reeves, Sierra Club Books, San Francisco, 1983.

**Bat illustrations courtesy of the National Museum of Natural Sciences. Excerpted from *Handbook of Canadian Mammals, Volume 2: Bats*, by C.G. van Zyll de Jong, National Museum of Natural Sciences, National Museums of Canada, Ottawa, 1985.

***Insectivore illustrations courtesy of the National Museum of Natural Sciences. Excerpted from *Handbook of Canadian Mammals, Volume 1: Marsupials and Insectivores*, by C.G. van Zyll de Jong, National Museum of Natural Sciences, National Museums of Canada, Ottawa, 1983

# totally cool
# ORIGAMI
# ANIMALS

# totally cool

# ORIGAMI
# ANIMALS

**Ann Kristen Krier**

Sterling Publishing Co., Inc.
New York

Prolific Impressions Production Staff:

Editor in Chief: Mickey Baskett
Copy Editor: Phyllis Mueller
Verses: Phyllis Mueller
Graphics: Dianne Miller, Karen Turpin
Styling: Lenos Key
Photography: Jerry Mucklow
Administration: Jim Baskett

Library of Congress Cataloging-in-Publication Data

Krier, Ann Kristen, 1962-
  Totally cool origami animals / Ann Kristen Krier.
       p. cm.
  Includes index.
  ISBN-13: 978-1-4027-2448-0
  ISBN-10: 1-4027-2448-9
1.  Origami.  2.  Animals in art.  I. Title.
TT870.K678 2007
736'.982--dc22

2006029593

2  4  6  8  10  9  7  5  3  1

Published by Sterling Publishing Co., Inc.
387 Park Avenue South, New York, NY 10016
© 2007 by Prolific Impressions, Inc.
Distributed in Canada by Sterling Publishing
c/o Canadian Manda Group, 165 Dufferin Street,
Toronto, Ontario, Canada M6K 3H6
Distributed in the United Kingdom by GMC Distribution Services,
Castle Place, 166 High Street, Lewes, East Sussex, England BN7 1XU
Distributed in Australia by Capricorn Link (Australia) Pty. Ltd.
P.O. Box 704, Windsor, NSW 2756, Australia

Printed in China
All rights reserved

ISBN-13: 978-1-4027-2448-0
ISBN-10: 1-4027-2448-9

For information about custom editions, special sales, premium and corporate purchases, please contact Sterling Special Sales Department at 800-805-5489 or specialsales@sterlingpub.com.

# About the Author

Ann Kristen Krier is a professional creative designer who specializes in developing new techniques for crafters. A seamstress since the age of 10, she maintains an extensive private resource library of creative journals filled with project ideas for paper, sewing, collage, and beading. This mixture expresses her innate ability for "cross-crafting." Her design work often includes many mediums used in harmony.

Ann has spent the majority of her professional business career in an industry that thrives on differentiation. From creative sales techniques to marketing the invisible, she is focused on sharing her creativity through writing. *Totally Cool Animal Origami* is her third book, joining two other paper titles. Ann's three books focus on designs that can be enjoyed by people of different skill levels, from children just beginning to craft to seasoned adult crafters.

Originally from upstate New York, Ann Kristen Krier lives in the Piedmont Region of North Carolina with her devoted husband, Jim, the younger two of her three children, and their golden retriever, Murphy. In addition to creative endeavors, Ann enjoys skiing, camping, hiking, and kayaking.

# CONTENTS

# ORIGAMI
# An Ancient Folding Art

Origami is as old as paper itself. Late in the 6th century, Buddhist monks brought papermaking to Japan and perhaps with it brought origami. While it is not known exactly where the paper folding art was invented or who invented it, it has become synonymous with the Japanese culture.

In the 8th century, Arabic cultures learned papermaking and brought their recipes for making paper to Spain in the 12th century. Since the Muslim religion forbade the creation of representational figures, Arabic paper folding forms existed as a means for mastering mathematics and geometry. When the Arabs left Spain, their geometric folded paper shapes remained. Those techniques evolved into the paper-folding art called *papiroflexia,* which remains popular in Spain and Argentina.

Origami, the common name used for the art of paper folding, took root in 1880. It is derived from two Japanese words, *oru* (to fold) and *kami* (paper). Yoshizawa Akira, a Japanese master of the art of origami, is considered by many to be the forefather of modern origami shapes. Akira organized traditional origami using the symbols that classify the art today, giving them names and assigning categories to take the art to its foundation, the folded base. This creates tasks that are easily learned.

This book uses the same principles, with forms that develop from simple beginner projects to advanced ones by building on fundamentals learned earlier. While the animals are categorized by perceived level of difficulty, some children may excel while others decide the art is not for them. Each person (and each child) perceives difficulty in his or her own way. The ratings are not a measure of ability, but rather a set of progressions.

# Origami Papers

Origami uses beautiful thin papers in a variety of patterns and solid colors. Their thinness allows you to fold them easily. Origami paper is generally found in sheets 7" or 5-7/8" square, though some sheets are as large as 10" square or as small as 2" square. The paper comes in packages of 20 to 50 sheets in a wide variety of colors and patterns. Unbleached and unsized, origami paper is one of the finest archival papers available.

Solid colors typically are packaged in color collections (jewel tones, pastels, bright neons). Most are colored on one side and white on the other; double-sided papers are colored on both sides. Patterned origami papers are available in a vast assortment of designs, including animal prints.

## ADDITIONAL SUPPLIES

In addition to origami paper, you need only a few additional supplies to create the projects: **paper scissors** for cutting and trimming, a **ruler** for measuring, and a **pencil** for marking.

# Basic Folding Techniques

All folds in the Projects section are defined with pictures. However, some folds that have names in traditional origami are explained here:

## BEND

Match the edges of the paper, but do not crease or mark. This will result in a soft curve.

## CREASE

To press along the fold with your fingers. This is done to smooth down the fold or to make a permanent line in the paper.

## FOLD

Match the edges of the paper, and eventually crease.

## FOLD DIAGONALLY

*Usually used in the beginning of a form.*
Fold across the paper from corner to corner. This turns a square into two triangles (one in front and one in back). Every square has two diagonals.

## FOLD IN HALF

Fold across the paper, meeting top to bottom or left to right. This creates two smaller rectangles or, if folded in both directions, creates four squares or quadrants. Every square has two sets of halves: top and bottom *or* left and right.

## REVERSE FOLD

*Used frequently for heads, beaks, tails, and legs or feet.*
Fold and crease the form where you wish the reverse fold to begin (change direction). When done

with two triangles and opened up, your form will show a diamond shape with a fold in the center. Push the center fold of the diamond in the opposite direction of its current fold. (Many times the area that is being used in a reverse fold has been previously folded in the opposite direction.). It becomes a fold in the reverse direction of its original fold.

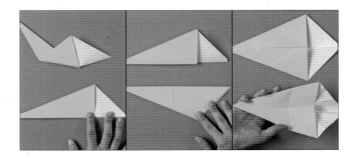

## SQUASH FOLD

*Used frequently for ears and appendages such as feet, flippers, and fins.*
Crease a triangle at its base in both directions. The longest folded edge of the triangle (not the base) will become the center of this fold. By pushing the longest side (fold) of the triangle and flattening it against the base form, a diamond shape is created. This is the squash fold.

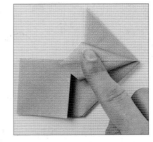

# Animal Origami Projects

**Animals, animals, large and small
From field and forest, sky and sea,
Animals, animals, you can make the all,
When you learn the art of origami.**

## Tips for Working with Children

- Patience, patience, patience!

- Try making the animals yourself before you begin working with children. Understanding the steps will make it easier for you to assist children as they learn.

- Allow children to try each step several times. If they become overwhelmed, use a piece of blank paper to cover the steps immediately following those they are working on. It will help them focus on the task at hand.

- If a child becomes upset, take a break!

- If a child becomes frustrated, switch to an easier project. Achieving good results at an easier level will help a child build confidence to attempt the more difficult folds.

The animal origami projects in this book are divided into three categories—beginner, intermediate, and advanced. Beginner projects are the most simple, intermediate projects are more difficult, and advanced projects are the most complicated. Projects for all three categories include step-by-step photos and instructions.

For most of the animals, 7" square origami paper is recommended, but paper sizes can be adjusted as you wish. If an animal is shown folded from a 7" square, in most cases it is perfectly fine to use a smaller or larger square, although most younger children will enjoy the experience more if they begin with a larger-size paper. (If a smaller square is not appropriate for the particular animal, it is noted in the instructions.)

# Piggy Head

The piggy's head is where we start—
It's easier than you think.
Just fold the face, then fold the ears;
Except for the snout, he's totally pink.

## 1

Fold a 7" square piece of pink origami paper in half in both directions.

Unfold.

Fold the top edge toward the center.

## 2

EARS:
To make the ears, begin at the center line and fold back on a diagonal toward the opposite corner.

## 3

Fold up the right bottom corner of paper square up toward the center, leaving 1" of space between the fold line of the ears and the turned-up corner.

Repeat on left side.

## 4

Turn form over.

## 5

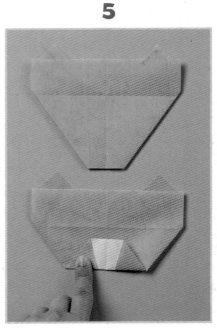

Fold up bottom to create the snout. Add google eyes, if desired.

# Cat Head

Try tiger-stripe paper in yellow and black
To make the head of a jungle cat.
Fold the pointed ears and the triangle mouth—
You'll be finished in no time flat!

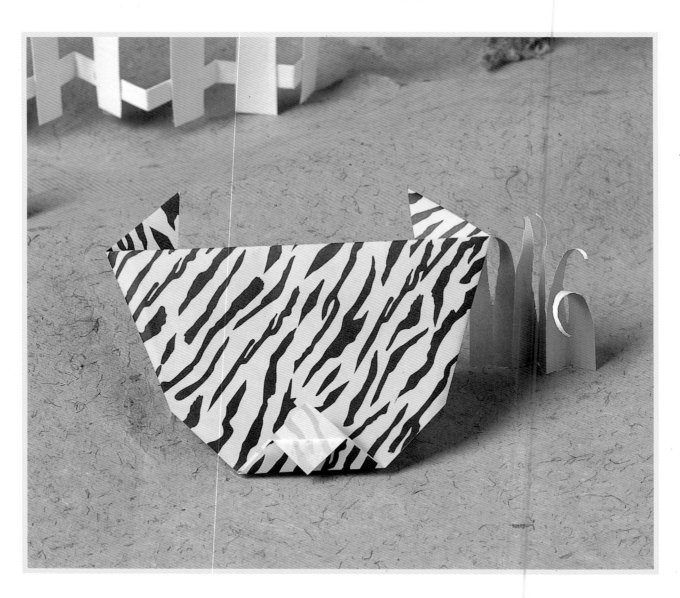

# CAT HEAD

**1**

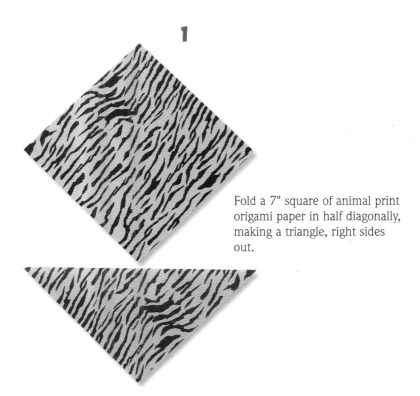

Fold a 7" square of animal print origami paper in half diagonally, making a triangle, right sides out.

**2**

Fold the right side up. (This is one ear.)

**3**

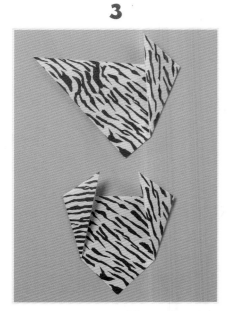

Fold the left side up. (This is the other ear.)

**4**

Turn over the form.

Fold up the lower part of the head, using both thicknesses of paper.

**5**

Fold down the top of the triangle. This makes the cat's nose and mouth.

Add whiskers and google eyes, if desired.

# Doggie Head

This doggie's head has long pointed ears
That cover the sides of her face.
The brown and white paper is creased to the points
So they stand up precisely in place.

# DOGGIE HEAD

## 1

Fold a 7" square of spotted origami paper in half diagonally, making a triangle, right sides out.

## 2

Fold down the right side. (This is one ear.)

## 3

Fold down the left side. (This is the other ear.)

## 4

On the front, fold a small triangle towards the wrong side (white side of the paper).

Turn the form over and fold in a small triangle towards the white side of the paper.

## 5

Open up the ears (the left and right triangles).

Make squash folds by holding on to the tops of the triangles and squashing them in place.

Add google eyes, if desired. 🐾

**1**

Follow instructions for Cat Head, steps 1 through 3, using a 7" square piece of origami paper, red on one side, white on the other.

Unfold the ears.

Fold back the top layer of the paper 1/4" on one side.

Repeat on the opposite side.

Fold the ears back into place.

Turn over the form.

**2**

# Fox Head

**Begin as you did for the head of the cat**
**To make a fox head, a bulldog, or cow**
**With different papers and finishing folds**
**You can master these variations now.**

◀ MOUTH:
To make the mouth, fold up the top layer of the head into a small triangle at the bottom. 🐾

20

# Variations

## Bull Dog Head

Use a 7" square of orange and white paper and follow the instructions for the Cat Head, but fold up a larger triangle at the bottom and fold down a smaller triangle for the mouth.

## Cow Head

Use spotted paper. Follow the instructions for the Cat Head, steps 1 through 4. Turn under the point of the triangle on the bottom.

# Rainbow Caterpillar

Cut strips of paper
And fold them just so
To make a caterpillar colored
Just like a rainbow.

## 1

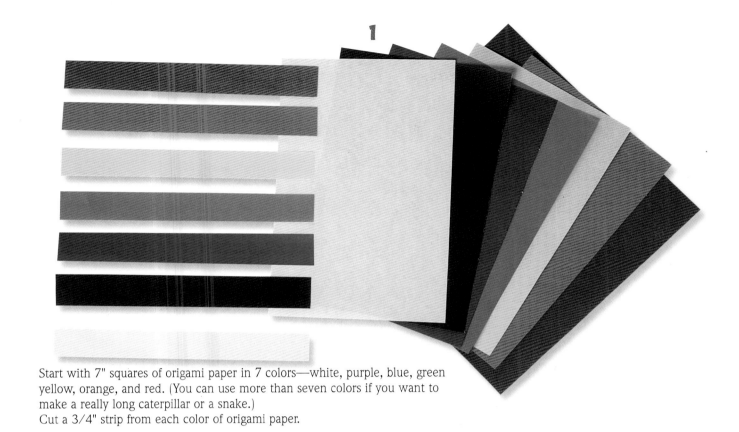

Start with 7" squares of origami paper in 7 colors—white, purple, blue, green yellow, orange, and red. (You can use more than seven colors if you want to make a really long caterpillar or a snake.)
Cut a 3/4" strip from each color of origami paper.

## 2

## 3

Bend strip in center, bringing ends toward one another. Holding the strip off the work surface, cross the left side over the right side.

Just as you would tie your shoelaces, tie the paper in a knot.

## 4

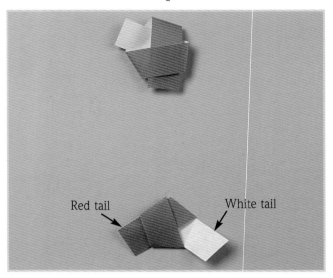

Red tail          White tail

Flatten the knot by creasing the edges.

Trim each end of the knot to 1/2".

Repeat steps 2 through 4 for each strip of paper.

## 5

To make the head, fold one tail back toward the shape and tuck it inside the knot to secure. (Our head is white.)

## 6

Place the knots in order on your work surface.

## 7

Insert the orange tail of the orange knot into the red knot over the white tail.

## 8

Repeat the process, inserting the yellow tail of the yellow knot into the orange knot.

## q

Repeat – adding the green, blue, and purple knots.

Turn over the caterpillar.

Tuck the tails of the knots into the folds of the connecting knots.

## 10

Add the head. Tails can be secured with glue if desired.

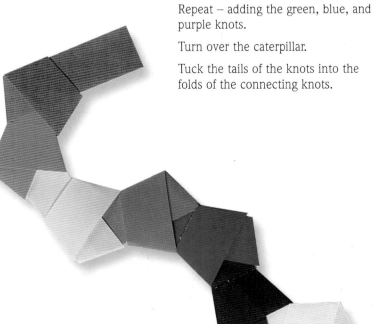

The caterpillar is complete!

# Clams

**Find clams of all sizes
On the ocean floor.
They are easy to fold
In colors galore.**

## Clam with Google Eyes

**Supplies**

Origami paper (1 piece for
   each clam)
2 google eyes
Scissors

**Instructions**

1. Make Clam following the folding instructions.
2. In the center of the top "shell," cut two V-shaped slits the size of the eyes, approximately 1" apart.
3. Fold up the V-shapes towards the front of the shell.
4. Apply the eyes.

**1**

Fold a 7" square of double-sided origami paper in half on the diagonal.

**2**

Fold in half again.

**3**

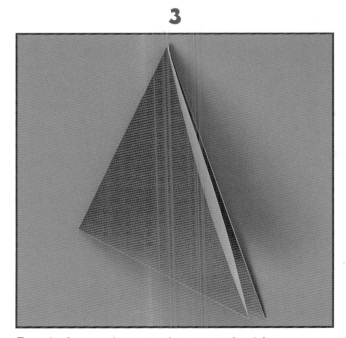

Turn the form so the open edges are on the right.

**4**

Open up form. The open edges are still on the right. Begin folding a fan pattern at top (back and forth) until the paper is used up.

**5**

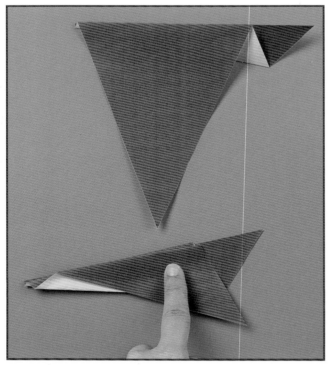

Here's another view of the folding process.

**6**

Round the two outside corners with scissors.

**7**

Cut off the tip on front, rounding the shape.

**8**

Open up the form and stretch gently to keep open.

*Pictured at right, top to bottom:* Clams of various sizes, Stingray

# Goldfish

**When you make this simple
Fish of gold,
You'll get to practice
The reverse fold.**

**1**

Fold a 7" square of origami paper diagonally.

Crease.

Unfold.

**2**

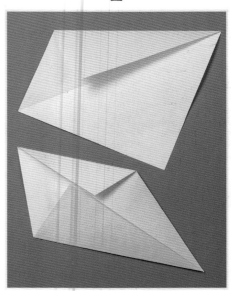

Fold down the top of the square.

Fold up the bottom of the square.

Fold down the left top.

30

### 3

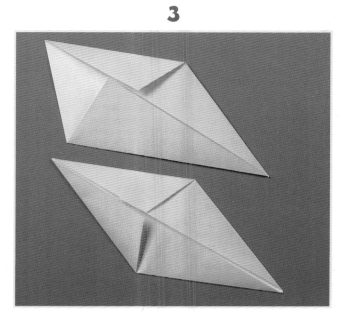

Fold up the bottom left.

### 4

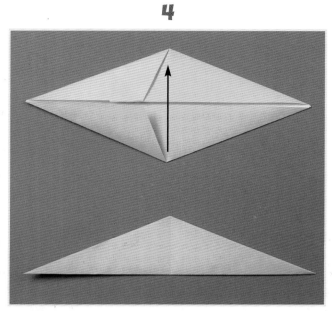

Fold the form in half by bringing the bottom half over the top half.

### 5

Fold the form in half, left to right.

Crease.

Unfold.

Fold up the left side to the center.

Crease.

### 6

Unfold.

Reverse fold.

Repeat on the right side—fold up, crease, unfold, and reverse fold.

### 7

Turn the form so the tails are on your right.

Reverse fold the top tail and crease.

Reverse fold the bottom tail and crease.

Your fish is ready to swim away!

# Grasshopper

A green paper grasshopper
Can be a fun toy.
Tap the end of its body,
Watch it jump for joy.

**1**

Fold a 7" square of green origami paper along the diagonal. Fold the triangle in half. (There are now two triangles, one on top of the other.)

**2**

Fold the top triangle in half.

**3**

Start at center of form and fold up the top two-thirds of the triangle.

**4**

Fold down the top of the triangle.

Line up the point of the triangle to the bottom of the fold.

Repeat steps 3 through 5 on the other (bottom) triangle.

# Mommy & Baby Penguins

To make this mommy and baby
Who live on the ice
Use different-sized paper
But fold the same—twice!

## 1

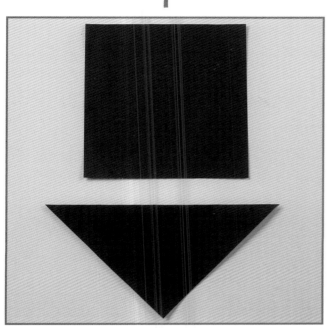

Use a 7" square for Mommy and a 4" square for baby. If you are using paper with different colored sides, fold it so the black is on the outside.

Fold the square of origami paper in half diagonally.

## 2

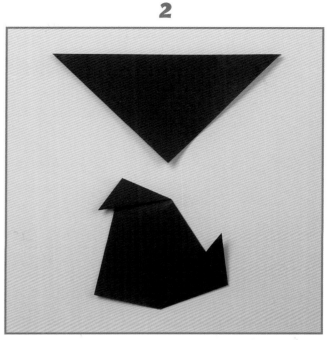

Fold down the top edge of the triangle to make the head.

Fold up the opposite end, creating the tail.

## 3

Unfold head.

Open up form.

Reverse fold head inside of the body.

## 4

With the form still open, fold the tail back toward the head.

Close the form.

Fold up the front corner on one side to create the belly.

## 5

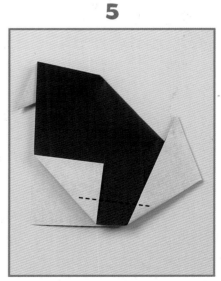

Fold up the bottom along the dotted line between the belly and the tail to create one foot.

Repeat 4 and 5 on the other side.

# Bat

Make this bat from a purple
Paper so deep
And hang upside down,
Like it does when it sleeps.

**1**

Fold a 7" square of origami paper in half. If you are using a paper with white on one side and dark on the other, fold with the white sides together.

Fold in half again, left to right.

**2**

Open.

Squash fold the left side, creating a triangle.

Turn over the form.

**3**

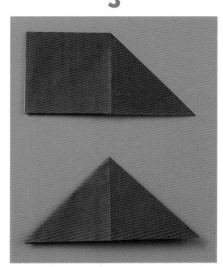

Squash fold the left side again. (This time you are working on the back side of the form.)

**4**

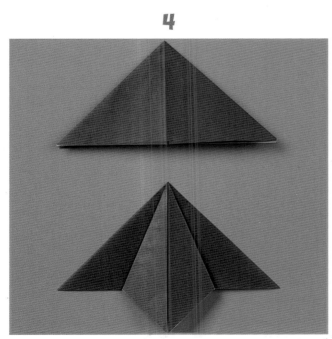

Fold the left and right sides of the top triangle toward the center so the outside edge lines up with the center fold. (This is the bat's body.)

**5**

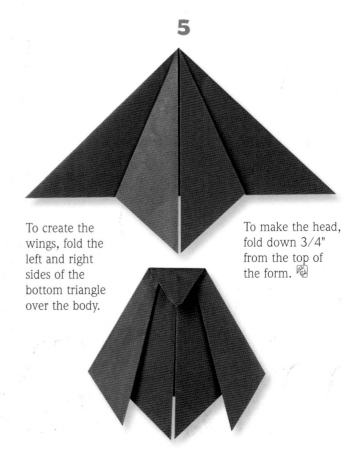

To create the wings, fold the left and right sides of the bottom triangle over the body.

To make the head, fold down 3/4" from the top of the form.

# Flying Butterfly

### This colorful butterfly
### Is ready to soar.
### When you've learned how to fold it,
### You'll want to make more.

### Playtime Ideas

• Make a small butterfly kite by threading a needle with clear monofilament fishing line. Sew through the center of a butterfly and tie to a piece of a dowel. Twirl in the air.

• Experiment with other types of folds on the wings (steps 11 and 12). Different types of folds will make the butterfly fly differently.

**1**

Begin with a 7" square of double-sided origami paper.

Cut it in half with scissors, creating two rectangles, each 3-1/2" x 7"

**2**

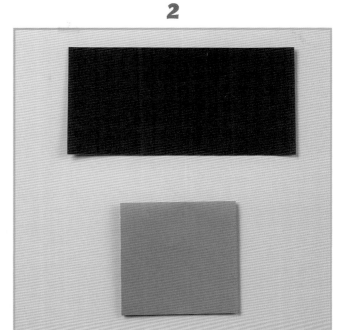

Fold one rectangle in half.

Crease.

**3**

Unfold.

Fold up the right side diagonally toward the center.

**4**

Fold up the left side diagonally toward the center. Turn over the form.

▶▶▶

## 5

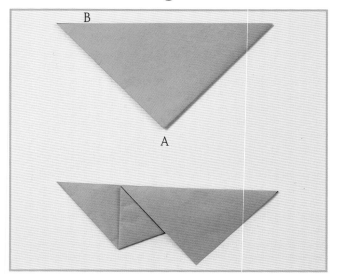

Hold the form in your hand.

Fold up the bottom point of the triangle (A) to meet the top edge (B), lining up the top edges.

A triangular flap from the back will come to the front.

Crease along the top edge and on the bottom **underneath** the triangular flap.

## 6

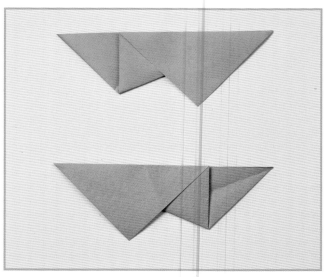

Unfold the last fold.

Repeat step 5 on the other side. (This also will form a flap.)

## 7

Pick up the form.

Gently pull the flap at the back right side toward the front. This will form a small triangle on the front of the form.

Fold and crease the small triangle to the left, as shown here.

Flip it to the right, as you would turn a page in a book.

Crease again.

## 8

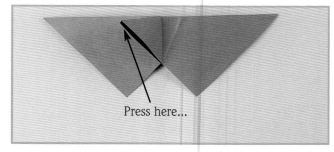

Press here...

Stand up the small triangle.

Squash fold by pressing on the triangle and forcing it open to make a diamond. The top butterfly in photo 9 shows the results of the squash fold.

Crease the edges.

## 9

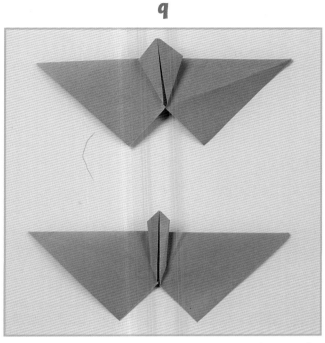

Fold under the edges of the diamond you created in step 8 to make the body of the butterfly.

## 10

Fold the entire form in half, with the body on top.

## 11

Crease

Fold the wings back to the front over the body.

Crease at the fold. This creates a little dimension between body and wings.

## 12

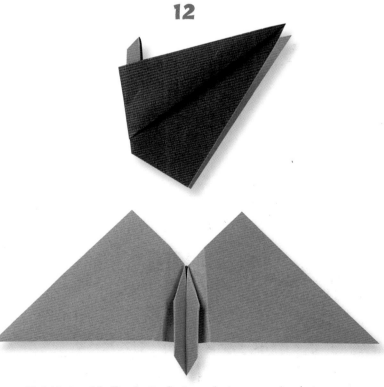

Unfold step 11. The butterfly is ready to soar—simply toss in the air as you would a paper airplane.

# Cardinal & Blue Jay

Fold the cardinal and jay,
Two fine feathered friends.
The steps are the same
Till you get to the end.

# CARDINAL & BLUE JAY

Steps 1 through 6 are the same for both birds.
Use red paper for the cardinal and blue paper for the blue jay.

**1**

Fold a square origami paper in half diagonally.

**2**

Unfold.

Fold the top half toward the center fold.

Fold the bottom half toward the center fold.

**3**

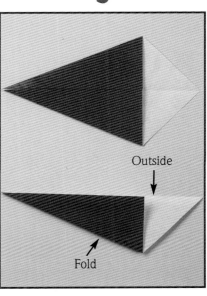

Fold on the center line so that the open edges of the paper are on the outside.

**4**

Reverse fold the tail so it is at a right angle to the body. See "Basic Folding."

**5**

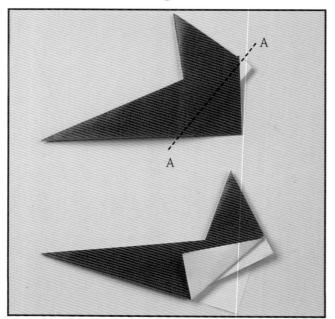

Fold up the top layer at A, creating a triangle for wings. Repeat on the other side.

**6**

Reverse fold the long pointed end, creating the head.

Reverse fold the small end of the head to create the beak.

*To complete the Cardinal,* go to step 7. *To complete the Blue Jay,* go to step 8.

**7**

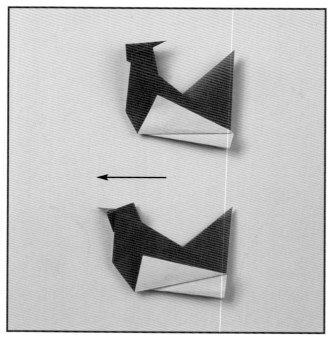

CARDINAL:
Reverse fold the beak one additional time and position to project straight from the body. This fold also will create the crest at the top of the head.

**8**

BLUE JAY:
Reverse fold the beak one additional time, positioning the beak so it points straight from the head.

Have an origami birthday party. Decorate presents and
cards for your friends with colorful origami animals.
You can also create one-of-a-kind party invitations
and decorations.

# Collie Dog

**The collie stands ready,**
**Guarding the farm,**
**Protecting livestock and children**
**From danger and harm.**

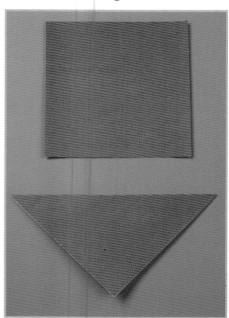

**1**

Fold a 7" square of origami paper in half diagonally. Fold it with the colored side out.

(A smaller collie can be created with a smaller 4" paper square.)

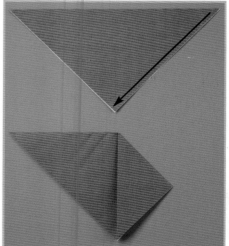

**2**

Fold the right side of the triangle toward the center. Match the point on the right side with the center point.

46

## 3

Fold the left side of the triangle toward the center, making a diamond.

Fold the diamond in half with the left side over the right side. The unfolded paper edges will be on the lower right.

## 4

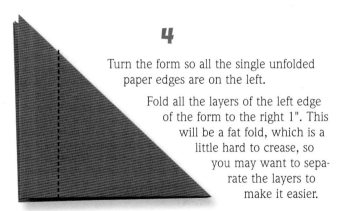

Turn the form so all the single unfolded paper edges are on the left.

Fold all the layers of the left edge of the form to the right 1". This will be a fat fold, which is a little hard to crease, so you may want to separate the layers to make it easier.

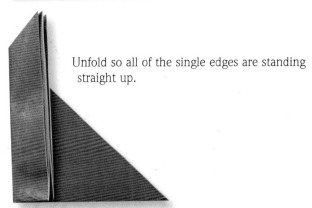

Unfold so all of the single edges are standing straight up.

## 5

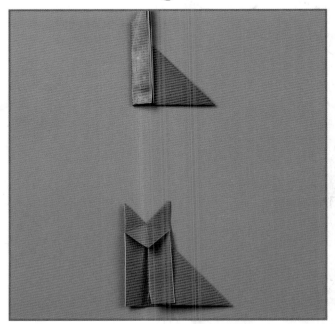

Open the left side and press flat with your finger.

Open the right side and press flat with your finger.

Squash fold the center to create the head.

## 6

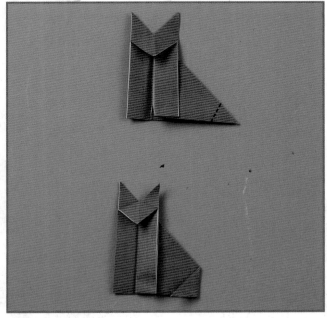

Roll the ears around a pencil to give them a slight curve.

Fold the end of the body to make the tail.

# House Mouse

A very long tail
Has this little mouse
Who may live in the field
Or live in the house.

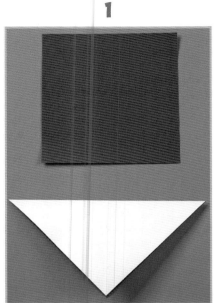

**1**

Fold a 7" square of origami paper in half in both directions.

Fold in half along both diagonals.

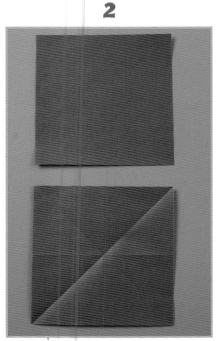

**2**

Crease and unfold.

## 3

Fold the paper in half at one center line with the right sides facing out and the open end at the bottom.

Reverse fold the right and left corners inside the form.

## 4

Fold the upper fold of the left side over the right side as though you were turning the page of a book. You will have 3 folded pages on the right.

Fold the top point to the back, lining up the edges along the bottom so the left side is the narrowest.

Fold the left side (the tail) to the right, creating a bend.

## 5

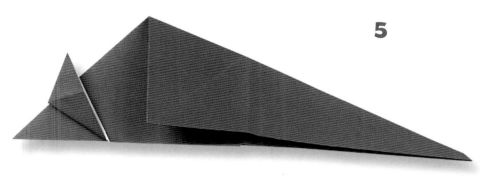

Turn the form over.

Fold up the left point to make one ear.

Squash fold the ear.

Fold the back point the same way to make the other ear. (The center point is the nose.)

# Stingray

Steer clear of the stingray,
Avoid without fail.
If you see one please don't touch
That venomous tail.

**1**

Fold a 7" square of origami paper along the diagonal, colored side in.

Fold in half.

Crease, then unfold the last fold.

Fold down the top on one side where shown by dotted line.

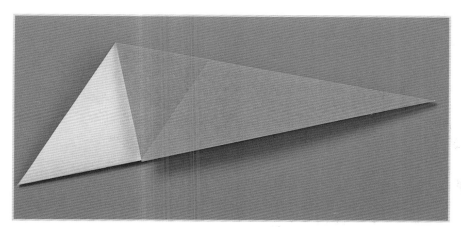

**2**

Turn over the form and repeat on the other side.

Edges line up at the bottom.

**3**

Open the center fold, placing it colored side up.

Fold the left edge to the right so that the point meets the crease. (The white side will show.)

Close the form on the center fold with the white part inside.

## 4

Fold the left end to the right where shown by dotted line, lining up with bottom edge.

Crease.

Unfold.

## 5

Fold down the top layer to the crease.

Crease.

Unfold.

Repeat on the bottom layer.

## 6

Lift the lower left corner of the form.

Reverse fold to the right.

**7**

Repeat on the other (back) side.

**8**

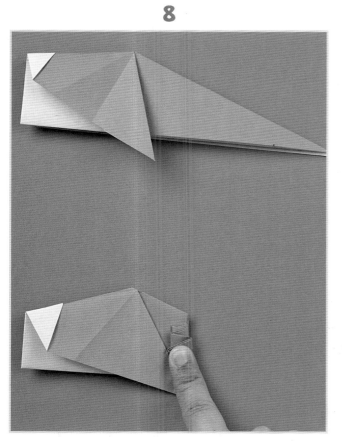

Fold the tail back and forth (like a fan).

**9**

Turn the form upright and gently pull on the end of the tail.
Pull up the rays, and he's ready to swim.

# Turtles

**A turtle's a reptile
That doesn't have teeth
The shell is on top
Feet, head, tail—they're beneath.**

**1**

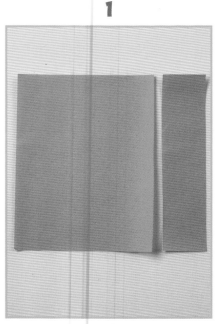

Cut 1-1/2" off one edge of a 7" square of origami paper.

You will begin folding with the large rectangle.

**2**

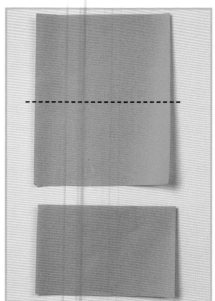

Fold the rectangle in half.

Crease.

**3**

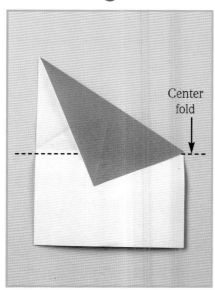

Unfold the rectangle.

Fold along the diagonal from one corner to the center fold line.

Crease.

Unfold.

**4**

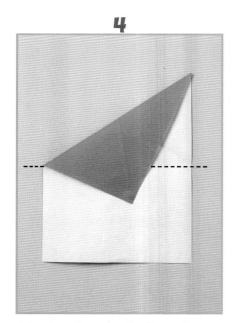

Fold along the opposite diagonal.

Crease.

Unfold.

Repeat on the second half of the rectangle.

**5**

Fold the form in half again along the original fold line.

**6**

Open the form.

Fold down the top half to the center fold.

Crease.

Unfold.

Fold the bottom half up to the center fold.

Crease. Unfold.

Turn the paper over.

Fold in half, white side out.

**7**

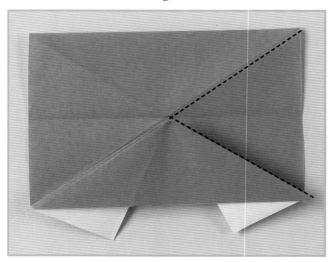

Reverse fold the ends of each half at the triangles of both ends. The colored side of the paper will be on the outside, and there will be two small white triangles.

Turn over the form.

Repeat the two reverse folds on either end of the other half.

**8**

Turn the form so the small white triangles are at the top.

Fold down the small white triangles on one side.

Crease.

Repeat on the other side.

**9**

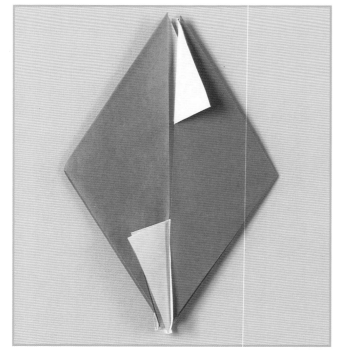

Open up the form.

Crease all the small white triangles on top.

**10**

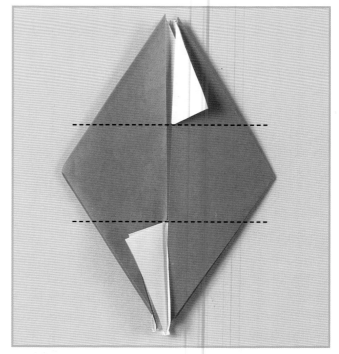

LEGS:
Lift up the left bottom and right bottom flaps.

Fold as shown on the dotted lines.

**11**

This photo shows the bottom flaps after folding.

**12**

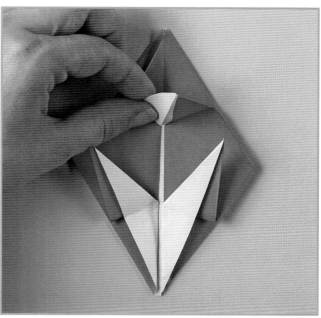

Fold down the left top flap.

**13**

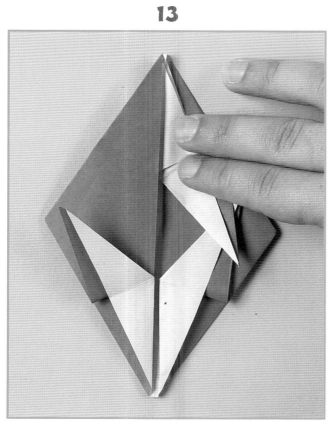

And fold down the right top flap.

**14**

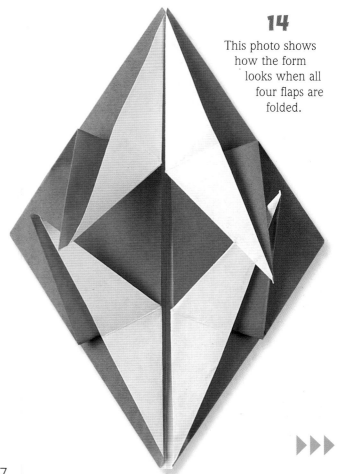

This photo shows how the form looks when all four flaps are folded.

▶▶▶

## 15

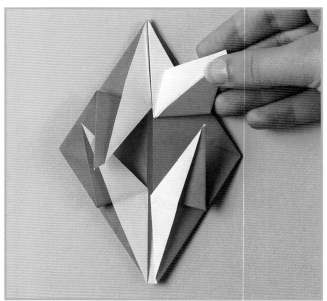

To complete the legs, pick up the right top flap and squash fold into place.

Repeat with the three remaining flaps to make the other three legs.

## 16

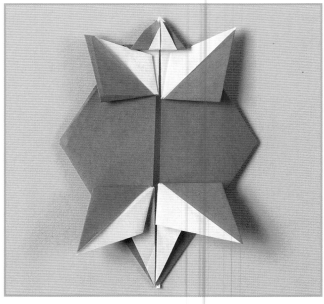

TAIL:
Fold down the top flap and crease.

Fold a small triangle from the same part up and crease.

## 17

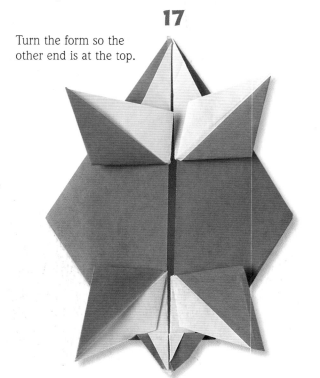

Turn the form so the other end is at the top.

HEAD:
Fold down the point at the top end and crease.

Fold a portion of the point back up and crease.

Turn over the turtle.

## 18

Crease the center to shape the shell.

Crease from the ends of that fold toward each of the four legs.

*Pictured clockwise from top:* Dragonfly, Turtle, Dragonfly, Turtle, Goldfish, Frog.

# Frogs

You can find frogs in ponds,
On rocks, and in trees.
With their camouflage colors
They're not easy to see.

**1**

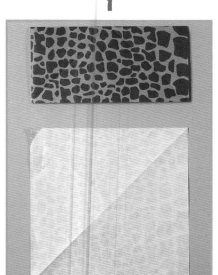

Fold a 7" square of animal print origami paper in half along one diagonal.

Unfold.

Fold the paper in half along the other diagonal.

Unfold.

**2**

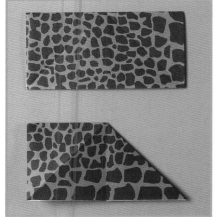

Fold in half across the middle.

Reverse fold the left side inside the form.

Reverse fold the right side.

**3**

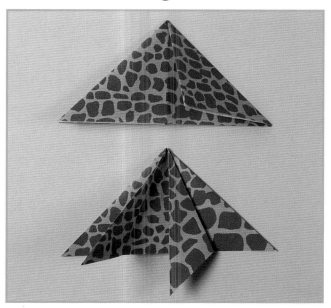

Fold one layer of the left side so the edges meet the center.

Repeat on the right side.

**4**

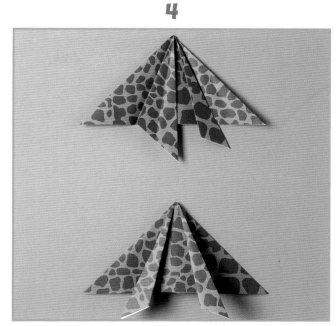

Fold back the right side in another triangle, aligning the edges. Repeat on the left.

**5**

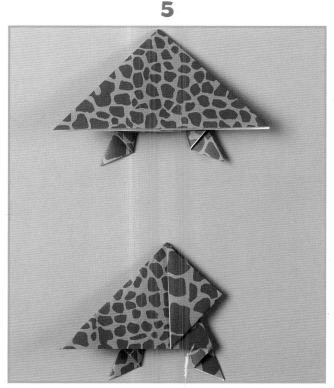

Turn over the form.

Fold up the right side toward the top along the center of the form.

**6**

Fold the left side the same way.

Fold back the top edge of the right triangle toward the legs.

Repeat on the left side.

Flip over the form, and your frog is ready to hop.

*Option:* Add eyes.

# Love Birds

Make two birds with paper
As blue as the sky.
When you spread their wings,
They're ready to fly.

**1**

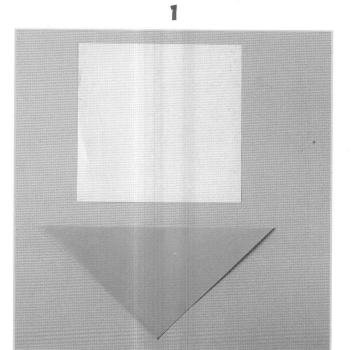

Fold a 7" square of origami paper in half diagonally, colored side out.

**2**

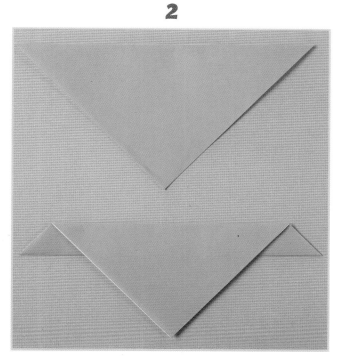

Fold down the top third of the triangle along the fold.

Crease.

Turn over the form.

**3**

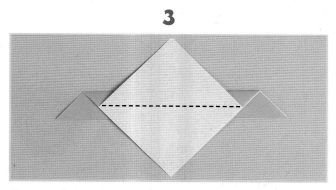

Open up the top layer of the paper.

Fold and crease. (The new fold you are making is in line with the edge of the fold below.)

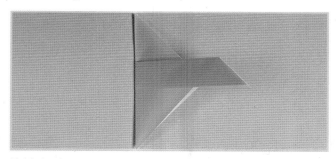

Fold the form in half.

**4**

WING FOLDS:
Fold back the top layer so the edge of the paper meets the center fold. Repeat on the other side. (This creates a small wing and a large wing.)

Small Wing

Large Wing

Tail

**5**

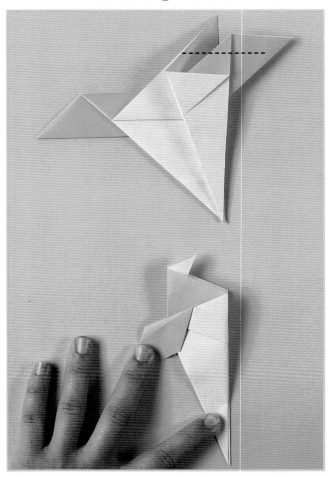

**6**

Fold the small wing on the right towards the tail (the point at the bottom), as indicated by the dotted line.

This creates a small diamond shape.

Repeat on the small wing on the other side.

Form the beak by creating a reverse fold down into the body.

**7**

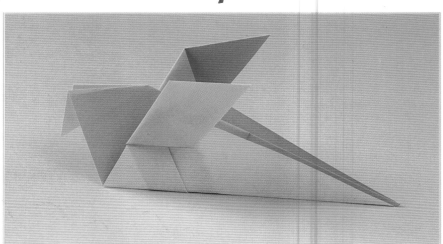

*Pictured on opposite page, top to bottom:* Love Birds, Cardinal, Peacock (on the left), Blue Jay (on the right).

Spread the bird's wings.

# Turkeys

For your Thanksgiving table
To delight and impress
Make turkeys from paper
One for each guest.

## 1

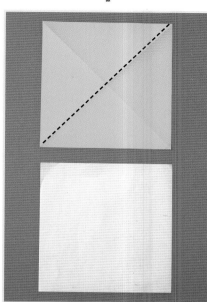

Fold a 7" square of origami paper in half along one diagonal.

Unfold.

Fold along the other diagonal.

Unfold and place the paper colored side down.

## 2

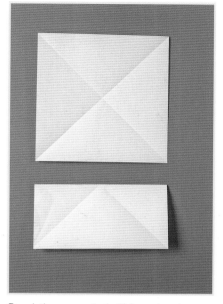

Bend the paper in half from top to bottom.

Crease **only** the right side from the center to the edge.

## 3

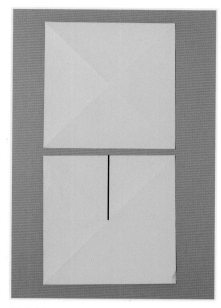

Unfold.

Place the paper colored side up with the crease on the right side.

Bend in half from top to bottom. Crease **only** the upper half from the center to the top.

## 4

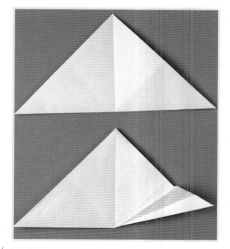

TAIL:

Fold the square in half along the diagonal with the colored side in and the creases on the right.

Fold as you would a fan (fold up, fold down, repeat) from the bottom until you reach the crease.

*Alternate Step 4:*

To make the tail, fold up the bottom to the crease line.

Unfold.

Fold up the bottom to the crease you just made. Unfold.

Fold under and over four times.

## 5

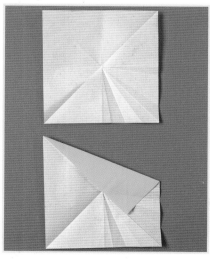

Unfold the form and place it white side up with the tail on your right.

Fold down the top point to meet the center diagonal fold.

**6**

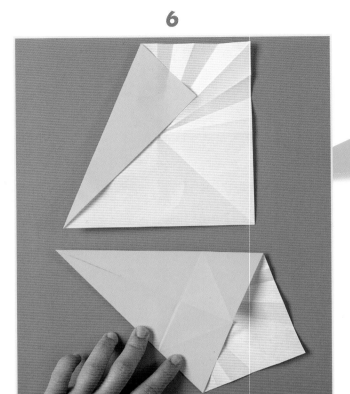

Fold up the bottom point to meet the center fold.

**7**

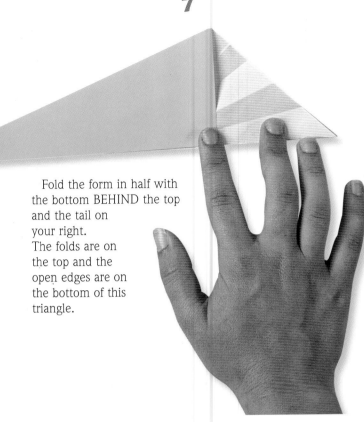

Fold the form in half with the bottom BEHIND the top and the tail on your right.
The folds are on the top and the open edges are on the bottom of this triangle.

**8**

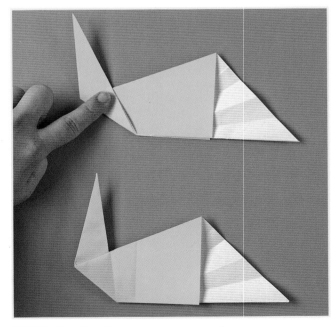

Fold the head as shown.
**Note:** The following photos show the neck and head *only* and demonstrate how to make a **reverse fold.**

**9**

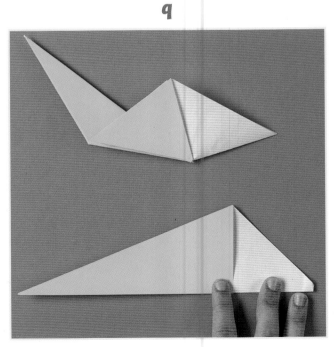

Unfold the head and neck.

## 10

Fold the head along the center so the white side is now inside and the single edges are inside.

Crease.

Fold along the neck fold again.

Crease and unfold.

## 11

This is how the inside of the head and neck will look. Notice the diamond shape created by the folds.

Pick up the form and gently push up on the center fold with your hand beneath the fold. (This will force the head and neck inside the turkey's body.)

## 12

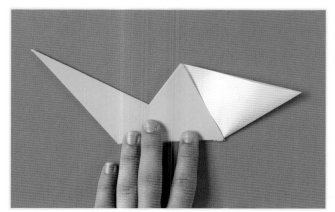

Crease. This is how your form will look after folding the head and neck.

## 13

To make the beak, open up the form.
Fold down the top to the halfway point of the neck.
Make another reverse fold at the end of the head.

## 14

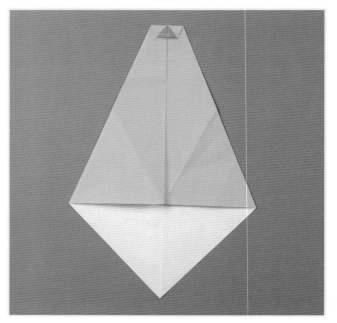

Fold up the tip of the beak so it stands up from the form at a 90-degree angle.

## 15

Close the neck by folding the beak inside. This creates the turkey's head.

## 16

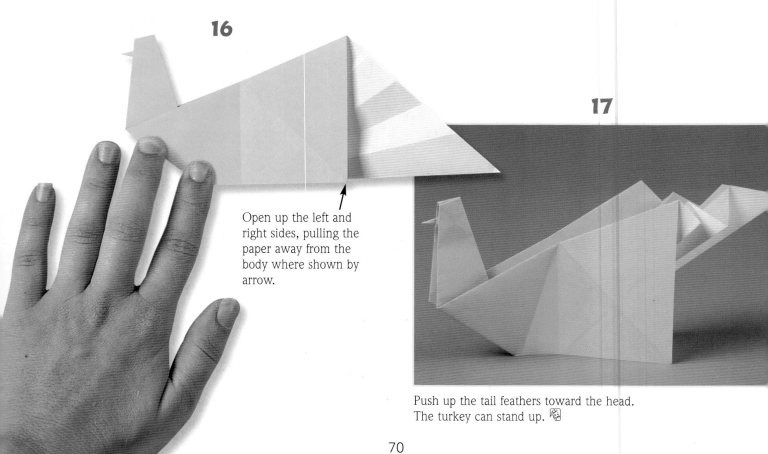

Open up the left and right sides, pulling the paper away from the body where shown by arrow.

## 17

Push up the tail feathers toward the head. The turkey can stand up.

# Peacock

**With stickers and eyes**
**This may come as a shock,**
**Turn your turkey**
**Into a peacock.**

### Supplies
7" square turquoise or green origami paper
Round blue stickers, 1/4"
Round green stickers, 1/8"
2 google eyes

### Instructions
1. Fold a turkey from turquoise or green origami paper, following the Turkey project instructions.
2. Using the photo as a guide for placement, apply blue 1/4" stickers to the tail.
3. Using Fig. 1 as a guide for placement, apply 1/8" green stickers on top of the blue stickers so that the bottoms of the stickers touch.
4. Add an eye on each side of the head. 🖼

Fig. 1 - Sticker placement

# Pot Bellied Pigs

**Pink piggies, pink piggies**
**With bellies so round,**
**When they walk their tummies**
**Are touching the ground.**

**1**

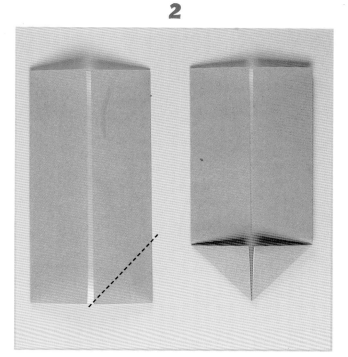

Use a 7" square of pink origami paper for an adult pig or a 4" square of pink origami paper for a baby pig.

Fold the square in half from left to right.

Unfold.

Fold the left side to the center fold.

Fold the right side to the center fold.

**2**

Fold up the bottom corners to the center fold.

**3**

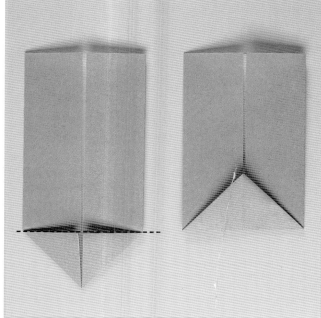

Fold up the bottom as shown.

**4**

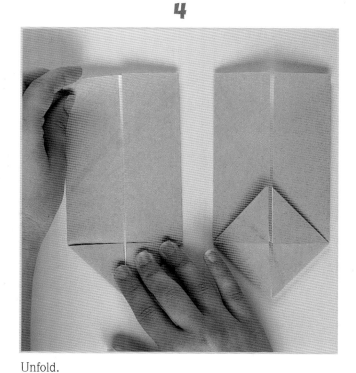

Unfold.

Squash fold the left and right sides of the bottom.

## 5

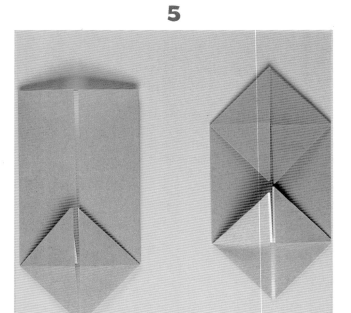

Repeat steps 2 through 4 on the top end of the form.

## 6

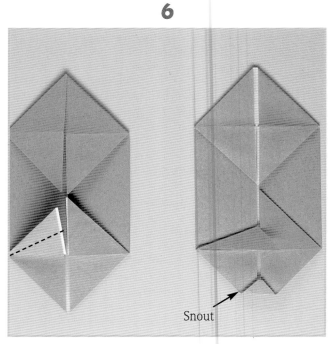

Snout

Fold down the top half of the bottom diamond on the left side to form one ear.

Fold up the tip to create the pig's snout.

## 7

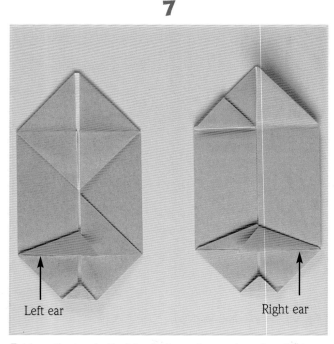

Left ear

Right ear

Fold up the top half of the bottom diamond on the right side to form the other ear.

## 8

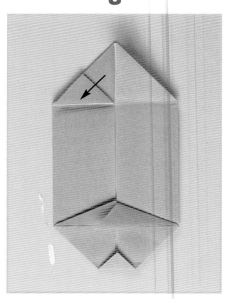

BACK SIDE LEGS:
Working at the top of the form, fold up the diamond point along the crease on the left side.

Fold over the newly formed triangle, creating a smaller triangle. This is one leg.

Repeat on the right side to form the other leg.

## 9

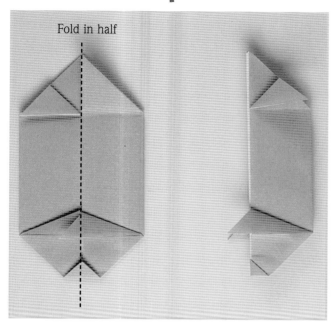

Fold in half

Fold the pig in half along the center line with the ears and the legs on the outside.

## 10

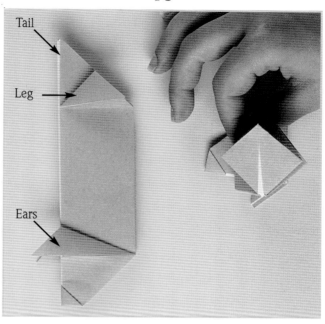

Tail

Leg

Ears

TAIL:
Reverse fold the end of the form, bringing the tip towards the belly.

## 11

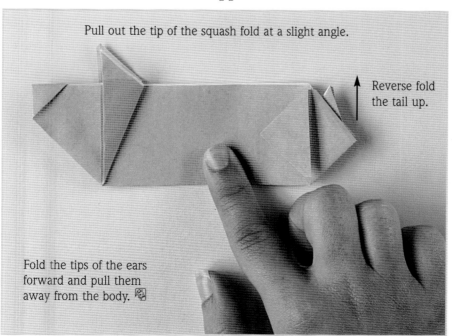

Pull out the tip of the squash fold at a slight angle.

Reverse fold the tail up.

Fold the tips of the ears forward and pull them away from the body.

# Whale

It's really a mammal
But it swims like a fish.
You can make your whale blue
Or any color you wish.

# WHALE

**1**

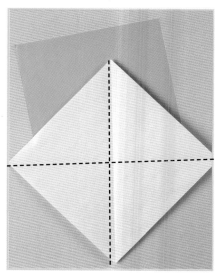

Fold a 7" square of origami paper in quarters across the diagonal.

Crease.

Unfold.

Place the paper white side up.

**2**

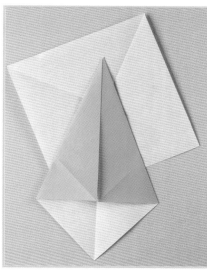

Fold the two upper corners towards the center fold.

Crease.

Open up the form.

**3**

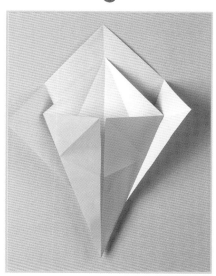

Fold the two lower corners toward the center.

Unfold.

**4**

Rotate the form sideways.

Fold up the paper along the fold lines from steps 2 and 3.

This creates small triangles in the center of the form.

Fold the two triangles to the right.

The two small triangles will become the whale's fins.

**5**

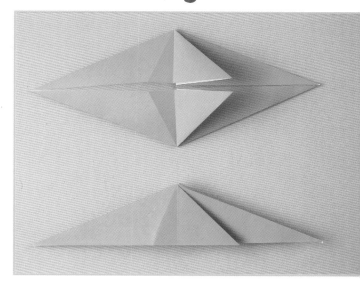

Fold the form in half with the fins on the outside.

## 6

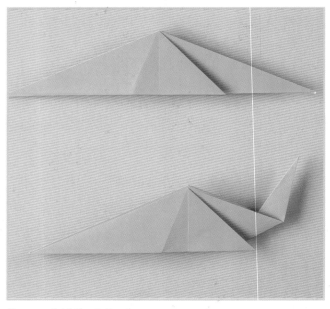

Reverse fold the tail.

## 7

Reverse fold the tip of the tail so it is parallel with the rest of the body.

## 8

Open up the form.

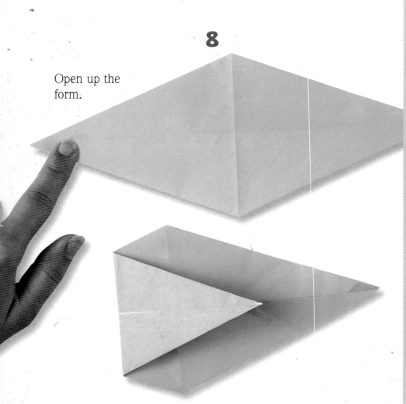

Work on the side with no fins.

Fold the left end towards the right with the fold roughly two-thirds of the way to the center.

Refold at the center, closing the body. This creates the head.

## q

Reverse fold the remainder of the "head" in an upright position. This creates the whale's spout.

## 10

Using paper scissors, cut the spout along the fold to a point just below the head.

Curl the spout by rolling the paper towards the head, then releasing it.

78

# Dragonfly

**Each dragonfly
Has two pairs of wings.
You're likely to see them
Near a pond, stream, or spring.**

**1**

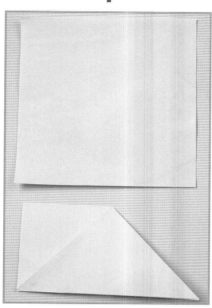

**2**

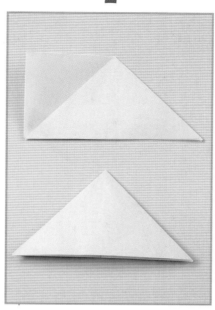

**3**

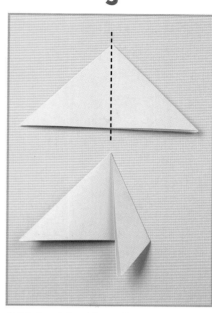

Fold a 7" square of origami paper in half. Crease.

Fold on one diagonal. Crease. Unfold.

Fold on the other diagonal. Crease. Unfold.

Reverse fold the left side. Crease.

Reverse fold the right side.

Crease.

Fold the right side to the center line.

Crease.

Unfold.

**4**

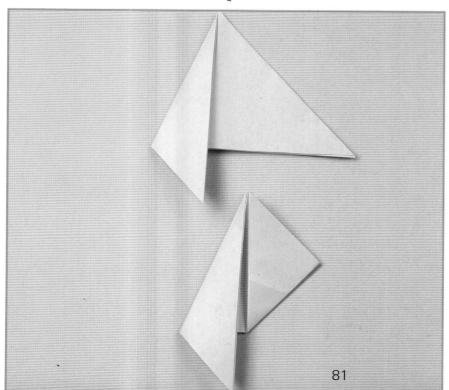

Fold the left side to the center line.

Crease.

Fold the right corner up to meet the top center point.

Crease.

**5**

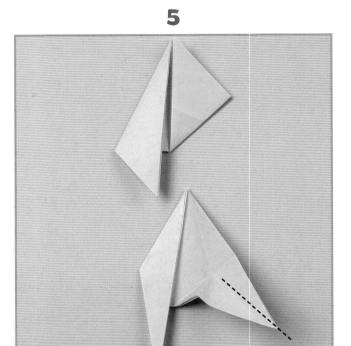

Unfold the right side.

Reverse fold the right side along the dotted line.

This will form the two sets of wings.

Repeat on the left side.

**6**

This photo shows how the form looks after step 5.

Notice the tips of the wings are pointed, not flat.

**7**

Fold up the right side.

**8**

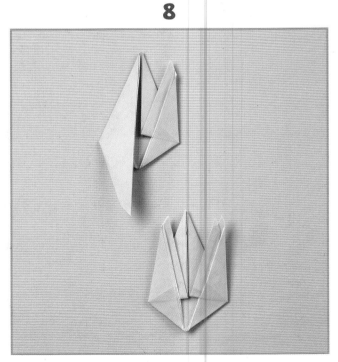

Repeat on the left side.

## 9

Turn the form so the wings are pointing down.

Fold out the wings on the right side.

Gently pull the inside set of wings away from the outside set.

Crease through all the layers.

Repeat on the wings on the left side.

## 10

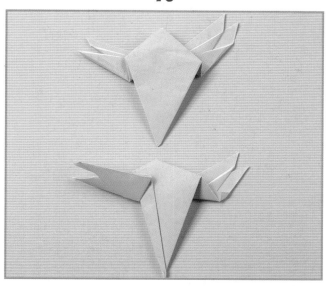

Turn over the form.

Fold the left side to the center line.

Crease. Since you are folding through eight thicknesses of paper, making a sharp crease may be hard. Do the best you can. A less-than-perfect crease is okay and adds body to the dragonfly.

## 11

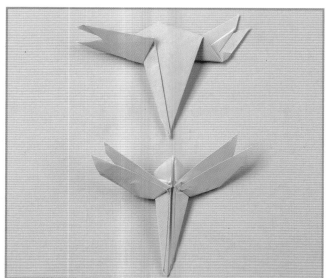

Repeat on the other side.

## 12

Fold back the top of the dragonfly's head and back.

Fold the dragonfly along the center line while you push down on the wings.

It will feel like a pinch with your fingers.

Crease. Release. 🐾

# Owl

The owl is nocturnal,
He sleeps in the day
And hunts in the nighttime
To capture his prey.

## 1

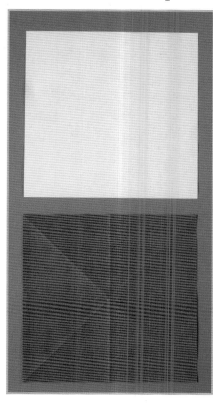

Place a 7" square of origami paper with the white side up.

Fold in half, left to right. Unfold.

Fold in half, top to bottom. Unfold.

Fold in half on one diagonal. Unfold.

Fold in half on the opposite diagonal.

Open the paper flat with the colored side up.

## 2

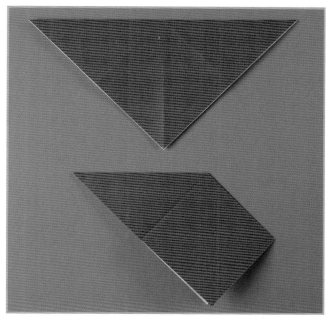

Fold the paper from corner to corner with the colored side out.

Lift the right corner and squash fold towards the center.

This makes a square on the top.

## 3

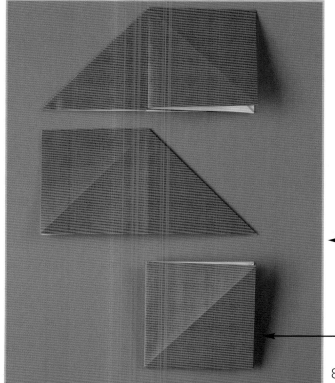

## 4

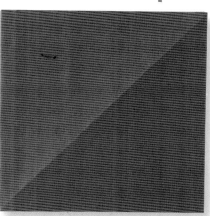

Turn the form so the single-thickness paper edges (not the fold) are at the top.

← Turn over the form.

Lift the left corner and squash fold.

Your form is now a square with the single-thickness paper edges on the bottom and the folded edges on the top.

Single-thickness edges

85

**5**

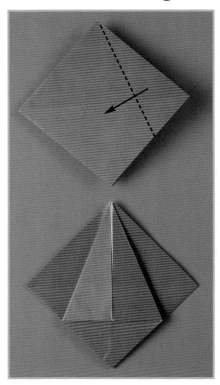

Fold the top layer of the right side to the center.

Repeat on the left side.

**6**

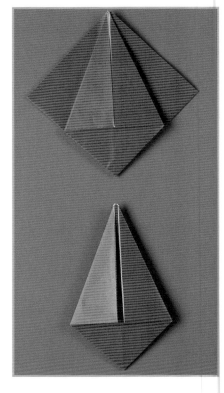

Flip over the form.

Fold the left and right sides towards the center.

This creates a diamond shape.

**7**

Fold up all the layers of the bottom part of the diamond shape towards the top.

Crease.

**8**

Unfold step 7.

## q

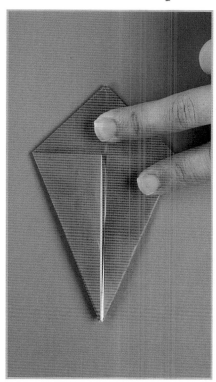

Turn the form so the longer point is at the bottom.

Unfold the two right and left flaps.

## 10

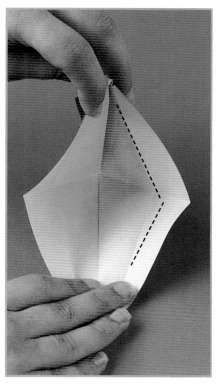

Lift the top layer at the bottom of the form and gently pull upwards.

As you pull, the form will follow the folds you made in steps 6 and 7. Continue to pull until the left and right sides meet in the center.

Crease.

You will have created the diamond shape shown.

Turn over the form and repeat the fold on the other side.

## 11

The form now has two free "legs" at the bottom end and two large triangles at the top end.

Fold down the top large triangle. It will cover the two small "legs."

Repeat on the other side.

## 12

Fold the top left and top right sides towards the center crease.

Turn over the form and repeat the folds on the back side.

The form will still be a diamond shape, but it will be a thinner diamond.

## 13

WINGS:
Between the bottom layer and top layer are two free "legs," one on the left and one on the right.

To form the right wing, pull the leg out gently, away from the body.

Crease. Repeat on the left side.

## 14

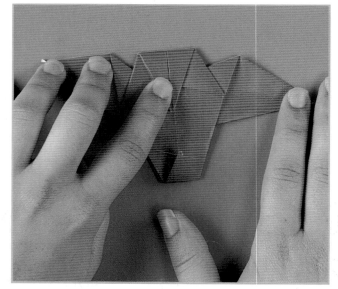

To make the feet, fold up 1/2" on both the front and back sides.

Fold down the top 3/4" on the front side to make the head.

## 15

Fold up the tip of the head to make the beak.

# Bat & Owl
# Halloween Garland

**Bats and owls are a scary combination.
Use them to make this Halloween decoration.
Hang on a window or doorway or wall
To greet trick-or-treaters coming to call.**

## Supplies

Origami paper, 7" square - 5 sheets
   purple, 4 sheets orange
2 yds. orange ribbon, 1/2" wide
Stapler and staples
Scissors
Computer and printer *or* black marker
*Optional:* Background rubber stamp
   and ink

## Instructions

1. Fold five purple origami bats and four orange origami owls.
2. Cut nine paper pieces, 2-1/2" square. Using a black marker, on each square write one letter to spell the word HALLOWEEN. *Option:* Print the letters for HALLOWEEN in the Chiller or other font at 144 points high with double spaces between each letter. Rubber stamp over the images, if desired. Cut out the letters, making 2-1/2" squares.
3. Place the orange ribbon on your work surface and arrange the bats, owls, and rectangles with letters, using the photo as a guide for placement.
4. Staple the paper pieces to the ribbon in sequence.

# Seal

## 1

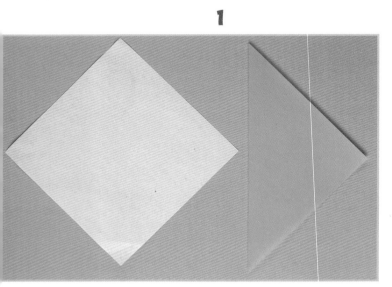

Start with a 7" square double-sided piece of origami paper.

Fold the square in half diagonally, colored side out.

## 2

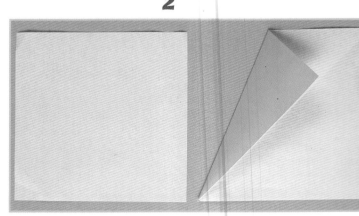

Unfold.

Fold up the left side to the center fold line.

Fold up the right side to the center fold line.

## 3

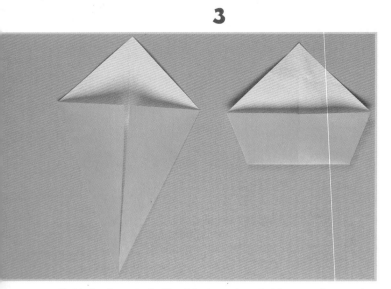

Fold the form in half, with the colored sides together so that the points meet at the top.

Turn so that you see the white part on the front as shown.

## 4

Gently lift the corner marked "A." Fold in place. Crease.

Repeat on the left side. The form will be a diamond shape.

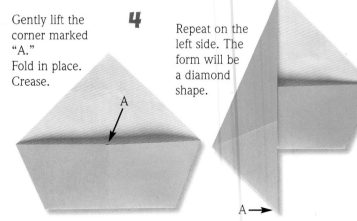

## 5

Fold down the top of the form. Crease. Fold back up.

Repeat on the other side. This will make the next few steps a little easier.

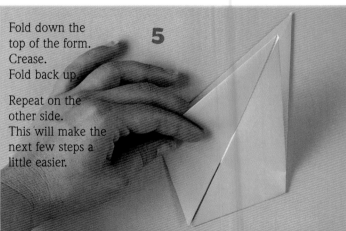

# SEAL

They have paddle-like flippers,
And are often in motion.
They like to eat fish,
And they live in the ocean.

**6**

Open the form and turn it sideways.

**7**

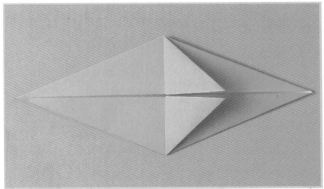

Turn over the form to the opposite side.

## 8

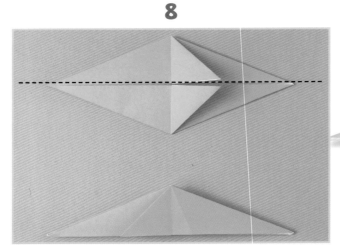

Fold in half along the center line.

## 9

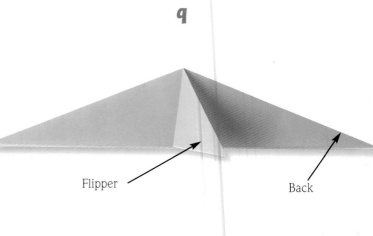

Flipper

Back

Fold the flippers towards the back.

## 10

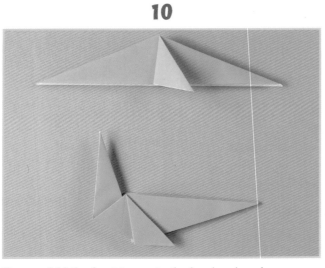

Reverse fold the front to create the head and neck.

## 11

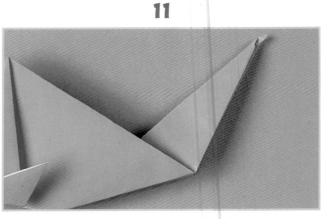

Reverse fold the back to create the tail.

## 13

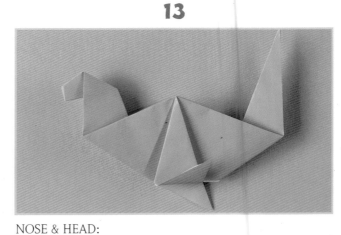

NOSE & HEAD:
Fold head forward (reverse fold inside and down).

Fold nose by folding back the end of the head into the head (reverse fold inside of head).

## 12

Fold up the flippers toward the body, front and back, so the form can stand up.

# Rabbit

**Rabbits have long legs
Intended for hopping,
Tiny noses, big ears
Some are straight and some flopping.**

**1**

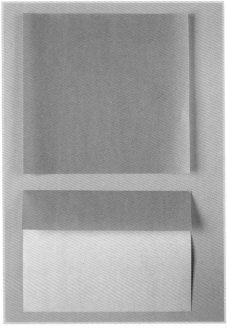

Fold a 7" square of origami paper in half.

Crease. Unfold.

Fold the top half to the center. Crease.

**2**

Fold up the bottom half.

Crease.

Unfold the top and the bottom.

93

## 3

Fold the entire sheet in half again.

Fold the top left corner to the opposite side on a diagonal. Crease.

Unfold.

## 4

Fold the bottom left corner to the top on a diagonal.

Crease.

## 5

Unfold.

Open up the paper.

Fold down the top half to the center and fold up the bottom half to the center again.

## 6

Turn over the form.

Fold the right end 1-1/2" to the left.

Crease.

## 7

Turn over the form.

Reverse fold the left top.

## 8

Reverse fold the bottom left corner.

These two points will become the ears.

## 9

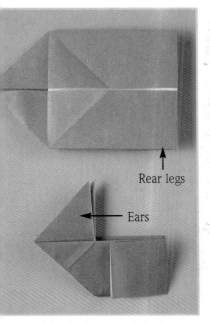

Rear legs

Ears

Fold the bottom of the form to the top along the center.

The back legs will be on the outside.

Reverse fold the ears into the body so they stand up.

## 10

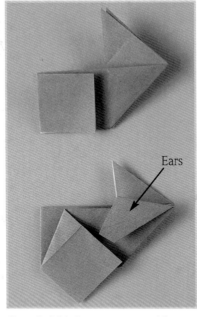

Ears

Squash fold the ear on one side to the body.

Fold the rear leg on that side on an angle.

Repeat on the ear and rear leg on the other side of the form.

## 11

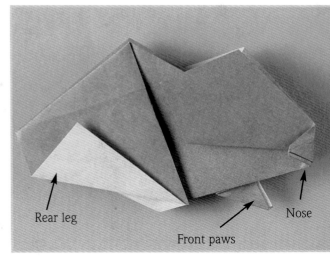

Rear leg

Front paws

Nose

Fold back the tip of the head to make the nose.

Reach into the front of the form below the nose and pull out the front paws as shown in the photo. Crease in place.

Fold up each rear leg to create the feet. 🐾

# Metric Conversion Chart

## Inches to Millimeters and Centimeters

| Inches | MM | CM | Inches | MM | CM |
|--------|-----|-----|--------|-----|------|
| 1/8 | 3 | .3 | 2 | 51 | 5.1 |
| 1/4 | 6 | .6 | 3 | 76 | 7.6 |
| 3/8 | 10 | 1.0 | 4 | 102 | 10.2 |
| 1/2 | 13 | 1.3 | 5 | 127 | 12.7 |
| 5/8 | 16 | 1.6 | 6 | 152 | 15.2 |
| 3/4 | 19 | 1.9 | 7 | 178 | 17.8 |
| 7/8 | 22 | 2.2 | 8 | 203 | 20.3 |
| 1 | 25 | 2.5 | 9 | 229 | 22.9 |
| 1-1/4 | 32 | 3.2 | 10 | 254 | 25.4 |
| 1-1/2 | 38 | 3.8 | 11 | 279 | 27.9 |
| 1-3/4 | 44 | 4.4 | 12 | 305 | 30.5 |

## Yards to Meters

| Yards | Meters | Yards | Meters |
|-------|--------|-------|--------|
| 1/8 | .11 | 3 | 2.74 |
| 1/4 | .23 | 4 | 3.66 |
| 3/8 | .34 | 5 | 4.57 |
| 1/2 | .46 | 6 | 5.49 |
| 5/8 | .57 | 7 | 6.40 |
| 3/4 | .69 | 8 | 7.32 |
| 7/8 | .80 | 9 | 8.23 |
| 1 | .91 | 10 | 9.14 |
| 2 | 1.83 | | |

# Index